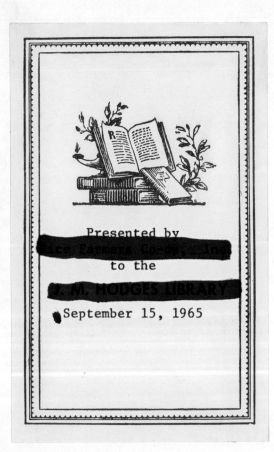

Presented by
~~Rice Farmers Co-op., Inc~~
to the

J. M. HODGES LIBRARY

September 15, 1965

SEEDS
THAT GREW

HOWARD EDWARD BABCOCK
1922-1937

JAMES A. McCONNELL
1937-1952

CHARLES N. SILCOX
1952-1957

EDMUND H. FALLON
1957-

GENERAL MANAGERS OF THE G.L.F. SINCE 1922

SEEDS
THAT GREW

*A History of the Cooperative
Grange League Federation
Exchange*

By JOSEPH G. KNAPP

ANDERSON HOUSE • HINSDALE, N.Y.
1960

Printed by

GEORGE BANTA COMPANY, INC.
MENASHA, WISCONSIN

TO
CAROL

Foreword

THE COOPERATIVE GRANGE LEAGUE FEDERATION EXCHANGE is a thoroughly unique institution of American business enterprise; a monument to "Yankee ingenuity" and rural independence. It has a distinguished ancestry, since one of its lines of descent derives from the post Civil War movement of farmers to better their lot through joint effort of the National Grange of the Patrons of Husbandry. Some of their buying and selling agencies were still alive in 1920 and, through the local and State Granges, ready to contribute the wisdom of long experience and the loyalty of conviction to a broadening cooperative endeavor. Not so old but yet no callow youth in the cooperative camp was the Dairymen's League, seasoned by many minor skirmishes and some major battles with powerful enemies of the farmers' desire to handle their own business. A somewhat younger brother, but one with excellent family connections, was the Farm Bureau, with its studious outlook and its close relationships with the Extension Service and the State Experiment Station.

These are superb materials out of which to build an edifice of farmer cooperative business adequate to the needs of modern agriculture. And Dr. Knapp was equipped as few indeed would be to record and interpret the G.L.F. experience. With the best of professional training and nationwide experience with all phases of cooperative business, he has been able to appreciate both the important goals to be achieved and the unexpected and persistent difficulties to be encountered in such a democratic undertaking. His pages show forbearance for the bad guesses and even stupidities of those who were striving, often with inadequate training, to keep a pioneering enterprise afloat and growing in service to its members.

Of course, a great body of knowledge about cooperatives in general and the nature of their special problems had come to "Joe" through his academic career, his travels, and his consultations as part of his official duties in the United States Department of Agriculture. But the time-consuming and thought-demanding task of getting the detailed history of the G.L.F., needed for the writing of this treatise, organizing and condensing this mass of material, filling in gaps, and distilling its meaning for the G.L.F. and many other cooperatives was a labor of love and of scholarship, done on his own time as he burned the midnight electricity at his home in Bethesda or embezzled precious hours—and days—from his all-too-brief "vacations" in his native Colorado.

The very fact of such richness of detail as he has given to the book will defeat the purpose of anyone who has the intention to read it in an evening or on a slack day at the office. But, by the same token, this gives it its enduring value as a reference-book of cooperative problems and business solutions not only for the new generations of G.L.F.ers but for farm leaders in other geographical areas and other product lines. A wealth of historic detail drives home the fact that in this dynamic world of ours we don't get pat and permanent "answers" to operative problems but should get skill and fortitude for dealing effectively with recurrent dilemmas and unpredictable changes. Dr. Knapp's long-time specialization in workaday problems of sound business structure and efficient business practice is reflected in his constant stressing and illumination of these phases of G.L.F.'s rich body of experience and experimentation.

One point that particularly impressed me as I followed these annals was the value of cooperative organization as a yard-stick on the performance of commercial agencies and as a pace setter in adopting or adapting new technological or business discoveries to local requirements and particular farming situations. This is clearly highlighted in the "viable seed" campaign, the scientifically flexible feed program, and the victory for "open formula" fertilizers. A large part of the explanation for success in the G.L.F. case is to be found in the fine partnership existing between farmers' business enterprise and the sources of scientific assistance or guidance available to them in their agricultural colleges and experiment stations. Also the broad avenue of communication furnished by local Granges and Farm Bureaus, county agents, and extension service.

It has been said that a business or social institution is, in last analysis, "the lengthened shadow of a man." The G.L.F. record does much to support such a concept. In the middle ground of that picture we see the towering figure of "Ed" Babcock, solidly flanked by his successors, "Jim" McConnell, and "Chuck" Silcox. But there were other men of strength and vision who bore the burden and heat of the day when G.L.F. was pioneering in new and often hostile business areas—such as Elmer Seth Savage, father of the "open formula" idea; R. D. Cooper, veteran of the "pooled feed orders" experiment of the Dairymen's League; W. L. Bean of Grange affiliation and wide practical experience; and Frank M. Smith, leading pure-bred dairy breeder and one of the founders of the American Farm Bureau Federation. He was a long-time president of the G.L.F. following such staunch leaders as Niles F. Webb and Fred L. Porter. Special mention should be made of Waldo G. Morse, who brought a profound knowledge of, and wide experience in, corporation law to the service of his farmer friends in shaping the structure of the cooperative association and devising business practices and legal instruments adapted to its distinctive needs.

At the other side of the stage we see the new leaders, in whose hands rests the future of the G.L.F.—Edmund H. Fallon, general manager and second-generation leader, whose father had been a long-time fighter for better milk marketing, and a Founding Father of the G.L.F.; and James C. Corwith, president and elder statesman, who helped sell the initial stock and to whom past is prologue.

There are other able generals in the several departments of the organization, but generals do not win battles singlehanded. They must have troops who believe in their cause and have been schooled in their duties. For the rank and file membership, not only in the G.L.F. but in all cooperatives, Dr. Knapp's book should be both an inspiration and a guide.

EDWIN G. NOURSE

Preface

THIS BOOK is a biography of a great cooperative enterprise. It is presented almost as a biological growth. The title, "Seeds That Grew," reflects the way the plant—that is, the G.L.F. idea—flourished from good seed and good care.

The G.L.F. has evolved experimentally to meet practical needs over a period of forty years. It has maintained its ideals while adapting its methods to great wars, depressions, prosperity, and a revolution in social, agricultural and industrial techniques.

Seeds That Grew has more than a symbolic significance. Many oldtimers believe that the early campaign to furnish reliable seed built the faith in good quality that has been a guiding principle in G.L.F. to this day.

This book will show that cooperation is not a simple form of business enterprise. G.L.F. experience makes clear that cooperation affords scope for great ingenuity and calls for character and leadership of the highest order. It indicates that cooperation is a method of business organization uniquely adapted to the needs of farmers for it can get for them as individual enterprisers the advantages of the modern large business corporation.

This book has been written over a period of years in the author's free time during weekends and vacations as a contribution to an understanding of the modern cooperative business corporation. While the G.L.F. has generously provided essential good will and information, the conception of the book and its preparation have been solely mine.

Appreciation to the many who have helped me so greatly in this effort is expressed in the *Acknowledgments,* at the end, page 525.

JOSEPH G. KNAPP

June, 1960

Contents

Illustrations

Charts

I. THE RISE OF THE G.L.F., 1900-1920

CHAPTER 1

The Underlying Trend

*It is of the greatest consequence that the people of the open country
should learn to work together, not only for the purpose of forwarding
their economic interests and of competing with other men who are organized, but also to develop themselves and to establish an effective
community spirit.*

Report of the Country Life Commission (1908)

THE ORIGINS of the Cooperative Grange League Federation Exchange,
Inc., reach far back in American Life—to the Mayflower compact, the
Declaration of Independence and the many other events which have fash-
ioned the spirit of self reliance ingrained in our people.

Working together to achieve group goals has been a common practice
since frontier days in G.L.F. land—the states of New York and New Jersey
and the northern tier of counties in Pennsylvania. Family records are re-
plete with references to log rollings, barn raisings, house warmings, and
quilting bees in which neighbors joined together for mutual pleasure and
benefit.

As the country settled and economic life became more organized, farmers set up more formal cooperative organizations to perform essential business services for themselves. Among the earliest forms of joint enterprise of
this type were the mutual fire insurance companies which sprang up more
than a hundred years ago. In the 1860's a group of farmers at Riverhead
on Long Island in New York bought jointly a shipload of guano fertilizer
and for many years continued this practice.

The real beginnings of cooperative marketing and purchasing in this
region came with the Granger Movement of the Seventies. Some of the
associations set up were significant in size and influence. For example, the
Union Grange Trade Association in Monroe County, New York, organized
to buy for cash necessary farm supplies at reduced rates, did a business
volume of over one million dollars in 1882 in 21 counties.

However, until 1912 the interest of farmers in cooperation in New York
and surrounding states was sporadic and intermittent. Some support was
given by the State Grange in New York State but this was a Grange program for Grange members and had little general effect.

In the early years of this century economic and social forces began to
change the situation rapidly.

The dairy industry was becoming intensively developed to serve the
growing needs of New York and other nearby urban markets and, as a

result, dairy farmers were finding themselves dependent for feed supplies upon a rapidly expanding commercial feed industry.[1]

In general, self-sufficient farming, in which farmers supplied themselves with feed, seed, and fertilizer in the form of manure, was being rapidly converted to commercial farming, with farmers buying a large part of their supplies from commercial agencies. Along with this change farmers became increasingly dependent upon sales to distant markets.

These changes were not limited to New York and surrounding States; they prevailed over the entire country. But they did not come painlessly. During the first decade of this century there was a growing concern throughout the nation over the rural life problem—the maintenance of a healthy rural community. This sentiment reached its peak in 1908 when President Theodore Roosevelt established the Country Life Commission. The report of this Commission placed great emphasis on ways farmers could help themselves by cooperative action. The Commission said:

> This effort should be a genuinely cooperative or common effort in which all the associated persons have a voice in the management of the organization and share proportionately in its benefits. Many of the so-called 'cooperative' organizations are really not such, for they are likely to be controlled in the interest of a few persons rather than for all and with no thought of the good of the community at large.
>
> While there are very many excellent agricultural cooperative organizations of many kinds, the farmers nearly everywhere complain that there is still a great dearth of associations that really help them in buying and selling and developing their communities. Naturally, the effective cooperative groups are in the most highly developed communities; the general farmer is yet insufficiently helped by the societies. The need is not so much for a greater number of societies as for a more complete organization within them and for a more continuous active work.

It is germane to our story that President Roosevelt selected Liberty Hyde Bailey, Dean of the New York College of Agriculture, to serve as Chairman of the Country Life Commission. Under his leadership the College of Agriculture had built a partnership with rural people in helping them solve their problems. Much of the philosophy and spirit to be embodied in the G.L.F. can be traced back to Bailey's vision and inspiration.[2]

---

[1] See Chapter III. At this time the commercial feed industry was in an emerging stage. It had not yet learned how to make products to help farmers feed scientifically although it was working toward this end. The G.L.F., Eastern States Farmers' Exchange, and other farmer cooperatives helped materially in this development. Many of the criticisms of the feed industry during this period were valid at the time but no longer apply. For an interesting account of the technical and commercial evolution of the American feed industry, see Larry Wherry, *The Golden Anniversary of Scientific Feeding*, 1947.

[2] In answer to my question, "Didn't cooperation grow naturally out of the forces changing rural life, which started about 1900?" Bailey replied, "Farmers couldn't avoid it." Interview November 30, 1945.

CHAPTER 2

New Impulses

If agriculture is to continue to prosper under a democratic form of government; if we are to be a nation of freemen of the soil; if we are to avoid coming to what all the older nations have come to—an agricultural peasantry—we must organize our industry, and that means cooperation.

DEAN BEVERLY T. GALLOWAY (*1915*)

THE GROWING IMPORTANCE of cooperation in New York State was significantly recognized by the New York State Agricultural Society in its annual meeting in January, 1912, when a resolution was passed which instructed its president to call a conference of "delegates of producers' and consumers' organizations" to bring producers and city consumers into closer relation by cooperative methods.

At the conference held in New York City on April 19, in compliance with this resolution, a State Standing-Committee on Cooperation was set up under the chairmanship of John J. Dillon, Editor of the *Rural New Yorker*, "to encourage cooperative action between consumer and producer." The conference also passed a resolution which requested the State Department of Agriculture "to assist in organizing cooperative societies among producers and shippers throughout the State by having competent organizers work with the Farmers Institute Bureau and by making cooperation a permanent feature of Institute work."

The chairman of the Standing Committee reported significant achievements when the New York State Agricultural Society held its annual meeting in early 1914. He declared: "For nearly two years we have worked to lay a foundation for a comprehensive cooperative structure, and we believe that we are now ready to raise the timbers." He then pointed out that:

During the preceding year we have succeeded in securing laws for the organization of cooperative purchasing and selling associations and credit unions. We also secured the appointment of an assistant commissioner in the Department of Agriculture to promote and help organize cooperative work in the State.

On May 9, 1913, the State Business Corporations Law had been amended by adding Article 3, Chapter 354, which provided for cooperative corporations for the purpose of conducting a general producing, manufacturing and merchandising business in articles of common use, including farm products, food supplies, farm machinery and supplies and arti-

cles of domestic and personal use. On the same date the Agricultural Law
was amended by adding a new Section 319, Chapter 235, which provided
for the creation of a Bureau of Supervision of Co-operative Associations
in the State Department of Agriculture. These acts were introduced as
bills by Franklin D. Roosevelt in the State Senate and by Marc W. Cole
in the State Assembly.

To carry on this work in the State Department of Agriculture a Bureau
of Cooperation had been organized under Marc W. Cole as superintendent. Mr. Cole reported to the Society that the work of the Bureau
was severely limited by meager appropriations. He was convinced that
the principal work of the Bureau "must be missionary in character. . . . It
must spread the gospel of cooperation and it must secure converts to the
cause."

A serious obstacle to cooperative advancement at this time was growing friction between organizations interested in cooperative development.
In particular, the leaders in the Grange were apprehensive that the farm
bureaus, which were rapidly spreading and getting into full swing, would
set up independent cooperative associations and thus interfere with
Grange-sponsored activities. There was also a conflict of interest and
viewpoint between supporters and advocates of producers' and consumers' organizations.

Sensing this sentiment the Superintendent of the Bureau of Cooperation called a conference of cooperative associations at Utica, New York,
in July, 1914. In a statement to this conference Mr. Dillon, the Chairman
of the State Standing-Committee on Cooperation, expressed the view that
ultimately "the local associations must have a central organization to
furnish information and execute the orders and transact the wholesale
business of both selling and buying for the local associations."

However, the conference discussion disclosed that the various groups
were not yet ready for a comprehensive plan of federation.

One group, composed largely of urban consumer cooperatives, favored
giving support to a consumers' wholesale society then being formed.
Grange representatives, on the other hand, maintained that the State
Grange purchasing agency was in position adequately to serve farmers'
needs. According to the Master of the State Grange, "its perfect success"
was dependent only upon "cooperation."

Although the conference refused to endorse any plan for federation,
it passed the following resolution which shows that the concept of federation was gaining adherents:

Resolved, that it is the sense of this meeting that considerable saving can be
made by a federation of the cooperative associations of this state for the purpose
of ordering supplies collectively directly from the producers and shippers, pref-
erably on specifications and analyses by contract.

Of more immediate and practical importance was a resolution which called upon "the Department of Agriculture to recommend to any association so desiring the service, a system of bookkeeping with a view toward uniformity of accounts by all associations." There was a growing belief that a sound program of federation could come only with the growth of strong local units set up on much the same pattern.

The meeting of the New York State Agricultural Society in January, 1915, makes clear that interest in cooperative organization was steadily developing. The report of the Committee on Cooperation, presented by Charles R. White, pointed out that many marketing and purchasing associations had been formed recently and were operating "with a very large degree of success." The Farm Bureau movement had taken hold—and county agents were aggressively promoting cooperative associations. While M. C. Burritt, the State Extension Leader, maintained that "we ought to keep in our minds more clearly that the Farm Bureaus are preeminently educational institutions," he asserted: "Nowhere is education and assistance more sorely needed than along the lines of cooperation in the purchasing of farm supplies and in the marketing of farm products. . . . No feature of Farm Bureau work is more important than this." At this meeting reports were given by Farm Bureau managers from six counties. Each indicated progress in cooperative organization. One of these reports was made by H. E. Babcock, then manager (county agent) of the Tompkins County Farm Bureau.

The spirit of the times was reflected in an address by the new Dean of Agriculture at Cornell, Beverly T. Galloway. He declared: "If agriculture is to continue to prosper under a democratic form of government, if we are to be a nation of freemen of the soil, if we are to avoid coming to what all the older nations have come to—an agricultural peasantry—we must organize our industry, and that means cooperation."

Strong support for cooperation came also from Dr. Raymond A. Pearson who had just completed a comprehensive study of cooperative organizations in Europe for the New York State Department of Agriculture. Pearson boldly asserted that the dairy problem "will never be settled until it is settled by the dairymen through having their own cooperative organization." He urged New York dairymen to organize cooperatively their milk business as the fruit growers of California had done for marketing their fruit.

THE FARM BUREAU INFLUENCE

In 1913 a new force in support of cooperative organization among farmers in New York State had begun to make itself felt—the county farm bureau associations. These organizations were formed to facilitate the work of county agents, and they soon became recognized as "the county groups of farmers cooperating with the agricultural colleges and the Department of Agriculture in carrying on county agent work."[1] This relationship is indicated by the fact that the county agents were then commonly called "farm bureau managers."[2]

While the first county farm bureau associations were conceived as educational organizations through which farmers could improve their efficiency in production, the county agents soon realized that "the better application of scientific and modern ideas to production" required the organization of farmers into groups or associations for cow testing, herd, seed or soil improvement, or similar purposes. Through such organizational activity the farmers came to look to the county agents for assistance in organization as well as for direct instruction on scientific agricultural practices. Work in organizing farmers to improve their methods of production led almost immediately to demands for help in organizing purchasing or marketing associations.[3]

The way in which the interest of county agents and county farm bureau

---

[1] See M. C. Burritt, *The County Agent and the Farm Bureau*, pp. 170-71. Prior to January 1, 1914, farm bureau work was being promoted and supported somewhat independently by the New York State Department of Agriculture, the United States Department of Agriculture, and by the State Agricultural College. On that date these three agencies coordinated their efforts by placing supervision into the hands of one person, and this gradually led to the administration of all funds for farm bureau work through the State College of Agriculture. The next two years saw a rapid expansion of county farm bureaus—from about 20 on January 1, 1914, to about 40 on January 1, 1916. By 1920 all of the 56 agricultural counties had farm bureau organizations. In 1917 the county farm bureaus federated to form the New York Federation of Farm Bureaus which took the name *New York State Farm Bureau Federation*, in 1920.

[2] "As he was, in a sense, the executive officer of the farm bureau, the county agent in New York was called its manager. This was an unfortunate term, as it implied a control which he did not possess and seemed to be contrary to the general policy of putting responsibility for the work on the operating farmers. It was out of line with the nomenclature adopted in other states where a similar officer was usually called a county agent." Alfred Charles True, *A History of Agricultural Extension Work in the United States*, 1795-1923, p. 84. M. C. Burritt in reviewing this chapter comments, "This name was an alternative one used by some but by no means by all. It gradually went out of use."

[3] The work of the first county farm bureaus was determined largely by the desires of the farmers themselves, as there was little agreement among sponsors as to what they "ought to do." The stated objectives of several of the county farm bureaus organized in New York State in 1913 and 1914 show that farmers expected assistance in forming marketing and purchasing associations. For example, the first of the declared objects of the Farm Improvement Association of Broome County (formed on October 10, 1913) was "to foster cooperation in the buying and selling operations necessary to farming." One of the objects of the Niagara County Farm Bureau, formed in January 1913, was to "aid in the organization of cooperative associations for the purchase of farm supplies and for packing and marketing fruit." Liberty Hyde Bailey, Director of the New York State College of Agriculture, in an address, March 17, 1914, held that county agents must facilitate buying and selling by aiding the organization and work of cooperatives. True, *Op. Cit.*, pp. 79, 82, 85.

associations shifted from production to economic problems is shown by the following passage from E. R. Eastman's novel, *The Trouble Maker* (1925) which portrays the conditions that led to the support of the Dairymen's League in 1916. The county agent is explaining his position to a group of farmers:

Two years ago, I came down to this country, happy and enthusiastic that at last I was in position to do something worthwhile for farmers. I had great dreams. . . . I saw the fields that needed drainage, the buildings that needed repairing, the crops that needed improvement. I saw what could be done with lime to make the clover grow and with spraying and pruning to rejuvenate the orchards, so I began to ride your hills and valleys and to talk with you at meetings, in your barns and in your lots about the gospel of better farming.

But something was wrong. . . . I finally saw what was the matter. . . . These many years all of us have been emphasizing and working to make two blades of grass grow where one grew before, without even trying to sell the first blade at a profit. . . . We should use better seed; we should study varieties; we should spray our orchards; we should weed out poor cattle. . . . But none of these things touched the greatest of all our problems, that of marketing. . . . It is our lack of study of our selling problem that has put farm people into the control of middlemen and is losing us our much vaunted independence.

Eastman was himself one of the pioneer county agents. In a later novel, *Tough Sod* (1944), he dealt with the complaint of farmers in buying their supplies that led to the formation of the G.L.F. These novels catch the spirit of frustration and bitterness in rural New York State from 1914 to 1920 that determined farmers to organize for their economic self-protection.

Looking back in 1922, M. C. Burritt, State Leader of County Agricultural Agents, 1914-1916, and Director of Extension, 1917-1924, said in his book, *The County Agent and the Farm Bureau*, "While organization among farmers had developed to a considerable extent previous to 1910 it has had its greatest and soundest development since the county agricultural agent came on the field. Many farmers have long felt the need for such organization but have lacked the leadership and initiative to effect it. These the county agent has supplied." (pp. 78-79) Later in the same book he said, "The greatest immediate demand for the application of the County Agent's organization and leadership abilities has proved to be that of cooperative buying and selling." (p. 84)

Writing in 1927, E. R. Eastman also declared:

The influence that the extension men and the county agents have had upon the rural social and economic life of the past decade is immeasurable. Many of these county agents recognized that the first problem of rural life was an economic one and they have been of invaluable service to farmers in helping to spread information about cooperative organizations, in encouraging organization and in helping farmers to get better markets for their products.[4]

[4] E. R. Eastman, *These Changing Times*, p. 156.

The support and encouragement that the county agents and county farm bureau associations gave to farmers' cooperative enterprises was bitterly resented by private business establishments. In self-interest they opposed farmers doing business for themselves. They contended that it was improper for county agents, as government employees, to participate in business activities in behalf of farmers.

Those in charge of county agent work recognized the force of this argument and soon took the attitude that it was proper for county agents to provide farmers with information and advisory assistance in organizing and operating cooperative associations, but improper to take an active part in their management or direction.

Although a conscientious effort was made by state officials to enforce this policy this was difficult to do, for assistance to farmers on their production problems led directly to buying responsibilities. Farmers demanded help from the county agents in pooling orders for feed, seed, and fertilizer and it was not possible for county agents to disassociate themselves from such activities. This situation gradually convinced the extension workers that farmers needed their own independent cooperative associations and it became established farm bureau policy in New York State to encourage the formation of cooperative marketing or purchasing associations—but not to participate in these as a farm bureau business activity. Thus the county agents and the county farm bureau associations played a highly significant role in fostering the organization of farmers into marketing and purchasing associations.[5]

However, one important commercial activity—seed distribution—could not be easily divorced from the educational activities of the Extension Service since no other agency could provide the service that farmers required to produce efficiently. This major exception to the rule of non-participation in commercial enterprise developed out of natural circumstances.

To understand this situation one must realize that when the county agents came on the field one of the greatest handicaps to efficient production was the inability of farmers to get dependable seed. The importance of good seed was then being stressed by the agricultural college, but farmers were unable to get from their local dealers the type and quality of seed recommended. In 1913, H. E. Babcock, then County Agent for Cattaraugus County, recognized this problem by forming a seed committee among the farmers in his county farm bureau association which soon became known as the "farm bureau seed committee." This committee, with the assistance of the county agent, proceeded to pool the seed orders of its members and obtain seed for them from a reliable source. The

[5] In reviewing this chapter, M. C. Burritt said of this sentence, "A true and exact statement."

beneficial results in yields obtained from this experiment soon led to the formation of similar farm bureau seed committees in other counties. In view of the close relationship of this program to the work of the College and County Agents, it was natural for these committees to turn to the State Office of the Extension Service for help in providing a source of supply. Within a few years this grew into a sizable volume of seed business. The expansion of such seed committees and the centralization of purchasing was indirectly encouraged by the fact that the organizer of the first committee, H. E. Babcock, was made Assistant State County Agent Leader (later called Assistant Farm Bureau Director) in 1914. In this influential position he naturally spread the idea and took responsibility for its successful development. From 1916 to 1920 Babcock was State County Agent Leader (also called State Director of Farm Bureaus).

Since the Extension Service was interested in this program only as a means of helping farmers obtain reliable seed, it was somewhat embarrassed as the activity grew in commercial scope. A way out of this difficulty came in late 1918 with the establishment of the State Grange Exchange to serve as a state-wide buying organization for local cooperatives. The task of securing seed to meet the pooled requirements of the farmers in the Farm Bureau Seed Committees was then entrusted to this organization. This partnership strengthened the Better Seed Committees and maintained the interest of the Federation of Farm Bureaus in state-wide buying service. It soon became three-cornered when some of the branches of the Dairymen's League, which were pooling seed orders, joined in this arrangement. Thus the three organizations which later were to sponsor the G.L.F. started to work together in pooling seed orders.

CHAPTER 3

The Demand for Better Feed

A wide field for fraudulent operation exists in the selling of concentrated feeding stuffs to the dairymen of this State. . . . Many gentlemen conceived the idea that by putting on the market concentrated dairy feeds of various ingredients or alleged ingredients useful for cattle feeds that large profits might be made by adulterating these feeds with inferior or worthless articles. The idea was followed by prompt and effective action.

The Wicks' Report (1917)

THE ECONOMIC FACTOR that was to contribute most to the development of cooperative buying in New York State was the commercialization of the dairy industry. By 1900 there had been a considerable expansion in the production of dairy products to meet the growing requirements of consumers in New York City and other urban centers, and this led dairy farmers to turn to commercial sources for grain and feed. At first farmers endeavored to mix their own feed on the farm, and the College of Agriculture, through farmer institutes and regular teaching courses, gave farmers and students instruction in "scientific feeding" and the best practices of "home mixing."

It was not long before certain concerns saw the advantages of compounding feeds in the form of "balanced rations" which farmers could use without mixing. As sales of such feed were supported by vigorous advertising and active solicitation, the mixed feed industry flourished.

If the service provided by the feed manufacturers had been satisfactory, there would have been little opportunity for feed buying cooperatives to develop. But the service was not generally good and dairy farmers could not rely on the nutritional values claimed for the feeds. They came increasingly to realize that prices charged were frequently too high and the quality inadequate.

This situation led farmers to again resort to home mixing and they turned naturally to their State College and County Agents for information on how they could provide themselves mixed feed with reliable feeding values.

T. E. Milliman gives us this graphic description of the situation as it prevailed when he came to Orange County, New York, as County Agent in 1915:

Because mixed feeds were poor, some of them loaded with junk, and all of them carrying low grade products of one kind or another, many dairymen were ingredient buyers and skilled mixers. . . . The 2,200 dairymen of the county had to purchase feed for their cows, since barely enough oats were raised to support the farm horses. Therefore, these dairymen were wholly dependent for dairy feed upon a high-cost, high profit set of feed dealers, far too numerous in number.[1]

This problem placed a great burden on the County Agricultural Agents who were expected to be authorities on feeds and feeding. Milliman recalls:

It fell to me as County Agent to make our home-mix formulas. . . . I had to keep up to date on the available ingredients and their various nutritive values as well as the economics of the ingredients in order to be able to compound on the spot, meaning the farm, as well as in the office, a formula to fit the farmers' needs. The only solution the farmer had to his problem of getting feed of good quality at a fair price was to buy straight cars of ingredients alone or with his neighbors and to compound his own formulas.[2]

THE BIRTH OF THE OPEN FORMULA IDEA

As the practice of using mixed commercial feeds grew because of the economy and convenience in the method, the College and County Agents found it increasingly difficult to instruct students and farmers in the nutritional values of commercial feeds.

Elmer Seth Savage, a young professor in the Animal Husbandry Department began to work on this problem as early as 1911.[3] He gradually became convinced that the closed formula method of selling feeds by proprietary brands was detrimental to the sound development of the dairy industry. It was obvious to him that dairymen could not buy mixed feed intelligently unless they knew the amount and quality of the various ingredients combined in a commercial brand.

A few feed manufacturers were interested in Savage's theories, notably F. A. McLellan of the Hales and Edwards Company, and through their influence Savage was invited to present his views at the Sixth Annual Meeting of the American Feed Manufacturers' Association in Chicago on May 22, 1914. Savage's talk, "The Attitude of the Teacher to the Mixed Feed Industry," which was to launch the idea of "open-formula feeds," proved to be the feature of the meeting. In pointing out the difficulties involved in trying to teach students how to feed most satisfactorily when the ingredients in a compounded feed were not known, Savage said:

My point is this. I want to bring out just how I wish to teach my students

[1] *The Record* (No. 1), Cooperative Grange League Federation Exchange, Inc., Ithaca, 1939, p. 5.

[2] Interview with author, April 4, 1947.

[3] In view of the close and significant friendship that developed between Babcock and Savage it is of interest that Babcock took the course in "Feeds and Feeding," given by Savage at the Cornell Agricultural Short Course during the summer of 1911.

—how shall I do it—to choose their feeds. That is what they are up against. Any farmer or student or any man handling cattle goes into a local feed store. The local feed dealer may have ten straight by-products and three or four mixed or compounded feeds on hand. The problem right before that farmer is how to select the four or five feeds that he may mean to mix together to make his ration or, which one of those compounded feeds will he select as his ration, if he doesn't want to mix his feed himself.

Realizing that he was treading on delicate ground, Savage asked that his ideas be examined with open minds. He declared that his only wish was "to help in bringing together the manufacturer and the consumer so that one may sell his product at a fair price, at a good profit, and the farmer purchase his necessary feeds as cheaply as possible."

Savage then presented several tables which had been prepared on the basis of information provided by Farm Bureau agents in 25 counties. He summarized these tables by saying, "I have checked up on compounded feeds in many localities at all times of year and I have failed to find one sold at a price which would make it a good investment."[4]

Savage then asked the manufacturers this question: "Why not guarantee a certain formula on every bag of feed sold so that I may teach all of my students to compute exactly the total nutrients in a ton of compounded feed. . . . Then as a feeder, when I see this feed at a feed dealer's I can compute its digestibility and check up closely whether I want to buy it or not." Savage granted the honesty of the feed manufacturers but he insisted, "We cannot study your compounded feed in any other way."

Such views were heretical to the assembled feed manufacturers and they were actively challenged by Roger W. Chapman, President of the American Feed Manufacturers' Association. "This mixed feed business is on a sufficiently stable basis for the agricultural colleges . . . to experiment with, to know their uniformity and place them on their regular teachings."

In the same issue of *Flour and Feed*, there was a lead article by President Chapman, entitled "Theory vs. Experience." Claiming that Savage's analysis was "primarily theoretical" and that "an ounce of fact is worth a pound of theory" he concluded: "For the present, at least, a manufacturer is giving known value in his ready-mixed ration, and that is something no hand-mixed ration based on a long-distance prescription can ever hope to do." Although the immediate response to Savage's suggestion was negative as far as the manufacturers were concerned, it heralded a new attitude among farmers toward feed manufacturers.

[4] These tables were omitted in the address as published in the June 1914 issue of *Flour and Feed*. An editorial note explained that the tables were not included "for the reason that after the discussion was ended it had been proved the tables did not give a true basis of figuring."

This was foreseen by one of the speakers on the program who good-humoredly made this prophetic observation, "It is very evident from the discussion on Professor Savage's paper that from now on, as a source of annoyance to the feed manufacturers, honors must be divided between the feed control officials and the teacher."

The immediate resistance to his proposal convinced Professor Savage that there was little reason to hope that the established feed manufacturers would adopt the "open formula" idea. Although he endeavored to find feed manufacturers who would give his plan a trial he recognized that it went against established practices and that the only real solution to the farmers' feed problem would come when the farmers themselves organized to provide themselves with the type of feed service needed. As Savage remarked many years later, "From that day on . . . I determined to do all I could to see that farmers had the opportunity to buy their feeds cooperatively."[5]

Unable to attract the interest of the commercial feed manufacturers and distributors, Savage finally persuaded the New York State Grange Purchasing Agency to try out his idea, and in 1916 this agency began to market an "open formula feed" using a formula provided by Cornell University. Adoption of the open formula idea by the Grange Purchasing Agency gave the idea wide publicity among farmers and demonstrated its practicability.

THE FEED INDUSTRY ATTACK ON COOPERATIVE BUYING

The support which the Federal and state governments and especially the county farm bureaus were trying to give cooperative purchasing was of great concern to the established feed manufacturers and distributors. This matter came to a head in May, 1916, when *Flour and Feed* published a four-page editorial under the title: "Feed Dealers Now Must Fight Uncle Sam on Direct Buying Proposition." This editorial quoted the following statement by Secretary of Agriculture Houston with deep disapproval:

The Department considers it a legitimate function of the County Agent to aid the Farmers in organizing associations for the cooperative purchase of farm commodities. The agent is expected to assist in an advisory way such associations in purchasing their farm supplies upon the best possible terms.

The editorial also complained of a letter that had been sent out in February, 1915, to county farm bureau presidents and managers by M. C. Burritt, State Director of Farm Bureaus in the State of New York. Bur-

[5] Excerpt from statement by E. S. Savage on *History of Open Formula Feeds*, October 17, 1936.

ritt had said: "Farm Bureau Managers may furnish information as to where lime, fertilizer, seeds and other supplies may be secured and if asked to do so, may quote wholesale and retail prices. . . . But the Managers should never personally take or transmit to shippers orders or money for supplies."

Flour and Feed was critical of this declared policy:

Feed dealers, manufacturers and jobbers don't care a whoop whether or not the agent actually handles the money in direct buying transactions. This is incidental to the main proposition. The trouble lies in the fact that the farm bureau man is expected to promote direct buying associations.

Maintaining that the Secretary's statement constituted a "dangerous menace to the feed dealers' business," feed dealers were urged to carry on a strong campaign to protect their interests. The editorial claimed that such a campaign a few years earlier had stopped the effectiveness of the work of the New York State Department of Agriculture in organizing cooperatives, and it proposed the same type of campaign to force a change in the policy of the United States Department of Agriculture.

During the next few months the organized feed trade waged aggressive warfare on the organizational work of the county agents. In the June issue of *Flour and Feed* an editorial entitled, "Must Plan for Big Fight," declared: "Feed dealers must not be satisfied with any halfway success in this campaign against the activities of the farm bureau managers . . . the vital point is as to whether or not the farm bureau managers still promote and help organize direct buying associations in any shape, manner or form. . . . There can be no halfway stand."

This same issue carried the annual address of the President, Roger W. Chapman, of the American Feed Manufacturers' Association. Finding promotion of cooperative buying associations to be both *"economically* and *morally"* wrong, he said:

There can be no question that these cooperative buying associations are doomed to failure just as has been the case with cooperative movements in the past. . . . There is clearly not room for all existing feed dealers and a competitor in the form of a cooperative buying association. . . . It is economically and morally wrong for the State or National Farm Bureaus to undertake to advise or assist in the formation of such associations. It will undermine established business and place nothing better in its place.

A more tolerant position was taken by *Flour and Feed* in its September, 1916, issue, in an editorial entitled, "Cure Rests with Dealer."

Despite the fact that we have been talking in heated terms of the practices of farm bureau managers in giving aid and comfort to cooperative buying enterprises organized among farmers . . . we fully recognize that the farm bureau man's effort in this connection is one of the effects rather than one of the causes of the trouble. . . . Perfect frankness and a proper recognition of the practical side of this proposition compel the statement that the chief cause for the direct and cooperative buying evil, so far as the feed industry is concerned, is to be found in the conditions that have surrounded the conduct of the retailers' business.

Although this editorial admitted that the dealers themselves, through the inefficiency of their services, encouraged direct buying by farmers, it was still felt that any measure to curb such efforts was justifiable.

The cooperative buying craze should convince every feed dealer in the country of the absolute necessity for the organization of a strong dealer's association. . . . Direct buying stabs right at the heart of the retail business and no stone should be left unturned to demonstrate its unsoundness.

Shortly after this was written the organized feed trade was placed on the defensive by the Report of the State Legislature's Wicks' Committee —which disclosed that it had gone beyond reason in its attack on cooperative buying. This official report found conditions in the feed trade so unsatisfactory that it urged farmers to protect themselves through the formation of their own buying associations.

THE REPORT OF THE WICKS' COMMITTEE

In the fall of 1916 an event occurred "which permanently altered the point of view of the entire farm population of the Northeast."[6] This was the successful milk strike of the Dairymen's League which welded into one solid block the dairy farmers of New York State. Success in this organized effort caused dairy farmers to focus their attention on ways to reduce their feed costs through cooperative action. This line of thinking was greatly stimulated by the findings of the Wicks' Committee, so called in honor of its chairman, State Senator Charles W. Wicks.

Aroused in 1916 by the struggle of the dairymen for fair prices, the Wicks' Committee had been jointly created by the Senate and Assembly of the State of New York to investigate marketing conditions for dairy products, poultry and eggs and livestock. This committee sought to determine, among other things, whether the distribution of milk and butter, eggs, poultry and livestock was "controlled by combination and monopoly of dealers and manipulation of prices. . . ."

Its carefully prepared report, transmitted on February 15, 1917, gave much encouragement to the development of cooperative marketing and purchasing organizations in New York State. It was the judgment of the committee that "cooperative agencies . . . are economic factors of great importance and should be permitted" and "legalized cooperation, publicly

[6] M. E. Campbell, *The Background and the Implications of the G.L.F. Idea,* Processed talk, (Undated), p. 3.

controlled, should be equally beneficial to producer, distributor, and consumer." The report frankly declared that "the milk industry at the present moment needs to be handled through cooperative effort."

However, the part of the report that aroused the most interest had to do with the quality of feed service then available to New York dairymen. It is doubtful whether any similar State legislative committee has ever been more outspoken in its criticism of conditions and practices found. Significant passages in this section of the report are quoted:

A wide field for fraudulent operation exists in the selling of concentrated feeding stuffs to the dairymen of this state. . . .

Many gentlemen conceived the idea that by putting on the market concentrated dairy foods of various ingredients or alleged ingredients useful for cattle feed that large profits might be made by adulterating those feeds with inferior or worthless articles. The idea was followed by prompt and effective action. The consequence has been that the dairy sections of the state were and are flooded with branded mixed dairy foods, a great number of which are shown upon analysis to contain a large amount of worthless material and are a fraud upon the dairyman who buys them. . . .

It is not going too far to assert that many thousands of dollars are yearly paid out by the dairymen of the State of New York for dirt, dust, straw and rubbish, permitted to be sold under some high-sounding name as a valuable cattle food, sure to increase the production of his dairy. An examination of the records of the Department of Agriculture and of the New York State Experiment Station leads to the conclusion that almost everything is used in these feeds, the nature of which can be successfully concealed. . . .

In the judgment of the committee it is no sufficient answer to this proposition to say that the dairymen should protect themselves from these frauds. . . . It is very doubtful if any class of men similarly situated without the effective action of the state could protect themselves.[7]

Much of the blame for the conditions described were attributed to the feed dealers associations which were singled out for special censure:

An examination of the record of these feed dealers associations discloses the most abhorrent and immoral practices, aims, and methods. . . . They sought by a system of blacklisting to frighten and terrorize all millers and wholesale dealers in grains from dealing in any way with the local grange, a co-operative society, or an individual dairyman. . . .

Naturally this made it difficult and in many instances absolutely impossible for the individual dairyman, grange or co-operative society to purchase cattle foods in the open market. In other words, this little group of men with a relatively insignificant capital sought to impose tribute on all the great dairy industry of the state of New York and made it difficult for the dairymen to do business except under their direction and control.[8]

This report could not go unanswered. Here was a challenge to arouse even the most lethargic. As H. E. Babcock remarked many years later,

---

[7] Preliminary Report of the New York Joint Legislative Committee on Dairy Products, Live-Stock and Poultry [Wicks' Report], pp. 784 ff.

[8] The same, pp. 790 ff.

"You can well imagine the reaction of the farmers of the State to such a report by a responsible legislative committee. You can also well imagine how tremendously this report increased the aggressiveness of men like Savage, County Farm Bureau Agents and other public officials who for years had been pointing out the abuses which the Committee disclosed."[9]

[9] Letter to author, July 1, 1946. J. A. McConnell, after reading this chapter, remarked: "We should not indict the entire retail feed industry of those days as if there were no community-minded citizens in it. What was lacking was research. When research findings became recognized, dealers sought leadership and many were glad to cooperate with the G.L.F." Interview, with author, June 13, 1959.

CHAPTER 4

Trial and Error

*No one thing receives so much discussion and in no one thing has
there been less accomplished than in rural cooperation. It is time
we developed a plan of true cooperation.*
S. J. LOWELL, *Master of the New York State Grange (January 1917)*

B Y SHOWING dramatically that farmers had no way of protecting themselves except through organization, the Wicks' report made organization imperative. The fact that the Dairymen's League was already in the
field as a militant champion of their rights in marketing led the farmers to
insist that it assume the responsibility of leadership in providing them with
the kind of feed service they required. In response to this pressure, President R. D. Cooper sent out a circular letter to the membership in early
1917 to get their ideas on what the League should do. The answers were
emphatic that some kind of effective Statewide feed purchasing program
be developed.

This mandate could not be ignored and President Cooper called for
assistance from H. E. Babcock, now State County Agent Leader and Secretary of the State Federation of Farm Bureaus, and from Professor E. S.
Savage, who had been most concerned with remedying the conditions so
dramatically disclosed by the Wicks' report. These men hammered out a
plan for providing feed service under the auspices of the Dairymen's
League. The plan proposed that feed of a definite quality be manufactured under contract by reputable commercial feed concerns in accordance with specifications set by Cornell University, and distributed
through approved local dealers for a fixed service charge.

Thus the success of this plan required cooperation from reliable manufacturers and local feed merchants. To work out the necessary arrangements the League officers called a conference to present the plan to interested feed manufacturers and distributors.

A report on this conference by S. T. Edwards, of the firm of Hales and
Edwards, was published in the September 1917 issue of *Flour and Feed.*
According to Mr. Edwards, "the general plans were discussed and approved by all present, the feed dealers declaring themselves glad of the
opportunity to cooperate with the League."[1] He considered the plan "a
splendid victory for mixed feeds" since it "recognized the ability of manu-

---

[1] However, the Editor observed in a note introducing the report that Mr. Edwards
was "speaking merely" for his company.

facturers of balanced rations to make . . . a better feed and at less price than could be done at home." He believed that the arrangement would benefit "manufacturers, consumers, and dealers alike," and would lead the colleges generally to give their endorsement to manufactured feeds "when balanced correctly and guaranteed to be up to a first-class standard." While Mr. Edwards admitted that there was some feeling on the part of the dealers that the commissions set by the League were low, he did not consider this a serious objection since the plan assured them "of their profits and of cash for goods sold."

With the apparent endorsement of important elements in the feed industry the League undertook to make arrangements for manufacture and local distribution. A contract was signed with Hales and Edwards, and negotiations were begun for similar contracts with other manufacturers.

In setting forth the plan in the August 1917 issue of the *Dairymen's League News*, it was pointed out that "feed bills have eaten up dairy profits" making "the average producer very despondent." While it was admitted that the League could not do everything to obtain cheaper feed, it was believed that "it can help shorten the road between producer and feeder."

It was explained that "through this plan a first-class, balanced ration for dairy cows has been developed" in cooperation with the New York State College of Agriculture. Under the plan "a number of the most reliable manufacturers" were to be selected "to manufacture feed upon this formula." Feed was to be sold "under individual brands" but the "authorization of the Dairymen's League" was to appear on every package.

The feed was to be distributed through established dealers acceptable to the local branches of the League. The names of these approved "purchasing agents" were to be forwarded to the Executive Committee which would turn them over to the authorized manufacturers. These purchasing agents were to "act as responsible representatives in handling matters of difference between the manufacturers and members of the local leagues." The plan was set forth in great detail. For example, it provided that:

1. The Dairymen's League shall establish and maintain a central feed office in connection with its central office in New York City. [This feed office] shall immediately arrange for the manufacture and sale of feeds according to formulas approved by the New York State College of Agriculture. The endorsement of the Dairymen's League shall appear upon all of the bags of all manufacturers authorized by the League. All orders for feed shall be approved and recorded in the central office. . . .

2. Feed shall be distributed by local purchasing agents, recommended by the local branches, acceptable to the manufacturer and approved by the Executive Committee of the Dairymen's League. The local purchasing agent shall solicit orders, make up the car, send in orders, collect money, pay for the car, notify members when car arrives, check out car and adjust local difficulties, etc. The

maximum price for feed shall be three dollars ($3.00) per ton above the whole-sale price at the time purchase is made.

League members in good standing were to receive the following dis-counts: $2.50 per ton was to be allowed when an entire carload was bought for one's own consumption, provided that feed was taken from the car and cash paid for it; $2 per ton was to be allowed on orders of less than carload lots where feed was taken from the car and cash was paid; $1 per ton was to be allowed provided that delivery was taken within five days after notification of car arrival and cash paid.

Without question, the plan was vulnerable as to its workability. If the League had been a strongly entrenched organization it might have been able to compel acceptance through power of boycott—but the League had no strong local organizations or strong central power. It was not a plan attractive to manufacturers or to local dealers for it was then a period of rising prices due to World War I, and dealers saw little advantage from a fixed profit margin. These difficulties might have been overcome if the cooperation anticipated from the manufacturers and feed dealers had been forthcoming.[2]

In the face of these problems, the reception of the plan was apparently all that could be asked for. The *Dairymen's League News* of September, 1917, stated that "the feed manufacturers under agreement with the Dairy-men's League are now in position to fill orders for Dairymen's League balanced ration feed as fast as their orders are received from local feed agents." Babcock at the time was optimistic. "The plan was launched at the New York State Fair at Syracuse in September. We had a big exhibit and there was a great deal of interest in the proposed service. At that time the dealers did not appear to fight it. Quite a number were named agent-buyers and a fair tonnage was shipped."[3]

The honeymoon was to be brief. Almost immediately *Flour and Feed* vociferously condemned the plan in a long editorial entitled, "Prussianizing the Feed Business," and no more effective title could be used to arouse business and public opinion against the plan for in 1917 the word "Prussian" was charged with great emotional bitterness.

This editorial charged that the scheme was "wholly atrocious and con-trary to sound economic practice." It described the plan as the "outgrowth

[2] A rumble of warning came from the *Rural New Yorker* of August 25, 1917, which anticipated difficulty in the use of local feed dealers as purchasing agents. "This may work out in some places, but in general it will be better for the League to get entirely away from the present system of distribution. . . . Working into the hands of the distributors and feed dealers is like playing with fire, and the dairymen already carry the scars of former burnings. Why not plan to do your own feed mixing."

[3] Letter to author, of July 1, 1946. The October 1917 issue of the *Dairymen's League News* reported that 300 League branches had appointed feed purchasing agents.

of all the various schemes for direct buying that have been promoted in the State of New York in recent years, with the added factor in this instance of an attempt to control the manufacture of feeds as well as to control their sale." Dealers were called upon to fight this "most brazen attempt to deliberately Prussianize a big element in our business life," and align every associated interest in opposition.

With the powerful feed trade stirred up it was impossible to make adequate local arrangements to get the plan under way. Even Hales and Edwards lost interest under threat of commercial ostracism and boycott.

Whether or not Babcock was right in believing that the New York State Retail Feed Dealers Association had "sprung a mouse-trap play" unquestionably it sabotaged the plan. According to him, most of its members when they got the feed "(1) talked it down, (2) offered other so-called better feed cheaper, or (3) hid it in the back of their warehouses."[4]

This ambitious program thus collapsed almost as soon as it was launched. Although it lingered on for several months, little mention of the plan was made after September in the *Dairymen's League News*.[5]

With the failure of its feed plan the League for a time contented itself with editorials on the advantage of open-formula feeds. However, its leadership was not willing to call the chapter closed. Professor Savage remarked in the *Dairymen's League News* one year after the inception of the plan, "During the last year the Dairymen's League Feed Formula 20 has been more or less successful. A good many tons were sold. Some even thought they liked it; others thought it unpalatable and dirty; others, including myself, thought the prices too high for the quality and character of the feed sold." To meet these objections a new formula was proposed. At least the League plan had done something to popularize the idea of an open-formula feed—and at least one manufacturer was finding that it was commercially feasible to produce and distribute feed in this way.

From this time down to 1920 the League did not actively attempt to provide feed service although it gave active support to the State Grange and State Farm Bureau Federation in their efforts to establish a workable program.

[4] H. E. Babcock, in letter to author, July 1, 1946. While Babcock admitted that the fixed margin—which limited profits on a rising market—contributed to these actions, he was positive that "the real reason the plan broke down was because the representatives of the feed manufacturers, working through the retail feed dealers, broke the plan up."

[5] Furthermore, economic conditions were becoming increasingly unfavorable for the success of a plan of this type. Feed prices and margins were steadily rising, and dealers were loath to have their margins restricted in any way. In March, 1918, dealers who had joined in the plan demanded successfully from the Food Administration that the allowed margin be increased from $3.00 to $5.00. This action in effect brought the plan to an end, although it had never achieved any promise of permanence.

FORMATION OF THE STATE GRANGE EXCHANGE

The early impulse given to cooperative purchasing by the Grange in
New York State in the 70's and 80's, which had never completely died out,
began to grow again in the early 1900's. To give it encouragement, the
Committee on Cooperation of the New York State Grange in March, 1912,
recommended:

That the New York Grange enter into a contract with some reliable parties
to conduct a business of supplying members of the Grange, through a representative selected by a subordinate or Pomona Grange, or a regularly organized
Grange "Cooperative association," with farm supplies that can be handled in car
loads on a cash basis, and to be delivered to any railroad station in the State.

A few weeks later an agreement was worked out whereby the firm of
Godfrey and Sloan, in Olean, would carry on a supply purchasing business
under the name of the New York State Grange Purchasing Agency, but
the State Grange was in no way to be financially liable for any purchase
made by Godfrey and Sloan. It is of interest that the senior partner, F. N.
Godfrey, was at this time Master of the State Grange. Thus the State
Grange Purchasing Agency was little more than a grange-endorsed private
agency—operated, however, by individuals prominent in Grange work.[6]

During the next few years the State Grange Purchasing Agency handled
a considerable quantity of supplies for local grange groups—mainly feeds,
fertilizers, flour, seeds, coal, lime, twine, fencing, and groceries. The volume of business amounted to $392,000 in 1913, and $439,000 in 1914.
Recognizing that a stronger type of organization was needed to meet most
effectively the needs of local grange members, the Committee on Cooperation and Trade recommended to the annual meeting of the New
York State Grange in February, 1913, that a committee prepare a general
plan for cooperative organization throughout the State. The plan, suggested by this Committee and approved by the Executive Committee in
August, 1913, proposed that "Cooperative Societies be organized and incorporated—under the New York Cooperative Law—in every locality producing for market any considerable quantity of farm produce, or buying
for the farm and house, feeds, fertilizers, and other supplies in considerable quantities." These local societies were to be set up with the minimum
of capital, with shares widely distributed and with provision that "all
dividends be credited on account of capital stock, and to be paid by a
stock dividend." These local societies were to be federated to form a

---

[6] In view of later developments, it is significant that H. E. Babcock's first job as
County Farm Bureau Manager in Cattaraugus County, brought him into close contact
with the Grange purchasing activities of Godfrey and Sloan in Olean. Godfrey was
at this time President of the Cattaraugus County Farm Bureau. See Campbell, *Op.
Cit.*, p. 2.

central selling and buying organization, and all dividends were to be credited to the local societies in accordance with "the volume of business done by them through the central organization."

As this ambitious cooperative program would have supplanted the State Grange Purchasing Agency which then had the support of influential grange leaders, it could not be put into effect.

The ineffectiveness of the State Grange Purchasing Agency was emphasized in late 1916 by the success of the Dairymen's League milk strike, and in early 1917 by the disclosures of the Wicks' Committee. Just at this time a special committee of the Grange found that the State Grange Purchasing Agency was taking an excessive profit in handling flour, and the support of the Grange was withdrawn.

The time was ripe for action and S. J. Lowell, Master of the New York State Grange, focused attention on the problem in his address at the Annual Meeting in January, 1917.

No one thing receives so much discussion and in no one thing has there been less accomplished than in real cooperation. It is time we developed a plan of true cooperation. Our purchasing agency has done some good work, but it is time this valuable factor were enlarged and brought into a full plan of cooperative buying, and later selling for every Grange member who desires to become one of its members. I am firmly convinced that the time has gone by for talking only, and that action must be taken. . . . It is OUR duty. . . . I rely on your calm deliberation over this subject at this session.

Later in the meeting a resolution presented by the Committee on Cooperation proposed the formation of a stock company, "to give to the members of the Grange such purchasing power as will supply the members with their supplies desired direct from the manufacturer at the lowest price possible." Consideration of this resolution led to the appointment of a committee to take the whole matter under consideration and report back to the next Annual Meeting.

This Committee, after much careful study and several meetings, presented its report to the Executive Committee on September 2, 1917, since it was felt by the Committee members that "the time is opportune for starting such an enterprise . . . without unnecessary delay."

The Committee unanimously recommended "the organization of a limited liability stock corporation . . . to be known as the New York Grange Exchange." This organization would have a capital stock of $100,000, "divided into small ($10) shares fully paid and nonassessable." The ownership of this stock was to be limited to members of the Grange, subordinate granges, Pomona granges, and the state grange. The Grange Exchange was to have power to engage in and conduct a general mercantile and manufacturing business. It was to be governed by a board of nine directors elected by the stockholders. Business was to be conducted on a "strictly cash basis and as close a margin as is possible consistent with prudent business foresight." Dividends on stock were to be limited to 6 percent and any further profits were to be divided among members "in proportion to their registered purchases or sales." Goods were to be sold at open prices to the general public as well as to members of the Grange.

The plan, as outlined, was unanimously approved at the next annual meeting of the Grange in February, 1918, and after several months of organization work, business offices were established at Syracuse under the management of Richard Hall.

Although the New York Grange Exchange was very much a "Grange affair" this was not a serious drawback since a large percentage of New York farmers were then active in grange work. The emerging county farm bureau organizations at this time were of the opinion that the Grange Exchange could facilitate their own efforts in promoting cooperative purchasing by serving as a central purchasing agency, especially for seed. Moreover, at this time the Dairymen's League was somewhat disillusioned by its efforts to establish its own feed buying plan and it saw in the Grange plan possibilities for serving the Dairymen's League members. Thus, the *Dairymen's League News* in describing the new plan (October 1918) said, "It is in reality the first State-wide opportunity offered the farmers for the purchase and sale of their farm supplies and products . . . under their own control."

The objectives of the new organization were set forth as follows by the newly designated manager, Richard Hall, in November, 1918.

The "purpose of the New York State Grange Exchange is to furnish the farmers of New York State all kinds of farm implements, feed, fertilizers, farm and garden seeds, and general house supplies." It was also to undertake marketing operations "when well established."

Hall pointed out that the new organization would not supplant any "cooperative association of farmers in the state that is doing legitimate work for the benefit of all the farmers of the state; rather it is the intent and purpose to concentrate the business of these small cooperative organizations whenever possible making the exchange a sort of clearing house or bureau for all; and the exchange proposes to work in harmony with them and hopes to give them a new impetus."

In brief, the exchange was to be "a bureau of concentration." The manager pointed out that "this is really the first state-wide effort that has ever been attempted to affiliate the various agricultural interests." The exchange proposed "to proceed step by step with the utmost conservatism," with the idea of laying "at least the foundation for the building up of an organization that would eventually have the full confidence of the people at large, not only the producers but consumers as well."

We have already seen that the Farm Bureau Better Seed Committees welcomed the opportunity to use the newly formed State Grange Exchange as a central source of seed supply. Therefore, as soon as the Grange Exchange was formed an arrangement was made to meet their pooled requirements. In general, the program gave satisfaction although Mr. Babcock recalled how he as Secretary of the New York State Farm Bureau Federation headed a group of county agents at the State Grange sessions in 1919 "who more or less put Richard Hall on the carpet because of what we thought was unsatisfactory cooperation and service to our Better Seed Committees."[7]

However, the New York Grange Exchange was handicapped from the beginning by lack of funds, for its initial paid-in capital amounted to only $3,000, not nearly enough for its ambitious objectives. With its capital so limited it could operate only as a broker. In the beginning it simply bought supplies to cover orders from its members, assembled mostly through the local granges. The only way it could obtain merchandise was to have it shipped with a sight draft bill of lading. Even so, the Grange Exchange had some success in obtaining supplies from a number of reputable concerns. Of particular interest was an arrangement under which a reputable feed manufacturer furnished an open-formula feed put out under the name "Grange Exchange Dairy Ration." This arrangement lasted only a few months for as soon as the feed began to gain popularity the manufacturer was boycotted by retail feed dealers, and he could not jeopardize his business for the small volume taken by Grangers. While the Grange Exchange was able to obtain feed from other sources, it was not sold on open-formula.

Although the Exchange was able to contract for a supply of fertilizer which it sold under its own "Star Brand," it was compelled to deal as a broker and sell at regular prices. The only savings possible were in the dealers' commissions, except for an allowance made by the fertilizer company for the sales service of the manager. To make matters worse, the fertilizer companies undersold the Grange Exchange by allowing farmers $1.50 or $2.00 a ton for fictitious warehousing service.

An attempt was made to handle farm machinery but supplies could not be obtained from any well-known company.

Notwithstanding such difficulties in arranging for sources of supply, the volume of business steadily expanded. The feeling of many farmers toward the venture was well expressed in an editorial in the *Dairymen's League News* in March, 1919, "We must support the Grange Exchange." This editorial declared:

As might be expected, it [the Grange Exchange] is meeting with bitter op-

---

[7] H. E. Babcock, *The G.L.F. Idea*, June 21, 1937. Mr. Babcock also recalled that he served as a member of a committee of three which was appointed by the Board of Directors to audit the records of the Grange Exchange.

position from dealers and others. We understand that many of the wholesale feed dealers are refusing to sell feed to this farmers' organization. This is simply a revival of what the organized feed dealers have tried to do before; that is, to make it impossible for farmers to buy grain or obtain supplies cooperatively. The fact remains, however, that it is impossible for the dealers to succeed, providing the farmers stand by themselves, that is, by organization. Not only every granger, but every farmer in New York State should get solidly back of the New York State Exchange and stay back of it.

In reporting back to the Annual Session of the New York State Grange in February, 1920, the General Manager reviewed the experience of the Exchange for its first full year of operations. In view of the difficulties encountered in getting started he was proud of the business volume for 1919 which totaled $529,694.

The manager held that "the principle of live cooperation among the farmers has triumphed in spite of bitter opposition by way of price cutting —indirect boycotts and the protected territory granted by some manufacturers and large distributors to certain dealers and brokers."

In reviewing the difficulties in obtaining feed for sale under open-formula brands the manager pointed out "we will not be able to give first-class service until we do our own milling, going direct to the farmers' elevators of the West for our supply of grain."

While it had so far been "impossible to break through the protected territory surrounding some lines such as farm machinery, coal and other supplies closely held in the monopoly of big financial interests," he hoped that a supply of farm machinery could be obtained during the forthcoming year. Pointing out that a good healthy start had been made he called for more financial support since "work of this kind cannot succeed without a large working capital. . . ." He held that "it is imperative that each one of you assume the financial responsibility of assisting us to put across the campaign to raise our entire capitalization of $100,000. . . ." Up to this time stock sales had totaled only $26,000.

Although the State Grange Exchange had begun to establish itself by early 1920, it was appreciated by many that a broader based organization was needed to attract the full support of all New York farmers. It was becoming clear that only a strong, well-financed, and well-supported organization could give them the type of statewide purchasing service called for by the times.

CHAPTER 5

The G.L.F. Emerges, 1918-20

The new movement has the approval and backing of every large farm organization, but it is one thing to talk about fine theories of co-operation on paper, and another thing to go down into our little old jeans and bring out the real cash to set the wheels in motion.
Dairymen's League News, June 10, 1920

T HE PRESSURE OF EVENTS was gradually forcing the various farm organizations of New York State to work together on common problems. The Dairymen's League needed the support of the Grange and the Farm Bureau on milk marketing and feed buying plans; the Grange was finding that its cooperative marketing and purchasing efforts could not be restricted to Grange members and be effective and the State Federation of Farm Bureau Associations, in view of its partial support by State and Federal funds as an educational agency, required the backing of all farmers, regardless of their other affiliations.

Although these state-wide organizations of farmers had much in common prior to 1918 there had been little coordination of effort. In fact, "it had become an established technique in New York State for legislative leaders to line up one farm organization against another and then say to farmers, "We can't give you any legislation because you aren't agreed as to what you want."[1]

COORDINATION THROUGH THE CONFERENCE BOARD

Although the need for some kind of coordinating center had long been obvious, it took a direct problem to bring one into being. In the winter of 1918 John J. Dillon, publisher of the *Rural New Yorker*—disgruntled by the unwillingness of existing organizations to accept his leadership—undertook "to establish an organization to be known as 'The New York Federation of Agriculture,' which would supersede all other farm organizations" in the state.[2] This aroused the existing state organizations into action and led to an informal meeting of their leaders in New York City.[3]

[1] H. E. Babcock, "The G.L.F. Idea" 1937.
[2] The same.
[3] According to Babcock, Dillon's scheme thoroughly alarmed the State Grange, which up to that time had insisted on "playing a lone hand. . . . Two of us, Ed Eastman and I, were quick to sense that resentment of the Grange toward Dillon gave us just the break we needed to bring the farm organizations of the state together." [Letter

At this meeting it was decided to form a conference board of farm organizations which subsequently became known as the New York State Agricultural Conference Board. The original members were the New York State Grange, The Dairymen's League, Inc., The New York State Federation of County Farm Bureau Associations, and the New York State Horticultural Society.[4]

As the primary objective of the Conference Board was to promote the common interests of its member organizations it was agreed that the Board would "speak for its members only when they were unanimous in their opinions."

During the next two years the Conference Board integrated the support of the various farm organizations on many problems of common concern. As we shall see later in this chapter, it was this body—rather than its constituent member organizations—which actually established the Cooperative Grange League Federation Exchange in 1920.[5]

ENCOURAGEMENT FROM STATE AGENCIES

Cooperative development in New York State was furthered, too, by the spirit of agricultural solidarity which came with World War I. The higher prices resulting from war inflation served as an inducement for organization. Large profits were being taken by marketing agencies on products marketed or on supplies distributed, and the services of such agencies were frequently unsatisfactory. It became fairly easy to form

---

to author, July 1, 1946.] Mr. E. R. Eastman, who was the first Secretary of the Conference Board, recalls how this first meeting was sponsored by the Dairymen's League. "I think I was largely responsible for the formation of the New York State Conference Board of Farm Organizations. At that time I was editor of the *Dairymen's League News*, and manager of their field operations. The League was still having all sorts of troubles with the dealers, and with all the newer problems of trying to market milk. As a result, I suggested to R. D. Cooper, then President of the League, that the milk marketing problem was everybody's job as well as that of the League, and the other organizations should share some of the responsibility. I suggested that we invite the other organizations to join in a conference to discuss current milk problems. R. D. approved, and I remember I wrote letters to various farm leaders in the state. We met in the old Murray Hill Hotel, New York City, and as a result of that preliminary conference the Conference Board of Farm Organizations was organized, and I acted as its secretary for several years." (Letter to author, of July 18, 1949.) See also E. R. Eastman, *Walking the Broad Highway*, pp. 92-93.

[4] The first meeting of record was held on May 25, 1918, under the name, "Joint Conference of the Agricultural Organizations of the State of New York." No minutes were kept of the early meetings because they were on a "superconfidential basis." (Letter, to author, from H. E. Babcock, July 1, 1946.)

[5] "It was the Conference Board which voted . . . to set up the G.L.F. and which named its incorporators." Babcock, "The G.L.F. Idea." Perhaps of equal importance, it was this body that knit the farm leadership of the State together into a team which could function as an entity.

cooperatives to correct such conditions and assure farmers of considerable savings.

By this time the State was served by a federated network of county farm bureaus closely related to the State College through Extension Service workers and county agricultural agents. Thus, the agricultural educational machinery of the State was geared to assist farmers in organizing and operating cooperative associations.[6]

In 1918 the work of the State Bureau of Co-operative Associations was invigorated by the enactment of a state law which provided for the incorporation of membership cooperative associations. This was carefully drawn by J. D. Miller, attorney for the Dairymen's League, assisted by Seward A. Miller, attorney for the Council of Farms and Markets, and it followed general lines advised by the Bureau of Markets, U. S. Department of Agriculture. It was drawn to conform with requirements of the Clayton Amendment to the Sherman Law, which allowed farmers to act together in non-stock cooperative associations and carry out their "legitimate objects" without the associations as such being held to be illegal combinations or conspiracies in restraint of trade.[7] Under the provisions of this law this Bureau, directed by Charles R. White, began actively to assist groups of farmers to establish cooperative associations. In September, 1918, the Bureau set forth its program:

The Bureau of Cooperative Associations will endeavor to apply to the farming industry of the state, those principles of cooperation that mark successful business operations of today. Instead of buying implements, livestock, seed, or fertilizers as an individual, and instead of trying to market his produce himself, the farmer will be induced to buy and sell cooperatively and collectively.

In New York State there exist numerous associations of one kind or another. The Bureau of Cooperative Associations will make a complete register of the organizations of this character operating in the State, study the weak points of those that are not progressing as they should, and give such aid and advice as may be necessary to put them on the road to success.

The Bureau will make a general survey of the state to determine where cooperative organizations are most needed or where the community is most ready for the introduction of this method of operation; to advise and aid such communities in organizing associations with suitable articles of incorporation and bylaws, and under efficient management; to assist in the installation of simple but adequate systems of bookkeeping and accounting; and in general, to afford advisory supervision and helpful cooperation to all organizations of this character in the state.[8]

The November issue of *Foods and Markets* was devoted entirely to

[6] It should be realized also that the United States Department of Agriculture was backing up the work of the State agencies and agricultural colleges by encouraging the development of cooperative marketing and purchasing.

[7] *Foods and Markets*, published by Division of Foods and Markets of New York State Department of Farms and Markets, November, 1918, (Volume 1, Number 3).

[8] *Foods and Markets*, Vol. 1, No. 1, p. 14.

"Cooperative Marketing." It listed 34 cooperative associations as having been organized and incorporated by the Bureau of Co-operative Associations since July. Apparently such rapid promotion of new associations was looked upon with some alarm, for Eugene H. Porter, the Commissioner of Foods and Markets, said at this time: "I have directed that for the present the bureau shall devote its attention to the consolidation of its work, and the strengthening of the associations already formed."

The Bureau of Cooperative Associations worked closely with the County Farm Bureaus. The initiative in forming cooperatives was usually taken by the farmers working through their local farm bureaus, while the Bureau of Cooperative Associations, and to some extent, the state agricultural colleges, provided technical assistance.[9]

Working together, the State college, the county farm bureaus, and the Bureau of Cooperative Associations contributed to a rapid advancement of agricultural cooperation in the years from mid-1918 to mid-1920 when the G.L.F. was coming into being. In this period several hundred local marketing and cooperative purchasing associations were formed and assisted. In *Foods and Markets*, for November 1920, the Bureau of Co-operative Associations reported: "Growth of cooperative marketing activities in this State has reached such a point that it requires the constant effort of the Bureau of Cooperative Associations to meet demands and properly direct the work." In the *Dairymen's League News* for January 25, 1921, H. E. Babcock recognized that the rapid development of co-operatives in New York State had been made possible by "the favorable attitude taken by the New York State government as shown by its legislative acts and by the work of its Department of Farms and Markets and its State College of Agriculture."

[9] In the March-April 1920 issue of *Foods and Markets* H. E. Babcock, then Director of Farm Bureaus, pointed out that "The position of the farm bureaus relative to the cooperative movement of the state should be an exceedingly modest one. . . . As I see the farm bureau system, it is simply a machine for doing things. I do not regard it as a machine for planning things. I assume that the planning is going to be done by the farmers themselves with the counsel of the specialists employed by the public institutions." In this same issue, Professor M. C. Burritt, then Director of Extension Service, pointed out how the various state agencies collaborated in helping farmers with their problems. In brief, he held that the college should foster research and education, the farm bureau development; and the Bureau of Cooperative Associations technical assistance in organization and operation. He defined the "primary function" of each agency as follows: "The primary function of the college is the gathering and distribution of agricultural information and the giving of instruction in fundamental agricultural principles. . . . The primary function of the farm bureaus is to assist in the preliminary organization and to give subsequent assistance in the development of the organization until it is firmly established. . . . The primary function of the [Bureau of Cooperative Associations] is the organization and supervision of the organizations formed under the laws of the state which come under the jurisdiction of their Department."

Formation of the G.L.F.

In February, 1920, shortly after the annual meeting of the Grange Exchange, W. L. Bean, the newly-elected president, called upon H. E. Babcock, then secretary of the New York State Federation of Farm Bureau Associations, to enlist his support for a plan designed to make the New York Grange Exchange a state-wide purchasing association for all farmers in New York State—whether or not grangers. Bean expressed the view that "the Grange Exchange was underfinanced, lacked the cooperation of farmers generally because of its close affiliation with the grange, and that the only solution . . . was to expand the organization so that it would have the support of farm organizations."[10]

Babcock was not immediately impressed with the soundness of the proposal. "I found so many holes in the plan that I talked him out of it and also thoroughly convinced myself of the folly of any such idea."[11] However, Babcock's "cold water" did not discourage Bean. In fact, it stimulated him to develop his idea more realistically with the enthusiastic assistance of Waldo G. Morse, attorney for the Grange Exchange.

Although the revised plan did not entirely convince Babcock, he saw its possibilities and agreed to call up the proposal for discussion at the spring meeting of the Agricultural Conference Board.

Before this meeting was held, however, an event occurred which made Babcock an earnest advocate of the plan. This event, unimportant in itself but symptomatic of a general condition, demonstrated that only a strong organization of farmers could protect farmers' interests.

At this time a "so-called cooperative" in Ithaca, New York, the Tompkins County Farmers Company, decided to handle spray materials. It was soon found that no responsible spray material manufacturer was willing to serve the farmers' association because it was "a cooperative." In this predicament the Tompkins County Farmers Company turned to Babcock for help, since he was secretary of the State Federation of Farm Bureaus. Babcock soon found that there was nothing that he or his organization could do to force manufacturers to recognize the right of a cooperative to serve the business needs of its members. In Babcock's words, "This situation swung me over completely and one hundred percent back of Bean's idea."[12]

The real beginning of the Cooperative Grange League Federation Exchange thus came at a meeting of the Conference Board in the Yates Hotel, Syracuse, on April 28, 1920. After Bean's proposal was carefully

[10] H. E. Babcock, "The G.L.F. Idea" 1937.
[11] The same.
[12] The same.

considered a decision was made by the farm organizations represented to form a state-wide purchasing cooperative designed to attract the support of all farmers in New York State.

To the credit of the participants, it was decided that the proposed organization would be on a large scale and formed in a manner that would insure the harmonious support of the sponsoring organizations. The imagination and foresight of the group was displayed in three vital decisions.

1. It was agreed that the authorized capital would be set at $1,000,000. A gasp went around the room when Mr. R. D. Cooper, then President of the Dairymen's League, moved that the authorized capital be set at this figure rather than the $500,000 which had been informally agreed upon. However, his prestige, and that of the organization he represented, carried the motion. This "bold stroke" served notice that the organization was to be "no piddling affair."

2. It was agreed that the new organization would be named the Cooperative Grange League Federation Exchange, a name which would show that the new organization had behind it the New York State *Grange*, the Dairymen's *League*, Inc., and the New York State *Federation* of Farm Bureau Associations. This name, which embraced the popular names of the three parent organizations, was to weld them together in support of a common enterprise. Although the name was awkward this seemed a small price to pay for the good will exerted.

No one seems to know who gave the G.L.F. its name. Someone suggested that part of the name of each organization be included in the name selected and this led to the adoption of the name, Cooperative Grange League Federation Exchange. The abbreviation, G.L.F., was also fortuitous. As a natural nickname it soon took hold.

3. It was agreed that responsibility for raising the capital required would be vested in H. E. Babcock, who had resigned in April as State County Agent Leader. He was given *carte blanche* to devise such plans as he might deem necessary. This decision could not have been bettered, for Babcock was a natural organizing genius. No one knew so well the rank and file of New York farmers nor had such a firm grip on their confidence. Given a free hand, Babcock would employ his unique gift of leadership without restraint.[13]

---

[13] Babcock, then 31, had been working closely with Burritt for the past five years in organizing the County Agent and Farm Bureau Systems in New York State, and they had taken a prominent part in setting up the American Farm Bureau Federation which was formed but a month earlier. (March 3-4, 1920). They combined the scholarly, serious-minded, dignified qualities of Mr. Burritt with the creative imagination and earnestness of Babcock. Both were hard workers. They drove themselves more severely than any who worked for them. See L. R. Simonds. *New York State's Contribution to the Organization and Development of the County Agent—Farm Bureau Movement*, Cornell Extension Bulletin 993, (1957) p. 15. M. C. Burritt recalls how Babcock was "a master at conferring with farmers and their committees, on laying

With these decisions made, the Grange Exchange was able to work out a plan acceptable to its stockholders for turning over its assets to the proposed new organization, and steps could be taken for drafting the organization papers for the Cooperative Grange League Federation Exchange.

The legal work involved was done largely by Waldo G. Morse, attorney for the New York Grange Exchange, in consultation with "Judge" John D. Miller, General Counsel for the Dairymen's League, Inc.[14] Many problems arose in getting the charter accepted in view of the fact that the Cooperative Grange League Federation Exchange, Inc., was the first cooperative to be formed under Article III of the Business Corporations Law. No one in the office of the Secretary of State had any precedent to follow and, moreover, Morse had woven into the certificate many novel provisions. "Among other things, the Secretary of State objected to writing into the charter the provisions for nominating directors from the Grange, the League and Farm Bureau Federation. In fact . . . the burden of proof was on Mr. Morse to justify practically the entire charter."[15]

The next important step in the formation of the G.L.F. came on May 25, when a meeting was held at Syracuse to launch the organization formally. At this meeting, which was attended by three representatives each from the State Grange, the Dairymen's League, and the Federation of Farm Bureaus, who had been selected to serve as initial directors, the G.L.F. was tentatively organized with W. L. Bean, President; Raymond C. Hitchings, Vice-President; H. E. Babcock, Secretary; and Arthur Smith, Treasurer.

Although the organization was not yet incorporated, Babcock was tentatively employed as campaign manager for the month of June at a salary of $1,000, to sell the 200,000 shares of stock at $5 a share. He accepted this job in the enthusiasm of the moment, but he soon found that he had "a bear by the tail." It was typical of Babcock to challenge himself with what appeared to be an impossible task.[16]

---

the groundwork in counties and in getting things done." Letter to author, September 1958.

[14] Mr. Morse (1859-1934), "the legal architect of the G.L.F., was a leading corporation lawyer in New York City who found both stimulus and relaxation in agricultural interests. The formation of the G.L.F. challenged both his creative imagination and fine intellect." Letter from Harold Greenwald, his colleague, to author, August 13, 1951. "Judge" John D. Miller, (1856-1946), a prominent figure in the creation of the Dairymen's League, and major draftsman of the Capper-Volstead [Cooperative] Act of 1922, was for many years President of the National Council of Farmer Cooperatives.

[15] "Principles, Legal and Otherwise, Underlying the G.L.F." Lecture given by Sherman Peer, General Counsel of the Cooperative Grange League Federation Exchange, Inc., G.L.F. School for Directors, April 12, 1939. See also Waldo G. Morse, "Legal Powers of the G.L.F.," *G.L.F. Shareholder*, January, 1929.

[16] Babcock at this time had an unannounced understanding with Dr. George F. Warren that he would join the staff of Cornell University as Professor of Marketing

Babcock lost no time in getting the campaign under way. He first called by long distance some 50 key farm leaders in the various counties of the state and got their assurance of support. With the top floor of an old office building in Syracuse for campaign headquarters, he then officially launched the stock-selling campaign with a big banquet in Syracuse.

Under his vigorous, determined and skillful direction, stock-selling campaigns were conducted in each community under the supervision of county committees comprised of the masters of county granges, the presidents of county farm bureaus, and the presidents of county branches of the Dairymen's League. County quotas were set up by the State campaign office, and stock was sold either for cash or with a definite arrangement for payment. Supported by effective publicity which blanketed the farming areas of the State, the campaign caught hold immediately and gave assurance that the capital essential for putting into effect the ambitious program contemplated would be forthcoming.[17]

The spirit with which the campaign was launched is shown by an article in the *Dairymen's League News* of June 10, 1920, entitled, "All Farmers Unite in Launching New Cooperative Exchange." This article, no doubt the work of Babcock, declared: "The beginning of the new farmers' exchange to be known as the Cooperative Grange League Federation Exchange, or the G.L.F. Exchange, for short, marks a new day in American farm affairs." It pointed out that "the State Grange Exchange was not large enough and did not have capital enough to serve the immense business that must be handled in order to get real results." The fact was stressed that the new organization had the full support of the agricultural leadership of New York State. "Great care has been taken . . . to get men on the board of directors who are bona-fide farmers and who at the same time have had the best experience and knowledge of cooperative affairs."

The article also emphasized that the G.L.F. was organized on the "correct cooperative principle of one-man one-vote. . . . No small clique can secure control." While it was admitted that plans for service could not be completed until policies were determined by the stockholders and the board of directors, it was believed that possibilities "were almost un-

---

in the fall. According to legend, Babcock, when offered the job, said that he didn't know much about the subject, while Warren rejoined by saying: "That's good. The buggy maker held back the development of the automobile for a fifth of a century." See Ruby Green Smith, *The People's Colleges*, Cornell University Press, 1949, p. 104.

[17] While historical accounts indicate that some 36,000 farmers bought shares with a value of $878,000 during the campaign, the financial records of the G.L.F. indicate that only $612,531 was paid in by December 31, 1921, and not more than $650,000 was eventually realized from this first stock-selling campaign. However, this magnificent achievement should not be minimized. Nothing like it had been done in the past. Moreover, the campaign created a personal interest on the part of leading farmers in every county to see the G.L.F. succeed.

limited." Both direct and indirect benefits were looked for, "the direct benefit being the actual saving made by each farmer . . . and the indirect benefit the effect this tremendous cooperative enterprise will have on other companies doing business with farmers."

"The biggest field" for the G.L.F. Exchange was expected to be in "the feed business," where "investigations have been made and conferences have been held looking toward the buying or renting of a great feed mill." Plans were being made "to send agents into the West to purchase grain direct from farmers cooperatives, bring that grain East to a mill controlled by the Exchange, grind it and sell it directly to farmers, saving the benefits that have heretofore been made by the dealers." Stress was also placed on the great opportunities which the G.L.F. would have in rendering seed and fertilizer service.

The article closed with the following paragraph which focused attention on the responsibility which farmers would have to assume if the plan was to be carried to success:

If the new company succeeds it cannot do business on a penny-ante shoe string capital. . . . During the last week of June a campaign will be put on to give every farmer an opportunity to test his spirit of cooperation. The size of the shares is made low purposely, so that no farmer has any excuse for refusing to take at least one share, to cost him $5.00. Few farmers should refuse to take less than twenty shares. . . . We should remember that it is an investment in the greatest business in the world, that of agriculture . . . an investment in our confidence in the greatest people in the world, our brother farmers.

The next meeting of the pre-organization board of directors was held on June 5. At this meeting the term of each director was settled by lot, and headquarters were established at Syracuse. Babcock reported on plans for the stock-selling campaign, and the arrangements made for publicity through the *Dairymen's League News,* the *American Agriculturist,* the *Rural New Yorker,* and the various county issues of the *Farm Bureau News.*

Although the problem of getting the organization established with adequate capital was of first importance, attention was directed simultaneously to a plan for inaugurating business service. When the board met on June 10, Professor Savage raised this question: "For this year's work would it not be best to lay particular stress upon the development of the selling end by establishing district warehouses and local retail stores with a set jobbing feed business to keep these warehouses filled and the retail stores going?" As a step toward deciding this question, Savage was requested to make a quick study of the merchandising practices of several large feed manufacturers.

Though the G.L.F. was practically formed, its legal birth occurred on June 22, 1920, when it received its Certificate of Incorporation. The incorporators were listed as follows: Frank W. Howe; William L. Bean; Niles F. Webb; Richard Hall; H. Edward Babcock; Raymond C. Hitchings; and Robert L. Speed. The nine directors who had tentatively organized on May 25 were listed as the directors for the first year and grouped according to their sponsoring organizations. (1) New York State Grange Order of Patrons of Industry; William L. Bean, Sherman J. Lowell, and Raymond C. Hitchings; (2) Dairymen's League Cooperative Association Inc.; Niles F. Webb, Harry Bull, and John C. Griffith; (3) New York State Federation of County Farm Bureau Associations; H. Edward Babcock, Arthur L. Smith, and Harry L. Brown.

The first official meeting of the board of directors was held on June 28, 1920, at the Yates Hotel in Syracuse.

With organization perfected it was now possible to acquire legally the business of the New York Grange Exchange in accordance with terms that had been agreed upon. In brief, the Cooperative Grange League Federation Exchange, Inc., took over the property, business and good will of the Grange Exchange by issuing to the New York Grange Exchange shares of its capital stock having a par value of $31,480, which the Grange Exchange transferred to its own stockholders in proportion to their stock holdings. In addition, the G.L.F. paid $750 in cash to be used for payment of 75 shares in the Grange Exchange which did not consent to the substitution.

The completion of these actions made the Cooperative Grange League Federation Exchange, Inc., a going concern.

II. ESTABLISHING THE IDEA, 1920-1930

CHAPTER 6

Inauguration of Business Service

Most businesses are a result of slow growth. In the case of the G.L.F. the board was faced with the complicated problem of organizing a large business all at once.

WHITON POWELL, *in "The Story of the G.L.F." (1933)*

WITH GREAT EXPECTATIONS being aroused by the stock-selling campaign, then in full swing, no time could be lost in establishing business facilities and procedures for the new organization. Professor Whiton Powell has well described the immense responsibility this imposed on the first G.L.F. board of directors:

Most businesses are a result of slow growth. In the case of the G.L.F. the board was faced with the complicated problem of organizing a large business all at once, together with the imperious demand that it be set up and ready to function almost immediately. Instead of having gradually acquired manufacturing and distributing facilities . . . this board had to obtain mills and warehouses . . .on short notice. Instead of gradually building up satisfactory relations with all the various concerns from which it must buy goods or services, it had to establish such relationships almost overnight. Instead of having gradually built up a network of smoothly functioning retail representatives, it had to bring into being an entire new system of retail distribution of farm supplies. Instead of slowly accumulating a staff of employees, each accustomed to his duties and to working with the others, it had to gather from where it might the necessary men to operate the organization. That this task was in some manner accomplished is a tribute to the courage and good judgment of the men to whom the task was entrusted.[1]

Professor Savage, having completed the study requested by the Board of Directors, was now ready to recommend a plan of operation. In his report to the Board of Directors on June 28, 1920, Savage concluded: "The first thing to do to make the distribution of feeds successful would be the proper organization of local feed stores which carry a stock of feed the year around, this feed to be purchased through the Cooperative Grange League Federation Exchange." He recommended that "these stores be fairly well standardized so far as their stock of feeds is concerned [and] owned locally by the farmers in the community [with] each local organization . . . [owning] stock in the parent exchange." It was his view that savings made either by the stores or by the G.L.F. would be divided among the shareholders proportional to their business. Writing in the *Dairymen's League News* of June 25, Savage had al-

[1] See "The Story of the G.L.F.," Cornell Farm Study Course (about 1933).

ready declared that "The G.L.F. Exchange must keep in mind that it has service to render. To me this means that the Exchange must see to it that bonafide stores are established in the country to give real service with stock on hand at all times of year and an appreciation of the purchase of goods by farmers, just the same as any store in the country existing as a proprietary store gives service and appreciates purchases."

Although Savage's recommendations were favorably received they could not be put into effect until a dependable supply of feed was available. Moreover, it was evident that the problem of organizing local cooperative feed services to meet the needs of farmer members was formidable.

Savage recognized these facts in an article in the July 10 issue of the *Dairymen's League News*. While he held that the ideal arrangement would be "the organization of retail stores in many communities to distribute feed and other commodities wanted in large quantities through the parent exchange," he admitted that "something [might] be done in the way of direct buying by individuals and groups of individuals" until these stores could be organized.

During this period the energies of the directors were largely devoted to the establishment of business service, as the stock-selling campaign was coming along smoothly. Babcock reported in the *Dairymen's League News* of July 25, that many counties were reporting daily on the success of the campaign and that about half of the counties had met their quotas. The campaign, however, was not all fair sailing. In two counties local farm leaders were effectively opposing the plan. Throughout the State "enemies of cooperation" were busy spreading the charge that "the New York Grange Exchange was a colossal failure, and that the new Exchange was organized to take it over and cover up the deficit." Babcock branded this statement "a malicious lie" as proved by the audit of certified public accountants available upon request. At about this time (July 24) an editorial in the *Rural New Yorker* declared:

The campaign in New York for putting over [the] big cooperative company has proved a great thing for the State organizations. . . . The time has long since passed when farmers can safely stand back and work as individuals. They must combine all their forces. This drive for a big co-operative exchange has united the Grange, Farm Bureaus and Dairymen's League for effective team work. We asked a man who was connected with this movement how these organizations compared. He said, after some thought, that the *Grange might be said to provide the sentiment*, the *Farm Bureau the organizing workers*, and the *League the fighters*. It is only natural that men and women should group themselves into the organization which best represents their nature and thought. Sentiment, organizing power and fighting! We need them all in the battle for common rights which lies ahead of us. We cannot win with either quality alone, or with any combination of two of them. We must have them all if we would win. The sentiment makes the mortar which binds individuals together, organizing power groups them to the best advantage, and fighting spirit gives them power.

In the pressure for results the board was determined not to be stampeded into premature decisions and was agreed on the need of making haste slowly. The burden of developing operating plans was largely delegated to the executive committee, comprised of W. L. Bean, President, Raymond Hitchings, Vice President, Arthur L. Smith, Treasurer, and H. E. Babcock, Secretary. On July 6 the following resolution was carried: "That the general policy of developing the corporation for the present under the direct management of the executive committee be continued."

The board at this time authorized this committee to buy a warehouse in Syracuse for $25,000 to serve as a feed depot. It established, under the direction of the Executive Committee, a commercial department to be managed by Richard Hall, the former manager of the Grange Exchange, and an educational department to be directed by the Secretary, H. E. Babcock.[2]

A policy of quoting two prices on feed was adopted at this time, "one to be its *warehouse price* to be made only to community representatives certified by county committees who furnish warehouse facilities and carry stocks of goods to serve the community; another to be its *car-door* price to be quoted to any farmer or groups of farmers." To encourage the development of local warehouse service it was declared to be "the policy of this cooperative to assist county committees in the organization of cooperative groups in communities where they are needed in order to get satisfactory service," and a committee of two, Messrs. Webb and Babcock, was asked to submit recommendations for putting this policy into effect.

As the primary concern of the G.L.F. was to get its feed service immediately established, little special attention was devoted to the improvement of services taken over from the Grange Exchange on fertilizer and other supplies which could be distributed from the Syracuse warehouse.

In an article in the *Dairyman's League News* of August 10, 1920, entitled, "G.L.F. Exchange is Now a Going Concern," Babcock summarized progress as of July 31:

Let me remind you that three months ago today the farmers of this State had no common project, no unity of interest; that two months ago today work was just begun on the articles of incorporation of the biggest farmers' cooperative company in the United States; that one month ago but $30,000 had been raised; and, finally, that today, July 31, 1920, the farmers of New York State stand advertised to the world that they can get together on a single project in

[2] Before Babcock joined the staff of Cornell University as Professor of Marketing on September 1, he persuaded E. C. "Curry" Weatherby to serve as Assistant Secretary and take over his educational and organizational work. Weatherby, with fine county agent experience and missionary zeal, was well suited for this job.

size worthy of the Empire State, that they can finance it, and that this company . . . can get on its feet and operate. . . .

Babcock also said:

I personally took hold of this proposition because my long experience as county agent leader had taught me the need of some such farmer-controlled and farmer-owned buying and selling agency to give service as a wholesaler to local cooperatives. I also felt that the time had come in June 1920 when such a company could be financed, if ever.

This last sentence was prophetic, for the post-war depression was just around the corner.

By this time stock subscriptions had been turned in for about $250,000, of which about $50,000 was in cash and the rest in obligated funds. It was believed that most of the 200,000 authorized shares would be placed as most of the county committees had not yet reported subscriptions. The directors had already adopted a plan for local organization under which, as soon as counties met their stock quotas, the G.L.F. would send a representative to meet with the County Exchange Committee to make definite plans for providing services.

The G.L.F. was gradually getting ready to give an effective service on feed. Grain was already being stored in the Syracuse warehouse purchased on July 10, and feed mill equipment had been ordered. Also, plans were under way to acquire a feed mill at Buffalo to serve farmers in western New York.

In his "G.L.F. Exchange Notes" for August 25, Mr. Babcock reported that the announced sales policy had been well received. The Exchange had taken "the right position in setting out to establish a system of permanent warehouse connections" and all indications pointed to "a rapid development of cooperatively owned or controlled warehouses."

In view of the fact that few cooperatives were in position to offer warehouse service, there was a demand for some plan that would permit the G.L.F. to give immediate service through private dealers. This problem was resolved by the Executive Committee on August 30. The Exchange agreed to "recognize established dealers . . . when the farmers served by those dealers . . . formed a cooperative association and entered into a contract with the dealers defining the service" to be performed for them. Under this plan the G.L.F. would "execute a contract with the cooperative association, thus provided with the dealer's services." The Executive Committee held that in this way, "the Exchange can develop without disturbing existing business organizations, [and] farmers can secure the services of local dealers, [while] . . . the cooperative control of farmers will be steadily increased."

Recognizing the need for a system of cooperative local distribution agencies the Executive Committee of the G.L.F., on the recommendation of Babcock, set up at this time a Field Organization department to help farmers form local cooperatives which would either perform warehouse service or enter into contracts with local dealers for such service. It was believed that the initiative for establishing local cooperatives should come from the farmers themselves and that assistance in organization should be provided only upon request.

With arrangements temporarily made with respect to sales and distribution policies the Board of Directors directed its attention to problems of management, internal organization, and provision of operating facilities. On August 23 the Executive Committee set up a feed department and employed Mr. Berend Burns, a Buffalo feed merchant, and friend of Director Arthur L. Smith, as manager.

The importance attached to this position is indicated by the fact that Mr. Burns was paid a salary of $15,000, while the Manager of the Commercial Department was paid but $5,000.

Soon afterward, on September 16, the Board authorized the buying of facilities for storage and feed manufacture at Buffalo. It was many months before this mill could be operated. In the haste to get started, it was bought at a high price and it didn't even have a siding. Although the initial cost was $110,000, subsequent improvements greatly raised this figure. In the meantime the G.L.F. obtained feed for its members through other concerns.

In the *Dairymen's League News* of September 10, Babcock explained how the Organization and Commercial Departments would work. E. C. Weatherby, as Manager of the Organization Department, would have charge of all matters relating to stock; the development of county exchange committees, agents and distributing agencies; the arrangement and scheduling of field work; and all publicity and advertising. Richard Hall, as Manager of the Commercial Department, would be in charge of all business operations. He was to be assisted by Berend Burns, manager of the Feed Division, and by E. C. Gardinier, Manager of the Traffic Division.

At this time Babcock reported that stock subscriptions totaled $456,640, of which $97,600 were in cash.

The *Dairymen's League News* of October 10, 1920, reported that the G.L.F. had acquired a large elevator with capacity of approximately 400,000 bushels, and a building on adjoining land which could be operated as a feed mill as soon as equipment could be installed. This mill was designed to supply as much as fifty cars of mixed feed a day. It was then intended to move all straight car shipments from Buffalo, and use the Syracuse warehouse largely for making mixed car shipments within its trade territory.

Experience in these early operations demonstrated that the G.L.F.'s form of organization did not provide enough operating flexibility. The State law under which it was chartered required that real estate mortgages and sales be approved by a majority of the stockholders, and it was not practicable to call a stockholders meeting whenever a real estate problem arose. Moreover, the G.L.F., as an organization, could not issue warehouse receipts on commodities stored, and this handicapped it in using capital to greatest advantage. Although the G.L.F. was desperately in need of working capital, it could not use its credit.

It was clear to General Counsel Waldo Morse that this problem called for the organization of a subsidiary warehouse corporation, and on October 22, the Board authorized him to develop plans for the Producers' Warehouse and Elevator Company, chartered under the Business Corporation Law on December 18, 1920.

The Exchange soon transferred its real estate, leases, fixtures and plants to the subsidiary in return for shares of stock. "The G.L.F. then had its facilities lodged in a wholly-owned subsidiary which the Board of Directors of the Exchange . . . could manage effectively and use to assist in financing Exchange operations by use of warehouse receipts."[3]

Thus, by the end of 1920 the G.L.F. had at least got started as a real business organization. Although its record of service up to that date was not impressive, it was beginning to get its services on feed, seed and fertilizer established. Its volume for the first six months was only $914,520 —or only double that done by the Grange Exchange, $454,830, during the preceding six months. But slow development was not unfortunate for the post-war agricultural depression had set in and feed and other prices were steadily falling. A larger volume at this time would probably have resulted in substantial losses from inventory holdings.

The plan of business organization—except for the formation of the Producers' Warehouse and Elevator Company—still differed little from that of the old State Grange Exchange. The principal change had been the establishment of the two coordinate general departments to carry on business and organizational affairs, and a feed department to provide specialized services on feed. Otherwise, except for seed, the methods of the old Grange Exchange were little modified.

The seed operations were amplified by the availability of the Syracuse warehouse for assembly and storage. As in the past, the "Better Seed Committees" pooled their orders so that supplies could be obtained from Michigan and other seed-producing regions. The successful operation of the seed pool brought credit to the new organization.

During this first six months the G.L.F. was really managed by the Executive Committee with Babcock as Secretary furnishing much of the vision, planning and drive for organization and service. The Executive

[3] Sherman Peer "G.L.F. Digest" p. 8.

Committee and many of the Directors gave a large part of their time to meetings and organizational work in their home communities. It is significant that the Executive Committee met 19 times though the full Board met only 5 times in this period.

In getting the plans of the organization under way the Executive Committee was largely dependent upon cash supplied through sales of stock. This served as a damper on grandiose dreams and encouraged careful use of available funds. Although the amount of stock subscriptions by the year end totaled $683,460, only $163,365 in cash had been received from the sale of stock. In November the G.L.F. was compelled to borrow $20,000 from the Syracuse Trust Company to meet current expenses. It was indeed fortunate that the G.L.F. stock-selling campaign was completed before farmers began to feel the full effect of the growing post-war agricultural depression.

With the organization established, Babcock in January gave up his membership on the Board of Directors and resigned as Secretary. He could not remain active in G.L.F. and also serve as Professor of Marketing at Cornell. However, as professor, he could continue his close contacts with the officers, board members, and operating personnel. His unofficial position as consultant also gave him an exceptional opportunity to influence the course of G.L.F. development without involving him in responsibility for management decisions and train himself for management of the G.L.F. should this contingency arise.[4]

Optimism at the end of the first six months was still high. This was evidenced at the annual meeting held in Utica on January 31, 1921, as a forerunner of the Convention of the New York State Grange. The *Dairymen's League News* of February 10, 1921, reported that "fully 500 farmers attended the inspiring session," and heard a "masterly address" by Professor George F. Warren, who said, "The New York College of Agriculture is interested in cooperation because it is interested in the fundamental welfare of all the people of the State."

Manager Hall declared there had been a saving of over $200,000 . . . besides many thousands more as a result of the influence which the Exchange exerted in lowering prices charged by dealers.[5] He also said:

---

[4] His college class in cooperative marketing gave him a working laboratory for trying out his ideas. He organized the students into dummy boards of directors for various cooperatives, arranged field contacts for them, and reviewed their recommendations. B. H. Staplin, who was on the "G.L.F. Board" in the spring of 1922, recalls the interest in better local distribution. Babcock later recruited several who had been students for G.L.F. work. Letter, to author, February 9, 1951.

[5] There was some justification for this statement. An article in the *Rural New Yorker* of January 22, signed "Dairyman," stated that "In our community retail feed dealers have lagged far behind wholesale reductions. . . . Up to a short time ago we were paying $70 a ton for oilmeal at retail. When the G.L.F. delivered price quotation of our section was $46, a few neighbors . . . got in a couple of cars of this G.L.F. Exchange feed and immediately local prices took a tumble."

"We believe that the Exchange is in excellent condition financially."

The more sober account of this meeting in the *Rural New Yorker* of February 19 stated that the meeting was "a good one 'full of pep and interest.'" However, this article revealed that the net loss for the year, 1920, was actually $10,543, largely from a decline in inventory values. It challenged the assertion of Mr. Hall that the Exchange had saved the farmers of New York State "at least $200,000" by saying: "It would, of course, be impossible to prove any such statement by actual figures."

While the article admitted that the Exchange represented "the largest and most successful attempt to cooperate on the part of New York farmers yet attempted" it cautioned, "The things for them to do are to decline to get a case of the 'Big Head' and to remember just what cooperation means."

CHAPTER 7

The Testing Period

The confidence of the farmers in G.L.F. has been shaken and they look to the Board of Directors to see that a degree of efficiency to insure success be maintained.
Report of JAY CORYELL *to Board of Directors, May 27, 1921*

DURING ITS FIRST SIX MONTHS the G.L.F. enjoyed the promise of a new organization. It was a time of projection—when plans were enthusiastically made with little appreciation of the difficulties involved in their execution. The testing period was to come in 1921 after the first flush of novelty was spent and the post-war agricultural depression had made itself felt.

THE PROBLEM OF LOCAL DISTRIBUTION

In early 1921 it was believed that the feed mill under construction at Buffalo would soon be able to supply the needs of G.L.F. members. Attention was thus directed to the problem of providing a system of local distribution. Here the problem was acute, as dealers were doing an effective job of obstructing the G.L.F. at the local points.

It was then believed that the best method for local distribution would be through independent cooperative associations formed and financed by the G.L.F. members in communities to be served. While the creation of such associations was being encouraged, the G.L.F. relied on the car-door method of distribution through groups of farmers who pooled orders and took delivery at the car door—the method employed by the State Grange Exchange. Although this was looked upon only as a stop-gap measure, it was the natural method for local distribution during this period while the G.L.F. was becoming established.

The progress of setting up local cooperatives to serve as distributing outlets was slow, for it largely depended upon local initiative. Even if the G.L.F. had desired to assist in the organization and financing of such local enterprises it could not do so because of limited personnel and financial strength. To set up a local association a considerable amount of capital was required and with the decline in agricultural prices farmers were less able and willing to invest in such enterprises.[1]

---

[1] The Executive Committee on December 30, 1920, authorized the employment of T. B. Clausen, Schenectady County Farm Bureau Manager, to work under Mr. Weatherby in organizing, signing up, and supervising local distributing agencies.

The G.L.F., therefore, endeavored to turn over the actual work of organizing local associations to the Agricultural Extension Service and the Division of Cooperation of the State Department of Farms and Markets. In January, 1921, the minutes indicate that the Board of Directors empowered Curry Weatherby—Assistant Secretary and head of the Organization Department—to draw up a memorandum of understanding with the State Department of Farms and Markets under which the latter would assist groups of farmers to form cooperative associations upon the request of the G.L.F. Exchange. This work, directed by Webster J. Birdsall, served an important function and also helped train a number of competent cooperative managers.[2] While this arrangement led to the formation of a number of associations, it was not possible to form them rapidly enough to serve the needs of the thousands of farmers who were looking to the G.L.F. for their supplies.[3]

The confusion which then existed as to how best to proceed is indicated in an article by Babcock in the *Dairymen's League News* of March 21, 1921, entitled: "How do you Want to Buy Your Farm Supplies?" After considering the advantages and disadvantages of using the local private feed dealers as distributing outlets for a state-wide organization of the G.L.F. type, Babcock said, "The arguments are especially pertinent in view of the very large present development of cooperative stores that are being put into the field to take advantage of such wholesale buying service as is furnished by the G.L.F. Exchange." Babcock pointed out that, "a very warm discussion, not untinged with bitterness and local prejudice, is being carried on in practically every farming community with regard to the best method for distributing farm supplies in local communities."

Apparently the problem was whether farmers should rely on local dealers for distribution or attempt to set up their own system through the formation of cooperative associations. Babcock did not offer a positive recommendation. He concluded by saying: "This article was never intended to get anywhere. It is simply written to get some more people thinking on a very perplexing problem."

Evidently the G.L.F. was losing confidence in the promotion of local cooperatives. Confronted with the practical problems involved in establishing wholesale service it was beginning to show more interest in distribution through those dealers who were friendly to its aspirations and who could relieve it of local distributing problems. For example, the directors on March 4, 1921, modified the sales policy of quoting a car-door price of $1 higher than the warehouse price by providing for quotation of one uniform price. Provision was made, however, for discounts "to local

[2] Interview with Curry Weatherby, June 17, 1951.
[3] The *Rural New Yorker* of February 19, 1921, reported that "contracts for 21 cooperative warehouses have been made, with 24 others on the way."

cooperative associations maintaining and operating efficient warehouses appointed by the Exchange to cooperate in its business."

On April 20 Weatherby reported to the Board that he had not been promoting actively the establishment of cooperative associations as it was difficult to assure them of good service. The Board, in commending this policy, said: "There is no use in promoting new sales agencies when we cannot give good service to those we have."

With the decline of interest in forming local distributing cooperatives the G.L.F. placed more reliance on distribution through car-door pooling groups and friendly local dealers. However, the G.L.F. did not actively promote distribution through local dealers until the summer of 1922, after Babcock took command of the G.L.F. as General Manager.[4]

THE PROBLEM OF FEED SERVICE

The rapid decline in feed prices which came in the summer and fall of 1920 taught the G.L.F. an expensive lesson. Inexperienced in the feed business at that time the Board of Directors had relied heavily on the judgment of Berend Burns, Manager of the Feed Department, who had built up large inventories of grain which could not be sold except at heavy loss. Moreover, he had encouraged the Board to invest heavily in costly feed milling equipment which was not adapted to the needs of the young organization.[5] Seeing that the situation could not go on, the Board, on April 11, discharged Mr. Burns and in his stead employed Mr. F. A. McLellan, a man experienced in feed manufacture and distribution and also a strong supporter of the cooperative way for handling feed.[6] This was an important decision for, in the words of Curry Weatherby, "McLellan brought to the G.L.F. the first glint of business thinking, and he knew how to get business cooperation."[7]

During the early months of 1921 the G.L.F. Board had been looking

[4] "The principal forms of distribution for the G.L.F. in its early years were Grange purchasing agents and farmer-members who became car-door distributors, also a few local cooperative associations." Letter of H. E. Babcock, February 22, 1950.

[5] According to H. E. Babcock, Mr. Burns "was trained in the grain trade, knew nothing about feeds. He was speculatively inclined also. Because he knew nothing about feed manufacture, he led the G.L.F. Board into the purchase of a totally unsuitable plant for that purpose. . . . He also loaded the organization up on grain while prices were declining rapidly. The net result was that he completely lost the confidence of everyone. . . ." Letter, to author, of February 22, 1950.

[6] Mr. McLellan had long been an advocate of the open formula method of feed distribution as promoted by Professor Savage. When the feed department was first set up, Professor Savage had urged the selection of McLellan as Manager. Mr. Babcock recalls "sitting in on the meeting at which it was decided to hire Mac. The main proponent of this action was Professor E. S. Savage. He had so convinced me of G.L.F.'s need for Mac that I threw my weight behind the deal also." Letter of February 22, 1950. Both Babcock and Savage were Cornell professors at this time.

[7] Interview June 17, 1951.

forward to the completion of its feed mill at Buffalo. It was therefore a heavy blow to morale when the feed plant was severely crippled by fire on April 14, before it could be placed in operation. The fire not only postponed the time when the G.L.F. could manufacture feed to meet its own requirements—one of the major objectives of the organization—but more importantly it destroyed the storage elevator upon which the G.L.F. was dependent as a depot for assembling, storing, and distributing feed. As the actual damage was only about half covered by insurance, the seriousness of the blow was compounded by this loss of storage and operating facilities.

While the fire was considered a calamity at the time, it soon proved to be a blessing in disguise in that it led to a commercial arrangement, worked out by McLellan, under which the American Milling Company provided an adequate supply of satisfactory feed. This made possible the rapid expansion of feed volume, reduced the burden of capital charges and freed the energies of management for the consideration of other important problems.

The Problem of Management

Little managerial discretion was permitted the Manager of the Commercial Department during the first year. In fact, the important feed operations were outside his jurisdiction, while the head of the Organization Department, who was largely in charge of local distribution, was an employee of equal rank. Under these circumstances, the Manager of the Commercial Department was little more than an office boy for the Executive Committee and the Board of Directors.

An important change occurred, however, in the composition of the Board of Directors and Executive Committee at the start of 1921. W. L. Bean, who had served as president, resigned and his place was taken by M. F. Webb. There was a great difference in the two men. Although Mr. Bean was conscientious in his duties, his horizon was limited by his Grange background to car-door operations.[8] Mr. Webb, a man of "unquestioned integrity and good judgment and courageous though not bold," to use the words of M. C. Burritt, brought to the G.L.F. "a steadying force." Without his firm hand at the controls it is doubtful whether the G.L.F. would have weathered the storms immediately ahead.

Another important change in the Board came with Babcock's resignation in January and his replacement, at Babcock's suggestion, by Fred

---

[8] "The great contribution of Mr. Bean was in aligning the Grange in support of the G.L.F. His initial leadership enabled the G.L.F. to get started." Interview with J. A. McConnell, July 19, 1958.

Porter, who was later to replace Mr. Webb as President. Porter brought to the Board practical business and legislative experience, a broad outlook, and a capacity to gain the support of farmers and business leaders. His selection gave prestige to the Board for it was a feather in the cap of G.L.F. to get a man of his standing to join it.[9]

The minutes of the Board of Directors' meeting of April 26, 1921, disclose the weaknesses in management at that time. There was no correlation of effort in selling methods, as evidenced by a complaint from Weatherby, head of the Organization Department, that "Mr. Oles goes out to sell fertilizer; Mr. Thompson, lime; and Mr. Rosenkrans, silos. Each works as he thinks best, and independently of the others. . . ."[10] Weatherby attributed "many of the mistakes" being made to the fact that "the Board of Directors does not make definite enough policies." He was answered by one of the directors who maintained that "It is each man's obligation to make out a plan of work and present it to the Board for their action."

The procedure being followed was illustrated at this same meeting. The Board was asked whether a garage should be built for the G.L.F. truck. The following resolution was unanimously passed: "That Mr. Hitchings [who also was a Director] be instructed to build a suitable garage for the truck as cheaply as possible."

Advice was also sought from the Board on methods that should be employed in selling goods from the warehouse—where part of the difficulty was attributed to "sending out price lists for goods we do not have." To meet this problem the Board appointed a committee of three of its members "to consult with Mr. Hall relative to an efficient method of handling these sales."

It is apparent from the foregoing that the Board was beginning to realize that full authority for management would need to be placed in an executive officer who would work under the Board's general, but not detailed, direction.

The weakness of G.L.F. management was again emphasized one month later, May 27, when Jay Coryell, the State Leader of County Agricultural Agents, reported to the Board of Directors on the standing of the G.L.F. in rural areas of the State. Coryell found "no compliments, but plenty of criticisms." The impact of his report is shown by the minutes of this Board meeting. "The summary shows that the situation is serious. The confidence of the farmers in G.L.F. has been shaken and they look to the Board of Directors to see that a degree of efficiency to insure success be maintained."

[9] Comment of J. A. McConnell, to author, July 7, 1958.
[10] The Board immediately passed a resolution "that Mr. Hall (the Manager of the Commercial Department) be called in and a plan be worked with him for the following of these salesmen," but it was decided that there was not enough time for this at the present meeting.

As a first step toward correcting this situation the Board immediately discharged the Manager of the Commercial Department and entrusted its affairs to the certified public accountant who had audited its books.[11] As will be seen later, it was a case of jumping from the frying pan into the fire.

ACCOMPLISHMENTS IN THE FIRST YEAR

When the G.L.F. came to the end of its second six-month period of operation, on June 30, results had failed to reach expectations. However, in spite of its many weaknesses as a business organization it was beginning to demonstrate power. During the first six months total sales amounted to only $911,981. In the second six months sales expanded to $2,423,314. These sales were divided as follows:

	First six months 7-1-20 to 12-31-20	Second six months 1-1-21 to 6-30-21	First year 7-1-20 to 6-30-21
Feed	$708,701	$1,771,739	$2,480,440
Fertilizer	37,887	229,037	266,924
Seed	10,285	345,242	355,527
Supplies	155,108	77,296	232,404
Total	911,981	2,423,314	3,335,295

The carry-over experience of the Grange Exchange was reflected in the type of supplies sold,—especially in the item of groceries—as here listed for their historical interest.

	First six months	Second six months	First year
Twine	$73,065	$38,543	$111,608
Groceries	58,994	5,617	64,611
Silos	17,645	231	17,876
Spray materials	518	23,436	23,954
Coal	605	738	1,343
Paints	1,559	1,895	3,454
Baskets	—	2,741	2,741
Harnesses	—	885	885
Miscellaneous	2,722	3,210	5,932
Total	155,108	77,296	232,404

The feed sales were handled from the Buffalo Office, while the other

[11] Mr. Hall, the Manager of the Commercial Department, was largely a victim of circumstances in that he had been given more responsibility than authority. He was, however, limited in his experience and it was felt that he was not equipped by training or temperament to manage a large organization of the type being planned.

supplies were distributed from Syracuse, the old location of the Grange Exchange.

The weak financial condition of the organization at that time is shown by its condensed balance sheet as of June 30, 1921.[12]

ASSETS

Current Assets

Cash	$ 40,870.18	
Stock Certificates at Banks and on hand	205,295.20	
Accounts Receivable	77,072.05	
Notes, Advances and Acceptances Receivable	28,291.94	
Advances on Purchases	26,349.61	
Inventories	79,598.99	
Total Current Assets		$457,477.97

Fixed Assets

Land, Buildings and Equipment-Cost	$264,505.41	
Less: Allowance for Depreciation	323.87	$264,181.54
Deferred Charges		57,535.34
Total Assets		$779,194.85

LIABILITIES, CAPITAL STOCK AND PATRONS' EQUITY

Current Liabilities

Accounts and Advances Payable	$ 20,887.14	
Notes Payable	42,500.00	
Notes Receivable Discounted	1,500.00	
Accrued Liabilities	1,900.00	
Total Current Liabilities		$ 66,787.14

Capital Stock and Patrons' Equity

Capital Stock—Issued	$553,004.80		
Subscriptions	205,295.20	758,300.00	
Undistributed Margins		45,892.29*	
Total Capital Stock & Patrons' Equity			$712,407.71
Total Liabilities, Capital Stock and Patrons' Equity			$779,194.85

* Denotes Red Figure.

It will be noted that over 40 percent of the "Current Assets" represented "Stock Certificates;" that about one third of the "Total Assets" represented investment in "Fixed Assets;" that "Deferred Charges," largely organiza-

[12] As revised by Will E. Morgan, Chief Reports Accountant of the G.L.F. This balance sheet differs slightly from the balance sheet issued in the *Dairymen's League News* of August 10, 1921 (p. 10). "Reclassifications account in part for the differences. Apparently, audit adjustments were made subsequent to the preparation of the published balance sheet, as indicated by an increase in the deficit from $35,346.96 to $45,892.29." Letter of W. E. Morgan, February 4, 1958.

tional expenses, amounted to $57,535.34; and that the admitted deficit stood at $45,892.29.

At the end of the first year the G.L.F. had several accomplishments to its credit. For example:

1. It had taken over and developed an efficient system for handling seed on a pool basis through the seed committees.
2. It had encouraged the formation of several cooperative warehouses for local distribution.
3. It had found out how to use the Producers' Warehouse and Elevator Company to obtain flexibility in financial operations.
4. It had found an efficient and successful way of getting G.L.F. feed into a community through its deal with the American Milling Company.

On the other hand, two serious weaknesses had begun to show up:

1. The dual system of management with actual control largely vested in the Board of Directors was not achieving organizational harmony or decisive administration.
2. The organization was beginning to realize that it was short of working capital and the trained manpower required to do the large jobs expected of it.

Thus the G.L.F. began its second year in a chastened mood. Most of the initial capital subscribed had been used for organization expense or had been tied up in fixed assets, with the result that capital for working purposes had to be borrowed increasingly. Moreover, the collapse of initial enthusiasm, with the abrupt fall in farm prices, and the poor showing to date reflected in an operating deficit, was making it almost impossible to sell more stock. These conditions had forced the Board to reduce all unnecessary expenditures while trying to increase efficiency. A more dynamic approach was needed.

CHAPTER 8

The Managerial Crisis

With the coming of more department heads selected to conduct special lines of business, different viewpoints have developed until the Exchange, as an organization, seems to be in some danger of individualism. . . . Someone must be arbitrator in case of differences of opinion, and this one should be the manager.

Report of Special Board Committee, June 22, 1922

IN THE FIRST MONTHS of its second year, however, conditions quickly went from bad to worse for the accountant acting as manager soon proved so totally inadequate that he had to be discharged.[1] In view of his effective work in the organization department, his energy and high ideals, the Board in October, appointed T. B. Clausen Acting General Manager with full authority over all departments.

Prior to Clausen's appointment, the G.L.F. had undertaken to buy for farmers almost anything they might require. It gradually became apparent to the Board of Directors that this policy, if persisted in, would make the G.L.F. but a mercantile agency, little different from its competitors.

At this time the brightest spot in the operations of the G.L.F. was the feed department, under the management of F. A. McLellan. He was steadily expanding sales volume under the plan which he had worked out with the American Milling Company. This experience showed the desirability of specialization in handling a major commodity, and led the G.L.F. to the conclusion that other major commodities, particularly seed and fertilizer, should be handled through specialized departments.

Clausen expressed this new line of thinking in an article in the November 1921 issue of the *Dairymen's League News* which carried this title, "What are the G.L.F.'s Plans?"

As far as the original plan is concerned, there will be no change except for this: Instead of the Syracuse office handling practically all the commodities that a farmer needs, it will tie itself up to the handling of six or seven commodities for which there is a great demand, and will put those commodities into various departments, grouping some of the commodities where possible. In charge of these departments we mean to place men who are *specialists* in the lines that they are handling. . . . I am fully convinced that with the specialists in charge of the various departments and with the supervision of correct costs and accounting, your Exchange can give you the service in the commodities that it handles, which you have so much desired.

[1] See Ruby Green Smith, *The People's Colleges*, p. 105.

I am submitting this plan to you . . . I am pledging our strict adherence to it, and I am furthermore stating that this Exchange will handle as expeditiously and efficiently as possible all orders and correspondence for our agents and friends.

Under Clausen's enthusiastic leadership progress was rapid. By the end of the year a Seed Department was set up, with A. L. Bibbins, Agronomist from Michigan Agricultural College, as Manager, and getting a man of such recognized competence gave standing to the G.L.F. Shortly afterward a new department was set up for fertilizers and spraying materials under W. L. Gay, a graduate of New Jersey State Agricultural College, with excellent sales and brokerage experience in handling fertilizer.

It appeared that the G.L.F. was at last becoming well organized and staffed. The Board was gaining competence with experience, and a number of employees were beginning to show real ability. Moreover, local distribution methods were giving more satisfaction. Weatherby reported in the *Dairymen's League News* of January 13, 1922, that it was the policy of the Exchange "to establish local warehouses and community agents as fast as possible. The local agencies should handle all the orders of the communities. We therefore recommend ordering through the agent instead of direct, unless there is no agent." The January 27 *News* reported that some "70 local cooperative associations have been established to manage local warehouses so the G.L.F. service will be permanent."

Significantly, at this time, Weatherby began issuing the *Warehousemen's Weekly News Letter* to provide warehousemen with current information on G.L.F. progress and advice from the department heads.[2]

Evidence was also accumulating that the G.L.F. was gaining in financial strength. This is reflected in an article by President Webb in the *Dairymen's League News* for February 17, 1922, in which he reviewed the reports presented at the second annual meeting.

Webb was not daunted by an operating deficit of nearly $24,000 for the year just closed which made it impossible to declare a dividend on stock for, as he pointed out, "Many well-established businesses have been forced to pass up dividends during this very trying year. . . It is evident from the bylaws that the directors have neither a legal nor moral right to declare any dividend whatever." He felt that the record was not bad when one took into consideration the developmental expenses involved in getting a statewide organization established, the general decline in values, and the loss from the fire at the Buffalo mill.

The basic objective of the Exchange remained unchanged—"the estab-

[2] In July, 1922, the name was changed to *Warehouse Managers' Weekly News Letter,* and its function was defined as follows: "Issued to furnish managers of local warehouses accurate market information and ideas for increasing the sale of G.L.F. goods." The last copy known to the author was issued November 11, 1922.

lishment of an organization that will unite the farms of this state into a business corporation in order that they may receive the advantage accruing from volume of merchandise handled." Farmers were urged to develop local service facilities to tie in with the services from the central G.L.F. However, Webb emphasized that: "It is not the intention of the Exchange to disturb the well-established distributive agencies of the State. Our policies are constructive and not destructive."

Pointing out that the Board of Directors had tried to be conservative, he promised that service would be confined to feed, fertilizer, seed, and a few related supplies until these departments were operating efficiently. He closed by saying: "It would appear that permanent success depends upon three essentials—quality, service and a reasonable price."

While sales of $1,248,028 for the last half of the year were down, as compared with the first half, they were higher than for the comparable period of the preceding year. Sales for the 6 months ending December 31, 1921, had been divided as follows:

Feed	$1,092,193
Fertilizer	42,427
Seed	5,190
Supplies	108,218

The change of emphasis was reflected in the composition of "supplies" sold. The two largest items sold were coal, $77,997, and twine, $21,413. Grocery sales fell to $559.

Prior to 1922 the G.L.F. was an idea groping for fulfillment. During the early months of 1922 it seemed that operations were at last under control. Then a set of unique circumstances brought on a managerial crisis which in turn led to the provision of strong management and the eventual establishment of the G.L.F. as a permanent cooperative institution.

With an operating profit of $19,000 for the first quarter, optimism was high. On April 26, Acting Manager Clausen proudly reported to the Board of Directors that the preceding four months had represented a period of "very constructive building." He continued:

We have not only picked men and placed them at the heads of the various departments but we have been going through the first shaking throes of having those men accustomed to business and business administration place their fingers on our weak spots and help us remedy them. We are pulling an organization, which has been groping around in the clouds, down to earth. . . . It is an exceptional fact to notice how marvelously well the farmers of New York State have rallied around their organization and have staged one of the greatest comebacks which I believe most of us have ever seen.

Clausen's full report indicated that the feed, seed, and fertilizer departments were becoming well organized, and that progress was being made in handling miscellaneous supplies. His major recommendation was that "the entire organization be departmentalized with each department with a budget, head, and a program, and with employees responsible to the head of the department."

Progress, however, was more apparent than real. In encouraging initiative, Clausen, as Acting General Manager, had gradually yielded almost full autonomy over operations to the department managers. This weakened the respect of the department heads toward the Manager to the extent that it threatened to destroy the unity of the organization as a whole. In fact, the department heads had already become so independent that they resented even Clausen's nominal authority.

This situation reached a crisis in May, when the department managers overplayed their hand and presented to the Board, without Clausen's prior knowledge, a plan for completely reorganizing the management of the G.L.F. This plan proposed to abolish the office of General Manager and to place management direction in a cabinet of department heads which was to report to the President of the Board of Directors. In justification of their plan the department heads said: "We are of the opinion that the Exchange must be more efficiently and economically operated."

As the seriousness of this revolt within the organization could not be ignored, a special committee of three Board members—A. L. Smith, Harry Bull, and G. A. Kirkland—was charged with the responsibility of examining the plan proposed by the department managers and recommending a course of action. The report of this committee, which was submitted on June 22, is one of the priceless documents of the G.L.F. for it cleared the ground for permanent growth.

The report of this committee is here quoted in some detail in view of its importance as a statement which shows how the principles essential to the successful administration of a large cooperative organization were becoming recognized.

With the coming of more department heads selected to conduct special lines of business, different viewpoints have developed until the Exchange, as an organization, seems to be in some danger of individualism. The peculiar nature of the Exchange as a cooperative body makes it necessary to take into consideration certain viewpoints, which may sometimes diverge from the usually accepted commercial policy and so it has seemed wise to have someone as manager to correlate the energies of the department heads and keep a proper balance between the commercial and cooperative lines.

Any man acting in the capacity of manager of such an organization, in order to succeed, must have the absolute confidence and cooperation of his department heads as well as the loyal support of the officers and Boards of Directors in his efforts to carry out the policies upon which they have determined. . . . Someone must be the arbitrator in case of differences of opinion and this one should be the manager, subject always to the Board of Directors which must be the court of last resort and final adjudication.

Your committee believes that it was a breach of business etiquette as well as good judgment for the commodity men to go over the head of the acting manager and without his knowledge propose such sweeping change in organization and policy. Such improprieties, if persisted in, would disintegrate the organization and destroy the morale of the office. . . .

The plan of reorganization as recommended by the commodity heads provided for the elimination of the central authority vested by resolutions of this Board and provided for in the bylaws of this organization. As a substitute they propose a business cabinet composed of commodity heads responsible to the president upon whom they have heaped such a multiplicity of duties and detail that any man occupying that position . . . would be unable properly to supervise the operations of the Exchange. Moreover, your committee believes that it would not be in accord with good business or parliamentary policies for the president to exercise the authority . . . ordinarily delegated to a general manager since in controversies on the board of directors affecting the propriety of some features of managerial execution the president would have a right to pass by ballot upon his own acts.

As a safety valve against radicalism which might develop with any department head, a general manager with broad vision, true perspective, and large executive ability should be employed to correlate the activities of the several departments. . . . Your committee wishes to state that this recommendation is [offered] . . . as a buffer and bulwark against contingencies which might arise in the future life of the Exchange. This Exchange is not being built for a year or a decade, but we hope for a century, and if this Board can set up the properly constituted authority . . . which shall endure and become as permanent as the constitutional authority which governs our national life, it will not have worked in vain.

Attention was then called to the fact that Clausen had been "given the position of acting manager pending the finding . . . of a general manager with qualifications of the type approved by this Board . . . Mr. Clausen has put his best service to work and has very materially helped to tide over a period very important in the life of the Exchange."

The report closed with these words: "Your committee believes it can suggest a man for general manager whom the board will approve and who will bring confidence both from the field as well as from financial centers."

Following the unanimous adoption of this report, H. E. Babcock, the *man* referred to, was offered the position of General Manager, which he accepted as of July 1, 1922.[3]

[3] When the report was submitted it was already understood that Babcock would accept the position. In fact, the report to a large extent represented Babcock's thinking as he served as principal adviser to the committee. Mr. Babcock gave me the following account of the circumstances which led him to accept this responsibility. "After I resigned as Director and Secretary of the G.L.F. Board [January 1921], I kept in very close touch with the organization through Fred Porter . . . through Mr. Webb with whom I was very close, and through Ted Clausen, who, when he was [acting] general manager, made a practice of coming over to Ithaca practically every week. From time to time these men and others urged me to come back into the organization. Three men, however, were responsible for my decision to do so. One was Harry Bull . . . [who] became the leading proponent on the Board to get me

back. He was a member of a special committee appointed to find a general manager. The second man was Professor G. F. Warren, head of the department of Farm Management at Cornell, in which I had accepted the professorship of marketing. Warren had great influence with me and told me that perhaps I owed it to the farmers of the state to see if I couldn't pull G.L.F. out of the hole. The third man was F. A. McLellan. When he accepted the management of the feed department I felt that his character and knowledge gave G.L.F. a chance to build a successful feed service." *Letter of February 22, 1950.* One other factor should be added—Mr. Babcock's high sense of personal responsibility. "Why, I felt that I really had to take the job was because I knew that it was the last thing I could do to make good with the thousands of farmers who had invested cash and high hopes in G.L.F." *The G.L.F. Idea,* October 1937 (an address to G.L.F. employees).

CHAPTER 9

Babcock to the Rescue

During this period I began to first appreciate the greatness of Ed Babcock. Never do I remember a time when he asked us to do a job that he himself would not do. If he found he was wrong, no matter whether it was a minor point or of great importance, he was a big enough man to acknowledge the fact at once and correct the error.
OBE SHELDEN, *Pioneer G.L.F. Fieldman.*
Letter to author, July 16, 1951.

WHEN BABCOCK assumed the direction of the G.L.F. on July 1, 1922, it had lost much of its original momentum. After starting out to acquire mills and other facilities, the G.L.F. had found that the costs were greater than its resources. As an alternative it had turned for supplies to a large milling company which it served as a jobber's agent. Likewise, it had found that the building of local distribution cooperatives could not be done simultaneously with the building of a wholesale procurement service. It had thus adopted a program of make-do, but the larger dream was not lost.

Babcock had little time to lay long-term plans. He was confronted with a fight for the organization's survival. He had to improvise—to work with what he had. The next two or three years was a training period for him as it was for the G.L.F. as an organization. His primary objective was to hang on—to build confidence and to build volume. Every step had to be an emergency decision.

Babcock lost no time in taking hold. He saw that his first problem was to create a team spirit and give the organization constructive leadership. To achieve this end immediately he called together his department heads and worked out with them an understanding as to their responsibilities and duties.

This meeting, which established without question that Babcock was going to be General Manager in fact as well as in name, also cleared the air on a number of matters which had caused confusion.

1. Department heads were to keep the central office informed on all matters of interest. "All the information of any *character whatsoever* which any member of the organization picks up which will be of interest—will be circulated." Moreover, copies of all complaints and correspondence bearing thereon were to be sent to the Manager's office immediately.

2. Fieldmen were to be representatives of the G.L.F. and not employees of the commodity departments. While the fieldmen were to be under the general supervision of the General Manager, they were to receive instructions from the

commodity department heads with respect to the sale of respective commodities. It was agreed that "the sole and only reason for the use of fieldmen is to increase the volume of G.L.F. sales. . . . In making sales, fieldmen will not only sell direct, but will establish and use agencies as a means of direct selling."

3. All publicity was to be handled through the central office and all advertising copy was to be written to carry a general G.L.F. message which would "make the consumer want to buy G.L.F. goods."

4. A plan was to be devised for the distribution of general overhead expense among the departments which would eliminate objections in advance "insofar as possible."[1]

With the fact accepted that he was to be the "boss," and with harmonious working procedures, Babcock turned to the most serious problem then confronting the Exchange—the raising of enough capital to keep the organization going. As Babcock later pointed out:

I was not long on the job before I discovered that the organization was in really worse financial straits than I had supposed from my inexpert reading of its statement, and by September I knew it could not continue unless it got a considerable block of additional capital. . . . An idea of how desperate the situation was may be gained from the fact that we employees were unable to draw our wages in the summer of 1922 and that to raise money to pay for seed which had been purchased, employees had to loan the corporation their personal funds, and Mr. Webb, who was then President, and I had to borrow $10,000 from the Tompkins County National Bank in Ithaca by personally endorsing the G.L.F.'s note.

The very lowest amount of new capital that I figured the G.L.F. would have to have in the fall of 1922, in order to continue in business, was $100,000. The only territory in which I figured there was a chance of raising any money at all was in the northern tier counties of Pennsylvania. In these counties the Dairymen's League was popular and I'd heard from friends in the area that they would like a cooperative purchasing service.[2]

Babcock grasped this straw. His first move was to persuade the directors of the Dairymen's League that G.L.F. service should be extended to its members in Northern Pennsylvania and New Jersey.[3] His next move was to persuade Ted Clausen, then G.L.F.'s "sole and only" fieldman, to take charge of the stockselling campaign.

[1] "Department Head Conference Report," presented to Board of Directors on July 27, 1922.

[2] The G.L.F. Idea, 1937. Babcock knew that a campaign to sell more stock to New York farmers would be a psychological blunder. Farmers were cynical over the value of their already large investment in G.L.F. stock which had not yet yielded expected service benefits and they had no disposition to send good money after bad.

[3] See Dairymen's League News, August 11, 1922. "Following Mr. Babcock's talk, J. D. Miller made the following motion which was adopted by the Board: 'I move that this Board recommend to its members in Pennsylvania and New Jersey that they subscribe to the stock of the G.L.F. and that they so keep in touch with the work of the G.L.F. that they may purchase through it from time to time as they desire.'" The fact that stock could be paid for by a "check-off" from the milk check greatly facilitated sale of stock.

The generous spirit with which Clausen accepted the assignment is shown by the following excerpts from a memorandum of "T.B.C. to H.E.B.," September 10, 1922:

1st. We will undertake the stock campaign job. I realize its size, yet I believe we can do it for I am convinced that the type of organization we have in mind will win if worked.

2nd. That commencing September 16, we will be glad to throw our lot with the Exchange for the next 15 months . . . for we want to see the organization win and succeed.

3rd. That we again pledge our absolute loyalty to the plan of strict departmentalization within the Exchange and to the Divisional development within the field.

4th. That no matter how lowly the job or how stiff the grade we will at all times give our very best to the service which we feel has truly and sincerely called us.

Clausen, with a few part-time helpers, including M. E. (Scotty) Campbell, Frank Naegely, and W. J. (Bill) Kuhrt, now Chief of the California Bureau of Markets, lost no time in getting started and, within a few weeks, stock subscriptions began to "pour in" first from Pennsylvania and then from New Jersey.[4]

Babcock's faith that $100,000 worth of shares could be thus sold was justified although the goal was not reached until January 1, 1924, as the stock was not issued until full payment was made. The stock record books show that about three fourths of the new capital was paid in during the last six months of 1923.

Clausen's method was to get first the support of a local branch of the Dairymen's League. He and his assistants then canvassed the local members and persuaded them to pay for a share of stock out of deductions from their milk checks. A major problem was to arrange for local distribution service on feed or other supplies. Sometimes it was possible to arrange for distribution through a local cooperative association, or through a reliable farmer who would arrange to pool neighborhood orders. More generally, it was found that the new members preferred to obtain service through their regular local dealers. As this was the quickest way and required less effort it soon was widely adopted by the groups of new members.[5]

Up to this time the G.L.F. had favored distribution through local co-

---

[4] It is of interest that this campaign brought into the G.L.F. two men—Campbell and Naegely—who were to make outstanding contributions to its later success.

[5] "There seems to be a tendency throughout this New Jersey territory for the retail dealer to serve farmers with G.L.F. supplies. Farmers decide who they want to handle the goods and the basis they will work on. In a great many cases the dealer who wants to be of real service will be just as willing to handle G.L.F. feeds, seeds, and fertilizer as any other brand providing the farmers of his community desire that service." T. B. Clausen in *Dairymen's League News,* March 30, 1923. (p. 10.)

operatives or car-door poolers. As the experience in Pennsylvania and New Jersey dramatically demonstrated the feasibility of distribution through dealers, the practice began to expand throughout all G.L.F. territory. Thus the G.L.F.'s unique system of using private agencies as distributive outlets was in the beginning a somewhat fortuitous development which grew out of the need to extend rapidly service as a means of selling stock to keep the organization going.

When Babcock came in as General Manager he realized that it would be necessary to develop a volume of business quickly. He perceived that the organization could not flourish without an efficient method of getting supplies into farmers' hands. One of his first acts, therefore, was to obtain authorization from the Board of Directors for the employment of up to six fieldmen. With this backing from the Board, Babcock began to quietly build up his field staff as men of the right type were found. Each fieldman was handpicked to meet the requirements of a given area, and each man had to be able to work with farmers on their own terms. Among the first of these early fieldmen were O. W. Sheldon, H. E. Aiken, B. H. Staplin, and J. A. McConnell.[6]

Babcock had immediately established the fact that the fieldmen were to represent the G.L.F. as a whole rather than separate departments as had been the practice. The effect of this policy was soon felt in increased activity and in better teamwork.

Babcock saw that the immediate responsibility of the field service lay in building up distributive outlets acceptable to the farmers in a locality. Later, Babcock was to say: "While Ted Clausen and his boys were selling stock I was making my own big contribution to G.L.F.—at least I so regard it—by establishing retail service agencies."[7]

At this time supplies were being distributed largely through car-door poolers and local cooperatives. The first efforts of the fieldmen, therefore, were to establish harmonious contacts with these distributing agencies and to develop similar ones in areas not then served. As in Pennsylvania and New Jersey, however, the fieldmen soon began to find from experience that the easiest and quickest way to build local service was through friendly dealers. In many communities the fieldmen worked with farmers in persuading a dealer to handle G.L.F. supplies for them, on an agreed-upon charge for his services. As J. A. McConnell recalls:

I . . . set up many local dealers during my first year as district manager. Very

---

[6] Obe Sheldon recalls how he was acting as a local Grange purchasing agent when he was employed by Curry Weatherby about July to work "on a per diem basis establishing cardoor agents for G.L.F. wherever it was possible to do so." Soon afterwards the fieldmen were given a weekly salary. "The work was to establish outlets wherever we could. Many times we were unable to get a farmer to act as our agent, but we could and did sell him a carload of Milkmaker." Letter of July 16, 1951.

[7] The G.L.F. Idea, 1937.

often, this was done after holding a local meeting of the leading men, but more often it was done by means of going from one leading farmer to another until I could get some suggestions as to who would serve the community and G.L.F. interests the best. If I remember right, it was the local farmers who first directed me toward the possibility of using local private dealers as a means of distribution. When I first started setting up distribution, my whole effort was directed to the farmer agent and to local cooperatives. [Letter, to author, of December 30, 1946.]

Because of its practicality, Babcock soon turned to the use of local dealers for distribution. It did not represent to him the ideal method but he saw that it could immediately increase volume and cut down the heavy overhead burden which was stifling the Exchange.[8]

When Babcock took charge, the G.L.F. was manufacturing only a small fraction of its members' feed requirements at its Buffalo mill. The great bulk of its feed supplies came from the American Milling Company of Peoria, Illinois, then making a strenuous effort to increase its business with cooperative associations. This company had overexpanded its facilities and needed volume to reduce overhead costs. It saw in the rapidly growing cooperatives an outlet which could answer its own problem and it agreed to manufacture feed of prescribed formulas at cost of ingredients plus manufacturing expenses and a small profit. This arrangement assured cooperatives a supply of feed manufactured to their own specifications at a favorable price, while it afforded the American Milling Company a potential outlet for a large volume of feed with practically no selling expense.

Earlier in the year the American Milling Company had worked out plans to supply feed to the Eastern States Farmers' Exchange for a New England-wide feed pool. Under this pool, farmers contracted with the Eastern States Farmers' Exchange for their feed requirements for the fall and winter months. In effect, then, this plan made the Eastern States Farmers' Exchange the buying agent for all the farmers who joined in the pool.

This pool plan was working so well with the Eastern States Farmers' Exchange that it encouraged the American Milling Company to promote a similar pool arrangement with the G.L.F. Babcock saw the possibilities in this approach, for Professor Savage had been pounding on the idea that farmers in the New York Milk Shed should pool their feed orders. In his column in the *Dairymen's League News* of June 23, 1922, Savage had declared:

[8] J. A. McConnell does not remember any definite policy to set up dealers. Ed simply said: "Get the business." He recalls how farmers would say to him, "Jim, let's go see Dealer X and get him to handle feed for us. He's a good fellow." The dealer would say: "I'll be glad to handle a few cars, etc." Interview with author, July 19, 1958.

From the standpoint of this column one of the most important questions that can be discussed by League branches is the question of buying feed. . . . The possibilities of the G.L.F. Exchange are not understood properly in this connection. In order to realize the opportunity to get feed at the lowest cost each branch should be ready to buy feed that it needs when that feed is low. What an opportunity to command a low price if the G.L.F. Exchange could pool the orders of 1,000 branches of the League. . . . Such an opportunity never before existed for cooperative enterprise on definite commodity lines if only leaders can be found who can make these units of branches function, and weld the organization into a smoothly revolving whole with immense buying and selling power.

The foundation for a G.L.F. pool plan was laid in Springfield, Massachusetts, on May 18, 1922, at a conference of college experts in feeding practices from the New England States and New York, called together by H. W. Selby, Manager of the Eastern States Farmers' Exchange. Professor Savage took a prominent part in this conference and served as its secretary.[9] This conference worked out a standard formula for dairy feed which was immediately adopted by the G.L.F., with slight modification. Savage, in reporting on this significant meeting in the *Dairymen's League News* of July 7, 1922, stated:

My whole opinion with regard to this feed is just this. The American Milling Company has gone a long way by making the formulas of their feeds public and should receive credit as the first big manufacturing company that is willing to meet its patrons half way by telling exactly what is in the feed. I am willing that this feed with its public formulas should take its natural place in the feeding operations in the eastern territory.

As these ideas appealed to Babcock he immediately made a deal with Mr. H. G. Atwood, the President of the American Milling Company, for a feed to be manufactured according to G.L.F. specifications and to be supplied at an agreed-upon price over a three-month delivery period in the fall months. This pool plan differed from that of the Eastern States Farmers' Exchange in that G.L.F. poolers were not legally obligated to take the feed ordered.

On August 19, Babcock addressed a circular letter to G.L.F. field representatives on the feed pool in which he said:

The weeks beginning August 20 and August 27 will determine the success of our Feed Pool. We have had only one real trial at it and that was up at Pulaski where our Raymond Hitchings pooled and contracted a little over seven cars in a day and a half, riding with the manager of the local cooperative. You must use every effort to get the agents busy throughout the territory.

[9] Out of this meeting grew the college conference feed boards which have performed a valuable function in establishing feed formulas for the use of G.L.F. and other cooperatives.

An advertisement in the *Dairymen's League News* of September 22 explained briefly how the plan would work:

> Under normal conditions it usually pays to buy the winter's supply of feed at late summer and fall prices, but the problem of storing the feeds thus bought and paying for them all at one time usually prevents the practice. Arrangements have, therefore, been made so that you may use the G.L.F. to buy for you Ready Mixed Feeds at prices now current for delivery during the coming months, as needed, *such feeds to be paid for only upon arrival.*

The State Fair, held in September, gave Babcock an opportunity to dramatize the G.L.F. feed program and pooling plan. With his cow "Jenny" as the center of attraction, with a sign on her pen reading "MORE MILK AND A BETTER COW LEFT" the G.L.F. exhibit emphasized the "Truth in Feeds" with a large sign showing the formula of "G.L.F. Milk Maker."[10] This exhibit attracted much farmer interest and, in the words of Babcock, kicked off the feed program.

As a result of the vigorous campaign to get farmers to order their feed requirements at a predetermined price, a substantial volume was attracted. The pool not only proved a practical method of distribution but it provided badly needed operating revenue.[11]

The fall of 1922 thus was a testing period for Babcock. Could he build volume through forced development of distribution outlets fast enough to insure profitable volume operations? The strain on the fieldmen was intense. In reporting to Babcock on November 21, Weatherby said:

> I find that the fieldmen are pretty tired—they need a little diversion. They have been hitting awful hard for the last couple of months and meeting some resistance, I'll tell you. The necessity of 'pepping' these men up a bit and getting them out of some of the ruts they are drifting into I think essential.

The pressure on Babcock during these early months was endless but he gloried in the job. In her diary Mrs. Babcock wrote on August 4, "Ed is due home at midnight. He loves his job, but the poor fellow is on a strain all of the time." Two months later, on October 5, she made this entry: "Ed was home today and yesterday and left tonight for Buffalo. The G.L.F. is coming fine under his management, but it is very strenuous."

On October 23, just when things were becoming a little more settled,

---

[10] According to W. J. Kuhrt, "It was my job to take care of the cow and explain the merits of the feeds to visitors and also on occasion to explain the G.L.F. organization." (Letter of March 30, 1951.)

[11] With feed operations running smoothly, F. A. McLellan resigned in September to become General Manager of the George Urban Milling Company. Harry J. Hannon, first assistant in the feed department since its organization, was then made Manager.

Babcock suffered a serious accident which laid him up until almost the end of the year.[12] Fortunately, lines of direction were set, and the entire organization rallied to support their chief during this ordeal.

At the end of his first six months as General Manager, Babcock could see real progress as revenue was beginning to exceed costs. Internal conflicts within the organization had been removed and a spirit of teamwork grown. The field service had begun to take shape and as a result a more effective system of distribution agenices was being developed. The pool method of handling feed had shown its possibilities, and farmers who had bought on the pool plan were generally pleased with results. Moreover, the desperate financial position of the organization had been greatly relieved by a long-term bank loan, and the stock campaign in Pennsylvania was bringing in new members as well as badly needed permanent capital.

On the other hand, operations during the first six months had been disappointing even when allowances were made. As compared with the first six months of the year, sales were off from $1,725,439 to $1,527,603, while a net margin of $5,203 for the first six months had been more than wiped out by a deficit of $62,521 for the last six months. This was disheartening even though it could be largely explained by the rise in distribution expense. The fieldmen were just beginning to show results as volume builders.

The balance sheet on January 1, 1923, showed further deterioration, since it reflected the loss from operations. While total assets had increased from $742,708 to $897,869, much of the increase was due to larger inventories, offset by a heavy increase in current liabilities. In fact, the net operating capital had fallen from $102,849 to $37,651, while the current ratio had declined from 2.70 to 1 to 1.14 to 1. Along with these measures of gloom the equity of the stockholders in the total assets had fallen from 91 to 69 percent.

In the face of this discouraging record there was little despondency in the G.L.F. camp. When the third annual meeting was held in February

[12] Mrs. Babcock graphically reported the accident in her diary. Babcock was riding his horse up to his farm, Sunnygables, "when a large Buick drove up from behind at a terrific speed. Ed's horse, 'Star,' bolted a bit or else thought he was going to turn in, and the car hit Ed. The horse kicked over with Ed under it, taking the force of the blow on his left shoulder. He was badly banged up, so the boys pulled him up unconscious and drove him to the hospital. . . . Dr. Tinker . . . worked on him for three hours. I am afraid he will be laid up several weeks before he can get back into his old stride." In her entry for November 17, Mrs. Babcock noted that Ed was "now home from the hospital but still confined to bed." By December 8, Ed was "up and around," but "his shoulder bothered him so much he had an X-Ray taken and they found a fracture of the scapula, and he will have to wear a sling until after Christmas." In her diary entry for December 19, Mrs. Babcock reported that Ed had gone back to his office in Syracuse on December 15 "not completely cured . . ." for his arm was still in the sling. However, "otherwise, he feels quite like himself."

1923, Babcock put the problem confronting the organization frankly up to the stockholders:

This great Statewide purchasing agency for farmers is in a position where it will either go forward to become an inspiring factor in the economic life of the farmers who support it, or will remain as it is at present—a finely equipped and organized business—but not taken full advantage of. . . . [It] is capable of handling treble the amount of supplies being handled.

The 200 stockholders present at the meeting responded enthusiastically to this challenge. At last G.L.F. had found a leader who was not scared and who could talk their language. The road ahead was wide open.

CHAPTER 10

Building the Organization

An organization is not an intangible proposition. It is made up of men. It goes ahead in proportion to the way the men discharge their duties. . . . I want to knit the whole organization together.
H. E. Babcock, *G.L.F. Fieldmen's School, April, 1924.*

WHILE PRIMARY ATTENTION had to be given to the feed problem, the other problems of the organization were not neglected, as we shall see in this chapter. Babcock realized that the feed, fertilizer, seed and other services of the G.L.F. were interrelated. The success of one was necessary to the success of all. He recognized that an effective field force and system of local distributive agencies were essential to the success of all of the commodity services.

Babcock also perceived that advertising was required, not only for the commodities handled, but for the Institution as a whole. He knew that the prestige of the G.L.F. depended upon the creation and satisfaction of demand for its commodities and services, and he was constantly striving to develop confidence in the minds of farmers that the G.L.F. was an organization concerned with their problems.

The campaign to increase volume was aggressively carried on by the fieldmen who were growing in number, and through advertisements in the *Dairymen's League News* and *American Agriculturist.* Typical advertisements urged farmers to "Feed G.L.F. Rations—High in Digestible Materials," and use "G.L.F. High Quality Known-Origin Seed," or "G.L.F. High Analysis Mixed Fertilizer."

As the year progressed, it was clear that the G.L.F. was catching hold. Volume of business began to expand. A surplus accumulated. Statements appeared in the farm press showing progress. But there was little false optimism in G.L.F. ranks. The G.L.F. was fighting for its life—the time for bragging could be postponed. While Clausen and his men were busy in New Jersey and Pennsylvania extending the operating territory and raising needed capital, Babcock was tightening up the entire organization.

During this period he continued to devote primary attention to the development of an aggressive field force who could work with farmers and get their loyal cooperation. The compelling need was for a system of local distributing agencies that would produce volume to spread costs and obtain advantages of mass buying.

Experience was showing that the quickest way to provide local facilities for distribution was to use those of local cooperatives or private feed dealers. If they were unwilling to serve as G.L.F. distributors there was no alternative but to establish car-door poolers—farmers who would order for their neighbors and arrange for local delivery at the car-door.

An important action, not considered significant at the time, was the transfer of the G.L.F. headquarters from Syracuse to Ithaca in April, 1923. Although this action was taken "in the interest of economy," Curry Weatherby explains the matter more simply by saying, "Ed wanted to be near his farm—and so we moved to Ithaca."[1]

The decision to move to Ithaca proved of tremendous long-run benefit. It placed the G.L.F. on the doorstep of Cornell University where authorities were available in the agricultural sciences, extension education, farm management, marketing, finance, and rural sociology. It made the G.L.F. in effect an experimental laboratory for the University in putting into commercial practice lessons from the laboratory and testing stations. This move, more than any one thing, was to foster a partnership of theory and practice in the business conduct of the G.L.F. The continuing high respect of the organization for scientific knowledge has been nourished by this close relationship.

At the end of December, 1923, the G.L.F. could look back on the accomplishments of the last year with satisfaction. The opening of new territory, the inauguration of the feed pool, and sustained field work had brought the volume of business to $5,919,361, or almost double that of the preceding year. The consolidated balance sheet also showed great improvement. The current ratio had increased from 1.1 to 1 to 1.6 to 1, and the deficit in the surplus account of $47,809 had been wiped out by a net increase for the year of $70,675.

Heartened by the savings, the Directors, in December, decided to pay a dividend on common stock in early 1924—to keep the faith of its stockholders and to build confidence in their investment. Financially, the dividend was probably unwarranted, but from a psychological point of view it was a strategic move, a demonstration to all that the G.L.F. had weathered its early difficulties and that the confidence of its thirty thousand stockholders was justified.

The G.L.F. used this payment to the full extent of its propaganda value. For years a sniping campaign had been alleging that the farmers' investments in the Exchange were of no value. But here—at a time when many financial firms were skipping dividends—the G.L.F. was distributing almost $50,000 to its stockholder members. Moreover, to dispel all doubt, the dividends were distributed at special meetings held throughout the territory to publicly demonstrate that G.L.F. stock was not "worthless"

[1] Conversation with E. C. Weatherby, June 17, 1951.

—but a "good investment." From this time forward, except for the following year, the G.L.F. has never failed to pay its 6 percent dividend on common stock.

The G.L.F. continued to make steady progress in the new year. Organizational efficiency and morale had been greatly improved by the better financial showing, and the field force under the direct leadership of the General Manager was creating a network of dependable local representatives. The power of the organization had been shown by its handling of the feed emergency which developed in September (see pp. 83-85), and farm supporters were also well pleased with improved fertilizer and seed services (see Chapter 12). Sources of supply were apparently secure and the Buffalo feed mill which had been a millstone around the G.L.F.'s neck was at last becoming productive.

With the feed, seed, and fertilizer departments performing efficiently, Babcock turned his attention to the miscellaneous supplies then handled more or less as convenience goods from the Syracuse seed warehouse. Since these supplies were largely handled on mail orders it was decided in February, 1924, to establish a "mail order department" under G. C. Gardinier to handle them in a more systematic way.[2]

As the staff grew, Babcock made more and more use of conferences as a means of pooling experience and developing common objectives. His college and extension service experience had taught him how to lead a group through meetings and the early staff conferences simply modified this technique to the needs of the G.L.F. These meetings were invaluable in keeping the staff pulling together and in developing trained men with G.L.F. *esprit de corps.*

The unique thing in the early conferences was Babcock's emphasis on educational techniques, and they quickly became known as "schools." He saw the fieldmen as a group of educators—similar to a group of county agents. He felt that it was their mission to teach farmers how to use their own organization.

The first conferences were quite informal. As experience was gained, however, more and more attention was given to the plans for such meetings. For example, considerable care was given in arranging for the Special Fieldmen's School, held in April, 1924, to start the feed pool campaign for 1924. This conference, unlike the one held a year before when representatives of the American Milling Company were present, was an inside affair for G.L.F. fieldmen and staff officers. It was the forerunner of systematic schools which soon became an accepted method of employee education within the G.L.F.

[2] Gardinier also replaced Babcock as Manager of the P.W. & E. Company at this time.

According to the announcement sent to fieldmen calling them for the school:

The purpose of this school is to bring you up to date on the present status of the Exchange, and to aid you in your work during the next four or five months. Particular emphasis will be given to the establishment and operation of local service stations, poultry feed order-getting, and to the 1924 feed pool.

In opening the school, Babcock declared:

An organization is not an intangible proposition. It is made up of men. It goes ahead in proportion to the way the men discharge their duties and it goes ahead smoothly and efficiently in proportion to the efficiency of its men.

Babcock wanted each man to feel his importance:

Our policy of decentralization fixes responsibility. It puts the blame on the fellow who deserves it. It puts the development of the sales service on you. You are the service directors for your territory. . . .

We have the means of measuring your success as fieldmen, and how near you come to the idea; how near you have come to installing local service in your territory; what percentage of your service stations are functioning.

Babcock was very frank and direct. He told the men just what he had in mind and how he planned to achieve his aims. "I want to knit the whole organization together."

He was direct in his criticisms. He listed common shortcomings which would have to be corrected. One lack was confidence. He saw that the men needed to strengthen their own confidence in the organization if they were to impart faith to others. Some were not aggressive enough. To these he said: "You do not know how to dig in and you have got to learn." Others were not orderly enough in their work. To those he said: "Lay out your contacts and plan your moves, then carry out your moves."

Babcock felt that the whole group was lacking in depth of understanding, and he asserted that they were not studying enough. He desired and demanded that every fieldman know the commodities being handled and the organization's methods and policies. He was trying to get them to accept responsibility—not as fieldmen—but as district executives.

Babcock placed each man on his mettle.

One thing is true in life—you either manage it or it manages you. . . . You men are going to be given a chance to build up the local service and have got to keep it going. Every man has until September 1 to make an appreciable dent on his job. This school is called now to help you. About September 1 we are going over your accomplishments very carefully and the man who seems unable to make progress with his territory is to get his 60-day notice then and be asked to help break in a man for that territory who we think can handle it. He will be given an opportunity to get something else with our help. . . .

A large part of the time of the school was devoted to methods of helping the fieldmen do a better job on their problems. They were not only given information that would help them in their work but these methods were demonstrated and discussed. The school was a laboratory as well as a class-room.

Although the G.L.F. was effectively telling its story through the *Dairymen's League News* and the *American Agriculturist*, Babcock felt that there was a need for a special membership publication which could periodically keep its farmer shareholders up to date on matters relating to their organization. The first issue of the *G.L.F. Shareholder* in May, 1924, was, in a way, a declaration of organizational independence, for it marked a new philosophy of taking members into partnership with management. Although Babcock drew on Mary Fennell and others for effective aid in getting out this publication it was primarily "his baby."[3]

The lead article of the first issue, "The G.L.F. on Its Feet," signed by President N. F. Webb, declared:

A successful farm cannot be built in a day nor can a useful service like that now rendered by the G.L.F. Competent men must be employed, facilities for doing business acquired, experience gained, an Institution developed. All of this takes time. . . .

Three years ago public formula feeds, sure supplies of domestic grown clover and alfalfa seed, public formula high analysis fertilizers were not available. G.L.F. service has put them in the reach of every farmer. . . .

Now has it saved us money? Can it? The first question most of you can answer out of your experience. If you will use the *correct measurement* of value your *answer must be yes*. Can it save more money? This you alone can answer. . . .

You can save much of the expense to which your management is now put to get your orders if you will order voluntarily, insist on G.L.F. goods, induce your neighbor to get them. . . . By still further increasing the volume of your ordering you can decrease the necessary assessment on each unit of overhead. Finally, if you will just remember that the G.L.F. Mills and warehouses are yours and that only by using them to capacity can you have their operations

[3] Mary Fennell (Mrs. Peter Kemper) was a gifted and ingenious writer in tune with Mr. Babcock. While a freshman at Cornell she got a job with Burritt and Babcock on an agricultural census. During her Junior and Senior years she worked part-time for the State Food Administration, then headed by Babcock. After graduation Babcock helped her get a job with Jerry Hammond, then editor of the *Dairymen's League News*, and she worked as his assistant on advertising. Later she became secretary to the League's President, and during this period she served as Babcock's assistant in the big G.L.F. stock-selling campaign. She then was employed by E. V. Underwood, President of the New York Farm Bureau Federation, to handle Farm Bureau publicity. After the G.L.F. moved to Ithaca in 1923 she joined Babcock as his assistant to handle advertising and information and in 1924 she was given the title, "Director of G.L.F. Information Service." In January 1926, with the encouragement of Babcock and Mr. Atwood, she established in Ithaca an independent advertising agency under the name, Agricultural Research and Advertising Service, to handle primarily the advertising and publicity for the G.L.F. and A.M.C. This arrangement gave the G.L.F. the services of a specialized advertising agency at a modest cost. In the late twenties W. D. McMillan joined the agency and took over direction of Research, and when Miss Fennell left the agency to get married, it was reorganized as Agricultural Advertising and Research Service, with Mr. McMillan as President.

efficient and cheap, you can save considerably on the cost of plant operations.

The big point is that when you make savings possible for the G.L.F. *you* benefit by them. . . .

The editorials in this first issue by Babcock, as Editor, made the aims of the publication clear. The first editorial entitled, "First-Hand Facts," stated:

You own the G.L.F. It is your right to know about it. It is your responsibility to meet situations as they develop as well as to take advantage of opportunities as they arise. The things which you will *read* here come from first-hand knowledge.

We should all be proud of what we have been able to accomplish. On the other hand, we should not mislead ourselves into feelings of false security. We still have some large problems to solve.

Babcock was concerned about the lying propaganda going around. He dealt with this in a second editorial:

On my desk is a pile of material several inches deep which is made up of lying, libelous, and vicious attacks on your management. . . . In the last analysis . . . it is you who own the G.L.F. who are injured by those seeking to destroy your organization. Your directors and your management stand ready to give you the facts. They should have your confidence or be changed. Tell the next man who says that the G.L.F. handles imported clover seed that he is a liar.

The rest of this issue presented information on developments of interest to G.L.F. patrons, such as plans for the 1924 feed pool, and the new service on flour for the farm home being developed in cooperation with the New York State Home Bureau Federation. Other articles and advertisements gave information on other G.L.F. services available through the fertilizer, seed and mail-order departments.

The need of the organization for stronger financial management, pointed up by the audit of W. L. Bradley, was recognized by the Board in early 1924, when, at the suggestion of Mr. Babcock, M. C. Burritt— who had recently resigned as Director of Extension for the State College of Agriculture and been elected to the G.L.F. Board of Directors—was named Comptroller and charged with the responsibility of strengthening the organization's financial position.[4] Burritt, by training and temperament, was ideally fitted for this post, and his long association with Babcock in Extension work guaranteed close working harmony.

With Burritt conscientiously watching finances, Babcock was free to devote his dynamic energies to promoting the program as a whole.

In the March 1924 issue of the *Shareholder* Burritt pointed out, "The best possible use of our capital and credit, together with the most rigid

---

[4] Babcock had urged Burritt to resign from the Board and work full time for the G.L.F. However, Burritt continued on the Board and worked on a part-time basis as Comptroller.

economy consistent with efficient operations are our immediate aims this season." He saw certain defects in the financial structure which "in the interest of further strengthening of the Exchange should be corrected." He referred to the $103,730.18 "appreciation" of plants in 1921 which was being carried on the balance sheet as undivided earnings, saying, "Although this item was fixed through disinterested public appraisal and was probably justified at the time it should as soon as possible be written off the books." He also felt that the "deferred charge for organization expense now carried as an asset" should be liquidated at an early date.[5] In addition to these actions, designed to squeeze the water out of the assets shown in the financial statement, he pointed out that "reserves for unexpected losses and unfavorable conditions, are inadequate and should be largely increased."

Burritt knew that these actions were necessary to get the organization on its feet financially, and faith in his judgment helped convince his associates and the shareholders that this view was sound.

In the haste to build volume the revenue to support the administrative expenses of the organization, including fieldmen's costs, came largely from assessments on the various departments in rough proportion to their earning ability. This method worked well during 1922 and 1923 when the G.L.F. was getting started but was not suited for permanent operations in that it penalized the efficient and subsidized the inefficient departments.

During the spring of 1924 the need of a more acceptable arrangement was stressed by the audit of W. L. Bradley and as a result the President appointed a committee of four to develop a better plan. The committee was comprised of Directors M. C. Burritt (Chairman), Henry Burden, and Raymond C. Hitchings, plus Dr. W. I. Myers of Cornell University.

The report of this committee, submitted on July 1, 1924, recommended that each commodity department support the executive budget according to its volume of business and its use of administrative services. The acceptance of this more equitable method of meeting executive expenses gave vigor to the executive office and reduced internal friction. This action recognized that financial planning was a total G.L.F. responsibility.

---

[5] Robert Dame, as Chief Accounting Officer, had strongly urged these actions to more clearly show the true financial position of the organization. During the early years when the G.L.F. was in desperate need of capital it did not hesitate to employ unorthodox accounting procedures if deemed necessary for survival.

CHAPTER 11

The Drive for Feed Volume

*As G.L.F. internal activity straightened out, and wholesale pro-
curement of farmer-ordered supplies began to run smoothly, farm
families cried for more service. One great call was FEED. Here was
a service challenge of tremendous magnitude. Nothing mediocre,
nothing picayune, nothing easy.*

T. B. CLAUSEN, *in letter to author, January 30, 1951*

I F THE G.L.F. was to make good it had to solve quickly the feed problem, for this represented the main economic interest of its farmer members. Babcock knew this and he never for a moment forgot it.

As feed prices rose appreciably during the fall of 1922 the farmers
who participated in the first feed pool enjoyed a "good buy."[1] Professor
Savage, in the *Dairymen's League News* of January 12, 1923, pointed
out how a farmer by buying feed in September for use in January could
have saved 75 percent on the money invested. He went on to say:

Now, these men who purchased feed on future delivery did not have to pay
for the feed until it was delivered so that they were able to make this saving
by giving their orders for future delivery. It seems to me that this is the proper
way to buy feed, to anticipate your needs and put in orders on at least the first
four months of the winter in advance.

The success of the pool resulted in a problem for after the pool tonnage was shipped it was impossible to get farmers to buy without a special price inducement.

To meet this problem Babcock arranged for a February pool which
was presented in a letter "To G.L.F. Agents," dated February 1. It illustrates how Babcock put over a proposition.

HERE IS A PROPOSITION THAT MERITS IMMEDIATE ACTION

It holds good until February 10, 1923.

Ever since last Fall we have kept the great plant of the American Milling
Company at Peoria running twenty hours a day. With the shipment of the last
of the pooled orders, however, the mill will have to close down to one shift
unless we keep the tonnage coming.

Realizing this, the American Milling Company has submitted us a contract
calling for an unusually low manufacturing cost on our ready mixed dairy rations provided we guarantee a certain minimum tonnage for February shipment. We must give them our answer immediately.

[1] This was a bit of good luck for G.L.F. According to J. A. McConnell, a fieldman
at the time: "This market appreciation saved the hide of G.L.F. If the market had
gone the other way, it would have been tough, for the fieldmen then were not trained
salesmen." Interview with author, July 19, 1958.

79

If we are able to pledge the required tonnage, and thus keep the mill running two shifts, we can make you some saving over the present quoted price on Milk Maker and Exchange Dairy.

These rations are already below competing rations of like quality.

Embargoes have slowed up the whole feed movement. It will pay to have some good feed rolling toward you.

Send your order . . . today and we will fill it for shipment any time you specify during February, at a price which will not exceed prices quoted on the February 1st quotation sheet and in addition give you the full benefit of any savings we are able to make in reduced manufacturing costs. . . .

Please give us the benefit of your immediate response.

The success of the February pool further demonstrated the practicability of this method of building feed volume and led to ambitious plans for a big pool to be started in the fall. Under the plan, as developed, the G.L.F., working with the assistance of the American Milling Company, would carry on a special campaign during the summer to get farmers to contract for their supply of feed for the fall and winter months.

The feed was to be manufactured by the American Milling Company, according to G.L.F. specifications, for the cost of ingredients and a charge for its services. The price to be paid by farmers was to be fixed in the fall. In theory it was expected that the feed would be bought at the low point of the market, to afford a speculative profit to the farmers.

At this time Babcock was working intimately with President Atwood of the American Milling Company, who saw in the G.L.F. a natural sales outlet for the feed manufactured by his company. As a result, his company not only gave the G.L.F. badly needed financial assistance but provided it with substantial funds for use in feed advertising. Atwood also made available the services of his plant superintendent to advise the G.L.F. on how it could reduce the operating costs of its Buffalo feed plant.

During the spring of 1923 the heart of the G.L.F. program was feed, and Savage, writing in the *Dairymen's League News,* kept up a continuous barrage of propaganda to encourage farmers' support. Babcock realized that if G.L.F. could really get its feed operations rolling this would build support for the rest of the program.

While plans were going forward for the fall pool, he was busy developing the field force which he had kept under his own direction. In late May, however, he decided to place the regular fieldmen under the supervision of Hannon—the head of the feed department. Although these men were to be primarily feed salesmen they were also expected to get business in seeds, fertilizers, binder twine, tires and coal.

At the same time he proposed to organize four temporary development teams of a few men each to:

(1) Resell the G.L.F. as an institution; (2) secure a stock subscription from

WILLIAM L. BEAN
1920-1921

NILES F. WEBB
1921-1930

FRED L. PORTER
1930-1938

LEIGH G. KIRKLAND
1938-1942

FRANK M. SMITH
1943-1953

JAMES C. CORWITH
1953-

PRESIDENTS OF THE G.L.F. SINCE 1920

LIBERTY HYDE BAILEY

GEORGE F. WARREN

ELMER S. SAVAGE

JAMES E. RICE

E. L. WORTHEN

JOHN H. BARRON

MAURICE C. BOND

WILLIAM I. MYERS

LEONARD A. MAYNARD

CORNELL FRIENDS

THE FIRST SERVICE STORE, 1925

EARLY WAREHOUSE DELIVERY, ABOUT 1925

SUNNY GABLES—BABCOCK'S FARM

every worthwhile farmer; (3) establish an agency or agencies at every shipping point; [and] (4) certify agencies, and in connection with the certificates show the shareholders served and the conditions that affect the sale of G.L.F. commodities in the community served.[2]

These teams were to be under Babcock's personal direction and captained by men who had shown capacity in developmental work. In presenting the plan, Babcock admitted that "it is an experiment but it at least provides for constructive and aggressive action." Although this proposed plan was not fully carried out, it served as a guide for developmental work during the next few years.[3]

Placing the regular fieldmen under Hannon did not turn out as hoped. Hannon was primarily a plant operator and had little experience or flair for the problems of distribution. Writing to Atwood on July 17, 1923, Babcock confessed, "I have shifted about shamefully this summer . . . but it has been a case of cast and try. First, I directed the fieldmen myself, then I put them under Hannon. . . . As a result, they ran wild and some very serious mistakes were made at the mill." To remedy this situation, Babcock gave Weatherby, who was steady and respected, complete direction of the fieldmen, along with advertising and publicity.

The 1923 feed pool was launched with a meeting at Ithaca on July 16. In writing to Atwood on July 17, Babcock said:

Yesterday we had your men here [A.M.C. salesmen who were assigned to assist in the campaign] and about 20 of our regular and per diem men. [The per diem men were employed only for the duration of the campaign.] We gave them a very thorough schooling at which Professor Savage was particularly valuable. They started this morning on the pool. We close it absolutely August 4.

We do not expect to get an enormous tonnage but do expect to get the easy business and create a situation whereby Weatherby with a few salesmen can continue to give us a regular dairy business of 10 to 15 cars a day in addition to the tonnage booked in the pool. This we believe is playing somewhat safer than it would be to oversell the pool. It also puts us in a position to keep our own mill operations on current business. The more I study the situation the more impressed I am with the point that our mill is and will remain considerably of a handicap unless we can develop a good poultry feed business.

Babcock did not forget the importance of protecting the G.L.F.'s investment in its Buffalo mill, badly in need of volume. He was beginning to see the possibilities of the poultry industry which was expanding rapidly as a result of the promotional efforts of Professor James E. Rice of Cornell University.

[2] As presented in memorandum to Department Heads, Messrs. Hannon, Weatherby, Bibbins, Gay and Gardinier, May 24, 1923.

[3] According to Obe Sheldon: "During 1922-23 Mr. Babcock tried out many ideas in the field. If they worked, everything was rosy; when they backfired he would reverse his thinking fast. This method I think accounted for a large percentage of our success."

Babcock took this occasion to call Atwood's attention to the need for closer cooperation with the American Milling Company as a means of reducing sales cost. "We must study to avoid duplication of sales personnel and expenses." He proposed that the G.L.F. should furnish its own salesmen and get from The American Milling Company only expert advice which could be given by its sales manager. Babcock had found from experience that the G.L.F.-trained fieldmen were better able to work with farmers since they looked upon themselves as representatives of the farmers.[4]

At this time Babcock was toying with Savage's idea of pricing all public formula dairy rations according to the cost of their digestible nutrients. "By doing this we would remove our feeds from the competitive field . . . in order to match our prices it would be necessary for the closed formula fellows to give out their formulas." He asked Atwood, "What do you think of the idea? It is the one point which we are playing up the most at the present time."

Writing to Atwood a few days later, July 20, 1923, Babcock reported that the pool sign-up was coming along well, promising a pool of about 50,000 tons, or about 10,000 more then had been expected. "I hope it won't go much over 50,000 tons because I don't want to put my eggs all in one basket. If the pool should ever go wrong it would cripple us indefinitely. . . . A fractional demonstration is just as effective in cutting the cost of getting the business . . . as a 100 percent demonstration."

In this letter Babcock again referred to the use of American Milling Company salesmen. Although he appreciated the contribution being made by the American Milling Company he was afraid of getting "our mutual overhead too high." He felt that the chief contribution of the American Milling Company should be "along the line of expert sales management." It was clear that Babcock was fast working toward independence in the field of distribution.

The plan of the 1923 pool followed the general pattern of those carried on during the preceding year. However, by this time the G.L.F. had more local distributing agents. The fieldmen, working with the local agents, solicited farmers, and the local agents placed orders received for feed to be shipped during the fall and winter months.

Under the deal with the American Milling Company the G.L.F. was to obtain an adequate supply of dairy feeds to meet the needs of its members, manufactured according to its specifications. The feed was to be delivered to the G.L.F. at prices which would cover ingredient costs, capital

---

[4] Jim McConnell recalls the problems that arose in using A.M.C. salesmen in 1922-23. "Ed was anxious to get away from this arrangement so as to have only cooperative fieldmen. The old-line salesmen had difficulty in understanding the open-formula idea." Interview with McConnell, June 22, 1951.

charge and a fee for manufacturing service. Under the plan farmers were to be solicited to place orders in the summer months for feed to be delivered during the six months from October through March, with the understanding that prices would be established monthly as feeds were delivered. Dealers were to be allowed a fixed margin for handling car-door deliveries.

Two types of public formula feed were to be distributed under the pool plan at prices fixed in accordance with the cost of ingredients before shipments were started. The theory of the pool was that as feed prices in the summer were customarily lower than during the feeding months, poolers would get the advantage of the normal price rise.[5] This theory had worked well through the fall of 1922, but conditions were to be quite different in the fall of 1923.

Almost before the pool was closed, there was a rapid increase in the cost of gluten meal, an important ingredient in the public formula feeds. Although the G.L.F. attributed this to antagonistic feed operators who were charged with trying to embarrass the cooperative feed pools by bidding up prices—in fact, the rise in price was due more to heavy demand for ingredients needed to produce the feed under the public formula rations, resulting from the G.L.F. and other cooperative pools. The success of the G.L.F. in getting a sign-up for the pool thus confronted it with a special problem. Since the pool called for the delivery of open formula feed with ingredients known, it set up an abnormal demand for certain ingredients—especially gluten feed. The feed trade, in turn, scrambled to get these ingredients and thus bid up prices for them with the result that the total costs for making feed under fixed formulas was greatly increased.

The G.L.F. had to make a practical operating decision. If it continued with its announced pool plan its feed prices would be out of line and cause much criticism among those who had joined the pool to obtain low-cost feed. At the same time, the G.L.F. was committed to the plan and had the responsibility of serving those who had signed up.

The G.L.F. met this situation with energetic action. Finding it possible to get a good deal on a large quantity of Canadian barley which could be substituted for the high priced gluten meal, Professor Savage then worked out an "Emergency Dairy Ration" based on the use of low cost barley. To inform farmers of the problem and get them to accept this new feed as a substitute for what they had ordered required a vigorous advertising campaign. In double-page spreads in the *Dairymen's League*

[5] An advertisement in the *Dairymen's League News,* July 20, 1923, stated that "The Cooperative G.L.F. Exchange is running its feed pool to buy your winter feed requirements for you at the prices which prevail between now and early fall—the lowest point usually. . . ."

News and the *American Agriculturist,* Savage commended the G.L.F. for its action. "I hope those who have ordered in the feed pool will cooperate with the G.L.F. in its fight for reasonable prices on public formula feeds." The advertisement also explained the problem and offered those who had signed up the option of taking delivery on "Emergency Dairy Feeds." A significant feature of the advertisement was a *facsimile* copy of the following resolution passed by the G.L.F. Board of Directors on September 1, 1923.

WHEREAS—The value and popularity of the public formula feeds heretofore originated by the Cooperative G.L.F. Exchange, Inc., have been so great as to stimulate extensive imitation on the part of competitors, and,

WHEREAS—The production of imitations has produced an extraordinary demand for the ingredients specified in said open formulae with the result of stimulating the market prices of such ingredients to unreasonable heights, and,

WHEREAS—It seems the part of sound economic policy to refuse to be a party to any action that will further increase prices of dairy feeds either now or in the immediate future, be it

RESOLVED that the Cooperative G.L.F. Exchange, Inc., suggests to its shareholders who have given orders for G.L.F. feeds for delivery during the six months from October 1923 to March 1924 inclusive, that they meet the situation by substituting for Milk Maker and Exchange Dairy a G.L.F. Emergency ration as made up under the direction of Professor E. S. Savage of Cornell University *and the price of which is hereby definitely set at $45.05 per ton Syracuse rate basis,* and be it further

RESOLVED that for those who feel that it is imperative that they have feeds mixed according to the established Milk Maker or Exchange Dairy formulae such feeds be priced for the month of October at $51.41 for Milk Maker and $48.41 for Exchange Dairy Syracuse rate basis.[6]

Regardless of whether the G.L.F.'s predicament was forced by the wickedness of its competitors, there was an overwhelming response to this appeal—and most of those who had signed up under the pool accepted delivery of the Emergency Dairy ration. Fortunately the new ration gave excellent satisfaction, for on October 30 Babcock wrote Atwood, "I feel we can congratulate ourselves relative to its qualities as a milk maker."

The ability of the G.L.F. to meet the crisis proved to be a boon to the organization. It was a dramatic achievement which demonstrated actual as well as potential power, and in rural communities it greatly strengthened the stature of the G.L.F. as a fighting organization. The lessons learned from this experience have been well stated by J. A. McConnell:

The first pool was fairly successful in that the feed market climbed about $10 a ton during the winter. Everybody figured that we had the key to prosperity as far as cost of feed was concerned. The second pool followed the same procedure. The bookings the second time of course were very, very heavy be-

[6] The *Dairymen's League News,* October 5, 1923.

cause of the experience that farmers had with the first pool. Lo and behold, when the various cooperatives, working through the American Milling Company, tried to cover the ingredients to make the formula which had been sold, with the maximum price, it couldn't be done. The co-op men were inclined to lay this to a squeeze by the sellers of feed ingredients. Actually, we know now that a big feed pool of this sort, based on a fixed formula, was bound to bull the market. We finally got out of that deal by making what was called '20% Emergency Dairy,' based on a very cheap purchase of barley which happened to be plentiful and low-priced that particular year. This experience pretty much wound up the feed pool idea and thus was born the flexible formula idea which G.L.F. has used ever since. From this experience also came G.L.F.'s policy of never booking feed to its members ahead. It was a very embarrassing situation, to say the least.[7]

By this time Babcock was already looking ahead. He confessed to Atwood in his letter of October 30, "I am concerned now about the next year and the next ten years. While you are worrying about deliveries on immediate business, I would like to lay plans to keep you worried."

He was then of the opinion that in view of the prospective shortage of protein:

We should build for the future on the basis of minimum protein content and maximum digestibility. With these two fundamentals in mind, we should then abandon the fixed formula, but not the public formula, and proceed to mix a feed that will hold a place for itself on the basis of economy.

He saw that this type of program would call "for more careful investigational work and thinking than we have put into our rations in the past" and he proposed that the G.L.F. establish under its own control a dairy feed research department to be supervised by Professor Savage, Dr. L. A. Maynard, Professor of Animal Nutrition at Cornell University, and himself.

Babcock believed that this work could be carried on with little expense. He had in mind a staff of two—a herdsman and a girl. The herdsman would feed different rations, test them out under practical conditions, and work with practical farmers feeding the same rations. For this work he had in mind William McMillan, who was then completing college work with a good training in food chemistry. The girl would "act as secretary and also keep track of retail prices throughout our territory, of the activities of our competitors, of propaganda of farmers where our rations are giving good results; in short, get together all of the material upon which our propaganda, advertising and sales talk would be based."[8]

---

[7] Letter to author, March 30, 1951.

[8] The research work proposed by Babcock was undertaken in a slightly modified form the following summer with a budget of about $5500 for a year's work with funds supplied by the American Milling Company, Corn Products, Linseed Crushers and the G.L.F.

Babcock concluded his letter to Atwood by saying: "when we have a lot of business is the time to plan to keep it coming."—a remark which throws much light on his management.

The power of the G.L.F. to carry through its 1923 feed pool in the face of the ingredient crisis and an unfavorable price trend served to establish it as an important feed distributing organization. Moreover, in operating this pool the G.L.F. learned the valuable lessons that prices as well as quality must be competitive, and that prices in the fall months could go down as well as up. As a result, G.L.F. began to give more attention to the development of regular round-the-year service, and to rely less on rising markets to show members the advantage of cooperative purchasing. The value of its growing network of local distributing agencies, and the key importance of the fieldmen in knitting the system together to make a smoothly operating machine was becoming apparent. In December, 1923, Babcock emphasized this fact by recommending to the Directors that they should pay fieldmen a commission for business produced in addition to regular salary to afford them a greater incentive.

The feed pools, however, had performed one highly important function by quickly establishing the G.L.F. as a major feed supplier. Through the pools, contracts had been made with dealers and agents who took on more and more responsibility for obtaining the orders of farmers. Imperceptibly, reliance on the pool as a method of distribution was giving way to a program of getting farmers to place regular orders with their representatives.

One of Babcock's worries during his first year as manager had been the operation of the Buffalo feed plant. Since it represented a large part of the G.L.F.'s fixed assets, there was a natural desire to make it pay. While some improvement was made in operational efficiency from recommendations made by the mill superintendent of the American Milling Company, performance—especially in the quality of feed produced and in the out-turn—did not satisfy Babcock.

In the summer of 1923 the criticism from farmers of the quality of feed produced at Buffalo became so insistent that something had to be done. Babcock decided to send J. A. McConnell to act as his personal representative at the plant to find out what the trouble was.[9] McConnell was the ideal man for this job. As a fieldman he had worked closely with farmers and knew the problem from their standpoint while, at the same time, his special training in animal nutrition at Cornell gave him an understanding of how the problem could be met. He was given the

---

[9] McConnell recalls how Babcock said to him at the time, "Jim, I am in trouble at Buffalo. There is a lot of criticism of our G.L.F. feed." Interview with J. A. McConnell, June 22, 1951.

official title of "Chemist" with the understanding that one of his first jobs would be to set up a quality control laboratory.[10]

It did not take McConnell long to find the major difficulty—primarily a lack of interest throughout the mill in producing the type of feed required. By getting the cooperation of the employees by showing them the importance of their work, he soon had the mill making feed according to the formulas, under a time record system.

Within a short time the Buffalo mill was on the road to profitable operation. In addressing a school for G.L.F. fieldmen in April, 1924, McConnell, who had been made Plant Superintendent a short time before, could say: "I feel that the G.L.F. has in the Buffalo Mill a real asset. . . . We put out more cars for the size of our mill and more economically than any mill in Buffalo. . . ."

It was at about this time that it was decided to make the mill strictly a poultry feed producing plant to cater to the growing poultry industry since the American Milling Company was providing an ample and satisfactory supply of mixed dairy feeds. At that time, as poultry feed was largely batch-mixed, it could be well produced by the Buffalo plant.

The feed pool plan for 1924 took advantage of the experience gained in 1923 and the formula was not fixed in advance. In the original plan for this pool the feed ingredients were to be bought by a joint buying committee representing the G.L.F., the Eastern States Farmers' Exchange, the Pennsylvania Cooperative Federation and the Michigan State Farm Bureau and their representative was to supervise manufacturing operations at the American Milling Company plant. It was announced in the *G.L.F. Shareholder* that the price to farmers would be based on costs of ingredients, of order-getting, of mixing, a general assessment for plant overhead, and enough saving to cover the 6 percent stock dividend requirements of the G.L.F. According to the announcement a large volume would mean a low mixing charge and a light overhead assessment.

Babcock was not entirely satisfied with this arrangement, for two reasons. He was skeptical of the ability of the joint buying committee, and he preferred to operate independently since G.L.F. volume was ade-

[10] This title, which gave McConnell free rein to solve an important problem without embarrassing his relations with the manager of the feed department, illustrates the acute psychological insight used by Mr. Babcock in making significant changes in organization so as not to upset morale. The laboratory was not installed until June, 1924, when McConnell, then Plant Superintendent, employed Fred H. Hessel as Chemist to design the laboratory, purchase the equipment and operate it. Hessel, who is now in charge of quality control for the Mills Division of the G.L.F., recalls how "Jim had to teach me the difference between corn, wheat, oats, barley and milo, also bran, meat scraps, dried milk, etc. The job was a challenge to me; it was a new world. Needless to say, when quality control was put into effect, better feeds were shipped." (Letter, to author, of July 6, 1951.)

quate to enlist interest on the part of the manufacturers. Moreover, he
was fearful of becoming too dependent on the American Milling Company as a source of supplies.

Ever since 1923 he had been quietly working to establish independent
G.L.F. feed operations. His first move was to take over full responsibility
for local distribution by dispensing with the assistance of A.M.C. salesmen in getting the 1923 pool sign-up. Independence was also furthered
by the aggressive steps taken by the G.L.F. to meet the emergency situation which had developed in 1923.

With control over a large bloc of tonnage assured by the feed pool
campaign of 1924, Babcock could negotiate with the American Milling
company for a more favorable arrangement.

At this time he was trying to find some way of reducing feed costs.
Since the American Milling Company owned a distillery—laid up by
the prohibition era—that could be fitted up as a feed manufacuring plant,
Babcock and Atwood conceived the idea of using it to serve the G.L.F.
and share the savings. This would also enable the G.L.F. to get away
from the cost-plus plan which caused endless controversies over what
were proper costs. Atwood was at first opposed, for under this plan the
American Milling Company would share buying or speculative profits,
hitherto retained, but Babcock convinced him that this plan was essential
to continuing relations.

By the deal finally worked out in September the G.L.F. arranged to
lease Mill No. 2—the old distillery—of the American Milling Company and
to employ the American Milling Company to operate the mill under the
supervision of a G.L.F. resident superintendent. Under this plan the
G.L.F. really went into partnership with the American Milling Company,
for savings after agreed-upon costs were split monthly.[11] By this arrangement the G.L.F. withdrew also from its partnership with the other cooperatives in joint buying and supervision. As soon as this plan was
agreed upon Babcock sent Jim McConnell to Peoria to serve as the G.L.F.
representative supervisor. This move gave McConnell an opportunity to
increase his knowledge and experience in large feed mill operations, and
it insured that the vital interests of the G.L.F. would be fully protected.

The acquirement of Plant No. 2 imposed the problem of its profitable
operation—and to get this it was necessary to keep the price of feed
attractive to farmers. With an upward trend of feed ingredient prices in
the fall, this problem gave Babcock much concern for, to cover costs of
ingredients, it was necessary to raise the price promised for pool de-

---

[11] This arrangement was terminated within a year, as there was some question of
the legality of splitting the profit. Babcock was afraid that the plan was non-cooperative. The plan was superseded by taking over the plant on a lease basis, although
buying was continued on a joint account. Interview with McConnell, June 22, 1951.

liveries. He did so with misgivings for he knew how desperately pressed farmers then were.

He set forth his views in a letter to Atwood on November 20. In particular he asked if it would not be a wise long-time policy to price feeds "so close as to drive our mixed feed competitors from the field, while at the same time taking reasonable precaution to get by with Plant No. 2."

Atwood's reply shows the close working harmony of the two, and the type of sound counsel given which meant so much to Babcock during this period when G.L.F. policies were being developed. It was Atwood's opinion that:

. . . it is absolutely impossible to work on a closer margin than the one . . . determined. It is not good business at any time to sell any product at cost or below to drive out anticipated competition. Your stockholders, as well as our own, will look for some returns on their investment at the end of the year, and there is nothing that puts a business concern in a stronger position than to have some earnings and a surplus at the end of that period.

Atwood closed his letter with this sentence: "In my opinion, you should not be alarmed over competition . . ."

The feed pool plan in 1925 was carried on as in previous years, but it had now become largely a matter of getting local dealers to place orders on the basis of orders obtained from their patrons. In addressing the Institute of Cooperation at Philadelphia in July 1925, Babcock said:

We are now out with a proposition to our farmers predicated on orders for a year ahead, which will place our dairy feed mill on a capacity ten-hour run for five months, and a capacity twenty-hour run for seven months. . . . This sign-up is coming along rather cheaply, so there will be a considerable saving in order-getting cost.

Later in his talk he declared: "We are now getting about 90 percent of our business in open price orders, which average about seven months ahead."

This plan required farmers to contract for a fixed amount of feed in the summer for delivery later in the fall and winter. It thus required farmers to store and finance feed when it was delivered.

The pool plan was entirely given up in 1926. Local representatives were given quotas based on past records. By this time the flow of demand was dependable.

In the summer of 1926 dairymen in the New York Milk Shed were greatly disturbed by the so-called "menace of western milk" and this gave the G.L.F. an opportunity to champion their cause. It was apparent that the market outlets for milk could not be held unless production in the fall and winter months was increased. To meet this situation the G.L.F. joined with the Dairymen's League and the New York College of Agriculture in a campaign to increase fall and winter milk production in New York State.

The unbalanced production of milk in New York State was a hangover from cheese factory, butter and condensory days when heavy production in the summer was desirable and light production in the winter normal. The efficient production of milk for the fluid market required a more even production throughout the year. Otherwise, heavy production in the summer would bring ruinous prices, while shortages in the fall and winter would widen the area from which milk was drawn, and intensify the summer surplus.

To expand fall production dairymen were urged to use more mixed feed in the summer to build up more milk production capacity for the fall. This program expanded feed volume and gave the Exchange an opportunity to prove that it could help its members on a major problem.

The G.L.F. was at this time demonstrating to its farmer members that volume operations could greatly lower their feed costs. In an article in the *Dairymen's League News,* November 26, 1926, J. A. McConnell, as Manager of the G.L.F. Dairy Feed Service, presented information from G.L.F. experience which showed that manufacturing costs per ton of dairy feed had been reduced from $5.30 from June, 1923, when 3,000 tons had been manufactured, to $1.68 per ton in December, 1925, when 12,000 tons had been produced. It was apparent that more even production throughout the year at full capacity operation could save many dollars in feed bills.

The achievement of the G.L.F. in establishing its position in the feed business in the years 1922 to 1926-27 was spectacular, as shown by wholesale dollar figures:

1922	$2,348,548
1923	$4,566,605
1924-25	$4,787,919
1925-26	$6,395,117
1926-27	$8,967,749

Much of this progress was due to the aggressive establishment in the minds of farmers that the G.L.F. was their servant in meeting their feed needs.

CHAPTER 12

Broadening the Base

The G.L.F. today is really a collection of service agencies. . . .
There must be a correlating agency, one that plans in common for
all and supervises the work of each. This is the function of the G.L.F.
Board of Directors. I am the agent of that body.
H. E. BABCOCK, *The G.L.F. Shareholder, November, 1925*

UNDER THE MANAGEMENT of Babcock, the G.L.F. rounded out its activities so that he could properly say in November, 1925, "The G.L.F.
today is really a collection of service agencies."

Although feed service was given precedence, attention had not been
entirely diverted from the problems involved in providing satisfactory
programs for seeds, fertilizers, and other farm supplies.

The difficulties involved in getting these programs going were comparable to those for feed, but they were different and can best be discussed separately. Take seed, for example.

THE SEED PROGRAM

The program on seed was fairly well established when the G.L.F.
acquired the business of the New York State Grange Exchange. At first
the G.L.F. had simply undertaken to get farmers to pool their seed orders
through the G.L.F. as they had formerly been doing through the Grange
Exchange. In some places local cooperatives and dealers placed orders
to serve farmers' needs, but most of the seed orders came from the local
seed pooling groups.

This program gave the Agronomy Department of Cornell University an
opportunity to put into effect its teachings on the need of using high
quality seed. As John Barron, in charge of Farm Crops Extension Teaching at Cornell, later said in the July 1924 issue of the *G.L.F. Shareholder,*
"The G.L.F. Exchange presented to me a medium through which this
work could be done." He went on to say:

The G.L.F. must do an honest business because it has no interest to do anything else, for it is the farmer, himself, doing business for himself.

One of the G.L.F.'s first actions had been to arrange for Barron to go
into the West with representatives from its Board of Directors, to obtain
supplies of native-grown clover and alfalfa seed of desired quality. The
interest of the college in this program is indicated by the following recol-
lections of C. N. Silcox, who was employed as Extension Specialist in

Farm Crops, under Barron in July, 1920. One of Silcox's jobs was to investigate complaints of farmers that their land was "clover-sick" or "alfalfa-sick." They reported how the fields were "as bare as a barn floor" in the spring, after they had carefully seeded and got beautiful stands of clover or alfalfa in the preceding summer or fall. The trouble was found to be that the seed used was usually of foreign origin—from southern France, Italy, Africa, and Argentina—and not hardy enough to stand the rigors of the northeastern climate. "I was so enthusiastic about this program," writes Silcox, "that at farm meetings I sometimes went beyond propriety, as a State College employee, in recommending that farmers buy their seed from the G.L.F. I remember being reprimanded by Professor Burritt, then Director of Extension work, because of complaints made by seed companies regarding some of my remarks."[1]

The effectiveness of the seed gave the farmers tangible goodwill toward the G.L.F. as an organization.

In the fall of 1921 the importance of the seed business was recognized by establishing a seed department with A. L. Bibbins, a trained agronomist from Michigan State College, in charge.[2]

Under the infectious leadership of Bibbins, the G.L.F. effectively developed a reputation for high quality "Known-Origin" seed. This did much to establish in the minds of farmers that the G.L.F. stood for quality products at a reasonable cost. Like Babcock, Bibbins was a born salesman, and his effective slogan, "Know What You Sow," soon became household words throughout G.L.F. territory.

The progress in seed was reflected in a statement in the *Dairymen's League News* of June 9, 1922, "This year twice the amount of G.L.F. seed sold last year, has been shipped. . . . How true is the slogan of the seed department 'Good Seed is Cheap at Any Cost. Poor Seed is Time and Money Lost.'"

Thus Babcock did not have to concern himself with the seed program when he came in as General Manager in July, 1922. In fact, its outstanding success largely carried the G.L.F. over this difficult period. According to the pioneer G.L.F. fieldman, Obe Sheldon: "The G.L.F. in making it possible for a farmer to obtain good seed adapted to the climate of New York State, Pennsylvania, and New Jersey, established the first confidence and goodwill of the farmers."[3]

[1] Letter of August 29, 1957. The seed dealers were confronted with a difficult problem, for they had no way then of obtaining "known origin" seed.
[2] Silcox had recommended his appointment in the light of the effective work done by Bibbins as Secretary of the Michigan Crop Improvement Association. He had also worked with Bibbins while he was a student at Michigan State Agricultural College. In the summer of 1922 Silcox joined the staff of the G.L.F. as assistant to Bibbins. Letter of C. N. Silcox, August 29, 1957.
[3] Letter of July 16, 1951. In this letter he listed this as the No. 1 G.L.F. accomplishment during his 30-year connection with the organization.

With the encouragement of Babcock, Bibbins succeeded in using every available media for getting over the idea that the G.L.F. was concerned with helping farmers on their seed problems. Effective use was made of advertising in the *Dairymen's League News*, the *American Agriculturist*, and its own publication, the *G.L.F. Shareholder*. This built a strong sense of confidence in the program.

During these early days the antagonism of competitors toward the seed program was vicious, and one of the most effective ways of countering it was the use of testimonials of growers who were satisfied users of G.L.F. seed. For example, an advertisement in the October 1924 *G.L.F. Shareholder*, headed, "G.L.F. Known-Origin Seeds Make Good," included endorsements from four county farm bureau presidents in northern New York.

This same issue of the *Shareholder* carried an article on misrepresentations in the seed trade, as disclosed by the State Commissioner of Agriculture. The Commissioner had called seedsmen to Albany and said: "There have been serious abuses in the vending of agricultural seeds . . . good seed is the foundation of agriculture. It is up to you to clean house." The article ended with this statement: "G.L.F. shareholders are fortunate in that they are assured of the absolute integrity of the tags on their G.L.F. seed. They know what they sow. They know its source. As far as the seed is a factor, they are sure of their crop."

One of the charges made against the G.L.F. by its competitors was that it did not live up to its own guarantees. The G.L.F. countered this by placing a $25,000 bond back of its guarantee. There is a full-page description of the bond in the *G.L.F. Shareholder* for January 20, 1925, supported by the following statement:

By insuring the origin of the seed you get through the G.L.F. to the extent of a $25,000 bond, the Fidelity and Deposit Company answers once and for all the claims of those malicious individuals who have slandered you and the manager of your seed department, that claims that you have gotten foreign seed through the G.L.F. . . . Where else can you buy clover and alfalfa seed that is known to be domestic, northern grown and which is selected by your own organization and backed by both word and bond?

The bond was made out in favor of F. L. Strivings, Master of the New York State Grange, as Trustee for G.L.F. Patrons.

In this same issue of the *G.L.F. Shareholder* is a full-page article on the seed program entitled "Performance is the Test of Seeds." It pointed out that 26,000 farmers had bought seed through the G.L.F. Seed Service and that their G.L.F. domestic northern grown clover and alfalfa seed had proved their worth. It called attention to the fact that the G.L.F. guaranteed its seed to be genuinely native-grown. This slogan ended the article: "Your G.L.F. will serve you but you must help yourself."

The seed program not only gained friends for the G.L.F. but it also helped to give the G.L.F. financial and business standing. It was the only activity in the black from the very beginning. Sales during these years reflect only a small portion of its significance:

1922	$490,554
1923	610,823
1924 (first 6 mo.)	652,390
1924-25	930,674
1925-26	881,439

In 1925 the G.L.F. Seed Department began to broaden its service by giving special attention to corn and feed grains. In the light of the experience of Cornell plant breeders in selecting or developing new varieties which were outyielding available commercial seed, the G.L.F. saw the opportunity of providing its grower-members with this type of seed which would help them increase their farm production and income.

THE FERTILIZER PROGRAM

When the G.L.F. was established, it took over the insignificant fertilizer business that had been developed by the State Grange Exchange. Little was accomplished in building up this business until late 1921 when a fertilizer department was set up, with W. L. Gay as manager.

Under Gay, the fertilizer department promoted, with the support of the State College, the sale of no-filler, open-formula, high-analysis fertilizer, but progress was disappointingly slow. Although Gay had good fertilizer experience he did not have the necessary spirit for farmers' interests found in Babcock and Bibbins. In fairness to him, however, it should be noted that conditions were not propitious for the new department, for the post-war agricultural depression had brought a great decline in fertilizer consumption and many fertilizer companies were desperately endeavoring to maintain volume by slashing prices or through giving special deals to large users.

When Babcock came in as General Manager, Gay energetically endeavored to build volume, but the program did not take hold in any vigorous way. Moreover, just when things were becoming a little brighter, in the spring of 1924, the fertilizer program was hard hit when 50 cars of green acid phosphate "hardened in farmers' hands." This gave Babcock much concern, and he wrote Maurice Burritt on May 13, 1924, "This is raising the very dickens. . . . We are agreed that the only thing for us to do is to get quickly to the men who have the hard acid and make a satisfactory adjustment even if it costs us several thousand dollars." Although G.L.F. met this problem courageously by recompensing those injured, it impaired farmer confidence in G.L.F. fertilizer service for many years to come.

Gay gradually became convinced and he, in turn, convinced Babcock and the Directors, that the G.L.F. needed its own fertilizer plant to insure a source of supply of good quality and increase savings from manufacture. Although the G.L.F. was not strong enough financially to invest heavily in this somewhat hazardous type of enterprise, Gay was alert to the situation and in the summer of 1924 he found an opportunity for the G.L.F., through an investment of a few thousand dollars, to acquire part ownership and a minority representation on the Board of Directors of the Summers Fertilizer Company in Baltimore—a firm he had been dealing with. The G.L.F. representatives on the Board were to be President N. F. Webb and W. L. Gay and Gay was also to be a member of the Executive Committee.

There is an enthusiastic account of this new development in the *G.L.F. Shareholder* for December 1924, under the title, "We become manufacturers of acid phosphate and mixed fertilizers." In this article Babcock said:

It has always been the policy of the Board of Directors of the G.L.F. to directly control the preparations and manufacturing of its goods whenever possible. This policy has been made necessary by the quality program . . . the Directors have felt that unless the grain and feed, seeds and fertilizers which you have bought through the Exchange were prepared and conditioned in Exchange plants exclusively there were too many opportunities for departing from the ideals of quality back of G.L.F. brands.

After describing the arrangement entered into with the Summers Company, Babcock continued:

All G.L.F. goods will be manfactured according to public formulas furnished by the colleges of agriculture and will be shipped under G.L.F. brands. This will include acid phosphate which will be acidulated at the plant. It is the present plan to carry a reserve of at least 5,000 tons of acid phosphate at all times so as to insure adequate curing period. No acid phosphate will leave the factory until it has passed a thorough inspection and is known to be thoroughly cured.

The *G.L.F. Shareholder* for January 20, 1925, went all out for the fertilizer program with a double-page spread article—advertisement headed: "For fertility, depend on G.L.F. High Analysis, No Filler, Open-Formula Fertilizer."

To overcome the memory of the hard fertilizer fiasco, it featured testimonials from satisfied growers and statements from dealers attesting to the good mechanical condition of G.L.F. fertilizers handled, "particularly the acid phosphate," and boasted that "G.L.F. fertilizers are now manufactured and mixed by the G.L.F. in its own plant at Baltimore."

A feature of this advertisement was a letter reproduced from E. L. Worthen, Extension Professor, Soil Technologist, of the New York State College of Agriculture. This letter, addressed to W. L. Gay, said:

I am pleased to learn that the G.L.F. will continue during 1925 its policy of high analysis fertilizers . . . the open-formula service should receive universal approval. Your formulas for 1925 are fully up to standard and agree very closely with those that we suggest be followed in home mixing. Also, I am glad you will continue your service in furnishing acid phosphate, nitrate of soda, and the other standard materials needed for separate application to the land for the home mixing of fertilizers.

G.L.F. members reacted favorably toward the new development and in early 1925 Babcock reported that it had done much to overcome the bad feeling that resulted from the sale of the hard acid phosphate.

However, the limited partnership arrangement did not prove entirely satisfactory for conflicts soon arose in the joint management of the Summers Company. Much of the difficulty came from the fact that Gay's personal interests often pulled against those of the G.L.F. In early 1925 he importuned the Board to let him and the manager of the Summers Company set up a non-cooperative fertilizer manufacturing company. He proposed that the G.L.F., in addition to these two, be "the remaining largest stockholder and financial backer." Later he asked the Board of Directors of the G.L.F. to lend him funds so that he could personally invest in the stock of the Summers Company. The Board met this situation by passing the following Resolution: "That the Board go on record as being opposed to both the principle and practice of employees being interested in companies which are doing or are designed to do business with the Exchange." However, the Board did not follow through on this policy, for it subsequently endorsed Gay's note for $2,500 to enable him to purchase stock in the Summers Company.

During this period Babcock was concerned over the way the Baltimore plant was running and on April 29 he wrote to Gay as follows:

There is one man in our organization who now has had better than two years plant training. This is McConnell. I think it would be a fine thing if you would write to him . . . and suggest that . . . he study with you and Mr. Tupman [the manager of the Summers company] the problems of your plant. There is no question but what you have got to bring this plant service up before you can develop this plant service up to its maximum capacity.

Gay did not follow up on this suggestion but continued to work unceasingly to increase the degree of control held by the G.L.F. To an extent, he succeeded, for the G.L.F. in mid-1925 increased its investment and obtained two more members on the Summers Board. (Burritt and Babcock.)

Even this arrangement did not give satisfaction, and Babcock toyed with the idea of forming another company to take over when the contract with the Summers Company expired.

It took Babcock and his associates some time to realize that Gay's personal interests might be adversely affecting the best interests of the G.L.F. For one thing, Gay attemped to do too much too fast. For example, before the service was well established to serve G.L.F. members, he set up a distributing agency in Puerto Rico. This hastily conceived arrangement to extend G.L.F.'s services to Puerto Rico was to result in an embarrassing loss.

Thus, the fertilizer program was a constant headache for Babcock and the directors throughout 1925. Babcock had confidence in Gay's ability but he was concerned over his personal ambitions. One problem was to pay Gay what he thought he was worth. Eventually a plan was worked out that provided him with bonus payments in addition to a substantial salary.

Babcock continued to hope that things would straighten out and that Gay would harmonize his interests with those of the G.L.F. He became more and more disillusioned. By the end of 1925 he was giving consideration to the employment of an understudy to have someone at hand to take over Gay's job if his replacement should be necessary.

Babcock did not place all of the blame on Gay for the troubles of the fertilizer department. On November 4 he wrote to Fred Porter that he was glad that he and Harry Bull, as a committee from the directors, were going to undertake to straighten out "our tangled fertilizer service affairs." Babcock admitted that he had been "a bit weak once or twice in handling them . . ." He recognized that he had been constantly pushed toward control of the Summers Company by Gay—but on this he said: "I am not blaming Gay. He honestly believed we should control Summers and I agreed with him."

One of the things that the G.L.F. learned from this experience was that it had to place a man in charge of the fertilizer program who was in tune with the distributing policies of the G.L.F. Gay temperamentally started from the top and worked down, while a man was needed who could start from the bottom and build up. While the G.L.F. did not get an effective fertilizer program under way until this was learned, Gay can be given credit for aggressively promoting the importance of open-formula fertilizer and the elimination of filler, which provided a good foundation for later progress.

A good commentary on Gay's management of the fertilizer service is the remark of one of his contemporaries, "At that time Bill Gay was running what you might call the 'Bill Gay fertilizer service.'"

The G.L.F. learned an important lesson from this partnership with a private concern—that dominant control was essential to safeguard co-operative interests. A partnership had been entered into without a definite arrangement for cooperative control, and soon the G.L.F. had found itself thwarted in obtaining the type of service it desired.

Although sales of fertilizer showed some increase during these years, the growth was not impressive:

1922	$405,002
1923	586,773
1924 (first 6 mo.)	470,896
1924-25	713,176
1925-26	673,201

THE MAIL ORDER SERVICE

The *G.L.F. Shareholder* of May 1924 announced the successful establishment of a Mail Order Service. This was not a brand new development, for the Grange Exchange had handled many miscellaneous supplies by mail order, and the G.L.F. had continued the practice. The new name for this service, adopted a few months earlier, was probably taken by Babcock because of the popularity at that time of the big mail order firms. It was, however, significant in that it gave this program recognition and indicated that it would be pushed.

The main products handled by the Mail Order Department were listed as tires and tubes, auto accessories, motor oils, house and barn paint, fly spray and, to a limited extent, household equipment. In the fall a "Truth-In-Fabric" service was added, and an arrangement was entered into with a tailor to make suits to measure from good virgin wool cloth. This program brought enthusiastic support from the sheep growers of the State.

The *G.L.F. Shareholder* of January 1925, called attention to the mail order service on groceries—mostly canned goods, staples of all kinds, dried fruits, and G.L.F. flours. Previous advertisements had featured Mail Order Service on rubber boots and binder twine.

A later article pointed out that "The worth of this Service to shareholders lies in the savings effected and in the convenience of having guaranteed products delivered at their door," and that it was set up by the G.L.F. to utilize its facilities to the fullest extent. Attention was called to the fact that it had no capital invested and that its overhead consisted of part of the salary of its manager, who was also manager of the Producers Warehouse and Elevator Company, and that a corner in the Seed Department at Syracuse sufficed to handle orders.[4]

This article claimed that no product was offered to G.L.F. patrons until

[4] The *G.L.F. Shareholder*, November, 1925.

the Directors of the G.L.F. were fully satisfied of its worth. It reported the following articles as then being handled: Tires, tubes, tire chains, and other automobile accessories, motor oil, house and barn paint, and roofing cement, working shoes, boots, milk-strainers, coolers and scales, dish strainers, and, in season, fly sprays, binder twine, hay and coal.

The volume of supplies sold by mail order amounted to $203,595 in 1924-25, and only $158,451 in 1925-26. The significance of this program lay more in the experience gained and the good will engendered than in volume or net savings.

Later chapters will show how this program evolved.

THE G.L.F. FLOUR PROGRAM

In 1923, a development occurred that brought the G.L.F. into the farm home. At that time, Elmer V. McCollum of Johns Hopkins University was gaining national attention through his advocacy of the use of whole wheat flour in the interests of better nutrition, and he had many adherents in the New York State School of Home Economics and the New York State Home Bureau Federation. This situation set up a demand for G.L.F. service on flour. This came to a head when the New York State Home Bureau Federation passed the following Resolution:

Resolved that the members of the New York State Home Bureau Federation request the Cooperative G.L.F. Exchange to set up a Statewide service in the distribution of G.L.F. Quality Flour and G.L.F. Whole Wheat Flour.

Babcock saw the desirability of meeting this demand.

To provide the type of white flour that would meet the needs of the farm home, various samples of flour were tested by the New York State School of Home Economics until one with satisfactory baking quality was found. The G.L.F. then arranged for its manufacture with the George Urban Milling Company whose manager was F. A. McLellan, the recent manager of the Feed Department of the G.L.F., and a man deeply interested in the objectives of the G.L.F.

While the service on white flour was assured, a search was made for a whole wheat flour with desired keeping qualities. The problem attracted the interest of McLellan. He put a chemist to work, and within three months a whole wheat flour was made which stood the test.

The problem of getting people to use whole wheat flour, in view of their unfamiliarity with the product, called for additional work. Miss Lucille Brewer, a gifted Extension worker of the New York State School of Home Economics, was called upon to work up some recipes calling for whole wheat flour, and these were published by the G.L.F. in a little pamphlet called "The Book of Breads."

It was arranged to distribute the flour through the Grain and Feed Department of the G.L.F. in Buffalo, and a considerable amount of publicity was given to the new service through the *G.L.F. Shareholder* and other farm publications in the State.

Although the flour business never reached a significant volume, it did much to build support for the G.L.F. in the farm home. It was a forerunner of Babcock's interest in the problem of human nutrition and the Family Foods program which played so prominent a part in later G.L.F. marketing developments.

Here was a program undertaken for the farm home because of an expressed need, and G.L.F. applied the same procedure that gave satisfaction in the development of its services on feed and other supplies.[5]

Although the progress of the G.L.F. in handling seed, fertilizer, mail-order supplies and flour was not spectacular as compared with feed, it had been substantial by the end of 1925, and together these services had broadened the base of the organization.

[5] For further information see Mary Fennell's article, "The G.L.F. Enters the Farm Home," in the *G.L.F. Shareholder* for May 1924, and the advertisement in the *G.L.F. Shareholder* of July 1924, page 15.

CHAPTER 13

Forging Ahead

*I wish that I could give every farmer in the New York Milk Shed
this vision: The G.L.F. is today an organization capitalized, equipped,
manned, and in running order, awaiting only the greater use by farmers to make possible substantial savings in the cost of farm supplies.*
H. E. BABCOCK, *G.L.F. Shareholder, March 1926*

DURING THE YEARS 1922 through 1925 the G.L.F., in Babcock's words,
"got on its feet."

On December 31, 1925, Babcock could say, "the original capital raised
is intact." The G.L.F. had plants, trained employees and buying power
which never before had been available to farmers.

The statement of financial condition, December 31, 1925, reflected the
growing strength of the organization. During the preceding year, increased volume and savings had permitted the G.L.F. to write down the
book value of its warehouse property by $103,730, the amount to which
assets had been appreciated in December, 1921, and to reduce prepaid
organization expenses to $50,059.

Thus, a net saving of $38,900 on December 31, 1925—and it should not
be overlooked that a dividend on common stock amounting to $45,994
had been paid in 1924—was an indication of the considerable achievement
made by the organization under Babcock's management since June 30,
1922, when its true deficit amounted to $72,658.

The course of G.L.F. development was now fairly well charted. The
Buffalo feed plant was rapidly becoming efficient, and the arrangement
with the American Milling Company (AMCO) was enabling the G.L.F.
to build a powerful system of local distribution. The seed program was
making spectacular progress, and the fertilizer plant operations were
slowly being improved. Moreover, through its house organ, the *G.L.F.
Shareholder*, the G.L.F. was vigorously building volume in miscellaneous
farm supplies through its mail order department.

With the feed, fertilizer, and seed programs doing well, the Board of
Directors in 1926 turned to motor oil, a supply of increasing interest to
farmers, with the growth of mechanized farming. Following the precedent established for feed and fertilizer, it was decided to request the
Rural Engineering Department of Cornell University to write specifications for motor oil suitable for farm use to insure quality service. This
program was soon established, and energetically promoted by the Mail

Order Service through the *G.L.F. Shareholder*.[1]

Another product beginning to draw special attention was paint. The Directors requested the President to check the quality of paint being sold, and to discontinue sales until satisfaction was assured.

The G.L.F. ceased handling virgin wool clothing at this time in view of a ruling of the Bureau of Internal Revenue that clothing could not be considered a farm supply. The G.L.F. did not wish to let a relatively unimportant supply item jeopardize its recently acquired exemption from Federal income tax.

However, the decision was not based entirely on tax considerations. The sale of suits from virgin wool had not proved either popular or profitable. It was believed that this service could best be developed as a specialty by Jay Gelder, the man who had largely promoted it for the G.L.F., and it was operated for a time, with G.L.F. encouragement, under the name, "Truth-in-Fabric Service." This venture had G.L.F.'s blessing but it was no longer a G.L.F. responsibility. It cost the G.L.F. a few thousand dollars before it was finally liquidated in 1929.

While the Mail Order Service was of minor importance at this time, compared with feed, seed, and fertilizer, it made many friends for the G.L.F. and provided experience in the handling of various farm supply items. Later chapters will show how this service paved the way for a more complete service on general farm supply items and petroleum products.

During the spring of 1926 the emphasis within the G.L.F. was on more complete utilization of services. Babcock expressed this spirit in an editorial in the *G.L.F. Shareholder* of March 1926, under the title, "Time for Action."

> For five years now we have been getting ready to buy cooperatively. . . . To fully capitalize what we have today we should at least double our purchases through the G.L.F. It is just like a pair of horses, bought, paid for, and broken to work. The more they do the less the cost of feed per hour of work and the better shape they keep in.

Every effort was being made to strengthen local arrangements for service, especially through local dealer agents. Although the five "experimental" retail service stores, described in the next chapter, were beginning to show promise, it was recognized that for the time being main reliance for maintaining and building volume had to be on cooperating dealers.

The appointment of James A. McConnell as head of the grain, feed, and service department in March also ushered in a more aggressive program of feed merchandising. Under his general supervision, mill operations both at Peoria and Buffalo were brought to a high state of efficiency which permitted lowering of prices.

---

[1] See *G.L.F. Shareholder* for March 1926.

Optimism Takes Hold

While the G.L.F. was getting into a solvent financial condition, Babcock had cautiously restrained promotion. Now the time had come to go forward, and to show a bold, confident attitude.

To explain fully his thinking, Babcock presented a written report to the Board of Directors for the year ending June 30, 1926. He apologized for presenting this report in writing, with this comment: "I do so now only because the G.L.F. has grown to such an extent that it may be helpful for all of us to pause for a moment to take stock of what and where we are." This report set the stage for the period of rapid expansion which was to continue until stopped by the great depression in 1930.

Babcock opened his report by calling attention to two fair measures of success for a cooperative organization:

(1) Its adaptability to operate without impairment of its capital, and to earn interest thereon.
(2) Its ability to serve satisfactorily its patrons.

He was pleased with the G.L.F.'s showing on both counts. With respect to the second point, he said:

I believe that it is fair to state that the quality of service rendered by the G.L.F. will, over a period of years, be measured by the volume of goods purchased through it.

It was thus with a considerable degree of satisfaction that he called attention to the increases in volume of seed, feed, and fertilizer during the preceding four years.

Babcock also took this occasion to consider the future prospects of the subsidiary corporations. Of these, the most important was the Producers' Warehouse and Elevator Company, since it held title to the G.L.F.'s operating facilities, and owned the capital stock of the New York Agricultural Credit Corporation and of the various G.L.F. service stores.

According to Babcock, the establishment of the P.W. & E. Company had accomplished three major objects. It had:

1. Placed the G.L.F.'s property in the hands of a warehousing corporation which could issue receipts for goods stored by the G.L.F.
2. Enabled the G.L.F. to acquire ownership in other companies, without going through the almost impossible procedure of getting the consent of a majority of its stockholders.
3. Made the real properties of the G.L.F. available for use as collateral in borrowing money—"since it is possible for the G.L.F. to support its note with the stock of the Producers' Warehouse and Elevator Company."

At this time the G.L.F. was making extensive use of the P.W. & E.

Company to provide local storage for grain and feed in connection with its distribution program. This program was handled through the Producers' Warehousing Corporation which was set up by the P.W. & E. Company.

The object of the Producers' Warehousing Corporation was to provide local warehousing facilities that would permit the G.L.F. to borrow on feed up to the time of sale to the farmer. The corporation leased space from local elevators and dealers where feed would be stored under a custodian arrangement which permitted feed to be used as collateral. Under this program the G.L.F. released feed secured by warehouse receipts as local dealers purchased it. Babcock's report indicated that the P.W. & E., through the Producers' Warehousing Corporation, then controlled by lease 47 warehouses outside of Buffalo and Syracuse. This program was very helpful at the time because the G.L.F. was then very short of capital. It was found unnecessary in subsequent years.

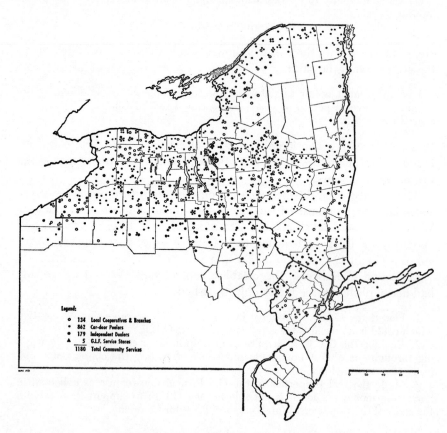

Legend:
o   134   Local Cooperatives & Branches
·   862   Car-door Poolers
●   179   Independent Dealers
▲   5   G.L.F. Service Stores
      1180 Total Community Services

FIGURE 1—G.L.F. COMMUNITY SERVICE AGENCIES, 1925

The G.L.F. had established the New York Agricultural Credit Corporation in 1924 primarily to provide a source of production credit to patrons. Babcock now felt that this corporation should be utilized to a greater extent "to furnish capital to G.L.F. agents and patrons who are good risks." Babcock felt that this would be desirable "because of the fact that when agents and patrons are loaned money for the specific purpose of purchasing through the G.L.F. their loyalty is much more to be depended upon."

In reviewing the policies which had proved successful, Babcock indicated that attention should now be devoted to improving existing services and building volume and support. This was to be done in two principal ways: By more aggressive field work and by establishment of more service stores. The time had come to discard the pool method of assembling orders in favor of continuous dealing through established agents, local cooperatives, and service stores.

Alert to the danger of becoming dependent upon private dealers, Babcock saw the service stores as a means of building a system of controlled retail distribution which could perform needed services and also keep dealers in line. He observed, however: "As farmers, we still lack the consciousness of ownership of our cooperative corporations which we must have if we are to protect and build them up."

In his report, Babcock declared. "It has been constantly my policy to so organize the G.L.F. as to be able to fix responsibility at all times," but he admitted being open to criticism for having let delegated authority in the case of one or two departments go too far. He went on to explain how he had recently corrected a situation of this type by placing James McConnell in charge of grain and feed service operations at both Peoria and Buffalo. Under this arrangement McConnell continued to supervise directly the dairy feed operations at Peoria while, under his direction, Otto Tanzer supervised poultry operations at Buffalo.

Babcock was greatly pleased with the results achieved from this arrangement. He declared:

The G.L.F. manufacturing of dairy feed stands out as probably the cheapest operation in the United States today due to the fact that we confine our activities to straight cars of dairy feed and because McConnell has introduced into mill management some of the farmer's common sense learned in the hay field and the threshing crew.

The change in management had provided also "an opportunity to work along lines [at Buffalo] which had developed through experience at Peoria" with the result "there had been the most remarkable growth which has ever taken place in a G.L.F. service." Babcock went on to say, "This . . . completes an attempt extending over the life of the Exchange, to put the Buffalo mill on a capacity basis."

Babcock was still not satisfied with the terms of the new contract recently entered into with the American Milling Company although it represented a major step forward. Believing that G.L.F. paid "too much rent" and "too large a service charge," he declared his intention to press for a reduction of the latter "as our volume in dairy feed grows until we get it down to 50 cents a ton."

Babcock was critical also of the lack of progress being made by the mail order department. He attributed the trouble with this service to the manager's lack of initiative and resourcefulness, and to his primary interest in savings rather than service to G.L.F. patrons. He was hopeful of more progress in the future since the manager had promised to operate the service "more along the lines of making savings for G.L.F. patrons than of making a showing by profits."

He also took this opportunity to recognize the importance of the field force. "It is my honest conviction that at the present time the G.L.F. field force . . . knows more about the problems of retailing and the factors which make for efficiency in handling farm supplies than any other similar body of men in the country." He went on to say, "I am ready to back them to the point of definitely ordering the fullest cooperation upon the part of the department heads, even though such orders mean the loss of men who do not share this confidence, or who do not see the problems of G.L.F. Field Service as I see them."

In closing his report, Babcock referred to a plan which he had put into effect to meet the growing pressure for higher salaries. Under this plan the G.L.F. paid the entire premium on a 20-year life insurance policy for key employees. While Babcock held that the type of men desired should be attracted by their desire to serve the objectives of the G.L.F. rather than through payment of high salaries, he recognized that employees must be given a sense of security for their families and a fair guarantee of permanency of employment. He looked upon this plan "as a forward step in establishing the G.L.F. on a permanent basis."

For some time the G.L.F. had been unhappy with the operations of its fertilizer service under its partnership agreement with the Summers Fertilizer Company. This program, which had been entered into hastily, had been a headache almost from the beginning, and more and more capital had been sunk without any significant benefits. In the fall of 1926, after careful study had been given to the problem by Professor Worthen and others from Cornell University, it was decided to withdraw from the existing arrangement and develop a program more closely related to the needs of its farmer members. With the resignation of Gay in early 1927, the Board of Directors moved the headquarters of the fertilizer service from New York City to Ithaca and placed L. J. Steele—a fieldman from western

New York with cooperative management experience—in charge. In announcing the change, in the October *G.L.F. Shareholder*, it was stated that "an important phase of Mr. Steele's work will be to develop local service on G.L.F. fertilizer."[2]

The rapid progress being made was reflected in the report for the fiscal year ending June 30, 1927. Volume was up from $8,208,208 to $10,778,174, or by 31 percent, largely due to the increase in feed volume from $6,391,249 to $8,967,749, an increase of 40 percent. While seed and mail order supplies had shown a slight volume increase, fertilizer sales were down from $673,220 to $547,220. Net margins from operations had increased from $46,654 to $193,601, largely reflecting savings in overhead expenses from the larger volume of feed business.

In addressing the New England Institute of Cooperation at Storrs, Connecticut, on August 18, 1927, Babcock expressed the opinion that "in the G.L.F. we have about reached the limit in saving on the cost of wholesale purchasing services we perform. Our orders are being secured for a cost of less than 1 percent on our volume." On the other hand, he saw great opportunities for saving in better retail service through the G.L.F. system of cooperative retail service agencies which "we are establishing as rapidly as possible." He closed his talk with this challenging paragraph:

> Cooperative retail service on farm supplies can be given, is being given, and will be given. Retail service should consist of cardoor service, warehouse service and accommodation credit at a total cost of not to exceed 5 percent on what you pay out for farm supplies and on the average today it is costing from 10 to 12 percent. In the efficient rendering of complete retail service lies the next opportunity of cooperative buying.[3]

While Babcock was enthusiastic over the possibilities of the service stores, he did not promote them at the expense of other activities. He realized that the bulk of G.L.F. supplies reached farmers through dealers and independent cooperatives, and he continued to concentrate the major effort of the field service department on serving these agencies. Moreover, he did not neglect study of how the feed and other wholesale operations could be made more effective.

---

[2] However, the G.L.F. continued to deal with the Summers Fertilizer Company on a commercial basis down to 1938, when the Summers plant was finally purchased by the Fertilizer Manufacturing Cooperative, Inc., set up jointly by the G.L.F. through its holding company, with the Southern States Cooperative, Inc., and (Ohio) Farm Bureau Cooperative Association.

[3] See E. A. Perregaux's *Economic Study of Retail Feed Stores in New York State.* (Cornell University Agricultural Experiment Station Bulletin 471, November 1928). Dr. Perregaux found that this margin in 1924 averaged 10.29 for cooperative stores and 12.24 for private dealers. None of the G.L.F. Service Stores was established when this study was made, but G.L.F. records indicate that some of these stores during the fiscal year 1926-27 operated close to the 5 percent margin figure given by Babcock.

At the close of 1927, the Directors could report in a statement in the January *G.L.F. Shareholder* that the Buffalo Mill was operating to full capacity night and day, and the leased mill at Peoria was just short of capacity, and that the volume on seed, fertilizer and mail order purchasing was materially cutting down the per unit expense of handling these items. Special satisfaction was expressed that this expansion of volume was coming from voluntary ordering in that two less fieldmen were employed than twelve months earlier.

IMPROVEMENT CONTINUES

On February 7, 1928, Babcock again presented a comprehensive report to the Board of Directors, primarily for the year 1927. He summed up the financial position of the Exchange as follows:

The original capital entrusted to you is intact. It is protected by a reserve and surplus equal to approximately 25 percent of the sum originally raised by the shareholders. Less capital is tied up in fixed assets than was originally invested in them.

Babcock thus took occasion to review the factors which he considered responsible for this satisfactory financial position, namely:

1. Absolute centralized authority of management.
2. A steady, persistent program of establishing low cost retail service agencies.
3. The constant stimulation of these agencies to produce volume.
4. A plan of setting prices which has passed on savings to patrons as fast as they have been accumulated.
5. General recognition of both the economic and human rights of employees, and
6. High standards of service to patrons.

Babcock proceeded to say:

Any story of our progress that does not take these policies into consideration deals only with the dusty documents and overlooks entirely the spirit that made possible the accomplishments they record.

He also emphasized this thought: *"The chief danger to a cooperative organization lies in a breaking-up from within. The chief protection is completely centralized authority that is held absolutely responsible for results."*

Babcock then turned to a consideration of "present conditions and problems," saying, "The G.L.F. is today a group of related activities."

The dairy feed service had experienced "a most remarkable extension," shipments from Peoria having increased from 119,760 tons of mixed dairy feed in 1926 to 184,064 tons in 1927, or an increase of 53.9 percent.

The contract with the American Milling Company was still in force, under which the G.L.F. paid 6 percent for the capital used, a rental for the plant based on 6 percent interest on the plant's book value plus 5 percent annual depreciation and a service fee of 75 cents a ton. However, "AMCO [was] being given an opportunity to adjust voluntarily this service fee downward in recognition of our increased tonnage and the increased contribution our men are making to management." Under the provisions of this contract, the G.L.F. was permitted to provide 50 percent of the working capital which now represented about $140,000.

Babcock summed up the situation by saying, "Without question, the major problem that is ahead of us consists of either working out permanent arrangements with AMCO for handling our dairy feed service or setting up to handle all or part of it independently of AMCO." However, Babcock did not look upon this as an immediate problem as the existing contract with AMCO would not expire until December 31, 1929.

Turning to the Poultry Feed Service at Buffalo, Babcock referred to it as "probably the most satisfactory service in which we are engaged." Although the mill had its physical limitations, it was operating very economically and effectively, and it was being financed without recourse to bank credit. By a low pricing policy capacity operation was being achieved and management was being pressed to apply ingenuity to increase capacity. The output of the mill had practically doubled during the year and, despite the low prices charged, operating efficiency had made possible a substantial net margin. He summed up by saying, ". . . the Buffalo plant is no longer a millstone around our necks."

Although the Buffalo plant was operating efficiently, it was apparent that "we must inevitably meet the problem of supplementing our mill capacity for what we know as Buffalo tonnage." Already some of the Buffalo orders were being diverted to Peoria. Babcock felt that this problem could not be separated "from the working out of [Buffalo] mill capacity on a more or less permanent basis for our dairy feed service as well."

This raised the whole perplexing problem of future relationship with Amco; whether in the long run it would be desirable for G.L.F. to break with Amco and operate its own mill. Babcock admitted that this question was a matter of constant correspondence and discussion between himself and McConnell, Tanzer, and Chase.[4]

During the preceding year the operations of the Seed Service had been brought into line with the Feed Service by establishment of better work-

[4] As indicated in the next chapter, Elwood Chase had been sent to Peoria to assist McConnell. His experience as Director of Field Service gave him a good basis for judgment.

ing relations with reliable "agent-buyers." Babcock was then promoting the plan which had given such good results on feed in getting orders with prices to be later fixed.

The death of L. J. Steele (See p. 130) had temporarily checked plans being worked out for the fertilizer department, but substantial progress had been made in developing more satisfactory sources of supply. The dry mixing plant established at Phelps was just emerging from the experimental stage and it was anticipated that "definite recommendations concerning the advisability of small-batch mixing plants" could be developed by June 30. T. E. (Tom) Milliman, the new manager, was getting hold of things.

The Mail Order Service was giving more satisfaction, but Babcock believed "that we have not yet touched the possibilities of this service." He urged that great precautions be taken to safeguard quality on supplies handled. A distinctive service on motor oils was already underway, and a program was being planned for paint. (See p. 131) In one year's time cod-liver oil sales had reached 30,000 gallons. He was still not satisfied with progress being made but as there was "no pressing need to build the department rapidly," he held that "we can well afford to take our time in bringing out its full possibilities."

Babcock felt that G.L.F. circulars and advertisements had set a new standard in the agricultural field, which demonstrated "the wisdom of our switch from the old line type of advertising agency to one capable of specializing in our field."

In referring to the Producers' Warehouse and Elevator Company, Babcock pointed out that it is "owned—lock, stock, and barrel—by the G.L.F." For purposes of administration its employees "are considered as directly responsible to the General Manager of the G.L.F." The principal subsidiaries of the P. W. & E. at this time were the 17 Service Store Corporations. Of the other two subsidiaries, the New York Agricultural Credit Corporation was being used "less and less," and the Producers' Warehousing Corporation, which had served a valuable function for a time in leasing local storage space, was now little needed in view of the growth of stores and stronger agencies.

In reporting to the Board on May 11, 1928, at Lake Placid, N.Y., Babcock referred to a change he had instituted to raise effectively funds for the support of the executive office, which covered salaries and expenses for himself, the accountant, attorney, and other general officers as well as the field force. Under the new plan, the wholesale departments were assessed one percent of sales, and the retail service stores one half of one percent of sales. He remarked, "The system of assessment is in line with the policy I have consistently followed of doing the theoretically correct thing even before it was strictly practical." While this was true, it should also be noted that Babcock never undertook a program without having a safety valve.

One of the major expenditures of the Executive Office was for advertising, which was then running to about $50,000 per year. Babcock was of the opinion that "probably no money we spend brings us any greater results in volume and therefore in attaining our objective of cutting down our costs of operation."

The 31 percent gain in volume during 1926-27 was far exceeded in 1927-28, rising from $10,778,174 to $19,066,118, or by 77 percent. Again, most of the increase was in feed which expanded from $8,967,749 in 1926-27 to $17,195,098 in 1927-28, or by 92 percent. While small gains were registered in fertilizer and other farm supplies, seed declined from $1,053,425 to $912,692, partially as a result of low seed prices.

The tremendous expansion in dollar feed volume—which was remarkable in that it was made without the benefit of price inflation—was accompanied by a rise in net income from $193,601 to $425,449, an increase of 120 percent. In fact, the savings in this one year—after generous allowance had been made for depreciation—just about equalled all of the savings which had been made up to that date.

This remarkable improvement in savings was reflected in a direct strengthening of the balance sheet. This is shown by comparing the balance sheet as of June 30, 1928, with the balance sheet at the end of the preceding year:

	June 30, 1927	*June 30, 1928*
Assets:		
Current assets	$ 677,172	$ 965,022
Fixed (net)	354,951	344,117
Other	155,824	184,912
Total assets	$1,187,947	$1,494,051
Liabilities:		
Current	$ 93,285	$ 45,020
Other	80,370	54,967
Total liabilities	$ 173,655	$ 99,987
Net Worth:		
Capital stock	$ 774,280	$ 774,220
Patrons' equity	240,012	619,844
Total net worth	1,014,292	1,394,064
Total liabilities and net worth	$1,187,947	$1,494,051

It will be observed that net operating capital had increased during the year from $583,887 to $920,002; that there was now $21.44 in current assets for each dollar of current liabilities; and that capital invested by members either invested in stock or represented by undistributed margins now amounted to 93.31 percent of total assets.

With this remarkable record, it is not surprising that G.L.F. leaders were ebullient, especially since the rate of growth in volume and savings was continuing upward. There were now funds available for expansion of the store program and to provide for the construction of a large feed mill in Buffalo should this action be deemed advisable. The more progressive thinking of G.L.F. officials during this period must be interpreted in the light of the new-found prosperity of the organization.

G.L.F. Fieldmen's Conference, January, 1934

Front Row: Jay Coryell; Fred H. Hessel; C. N. Silcox; H. E. Babcock; E. V. Underwood; J. A. McConnell; Harlo P. Beals; Merritt H. Crouch.

Second Row: Joseph L. Batty; Norval G. Budd; E. H. Fallon; S. C. Tarbell; M. E. Campbell; Herbert J. Aiken; Charles W. Skeele; Dean W. Kelsey; T. B. Clausen.

Third Row: F. A. McLellan; W. D. McMillan; O. W. Sheldon; Britt Cooper; Frank Fallon; Milton P. Royce; Al Coleman; T. J. McInerney; Stanley Griffith; C. W. Sadd; A. L. Bibbins.

Fourth Row: C. E. Dayton; V. A. Fogg; Russ Rafferty; Frank Naegely; Fred Naegely; J. W. Stiles; Henry Moore; A. J. Masterman; Bayard H. Staplin; W. S. Miller.

THE BOARD OF DIRECTORS, 1921

Top Row: J. C. GRIFFITH; FRED PORTER; S. J. LOWELL; RICHARD HALL, *Manager;* HARRY BROWN.

Bottom Row: W. L. BEAN, *President;* HARRY BULL; N. F. WEBB; E. C. WEATHERBY; *Assistant Secretary;* RAYMOND HITCHINGS; A. L. SMITH.

THE BOARD OF DIRECTORS, 1960

Standing: HOWARD G. SOPER; HOWARD A. GILES; ORRIN F. ROSS; HENRY W. BIBUS, JR.; MORRIS T. JOHNSON; CLAYTON G. WHITE; WALLACE H. RICH; MILBURN J. HUNTLEY; ROY S. BOWEN.

Seated: RALPH L. CULVER; CLIFFORD E. SNYDER; JAMES C. CORWITH, *President;* EARL B. CLARK; HAROLD L. CREAL.

Background picture: Ithaca business district with G.L.F. buildings on Terrace Hill in upper left. *Upper inset picture:* Babcock Hall. *Center inset picture:* Administration Building. *Lower inset picture:* G.L.F. School of Cooperative Administration.

BUFFALO FEED MILL

DIRECTORS INSPECT MARINE LEG AT BUFFALO MILL

CHAPTER 14

The Store Experiment

*It is my honest conviction that the G.L.F. owes its future existence
and its opportunity for service to a system of retail service.*

H. E. BABCOCK, *June 30, 1926.*

I N JUNE, 1923, while Babcock was pragmatically feeling his way in building distribution outlets, a situation developed at Ithaca which was
destined to have a considerable effect on the trend of G.L.F. development.
With the failure of the Tompkins County Cooperative, primarily because
of meager capital and weak management, farmers in Tompkins County—
the home county of the G.L.F.—had no means of obtaining G.L.F. service.
This event, which impaired the local prestige of the G.L.F., gave Babcock
just the opportunity he was looking for to experiment in the field of local
distribution. At this time the G.L.F. was turning more and more to local
dealers as distributive outlets. While Babcock recognized the value of
such distributive outlets as a means of building volume quickly, he also
realized that as long as local dealers controlled local service, G.L.F. objectives could be but partially achieved.[1]

To correct this local situation Babcock persuaded V. B. Blatchley, the
popular county agent of Tompkins County, that he could make more
money as exclusive agent for the G.L.F. in Tompkins County than as
county agent. In undertaking this arrangement Babcock also hoped to increase the use of poultry feed being manufactured by the G.L.F. at its
Buffalo plant. To insure success Babcock promised Blatchley the financial
backing and considerable moral support of the G.L.F.

To help Blatchley get the new service started Babcock sent out, in July,
a letter to all G.L.F. shareholders in Tompkins County in which he said:

> The big handicap which you have faced in the past in using G.L.F. has been
> the absence of local service arrangements. The chief object of this letter is to
> announce that this then is now overcome. On July 1st, Mr. V. B. Blatchley
> . . . took over the business of the Tompkins County Farmers Company. . . .
> You will know at all times just what G.L.F. goods cost Mr. Blatchley. You will
> know the pay he receives for the work he does. The amount of this pay, as does
> the price of G.L.F. goods, depends on the volume of business done. Will you
> cooperate to build up your own business?

Although a considerable volume of business was developed, it gradually
became clear that the arrangement was weak in that it gave G.L.F. no

[1] It will be recalled that Professor Savage had advocated a system of retail store
outlets when plans for the G.L.F. were being worked out in 1920. (See p. 41.)

direct supervision over the retail service. The G.L.F. could assist and advise but it could not administer. This situation led naturally to the conception of a local service center under the direct management of the G.L.F.

As the *G.L.F. Week* reported some years later, April 1, 1946:

This agency was the first step toward a local community service. Blatchley operated from the Tompkins County Farmers warehouse, and put in a line of G.L.F. commodities, taking orders from farmers over the entire county. Seed, feed, and fertilizer orders were pooled, as was the custom at that time. Delivery was made by railroad car to eleven different sidings throughout the county.

Babcock's correspondence with Hannon, Manager of the Feed Department at Buffalo, also shows how this conception was broadening. On August 4, 1924, Hannon had written him as follows:

The more I see of the operations of this Department, I am forced to the conclusion that there is only one way in which we can deliver the best and greatest amount of cooperative service at a reasonable figure, and that is through a chain-store arrangement whereby we will control the warehouses, employ the manager, and pay him a regular salary for his service, based, perhaps, upon a minimum with a bonus for increased sales.

On the margin of this letter which was returned to Hannon, Babcock had written:

Right—a subject very dear to my heart.

For some time Babcock had been toying with the possibilities of distributing farm supplies through a system of local warehouses, managed through a central warehousing corporation. Under this plan stocks of feed and other items that could be handled in bulk were to be stored in local communities and financed largely by borrowing on the commodities stored. It was thought that this would provide the capital needed to facilitate a rapid expansion of farm supply volume.

In a memorandum dated June 14, 1924, Babcock gave Burritt his "suggestions" on "operation of the warehouse corporation in the distribution of farm supplies." These are quoted in detail, as they show how Babcock's mind was working on this problem.

(1) The local superintendents should be employed by the central warehousing corporation controlled by it.
(2) They should operate in the role of order-takers and never be permitted to go into a general merchandising business which will result in their accumulating speculative stocks.
(3) The local warehousing men should be guaranteed a flat salary by the central organization and given an opportunity to add to the same through the operation of a commission schedule which would automatically recognize their efforts in building up volume . . .
(4) Local superintendents should have nothing but retail prices to deal with.
(5) Finances for lifting the draft should be provided by local institutions.

All of the above is based *on cardoor, or practically cardoor,* deliveries, and I want to say right here that this is the safest kind of service *to begin with.* You will get into a general warehousing service fast enough without planning to do it.

To arrange for the capital on a practical basis I would *go to a local bank* and arrange for the local superintendent to have a line of credit up to some agreed-upon sum.

Four months later, on October 18, 1924, Babcock reported to the Executive Committee:

I feel that I'm now free to develop local G.L.F. Service. In the development of that service I am sure the P. W. and E. Company and the New York Agricultural Credit Corporation will play a big role. With the P. W. and E. Company we can rent warehouses, ship goods into those warehouses, and issue warehouse receipts. With the New York Agricultural Credit Corporation we can take groups of farmers and furnish them with capital to use in direct purchases. We are so set that we can go into a community and offer financial assistance without a very great risk ourselves.

We are now operating at the rate of $8,000,000 a year, $2,000,000 over last year. With 100 financed farmer groups we can distribute an additional $1,000,000 worth of supplies. Ten stores in which we participate in the management through the P. W. and E. Company are easily good for another $1,000,000. It is my thought to try to hold our eight million with our present distributors and go out and locate the other two million in these two groups. When we are handling $10,000,000 we will be in good shape.

On October 15, 1924, while the G.L.F. was moving toward the formation of a warehouse corporation—which was made use of in 1926 and 1927, (p. 104) the organization moved a step closer toward control of retail distribution at Ithaca when it took over Blatchley's operations and employed him as manager. The immediate cause for this action was the impairment of G.L.F.'s investment by overextension of credit to farmers. Since the G.L.F. was so far committed, it was logical to take the next step and acquire complete control so that it could enforce measures essential to success. This action was taken by Babcock with Executive Committee approval. Thus, the first of the G.L.F. Service Stores began to operate under the sign "Ithaca G.L.F. Service."

A handwritten letter in the G.L.F. files, drafted by Babcock, for circulation to Exchange supporters in Tompkins County after this arrangement had been consummated, shows how Babcock was feeling his way.

On October 15, 1924, the G.L.F. took over the business . . . with the view of determining whether a chain type of store could be made to pay and, if so, use this store to gain experience for the establishment of others. . . . We are now facing a problem of a new location. . . . Gather as much sentiment as possible on the following questions. . . . Would our Ithaca store, if accompanied by truck service, goods in storage at all times, and a good agent to handle cardooor shipments be a greater service than present method? Or bring a diversion of opportunity of getting first quality goods through our agency?

However, Babcock moved forward cautiously. Little was said of the Ithaca experiment, although the cover page of the *G.L.F. Shareholder* for January 1925 carried a photograph of the Ithaca G.L.F. Service Store over this legend: "The first local service station to be owned and managed by the G.L.F. Exchange devoted exclusively to the handling of G.L.F. goods, located at Ithaca, New York. Visit it Farmers Week."

Babcock gave his thinking in a letter dated February 25, 1925:

Blatchley operated along several months very successfully from our point of view; that is, he developed a good demand for G.L.F. goods here and gave good service. However, everybody knew Blatchley and, in addition, he is very easy going so that the first thing he knew he had all his capital tied up in accounts receivable. I then took the matter up with our Executive Committee and suggested that we take over the operation of the store with the idea of studying out a system of bookkeeping and operation and of establishing a base at which we could train store managers. They approved and we have been running the store on Executive Office funds. . . . We have run into a lot of problems but are gradually solving them. . . . We are working out a set of incorporation papers for stores. . . . As soon as the papers are all completed I want to call a directors' meeting at which the major portion of the discussion will be devoted to this chain store proposition. . . .

Then on March 11, 1925, Babcock recommended to the Board of Directors the establishment of a policy with respect to the formation and operation of stores. He saw the present problem of the G.L.F. as that of "giving service as cheaply and efficiently as possible and obtaining the desired volume to do so." To increase volume he proposed:

to set up a series of local distributing stores under Article 12 of the Business Corporation Law which provides for the issuance of preferred and common stock. Local people are to subscribe to the preferred stock which will provide means of obtaining a building and other necessary equipment. The G.L.F., through its P.W.E. Company, is to purchase the common stock and thereby control the voting power of the company.

The record of this meeting indicates that the directors were most concerned over the ability of the stores to control retail credit. To assure control on this matter the directors stipulated that the stores should be located only at such points where "a strictly 30-day credit system" could be effectively operated. At the end of this discussion it was: "Resolved that Mr. Babcock be authorized to establish local services at Afton and Cincinnatus by means of local G.L.F. stores set up as outlined and unanimously agreed upon by the directors."

With this policy established, stores were soon established at Afton (April 9), Cincinnatus (April 14), Honesdale, Pennsylvania, (May 27), and Walton (July 9). In the first two the stores took over the business of insolvent cooperatives which made difficult the re-establishment of cooperative service.

It was a period of trial and error—for there was little real experience to go on.[2]

To obtain a store, local farmers were required to subscribe for a minimum of $2500 in preferred stock and set up an Auditing and Advisory Committee. The G.L.F. was to provide management and capital for operations. The "proposition presented to the Walton Farmers' Cooperative relative to establishing G.L.F. Service at Walton" is here given in full to illustrate the plan basis on which these first stores were set up:

1. The G.L.F. agrees to establish and incorporate a Cooperative Stock Corporation to be known as the Walton Cooperative G.L.F. Service, Inc., provided that the farmers in the vicinity of Walton purchase a thousand shares of Preferred Stock, with a par value of $5.00 per share, of the Corporation. This will be incorporated under Article 12 of the Business Corporation's Law.

2. The 6% Preferred Stock will be fully paid, non-assessable and cumulative and will be preferred as to assets and dividends.

3. The Cooperative G.L.F. Exchange agrees to purchase the common stock up to the amount of 1000 shares with a par value of $5.00 each, of the corporation.

4. It is mutually understood that the proposed Walton Cooperative G.L.F. Service will purchase the present warehouse of the Walton Farmers' Cooperative Association for $2500 provided the Walton Farmers' Cooperative will accept preferred stock of the proposed Walton Cooperative G.L.F. Service, Inc., in payment for the building.

5. Grange League Federation Exchange, Inc., will be the holder of the common stock and the directors of the Cooperative G.L.F. Exchange will be the directors of the Walton Cooperative G.L.F. Service, Inc., and will have control of the corporation and manage the same.

6. The preferred stockholders will select from among their number an auditing and advisory committee of three whose duty it will be to secure proper audits of the Walton Cooperative G.L.F. Service, Inc., at stated periods and to advise with the Cooperative G.L.F. Exchange and the local manager of the Walton Cooperative G.L.F. Service, Inc., regarding local policies of management.

7. It is distinctly understood that the store will be operated on a strictly cash basis.

Setting up a store usually consisted of renting a building, furnishing it with an inventory of G.L.F. supplies, and placing a manager in charge to sink or swim. No elaborate accounting records were necessary, for the manager was required to deposit all proceeds daily for the account of the G.L.F. at a local bank, and credit business was not permitted. Methods of operation had to be improvised until a system could be worked out.

The experience of Frank Naegely in opening the store at Honesdale brings out this point. Naegely had been sent to Honesdale by the G.L.F. to

---

[2] It is of interest that the first retail stores of Sears, Roebuck & Company were not opened until later in this year, while the local retail stores of Montgomery Ward & Company were not started until a year later. For an account of early Sears' experience see Boris Emmet and John E. Jeuck, *Catalogues and Counters*, 1949, pp. 341-343.

help the local agent get more feed orders. Finding the agent little interested in promoting the G.L.F.—"that dollar-a-ton feed company"—Naegely requested the opportunity of organizing one of the new G.L.F. stores when the agent's contract expired in April. Naegely writes:

My dream came true the last Monday in April 1925. Elwood Chase instructed me to go to Honesdale and call a meeting of dairymen for Wednesday night. Those at the meeting had no objections and neither did the agent-buyer to our selling stock and starting a local farmers' cooperative. The promise was that as soon as I had collected $2500.00 in store stock we would start retail service. This was done in about 10 days, and I ordered a supply of feed. No system of store operations had been explained to me so I purchased several sales pads and listed each purchase. Then at the end of the day I deposited the day's cash receipts in the bank in my own name and wrote a check of equal amount and mailed it to Ithaca, attention E. L. Chase.

The first visitor from Ithaca, I recall, was Mr. Townsend, and it must have been early in July as farmers had just started to harvest hay. He was to help me set up some books, but we went out to sign up the coming winter's feed supply. It was probably August when Mr. Chase, in charge of Retail, brought Alice MacAniff down from Ithaca and told me the store was in the red and that Alice would find out what I did with the money. After Alice looked things over she discovered my mark-up was $1.00 per ton off car and $2.00 in warehouse, and being summer and no feed business, we could show no profit. However, this showing did slacken the pressure—for we all went up to $1.50 per ton off car. As I recall, we inaugurated some kind of system of a short daily report at that time and set up a store bank account.[3]

This account shows how little overhead direction was given in starting these early stores. Mr. Babcock had placed Elwood Chase in charge of field service on January 1, and the stores came under his general direction, but his major energies were devoted to the building of needed business volume. As it had early become apparent that specialized assistance was required, Jay Gelder and G. B. Townsend were given the job of helping get the stores established. In the summer of 1925 William McMillan was placed in direct charge, with Alice MacAniff providing needed assistance in store accounting and business methods.

Fortunately Miss MacAniff quickly recognized the necessity of a uniform accounting system for the service stores, and in a short time all of the stores had standardized their business records. This was essential to the development of a system of G.L.F. retail stores.[4]

In view of the shortage of G.L.F. capital no additional stores were

[3] Letter to author, March 14, 1951.
[4] Instruction Sheet A, G.L.F. Service Store Accounting Rules, issued in September 1925, prescribed definite procedures for handling orders, inventories, sales slips, and deposits, reports, and similar matters. Under the plan the local managers simply provided reports to the central office where the accounting for each store was done. This simplified the management and control of a store and provided low-cost accounting service.

formed in the last six months of 1925. Thus, the G.L.F. had an opportunity to concentrate attention on learning how to operate the five stores already set up. One of the most difficult problems to overcome was the over-extension of credit, which reflected the go-easy management methods then common. Nowhere was this problem more acute than at the Ithaca store where the credit practice was deeply ingrained. With Babcock's firm support Chase planned to sell there only for cash and ordered Manager Blatchley to collect the outstanding accounts without delay. This action seemed drastic at the time, but no temporizing could be permitted.[5]

Although the stores had got off to a slow start, Babcock declared, in addressing the American Institute of Cooperation in the summer of 1925, "These chain stores . . . promise well."

In August, 1925, Babcock gave the store idea a further boost when the *G.L.F. Shareholder* carried an article by G. B. Townsend on "A new G.L.F. Development—Local Stores Complete the Service," illustrated by a new model store and warehouse at Cincinnatus, New York.

The article, which reflects the mind of Babcock, tersely described how the new stores were organized and operated, and closed with this sentence: "It is not contemplated to organize these stores where adequate G.L.F. service is being given either by local cooperatives or established dealers."

The *G.L.F. Shareholder* for November 1925 carried an article on the work of the G.L.F. Field Service by its Manager, E. L. Chase, which made clear the attitude of the G.L.F. toward established dealers while it was trying to get the stores established. "There is," he said, "no reason why the local dealer in farm supplies should not perform the local G.L.F. service. Many of the most progressive dealers are now doing it to their own satisfaction as well as to that of the local G.L.F. Shareholders."

He went on to say:

As an endeavor to establish cooperative purchasing clear through from the point of origin to the ultimate user of farm supplies, the G.L.F. Field Service is now operating several chain stores. These stores are owned jointly on a cooperative basis by the local shareholders and the G.L.F. Field Service, the local

---

[5] This is shown by letter of E. L. Chase to V. B. Blatchley of July 24, 1925 and Babcock's letter to Blatchley of July 27, 1925, in which he said, "I am convinced that unless this is done, the Ithaca store will have to be closed." In a later letter, November 9, 1925, Babcock indicated to Blatchley (Who was trying to carry on extensive business operations in addition to his work for G.L.F.) that he was "not at all pleased with the progress that is being made" and he gave him "friendly but nevertheless a firm warning that by the first of December, you are to be so fixed as to give all of your time and energies to the store, or we will either close the store or effect a change in management." These quotations reflect the difficulty of changing old habits, especially those of friends. It is significant that Blatchley weathered this storm and became one of the outstanding managers in the G.L.F.

shareholders electing an auditing committee which also serves in an advisory capacity in solving the problems of store management.

These auditing committees were the forerunners of the advisory committee system later to become a dominant feature of G.L.F. organization.

The use of the advisory committee idea to give shareholders a say in the management of their store was no doubt an adaptation of the concept of an independent board of directors to the needs of a centrally directed system of stores. Farmers liked to be on boards of directors and the advisory committee idea recognized this, while it maintained a general control for the stores as a group.

The need for advisory committees was recognized by V. A. Fogg, then one of the fieldmen, who, with Babcock's encouragement made a study to analyze why local cooperatives failed in order to find out how to make the G.L.F. stores "click." His conclusions helped set a course that would work in practice. His main recommendation was that over-all management should be taken from the community and placed in an organization whose only business was to manage for a set fee.[6]

On December 31, 1925, the G.L.F. had $30,000 invested in the five stores represented by P. W. & E. Company holdings of their common stock. These five stores showed total sales of $186,356.36 and total net saving of only $491.45 for the six months operations ending December 31. In commenting on this Maurice Burritt, Treasurer, said:

> There are many opportunities for additional stores and many local situations where it would be very easy to take over the business of cooperatives and put stores in operation. These stores are a very great asset—however, we are not yet out of the experimental stage and the establishment of more than five additional stores should await further experience. When these stores are authorized we should not begin business until the local funds subscribed are paid in the full amount of the preferred stock required.

The G.L.F. was wisely holding back on the development of the stores —until more capital was available and experience could be gained on how best to operate them.

However, by June 30, 1926, when he reported to the Board of Directors for the preceding 12 months, Babcock had become concerned over the need for more service stores. There were then seven "either operating or soon to be in the field." The first three had picked up and continued the business of farm organizations which had failed. The fourth had got off to a late start whereas the fifth was "one of the worst messes the G.L.F. has ever got into." The two remaining were just getting under way.

Babcock's analysis indicated that the G.L.F. was learning how to operate retail service stores. It was becoming clear that such stores re-

[6] Letter, to author, March 14, 1951.

quired good local managers, strict control over credit, favorable location, adequate capital and assured local support. Babcock thought that "the chief development to date had been the organization of an accounting system and the training of an organization under the general supervision of Elwood Chase and the direct management of William McMillan for the handling of store service." He believed that:

This organization is particularly capable in the matter of looking after the investment in the stores and the handling of the accounts, credits, etc. It is still not satisfactorily developed as to its correlation with department heads in the matter of purchasing, its use of fieldmen, and in its abilities to develop volume around the stores themselves.

Later in the report he said:

It is my honest conviction that the G.L.F. owes its future existence and its opportunity for service to a system of retail service.

In October, 1926, Babcock gave the service store program an aggressive push with a lead article in the *G.L.F. Shareholder*, entitled, "The First Step—Local G.L.F. Service." This article pointed out that:

The longer the G.L.F. operates the more certain it becomes that the wholesale buying service it renders must be connected with local retail purchasing. Otherwise, no matter how efficient the wholesale purchasing business is, the savings it makes may fail entirely to reach a farmer because of excessive retail handling costs. In fact, just this thing is happening today at a number of points in G.L.F. territory.

This situation led Babcock to the conclusion that if dealers would not cooperate with the G.L.F. in giving efficient and low cost service the G.L.F. would have to provide it through its system of "cooperative chain stores." He made it clear that there was no desire to set up such stores where adequate service was available but he also made it clear that the G.L.F. was ready to do so if necessary to protect the interests of its members.

About this time President Webb furnished Babcock with his impressions of the chain stores. Webb thought they would result in great benefit to the G.L.F. if properly developed. He believed their sound development required "sufficient finances, good management, and a good local committee who take an interest in the welfare of all farmers rather than getting benefits for themselves." He also emphasized need of good location, an adequate supply of goods, and control of credit. He concluded by saying: "I do not favor development of the stores any faster than the above requirements can be met. However, the G.L.F. must be prepared to offer service as soon as they are set up."[7]

These views were in accord with Babcock's thinking that "one should

[7] Letter of November 30, 1926.

not get more hay down than can be raked up," and he was not yet ready to embark on a program of vigorous store expansion until the techniques of successful management and operation were more fully tested.

Babcock's faith at this time in the future of the "chain stores" was unlimited, but he wisely knew that their ultimate future depended upon the success of each store as it was established. Fortunately, the G.L.F. was short of capital for investment in such stores, so each new store had to be able to largely pay its own way. It is significant that there were only ten stores in operation in early 1927, two full years after the Ithaca store was established.

Up to this time the stores had been developed more or less independently of the fieldmen in the territory, although the fieldmen had helped set them up and had assisted on store problems. As store development and management was considered a specialist problem, it had been centered largely under Babcock's direct attention. Now he saw that the time was ripe to use the fieldmen in more vigorously promoting the establishment of new stores.

He therefore placed responsibility for store development and management in the field man who supervised the territory in which a store was needed or located. The fieldmen were expected to get new stores established where the lack of a store was holding back G.L.F. progress. This plan resulted in the establishment of several new stores during 1927, bringing the total number to seventeen by the end of the year.

Babcock's thinking at this time on the potential value of service stores was fully presented at the Institute of Cooperative Marketing, held at Storrs, Connecticut, August 18, 1927. In this talk on "Factors of Efficiency in Rendering Retail Service on Farm Supplies" he pointed out that: "In the G.L.F. we have about reached the limit in saving on the cost of wholesale purchasing services we perform." However, on the other phase of cooperative buying—the performance of cooperative retail services, he said:

> Cooperative retail service on farm supplies can be given, is being given, and will be given. Retail service should consist of car-door service, warehouse service, and accommodation credit at a total cost of not to exceed 5 percent on what you pay out for farm supplies and on the average today it is costing from 10 to 12 percent. In the efficient rendering of complete retail service lies the next opportunity of cooperative buying.

Babcock's position was supported by Dr. E. A. Perregaux's study of retail feed stores in New York State. W. I. Myers writes me, January 5, 1959, "It is my opinion that a good deal of credit for dramatizing the high cost and inefficiency of retail distribution of feed in New York goes to Perregaux's study of this problem. . . . Ed Babcock may have had some general ideas about this matter before Perregaux's study became available [as a doctoral dissertation in 1926] but Perregaux's work gave definite proof."[8]

Up to now, the G.L.F.'s financial control over stores was vested in its subsidiary corporation, the Producers' Warehouse and Elevator Corporation. As the capital investment in such stores grew with the addition of more stores, Babcock decided in June, 1927, to make Elwood Chase manager of the P. W. & E. Corporation to achieve a better administrative control over the store program and he, himself, resumed direction of the field force.

To make clear administrative lines of responsibility under the new arrangement, Babcock issued a memorandum to "Managers of G.L.F. Chain Stores" on June 28, 1927, which stated:

As I believe you are all aware, the G.L.F. Exchange proper owns a subsidiary corporation, the Producers' Warehouse and Elevator Company which, in turn, holds title to all real estate, commonly supposed to be owned by the G.L.F., and to the common stock in G.L.F. Service Store Corporation, commonly supposed to be owned by the G.L.F.

The manager of this subsidiary corporation which is the Producers' Warehouse and Elevator Company, Inc., is Mr. E. L. Chase who, therefore, is the manager of the Company which owns the common stock of the G.L.F. Service Store Corporation. This makes Mr. Chase responsible for the financial welfare of the stores and also responsible for their management and operation.

To assist himself, Mr. Chase has appointed Arthur Masterman assistant manager of the Producers' Warehouse and Elevator Company, with particular responsibility for the operation of Service Store Cooperatives. This means that Mr. Masterman is your immediate supervisor, and that Mr. Chase is Mr. Masterman's supervisor. Mr. Chase, of course, reports to myself as the General Manager of the parent company which owns the Producers' Warehouse and Elevator Company.

I am giving you these facts so that you may know to whom you are responsible and who the G.L.F. holds responsible for the success of the stores.

Later in the fall, Chase was made assistant to McConnell who was burdened by the growing problems of administering the feed service program.[9] Miss MacAniff, who had largely developed the accounting system used by the service stores, was thereupon made manager of the Producers' Warehouse and Elevator Corporation.

To assist Miss MacAniff in directing the store program, Babcock on January 27, 1928, made the district managers of field service into an advisory board of directors for the stores.

---

[8] See E. A. Perregaux, *An Economic Study of Retail Feed Stores in New York State;* Cornell University, Agricultural Experiment Station Bulletin 471, November 1928.

[9] By shifting Chase to Peoria, Babcock not only provided McConnell with a competent assistant and understudy, who knew field conditions, but he thus widened the executive experience of Chase. At this time Babcock was endeavoring to develop a corps of able executives who were widely experienced in G.L.F. operations and responsibilities.

Babcock explained this action in his general report to the directors of February 7, 1928:

At our last fieldmen's meeting on January 27th, I organized our eight field-men into what amounts to an advisory board of directors for our chain stores with Miss MacAniff as secretary of the board. My idea in doing this was to create a body of experts which would be able to go over situations and sort out facts for presentation to the board of directors of the Producers' Warehouse and Elevator Company and which in addition would take real management responsibility.

It was apparent that Babcock had at last become convinced that the time was approaching for a more vigorous expansion of the store program. He said:

Before I close this discussion of our service stores I want to emphasize that in my judgment the development of one hundred strategically located, economically operated, retail service agencies which are run on a cooperative non-profit basis will save at least 5 percent for farmers on what they are now paying for farm supplies. . . . Furthermore, the possession of these stores will do more to give stability and make effective our wholesale purchasing services than any other means I can think of.

However, conditions were not yet favorable for rapid promotion, and only three new stores were started during the next six months. This brought the total to 21 on July 1, 1928. In its meeting of May 12, 1928, the Board of Directors went on record as follows:

Resolved that in the development of our service stores we should now work toward replacing independent agencies which are not satisfactory with service stores rather than toward opening up new communities with such stores.

While Babcock was "laid up" by tuberculosis at Lake Placid during the winter of 1928, he conceived the idea of reorganizing the G.L.F. into two major divisions—Wholesale and Retail. The Wholesale Division was to be managed by Assistant Manager McConnell, who would be responsible for all procurement and manufacturing functions, while the Retail Division would take charge of all distribution and field service functions. Babcock felt that Fogg had the temperament, ability and experience to give leadership and direction to the Retail Division, and he called Fogg to Lake Placid to develop plans for the new Division, with emphasis on the expansion of service stores.

The new plan of organization, with two major divisions, became effective on July 1, 1928. It opened the door for vigorous store expansion with the result that the number increased to 31 by July 1, 1929, and to 65 by July 1, 1930. On April 16, 1929, Babcock made this statement:

If I were to place my own valuation on the best job I have done since I have been with the G.L.F. I would unhesitatingly state it to be my final, though belated, recognition of the fact that retail service is as important to farmers as wholesale service, and my subsequent creation of a division of Retail Service on a par with the division of Wholesale Service. Also, I would pat myself on the back over the selection of the men I secured to handle this division.

In Mr. Fogg, Mr. Campbell, in the eight division managers of Retail Service, and in the fifty or sixty men employed in our Retail Service Stores, we have a group of men who know more about rendering of retail service on farm supplies in both its theoretical and practical phases than any other group of people in the country. It is well that these men do know their job, because almost more rapidly than we shall be prepared for it, or wish to take the responsibility, the G.L.F. will have to take over the ownership and management of a state-wide system of retail service stores. I vision at least 400 of these stores.

The service stores had now become a fixed part of the G.L.F.

CHAPTER 15

Diversification Takes Hold

Stated in farm terms, the G.L.F. is like a silo filling rig which could handle three more loads of corn an hour if there were men enough in the field picking it up so as to get it there that fast.
H. E. BABCOCK, *G.L.F. Shareholder, January 1928*

WHILE THE SPECTACULAR EXPANSION of feed volume and the development of service stores were the dominant features of G.L.F. growth from 1926 to 1930, substantial progress was being made in service on seeds, fertilizers and other farm supplies. It was during this period that the feed and fertilizer services firmly established themselves, and experience was gained for future use in handling farm supplies.

SEED

The seed program was moving along satisfactorily in March, 1926, as evidenced by an article in the *G.L.F. Shareholder,* entitled, "Why 35,000 Farmers Use G.L.F. Seeds." This number had increased several thousand during the preceding year. The article made these points: That the origin of G.L.F. seed was unquestioned; that its hardiness, productivity and adaptability were established; that its original vitality and vigor were preserved; and that it represented a high degree of priority. "Know What You Sow," was becoming an accepted practice among good farmers.

At this time the seed department was extending its operations for corn and grain seeds. Much of the commercial seed was then simply good looking corn, wheat, oats, and barley which had been well cleaned up and given a fancy name such as "Pride of the North," and yields were light compared with those of new varieties developed by the Cornell plant breeders. The G.L.F. seed department saw an opportunity to put the Cornell findings into practical use and proceeded to have "True-to-Name Seed" increased under contracts with reliable growers in the Northeast. It was found, however, that growing conditions were not favorable for the maturing of seed, so stock seed was taken to the Mid-West where farmers grew it under contract for a premium over cornbelt varieties.[1] This prac-

---

[1] C. N. Silcox recalls the first contract he signed for seed corn, sitting on the Court House steps at Havana, Illinois. "The farmer didn't have enough money to buy seed corn and was glad to sign a contract with G.L.F. He became the leader of a group of farmers who later grew several hundred acres per year of seed corn for G.L.F. farmers." Letter, to author of August 29, 1957.

Why 35,000 Farmers
USE G.L.F. SEEDS

1 ORIGIN IS UNQUESTIONED. G. L. F. seed comes from the best northern growing regions of North America.

2 HARDINESS, PRODUCTIVITY AND ADAPTABILITY ARE ESTABLISHED by the inheritance of these qualities from the parent plants.

3 ORIGINAL VITALITY AND VIGOR IS PRESERVED by careful harvesting and storing.

4 92 TO 99% QUICK VIGOROUS GROWING SPROUTS ARE ASSURED by double scarification of alfalfa, sweet clover and the North Western red clover seed.

5 A HIGH DEGREE OF PURITY IS SECURED by thoroughly recleaning and refining in the G. L. F. warehouse.

6 A $25,000 BOND FURNISHES FULL PROTECTION AGAINST POSSIBILITY OF BLENDS of G. L. F. seed with foreign or southern grown seed. No other seed available to farmers has such a backing.

7 SEED IS SELECTED ON A SERVICE BASIS. The G. L. F. being coopertive and non-profit, the seed service is operated solely to select the best possible seeds for G. L. F. patrons and friends, not to make a profit by merchandising

The G.L.F.

K N O W   W H A T   Y O U   S O W

ADVERTISEMENT USED IN MARCH, 1926

tice met with opposition from some New York State farmers who brought pressure on Cornell officials to prohibit the G.L.F. from taking its stock seed outside of the state, but the practice gradually gained acceptance as being in the best interests of farmers.

The G.L.F. Shareholder for October 1926 carried information on the new staining law—the Federal seed act which required "that seeds imported into this country from certain foreign sources shall be stained a definite distinctive color." This article pointed out that the original sug-

gestions for the seed act were drafted by the G.L.F. and presented to
the Resolutions Committee of the American Farm Bureau Federation.
" 'Known-origin Seed,' the slogan originated by G.L.F. Seed Service, was
the purpose of this legislation," and the article went on to say that there
would still be a need for selective buying by their own organization as the
new law would not solve all of the farmer's seed problems.

The high standing of the G.L.F. in its seed operations was also attested
by M. C. Maughan, then in charge of the Seed Laboratory of the New York
State Agricultural Experiment Station:

> . . . May I take this opportunity to express to you, as one of the managers of
> the Cooperative G.L.F. Exchange, Inc., my personal appreciation of the serv-
> ice in seeds for planting which you have rendered to the farmers of this State.
> I am glad to say that to date in no instance have we ever found an occasion or
> opportunity to question any statements made about the origin of seeds sold by
> this cooperative organization.

During the next few years seed operations continued to expand. By
January, 1928, the number of farmers buying seed had increased to 42,000.
Many endorsements of the Seed Service were carried in various issues of
the *Shareholder*. One farmer wrote, "If the G.L.F. had only a seed service
its existence would be justified."

The outstanding success of the seed program, under the enthusiastic,
temperamental and strong-willed leadership of Arthur Leal Bibbins, gave
Babcock one of his most vexing managerial problems. "Bib" was dedicated
to the seed program, and he devoted all his gifted energies to its success.
He found it hard to accept the idea that seed could be handled through the
local agencies of the G.L.F., while Babcock was convinced that all commodities could be best handled this way. Bibbins had built his program
with the help of the seed poolers, and was convinced that the program
should center in serving them. This conflict in thinking was not settled
until Babcock, in 1927, insisted that the seed program be brought in line
with the other programs. One thing could not be countenanced—the establishment of an independent empire by any department manager. The up-
rising of the department heads in 1922 had demonstrated that the parts
could not be co-equal with the whole.

In his report to the Board on February 7, 1928, Babcock explained his
position:

> There was perhaps less expansion in our Seed Service during 1927 than in
> any other department. This, I believe, was largely due to the fact that for the
> last three or four years we have been attempting to give retail service on seeds
> in three ways: (1) Through agent-buyers who buy in full bag lots; (2) through
> poolers who buy in broken package lots; (3) direct to consumers.

*   *   *

> During the year 1927 it was my policy to try and swing our Seed Service

into line with our Dairy [feed] Service so far as cooperation with, and dependence upon, established retail service agencies is concerned. . . .

All in all, the year 1927 has been significant in our Seed Service in that during it we have put it more definitely on a retail agency basis. . . .

Experience was to demonstrate the soundness of Babcock's position. Seed sales for the years from 1925-26 to 1929-30 are here given:

1925-26	$ 981,439
1926-27	1,053,425
1927-28	912,692
1928-29	1,134,724
1929-30	1,065,390

Fertilizer

The fertilizer program had been disappointing prior to 1926. Much had been learned, and some progress had been made in raising standards of fertilizer quality and usage, but much remained to be done to make the program really successful. The partnership arrangement with the Summers Company had, if anything, a negative benefit in that it demonstrated how not to engage in manufacturing.

Babcock had been glad to share the responsibility of improving the fertilizer program with Directors Fred Porter and Harry Bull, along with Comptroller M. C. Burritt. As a result of their examination of the problem, the G.L.F. in the fall of 1926, decided to cut loose from the Summers Company, to the extent possible, and replace Gay, the manager of the Fertilizer Department, with L. J. Steele, a man who understood field conditions and problems. Steele's experience as a County Agent and District Fieldman gave him an understanding of distributive needs in G.L.F. territory. The G.L.F. also decided to tie in more closely with the recommendations of Professor E. L. Worthen of Cornell University, who advocated greater use of phosphate in the Northeast.[2]

An editorial in the *G.L.F. Shareholder* for October 1926 on "G.L.F. Fertilizers" announced Steele's appointment as manager and indicated that the headquarters of the Fertilizer Department were being moved from New York City to Ithaca. The editorial stressed that an important phase of Mr. Steele's work would be to develop better local service on G.L.F. fertilizer; and it closed with this sentence, "In naming Mr. Steele to head the G.L.F. Fertilizer Service, the G.L.F. has followed the policy inaugurated with the appointment of Mr. McConnell of heading its Service Departments with men of first-hand experience with the G.L.F. patrons, and trained in its ideals."

[2] The *G.L.F. Shareholder* for October 1926 carried a two-page article entitled, "Why Not Apply Acid Phosphate with Manure." It featured a statement from the New York College of Agriculture in favor of the practice.

Although Steele had to learn the fertilizer business almost from scratch, this was probably an advantage in that his mind was not cluttered with industry experience. He soon established satisfactory arrangements for needed supplies while plans could be developed for a more permanent program. Under his leadership the G.L.F. acquired a dry-mixing fertilizer plant at Phelps, New York, to serve nearby counties and reduce freight and hauling costs.

This plant was just emerging from the experimental stage when Steele died from pneumonia on January 8, 1928. Babcock, in reporting to the Board a month later, said:

The tragic and untimely death of the manager of our fertilizer department has but temporarily checked the development of a service which . . . gave every indication of being as worthwhile and far-reaching as our Feed Service. . . .

Had Mr. Steele lived, he would have been able to have made definite recommendations concerning the advisability of small batch mixing plants by the end of the present fiscal year. It may be that we shall be able to do this.

The loss of Steele was a heavy blow. He was a terrific worker and his death was attributable to his overzealous efforts to get the fertilizer program going on a firm basis.

The man who replaced Steele was T. E. Milliman who had been employed by Babcock on December 1, 1927, to start a spray material business with headquarters at Rochester. Although Milliman had no direct experience in handling fertilizer he had long worked closely with farmers as a County Agent, as Director of Field Service for the Dairymen's League and, more recently, as Manager of a fruit growers' cooperative. Milliman found the general fertilizer industry

in the doldrums in which it had been wallowing since 1921. . . . In spite of the fact that the materials for the production of superphosphate were cheap and superphosphate itself was in excess supply, the fertilizer industry had made no effort to sell this commodity to farmers as a separate ingredient. [They thought] . . . more money could be made from complete fertilizer and that only enough superphosphate should be produced to supply the demand for mixed goods. Such a curious situation persisted all during the twenties and well up into the thirties—when various land-grant colleges, Cornell in particular, had been advocating the use of superphosphate as such on dairy farms.[3]

Milliman was soon working closely with Professor E. L. Worthen, Extension Agronomist of Cornell, "America's chief promoter and salesman of the superphosphate idea," and sales of G.L.F. superphosphate began to climb. From 10,995 tons in 1927-28 they were stepped up to 17,665 tons in 1930-31.

It was also soon apparent from the Phelps' experience that G.L.F. should expand its business by acquisition of an upstate mixing plant west of

[3] Letter, to author, of March 3, 1952.

Phelps. After seeing the agricultural potential an old gypsum board plant was found at Batavia late in 1928, which could be "revamped into a make-shift but reasonably efficient dry-mix mixing operation." The next mixing plant, at North Collins, "was built from the ground up and opened for business in the spring of 1930."

The sales of fertilizer from 1925-26 to 1929-30 reflect the changes and progress in fertilizer operations:

1925-26	$ 673,201
1926-27	547,220
1927-28	726,036
1928-29	1,036,582
1929-30	1,217,639

Milliman had just begun to make trade connections for spray materials when he was placed in charge of the fertilizer department. Although some spray materials were handled in 1928, little was accomplished until 1929 when Jay Coryell, who had resigned as County Agent leader, was placed in charge of spray materials. The G.L.F. began to manufacture dusts as early as 1929, at Batavia.

As indicated earlier, the G.L.F. had been concerned with the problem of paint quality. Babcock was convinced that the fertilizer department could manufacture it and in 1928 information on paint production was obtained from Professor B. B. Robb of the Department of Rural Engineering at Cornell, U. S. Bureau of Standards, and industry sources. Within a short time paint of good quality was being produced by a simple process at the Phelps fertilizer plant.

These developments were significant in that they both led to manufacturing operations to provide products of known quality.

MAIL ORDER

On May 13, 1925, the G.L.F. filed its application for federal income tax exemption. While the application was pending, Babcock and the Directors began to examine more closely the type of supplies and patronage of the Mail Order Service under the requirement that not more than 15 percent of the business could be done with persons not farmers. Would some of the items handled by the Mail Order Service such as tea wagons and men's suits jeopardize the Exchange's right to exemption? Although the exemption was granted on July 3, 1926, the consideration of the problem led the G.L.F. to restrict the service of the Mail Order Service to items of bona fide farm use. This desire to keep the record clear was partly responsible for the discontinuance of the G.L.F. Truth-in-Fabric Service in early 1926.[4]

[4] This business was turned over to a new cooperative known as "Truth-in-Fabric Service," with G.L.F.'s blessing and financial encouragement.

During the next few years the Mail Order Service continued to expand modestly with the considerable advertising assistance of the *G.L.F. Shareholder*. An example of how a new line of service was introduced is given in a letter of the Manager, G. C. Gardinier, to W. G. Wysor, Manager of the Virginia Seed Service, Richmond, Va., of December 30, 1927:

> On the recommendation of the College Feed Conference Board, the distribution of red cod liver oil for poultry feeds, was announced in our January *Shareholder*. Since that time we have received 1319 orders covering a total of 27,203 gallons.

Gardinier also reported how the Mail Order Service was handling other farm supply items such as tires, roll roofing, paint, fly spray, coal, and motor oil on an open-formula basis.[5] All of these basic commodities, except binder twine, which was distributed from the Syracuse Office, were shipped direct from the supplier firm, thus eliminating the expense of stocking and handling goods. The cost of the service was low as it required little more than bookkeeping. Although operated more for service than for savings it yielded a net margin of about $10,000 in 1927.

In his report to the Directors on February 7, 1928, Babcock said:

> I believe we have not yet touched the possibilities in this service. We must, however, as we develop it, take great precautions to safeguard the quality of the supplies our patrons purchase in this way.

However, he saw no pressing need to build the department rapidly; he favored taking time to bring out its fullest opportunities.

The *G.L.F. Shareholder* for January, 1929, carried an article, "Mail Order Service Announces a Steady Growth in Volume." It showed the increase in number of orders and sales, as follows:

	Orders	
1924	3,112	$167,457
1925	4,749	198,928
1926	4,003	192,896
1927	7,606	222,503
1928	9,036	239,131

An organization chart in this same issue carried this note: G.L.F. Mail Order Service is operated as a separate and distinct activity under the direct supervision of the General Manager."

As will be explained later (p. 144) the Mail Order Service was discontinued in 1930 when service was stopped on all non-agricultural commodi-

---

[5] In the *G.L.F. Shareholder* of March, 1926, there is a full-spread advertisement telling how representatives of the Department of Rural Engineering at Cornell had approved the specifications for G.L.F. motor oils.

ties, and service on such farm supplies as spray materials, motor oil, binder twine, paint and cod-liver oil was transferred to the Fertilizer, Chemical and Paint Service. During its brief career the Mail Order Service made many friends for the G.L.F. and helped broaden the character of G.L.F. services. By its advocacy of specification buying and high quality standards it paved the way for a more comprehensive farm supply service in the years ahead.

CHAPTER 16

The Big Mill

*No one hated to go into the large investment of the Buffalo Mill
more than Babcock and myself, but the market structure forced us.*
JAMES A. McCONNELL, *January 29, 1951*

A s THE VOLUME of feed obtained through the American Milling Company steadily expanded, the G.L.F. began to think it might be desirable to own and operate its own mill.

In May, 1926, Babcock took advantage of G.L.F.'s growing strength to negotiate a new contract which provided that the G.L.F. would pay AMCO "not to exceed $1.00 a ton, the amount to be agreed upon from time to time," for manufacturing G.L.F. dairy feeds. This new arrangement limited the charges paid to AMCO and gave the G.L.F. greater freedom of action in establishing feed prices. Prior to this, the G.L.F. had been in effect a partner in the operation of Plant No. 2 of the American Milling Company. Babcock saw the desirability of making G.L.F. operations more independent.

Under the provisions of this contract: Plant No. 2 of the American Milling Company was to operate under the management of a resident representative of the G.L.F.; the G.L.F. was to manufacture all its dairy feed in this plant, other than that mixed at its own Buffalo plant; the American Milling Company was to furnish all necessary capital, and for all such capital was to be paid 6 percent. However, the G.L.F. could furnish up to 50 percent of the capital needed on the same terms; and the raw materials for the mixing of feed were to be bought by either party to the agreement, subject to confirmation by the other party.

This arrangement improved the G.L.F.'s position but, with continuing growth of volume, it did not satisfy Babcock and McConnell.

On August 11, 1927, McConnell wrote to Babcock as follows:

. . . In regard to your two questions: (1) Can we better this deal with AMCO? It might be possible to get AMCO to throw 50 cents off mill cost which we are now giving them. Personally, I doubt it. (2) Has the time come to proceed with definite plans for a large Buffalo mill? Personally, I believe yes. I expect to be in position to answer that question without any reservations when we meet in September.

In a memorandum to the Board of Directors on September 16, 1927, Babcock stated:

I submit that the G.L.F. is in an easy financial position as long as the present arrangement with AMCO is in effect, and if it does not continue, then we face a problem of new financing which would involve the raising of about one million dollars and which is a bridge that can be crossed when we come to it.

McConnell continued to work on the problem. On December 6, 1927, he wrote as follows to Babcock:

We are doing some work on what it will actually cost us to set up an organization here [Peoria] and handle all our tonnage. This information should be a good basis to arrive at a good service fee.

He went on to say,

I think our first decision must be whether or not we are to continue on the present policy of holding G.L.F. assets in liquid form, or whether we are, at some time in the near future, to own and operate our own plants. If the decision is against fixed assets, and I believe our thinking is that way for the present, then certainly a permanent formula for working out a service fee should be agreed upon.

The information sent Babcock on the following day indicated that the G.L.F. could perform all the services of the American Milling Company at a cost of 22.5 cents per ton as compared to the 75 cents per ton then being assessed. McConnell observed: "It is my opinion that our simplified business is being made to bear the cost of a complex system built to take care of a complex business."

In view of the G.L.F.'s costly early experience in overexpansion of fixed assets, Babcock and McConnell preferred to hold back on ownership of a large mill until volume, capital, and trained manpower were adequate to insure its economical operation. They therefore followed a strategy of pushing the American Milling Company to give increasingly better service at increasingly lower cost. This approach worked well, for Atwood, fearful of losing this large block of business, knew that G.L.F. could make other arrangements if the need should arise. He realized that it would be wiser to yield than to lose all.

In a report to the Board on February 7, 1928, Babcock indicated that an effort was being made to persuade AMCO to reduce again the service fee. He went on to say,

We must inevitably meet the problem of supplying more mill capacity for what we now know as Buffalo tonnage. . . . The problem cannot be separated and should not be separated from the working out of mill capacity on a more or less permanent basis for our dairy feed service as well.

It should here be kept in mind that the Buffalo mill then being used exclusively for manufacturing poultry feed was operating very successfully and that this experience was indicating the desirability of an expansion of operations in Buffalo. In fact, in this same report Babcock referred to this operation as "probably our most satisfactory service."

While asserting that he had "no tangible suggestions on the perplexing problems related to possible mill ownership," Babcock saw the facts as follows:

1. As a matter of fundamental policy, we must proceed very carefully in acquiring fixed assets—that is, mills.
2. Should we purchase mills the amount of money involved would be so large as to require new financing. This, I recognize, can be secured.
3. If we lease mills we can finance their operations from our present resources. That is, were there need to do so, we could now replace AMCO financing with our own money.
4. We probably are now established in our own right in a position where we can make commitments as the G.L.F. for almost unlimited quantities of ingredients. . . .
5. Our men, McConnell, Tanzer, and Chase, seem to approach the ability of the executives of other milling companies.

Although this analysis pointed toward the "practicability of our setting up our feed service entirely independent of the American Milling Company, especially if this company tends to overvalue its services," Babcock recognized that "in union there is strength," and was loath to break up an arrangement which had worked so well—especially in view of "a strong bond of personal friendship between our respective staffs." He thought it likely that AMCO might be able to permit a working arrangement more satisfactory all around. He thought that:

There is more likelihood of their doing this because they undoubtedly need the prestige of our tonnage and our experience in securing and servicing volume in a retail way.

In view of this probability, Babcock concluded:

While we are working out the problems of our feed service . . . we should not attempt to expand our volume too rapidly, but instead . . . endeavor to make a little wider net margins . . . to the end that we may not over-reach ourselves, and instead may strengthen our financial position against the days that are ahead.

Thus Babcock recommended playing it both ways, to be able to move in either direction. Atwood, seeing the handwriting on the wall, soon agreed to a reduction of the service fee to 50 cents per ton but this did not settle the problem. This is shown by a handwritten letter that Babcock sent to Sherman Peer[1] from Lake Placid on March 21, 1928, with instructions that it be shown to Webb, McConnell, and Burritt, for he wished to be assured of their support. In this letter he said:

I am now planning to finance the mill when needed by the sale of the unissued G.L.F. finance stock to farmers and the sale of . . . P.W. & E. preferred stock to wealthy agriculturists.

---

[1] Sherman Peer, of Ithaca, N.Y., had joined the legal staff of the G.L.F. in 1925, as assistant to Waldo Morse.

He also took into account that some capital could be raised from the old mill.

When the Board met on May 11, 1928, Babcock was still hesitant in showing his hand. Knowing that a major decision was involved he wanted it made from a full recognition of all the factors to be considered. Although confident that the mill could be financed along sound lines he was not sure that the time was ripe for the undertaking. He pointed out that the G.L.F. was undercapitalized and only "beginning to achieve a measure of independence from the American Milling Company." On the other hand he admitted that the G.L.F. had demonstrated the safety of its program and management, and that there was a surplus of capital in the country seeking safe investment, which could be brought in without jeopardizing the control of the Exchange.

Babcock wished to proceed cautiously:

I recommend that any expansion in the ownership of fixed assets which the Board may authorize be made only from an increase of our permanent capital. I am against the financing of fixed assets from earnings because I believe that such procedure is contrary to the spirit and practice of the cooperative, non-profit service our patrons expect from us.

In line with this thinking, he declared: "I am emphatically against the building of a mill at Buffalo before 1930 under any conditions," for four main reasons: (1) "We are short of manpower. . . ." (2) "Our growth isn't proven yet. . . ." (3) "We are dangerously near the point of diminishing returns. . . ." (4) "Our retail service opportunity . . . is largely under-developed."

For the immediate future he advocated a more aggressive development of retail service:

As I see things now, I had rather make sure of saving another 5 percent through improved retail service on 20 million dollars worth of farm supplies than to take a chance on an expansion which might jeopardize all of the progress we have made.

Babcock's statement set the stage for a full discussion of the problem by the Board on the following day.

To McConnell it had become clear that the building of the mill could no longer be postponed. At this meeting the Board appointed a committee comprised of McConnell, Tanzer, and Atwood (of AMCO) to find a Buffalo site as soon as possible.

In moving forward on the mill proposition the G.L.F. was careful not to burn its bridges with the American Milling Company. At this time it was recognized that the G.L.F. would need the services of the American Milling Company for several years even if it should acquire a large mill. Apparently it was then believed that the mill being planned could not fully meet the needs of G.L.F. patrons.

In reporting to the Board on July 1, 1928, McConnell indicated that, with expected growth of tonnage, "it would be possible to operate not only the Peoria plant on dairy feed but also a large Buffalo plant on poultry and assorted cars." For this reason the contract with the American Milling Company was renewed at this time to safeguard the dairy feed operation.

The new contract, to be effective for six years from January 1, 1929, was described as "an entirely different form of contract. [It] is purely and simply a lease, and distinctly establishes the identity of the G.L.F. It will give G.L.F. much freedom of action, both in financing and in operation, and the service fee is reduced from 42 cents to 30 cents a ton, with a minimum charge of $75,000 a year."

McConnell further reported that, in line with the decision to acquire a Buffalo mill as soon as possible, three locations had been studied, and that an offer had been made on the one considered most favorable. The close tie of the G.L.F. and the American Milling Company at this time is indicated by the fact that Atwood actively helped on this matter. However, several months elapsed before the land for the mill was formally acquired in January, 1929. During this period only those on the inside knew that plans were going forward for the Buffalo mill. In fact, little publicity was given to the new mill until it was nearly a going concern.

Several more months passed before the plans for the new mill could be completed and construction begun. It commenced operations in February, 1930. To provide financing, the P. W. & E. Company issued $1,000,000 in 7 percent preferred stock.

It was soon found that the mill was able to handle a larger capacity of G.L.F. feed tonnage than had been expected. On November 5, 1930, Babcock reported that it was thoroughly broken in and was gradually approaching capacity. He indicated that the Peoria plant was organized for day-runs and that the smaller, old mill at Buffalo was also available in reserve.

When the G.L.F. plant was built it was hoped that both the Buffalo and Peoria mills would be operated. The next several months demonstrated, however, that the G.L.F. could operate the Buffalo plant so efficiently that it could afford to close down the Peoria plant and continue to pay rent on it.

The minutes of December 11, 1930, indicate that the Peoria plant would be closed on January 1, 1931, and that all dairy and poultry feeds would be henceforth manufactured in Buffalo. Thus, within a relatively short time, the dream of having the big mill had become a reality, and there was no longer any need for the continuation of the arrangement with AMCO. Had this result been foreseen, the G.L.F. might have relieved itself of the burden of paying several hundred thousand dollars in compliance with its contract.

The decision to build the big mill was based on sound economic reasoning. During the twenties, Buffalo had become a great milling center which insured supplies of all mill feeds. Ingredients could be moved to it at low cost by boat. The cost of shipping mixed feed by rail from Peoria into G.L.F. territory made such feed non-competitive with feed produced at Buffalo.

This situation was not at the time fully recognized, and it took some time for the facts to become clear. During the late twenties feed prices were rising and with the reduction of charges for American Milling Company services savings made the arrangement with that company seem more advantageous than it really was.

McConnell believes that one of the big milestones in G.L.F. progress came with the understanding of the economic factors behind the feed business which resulted, not only in the building of the large plant at Buffalo, but in the rapid acquisition soon afterward of mills at Albany and Bordentown.[2] "We were finally forced to move into Buffalo so that we could buy out of all the major markets of the country. The American Milling Company deal was not an expedient. No one hated to go into the large investment of the Buffalo mill any worse than Babcock and myself, but the market structure forced us."[3]

Thus the G.L.F. acquired its own mill because the Peoria operation gradually became uneconomic. By the late 1920's the G.L.F. had developed a business of 300,000 tons a year for shipment out of Peoria. According to McConnell, this meant "We had to buy all of the raw materials at the Minneapolis-Peoria-Chicago-St. Louis and Kansas City markets. It also meant all-rail shipment to the East, cutting off the opportunity to use any of the cheaper grains which were shipped to the big Buffalo terminal by lake."[4]

This situation developed so quickly, recalls McConnell,

that it caught us with a fairly long-time lease on the Peoria plant. . . . I think it cost us over a half million dollars, over a period of years, to carry the closed Peoria plant. This coming at the time of a deep depression made it difficult. We, however, never missed a year of meeting our schedule, and the move turned out to be the smartest thing, from a feed standpoint, that we ever did.[5]

Although Babcock saw the possibilities of the Buffalo feed mill, it was McConnell who was the driving force behind the mill purchase. In his operating relationships to the American Milling Company and the milling industry McConnell perceived the changes taking place in the industry and the longtime difficulties inherent in a permanent contractual rela-

[2] Letter, to author, of May 27, 1950.
[3] Letter, to author, of January 29, 1951.
[4] Letter, to author, of March 30, 1951.
[5] Letter, to author, of March 30, 1951.

tionship with the American Milling Company. Although he personally enjoyed a cordial understanding with Mr. Atwood and the American Milling Company, he saw that long run circumstances would force the G.L.F. to assert its independence. The farmers in the G.L.F. represented the largest concentrated volume of feed business in the world and with this volume it was unthinkable to continue for long an arrangement whereby toll was paid to another company for manufacturing services.

There were also psychological advantages from having the mill at Buffalo where it could be seen by G.L.F. members. It would give the members what they had always wanted—their own mill, under their own direction. It would give an outlet in G.L.F. to staff energies and afford opportunities for advancement. These considerations, plus the economic facts, made the decision obvious.

The Buffalo Mill was something more than a mixed feed plant. It was a symbol of progress and success—a tremendous monument of achievement. Babcock made the most of this fact.

III. DEVELOPING THE ENTERPRISE, 1930-1940

CHAPTER 17

Riding The Storm

*We must put the farmers of the New York Milkshed behind the
G.L.F. . . . The organization is challenged as never before to cut its
expenses in order to meet new conditions.*
H. E. BABCOCK, *Talk to Fieldmen, October 20, 1931*

CHANGE WAS IN THE AIR as the G.L.F. moved into 1930. The big mill
would soon be in operation. The economic situation was uncertain,
and it was realized that a period of testing was ahead. With the fall in
commodity prices which had set in after the stock market crash, the long
record of accumulating savings had come to an end, just as the organization had obligated itself for a heavy investment in fixed assets. To maintain service for its members, large inventories had to be held, and losses
from their depreciation could not be avoided.

Yet there was little anxiety for the future. The record of the past ten
years had built a great reservoir of confidence that the G.L.F. could meet
any situation as well as its competitors. Farmers were showing their faith
in the organization by buying the preferred stock of the P. W. & E. Company, and adequate operating capital seemed assured from current savings, plus ability to borrow from the American Milling Company.

A NEW PERIOD OPENS

The closing of one period in the life of the G.L.F. and the opening of
another was marked by the death of N. F. Webb on January 10, 1930, one
of the original directors and the president of the organization since January, 1921. Under his presidency the G.L.F. had largely overcome its early
difficulties and placed itself in position to go forward. Up to this point
there had been little change in the membership of the Board. It was a
little group of determined men.

The election of Fred Porter as President brought a new type of leader
to the Board. Webb had been deeply conscious of the Board's responsibility as guardian of the interests of stockholders, and as president he
had conscientiously endeavored to keep himself informed on detailed
matters.[1] Porter, on the other hand, although acutely conscious of the

[1] In paying tribute to Mr. Webb in the February, 1930, *G.L.F. Shareholder* Mr.
Babcock said: "For a period of nearly ten years Mr. Webb sat at his desk in the G.L.F.
office twice a week. Into a tray on his desk went copies of all important letters and
documents. These Mr. Webb painstakingly read. The awareness that his scrutiny was

Board's responsibilities to its stockholders, looked at things as a business man and as a politician as well as a farmer, and he was more inclined to follow Babcock's lead in striking out on new paths.

The aggressive spirit in the organization at this time was reflected in the decision to issue the *G.L.F. Shareholder* each month to all of the 90,000 "patrons." In the first issue (February 1930) under the new plan, Babcock explained that "this method of contact between the management of the G.L.F. and those of you who own and use it is cheaper and more efficient than the circulars used in the past."

Strategically it was a good time for this decision. The G.L.F. had assumed heavy financial responsibilities and it was important that its volume be maintained. The G.L.F. needed the support and understanding of its membership, and periods of transition call for more explanation of organizational objectives.

It is also significant that fiscal and accounting controls were also strengthened at this time by bringing into the organization E. Victor Underwood and M. Lyle Holmes. To some extent these men replaced Maurice Burritt, part-time Controller, and Robert Dame, Chief Accountant, who had left the organization in 1929, but they were given more general responsibilities. Underwood, as Secretary of the New York Farm Bureau Federation, was well known for his administrative ability and general competence in agricultural affairs. Holmes, as Professor of Business Management in the College of Agriculture at Cornell, was well qualified to bring about needed changes in accounting systems and procedures as the organization grew in size and complexity. Their appointments increased business respect for the G.L.F.

Another intimation of change was an announcement in the February *Shareholder* that "effective February 3, 1930, G.L.F. Mail Order Service as such, was discontinued. . . . Part of the Mail Order Service will be continued out of the Rochester Office . . . Service on all non-agricultural commodities, however, will be discontinued."

Several reasons explain why the Mail Order Service was closed. For some time it had been a "fifth wheel" which could not be fitted into the general plan of the G.L.F. as a farm supply procurement agency. With the energies of the G.L.F. focused on feed and basic farm supplies there was less enthusiasm for this marginal business. In fact, many agent-buyers and service store managers held that sales of consumer goods antagonized business interests to the disadvantage of basic farm supply operations. In

---

to follow made stenographers mindful of *their* punctuation and department heads watchful of *their* pennies. When 'O.K. N.F.W.' was written, it meant that the action approved checked with the interests of farmers. No substitute or evasion could get by him."

a letter to J. M. Burmeister, December 7, 1929, Babcock recognized the force of this opposition: "You have probably seen the petition which is being circulated by the Eastern Federation of Feed Merchants, in which they claim that the G.L.F. handles boots, tires, etc., which are not strictly agricultural products . . . I am now engaged in reorganizing our Mail Order Service so that it will only handle strictly agricultural commodities."

Moreover, the term "mail order" had a connotation of consumer as opposed to farm supply business, and was a vestigial reminder of the old Grange Exchange. There was also a tendency for the mail order service to increase business with nonfarmers so as to impair the G.L.F.'s income-tax exemption. Furthermore, discontinuance was recommended by the Federal Farm Loan Board—which was discounting the agricultural paper of the G.L.F.'s credit corporation. In view of these considerations, Babcock and the board of directors had gradually come to the opinion that the benefits from continuing the service were slight compared to the disadvantages. In liquidating it, the G.L.F. thus freed itself from various embarrassments while it kept the parts which fitted in with G.L.F.'s major function of being a procurement agency for farmers on their basic farm supplies.

For some time the G.L.F. had been concerned with the tendency of Agent-buyers to charge what the traffic would bear on supplies furnished them by the G.L.F. Savings from efficient mill operations, made available through lower wholesale prices, were being absorbed by the Agent-buyers and were not being passed on to farmers. It was quite clear that this situation, if not corrected, would tend to dry up farmer support.

Babcock met this problem head-on by providing full information to farmers on what they should expect to pay for feed from the G.L.F.[2]

Highly pleased with the response to this experiment which gave the G.L.F. a simple but effective method of control over retail margins, Babcock took advantage of the opportunity to strengthen ties with the Agent-buyers by expressing appreciation for their cooperation in the April *G.L.F. Shareholder:*

It was with considerable misgiving that we began publishing consumer cash off the car prices for feed in the *Shareholder*. . . . You can imagine our pride, therefore, in being able to report that out of approximately 700 G.L.F. agents handling feed, only four have objected to the G.L.F. publishing the facts about what the feed costs them.

During this time when the G.L.F. was getting the new mill into operation the economic situation worsened. Prior to January 1, the effect of the drop in grain prices which had begun in October 1929 was not serious. However, in January and February, significant losses, especially in the

[2] See February, 1930, issue of the *G.L.F. Shareholder.*

feed operations at Peoria, began to show up, and on March 20, Babcock reported to the Board that the loss to date amounted to $11,000.

The G.L.F., however, had learned an important lesson from the abrupt decline in prices in 1920. Instead of trying to sell inventories without loss as it had done then, the G.L.F. decided to follow the market down, and to offset inventory losses with gains from operating efficiency. In this way consumer demand could be kept strong by passing on price drops as they occurred.

Babcock reported on the results of this policy to the Board of Directors on May 22. The net for April alone was "in excess of $115,000," and "assured net margins for May and June" promised "the best prospects ever for the next fiscal year." "Moreover," he went on to say, "while this progress has been made, the G.L.F. has carried the dead financial load of our investment of close to one million five hundred thousand dollars ($1,500,000) in a new mill and elevator for which it has had no profitable use." This achievement in weathering the drastic economic decline had been obtained "by a reversal of the policy of ten years ago and because of this the organization has constantly met inventory declines with increased operating earnings until today it is in the best earning position of its career."

Although the achievement in meeting the impact of falling prices could be looked upon with pride, the results of the year's operations on June 30 gave cause for concern. Although sales for the year totaled $29,239,098, the highest volume yet reached, there was a year-end deficit of $6,423 in contrast to the net operating margin of $567,367 for the preceding year. This poor showing for the year as a whole was largely due to a heavy trading loss on options during the spring months which could not be fully recouped from operating savings. As a result, it was necessary to draw on surplus to pay the dividends on stock of $83,162.

During this difficult period the G.L.F. was carrying on its campaign to sell P. W. & E. preferred stock to finance the investment in the new mill.[3] Fortunately, at this time of financial stringency it was possible to borrow operating funds from the American Milling Company.

Babcock was alert to the importance of maintaining confidence. In the May issue of the G.L.F. Shareholder he called attention to the sales pressure being generated by competitors who were making a desperate drive for business. He urged patrons to do some remembering.

Remember that you have your own organization through which to purchase your farm supplies. Remember that these supplies give results. Remember that

[3] "By March 10, 1930, from an original 10,000 shares authorized, there were 3,000 shares left. By July 7, 1930, there were 2,000 shares left and by September 4, 1930, there were 1,500 shares left." Most of the stock was sold by two or three fieldmen who largely concentrated on this work. (Letter of E. V. Underwood, March 20, 1952.)

the cost of the salesman is *always* included in the price you pay for the goods, or taken out of their quality.

The July issue of the *Shareholder* presented a detailed breakdown of expenses to show that overhead costs of G.L.F. were not excessive in that they amounted to but 1.1 percent of the value of purchases. In this way, Babcock appealed to the farmer's common sense knowledge that services cost money.

CREATION OF FARM SERVICE MANAGEMENT

For some time prior to July, 1930, Babcock had been concerned with two problems: (1) how to strengthen the distributive services of the organization and (2) how best to promote cooperative marketing operations in connection with other G.L.F. activities. He gradually came to the belief that both problems could be solved by the creation of a corporation to be known as "Cooperative Farm Service Management."

The new organization, incorporated on July 30, 1930, carried forward Babcock's action in 1928 of separating retail from wholesale functions, and represented a basic change in G.L.F. structure. Cooperative Farm Service Management was designed to take over "the retail service heretofore conducted by the G.L.F." with the result that "hereafter the G.L.F. will be a wholesale purchasing and manufacturing organization for feed, seed, and fertilizer."[4]

Babcock believed that this centering of responsibilities would permit greater specialization of functions, increase the scope of initiative, reduce internal frictions, and make both wholesale and retail services more pliable for experiment.

Under the plan for Cooperative Farm Service Management, which was the first agency-type cooperative corporation to be formed under the recently enacted Article 8a of the New York Cooperative Corporations Law, the members were to be local G.L.F. Service Stores which were each to hold $25 in common stock.[5] Cooperative Farm Service Management was

---

[4] G.L.F. announcement, August 4, 1930.

[5] Article 8a, which became law on March 29, 1930, had been sponsored by the Dairymen's League Cooperative Association, Inc., for use in organizing subsidiary corporations. However, the League never made use of the law while the G.L.F. found that it could be used very effectively in many operations. (Letter of W. I. Myers, March 24, 1929.) According to Sherman Peer who, as counsel for the G.L.F., drew up the legal papers for Cooperative Farm Service Management, and most of the other G.L.F.'s "8a Agency Corporations," this law provided for a "hybrid type of cooperative" with certain characteristics of an ordinary business corporation. A cooperative corporation formed under Article 8a could be "unlimited and unfettered by special cooperative laws except its common stock could be owned only by a truly cooperative organization responsible to its members." Thus, Cooperative Farm Service Manage-

to perform management and accounting service for them at a charge of one-half of 1 percent of their volume of business, and savings were to be pro-rated back to them according to patronage.[6]

According to Babcock, the significance of the plan lay in the fact that "the grouping of the local cooperative agencies under a single unit gives all the advantages of central control, but leaves the ownership and reflection of savings and profits on a local shipping point basis as far as your supplies are concerned."

Cooperative Farm Service Management was not only designed to manage the Stores—which were henceforth to be considered cooperative farm service agencies—but it was also intended that it would supervise the activities of fieldmen in working with stores and agent-buyers. For such general field service as delegated to Cooperative Farm Service Management the G.L.F. was to pay a fee of half of one percent on the volume of business furnished by the agencies. To effectuate this program all G.L.F. field service employees were transferred to the pay roll of the Cooperative Farm Service Management.[7]

Although, strictly speaking, Cooperative Farm Service Management was not a subsidiary of the G.L.F. in actual fact, control by the G.L.F. was assured by its ownership through the P.W. & E. Company of the common stock of the individual service agencies and by its dependence on the G.L.F. for fees to be paid for field service.

---

ment was set up as an agency of the separate local G.L.F. Service Stores to perform accounting and management service for them. According to Sherman Peer, the advantage of the 8a type of corporation is that "it can be administered by a board of directors subservient to the board of an Article 7 cooperative without the necessity of consulting the latter's stockholders because the stockholders of an Article 8a cooperative is or are one or more cooperatives formed under Article 7." (Letter of January 8, 1952.)

[6] V. A. Fogg, one of the chief promoters of Farm Service Management, adds this comment: "It was also set up to provide experienced supervision, to provide a central control of funds, to take advantage of floats, to make it possible to train and fairly pay store personnel. It was a method of getting standard bookkeeping and analysis and saving on the cost, of making it possible to get records faster and provided a method of central supervision, making possible quick action." Letter, to author, of February 12, 1959.

[7] William I. Myers, while Professor of Agricultural Economics at Cornell University, served also as a director for Cooperative Farm Service Management, and as Assistant Treasurer of the G.L.F. from 1930 until he left for Washington in March, 1933, to be Deputy Governor, and then Governor of the newly formed Farm Credit Administration. Relative to his experience with G.L.F. he says: "Ed Babcock knew that I favored conservative financing and he asked me to serve in both of these posts in order to give the G.L.F. directors a better balanced program. As we all know, Ed was a salesman, always ready to take risks, but his greatest strength lay in the fact that he invited others who differed with him to take part in discussions before a decision was reached. My job as Assistant Treasurer was really to explain the balance sheet and operating statement to the directors so they could employ their good business judgment to G.L.F. financial problems. My worth was not important but Babcock's attitude was." Letter, to author, of January 5, 1959.

In announcing the plan the G.L.F. stressed the voluntary character of the new organization. "Local service agencies may be said to have united in employing the Management Corporation to run their business. . . . Each cooperative is free to withdraw from the combination by giving notice of its intention to do so."

To emphasize further the independence of the new organization it was announced that Cooperative Farm Service Management would make contracts in behalf of its member cooperatives with manufacturers for whom it would act as agent, and that a contract of this type for silos had been signed following incorporation. The new organization was thus given encouragement to strike out on its own in handling such commodities as might not be available through the G.L.F.—a policy which was bound to lead to jurisdictional disputes with the parent organization. The aim was to control and consolidate outside buying.

The real significance of the plan from the standpoint of G.L.F. structure was in its recognition of the functional division of wholesale and retail activities. By emphasizing the importance attached to retail distribution at a time when interest in wholesale and manufacturing functions were dominant due to the heavy investments recently made in feed and fertilizer plants, it corrected the balance by pointing out that economical operation of the wholesale and manufacturing services depended upon the efficient performance of the retail distributive function.[8]

PROMOTION OF MARKETING

Although the formation of Cooperative Farm Service Management was a logical extension of the "retail division" idea, the immediate objective was to facilitate promotion of cooperative marketing enterprises within the G.L.F. System. This is evident from the statement by Babcock in the public announcement that "the new company . . . is a definite step in putting into effect a plan for the marketing of farm products that the G.L.F. outlined to the Federal Farm Board a year ago." To understand this situation one must review the developments in marketing which had come to a head during the preceding year.

Although the Articles of Incorporation, as drafted by Waldo Morse in 1920, permitted the G.L.F. to engage in marketing operations, the full energies of the G.L.F. during the early years were absorbed in getting the buying operations soundly established. Moreover, during the twenties, farmers in the New York Milk Shed were not seriously concerned about

---

[8] According to J. A. McConnell: "The plan was partly designed to dilute power of the wholesale divisions. Babcock feared subjection of local communities to strong wholesale power." Interview with author, July 1958.

their marketing problems, except for milk then being capably handled by the Dairymen's League.[9]

In the late twenties, however, farmers were beginning to ask, "Since the G.L.F. has helped us so much on our purchasing problems, why can't it also help us in marketing our products other than milk?"

As if to answer this question, Mr. Morse, writing in the *G.L.F. Shareholder* for January, 1929, pointed out: "All of our powers may be directed toward the marketing of farm products as well as toward the purchasing of supplies, in that manner providing for the gathering up in our territory of such miscellaneous products as lack, at present, organized facilities for their orderly marketing."

For some time prior to the establishment of Cooperative Farm Service Management, Babcock had been giving attention to the possibilities of extending G.L.F. Service into the field of marketing. The problem was arising naturally as several of the local service stores were being called upon to handle poultry and eggs and other commodities in connection with their buying operations.

When the Federal Farm Board was established in the summer of 1929 to give national encouragement to the development of cooperative marketing, Babcock saw this as an opportunity to test his theories on how cooperative marketing might be tied in with other G.L.F. operations. As early as October 25, 1929, he had reported to the Board of Directors on an arrangement made to borrow $50,000 at 4 percent from the Federal Farm Board "for the purpose of assisting the P.W. & E. Co., Inc., in financing the purchasing of additional facilities providing for its program of marketing farm products." However, no money was borrowed from the Federal Farm Board before January 1931.

With several of the local service stores beginning to market eggs and other miscellaneous products for their patrons the desirability of correlating these local marketing activities was apparent. Thus the problem of providing for marketing within the G.L.F. system was met by the formation of Cooperative Farm Service Management which could federate all the service stores into one organization to offer marketing service. This would give G.L.F. adequate power to develop wholesale marketing enterprises should this be found desirable.

---

[9] This is shown by the fact that only 55 marketing associations were started in New York State in the seven years from 1923 to 1929, inclusive, while in the three years from 1920 to 1922, inclusive, 328 associations of this type were formed; although most of these early associations were short-lived. There was a considerable improvement in the index of prices paid to farmers for their produce, while on the other hand there was an even greater rise in the prices paid by farmers for farm supplies. This placed more relative emphasis on cooperative purchasing than cooperative marketing. See F. A. Harper, *Cooperative Purchasing and Marketing in New York State,* Cornell University Agr. Exp. Station Bulletin 554 (October, 1932) pp. 12-13.

At this time it was expected that the immediate problem in marketing would be to work out satisfactory plans for handling local products, leaving for later development the establishment of central selling agencies. The immediate aim of Cooperative Farm Service Management was to help the local cooperative service agencies in such matters as the training of employees, devising record forms and in facilitating business contacts. Loans could also be made to them for marketing programs through the P. W. & E. which, in turn, was to obtain funds for the purpose through the G.L.F. from the Federal Farm Board.

Babcock revealed his thinking with respect to marketing in July, 1930, in an address to the American Institute of Cooperation:

> I hope, and rather believe, that the same agencies which give retail service on incoming farm supplies . . . can become effective agencies for the working out of a little better marketing system for the miscellaneous produce in the New York Milk Shed. We can use the same capital, the same employees, the same set of books and the same management, to receive the outgoing produce from the farm and put it in shape for shipment.

To show the practical possibilities of this plan Babcock described how the service store at Cortland had loaded during the preceding year 1,200 tons of cabbage on which a service fee of $1.50 per ton had been received. He felt, however, that the development of a real marketing program would depend upon having products worth shipping, and that it would take time to teach farmers how to produce for market. He summed up by saying, "So, while the Farm Board is very friendly toward our marketing plan and ready to go ahead and support us in this type of marketing, it will be three or four years before we are ready to step out."[10]

EMPLOYEE EDUCATION RECOGNIZED

The formation of Cooperative Farm Service Management, the new emphasis on marketing, the establishment of service by the Buffalo Mill, and the many other changes taking place within the organization led the G.L.F. in July to inaugurate a series of monthly schools at selected points better to inform the 200 men then employed in retail service work on the policies and aims of the organization. This was the first systematic educational program to be carried on for the field employees of the organization as a whole, and it paved the way for later employee educational experiments which culminated in the establishment of the G.L.F. School of Cooperative Administration, in 1941.

It is significant that the first series of schools centered on an analysis of the G.L.F. as an organization. This series featured a talk by Babcock on

[10] *American Cooperation*, 1930, Vol. I, pp. 245-355.

the corporate structure of the G.L.F. and its subsidiaries, while men from within the organization imparted information based on their commodity or functional specialty.

Babcock emphasized the fact that the G.L.F. was a corporation of cooperative form. He explained how the directors of the G.L.F. had set up the P. W. & E. Company as a straight stock corporation to perform certain landlord and financial functions that the G.L.F. could not perform under its legal authority. He then described briefly how Cooperative Farm Service Management was being formed to strengthen the retail service and provide for the extension of marketing. The organization chart used to illustrate his lecture shows the G.L.F. structure as still quite simple. There was little indication of the extent and character of the important functional changes in the offing which were to increase greatly its complexity.

BIRTH OF THE HOLDING CORPORATION

The first of these significant changes came with the formation of the Cooperative G.L.F. Holding Corporation in the fall of 1930, which in turn facilitated other corporate changes.

With the great expansion of the G.L.F. into mills and other expensive facilities, the need for permanent and operating capital was greatly increased. This made clear that the authorized capital stock of the P. W. & E. would soon have to be increased again. Rather than patch up the old corporation it was decided to replace it with a new corporation to meet more specifically G.L.F. needs and be itself fully cooperative in name and fact.

In making the decision, it was also appreciated that it would be comparatively easy to reorganize the P. W. & E. Company at this time as the stock was not yet widely dispersed—while it could become much more difficult later when the preferred stock had been greatly expanded, since consent of fully two-thirds of the stockholders, common or preferred, was necessary for reorganization.

It will be recalled that the P. W. & E. Company had been formed in 1920 as a stock corporation, since no cooperative law then permitted formation of corporations of the type required. With the amendment of the Cooperative Corporations Law in 1930 it became possible under Article 8a to reorganize the P. W. & E. Company as a cooperative of the agency type, possessing all of the flexibility of a stock corporation.[11]

[11] The conversion was strongly advocated by Assistant Treasurer W. I. Myers who wrote Babcock on October 10, 1930, that: "It is apparent that it would be desirable to sell more P. W. & E. preferred stock as soon as the present issue is disposed of.

In a memo to department heads on October 13, Babcock stated that he and McConnell were greatly interested in this proposal but that they were reserving decision until Counsel Sherman Peer and W. I. Myers could fully examine its possibilities. On November 4, Babcock in a memo to McConnell, reported that "I have finished a long conference attended by Peer, Myers, Fogg, Crissey, Holmes, and Underwood, at which agreement was reached to change over the P. W. & E. to a cooperative finance corporation . . . immediately."

According to Sherman Peer who, as Counsel for the G.L.F., drafted the organization papers, the new corporation—the Cooperative G.L.F. Holding Corporation, Inc.—had the following advantages over the P. W. & E. Company: (1) It was a cooperative; (2) It was eligible for exemption from Federal Income and other Federal taxes: (3) It saved on state organization taxes; (4) It could pay dividends quarterly instead of semi-annually; and (5) It would start business with an authorized issue of preferred stock of $5,000,000 instead of $1,000,000—and thus have elbow room.[12]

Moreover, the change had the advantage of relating the name of the Holding Company to the parent organization, a fact of considerable importance, for the ambiguous relationship of the P. W. & E. Company to the G.L.F. had been a source of continuous confusion. The new name made it clear that the new company would serve as an exclusive holding corporation for the G.L.F.

The decision to form the Cooperative G.L.F. Holding Corporation, Inc., was approved by the Directors on November 5, and incorporation took place on November 20. However, the actual transition occurred on December 11 when stockholders of the P. W. & E. Company met and agreed to the conversion.

With the change-over from the P. W. & E., the Holding Company acquired responsibility for handling all financial matters for the G.L.F. Exchange as well as for all of its subsidiaries. All borrowing, financing,

---

Before this is done, I think it will be wise to change the P. W. & E. from a business corporation to a cooperative agency corporation under Article 8a of the Cooperative Corporation Law. This will be a benefit in several ways. It will answer the criticism of those who attack the cooperative position of the (present) agency corporation because it owns a business corporation. Much more important than this, it will safeguard the ownership of the [new] agency corporation by the G.L.F. even though it should be necessary to use the common stock as collateral for a loan. This particular cooperative law stipulates that all of the common stock of such a cooperative agency corporation must be owned by a cooperative organization. Hence, even though it were impossible to repay a loan on which this common stock was used as collateral, control of this indispensable arm of the G.L.F. would remain with it. The longer this change is delayed the more difficult it will be. It seems to me that the logical time to make the change is not later than the time when the present issue of preferred stock will be sold. . . ."

[12] *G.L.F. Digest*, p. 66.

and investing for the G.L.F. System was to be done by and in the name of the Holding Corporation. The Cooperative G.L.F. Exchange thus divested itself of all assets other than the common stock of the Holding Corporation which gave it the right to "dictate management of the G.L.F. family group," and direct policies.

The control of the new corporation was similar to that of its predecessor. Its Board of Directors consisted of the Board of Directors of the G.L.F. Exchange, plus the addition of two selected from management, H. E. Babcock and E. V. Underwood, who were also to serve as President and Secretary-Treasurer, respectively.

The formation of the Holding Company was a spectacular event in cooperative business organization. Here was a cooperative organization which had frankly adopted the organizational pattern and terminology of big business. As we shall see, the Holding Corporation was to have a significant effect on G.L.F. organizational structure during the next few years, for it stimulated and facilitated the formation of separate operating corporations.[13]

DEPRESSION MEASURES

While the Holding Corporation was being set up in the fall of 1930 the G.L.F. was feeling the full force of the depression, and the need for capital was becoming acute. In his September report W. I. Myers declared to the Board that "The G.L.F. needs about $1,000,000 of additional working capital. This is the most important financial problem now confronting the management." In the next few months the situation worsened, with a serious decline in feed volume due to larger crops at home, more careful feeding, stiffer competition, along with further losses in grain options.

The steady decline in grain prices confronted the management with a difficult problem, well expressed by W. I. Myers in a memorandum to Babcock on October 10, 1930: "If we decide to confine our buying to a

[13] At this time the term "Holding Company" was not in disrepute as it was a few years later, and it seemed to be most descriptive of the function to be performed. Although at this time the holding corporation device was being used by many large business organizations to achieve administrative decentralization and flexibility this does not appear to have been a major G.L.F. motive. However, we shall see how this use of the G.L.F. Holding Company to facilitate administration soon became apparent. For a contemporary discussion of business thinking with regard to the use of holding companies see article on "Holding Companies" by James C. Bonbright and Gardiner C. Means in the *Encyclopedia of Social Sciences* (1931). See also James C. Bonbright and Gardiner C. Means, *The Holding Company, Its Public Significance and its Regulation*, especially pp. 83-85.

30-day basis there is no question in my mind but what our costs would carry us through and not only hold but build volume." "On the other hand," he went on to say, "if these markets shift rapidly now or twelve months from now, our whole organization, including myself, would be heartsick to think that we had not been on to our job sufficiently to take advantage of this situation." He concluded, "Probably a middle course is the answer."

It should be recalled that at this time the Federal Farm Board was bullish on the market outlook. Betting heavily on the ability of the Federal Farm Board to at least arrest the market decline, Babcock declared to the G.L.F. Board on November 5 that the only way to get the $500,000 then urgently needed was "to earn it—and the only way to earn it is to try to break even and own necessary amounts of inventory until the market turns. . . . We are, therefore, following the policy of accumulating long lines of wheat and oats as the market goes down."

At this time the G.L.F. was fighting for its life. In speaking to a conference of the fieldmen on October 20, Babcock put the problem squarely up to them. He recalled the summer of 1922 when the G.L.F. was in desperate straits when "certain men in this room came to the rescue." He went on to say: "Today the situation is just as desperate because so much more is involved," and he called again "on the same men and a few more to help me out." He declared, *"We must put the farmer of the New York Milkshed behind the G.L.F. We have got to get him in a fighting mood for it. As a result, we will get the volume we need. I know of no other way to do it."*

During the next few months a strenuous campaign was carried on to maintain and build volume, and a more cautious policy of watching the market was adopted. On December 11 when Babcock again reported to the Board, the position of the Exchange was a little brighter. "As prices have gone down, we have increased our inventories, thus broadening our base." However, he warned, "The organization is challenged as never before to cut its expenses to meet new conditions." In a memo to department heads on January 21, 1931, Babcock and McConnell stated, "We have heavy commitments on future years [but] it was agreed some time ago that these would be the only speculative risks taken by the Exchange. They will be watched closely and no chance will be taken with them. This is said merely for the peace of mind of those who are not directly in touch with this activity."

The losses in grain futures which had totaled about a million dollars during 1930 gave the management and Board of Directors great concern. Part of the difficulty had been from lack of experience and fixed responsibility in handling option sales. To remedy this situation the directors adopted on April 22 a recommendation of the General Manager which centered authority for all purchases of futures in the hands of the Manager, Assistant Manager, and Hard Grain Buyer. It was further agreed that "No purchases of future grains shall be made except when two of the above three are in accord as to a particular transaction and all three as to policy."

The financial position of the Exchange began to improve about this time and, in the next few months, substantial savings were made. As a result, at the year end a net saving of $29,927 could be recorded in the face of a loss on options of $448,656 and losses in inventory valuations of approximately $162,229. Thus, net gains in operations were more than sufficient to cover the burden of these unusual losses caused mainly by the rapid decline of prices.

Marketing Encouraged

While interest in cooperative marketing did not entirely subside during this period it was subordinated to the problem of survival, for the energies of G.L.F. management were largely absorbed in meeting problems that came from the continuing fall of commodity prices.

At this time the Ithaca G.L.F. Service Store was carrying on an interesting experiment in egg marketing which demonstrated that the western system of marketing graded eggs in large quantities was not adapted to a region close to terminal markets. In other communities local service stores were carrying on similar experiments in assembling eggs, cabbage, buckwheat and other produce, with varying degrees of success.

With the continuing fall of commodity prices and increasing financial stringency,[14] the G.L.F. turned to the Federal Farm Board for help. Although the Federal Farm Board was not empowered to lend funds for cooperative purchasing operations it could provide them for cooperative marketing operations. This would serve the same purpose, for funds for any specific purpose could relieve the general strain.

In granting the G.L.F. a loan of $250,000 on January 7, 1931, the Federal Farm Board stipulated: "The purpose of the loan shall be for the effective merchandising of agricultural commodities produced by the members and for stockholders of the former [the Cooperative G.L.F. Exchange, Inc.] and of its subsidiaries and affiliates."[15]

[14] The G.L.F. was severely jolted about this time when a prominent Buffalo Bank called for immediate payment on notes used to finance the mill.

[15] This loan, as indicated by the minutes of the Federal Farm Board for December 9, 1930, was secured by common stock of the G.L.F. Holding Corporation owned by the Exchange and was repayable $25,000 semi-annually.

Expanding the Stores

The slump in sales volume came with the inauguration of the new arrangement under which all fieldmen were supervised by the Cooperative Farm Service Management. These fieldmen were responsible not only for organizing new stores and assisting the old ones but they were also expected to work with agent-buyers and perform general field services.

With the great interest in expanding stores, problems of stores took an increasing part of the fieldmens' attention. To remedy this situation W. I. Myers had proposed that the district agents be divided into two groups. The first group would supervise the store system and be employed by the Management Corporation. The second would be salesmen and they would be direct employees of the G.L.F.

This proposal met with stiff resistance from V. A. Fogg, President of Cooperative Farm Service Management. In a memorandum to Babcock on January 31, 1931, Fogg said:

I feel that the retail service has been undermanned both in numbers and in ability. . . . As a fundamental principle I am against duplication of effort in territories. I think it is sound to put a particular territory under one man and to hold him responsible for getting the business for the G.L.F. in that territory, whether it be through stores, agents, or poolers. . . .

While Babcock was not entirely convinced—for he noted on the margin of Fogg's memorandum that "the specialist has his place and may be the cheapest operator in his field"—the system then being followed was continued without significant change until November, 1935.

It was at this time that the energies of the field service became increasingly concerned with the establishment of stores. Babcock had been impressed with the ability of the existing stores to maintain volume and he was anxious to expand their number. In a memorandum to department heads, he and McConnell said on January 22, 1931: "We have funds available for thirty more stores. If possible, we hope to have 100 stores operating by the time cows go on grass so that these agencies may be depended upon to furnish volume to the feed plant during the summer season." Although the record did not come up to this aspiration, seven new stores were started during the first six months of 1931 and fourteen more during the last half of the year, bringing the total to 86 at the beginning of 1932.

The Problem of Control

At the first meeting of the Board on February 12, 1931, following the formation of the Holding Company, a number of important policy decisions were made. It was agreed that the Holding Company would handle all financial matters for the G.L.F. subsidiaries as well as for the Exchange. It would borrow all money and finance the institution. It would own all investments and properties for the G.L.F.

In the interest of efficiency it was also decided to consolidate at Buffalo the various wholesale services, and to continue supervision of all G.L.F. retail cooperatives and agent-buyers as well by the Farm Service Management Corporation from Ithaca.

The delegation of much of its power to the Cooperative G.L.F. Holding Corporation emphasized the importance of the G.L.F. as the controlling institution and the need of keeping the control of the Exchange in safe hands. This problem was recognized by the General Manager who called attention to the fact that whoever controlled the Exchange controlled also the Holding Corporation and all G.L.F. subsidiaries. Babcock perceived a danger in possible control by a bloc of unfriendly stockholders representing but a fraction of the patrons, and he saw the need of a plan that would place active control in the hands of those who used its services. To safeguard against the possible misuse of central power by the stockholders, Babcock proposed that each G.L.F. retail cooperative own a block of G.L.F. common stock.[16]

This would have little effect on the number of stockholders which then totaled 34,000, since each cooperative could have only one vote from its common stock under existing law, but a bloc of about 125 stockholders attending an annual meeting as representatives of their local cooperatives could be expected to exert a significant effect, since only a small fraction of the total number of stockholders usually attended the annual meeting.

While at that time nothing came of Babcock's proposal, it foreshadowed the adoption of an enlarged plan of this same type following the attempt of a faction to gain control at the next annual stockholders meeting, and thus demonstrated Babcock's foresight in recognizing danger in advance.

Corporate Accountability Expanded

Prior to July 24, 1931, the G.L.F. carried on all wholesale operations (including manufacturing) through its Wholesale Division. At this time

[16] V. A. Fogg had also been thinking about this problem. In a memo to Babcock on January 31, 1931, he had observed, "I would like to see the farm service agencies become even more of a local institution than they have in the past, and would like to see ways and means developed whereby every patron becomes at least slightly interested in the ownership of preferred stock. I would like to see the service stores in time own the common stock of the G.L.F. and the common stock of the Holding Corporation. This I would like to see done solely from the standpoint of building a true cooperative. . . . I believe that this stock policy . . . would fundamentally build our cooperative from the ground up in such a way that it should be self-perpetuating."

it was decided to set up under Article 8a a separate agency corporation —the Cooperative G.L.F. Mills, Inc.—with control vested in the Cooperative G.L.F. Holding Corporation through stock ownership for the purpose of handling all feed, fertilizer and seed operations. It was anticipated that this action would achieve more flexible operations and better fix administrative responsibility.[17]

Babcock and his associates were then becoming enamoured with the idea that administrative decentralization and greater scope for managerial initiative could be achieved through the use of subsidiary corporations financially controlled through the Holding Corporation with the G.L.F. in indirect control of all institutional policies. Thus Mills continued the trend toward separate corporate accountability which had been started with the formation of Farm Management Service, Inc., and the Cooperative G.L.F. Holding Corporation.[18]

With the incorporation of Cooperative G.L.F. Mills, the Cooperative G.L.F. Exchange divested itself of all operating responsibilities and became in effect the policy and control center for the G.L.F. system. The directors of the new corporation were selected by the directors of the Holding Corporation, with the approval of the G.L.F. Board of Directors, from the managerial staff, and J. A. McConnell, the Assistant Manager in charge of the purchasing division, became the first Mills President.

As the Holding Corporation grew in power within the G.L.F. structure after the establishment of the Mills Corporation, confusion began to develop in lines of authority. This question was settled to some extent by the G.L.F. Board of Directors at its September meeting. It was the consensus "that the G.L.F. Board, being elected by the farmer stockholders,

[17] Babcock's general thinking which led up to this decision was reflected in a paper, "Elements of Success in Cooperative Purchasing," which he presented at the annual meeting of the American Farm Economic Association in December 1930. He pointed out that "the one big lesson" he had learned "as the fundamental of first importance" was to recognize "the fact that there are two separate and distinct functions to be performed in cooperative purchasing. . . . One of these functions is distinctly a community enterprise which I shall call 'retail purchasing service.' The other is a regional activity which I shall call 'wholesale purchasing service.'" Believing that "the two jobs must be reviewed separately and each one worked out for what it is," the formation of G.L.F. Mills naturally followed the establishment of Cooperative Farm Service Management, Inc.

In Fogg's memo to Babcock of January 21, 1931, he had advocated the consolidation of wholesale service at one central point. "Such a plan would prevent mistakes of the retail service going out on a plan before wholesale was ready to cooperate or vice versa. I believe also that such a plan would do much to better coordinate within our own organization the spirit of working together, and would also eliminate any tendency or feeling of playing one group against another."

[18] Strictly speaking, this trend was begun early in the life of the G.L.F. when certain activities such as the Service Stores were controlled through the P. W. & E. Company. However, the significance of this principle of administration was not fully recognized until it was employed in the organization of Cooperative Farm Service Management.

was morally, if not legally, responsible for the acts of the Holding Corporation and its subsidiaries." It was therefore resolved: "That all reports and all matters pertaining to policies of the G.L.F. or subsidiaries of the Holding Corporation be brought before this, the G.L.F. Board of Directors."

The formation of G.L.F. Mills was attended by difficulties. Economic conditions were far from favorable and it required some time for management staff of the new corporation to adjust to the revamped set-up. During the first few months of the new fiscal year, with prices uncertain, farmers resorted to hand-to-mouth buying and volume fell off appreciably, giving the directors considerable concern. In his November report to the Board, Babcock said:

> Since the first of July our major problem has been to . . . bring to full operating strength the Mills Company. No enterprise could have gotten off to a worse start. . . . From July 1 to mid-October the drop in feed and grain volume was terrific. . . . At one time early in October the Mills Company, capitalized at $600,000, figured it had lost ⅔ of the original capital. Nor is it any wonder that the men who were fighting this condition temporarily lost their feel for field conditions. . . . In early October, however, several conditions set in to correct this situation. Grain and feed sales hit bottom and firmed. Volume of feed and grain purchases by our patrons picked up. This enabled the Mills to run out high cost goods. Most important of all, the Mills personnel under McConnell's leadership, began to find itself as an operating unit.

The experience of the G.L.F. during the depression made it more and more apparent that the real strength of G.L.F. lay in support from the farmers who used its services. This fact was recognized in November with the re-emergence of the house organ as the *G.L.F. Patron* rather than as the *G.L.F. Shareholder*. The emphasis in the organization was fast shifting from *shareholders* to *patrons*.

HARLO P. BEALS   A. L. BIBBINS   WALTER L. BRADLEY

MAURICE C. BURRITT   M. E. CAMPBELL   ELWOOD L. CHASE

T. B. CLAUSEN   JAY CORYELL   C. E. DAYTON

SOME BUILDERS OF G.L.F.

CHARLES L. DICKINSON   CHARLES E. DYKES   E. R. EASTMAN

VERNE A. FOGG   FRED H. HESSEL   MILTON LYLE HOLMES

FREDERICK A. McLELLAN   WILLIAM D. McMILLAN   THOMAS E. MILLIMAN

SOME BUILDERS OF G.L.F.

WALDO MORSE   FRANK K. NAEGELY   SHERMAN PEER

MILTON P. ROYCE   C. W. SADD   B. H. STAPLIN

PAUL TABER   E. VICTOR UNDERWOOD   E. C. WEATHERBY

SOME BUILDERS OF G.L.F.

CROP DEMONSTRATION WORK

LIME SPREADER AT WORK

CHAPTER 18

Redevelopment, 1932-35

It is my personal opinion that it is more important to know why we have the G.L.F. and why it proceeds according to certain policies than it is to know when it was incorporated, how much capital is issued, or its current financial position. It is much harder, and therefore much more worthwhile, to grasp the spirit of the Institution and to get the "feel" of it in operation.

H. E. BABCOCK, *July 1934.*

THE GROWING CORPORATE COMPLEXITY of the G.L.F., with its Holding Company and related subsidiary corporations, gave emphasis to the importance of membership control. The aims of the G.L.F. pioneers had been to obtain needed supplies and services through their own organization at cost. The problem of membership control did not particularly concern them as it was largely assumed that stockholder and membership control were synonymous. It was taken for granted that control by stockholders would serve also the great body of farmer patrons. While provision was made for payment of patronage refunds, the more immediate concern was to pay dividends on the large amount of outstanding common stock. Thus for many years the G.L.F. was in fact a farmers' stock company chartered under the cooperative law rather than a true operating cooperative organization.

By 1932 the G.L.F. had become a huge corporate conglomeration—more or less cooperative in form. It is true that the control was vested in directors elected by stockholders—but the directors were nominated in the first instance by the three major sponsoring organizations. Seldom more than a hundred stockholders troubled to come to the annual stockholders' meetings, yet these stockholders in the final result had full control.

If any adverse group were to take the trouble to get a large group of stockholders to a meeting, and proxies from many more—not an impossibility—control might be wrested from the directors nominated by the founding organizations. This was deemed to be only a theoretical hazard until the annual stockholders' meeting in February, 1932, demonstrated that such a situation could easily arise.

As if to prove the claim made the year before that the method of membership control for the G.L.F. was vulnerable, an attempt was then made by a few disgruntled individuals, sparked by Robert E. Dame,[1] the former

---

[1] Dame had long been critical of Babcock's leadership of G.L.F. and he resented his dismissal in 1929. The two were not compatible.

Chief Accountant, to upset the election of the three nominees from the three sponsoring organizations. Three other persons were nominated from the floor and might have been elected by the use of some 500 proxies had the proxies not been altered, making them invalid. This attempt to wrest control of the organization from its established supporters had been engineered so quietly that it came as a complete surprise and something of a shock. Its near success shook the equanimity of those who had long considered themselves responsible for the organization's welfare.

This annual meeting also demonstrated that a small group of stockholders with shrewd leadership could subvert policies into their selfish interests at the expense of the larger needs and responsibilities of the organization. A resolution was proposed and, by the use of proxies, passed, which would have milked the organization of savings as made for the benefit of stockholders, regardless of the organization's financial needs, if it had not been disregarded by the Directors upon advice of legal counsel.[2]

This scare was fortunate. After the annual meeting, immediate steps were taken to safeguard the organization from such future attacks. Recognizing that the problem called for a fundamental change in the plan of organization, a bill was drafted with the assistance of Professor W. I. Myers of Cornell University and passed with the support of the farm organizations of the state which amended the Cooperative Corporations Law in two important respects.

The amended law gave member cooperatives of the G.L.F. the right to vote one share for each accredited delegate, not exceeding the number of shares owned by the cooperative. It also permitted a cooperative to revise its documents of organization by a two-thirds majority of its stockholders present at a regularly called stockholders' meeting.

With this law in force the G.L.F. called a special meeting of stockholders for November 15 to amend its certificate of incorporation and by-laws. In anticipation of this meeting, six shares of stock were issued to each local G.L.F. cooperative so that each member of its advisory committee could serve as a delegate at the annual meeting, and special meetings were held with the committee members to acquaint them with their new responsibilities as representatives of patrons. As there were then about 100 cooperative service stores, this assured that there would be several hundred delegates at the special meeting who were interested primarily in the organization as representatives of the patrons. It is significant that

---

[2] The law under which the Exchange was chartered provided for distribution of net earnings "once every twelve months." If strictly followed this would have prohibited the G.L.F. from using savings to develop the organization. With the heavy investment of the G.L.F. in plants at this time, strict compliance would have been disastrous.

542 stockholders were present in person and 836 by proxy, and that all votes were cast in favor of the changes recommended.

At this special meeting the documents of organization were revised to provide for:

1. delegate representation by advisory committeemen of local cooperatives at the annual stockholders' meetings.
2. discontinuance of proxy voting while permitting voting by mail.
3. an increase in the number of directors from 9 to 13, to provide for representation of G.L.F. members in Pennsylvania and New Jersey. This change also provided for direct nominations of directors by the members of local G.L.F. affiliates in Pennsylvania and New Jersey rather than by sponsoring organizations.

This modified the structure of the organization by giving a select group of patrons a certain degree of control through placing voting stock in their hands. With upwards of 500 patron representatives, with full stockholders privileges, present at a stockholders' meeting, there would be little chance of an opposing faction gaining control or upsetting policies, especially with the machinery of the organization working to obtain written votes on policies and services submitted to stockholders in advance of a meeting.[3]

Of significance also was the provision for nomination of directors to represent G.L.F. patrons direct in Pennsylvania and New Jersey. This was a step toward giving those who used the organization the right to nominate its directors—as recommended three years earlier by the Dairymen's League.[4]

MANAGEMENT BY HOLDING CORPORATION

In March, 1932—while plans were being made for the revision of the articles of incorporation and bylaws—Babcock resigned as General Manager, but continued to hold his position as President of the Holding Corporation. He apparently thought that this would simplify executive direction and give him as President of the Holding Corporation the de-

---

[3] While this arrangement gave the G.L.F. a large measure of protection against dissident groups, it set up an organization imbalance in that it did not recognize the interests of the large group of patrons who were served by agent-buyers. This condition was corrected in 1935, when the G.L.F. moved to treat all patrons alike by giving the advisory committees of the agent-buyers similar representation. (See pp. 182, 184.)

[4] During the formative years, the three sponsoring organizations had nominated the directors who were thereupon formally elected at the annual stockholders' meeting. In early 1928 the Board of Directors of the Dairymen's League had passed a resolution recommending "that the G.L.F. should develop some machinery whereby the stockholders of the organization will have a direct voice in naming their own directors." This resolution laid the ground for the electoral changes in 1932 and in later years.

gree of control necessary, since the recent organizational changes placed responsibility for operations in the corporations financially controlled by the Holding Company.

Babcock gave his reasons for resigning in a personal letter sent to each member of the Board of Directors on March 17. He declared that as far as he could foresee "the G.L.F. is adequately organized to render efficient service to the farmers of the New York Milk Shed." He went on to say: "Since all the purely business activities of the Exchange are now entirely handled by subsidiary corporations, with control ultimately resting in the Holding Corporation, a General Manager of the G.L.F. may well be dispensed with and some expense saved."

He therefore proposed that his resignation as General Manager be accepted with the understanding that he would be willing to continue on part time as President of the Holding Corporation "in order that the Exchange may not lose out on the investment it has made in my experience."

It was then Babcock's view that even the job of being President of the Holding Corporation would require but a small part of his time, as he gave the following personal reasons for wishing to be relieved of the responsibility of being General Manager:

1. I desire more time at home and more time for my farm.
2. Since my breakdown four years ago, I have not taken a day's vacation, and my nights and Sundays have literally been my busiest hours. I feel it unwise to continue such a pace.
3. While I can still be available for emergencies I want to make certain we have built an Institution which can go on indefinitely serving farmers of the New York Milk Shed without depending too much on any one individual.
4. I want some time for serious study and observation of the cooperative movement, and for writing about it, especially in the field of local marketing service, in which I am convinced there will be major developments during the next ten years.

On March 22 the Board accepted the resignation with the understanding that Babcock's services would be still available as President of the Holding Company.

Thus, Babcock continued to direct the affairs of the G.L.F. by virtue of his presidency of the Holding Corporation. This made the Holding Corporation Board the directing center for the affairs of the G.L.F. for the Board of the G.L.F. controlled the Institution only in the nominal sense that it rubber stamped the decisions made by the Board of the Holding Corporation.

This development greatly increased the sense of operating independence of the subsidiary corporations—particularly G.L.F. Mills, Inc., and Cooperative Farm Service Management, Inc. To meet the obvious need of coordination, Babcock set up a correlating committee composed of himself as President of the Holding Corporation; Underwood, the Secretary-Treasurer of the Holding Corporation; McConnell, the President of Mills; Fogg, the President of Farm Service Management; Holmes, the Chief Accountant; and Peer, the Attorney—but, as he later reported, the arrangement never gave complete satisfaction.[5]

In resigning as General Manager Babcock apparently believed that his days of active management were over and that he could assume the mantle of Elder Statesman, although he was then but 42 years of age. Experience during the next twelve months proved the contrary.

The completion of his ten years of active management was celebrated with a dinner given in his honor at the Onondago Hotel, Syracuse. As a token of esteem, his friends and associates presented Mr. and Mrs. Babcock with tickets and all expenses for a trip to Europe.[6]

Soon after Babcock returned in the fall, the national election ushered in a change in agricultural policies which required his close attention. With the inauguration of Franklin D. Roosevelt as President in March, 1933, his old friend, Henry Morganthau, Jr., became Chairman of the Federal Farm Board, and later the first Governor of the Farm Credit Administration. It was natural that Morganthau would draw heavily for assistance on his New York State friends—Professors George F. Warren, W. I. Myers, and H. E. Babcock. Thus for a period of three months in the spring of 1933 Babcock spent 4 days each week in Washington, primarily assisting in the liquidation of Federal Farm Board loans.

INTERNAL RIVALRIES DEVELOP

As a result of these activities not related to G.L.F. business, Babcock was unable to give adequate time to G.L.F. administrative affairs and there resulted a battle for dominance within the G.L.F. structure. The clash was principally over the relative importance of retail distribution as opposed to wholesaling and manufacturing. Those working directly with farmers in the field were inclined to overemphasize the importance of a strong distribution system. The Mills organization, on the other hand, having control of the supplies, was just as determined not to relinquish power to those in the field.

[5] It might have worked better, according to one of its members, if Babcock had always been there to preside over committee meetings. It led to a situation where there was responsibility without authority.

[6] "Over 300 of our friends were there, many unknown to me, but everyone a personal acquaintance of Ed's. Representatives from all the farm organizations, G.L.F. officers, employees from Jim McConnell down to office girls, old school friends of Ed's, those he had worked with in County Agent days. . . . The speeches were full of compliments for Ed with an occasional bouquet for me." Journal of Mrs. H. E. Babcock, September 1932.

This trend was noted with concern by close observers who felt that the resumption of active forceful management by Babcock was imperative. One friend wrote to him in July, 1933, that "a strong coordinating head is required to synchronize the operations of the wholesale and retail divisions" and make them "realize that the G.L.F. [is] an Institution of many ramifications but with one single purpose—that of maximum service to the farmer at the lowest cost. . . . I am afraid it is going to take your influence and your reasoning and logic to safely steer the ship."

There is evidence that Babcock recognized this situation although no positive steps were immediately taken to change it. However, this situation soon began to clear as he withdrew from various outside activities and gave more attention to administering G.L.F. affairs.

Let us examine the direction in which the G.L.F. was then moving. The separation of the wholesale and the retail supply divisions of the organization into two semi-autonomous corporations—Cooperative Farm Service Management and G.L.F. Mills—was beginning to create a rift in the G.L.F. as a whole.

In the aggressive development of its retail program Cooperative Farm Service Management was gradually becoming a strong self-centered organization. Within the staff of Cooperative Farm Service Management there was building up pressure that G.L.F. should extend its service beyond the basic farm supplies available through the G.L.F. Mills Corporation. This raised a serious problem since G.L.F. Mills was a specialized functional organization which could not easily handle miscellaneous commodities.

Sensing the seriousness of this problem, Babcock brought it out into the open for discussion at a staff conference. He asked:

Should G.L.F. Mills add the purchase of other products to its line or should Farm Service Management make independent arrangements for the purchase of such miscellaneous commodities? Should Farm Service Management contract with private concerns for the handling of other well-known brands of feed, seed and fertilizer to their stores and agents?

An affirmative answer to the second question would have placed Cooperative Farm Service Management in direct competition with the G.L.F. Mills—a logical outcome of the trend toward complete corporate independence in Cooperative Farm Service Management.

The first question was more difficult. Although it was logical that all buying should be centered, Mills had little direct interest in building a business in miscellaneous supplies. On the other hand, to turn over such business to Cooperative Farm Service Management would break down the functional distinction between retail and wholesale which had been found essential to operating efficiency.

Although these questions were not immediately resolved, their consideration was healthy in that the trend toward fission was recognized and arrested.

At this time there were two schools of thought in the upper management circles of the G.L.F. One favored restricting service to the basic farm supplies: Primarily feed, seed and fertilizer. The other recognized the growing demand of farmers for service on miscellaneous farm supplies and equipment, and thought that the organization should recognize this demand.

At the Board meeting on September 7, 1933, Babcock asked:

Should it be the policy for G.L.F. Mills to move toward the objective of confining its wholesale purchasing and processing services on such various items as feed, seed, and fertilizer and even on simpler programs for service on these items.

At the same time he asked also whether the marketing service should be expanded, or discontinued entirely.

It was apparently the thinking of Babcock and the Board that service should be restricted to the basic farm supplies insofar as possible and that marketing operations should be limited in scope to those that could be conducted advantageously. It should be recalled that at this time economic conditions were still depressed, and that this tended to make management unduly conservative. So, for the time being, the basic issue was left unresolved.

Dangerous Trends Recognized

On January 16, Babcock expressed concern to the directors over certain trends within the organization "that should be arrested." He feared that the G.L.F. was "losing contact with the rank and file of farmers who are to be served and consequently losing a knowledge of their needs." Along with this he saw a tendency toward "extravagance in operations, a danger which creeps up on an organization by age and success, and speculation."

This talk set the stage for remedies which were to be put into effect later in the year. As the problem of speculation called for immediate action the Holding Corporation prescribed procedures for the purchase of futures options and holding of physical inventories to be enforced by the President of the Holding Corporation.

Babcock's report to the Board indicated also that the problem of executive control was giving him some concern. The tension within the top command of the G.L.F. during the period while management responsibilities were decentralized through the device of autonomous operating corporations, had finally persuaded him that loose control through the Holding Corporation was not sufficient to achieve integrated operation for the system as a whole. At the meeting of the Holding Corporation Board on February 16, 1934, he indicated that the use of committees through which he had undertaken to coordinate the Institution had not proved practical. Although "the committees are faithful they are unable to furnish the final, alert, firm and intelligent leadership which is required in the management of as large an organization as the G.L.F." He had therefore come to the conclusion that the President of the Holding Corporation, himself or someone else, "must accept the responsibility of [being] the Chief Executive of the G.L.F. System."

EXECUTIVE DIRECTION CENTERED

The Holding Corporation Board—which comprised within itself the G.L.F. Board—thereupon designated Babcock to be the executive head of the G.L.F. System. As he was already in fact the chief executive—as President of the G.L.F. Holding Corporation—this action simply recorded Babcock's decision to take over more active direction of the G.L.F. It made clear that he was to be recognized as "Chief Executive," with full personal power over all other employees in the organization.[7]

Babcock immediately opened an office in the headquarters building where he could keep in intimate touch with all operations. He at this time stated that in the near future he hoped to turn over the responsibilities of executive direction for the G.L.F. System to a qualified successor. He also reserved to himself the right to "do another job—that of directing the G.L.F. publicity, public relationships, and educational activities." He declared *It is the job to which I hope eventually to devote all of my time.*"[8]

Babcock lost little time in re-establishing his active—as opposed to passive—leadership. After a few weeks of sizing up the situation he presented his views to the operating heads in a memorandum of April 25, 1934. In this memo he expressed concern over the growing competition from commercial organizations which was developing as a result of certain governmental policies and economic conditions, and recommended a course of action to meet this situation, since "obviously we cannot afford to stand still."

[7] Apparently Babcock believed that the informal control he had as President of the Holding Corporation did not provide for continuing supervision and the making of executive decisions as they were called for in day-to-day operations. Babcock thus wanted the *right* to manage without being responsible for *direct management.*

[8] Letter to G.L.F. Directors of Feb. 19, 1934.

Babcock offered three "constructive suggestions as to how to extricate the G.L.F. System from its speculative bogdown and its imminent loss of tonnage."

His first concern was to change the attitude of the District Managers who, "despite the wonderful job they have done . . . [were] (1) lacking in commodity enthusiasm, (2) short of commodity knowledge, (3) deficient in commodity confidence and (4) increasingly lacking in institutional spirit and zeal."

To remedy this condition Babcock proposed to "increase the number of District Managers by subdividing the territory." This would concentrate responsibility.

His second "constructive suggestion" was that G.L.F. take over and expand the work performed by Agricultural Research.

The third suggestion was that direct circularization by stores and agencies be decentralized in accordance with "established G.L.F. policy of permitting each community to determine its own retail distribution costs by its own cooperative efforts."

To effectuate the program of tightening up, Babcock set up a committee of three to work with him, composed of McConnell, the President of Mills, Fogg, the President of the Management Cooperative, and Underwood, the Secretary-Treasurer of the Holding Company. Declaring that "this group must be at all times institutionally minded, Babcock diagnosed the whole G.L.F. System as follows:

I am convinced (1) that the Mills Corporation is suffering from overexpansion, some of it not thought through, and from a too free attitude toward expenditure which has been largely corrected this winter. I do not believe that Mills' operators are very far removed from the commodity problems of the field but I doubt if they fully realize the economic conditions under which G.L.F. patrons are laboring; (2) I am convinced that the introduction of the administrative manager type of District Manager into the field force has killed off something in the way of commodity appreciation and belief in the G.L.F. program. If anything, the management corporation is overimpressed with the economic condition of prices and underimpressed with what the G.L.F. is doing in the way of reducing service on commodities. (3) There has developed throughout the G.L.F. System some internal friction. I intend to iron it out.

The resumption of active leadership immediately arrested the lethargy and confusion growing up in the organization. The old Babcock of 1922 was back in the saddle—calling the shots and seeing that they were made.

During the past few years Babcock had come to realize that the ultimate control of the G.L.F. and its ideals largely depended upon the cooperation of the advisory committeemen. On June 5, he took them into his confidence in a special memorandum.

He proposed that "we begin to look forward to the following set-up" in which:

1. Much of the stock of the G.L.F. would be owned by the local cooperatives, which would insure a G.L.F. Board that knows the problems and needs of local purchasing and marketing cooperatives.

2. The Cooperative G.L.F. Holding Corporation would cease to draw common stock dividends from the Cooperative G.L.F. Mills, the Cooperative G.L.F. Marketing Corporation, and the Cooperative G.L.F. Credit Corporation after it has a sufficiently strong financial statement to permit it to finance the entire G.L.F. system as cheaply as possible.

3. The Cooperative G.L.F. Mills and other wholesale corporations should look forward to the time when no common stock dividends will be paid the Holding Corporation. "When this point is reached," and Babcock thought it might be reached "within a comparatively few years," he proposed that "every dollar of earnings should be paid out in patronage dividends to the G.L.F. Stores and independent cooperatives which are its patrons." He indicated that a start was made in this direction the preceding August when $50,000, resulting from appreciation of inventories, had been so distributed.

The prospect of paying patronage refunds emphasized the importance of the advisory committees in helping locals get in shape to pay them to patron-members. Babcock clearly saw that this whole trend would lead to the recognition of the importance of patron-members as contrasted with shareholders.

His thinking represented a complete change-over from the early emphasis on stockholder control. From now on—the patron—the user of G.L.F. services—was to control and enjoy the benefits resulting from his patronage. The G.L.F. was coming to recognize that those who use the service should control it, and receive the benefits arising.

CONTROL SHIFTS TO PATRONS

On June 28 Babcock gave the Directors his views on trends within the G.L.F. and their significance, stating that "The foundation and methods to be followed in changing the ownership of the G.L.F. system from stockholders to patrons has been laid and gotten underway." He went on to explain, "This means that eventually the farmer doing $100 worth of business through the system will name its directors rather than the men who own $5.00 shares of stock." He also pointed out that:

We have demonstrated in the system what type of cooperative subsidiary upon which I believe we must rely in the future for safety and flexibility. I refer to the Cooperative Corporation which has been established to do some definite job as a part of the system and which has been consistently financed out of its own earnings. *It is my considered judgment that as soon as possible the G.L.F. itself and all corporate units in the system must be thus financed.*

In no other way can we have a 100 percent adaptable system, that is, a system which can set up a new service or discard an old service without jeopardizing the financial situation or hamstringing the operations of the Institution as a whole.

At that time Babcock saw three fundamentals which must dominate the policies of the G.L.F. System from "now on." (1) Emphasis on service to patrons rather than to non-patrons. (2) Emphasis on financing all services out of savings. (3) Taking steps to keep open channels which would permit each individual patron to make his contribution to the G.L.F.

He stated that he resigned as Manager in 1932 because he doubted "if the centralization of administrative authority in the hands of a single individual was the way to run the Institution." The experience during the past two years had made it clear to the Board of Directors and the principal executives "that in order for the Institution to run smoothly *there must be centralization of final authority in the hands of one man,* and that this official should be the President of the Holding Corporation."

Babcock went on to say that he didn't want the job, that his resignation was on the table "while the field is being canvassed for a satisfactory man to take my place." In the meantime, he insisted, "While I am on the job, . . . I intend so far as humanly possible, to see that the G.L.F. is properly run, its future safeguarded, and its usefulness continually developed."

With this preamble "to show the spirit back of what I write," Babcock proceeded to discuss "some of the fundamentals concerning the operation of the G.L.F. system."

He first directed his attention to the importance of protecting the investment of various types of G.L.F. shareholders. He then turned to the importance of protection of Patrons' interests. To do this he proposed "to finish up every G.L.F. service corporation" by setting up adequate reserves to protect capital, writing down their fixed assets to $1, providing 100% reserves on accounts receivable and providing all the working capital they need. Thereafter, the question of distribution of savings by means of patronage dividends would become a live one.

Babcock also reported to the Board on national developments as they related to the work of agricultural cooperatives. He thought it was at last becoming recognized in governmental programs that cooperatives were not "primarily great social forces, but simply another means of doing business." He was glad that they were no longer expected to carry the "burdens of industry representation," and could proceed to strengthen their efficiency as business organizations.

At this time Babcock was trying hard to give employees his conception of the G.L.F. In July he issued a brief document, for the exclusive use of employees, designed to present "the philosophical background of the G.L.F." In the foreword he observed:

It is my personal opinion that it is more important to know why we have the G.L.F. and why it proceeds according to certain policies than it is to know when it was incorporated, how much capital is issued, or its current financial position. There are many facts about it which can easily be looked up. It is much harder, and therefore much more worthwhile, to grasp the spirit of the Institution and to get the "feel" of it in operation.[9]

The growing Institutional significance of the G.L.F. was emphasized in the *G.L.F. Patron* issued in November. The President's message was keyed to the patron—under the heading, "Your G.L.F." Moreover, in Babcock's report as President of the Holding Corporation he played down the importance of the Holding Corporation by saying, "The real holding company in the G.L.F. System is the G.L.F. itself. It owns all the common stock of the holding corporation."

He was not yet ready to take the next step and make the Holding Corporation fully subordinate to the G.L.F. He still tried to marry the two.

When the stockholders met on November 12 Babcock reported that, "The influence of the patron-member will steadily grow." He expressed the conviction that, "The patron-members and the advisory committeemen elected by the patron-members are the foundation of the G.L.F. of the future."

The organization at this time was in a healthy economic condition. In the face of the general agricultural depression, volume had increased from $16,044,835 in 1932-33 to $23,673,283 in 1933-34. Although savings were down slightly from the year before they amounted to $739,138 in 1933-34.

As the G.L.F. entered 1935 the principal problem was one of achieving better internal coordination. While Babcock had taken vigorous steps during the preceding year to give the organization single direction there were still rivalries among the operating divisions which were imperiling organizational harmony.

[9] The significance of the document was in the emphasis which it placed on G.L.F. as an Institution. As a handbook for G.L.F. employees it did much to impart to them Babcock's conception of the G.L.F.

CHAPTER 19

Babcock Resumes Active Control

I am willing for the time being to get back into the collar because the enemies of the G.L.F. are becoming very active. They have met and planned and plotted all winter. They know what they are going to do. So do I.

H. E. Babcock, *May 9, 1935*

ON JANUARY 2, 1935, Babcock called the attention of the Executive Committee to the plan he had presented on December 21, 1933, to develop a greater feeling of responsibility upon the part of the real owners of the G.L.F. "This plan," he said, "called for better organized directors' meetings, and patrons' commodity meetings to culminate in the patrons' annual meetings." He could now say: "during 1934 the cooperative base of the G.L.F. was broadened and strengthened by means of the meetings mentioned above. This strengthening of the G.L.F. was the most significant accomplishment of the year."

A second part of the plan called for "the education and development of personnel." While "great progress had been made in this respect, there was much room for improvement by the directors of Farm Service Management and in the marketing services."

The third part of the plan called for tightening up of operations (1) by appointing comptrollers for the various corporations; (2) by controlling futures' trading, and (3) by having stores cooperate more closely with Mills in ordering." On this part he was "not satisfied with the progress made."

Babcock then directed attention to plans he had presented some six months later.

By June 4, 1934, after watching operations more closely than I had during the previous two years, I came to the conclusion that even more emphasis should be put upon patrons members' relationship to the G.L.F. and at this point there was introduced into our thinking a new idea that promised much. I refer to the plan of selling patron members, both of locals and the G.L.F. system as a whole, on an idea of so-called "finished" cooperatives. This idea was presented at patron committee meetings and in advisory committee meetings. It is so valuable that it should not be lost sight of, particularly since we are really "finishing" the Institution at quite a rapid rate. . . .

He was still not satisfied.

By November 1, 1934, I began to feel quite certain that the G.L.F. System, for some reason or other, was on dead center and that it had arrived there following some grinding of the gears.

My first diagnosis of the situation convinced me that a proper relationship did not exist between the Mills and other wholesale services in the field. My first conclusion was that this was due to an ineffective attitude upon the part of Mills toward volume building. I, therefore, urged that Mills recognize the natural urge in the field upon locals to build volume and that instead of driving for volume, Mills' executives substitute a leadership in aids for building volume. Continuing with my study of the situation, on December 18, 1934, I sent a memorandum to Fogg which expressed a further doubt in my mind regarding the G.L.F. situation as a whole. In this memorandum I raised the question which I consider to be a vital one, of the possibility of G.L.F. Division Managers being so dominated by the Store Board that they no longer represented the Institution as a whole.

From this background Babcock turned to the immediate problems at hand.

He first dealt with the problem of outside purchases by locals from other firms of supplies handled by G.L.F. Mills. In the future, copies of all orders of this type "must be sent to Mills" at the time executed. "Where practical, purchase must be for account of Mills which will pay for it and re-bill the local." This recognized Mills as the sole Purchasing Agent for G.L.F. and halted buying independently. Moreover, the mill at Vineland had been manufacturing for the account of other stores and agents. If this was to continue Babcock decreed "it must be returned to Mills ownership and administration."

He then asked the Executive Committee for help in settling two questions.

1. Should Division Managers be transferred from Farm Service Management to the Holding Corporation?
2. Should the Board of Farm Service Management be the same as for the Store Board?

These questions clearly show Babcock's mind at work on the vexing problem of the best form of field organization.

At this time he was greatly concerned by the stiff competition on feeds. In a confidential letter to G.L.F. Division Managers on January 1, 1935, he dealt with this problem: "This letter is intended to get action. Quit trying to be batch mixers and amateur purchasing agents. Quit writing in about competition. Meet your situations yourself with G.L.F. Formula Feeds . . . the best feeds for the farmer in the world."

Babcock again reported to the G.L.F. directors on January 31, 1935. Vic Underwood had done "a marvelous job" in keeping down the cost of borrowed money. Moreover, the fortunes of "the undernourished members of the G.L.F. family"—G.L.F. Products, Inc., and G.L.F. Marketing Corporation—were both looking up. Products had reduced its accumulated deficit and Babcock was enthusiastic over its possibilities now that it was placed under the management of C. N. Silcox. "It will be used in the future to market, throughout the East, such G.L.F. products as rein-forced cereals, pancake flours, etc. A substantial government contract is just now in prospect which alone should pull it out of the red by June 30." G.L.F. had already supplied the government (for relief purposes) considerable quantities of reinforced cereals and eggs. Although G.L.F. Marketing Corporation was in the red this did not seriously worry Bab-cock since a slight increase in bean volume would put it in the black.

At this time Babcock announced several important personnel actions. Jim McConnell, who had spent the last ten weeks in Washington and New York City on special assignments, was being granted a leave of absence for one year to work with the Commercial Molasses Company.[1] In McConnell's absence, T. E. Milliman would act as head of Mills, with Otto Tanzer in charge of all feed services. Ted Clausen was to serve Babcock as special assistant in developing membership relations. At this point Babcock brought up an important matter.

I will ask you to confirm at your meeting the direct employment of the G.L.F. Division Managers and their supervisors, Fogg, Frank Naegely, Harlo Beals, and Jay Coryell, by the G.L.F. Holding Corporation, under my direct super-vision. I have already taken this step. I could not have made the move without discussing it with you had I not come to the conclusion that Division Managers and their supervisors—Fogg, you know is President of all store corporations—were judged to be so "storeminded" by others in the Exchange that they no longer represented the Institution. Whether or not this view of the situation was correct, it had to be summarily dealt with and *I accordingly, moved.* This throws more work and direct responsibility on me than I like but, just as I decided last summer that there must be a single executive operating head of the G.L.F., I reluctantly had to decide a few weeks ago that those who repre-sent the Institution in the field must head up to this man.

Babcock closed his report by posing two important questions of policy:

Question No. 1: Is the G.L.F. set-up with both the Holding Corporation and the Exchange too complicated? Is the time approaching when we might con-sider (a) liquidating the Holding Company; (b) issuing a G.L.F. preferred stock carrying a lower dividend than the present Holding Company 7 percent pre-ferred?

Question No. 2: The charge is being vigorously pushed by the *Rural New*

---

[1] The relationship of this matter to G.L.F. deserves brief mention. Babcock ex-plained how McConnell had been called to Washington to advise the government on its purchases of feed for livestock relief. "He was instrumental in keeping the Gov-ernment from going into the feed business, saving it millions of dollars. He was then asked to form a syndicate of molasses companies to handle enormous quantities of government molasses. This resulted in the organization of a great new molasses company which will be known as the Commercial Molasses Company." It should be noted that G.L.F. had a definite interest in an economical source of molasses, an im-portant ingredient in mixed feeds, and that the Holding Company soon afterward purchased a substantial interest in the new company.

Yorker . . . that our annual meetings are cut and dried affairs. Of course, this is not so. Should we, however, recognize the situation and make some move to forestall the criticism?

THE NEW ADMINISTRATIVE SET-UP

On March 15, 1935, Babcock established a new administrative set-up to become effective on March 18. Its most significant feature was the realignment of retail service work under F. K. Naegely, as President of G.L.F. Service Stores, and Jay Coryell as President of Farm Service Management. V. A. Fogg became "Controller" responsible for the efficiency of the Holding Corporation and all subsidiaries. Division executives in serving the territory were to be under the direct supervision of Babcock as President of the Holding Corporation, assisted by Controller Fogg.

Under the new arrangement Babcock took over the direction of the Division Executives in the field. T. B. Clausen became responsible for membership work and Harlo Beals for employee education.

To achieve coordination two committees were set up:

(1) A "Long-Time Planning Committee" to meet at least quarterly with H. E. Babcock, as Chairman and V. A. Fogg as Secretary. This committee included all operating and Division executives.

(2) A "Current Planning and Control Committee" to meet monthly when statements were ready, with H. E. Babcock, Chairman and V. A. Fogg, Secretary.

The execution and correlation of plans both within the organization and in the field was to be the responsibility of President H. E. Babcock.

In a letter to the Directors on March 25, Babcock called attention to the new administrative set-up which he had put into effect. He invited them to sit in on the first meeting of the Long-Time Planning Committee "as observers."

On April 11, he again wrote to the Directors, with copies to operating heads, to point out "essential policies to guide us through the spring, summer and fall." He proposed:

1. To put into effect the tightest budget in the history of the G.L.F. . . . I am asking Controller Fogg to address himself to this problem above everything else.

2. To increase the volume of processed feed, seed, and fertilizer . . . which is handled through our plants. I plan to give this problem my own major attention.

3. To bring about in the field an appreciation of the cooperative nature of the G.L.F. This is a challenge to everyone connected with the G.L.F.

It is apparent that Babcock was gradually resuming active management. On May 2 the Directors recognized this fact by again appointing him General Manager. At the same time E. V. Underwood was made President and V. A. Fogg, Secretary-Treasurer of the Holding Corporation.[2]

Although Babcock had been, in effect, General Manager of the G.L.F. during the period while he was President of the Holding Corporation, he was *in fact only* the executive officer of the Holding Corporation. This situation had been remedied to some extent in February, 1934, when he was made Chief Executive Officer of the G.L.F. System—but there was still a twilight zone of divided executive responsibility. It had finally become clear that the situation required that he become again in name and fact the General Manager of the G.L.F., responsible for the execution of Board policies, including the control of personnel in the Holding Company and its subsidiary corporations.

It should be recognized that the dominance of the Holding Corporation, while effective in giving financial power to the G.L.F., had also tended to set up a barrier between the membership and the Institution itself. The Holding Company had become so complex and management-controlled— that farmers lost their sense of participation and responsibility. It was management *for* them, not *by* them. Moreover, the term "Holding Corporation" with its connotations of Big Business and monopoly was hard for farmers to swallow. It was time to play down the Holding Corporation and center effort on building support for the G.L.F. as the parent organization.

Soon after Babcock resumed the position of General Manager, he explained his action in a memorandum to G.L.F. Advisory Committeemen, Division Executives, Store Managers, and Agent-Buyers.

Experience proves that the G.L.F. can best be operated by a single individual who is *directly responsible* to the Board of Directors and who is known to everybody.

Apparently he had come to realize that as President of the Holding Company his responsibilities to the Board were indirect. A personal consideration also led to his decision. The G.L.F. then was being vigorously attacked by its enemies who distorted his relationship to the organization. Babcock felt that he could fight back better under the title of General Manager. He explained this in his memorandum:

I am willing for the time being to get back into the collar because the enemies of the G.L.F. are becoming very active. They have met and planned and plotted all winter. They know what they are going to do. So do I.

(1) They are trying to make effective the age-old strategy of creating suspicion, lack of confidence among patrons, stockholders, directors and employees of the G.L.F.

---

[2] Fogg was in the position of Controller for only a few months. During this time he submitted a proposed budget for 1935-36 which "represented the best judgment of the executives as to what should be spent and earned next year." In submitting it he expressed the hope that it would "lay the basis of an easier understood, more complete, more accurate, and more valuable budget in the future."

(2) They are trying to stop your Board of Directors from "finishing off" the G.L.F. with earnings so that it is independent of borrowed money. They know that when the G.L.F. reaches that enviable position—it is only two or three years off—it will handle farm supplies so much more cheaply than it does now that they don't want to face its competition.

Babcock proposed "a fight to the finish." He said:

The present attack against the G.L.F. is carefully planned and has no other purpose than to break up the Institution. It will be waged relentlessly. Under no consideration let anyone kid you into believing that your G.L.F. is not a competent business organization, 100 percent farmer-owned and farmer-controlled.

At this time he also sent preferred stock owners a memorandum to warn them of the "very active campaign being conducted . . . to discredit the Institution"—[which]—"jeopardizes your investment." He went on to say:

. . . I want you to know that I personally have accepted a job I don't want for the sole purpose of putting myself in the most effective position possible to protect your investment in G.L.F. Holding Corporation stock. *I feel a personal responsibility for this investment.*

Babcock's return as General Manager gave a charge of electricity to the organization. If there had been any doubt who was in fact General Manager it was now removed.

Strong Management Reasserted

On May 22, Babcock informed his Division Executives that:

Big organizations always tend to get sloppy and to be slow in making moves. *This will not be permitted in the G.L.F. System.* . . . I know that you will all agree with me on two things:
(1) That moves which call for concerted action be kept to a minimum.
(2) *That when any action is called for, immediate and 100 percent response be demanded.*
The only way I can see to apply the necessary discipline is to correlate the promptness with which an individual, Division Executive or Store Manager, responds with the sending out of the salary check. I think you get the point. Don't be surprised or peeved if there is some action along this line before very long.

Babcock's changes required time for adjustment. Sensing the need for a fuller explanation of how the new set-up would work, Babcock said in a memorandum to Mills Directors on June 25:

I doubt if you have all caught the full significance of the changed G.L.F. line-up.
For a period of about three years, G.L.F. fieldmen concentrated on the development of retail service stores. Eventually, while doing a splendid store job,

they became 100% store-minded even to the point of becoming competitive with Mills. *All this is changed.*

In the new budget, all store machinery, including Naegely and Coryell's offices, are supported by the assessment of one half of one percent on store dollar volume.

Under the new set-up, Naegely, President of the store board, . . . and Coryell, President of Farm Service Management, and their assistants Ed Fallon and McInerney, are responsible for the characters, training in store management, and work of all store employees, but not for Division Executives.

The new budget provides for 20 division executives. . . .

Division Executives will be supported by a 25¢ a ton assessment on *open* formula feeds and fertilizers. . . . You should note carefully that stores will no longer be the primary responsibility of Division Executives. Stores will be just one of their service tools. Mills feed, seed, or fertilizer services will be tools of equal value and importance as will Crissey's egg marketing service.

At the same time Babcock informed Naegely and Coryell that he did not hold them responsible for the work of Division Executives.

Rather you are to hold division executives responsible *for giving you* the kind and quality of cooperation that is necessary if you are to make a success of your stores.

Please take up with me personally the cases of division executives who do not competently handle stores for you.

I do hold you responsible for the characters, training in store management, work, and spirit of all employees of Coop. Farm Service Management, Inc., and of stores. Commodity training schools from now on will be planned, manned, and managed by Mills.

Your job is to make a success of store management and to support Farm Service Management on the half of one percent assessment on store dollar volume.

In a companion memorandum to G.L.F. Division Executives, Babcock said:

You are in effect assistant General Managers. . . .

Under the set-up I am putting into effect, I am your boss, *yet you must render satisfactory service to a number of executives*—Naegely on stores—Bibbins on seed—Clausen on advisory committees, patrons', and annual meetings, etc., etc.

Your job calls for an all around man, level-headed, cooperative, spirited. One who does not need supervision. Under me you will be given a minimum of supervision, a maximum of cooperation. *You are expected to work harmoniously and effectively with everyone.* If any executives are unreasonable or unfair in what they expect, if they don't give you cooperation, take such cases up with me.

In view of the basic changes made within the organization while competition was intense it is not surprising that G.L.F. tonnage volume declined from 820,453 in 1933-34 to 727,214 tons in 1934-35. However, with slightly higher prices, total dollar volume increased from $23,673,289 to $24,261,900. Net margins after dividends amounted to $499,299 compared with $626,144 for the year before. Retail volume done by G.L.F. Stores increased from $12,511,456 to $16,011,107, due partly to an increase in tonnage handled.

The vigorous cooperative philosophy of Babcock at this time cropped out in his address to the American Institute of Cooperation in July, 1935. Speaking under the title, "Cooperatives as a Means of Doing Business Practically," he recalled that as a boy he had learned a valuable lesson as the result of a rooster fight. The story catches his indomitable spirit.

One day I craved excitement; so I decided to run an elimination tournament for the roosters on the place. . . . I rigged up a pit in the hay mow. For my first match I selected one under-sized Game rooster and a big Plymouth Rock. The battle did not last long. There was a flurry or two, then a tell-tale squawk and the big Plymouth Rock ran and stuck his head in the corner. . . .

For my next bout I got a White Leghorn rooster. As I carried him through the barn to the tired little Game cock I was struck with what a strong lovely bird he was, how proud he seemed, how cruel and capable his spurs looked. . . . Would he lick the Game cock or wouldn't he? . . . I dropped him in the hay mow. There were the usual flurries of fighting. Then a few white feathers floated in the air. Instead of running squawking to a corner, the white rooster fled around the hay mow with a wild beating of wings. I caught him and looked him over. He was not marked, apparently he was not hurt much, but he did not have any use for any more fighting.

. . . *The most important thing in life is the point of view of a man,* your point of·view or mine. I am sure that if that White Leghorn had had the same point of view toward a fight the Game cock had, he could have won the battle easily. . . .

The same strategy will work in the operation of cooperatives with members and executives who have the proper point of view.

In the ensuing months Babcock gave close attention to every activity. His zeal in reinvigorating the organization is shown in the following memorandum to G.L.F. business executives of August 13:

There is no question and should be no confusion about the main job ahead of me and ahead of you men who are my assistants. It is to land on the farms of G.L.F. patrons the highest quality mixed poultry and dairy feeds and mixed fertilizers for the least possible money. The same goes for seeds and for a unit of phosphoric acid.

There are three ways to push our program forward:

1. Keep down expenses all along the line.
2. Spread expenses over a broader base. . . .
3. Build the volume on the essential lines.

Babcock was at this time alert to all possible economies. On August 27 in a memorandum to Directors he urged replacing 7 percent preferred stock of the Holding Company by a 5 percent non-cumulative stock, since refinancing "conditions may not be as favorable again for years." He also proposed that McConnell be brought back to G.L.F. as Assistant General Manager.

The continuing pressure of competition was reflected in a memorandum to Directors on September 26:

If we continue, as I feel we must, to furnish rations to the field at a loss or at best a "break-even" basis—*I am in favor of doing it. . . .*—We must meet the situation. There are two ways to do it: (1) Internal economies. (2) Increased earnings from other farm services.

I can take $100,000 out of operating expenses. *This will mean letting some men go, cutting the salaries of others.* I am about ready to do this.

At the same time Babcock let the G.L.F. Division Executives in on his thinking. He told them "I've got to take $100,000 out of operating expenses. You've got to increase volume at least 25%. Fit the two ideas together and you'll note they make sense."

At the annual meeting on October 21, 1935, Babcock announced to the 1000 stockholders present that he was going to divide the field force into two parts—one group to work in the G.L.F. Stores and the other to work with independent cooperatives and dealers. This idea had been incubating in his mind for several years and he was at last ready to put it into effect.

He also raised the question as to whether the G.L.F. should continue its open-formula policy with respect to feed and fertilizer. In response a committee was appointed to report back on the matter at the next annual stockholders' meeting.[3]

Babcock Separates Sheep from the Goats

For some time Babcock had been concerned with the performance of the fieldmen. Since he had personally built the original field force in 1922 and made it the dynamo for G.L.F. expansion, he sought to find out why

---

[3] The *Rural New Yorker* was then putting the heat on the G.L.F. and this no doubt influenced Babcock's thinking on this question. In a printed statement entitled, "The Record of a Racket," it alleged that the quality of G.L.F. feed was below specifications. It went on to say: "The G.L.F. management makes a virtue out of its 'open-formula' but many dairymen have now come to look at it as an adroit stunt. It gives the G.L.F. opportunity to increase its profits by substituting low-priced substitutes for better and more expensive feed ingredients." Although the G.L.F. circulated a letter from Peter G. Ten Eyck, Commissioner of the New York State Department of Agriculture and Markets, to the effect that the article as a whole was misleading, it was not possible to entirely undo the harm done. This statement also alleged that the stock issued by the G.L.F. was practically worthless, and that the "most widespread deception" of the G.L.F. "is the publication of a magazine under the mask of a house organ." That the G.L.F. was giving the *American Agriculturist* financial support at this time was a matter of public knowledge. On October 16, the *American Agriculturist* announced the formation of the "American Agriculturist Foundation, Inc.," under which the paper would be placed "under direction of its readers" and its profits would be devoted "to the service of agriculture and homemaking." This action removed any doubt as to the ownership and policies of this publication.

it had lost its oldtime vigor. He came to the conclusion that the system of organization was wrong, that the responsibilities of the fieldmen were becoming too diverse and scattered. He was now ready to act.

The result was a dramatic fieldmen's conference on November 1, 1935, at which he separated the "sheep from the goats."

Babcock's designation of half of the fieldmen as "sheep" and the other half as "goats" implied no personal criticism and no one has ever known which were which. It was his way of dividing the force into two groups under separate direction, one to work with the service stores, the other to work with the Agent-Buyers.

Babcock felt that the fieldmen were becoming "store-minded" and that this was not building the maximum degree of cooperation from Agent-Buyers. He held that one group of fieldmen, giving full attention to the needs of the Agent-Buyers, could expand volume and that the remaining group, freed of other responsibilities, could do an even better job on store problems.

This separation also reflected his "game-cock" philosophy. He counted on the challenge from pitting one group against the other.

There was another important factor involved. For some time the G.L.F. had been planning to extend its system of advisory committees to Agent-Buyers and get their records in shape to pay patronage refunds. This called for a special job in organizing each local community and this could be done only through concentrated attention. Thus Babcock not only divided the field force in order to get more drive, but in doing so he had a special job in mind that could best be done by a specialized group.

The new line-up was announced in a memo to the directors on October 29. Under Frank Naegely, President of Cooperative Farm Service Management, were placed those who would work with Service Stores. This group consisted of Jay Coryell (Office Manager), Fran MacAniff (Treasurer and Chief Accountant); E. H. Fallon, C. W. Sadd, J. W. Stiles, D. W. Kelsey, Fred A. Naegely, and Russell Rafferty.

Under M. E. Campbell were placed those who would have "the job of building up the retail service on supplies which farmers buy from the G.L.F. through independent cooperatives and regular dealers." This latter group was again to be called "Fieldmen." This group consisted of H. E. Aiken, Harlo Beals, O. W. Shelden, B. H. Staplin, C. W. Skeele, T. J. Mc-Inery, and M. P. Royce. Babcock remarked that "a study of the personalities of the above men will convince you that they are the fellows who have gotten results in the past through dealers."

This action indicated that a brake was being put on "store business" and that the throttle was being opened on business with agent-buyers. Babcock explained:

My own personal feeling is that from this point on G.L.F. should proceed rather slowly in the development of stores. We now have half our volume through our own managed retail agencies. Carrying these agencies constitutes a very heavy financial load and an even greater responsibility in management. With your approval, my policy now is to refine and tighten the management of stores to eliminate stores which are not holding their own and take on new stores only where the support and volume of a community practically guarantees their successful operation from the start.

He closed in a jubilant vein, "By reorganizing the field force, and by calling the Holding Corporation 7% Preferred Stock, we are saving $50,000 a year on operation expenses. By some reorganization in Mills . . . we can save thousands of dollars in operating costs. . . . My job is very clearly to lead in making these savings. I do not think it is going to be too difficult. I never saw G.L.F. spirits higher."

Babcock was well pleased with the way the organization was moving on November 15, as evidenced by a letter which was sent to President Fred Porter, with copies to all Directors and key executives. This letter is here summarized in some detail, not only for its content but to show the close working harmony of the General Manager and the President of the G.L.F. In it Babcock listed a number of recent organizational changes which were proving constructive.

1. Moving Mills' accounting and traffic headquarters to Ithaca gives a badly needed control and better working harmony.
2. Moving the fertilizer department to New York locates it "where its business is."
3. Arranging for Jim McConnell to come back provides for a man who can devote his full time to watching and developing our buying connections, "a job for which Jim is peculiarly well fitted."
4. Freeing Vic Underwood from internal duties and making him President of the Holding Company provides a "roving landlord" for G.L.F. properties and enables him to "buy" loans to best advantage.
5. Centralizing all members' corporate accounts, taxes, insurance, bonds, and the control of loans to subsidiaries in the office of the Secretary-Treasurer gives "Misty" Fogg an opportunity to render an invaluable service.
6. Dividing the field force was timely, and "the reaction of agents has been fine. . . . We can now take the fieldmen and use them to organize patrons of agent buyers for advice and cooperation, and to get the agents' records in shape so they can hand on patronage dividends when paid them by Mills."

Babcock also indicated that *Products* was steadily moving ahead both in volume of service and profits. "It is a great hit for the long pull." He also indicated that the recent establishment of the American Agriculturist Research Foundation had "about driven nuts" the publisher of the *Rural New Yorker*.[4]

[4] See footnote above, p. 181. The reactions of the *Rural New Yorker* to this action were expressed in an article in the issue of November 9, 1935, entitled, "A Racket Masked as a Gift."

In a memo to G.L.F. agent-buyers on November 21, Babcock informed them that the day was coming when G.L.F. Mills would distribute its savings to stores, independent cooperatives and agent-buyers. To participate in patronage refunds, independent dealers must set up advisory committees and keep their records in a prescribed way so that G.L.F. could pay patronage refunds to its members. He announced that all agency agreements would be canceled on January 1, and new ones entered into only with agents recertified who agreed to conform under the new plan.

In a letter to G.L.F. fieldmen, on December 14, Babcock urged them to "multiply efforts . . . to galvanize into action your agents . . . to focus your attention on the non-buyer and then see that he is gotten either by the store or an agent." When Babcock was in a struggle he never let down on the pressure.

CHAPTER 20

Transition

*I hope all of us will think of the opening of the new G.L.F. official
headquarters on May 6 as marking a new era in G.L.F. service.*

H. E. BABCOCK, *May 13, 1936*

T HE G.L.F. was running more smoothly as it entered 1936.

In a memo to directors on January 7, Babcock called attention to
the present financial strength of the organization as attested by: "(1) the
ease with which the 7% Holding Company preferred has been exchanged
for a 5% preferred; (2) the number of unfilled applications for preferred
stock; (3) the acceptance by the market of G.L.F. 'street paper.'"

In view of the improved conditions, he believed that it would be desirable to pay out part of the net margin on June 30 "as a cash patronage
dividend."

"In a broad sense," he said, "the physical set-up of the G.L.F. System
is now complete. A few small plants may have to be built, but *by and
large, G.L.F. is through investing large sums in physical assets.*"

Babcock was more concerned with the internal problems of the organization. "I remember once saying that the G.L.F. would be more likely to
break up from within than from outside pressure. I still think internal
hazards are the chief ones we face in G.L.F."

He then said: "Our experience has shown that nothing would so handicap the Institution as to have a man appointed general manager who was
one-sided in his interests or sympathies. Always keep a man in training
for general manager. My understanding is that this man, at present, is
Jim McConnell."[1]

On January 1, 1936, G.L.F. Bean Marketing was combined with Cooperative G.L.F. Products, Inc., under C. N. Silcox as Manager. In a letter
to G.L.F. Directors, on January 14, Babcock explained that he had "taken
the liberty of merging our bean marketing corporation, which was not
getting anywhere fast, with Cooperative G.L.F. Products, Inc., which has
been going like a 'house afire.' I did this for two reasons: (1) I wanted to
get the benefit of the management of C. N. Silcox for our bean marketing;
(2) I wanted to effect some economies now and in the future."

All marketing operations except for eggs and poultry were now centered in Products. The five egg auctions, and egg and poultry sales were
being directed by J. C. Crissey.

[1] On February 12, 1936, the Board of Directors approved the employment of
McConnell as Assistant General Manager, to take effect July 1.

Babcock was less satisfied with general corporate administration. To improve it he proposed that greater responsibility be placed in E. V. Underwood, President of the G.L.F. Holding Corporation, and more careful attention be given to budget preparation.

THE SHIFT TO PATRONAGE REFUNDS

As already indicated, Babcock was paving the way for the payment of patronage refunds should there be substantial savings for the fiscal year. On January 10, 1936, in a letter to members of the G.L.F. Store Advisory Committees, he said:

The G.L.F. Board of Directors will meet here in Ithaca, February 11 and 12. . . . There will be a discussion of the patronage dividend policy of the G.L.F. Mills from now on.

The point to be settled is whether the G.L.F. should retain all the earnings of G.L.F. Mills, Inc., until all G.L.F. properties are charged down to $1.00 or whether it should pay out part of these earnings in patronage dividends from time to time.

While this is a matter wholly within the jurisdiction of G.L.F. directors I would be interested in your views on the subject if you will be so kind as to write me. Please do.

When the Board of Directors met on February 12, 1936, Babcock reported that replies on patronage refund policy had been received from 143 committeemen, which he summarized as follows: Sixty-six were in favor of paying patronage refunds, while 77 were in favor of retaining all margins until the G.L.F. plants were written down to $1.00. At this meeting the Board decided to pay a patronage refund at the end of the fiscal year, should savings be adequate.

The G.L.F. was now making steady improvement in plant operating efficiency. On March 2, Babcock informed the Directors that the objective of getting overhead expense down to $1.00 a ton had been reached, and progress was being made in getting plant costs down to $1.50 a ton.

But Babcock was far from satisfied. In a memo to key officials on March 12, he declared, "We cost too much for what we do. . . . We may easily drift into being 'stuffed shirts.'" To remedy the situation he proposed that administrative responsibilities be sharpened. For himself he would "personally direct research, advertising, publicity, internal and external education, all volume building activities." McConnell was to understudy the General Manager, "contact, maintain, and cultivate all outside connections," while working with Fogg "on the *development of a self-supporting, G.L.F. Liquid Products service.*" This service was to handle gas, oil, molasses, alcohol, paint, fly-spray, liquid lime-sulphur. Underwood was to control finances and budgets, and be responsible for all real estate investments. He would also actively manage the Ithaca office building, supervise the Chief Accountant and Director of Traffic, operate a central purchasing service for printing and office supplies, supervise the mailing and central filing rooms and handle all legislative contacts.

He closed the memo with the challenge, "Make the 1936-37 budget the expression of better planning, better meaning, and more definite, harder hitting leadership."

Babcock's avowed aim was to get the organization smoothly operating so that he could conscientiously retire from active management.

On March 24, in a letter to the Board of Directors, he said:

This is intended to be a more thoughtful letter than I have written you for some time. Won't you please do me the honor of reading and re-reading it and of thinking how the situation I describe may be best met.

You G.L.F. Directors have never functioned with reference to the budget to the degree to which I am convinced you are going to have to function in the future. . . . I am coming to the conclusion that I am not heavy enough personally to resist the continuous upward thrust of increasing expenses, particularly the steady pressure to increase salaries. . . . I see no solution for this situation but for you Directors who are the direct representatives of the patrons to take more responsibility than you have yet taken on budget making and enforcement.

Babcock was anxious that he not be misunderstood. He declared:

G.L.F. is going swell. The general manager method of direction is the correct one for G.L.F. I believe this so thoroughly that, without the slightest trace of egotism, I can say that I should hate like the devil to leave this job unless there was an assistant general manager trained to slip into my shoes the moment I left it.

On the other hand, I do not believe that any general manager can keep down expenses in this organization, particularly the salary item and certain other items of overhead, single-handed. Back of him must be a Board of Directors, understanding the budget in detail and enforcing it in detail.

In a postscript he added, "I think I wrote the above letter because I foresee certain adjustments which must be made effective with the next budget."

THE BIRTH OF NEW SERVICES

On April 8, in a memorandum to the Board, Babcock proposed two major changes in G.L.F. structure. A new corporation, G.L.F. Soil Building Service, Inc., was to be set up on the pattern of the Mills Corporation to handle fertilizer, insecticides and similar supplies, with T. E. Milliman as Vice President and Manager. This would limit Mills to feed and seed operations.

Another new corporation which he tentatively called "G.L.F. Community Services, Inc.," also was to be patterned after Mills. It would provide oil and gas and miscellaneous purchasing services. V. A. Fogg was to be vice-president and manager.

With these changes, he pointed out:

> Five corporations—Mills, Products [for marketing], Credit, Soil Building, and Gas and Oil, will be held together through three common officers; the same Secretary-Treasurer (also attorney) the same Comptroller, and the same Director of Traffic. These men will hold the same offices in the Holding Corporation. All five corporations will be financed by the President of the Holding Corporation. All five will have their accounting correlated and be audited by the same Chief Accountant.

> The above program more clearly fixes responsibilities, provides for economies, and lays the basis for the expansion of certain G.L.F. services.

On May 6, 1936, the G.L.F. officially opened its newly constructed head-quarters building in Ithaca. Babcock believed that this would bring a new era in G.L.F. service in which the main objective would be "the rendering of distinctive services to farmers, services they cannot get from any other Institution."[2] He went on to say:

> No. 1 of these services is to be that of presenting the idea of cooperation more effectively than it has yet been presented to farmers.

> No. 2 of these distinctive services is to be the advancement of such special items as G.L.F. calf-starter, reinforced cereals, Kem Fee treated seeds, granular superphosphate, etc., commodities in which G.L.F. has no rivals.

> No. 3 is to be the use of the whole Institution, at times,—patrons, committee-men, store managers and agent-buyers, and employed personnel—for the making of "team plays" designed to advance the position of the Institution in some particular field of service quickly and smoothly. . . .

In the new era, prices would be played down as a method of building support.

> During past periods in G.L.F. development, we tended to capitalize, equip and man the Institution. We have had to build a distribution system, devise and install a record-keeping system and build a going business.

> Probably too often in the past we have built volume by price appeal alone. Better prices and better service will not be forgotten in the era that is ahead but we will try to use a more intelligent technique in applying the price factor than we have sometimes used in the past.

Babcock took advantage of the "new era" idea by writing the Directors on May 13 that "one mark of this new era is to be a greater participation in the conduct of the Exchange by its farmer directors." In this connection Babcock took occasion to congratulate the Board on its "smart and timely move" in appointing a budget committee at its last Directors' meeting, an action which he had been vigorously advocating.

During the winter and spring the work of organizing committeemen

---

[2] Memo to G.L.F. Fieldmen and Farm Service Management Vice Presidents, with copies to directors, May 13, 1936.

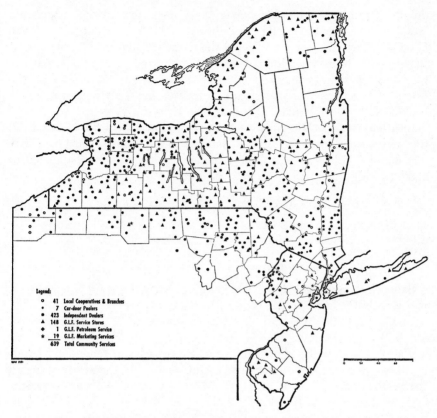

Legend:
○ 41 Local Cooperatives & Branches
• 7 Car-door Poolers
● 423 Independent Dealers
▲ 148 G.L.F. Service Stores
◆ 1 G.L.F. Petroleum Service
★ 19 G.L.F. Marketing Services
639 Total Community Services

FIGURE 2—G.L.F. COMMUNITY SERVICE AGENCIES, 1936

for G.L.F. Agent-buyers had been completed, with the result that by June there were 2,778 committeemen (901 for stores and egg auctions and 1,877 for Agent-buyers)—all qualified to vote as stockholders at the G.L.F. annual meeting to be held on October 19, 1936.

Babcock considered it a primary responsibility to keep these committeemen intelligently informed so that they would be in position to safely administer G.L.F. affairs. On June 10, he wrote to the committeemen that the problem of whether the G.L.F. should pay patronage refunds on this year's savings would come up for discussion at the annual meeting, and gave them pertinent information on the progress being made. He used this letter to stress that "ultimately, all G.L.F. Agent-buyers must keep patronage records and work closely with Advisory Committees of their patrons. They must also cooperate with G.L.F. directors in seeing that patrons on their committees are represented at the G.L.F. annual meeting."

It is evident from these various communications that Babcock was doing everything within his power to develop institutional teamwork, based on an acceptance of responsibility by all component parts of the G.L.F. System. He never neglected the Board of Directors in his educational efforts to improve the G.L.F., for he realized that in the last resort the Board was the primary source of G.L.F. power. His respect for the Board of Directors was sincere and he missed no opportunity to get the benefit of their combined—and more objective—judgment.

In a letter to the Directors on June 26, he gave them his ideas on the proper relationship of the G.L.F. Manager to the G.L.F. Board of Directors. He pointed out that as Manager he was "continually challenged to make two absolutely contradictory adaptations."

One of these is to keep in touch with all of the operations in such a manner that I am currently familiar with everything which is going on to see to it that all of the activities of the Exchange are correlated. My other big responsibility is to keep far enough away from individual activities and from the Exchange as a whole, so that I may have the proper perspective from which to view the Institution as a whole and from which to project my planning for the future.

Babcock then proceded to place before the Board several "Institutional problems in the largest sense" upon which advice was desired.

The first question had to do with the inauguration of the policy of paying patronage refunds. Should patronage refunds be distributed immediately, or after the annual meeting, or next year or thereafter? In introducing this question he reviewed the history of the organization during the past 15 years when all savings had to be conserved for development and expansion. He emphasized the fact that "because we had to do all these things, we have never yet been able actually to operate a farmer-owned, farmer-controlled cooperative which made savings for farmers, and distributed such savings to them in the form of patronage dividends."

Now the day was here and the ideal could become a reality.

Babcock was now ready to act.

After sleeping with the question, driving hundreds of miles with it, settling it one way one day and another way the next, I come to you with a definite recommendation. This recommendation is entirely my own. It represents Institutional as well as seasoned thinking on my part. It is this:

I recommend that you, as the Board of Directors of the G.L.F. Exchange, pass a resolution today directing the Board of Directors of G.L.F. Mills to pay, not later than August 10th, a 2% patronage dividend on the dollar value of all purchases from the Mills of Formula Feed, Formula Fertilizer, and G.L.F. Seed by G.L.F. Agent-buyers and G.L.F. Stores, during the period January 1st through June 30, 1936. That you make this distribution of a patronage refund, as described above, subject to the approval of a majority of all G.L.F. Advisory Committeemen; and that, for the purpose of securing such approval, your recommendation that such a dividend be paid be made the subject of a referendum to Advisory Committeemen early in July.

He saw several advantages from this proposed procedure. It would not cost more than $200,000. The referendum would be considered an act of good faith by Advisory Committeemen, and would give significance to their office. Moreover, it would give added publicity to the payment of the refund and thus would increase the volume of business.

He turned then to the importance of the budget as a tool in management. After expressing delight with the way the recently appointed budget committee was functioning, be emphasized that "a committee of G.L.F. directors is in position to take responsibility for economy measures which it might be difficult for your managing executives to make."

He then went on to say that in his opinion the responsibilities of G.L.F. Directors were greater than many of them yet realized. They were now in the "spotlight" in proving whether they could be as effective in actually operating a cooperative as successfully as they had been in building it. He felt that as Directors they should recognize that:

. . . the minute you pay a patronage dividend and become the Director of a farmer-owned and controlled cooperative in practice as well as in theory you establish yourselves in an entirely different relationship with the stockholders, patrons, and committeemen of the organization. Every move that you make in the future must take these forces into consideration; unless you handle them they will handle you.

With this admonition Babcock turned to two immediate problems.

This Institution must digest into the G.L.F. System the Advisory Committeemen which have been recently appointed to supervise Agent-Buyers' service. Second, we must stage an annual meeting which will give to stockholders, every patron, and every committeeman who attends, a practical demonstration of the application of control by farmers.

In summing up, Babcock urged the Board to recognize that [when] the G.L.F. "pays a patronage dividend and becomes . . . a cooperative which is operating in fact as well as in theory, it will experience an increase in the interest taken in the personalities on the Board, the competency of the Board, and the relationship between the member and the Board, which has not yet been faced."

In response to Babcock's recommendation, the Board authorized the referendum to get the views of committeemen on patronage refunds. In early July by postal card ballots they unanimously endorsed such payments.

Effective on July 1, Cooperative G.L.F. Mills, Inc., was divided into three wholesale service corporations.

1. Cooperative G.L.F. Mills
2. Cooperative G.L.F. Soil Building Service, Inc.
3. Cooperative G.L.F. Farm Supplies.

This simplified structure recognized that procurement, processing and wholesale services for feed and seed; fertilizers and insecticides; and various farm supply items could best be given specialized attention through separate specialized corporations.

The most important change lay in the decision to establish Cooperative G.L.F. Farm Supplies. There had been a growing demand for a service of this sort, and this action gave the "go ahead signal."[3]

The G.L.F. was in excellent condition as it entered the new fiscal year on July 1, 1936. Net purchases by patrons for the preceding fiscal year amounted to $25,313,022, the highest figure since 1929-30, and net margins of $815,551 exceeded all previous years.

All parts of the organization, even marketing, were operating quite well, and the functions were better coordinated than ever before by the formation of the separate corporations.

The payment of a cash patronage refund was also an indication that the organization was beginning to function as a "cooperative" institution.

On September 10 Babcock addressed the Board of Directors on the problems of the organization as he saw them.

"At the present time G.L.F. has no financial worries nor does it need orders. Thus it is possible to pass very quickly over two of the matters which have taken up nine tenths of your time and energy and the time and energy of your management in past years."

He attributed this lucky situation to four factors: "1. The generally improved business conditions which come about as a result of raising the price of gold. 2. The enthusiastic cooperation which G.L.F. is receiving at the present time from between four and five hundred independent dealers in farm supplies. This improved cooperation of the group is due entirely to dividing the field force last spring. 3. The drought. 4. The payment of a patronage dividend by G.L.F. Mills." He continued:

To the above . . . might also be added the appointment of agent-buyer patrons' committees. The function of these committees has brought into the G.L.F. picture some 2,500 leading farmers whose influence with and effect upon the Institution is bound to be great. The Institution, at the present time, may be said to be in the process of assimilating this new group. When all worthwhile agent-buyers are brought under the supervision of patrons' committees the total of store committeemen and agent-buyers committeemen and marketing committeemen will be right around 4,000 individuals. A majority of these 4,000 committeemen will be in Syracuse on October 19th for the G.L.F. Annual Meeting.

Babcock considered the coming annual meeting of the greatest importance. Since it would greatly expand the franchise of patrons' committee-

[3] In Babcock's memorandum to the Board of April 8, he had proposed this service under the tentative name, "G.L.F. Community Services, Inc.," and it was then thought that its primary function would be to handle oil and gas. Since then the objectives were generalized and the more descriptive title chosen for the service to be performed.

men, he urged that full opportunity be taken to acquaint committeemen
with their responsibilities in helping guide the destiny of the G.L.F. He
proposed that certain policy questions be presented for open discussion
and that votes be taken "for the guidance of the directors." Babcock recommended this procedure as "absolutely necessary to provide a safety
valve for the opinions of committeemen."

In summing up Babcock said: "G.L.F., and in fact, any institution goes
forward through those responsible for it committing it from time to time
to courses of action. Direction is given to the thinking and action of men
and women associated with an Institution when they all understand the
program to which it is committed."

The annual meeting of the G.L.F. held at Syracuse on October 19, 1936,
was the largest gathering in G.L.F. history. It was attended by some 2,370
stockholders, most of whom were patrons' committeemen.

It was a signficant gathering for another reason. It was the last time
that Babcock was to address the annual meeting as the manager of the
G.L.F., for he was to announce his resignation the following day.[4]

Babcock's farewell address to the stockholders was designed to emphasize those principles which he held[5] of greatest importance. Of particular interest were the following points:

In the operation of this cooperative there is no place for partisan politics,
religious issues, competition with other cooperatives, or intolerance.

It will be impossible to run this organization at all times so as to receive the
unanimous approval of all patrons. If you happen to be in the minority, be big
enough to stay with the organization even though temporarily you may not
approve of what it is doing.

In a growing organization like the G.L.F. it is well to guard against overexpansion. There is danger that an aggressive and ambitious management may
undertake to render service on more fields of activity than it can successfully
handle. Such ambitions will tend to overload your organization financially, to
put too great a load on your general manager, and to involve your organization
in unnecessary complications and competition. . . . As I see it, your organization
has plenty of hay down right now.

❖   ❖   ❖

Care should be taken to see that G.L.F. executives do not overstay their time,
and that they do not load the payroll of the organization with their relatives.
The best guarantee that your organization will never become a haven for job-

---

[4] In a letter to all committeemen dated October 20, Babcock closed with the following paragraph headed "MEET JIM McCONNELL."

"At a meeting held the evening of the Annual Stockholders' Meeting . . . your
G.L.F. Directors granted me an indefinite leave of absence. Jim McConnell was named
Acting General Manager to carry on. May I recommend for Jim the same hearty
support and cooperation you have always given me. Jim has worked up from the
ranks. . . . You will find that he is idealistic but also practical and level-headed. He
has courage, and above everything else he is always fair. I know the G.L.F. will go
forward under his leadership. He will write you the next letter."

[5] The full address was printed in the *American Agriculturist* of November 7, 1936.

holders is to develop your younger employees so that they will push the older fellows like myself out of the picture.

❉   ❉   ❉

Some of you folks in the past have thought that the Government would solve your economic and spiritual problems. It can't and it shouldn't. Others of you have tried to work out your destiny as individuals. Gradually the operations of the capitalistic competitive society in which you live have tended to grind you down. An individual forever working alone in such a society cannot long maintain his standard of living, his happiness, and his freedom of spirit. Fortunately, he doesn't have to work alone.

Farmers working together through adequately financed, well managed, aggressively supported cooperative organizations can protect their economic rights and through them, their standards of living. They can and should enhance their happiness and the happiness of their families. Above all, they can attain the freedom of spirit and be men among men.

I challenge you to do it!

It will be recalled that Babcock proposed that certain questions be presented to the stockholders for discussion and vote.

These questions and the votes recorded are here presented.

1. Should the Directors reduce the annual dividend on G.L.F. common stock if earned from six percent to five percent? "*Yes*—536; *No*—733."

2. Do you approve the policy of retaining a part of each year's net earnings until your directors are satisfied that the capital assets of the Exchange are adequate? "*Yes*—1239; *No*—46."

3. Should the G.L.F. continue to experiment with the development of Cooperative Marketing Service even though in their early stages these services may operate at a loss? "*Yes*—1142; *No*—46."

4. Your Directors believe that the best way to reduce the cost of feed, seed, fertilizer, lime and spray materials is for G.L.F. to handle more supplies like paint, roofing, human foods, fencing, gasoline, and oil, etc.

(a) Does this policy of diversification of G.L.F. purchasing power meet with your approval? "*Yes*—1230; *No*—25."

(b) Will you support the policy of buying such supplies through the G.L.F. and encourage your neighbors to do likewise? "*Yes*—1221; *No*—18."

At the annual meeting the year before, Babcock had raised the question whether the "open formula policy" on feeds be discontinued. The committee consisting of Walter A. Smith, William B. O'Neil, Herbert Rose, F. J. Walton, J. M. Burdick, which had been set up by President Fred L. Porter to consider this question, reported back to the 1936 annual meeting. It unanimously endorsed the principle of the open formula and recommended the continuance of the present policy of publishing the formula of all G.L.F. feeds, and the stockholders adopted the report. This decision was supported by the answers to a questionnaire which had been sent to the Advisory Committeemen of all G.L.F. Service Stores.

They were "practically unanimous that the present policy of open formulas for G.L.F. feeds shall be continued."

The report of the committee pointed out that:

1. G.L.F. Feed service was founded on the principle that the purchaser of a ready-mixed feed is entitled to know the formula so that he can judge the feed intelligently.

2. G.L.F. depends on and enjoys the close cooperation of feeding authorities of state agricultural experiment stations in building and improving G.L.F. feed formulas. This valuable assistance to G.L.F. feeders would be lost if the formulas were closed because these college men cannot recommend and approve closed formulas.

3. G.L.F. open formula Feed Service has been a tremendous force for education of feeders and improvement of competitive feeds so that all dairymen and poultrymen in G.L.F. territory have benefited from this service whether they have used G.L.F. feeds or not.

4. G.L.F. open formula feeds have been outstandingly successful and a tremendous volume has been built up in competition with all types of closed formula feeds.

Babcock had sent out a statement to patron committeemen a few days before the meeting (Oct. 17, 1936) to acquaint them with the conditions which had led to the consideration of this question. He indicated that when he raised the question he had good reason to believe that competitors were using the open formulas to determine what G.L.F. was paying suppliers for raw materials, but that he couldn't explain this adequately in the open meeting. As an alternative, he had temporarily withdrawn all price lists from the field and this had accomplished the same objective "of confusing the competitors." He closed his statement by saying: "While the present situation of open formulas, open costs, and open prices is not worrisome, I for one do not know when it might become so."

Although Babcock gave up active management in October he continued to give active interest to certain G.L.F. affairs. In particular, he was anxious to have the patrons' committeemen system working well. To give them guidance he assembled the best thinking in the organization for a statement entitled "The G.L.F. Policy in regard to Agent-Buyers' Patron Committeemen" which he respectfully submitted, for consideration on January 1, 1937, as "General Manager (on leave)."[6]

The preparation of this statement represented Babcock's final job, while nominally General Manager. Thus it is of particular interest.

[6] The reader may be confused by the change in designation of the Advisory Committees. During 1936 they came to be called "Patron Committees," although the term, "Advisory Committee," is still infrequently used. In 1948, "Patron Committees" gave way to "Member-Patron Committees," and since 1949 "Member Committees" has prevailed. Since July 1, 1948, the Bylaws have designated such committees as "Member Committees."

The most important challenge the G.L.F. faces in its patron-member relations during 1937 is to continue the development of agent-buyers' patron committees, and the relationship with dealers which they sponsor.

In order to see the problem in true perspective, we first must recognize what G.L.F. is trying to accomplish by means of agent-buyers' committees. Some of you will say that through these committees G.L.F. is attempting to secure a widespread, representative delegate body which will attend the annual meeting and elect directors. This is true. Others will say the purpose of the patron committees is to establish throughout the territory men who will be leaders in their respective communities in forwarding the interests of the G.L.F. as a cooperative service. This also is true.

There remains, however, a third use for agent-buyers' patrons' committees which is fundamentally of much more importance than the two mentioned. A cooperative (G.L.F.) is attempting to establish and maintain a practical working relationship with profit-keeping units of service (dealers). *The test of this partnership is of the utmost importance not only to the G.L.F. but to the entire cooperative movement in the United States.* If G.L.F.'s plan works, we in the G.L.F. shall not look forward to a cooperative monopoly nor to basic changes in the present economic order. Here we shall find ourselves at odds with the movement. We shall be attempting to operate in harmony with and even in partnership with agencies run to make a profit on capital.

Such relationships already exist in the arrangements between a number of wholesale cooperatives and their sources of outlet or supply. No cooperative in the United States, however, has tried out such a plan of cooperation with capitalistic interests right under the nose of its patrons. The really important job, therefore, of agent-buyer patron committees becomes that of making a fair test of a fundamental policy and of deciding whether or not this policy of a cooperative's going into partnership with a profit-keeping agency is sound and whether or not it works.

Because our patron committee set-up is so new and so imperfect, a very large percentage of committeemen not only have failed to realize their responsibility in the local testing out of the G.L.F. policy of partnership with dealers, but have also failed to grasp the importance of their responsibility in maintaining a competent board of G.L.F. directors, and in protecting and furthering the interests of the G.L.F. in their localities.

This situation gives us the clue as to what we must do as employees to carry out the policy of the Board of Directors for whom we work. First, we must go boldly out with the declaration that it is G.L.F.'s policy to work out a partnership relationship for retail service, in a large percentage of the communities it serves, through established retailers. *There must be no pulling of our punch either in stating this policy or in establishing it.* Otherwise the policy will not get a fair trial, and a great experiment in cooperative relationship will go by the boards. Second, we must impress on patron committeemen their responsibility to all the patrons of the G.L.F. for maintaining a competent board of directors to direct the affairs of the Institution. Third, we must inspire *and mobilize* patron committeemen to a greater local support of the G.L.F. as an institution of service.

On February 17, 1937, Babcock urged the Board of Directors to immediately designate James A. McConnell General Manager, since he had fully justified the faith placed in him in his work as acting General Manager. This would permit Babcock to devote his time to "directing G.L.F.'s whole program of research, education, advertising and publicity," which he considered the area of "G.L.F.'s greatest weakness." McConnell was thereupon made "General Manager of the G.L.F. Exchange and of each and all subsidiary corporations."

A new era had begun.

CHAPTER 21

Refining The Institution

Today the job is one of conserving the inventory; of carrying out the original purposes of the founders better than it has been done—better because of accumulated experience and adequate facilities. . . . In short, we might say a job of refining the Institution.
JAMES A. McCONNELL, *Report to Stockholders, November, 1937.*

T HE TRANSFERENCE of management power from Babcock to McConnell marked a new epoch in the life of the G.L.F. McConnell moved into his new position so unobtrusively that it was some time before it was fully appreciated that he was now calling the signals as well as following through on the plays. While Babcock's influence continued to permeate the organization, a new driver had the reins and he held them firmly.[1]

McConnell recognized that his immediate problem was to establish his position of leadership throughout the entire organization and the 40 regional conferences scheduled for early spring with the advisory committeemen of local G.L.F. service agencies ideally suited this purpose. At each meeting he stressed the stability of G.L.F. operations and gave assurance of their continuance and development without interruption. He emphasized the importance of the advisory committeemen by calling them "the guardians" of the G.L.F. "Yours is the responsibility to advise and guide Agent-Buyers and Store Managers in giving service to patrons; to help with surveys; to protect G.L.F.'s interests in your communities; and to attend the G.L.F. annual meeting as a voting delegate."

Although the strings had not been taken from his title until February 18, McConnell had been carrying the actual burdens of management for several months, and in a memorandum to Vice Presidents on January 14, 1937, he had made known his "own conception of how management must look at a successful cooperative business."

There are, so to speak, three legs on the G.L.F. stool. The Distribution System, the Wholesale end of the business, and a third leg which might be called the management of patrons' relations, or teaching members about their Institution and good economic philosophy. Along with this last goes proper information enabling patrons to use their organization intelligently.

[1] In the announcement of McConnell's appointment, February 8, 1937, President Porter pointed out that the Board of Directors of the G.L.F. had made an arrangement with Mr. Babcock under which he "is relieved of administrative responsibilities but will continue to help the Directors and management in the working-out of certain policies of importance to the membership of the Exchange. This arrangement, according to Porter, "Puts the G.L.F. in position of having an experienced general manager in reserve. . . ." For a time Mr. Babcock used the title, "Reserve General Manager."

McConnell felt that the wholesale and retail legs of the Institution were in good shape. As to the third leg, he said:

Probably one of the biggest jobs ahead of this cooperative is the proper handling of its membership relations. Not only the Patron Members must be fully informed so that they may effectively use and effectively control the Institution, but the thinking of the employees must be kept sound and straight. Keeping this leg of the Institution in its proper proportion with the other two is becoming more and more a problem of major importance.

At this time McConnell announced that Babcock had volunteered to supervise this phase of operations. He then said: "No man within the organization, or without . . . is so capable of doing it. If this Institution is to maintain its present economic status and increase its worth to patrons it is important to train personnel soundly, not only in good business methods but in good cooperative philosophy. . . . The device which Mr. Babcock will use in this job is the *Patron.*"

The *G.L.F. Patron* was to be issued in four editions to serve (1) Employees, (2) Distributors (Service Agencies), (3) Committeemen, and (4) Patrons; each to come out as often as needed.

In this way McConnell ushered in an intense period of educational activity which soon permeated all parts of the G.L.F. system. Both he and Babcock were in happy accord on the need for this work, and Babcock was to be given full play for his genius in this field.

For some time G.L.F. officials had been so busy shaping policies that little time was left to explain the significance of these policies to employees, patrons and the public. Now the G.L.F. undertook a program designed to make its views and methods clear to all through publications and intensive educational meetings.

The *G.L.F. Patron* for April reflected this campaign for broadening the G.L.F. outlook. Along with articles explaining G.L.F. commodities and services there were editorial expressions by Babcock, McConnell, and President Porter.

In his statement McConnell observed:

The G.L.F. is classed as a competitive cooperative. That is, it operates not as a monopoly but alongside private industry, in the same field. . . . Competitors in general must sell at G.L.F. prices in order to do business. Thus G.L.F. affects directly or indirectly practically every feed buyer in the New York Milk Shed.

President Porter was concerned with laying the charges that the G.L.F. Board of Directors was a rubber-stamping body. He explained how the resolutions passed by the Directors over a long period of years had gradually built up "a body of law to govern the G.L.F." He also pointed out how the Directors in recent years had developed budget-making "to a fine degree of comprehensiveness and accuracy." He made clear how

Certified Public Accountants audited all financial records and reported independently to the Board.

"I hope I have satisfied you, as I have satisfied myself," said Mr. Porter, "that it is possible and practical for a farmer-director of a cooperative—even of a cooperative doing an annual business of $50,000,000 a year—to be effective in molding the destiny of the organization, controlling its finances, and insuring the honesty of its operations."

THE UNIVERSITY OF THE G.L.F.

The new emphasis on employee education was dramatized by the establishment of "The University of the G.L.F." This was no formal degree-granting institution of research and higher learning. It was simply the name under which an ambitious executive and employee-training program was conducted. Under the plan, special schools lasting usually four days were held for different groups of executives and employees. The subject matter for each school was fitted to the particular needs of those in attendance. While a few of the "Professors" were from the Cornell University Faculty—men like Professors Savage or Warren who had long and intimate association with the G.L.F.—most were drawn from G.L.F. executive ranks.

The fiction of a University was maintained by referring to the program director, C. W. "Hap" Sadd, as "Dean." The writer can attest from attendance at several of the Schools that a real University atmosphere was created. The professors carefully prepared their lectures and the "students" responded to the sense of high purpose that was imparted by McConnell and Babcock.

The first school held in June, 1937, was designed for Fieldmen and District Managers. This was followed by Schools for Store Managers, for Agent-Buyers, for Wholesale Operators, for Office Employees, and for G.L.F. Directors. In some cases it was necessary to repeat the same School to meet the needs of all members in a group. For example, recurring sessions were required to serve the hundreds of store managers and agent-buyers since not more than 50 could be accommodated at one time, and one of the objectives of the schools was to establish intimate contact between the "students" and the "faculty."

The content of the Schools was tailored to the special group served. Generally, McConnell started a School off with a brief talk on the importance attributed to it by top management, and reviewed its contributions at the end. An important feature of many of the early schools was a series of intimate lectures by Babcock on "the G.L.F. idea." In these he told the story of how the G.L.F. had come into existence and what it meant to him. These talks were highly inspirational for they were made by the man who had done more than any other to fashion the G.L.F., and he had the gift of being able to impart to others much of his vision and philosophy.

Other executives gave lectures on the work of the G.L.F. in areas of their particular fitness. For illustration, at several Schools, General Counsel Sherman Peer explained the G.L.F.'s corporate structure. M. E. Campbell, in charge of Agent-Buyers, explained the Agent-buyer program, while Frank Naegely, in charge of G.L.F. Stores, explained the store program. The men in charge of various wholesale operations—A. L. Bibbins, T. E. Milliman, B. H. Staplin, and V. A. Fogg—explained objectives and dealt with associated problems. Taking the Schools as a group, the lectures, which were frequently mimeographed for study use, covered practically every aspect of G.L.F. organization and operation, and provided a fund of information unique for any business organization.

The aims of the Schools conducted by the University of the G.L.F. were well expressed by McConnell in his introductory or concluding messages. At the first school he said: "Our goal is to have every man who contacts the public so well informed that he can accurately reflect the facts concerning G.L.F. and discuss with assurance that comes from real knowledge, any phase of G.L.F."

McConnell at this time was concerned over the misconceptions which business concerns, and even other cooperatives, had regarding the G.L.F. He saw in the University of the G.L.F. a device through which such misconceptions could be overcome.

There is no question but that the University of the G.L.F. idea if carried through, will produce so many points of contact with the public outside of the Institution as represented by employees, which points of contact sparking correctly, so to speak, will produce a knowledge, understanding and philosophy that will drive the roots of this Institution into the hearts and minds and habits of communities which use it to a point that even an earthquake can't shake it loose. . . . You can begin to see what Babcock has been visualizing for the last few years and which is only now beginning to crystallize.

McConnell maintained that "consciously or unconsciously, all G.L.F. men are educators." The example of top officials serving as "Professors" in the University of the G.L.F. emphasized this fact and gave to education as much place in the thinking of G.L.F. executives as the distribution of feed or fertilizer.

Although this program of instruction was not academic in the usual sense, it gave those who attended the sessions an unusual opportunity to know the men who were managing the organization and to gain from them the advantages of their experience and knowledge. As McConnell said, "Nowhere would you find men better qualified to talk on the subjects covered. . . . In fact, on many of the subjects the knowledge doesn't exist elsewhere."

In the second School—for wholesale plant operators—Mr. McConnell stressed another pressing object of the Schools—"to give you information which will aid you in the performance of your day-to-day duties." He also observed:

In my fifteen years' work with G.L.F. I have become impressed with three things which immeasurably make for the success of the individual in G.L.F. The first of these is knowledge. The second is the ability to work with other people in a harmonious relationship, and the third is just plain hard work. I am inclined to rate the second as the most important because an organization is a group of people working together. Work and knowledge are impossible without the ability to get along harmoniously with others.

At the third School—for Ithaca office workers—held in late August, McConnell said, "As the Institution has grown in size and therefore in the number of employees, the need of internal education has become more and more necessary. This need finally brought about the organization of the University of the G.L.F."

As school followed school the objectives desired by McConnell and Babcock were largely realized. Employees caught a new vision of the organization they worked for, and a desire to render it maximum service. The schools not only informed: they also inspired the employees with a team spirit founded on high individual performance standards.

Perhaps of even greater value the Schools made the employees think. In June, 1938, after John Daniels, author of *Cooperation—an American Way*, and an all-out advocate of the democratic process, addressed a session, McConnell said:

Mr. Daniels was brought here with a purpose. When he . . . challenged the Institution you could have heard a pin drop. I am telling you this: We in G.L.F. have got to begin to square our thinking and public actions with public thinking. . . . Daniels and several hundred others are beginning to see G.L.F. . . . We are going to be hit by a bunch of men like Daniels. I'll bet there hasn't been anything discussed more this week than whether this is or is not a democratic institution.

Earlier in this same School, Babcock had said: "What I like about Jim's administration at the present time is that he is continually sticking his fingers through the bubbles we all blow." Babcock did not go all the way with Daniels "that it [the G.L.F.] does not satisfy the spiritual needs of its members because its voluntary control and management are too centralized." On this Babcock said: "When you trace the ownership and control of G.L.F. you find a technical situation that over a period of time can and shall be corrected." He then added, "Most G.L.F. patrons, according to my observations, prefer not to monkey too much with G.L.F. voting control or management. . . ." No doubt Babcock was right, but up to this time patrons had been given little opportunity to participate in policy decisions and they thus had little experience in making their views known to management.

Although the University of the G.L.F. continued to function until it was superseded by the G.L.F. School of Cooperative Administration in 1940, it reached its heyday during 1938. A report in December of that year by McConnell stated that:

During the last sixteen months nearly every employee . . . [has] had an opportunity to attend at least one of the thirty-six schools held. Two hundred sixty two teachers have delivered 513 lectures. . . . This educational program gives to G.L.F. employees the opportunity of becoming the best trained co-operative workers in the country.

THE SERVICE SCHEDULE

Another step in improving communications within the G.L.F. was taken in September, 1937, when McConnell placed Babcock in charge of the *G.L.F. Service Schedule* which provided essential price and commodity information bi-monthly to employees. Some idea of the verve with which Babcock proceeded to "pep up" this essential informational organ is indicated by this letter, published on the front cover of the *Schedule* for October 22:

TO MANAGERS OF G.L.F. RETAIL SERVICES

I have never gotten into a job which interested me more or that was tougher than this one of trying to make the *Service Schedule* of use to you.
The trouble is that most of you don't read the darn thing.
Now listen, there are a lot of things connected with the retail handling of farm supplies which if you only knew them would help you improve your store, and safeguard your capital which is being used for very necessary services in your country.
I don't know what these things are, but if you will only work with me I can dig them up out of the experience of G.L.F. Agent-Buyers and Stores. First, however, you need to read carefully each issue of the SERVICE SCHEDULE; then you need to tell me about the information you would like included in it, and finally you must help make it a success by your own contributions. . . .
Respectfully yours,
H. E. Babcock

Babcock was especially interested in this job for it gave him a very important vehicle to promote the marketing and G.L.F. Family Foods programs that were fast becoming his major interest. In his first Editor's Note in the issue of September 25, 1937, he said: "Many managers of G.L.F. retail service agencies do not realize that the charter of the G.L.F. authorizes it to market for its members as well as to purchase and process for them. Furthermore, the extent to which G.L.F. is pushing forward programs of complete service for its members is not generally appreciated."

In his Editor's Note of November 19, 1937, he said:

I want to thank all of you fellows for your splendid work in increasing our volume of Family Foods. Jim McConnell was just in to see me and during the course of our conversation he mentioned that our growing flour volume is helping Mills tremendously in its purchase of wheat feeds. Both *Jim and I look forward to the time when Family Foods, in addition to furnishing farm families with better nutrition foods will carry a considerable portion of G.L.F. overhead.*

The Patron Committees

McConnell was in complete accord with Babcock's policy declaration on patron committeemen (see p. 195) and was fully aware that the burden of making the policy effective lay with G.L.F. top management. In his regional conferences with G.L.F. committeemen he endeavored to create in all committeemen a sense of their ownership interest and responsibility. To achieve this end he distributed at these conferences a circular to show the administrative set-up of the G.L.F., as of March 1, 1937, so that all could know how the system was organized to serve its 77,729 patrons through 148 Service Stores, 406 agent-buyers and 48 independent local cooperatives.

McConnell lost no opportunity to stress the importance of the patrons' committees. In April he emphasized their role in an editorial in the *Patron.* He reverted to this theme in a full article in a special committeemen's edition of the *Patron* issued in October. In this article, entitled, "Your Job as G.L.F. Committeemen," McConnell said that he had become more and more sure of the soundness of the plan of patrons' representation through committeemen, but that both management and the committeemen had yet to learn how to work together effectively. He pointed out that "under the committee system any community in G.L.F. territory can make direct contact in an organized way with the management of the G.L.F."

The 17th Annual G.L.F. Stockholders' Delegate Meeting was a test of the effectiveness of the committeemen system for it brought in as full partners for the first time the Patron Committeemen organized in communities served by Agent-Buyers. One thousand six hundred eighty-four committeemen were present as compared to 853 the year before, and the spirit of the gathering demonstrated that they recognized their power and responsibility.

Immediately following this meeting plans were announced in the *Service Schedule* of December 3, 1937, for a series of winter regional conferences to acquaint committeemen with "Institutional control factors by which they can determine whether G.L.F. is being operated efficiently and in their interest."

"These meetings," said the announcement, "are probably the most valuable series of meetings ever held in the country as far as giving patrons actual information about the progress and control of their organization."

The three main control factors which McConnell emphasized in the series of meetings were I. Volume, II. Earnings, and III. Costs.

With regard to the first, he said, "The first and most important control factor is volume. To a purchasing institution a certain amount of volume insures its basic success. . . . When [volume] is slipping you can ask the Board of Directors or Management what has happened."

"Earnings are another control factor which is usually, I think, second in importance. If this Institution is run so that it makes money it means that the original investment will be protected. . . . If we ever lose control of G.L.F. it will be because of overexpansion and lack of earnings. . . ."

The importance of the third control factor, costs, needed no special emphasis, for costs showed whether the organization was getting out of line.

During the next few years McConnell stressed these control factors until they became barometers for employees and patrons.[2]

NEW SERVICES

As late as 1935, Babcock and his associates thought largely in terms of feed, seed and fertilizer service. Gradually, as we have observed, the idea had grown that the lines of supplies handled should be widened to meet the demands of farmers for other supplies.

The establishment of Cooperative G.L.F. Farm Supplies thus represented a pronounced break with the past. It recognized the feeling within G.L.F. ranks that a real development of the farm supply business in the G.L.F. required independence from the Mills Corporation and a dynamic leadership appreciative of the opportunities in this unexploited field. V. A. "Misty" Fogg, who was placed in charge, had long advocated that the Exchange move faster in this area of service, and his long and broad experience in the G.L.F. made him the ideal man for this post.

The management of the new Service met with favor from the patrons. The *Patron* for April, 1937, stated that some thirty different lines of commodities were already being handled. Nearly 80 carloads of steel roofing and wire had been ordered for spring delivery, and 250 electric milk

[2] The first *Control Factors Report* was presented by Chief Accountant Lyle Holmes to the budget committee in July 1935, at the request of Babcock. It showed only 4 wholesale figures: Total net margin, total tonnage, overhead per ton, and plant unit cost per ton. The objective then set was respectively $2,000,000; 1,000,000 ton; $1.00 per ton, and $1.50 per ton. McConnell used the report to dramatize goals and progress.

coolers were "out in the territory." Stress was placed on the fact that all supplies handled were being manufactured or purchased according to specifications.

Among the new lines of supplies handled, none attracted more interest than petroleum products. Motor oil had long been handled on a specification buying basis, but it was distributed in cans of conventional type. The first experiment in handling gasoline was initiated at Ithaca in August, 1936. A filling station was located across the street from the Ithaca Service Store and a few delivery trucks began to deliver petroleum to patrons in its trade territory. The popularity of this service, set up as the Tompkins G.L.F. Cooperative, Inc., to furnish farmer-patrons with gasoline and oil in the Ithaca trade area, soon led to similar incorporated petroleum units in other areas. (See Chapter 23.)

The progress being made in handling farm supplies under the new program was discussed by Mr. Fogg in a session of the University of the G.L.F. for Agent-Buyers in October, 1937. He indicated how the service had gradually been expanded to include milk coolers, barbed wire, fencing, poultry equipment, small tools and asphalt roofing.

He expressed the view that the farmer was going to demand that the G.L.F. "do more and more things for him." He believed that farmers wanted to buy at a one-stop agency. "Give him an opportunity to purchase his tools, his paint, his roofing, his small equipment, or any of the many ordinary, everyday supplies at the same place where he buys his feed and he will do it."

Fogg was aware that there were many problems in getting service on farm supplies well established. He stated that service agencies had to learn how to display items they were not accustomed to handle. He counseled that it was sound procedure to build one line of supply service at a time.

Fogg termed the distribution of gasoline and kerosene a brand new field, with "tremendous possibilities. This business" he predicted, "can easily become one of the large departments of the G.L.F."

Fogg summarized his remarks with this admonition, "As you get into gasoline and oil and other miscellaneous farm supplies . . . you will need to pick better men to work with you than you have had . . . in the feed business . . . Your competition will be keener."

When Fogg addressed a session of the University of the G.L.F. nine months later (June 20, 1938), the service on farm supplies was growing at a phenomenal rate. Volume had reached 1-½ million dollars during the past year, or 50 percent more than the preceding year. Fogg believed that a volume of 10 million dollars in this field in G.L.F. territory was easily possible and practical, and was coming faster than most people realized.

The new service was affecting the thinking of the service agencies and turning their attention to the importance of good merchandising. Fogg urged: "Let us keep our main objectives clear and not get side-tracked on volume for volume's sake. Let us study the methods of handling these new services. They are different."

PATRONAGE REFUNDS AND PRICE POLICY

G.L.F. policies on patronage refunds were largely formulated in the years from 1937 to 1940. Before McConnell became General Manager the G.L.F. had been little concerned with the problems of patronage refunds. Savings were needed for the expansion of services, and Babcock had favored a policy of keeping margins narrow and prices low to build volume operations necessary to achieve cost economies. As the G.L.F. grew stronger financially there was less need for retaining margins and more to be gained in building local support through returning savings to those who patronized the organization.

On May 10, 1937, the Board authorized payment of patronage refunds as follows: 60 cents a ton on mixed fertilizer, 80 cents on each ton of mixed formula feeds, and 2 percent on each dollar volume of seed purchased. The total amount so distributed amounted to $465,000.

In his report to the annual meeting on October 28, 1937, McConnell expressed his views on the role of patronage refunds in the operation of the G.L.F. He said:

In a cooperative business, the patronage dividend is only an incident. Its purposes are twofold:
1. To pay out to the patrons surplus funds or surplus earnings any particular year which are not needed for good, safe, economical operations.
2. To permit a safe, sound, and intelligent pricing program which takes into consideration the control of volume, the competitive situation, the up and down movement of commodity prices, and the proper balancing of working capital to the needs of the Institution.

He then said:

Since the Institution should always attempt to operate on a profit-making basis, and will over a period of years under efficient management produce earnings more than adequate for its needs, the corrective measure is to pay out the surplus as patronage dividends. We should, however, never forget, in determining what surplus moneys are, the credit rating of the Institution. It should always come ahead of patrons' needs for patronage dividends.

The interest that rapidly developed in patronage refund payments was a matter of concern to G.L.F. management. In his talks given at the regional meetings of G.L.F. Patron Committees in March and April, 1938, McConnell cautioned against overemphasizing the importance of patronage refunds. He said:

I want to make a statement about patronage dividends because patronage dividends are a fairly hot subject at times. . . . In my report to stockholders at the annual meeting . . . I was fearful that a false philosophy was growing up regarding patronage dividends. I think this is particularly true among employees—probably more so than with farmers. There is nothing that employees like better than paying a patronage dividend. . . . I am told that [certain cooperatives] measure their success by the amount of patronage dividends they pay. Correct specification, research and low handling costs have been neglected because the patronage dividend must be paid. I think this is a false philosophy and that patronage dividends are a by-product of doing business. . . . Again, I want to say that I am not against patronage dividends but that I think they are far from the main objective.

The mechanics for handling the patronage refund payments were gradually smoothed out. Each local service agency sent in to Ithaca forms showing amount of purchases by patrons. Patronage refunds were then calculated and checks for the amount were sent back to the local service agency for distribution to the individual patron. Patronage refunds of less than $1.00 were paid in cash by the local service agency as the agent of the G.L.F.

With over $1,000,000 paid out in the past three years in patronage refunds, McConnell could say at the next Annual Meeting on November 1, 1938, "G.L.F. has definitely reached a position in its volume and financial set-up where it will, from time to time, have surplus moneys to pay out as patronage refunds."

However, McConnell was concerned with having it understood that patronage refunds were dependent upon price policy. On this he said:

There is another system of paying dividends, which is used from time to time, and that is in pricing commodities at just as near cost as we are able to figure them. This method of paying dividends was used this summer on feeds. Through the months of August, September, and October, dairy and mash feeds in G.L.F. were priced just as near cost as possible. This method of paying patronage dividends is very effective as a price-setting measure, which affects beneficially all buyers in the area, whether or not purchases are made through G.L.F.

McConnell pointed out that this question of determining how to pay patronage refunds is "a ticklish one for management to handle. . . . If it pays out big cash dividends, its critics will say that it overcharges and then pays it back in order to make farmers feel good. On the other hand, if it sells with no margins above costs, its critics will say that it is trying to drive out all competition so as to build up a virtual cooperative monopoly."

McConnell concluded by saying, "Personally, I think both methods should be used, as the occasion would seem to warrant."

Several months later the G.L.F. was still feeling its way in its pricing policies. A Memo to Retail Service Agencies, August 7, 1939, announced that:

During this period of ruinous milk prices to farmers, the G.L.F. will for a time operate without its usual profit margin. . . . This will mean that during this time there will be no accumulation of reserves to protect investment, to furnish new working capital or to provide a source of cash dividends to patrons. . . . These low prices are in no way intended to attract new patrons. Should non-patrons be attracted . . . to the extent that business can't be handled properly with present facilities, a policy of serving only now-established patrons will be put into effect.

Up to now no comprehensive policy on patronage refunds had been established. On February 15, 1935, the importance of having an Institutional policy was recognized by the Board of Directors, and they recommended that the subsidiary corporations "should adopt resolutions" embodying the following:

That it become the settled policy of said subsidiary to eventually pay out all net margins as patronage dividends, after ample deductions have been made for dividends on stock, extraordinary write-offs, and other reserves for various corporate purposes. . . .

In a brochure, *How the G.L.F. Operates,* issued in June, 1939, McConnell said, "No discussion of G.L.F. will be complete without a consideration of the place of the patronage dividend." Again, McConnell reiterated his view that patronage refunds were incidental to service and quality and that in order to build and hold volume "G.L.F. prices must never for any long period be above the market. In order to go down with the market, which usually means losses, it is apparent that prices must also go up with the market, which usually means gains."

McConnell held that pricing according to market trends was "the only safe way to protect regular patrons from being deprived of their just share of savings by the intermittent user whose business in the aggregate is large and desirable." He also held that it was "the only sure way of protecting the pool of capital which has been built up in G.L.F. for the purpose of rendering and continuing to render service to patrons."

McConnell also recognized that there was less ability to adjust prices for a commodity like petroleum or fertilizer where prices were more or less set by the industry. On these commodities the G.L.F. priced with the industry and sought to accumulate needed capital and savings. McConnell made it clear that pricing policy must protect capital, and that at times "it is necessary to adopt a pricing policy on feeds and grains which allows for little or no earnings." He said:

On occasions, it may even be necessary for a short period, to actually price out reserves in order to build business or protect already established business against competition. There are other times when it is desirable to do this when farmers are in more than ordinary economic distress and need the benefit of the lowest possible prices. When an aggressive pricing policy of this sort is followed, it benefits all farmers in the territory whether or not they purchase through G.L.F.

McConnell then believed that the G.L.F. practice of paying patronage refunds by commodity was sound as "this assured each individual user of his just share of the earnings or savings."

The foregoing discussion indicates how rapidly the G.L.F. developed clear-cut views regarding the relationship of patronage refunds to price policy and the maintenance of Institutional stability.

Moreover, the payment of patronage refunds gave a new charge of energy to the organization. It gave patrons a greater sense of partnership. They could see the strength of the G.L.F. in their patronage refund checks. This encouraged support to the organization. As patronage refunds grew, volume expanded, and as costs were reduced with increased volume, the refunds grew.

CHAPTER 22

On with Marketing

Marketing cooperatively is a much harder job than buying coopera-
tively. It is going to be a slow, long, hard pull.

JAMES A. McCONNELL, *July 1, 1938*

WHEN McCONNELL made the above statement he was speaking on the basis of some seven years of G.L.F. experience in the field of marketing. Now the time had come when the lessons from this past could be effectively used.

As noted above (p. 150), the first experiments in marketing eggs, cabbage, potatoes, fruit and other commodities in 1929 and 1930 were largely carried on by the service stores working in cooperation with the staff of Cooperative Farm Service Management, Inc. It was soon found that progress would be slow. On January 7, 1931, J. C. Crissey, then charged with the responsibility of developing the marketing program, as Vice-President of Cooperative Farm Service Management, declared in an address to the Annual Meeting of the New York Vegetable Growers Association: "I wish to say emphatically that we do not expect the G.L.F. Marketing Plan to revolutionize the produce business of this territory. It will be a 5 to 10 year program starting with careful conservative experiments."

Crissey pointed out that six months' experience in handling eggs "has taught us a basic principle which must be adhered to throughout the whole program," namely, "that, we cannot buy and grade, pack and sell farmers' eggs and return them more money unless the producer will give us his eggs consistently. The plan must be changed to a cooperative marketing service on a service basis." He went on to set forth the marketing policy of the G.L.F. at that time:

Farm Service Agencies will not buy or sell any produce. They will pack and grade for the patrons or for the buyers on a unit packing charge basis. . . . When ready for market, disposal will be made by the patron or buyer. The agencies will sell nothing. They will take no risk, neither will they speculate with the farmers' produce. . . . The G.L.F. will bend every effort to improve the present outlets for produce, will counsel with the shippers, and do everything possible to build a cooperative outlet that means a greater return to the farmers.

Crissey was confident that this objective could be achieved but he recognized that "it must be a slow, sound policy." He then said: "Just how the G.L.F. will accomplish these things is not known. We do know that

211

this service will not be set up in any community unless the local producers are willing to cooperate and demand it. The G.L.F. will do everything possible to assist in the development of these units."

This program was just getting under way for eggs in November, 1931, when the failure of the largest receiver forced the G.L.F. to rent a store in the wholesale egg marketing district of New York City to receive and sell eggs for it.

On November 27, 1931, the Cooperative G.L.F. Marketing Corporation was set up to supervise all marketing of farm products for G.L.F. patrons. However, this corporation never attained this objective for one year later, in December, 1932, the New York depot was incorporated as a separate agency to handle eggs—the Cooperative G.L.F. Egg Marketing Service, Inc. Shortly afterward, in February, 1933, a separate agency was formed to handle beans—the Cooperative G.L.F. Bean Marketing Corporation. These two corporations supervised marketing from the farmer producer to the brokers or wholesalers in the large consuming markets.

With specialized corporations handling the principal commodities, the Marketing Corporation had left responsibility only for potatoes, cabbage, hay, and fruit.

At this time Babcock favored separate corporations wherever possible to center interest and managerial responsibility. He therefore encouraged the organization of local cooperative marketing corporations whenever justified by local marketing conditions. The first was set up to auction eggs in the fall of 1932. It was followed by others for marketing specialty crops.

During this period, while the great agricultural depression wore on, there was doubt on how marketing work should be conducted.

Babcock on September 7, 1933, asked the Board of Directors:

Should [G.L.F.] . . . look forward to expanding its marketing services or should [they] be entirely discontinued?
Is the G.L.F. Egg Marketing Service worth while?
Should the Egg auctions be discontinued?
Is it fair to assess the wholesale purchasing service to support marketing and credit services?
Will marketing and credit services unsatisfactorily performed jeopardize the standing and usefulness of the purchasing service? Have they?

These questions were largely rhetorical, for Babcock had no intention of dropping the marketing program. However, they did emphasize the issues that had to be faced. The marketing program was floundering and something had to be done to put it on a self-supporting basis.

In connection with its marketing operations considerable stocks of eggs and beans had been acquired which could not be sold at profitable prices.

To free the hands of the marketing corporation on these operations Co-operative G.L.F. Products, Inc., was set up on March 2, 1933, as an agency corporation of the G.L.F. Holding Corporation to acquire these surplus commodities and liquidate them as market conditions warranted.

There was little opportunity for this corporation to make a saving with prevailing market trends. This situation changed in January, 1934, when the G.L.F. undertook to furnish the government reinforced cereals for relief purposes. These products, developed by the College of Home Economics at Cornell University to form the basis of a healthful diet at low cost, were manufactured under license by the Cornell Research Foundation in the G.L.F. mill at Buffalo. This transaction netted the G.L.F. a considerable return as the price of raw materials declined after the selling price had been set. Of more importance, it encouraged the G.L.F. to step up its interest in cereals, and to place this program under the supervision of Products.

During 1934 the G.L.F. struggled valiantly to get its marketing operations in the black, and with some success. Although losses were sustained, some of the individual enterprises made comparatively good showings.

Touch and Go

On January 2, 1935, Babcock gave the Executive Committee his views on the problems which appeared to need the most attention for the year ahead. He had come to the conclusion that "directors for egg marketing and bean plants need to be selected who can contribute more to these activities. ..."

Babcock felt that the following marketing questions warranted consideration:

1. Should the New York City egg marketing service become the mother service for all egg marketing activities including egg auctions?
2. Has the time come to advance Jack Crissey from Executive Vice-President to President of all egg marketing services?
3. Has the time come to broaden the base of marketing and bean marketing plant directorships by drawing on Mills' experience?

On January 31, Babcock reported to G.L.F. directors that Marketing was the only corporation in the main family group with a red figure. He said:

Two corporations, Products and Marketing, you will recall, are the undernourished members of the G.L.F. family. Products started in the year with an accumulated deficit of $37,000. During the first six months $12,000 was earned through market operations which leaves it but $25,000 in the red.

You will be asked to confirm a new Board of Directors for this [Products] corporation—President F. A. McLellan, Vice-President Elwood Chase, and

Secretary-Treasurer E. V. Underwood. Also the following employees without salaries—Assistant Secretary-Treasurer and Manager C. N. Silcox . . . I have transferred the headquarters of the corporation to Buffalo. [Products] will be used in the future to market, I hope extensively, throughout the East, such G.L.F. products as reinforced cereals, pancake flour, etc. A substantial government contract is just now in prospect. . . . I have every expectation that this corporation, in addition to performing some valuable marketing functions in selling dry skim milk, buckwheat flour, etc., will eventually become a good earner and absorb at least a good part of the salaries of its employees. Just give it a year or two.

At this time the New York State Grange was enthusiastically cooperating with Babcock in acquainting its members with reinforced cereals by means of a membership contest. To build up farm home demand for flours and reinforced cereals a G.L.F. booklet on Foods was being issued, based upon Cornell recipes, "kitchen-tested" in farm homes.

In a statement listing the present objectives of G.L.F. Management, dated February 2, 1935, the future of marketing operations was realistically appraised. The poor showing was held to be largely "a matter of the price of beans" while the future of Products "depends on market trading and farm family foods." It was believed that the egg marketing service and the bean plants could be made profitable within five years.

In a memo to G.L.F. directors of August 28, 1935, Babcock indicated that the bean situation was being satisfactorily worked out by George Tyler "upon whom I have placed the entire responsibility for moving our present inventory and for operations this coming season. . . . Tyler should be supported, not criticized."

With growing interest developing in marketing, Babcock raised this question at the annual meeting on October 19, 1935:

Should the G.L.F. continue to experiment with the development of cooperative marketing services even though in their early stages these services may operate at a loss?

The replies were "Yes"—1142; and "No"—125.

The die was cast to go forward in marketing.

In a letter to President Porter, dated November 15, 1935, Babcock indicated that Products was "steadily moving ahead both in volume of service and profits [and] . . . is a great bet for the long pull."

A G.L.F. organization chart, dated December 12, 1935, showed F. A. McLellan as President of Products, with C. N. Silcox as Manager and Assistant Secretary.

The same chart showed G. M. Tyler as President of the G.L.F. Bean Marketing Corporation. According to this chart, the G.L.F. Egg Marketing Service then was "composed of five auctions which purchase and sell eggs for farmers." J. C. Crissey at New York City was supervisor and maintained all accounting records.

On January 7, 1936, Babcock, in reporting to the Board, said:

On January 1st I combined G.L.F. Bean Marketing with G.L.F. Products, Inc. C. N. Silcox, as Manager of Cooperative G.L.F. Products, Inc., now markets all sorts of things, from reinforced cereals to beans.

Applying his immediate attention to the bean marketing problem, Silcox satisfied himself that its greatest weakness was in selling rather than in the plant operations. He therefore decided to devote his full energies to the selling job. On January 10, 1936, he wrote Babcock:

After studying the monthly and annual operating statements of the Bean Marketing Corporation for the last three years, the job looked terribly discouraging. These operating statements, however, did bring out the fact that George Tyler has done a good job in the operation of plants and getting the costs per bag down to a reasonable basis. Both George and I believe that further progress can be made along these lines, but it will be limited.

The second thing I have learned from talking with a few bean brokers and jobbers is that the G.L.F. has established a good reputation in the trade for packing a high quality of beans. They are unanimous in the opinion, however, that we have not cashed in on this reputation because of certain sales policies— or lack of policy—in the past.

＊　　＊　　＊

While we are a cooperative organization and should at all times work with the idea in mind of helping the bean growers, I believe we will fail to accomplish our purpose if we do not make a fair and reasonable profit so that we have a right to stay in business.

The views expressed by Silcox reflected a new and more practical attitude in G.L.F. thinking as applied to marketing. With this change in organization, management and viewpoint, progress became apparent.

An article in the *G.L.F. Patron* for March, 1936, indicates that the G.L.F. Egg Marketing Service also was at last beginning to give results. This article gave a good picture of the egg and poultry marketing program then being carried on under the general supervision of J. C. Crissey. Each of the egg and poultry services was set up similarly to the G.L.F. Service Stores, as a separate corporation, with the idea that the patrons of each service would profit in proportion to its success. All accounting was centralized and capital for initial financing of auctions and sales rooms was provided through the Cooperative G.L.F. Holding Corporation.

This article concluded:

It has taken G.L.F. four years to establish the Egg and Poultry Marketing Services. Major emphasis to date has been along the lines of working out locations in which the services should be established, selecting and training managers to operate the units, developing accounting practices, and deciding upon the problems which it is most important to solve in order to get producers of high-class eggs . . . the highest possible return.

This issue of the *Patron* also reported progress in the marketing of beans, buckwheat and wheat, but called attention to the fact that "the scope of G.L.F. Marketing Services to date is modest." It pointed out that:

The principal operations are the buckwheat flour mill at Coudersport, Pa., and the bean plant at Phelps, N.Y. Each G.L.F. store and agent-buyer, however, is a potential marketing agency and is already an actual user of the three products—beans—buckwheat and wheat—with which G.L.F. is feeling its way in an attempt to inaugurate some fundamental and far-reaching improvements in the marketing procedure for these products.

This issue also devoted three illustrated pages to "G.L.F. Foods for Farm Families." They showed how this program had grown from a small service on whole wheat flour which had been started in 1924 at the suggestion of the New York State Home Bureau Federation to supplement a small service then being given on patent flours.

From this small beginning G.L.F. has developed a "specification" buying and pricing service on foods for the farm home which rivals in usefulness its service in buying and processing feeds for farm animals and poultry. This service is carried on by a wholly owned subsidiary . . . known as Cooperative G.L.F. Products, Inc. This corporation seeks (1) to improve the quality and save on the expense of foods used by farm families; (2) to utilize, by making them readily available to farm families, such agricultural products, raised in G.L.F. territory as buckwheat, soft winter wheat, dried skim milk, beans, et cetera.

To better direct and coordinate the services of the separately incorporated egg, poultry and fruit marketing units scattered throughout G.L.F. territory an overhead organization, Cooperative G.L.F. Marketing Management, Inc., was set up on June 8, 1936, with J. C. Crissey as President and Manager. This organization, patterned on the experience of Cooperative Farm Service Management in serving G.L.F. Stores, was designed to provide Management Service for its member marketing units who were to own and control it.

On this same date three more local produce marketing units for berries, cherries, cauliflower and similar products were set up, giving Cooperative G.L.F. Marketing Management a total of ten member associations. The produce units were simple auctions in which the producer reserved the right to turn down the sale.

When the fiscal year closed on June 30, 1936, it was found that considerable progress had been made. For 1935-36 the losses on marketing were only $33,003, while they had been $74,143 for 1934-35. The volume of products marketed remained about the same—$2,442,081 in 1935-36 as compared to $2,577,284 in 1934-35.

In December, 1936, a new organization—Cooperative G.L.F. Produce, Inc., was set up for the purpose of centralizing the activities of the Cooperative Egg Marketing Service and the Cooperative G.L.F. Bean Marketing Corporation, along with Cooperative G.L.F. Products, Inc. A month or so later Cooperative G.L.F. Produce, Inc., became Cooperative G.L.F. Products, Inc.[1]

DIAGNOSIS AND PRESCRIPTION

At this time McConnell became General Manager and no problem was giving G.L.F. more concern than marketing. Fortunately, he had a good understanding of marketing experience and he was able to draw on the abilities of Babcock who, freed at last from administrative responsibilities, was in position to devote a large part of his imagination and energy to the solution of this problem.

In March, 1937, McConnell called Silcox to Ithaca as Secretary of the G.L.F. Holding Corporation, and made B. F. Staplin Manager of Cooperative G.L.F. Products. As marketing losses were a matter of grave concern Silcox gave them special study. For the next several months Silcox advised McConnell closely on marketing problems although he had no authority over marketing operations.

By now Babcock had developed a great interest in the possibilities of Products as a means of marketing farm products through building up a market with farm families. Babcock and Silcox saw eye to eye on this matter, and Staplin was in close accord with their thinking.[2] At this juncture they persuaded Miss Lucille Brewer to join the staff of Products and set up a testing kitchen for food products. Miss Brewer, long in touch with G.L.F. through her work as Food Specialist at Cornell University, was not only technically competent but she had a wide following that attracted interest in the new program.

On June 4, 1937, McConnell appointed Babcock President of G.L.F. Products. His plans for Products were announced on October 19. The

---

[1] The names of the corporations used for marketing were very confusing, both within and outside the Exchange. After reading this chapter J. A. McConnell remarked, "That was always one of G.L.F.'s faults—using descriptive names rather than euphonious ones." Letter, to author, of December 22, 1958.

[2] In the spring of 1937 the G.L.F. was featuring a "housewives' dividend" to popularize its products in the farm home. With every purchase of G.L.F. Quality Patent Flour at the regular price the purchaser received a dividend in the form of 1 pint can of G.L.F. Old Jug Molasses, ½ pint of G.L.F. White Enamel, and a 2-ounce package of G.L.F. Golden Cross Bantam Sweet Corn, the retail price of which was 50 cents. In April, G.L.F. Products added G.L.F. Dog Food to its line, as this product could be economically manufactured along with dairy and poultry feeds and as there were many patrons who desired this product.

food line was to be known as "G.L.F. Family Foods," and a display of the food line was to feature the annual meeting in November.

Babcock stressed three points:

1. Only a single line of food products was to be handled.
2. Interest was to be built point by point.
3. The program was to feature the repetition of a simple story on each product.

Babcock saw in the program an opportunity to mobilize farm women behind the G.L.F., reduce retail costs on feed, seed, and fertilizer as food product volume assumed a share of the cost burden, increase earnings for store and dealer operators, and develop outlets for the farm products of G.L.F. patrons.

Back in Babcock's mind was a deeper objective—which he expressed as follows in the *Service Schedule* of December 21, 1937:

> It has griped me for years to see the baby chicks and even the old dairy cows on many a farm fed better than the babies and the growing boys and girls. . . . There can be no more interesting work, and certainly there can be no finer service, than to raise the level of human nutrition among G.L.F. patrons.

While Babcock and Staplin were pushing the family foods program, Silcox was concerning himself with the problem of how to make the G.L.F. marketing program for farm products tick.

The fruit of his study was presented in a report to the Board of Directors on December 29, 1937, designed primarily to improve the egg marketing operations. He made a separate report at about the same time to General Manager McConnell on the Marketing Program as a whole. These reports are of special interest in that they helped "shore up" thinking on marketing and provided a basis for its stronger development. Some of the recommendations were ahead of the times and it took almost a dozen years for them to be made effective.

In the first report Silcox pointed out that the all-time losses on G.L.F. marketing operations as of June 30, 1937, amounted to a minimum of $190,000. For the preceding year the net losses on the thirteen active marketing operations were only $2,093, and seven of the units had operated in the black. Bean marketing savings were $13,032.

Silcox devoted special attention to the New York Egg Marketing operations as they were responsible for the heaviest losses. Silcox referred to this experience as

> one of sincere effort on the part of its officers to promote and develop a marketing service offset by mismanagement, dishonesty, inventory losses and racketeering.

Silcox then said:

> If we had arrived at this point without knowing *how* we got here, or *where* we are going from here, it would be a most discouraging situation.

From his study Silcox concluded: "(1) We must improve and increase outlets for eggs, (2) control credit, (3) control inventories, (4) select and train better personnel, (5) cut costs, and (6) make use of the G.L.F. Institution in relation to patrons."

The tenor of this report indicated that the G.L.F. was at last coming to apply the same principles of good management to its marketing operations which had been so successfully employed in its farm supply purchasing operations.

Silcox's second report, entitled, "G.L.F. Marketing Program," was to set the stage for subsequent advances in the field of marketing. He began:

There should be presented to the G.L.F. Exchange Board of Directors a general program of G.L.F. marketing activities. The Board should either take a stand against the future development of marketing activities or approve a G.L.F. marketing policy. . . . No firm policy has ever been adopted in marketing. The Board has simply acted on individual marketing units as brought to its attention.

Silcox gave two major reasons for G.L.F. activities in marketing:

1. Giving aid to G.L.F. patrons in disposing of farm produce will react in increased purchasing of G.L.F. supplies.
2. It seems wise for G.L.F. to assume the sponsorship of marketing to prevent some other organization from stepping in and later developing a purchasing service on farm supplies to support the marketing program.

He then said:

If these reasons are accepted, marketing is not a primary G.L.F. activity but an institutional necessity which should be closely controlled and kept in line with institutional policies.

Silcox proposed that "the men in charge of investigating requests for marketing services and developing and promoting their organization when approved" should work out of the Ithaca office. Thus close contacts with the regular G.L.F. fieldmen working out of the Ithaca office would make "available the all important first-hand information regarding the community."

Silcox believed that the regular field force could aid in the handling of community and patron relations. He strongly favored, wherever possible, tying in the marketing operation with the existing local purchasing service and keeping it under the control of the store manager and district manager. He gave several illustrations to show how the same management could efficiently supervise both supply distribution and marketing. He said this "makes the local G.L.F. Service a complete agricultural community center which buys and sells for patrons. This set-up cuts down local overhead costs and prevents duplication of personnel."

One of G.L.F.'s problems in marketing was to withstand pressure from special groups desiring "services to market this or that product." Silcox believed that marketing should not be undertaken unless 50 percent of those desiring such service were bona fide G.L.F. patrons.

Believing that marketing should be looked upon as an institutional service "with indirect benefits flowing back to the wholesale purchasing divisions" Silcox thought that these divisions should pay a portion of the cost of maintaining the marketing service. However, where a special marketing service was needed at a local point, it was recommended that the prospective patrons should "buy preferred stock in the G.L.F. Holding Corporation sufficient for fixed assets and organization expenses."

The report closed with these strong statements:

> The selling job is the most important part of the marketing program and we need good salesmen who can in season as needed visit the trade and develop new outlets in a wide variety of G.L.F. produce. I believe this is where the G.L.F. has fallen down badly in marketing because we have given our attention to the accumulation and physical handling of supplies while our competitors in this line of work have given their attention to selling.

> In our marketing services the operation should carry the product through as many steps as possible from the producer to the consumer.

Marketing Stabilized

During 1937 G.L.F. marketing operations had been studied and stabilized. In 1938 the marketing program was beginning to find itself. The *G.L.F. Patron* for March 1938 reflected this new positive approach:

> G.L.F. patrons have marketing services available on beans, eggs, buckwheat, wheat, fruits, vegetables, potatoes, and poultry. . . . These marketing activities have been started because a great many groups of G.L.F. patrons insisted on them.

The *Patron* also indicated that nineteen marketing units had been operated in 1937, of which "10—check fair to good; 7—are on probation; 1—checks bad; and 1—was closed."

McConnell also gave support to marketing in the spring series of regional meetings with G.L.F. Patron Committees. He said:

> Let's discuss marketing. Most of our membership is today marketing minded. This is probably due to a declining price level and farmers are turning to the G.L.F. . . .

McConnell then referred to the lessons learned in five years of experimental marketing effort: "We have discovered that there are few men available who really know marketing. . . ." He pointed out that "supposedly experienced men" have been "robbing us blind." He had no illusions. "It is going to be a slow, long, hard pull."

On August 1, 1938, McConnell made C. W. Sadd President of G.L.F. Marketing Management and placed him in charge of the entire marketing operation. He also appointed H. E. Babcock and C. N. Silcox to work with him on a marketing committee. In setting up this important committee McConnell said:

. . . I am asking Sadd to attempt the correlation of all marketing operations of the G.L.F. into the other activities of the organization. He is well qualified to do this as a result of his years of experience in successfully supervising G.L.F. Service Agencies and because he understands human nature pretty well.

At this time the Family Foods program was running in high gear. Babcock used it to dramatize the importance of marketing as of equal importance with purchasing. In addressing the Field Force, in October, he pointed out that Products had three fundamental objectives:

1. Specification buying of family foods for G.L.F. patrons.
2. To perform as far as possible the services needed for a complete marketing operation from producer to consumer.
3. To distribute all savings to the retail distribution system and to G.L.F. patrons.

Babcock illustrated his hope for marketing with buckwheat, starting with furnishing of buckwheat seed to the grower and controlling every step of its marketing through the mills and on to the consumer's plate in the form of a pancake.

On December 23 Babcock announced that the Supplementary Distribution of Family Foods is a "bouncing baby right now. About 195 G.L.F. Service Agencies are signed up as Products representatives."

In February, 1939, he reported to the Board of Directors:

I am pushing very hard for the building up of a system of retail stores which will supplement our present retail agencies in the distribution of Family Foods and possibly as time goes on, of certain items which G.L.F. will market. . . . The building of a system of supplementary retail services by G.L.F. will not only increase the sphere of its influence, but will give its field force a good healthy workout on a challenging job—and if the job is well handled G.L.F. will have a volume of Family Foods on which might be earned substantial sums each year to accrue to the benefit of the retail service agencies.

When he presented his annual report on November 1, 1938, McConnell could be more confident of the future of marketing. C. W. Sadd was giving the program energy and direction. McConnell said:

Considerable progress has been made this last year in getting all marketing units on a self-sustaining basis. A good marketing personnel is being gradually trained, and the results of this are beginning to show up. The Board has directed me to continue cautiously with experimentation in marketing but to expand it only in those fields where it can be self-sustaining and render a definite service to patrons. . . .

In a special report to G.L.F. Committeemen on December 7, McConnell reviewed G.L.F.'s experience in marketing to date. Marketing volume had changed as follows in the preceding five fiscal years:

1933-4	$1,579,000
1934-5	2,577,000
1935-6	2,442,000
1936-7	3,315,000
1937-8	2,733,000

He attributed the last year's decline largely to the lower price level as quantities of most products marketed had expanded.

A significant new development had been the establishment of a wheat marketing pool to handle wheat through 20 G.L.F. Service Agencies."

McConnell indicated that there were two distinct jobs to be done:

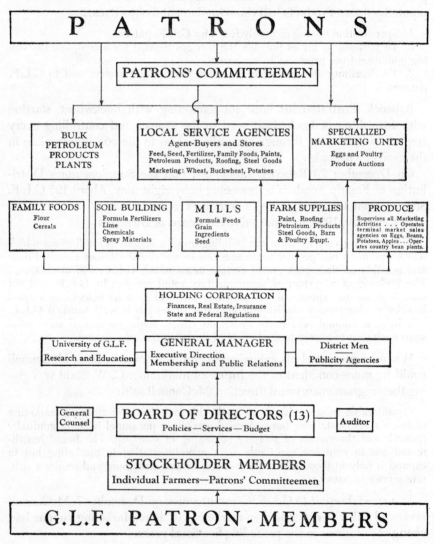

FIGURE 3—CHART SHOWING USE AND CONTROL OF G.L.F., 1939

(1) to build a sales program in terminal markets, which may involve some terminal warehousing.

(2) to work out a sound plan for purchasing the produce of patrons in the country, which in some cases may require processing and grading.

He pointed out that in the opinion of Sadd, distribution was the biggest problem facing marketing, and that Sadd hoped this could be solved "by controlling the commodities all the way from producer to the consumer wherever possible."

"Most marketing cooperatives," said McConnell, "have concerned themselves with just two or three phases of the program, with the result that the old line agencies narrowed their margins in those steps in which the cooperative operated and broadened them in other fields."

Soon after this McConnell issued the following statement:

I believe it is accurate to state that most rural communities and areas lack adequate marketing machinery to do a good job of grading and selling. The only way I know to remedy this is for farmers to do it themselves, and I see no reason why they shouldn't look to G.L.F. to undertake the job.

That is . . . why G.L.F. is in marketing. . . . So far it has been largely experimental; but we are rapidly accumulating a force of trained men and considerable experience. . . . Sooner or later, this manpower and experience cannot help but produce results.

McConnell was right. From that date, marketing began to move steadily forward, although the volume of products marketed increased only from $2,733,000 in 1937-38 to $2,875,387 in 1938-39.

On January 31, 1939, the various marketing enterprises in the G.L.F. System were brought together into a new organization—Cooperative G.L.F. Produce, Inc.

According to Sherman Peer, "This step [was] made to tie marketing into a uniform pattern with respect to urban terminal markets." Under the new plan Cooperative G.L.F. Market Management, Inc., became the Management Department of Cooperative G.L.F. Produce, Inc., and the Egg and Bean Corporations became the Egg and Bean Departments.

A week or so earlier (January 18, 1939) Cooperative G.L.F. Farm Products was set up to market the produce of G.L.F. farms, such as eggs, beans, fresh vegetables and canning crops. At the same time the flour and cereal business was turned back to G.L.F. Mills.

This arrangement continued until January 29, 1941, when Cooperative G.L.F. Produce was merged into Cooperative G.L.F. Farm Products, Inc. Thus, the special purpose marketing corporations within the G.L.F. were integrated at last into one organization for marketing.

By this time marketing in G.L.F. had passed the experimental stage. This is shown by the fact that the value of all products marketed for patrons increased from $3,082,157 in 1939-40 to $4,189,576 in 1940-41. Marketings were to double in 1941-42 and almost redouble the following year.

CHAPTER 23

Installing the Petroleum Service

Resolved: That the G.L.F. policy relating to gasoline distribution be one of deliberate to slow movement . . . and that the general procedure be to develop one bulk station in each district of the G.L.F. territory. . . .

G.L.F. Board of Directors, February 18, 1937

T HE WAY in which the petroleum program was developed is of special interest in that it called for entirely new methods of distribution.

Although the program did not get really started until June 4, 1936, when the Board authorized the establishment of the Tompkins G.L.F. Cooperative, Inc., to furnish farmer patrons near Ithaca with gasoline and oil, it had been a matter under consideration for some time. As early as June 10, 1931, Babcock had written to General Counsel Waldo G. Morse, "When it comes to the oil and gas business I am puzzled."

It should also be remembered that the G.L.F. handled lubricating oils in cans on a mail order basis in its early days, and that G.L.F. specifications for motor oils were established in 1927. This business had grown appreciably by 1936, indicating that, increasingly, farmers were buying mechanized equipment. Thus, there was good reason to examine the possibility of broadening services on petroleum products to include motor fuels.

Moreover, farmers were beginning to demand this service from the G.L.F. At the Stockholders' Meeting in October, 1936, over 98 percent voted in favor of the G.L.F. handling gasoline and oil, along with general farm supplies. It was believed that the spread between the price paid by farmers and that paid by the distributor was too high, and that an efficient system of distribution by G.L.F. would provide substantial savings for farmers, while improving the character of services performed.

In the early thirties G.L.F. officials also were watching with interest the rapid development of petroleum business by cooperatives in the Middle West. With the formation in 1934 of the Pennsylvania Farm Bureau Cooperative Association to handle petroleum and other supplies, petroleum operations were beginning to demonstrate their appeal to farmers very near home. It became apparent that if G.L.F. did not enter this field the demand from its farmer patrons for this service would encourage the establishment of cooperatives to provide it. This the G.L.F. could not afford to have happen, for the establishment of a cooperative purchasing service on petroleum products might lead to duplicate purchasing service on feed and other supplies.

V. A. Fogg, who had the responsibility of starting the Petroleum Service in G.L.F. Farm Supplies, has given me this account of its beginnings.

G.L.F. at this time was looking for new fields to conquer. There was much interest in petroleum since the mid-west coops were successful in this field. One day Ed Babcock said to me 'Let's experiment.' I suggested that Harvey Hull, General Manager of the Indiana Farm Bureau Cooperative Association and President of the Farm Bureau Oil Company would be a good man to contact for information. Ed grabbed the phone and put in a long distance call to Harvey. After a good talk Harvey said 'Why don't you come out and we'll talk it over.' As a result Ed and I went out and saw Harvey. Harvey explained that the mid-west coops were looking for a good chance to work with us on petroleum or in similar fields. He suggested that G.L.F. might join the Farm Bureau Oil Company and get petroleum supplies through it. We pointed out to Harvey that G.L.F. could not join an organization having a Farm Bureau name as the G.L.F. was not particularly a Farm Bureau Organization. Harvey said: 'If that's the only problem we will change it's name.' Ed said 'O.K.' That was how the G.L.F. became a charter member of United Cooperatives. (September, 1936). This helped us get the program under way. Vory Everson, the manager of United, helped us get a reasonable contract for petroleum supplies with Sinclair. He sent a man out to help Stuart Miller set up the Ithaca Installation. (Interview June 3, 1958)

The Ithaca G.L.F. Store had long operated a gasoline pump for the convenience of its patrons. Thus the decision to organize the Tompkins G.L.F. Cooperative, Inc., as a separate service represented a positive step forward. It set out petroleum operations for experimental study, and disassociated the program from the other operations of the G.L.F. Store. Although it was organized as a subsidiary of the Ithaca Cooperative G.L.F. Service, Inc., it was not entirely a local venture. It was in reality a pilot plant operation. This is shown by the Minutes of the Cooperative G.L.F. Holding Corporation, May 6, 1936.

Resolved: That this Board go on record in favor of the organization of a local cooperative to be known as Tompkins G.L.F. Cooperative, Inc., for the purpose of enabling farmers in the Tompkins County area to purchase gasoline and other petroleum products cooperatively; and that Ithaca Cooperative, be authorized to invest $75.00 in common stock of the new cooperative in its organization.

The Tompkins G.L.F. Cooperative, Inc., was soon operating a bulk plant and filling station, with two trucks to deliver petroleum products direct to farmers in the Ithaca trade area. It started out to serve farmers from a service station, with the idea that they would come in with drums and cans to pick up what was wanted, but it was soon found that farmers desired delivery to their farms.

This raised another problem—how should delivery be made? By owned, or hired trucks? An arrangement was worked out to hire this service from Crispell Brothers. They owned and manned their own trucks and made deliveries whenever called on by the Association.

The favorable response of farmers for the service provided by the Tompkins G.L.F. Cooperative, Inc., led to a rapid demand for similar service in other parts of the G.L.F. territory. However, one problem concerned G.L.F. leaders—how could the program be developed so that it would not endanger the income tax exemption enjoyed by the G.L.F.? As long as a retail service was provided could the service be restricted to farmers?

To meet this problem the G.L.F. decided that new petroleum units would be set up to serve farmers only from tank wagons, operated in connection with bulk plants. As a result, the new units formed were of this type.

The problem of how to make delivery was still not settled. At Fort Plain, New York, a couple of skid tanks were bought and a local trucker was hired to make deliveries. At Greene, New York, the product was sold from the bulk plant to a firm which distributed it by truck on its own account. These experiments proved that a good job could not be done in distribution without ownership and operation of delivery trucks. By the summer of 1937 all of the seven bulk plants in operation were equipped with single trucks.

The first trucks were very simple by today's standards. They consisted generally of an 800-gallon, four compartment tank mounted on a one-and-a-half-ton chassis. All gallonage had to be bucketed. When in early 1939 the Bowser Company came out with a small pumping unit, all trucks were so equipped for gasoline deliveries.

In these early days, farm storage and dispensing equipment were not available. Most equipment then being loaned farmers by the major companies was obsolete equipment taken from service stations. The G.L.F. met this problem by loaning farmers 55-gallon drums, which were not too satisfactory to larger users, particularly, as mechanized farm equipment was steadily calling for more fuel. This problem was solved by persuading manufacturers of tanks for other purposes to adapt them for gasoline storage. Also, manufacturers were persuaded to make one-gallon pumps for farm use.[1]

While the G.L.F. was still "fumbling" as to how to get the new service working, it also became evident that some kind of plan for deliveries was needed. Delivery on call resulted in a truck being in the same neigh-

---

[1] As reported by Ray Wolf, who helped establish G.L.F. petroleum operations, in memorandum, to author, of April 29, 1958. For illustrations of simple farm storage equipment used in the early days see the Petroleum Service Edition of the *G.L.F. Patron,* for June, 1941, page 15.

borhood several times a week or even in a day. As a result of this experience a two-week route system of delivery was installed when the decision
was made to own and operate the trucks. This system proved satisfactory,
economical, and, with modifications to meet changed conditions, is still
used.

From the beginning—except for the experimental operations above mentioned—the farm service men on the trucks were paid straight salaries,
and the trucks were owned by the G.L.F. This was in contrast to the procedures then being followed by most other petroleum cooperatives of paying on commission, with the farm service men owning the trucks. For a
period in 1938 the G.L.F. paid farm service men on a per-gallon basis
while continuing to own the trucks, but this experiment was given up as
being not in accord with G.L.F. philosophy.[2] There is this to be said for
the G.L.F.'s practice of owning and operating its own petroleum delivery
equipment. It gave G.L.F. complete control over its program and freed
it from the problem of vested interests in distribution territory.

When the G.L.F. entered the field of petroleum distribution many farmers, located off the main hard roads, could not get petroleum service from
existing companies. Farmers on the side roads and on dirt roads were
forced to go after their own supplies. From the beginning, the G.L.F.
made delivery to farms regardless of their location in the area of the bulk
plant. This practice proved very popular with farmers and did much to
build initial support.[3]

The location of bulk plants was not part of a master plan. Usually plants
were located through the expressed interest of farmers in a general area.
The Patrons' Committee of the ten to fifteen service agencies in that area
were then called together and consideration was given to such factors as
the volume needed, the cost of a plant and service desired.

If the committee men present voted for a plant, the G.L.F. then made a
careful survey of the potential farm volume and best possible location. In
selecting location, consideration was given to zone price, transportation
rates, geographic factors, and availability of both truck and rail transportation.

In October, 1937, V. A. Fogg, President of G.L.F. Farm Supplies, reported on progress in this "brand new field" to a G.L.F. School. He used

---

[2] It was believed that payment on commission would encourage farm service men
to think of themselves as salesmen rather than as G.L.F. servicemen for farmers.
G.L.F. feared that paying commissions would weaken the loyalty of the employees
to the Institution.

[3] The practice of serving all G.L.F. farmers regardless of their accessibility, to the
extent that this was economically feasible, did not call for a policy decision as this
was implied in the general principles of the G.L.F. It gave impetus to volume building as "it was easier to build business" on these side roads where farmers generally
could not obtain service. (R. J. Wolf in memorandum, to author, of May 5, 1958.)

a map to show 16 locations where gasoline was being handled in carload lots and said: "In each location where the distribution has been started the G.L.F. has sent a man to estimate the cost of the equipment, has purchased the equipment, and supervised the installation."

He saw "tremendous opportunities in this field," and declared: "This business can easily become one of the largest departments of the G.L.F."

The rapid development of this program raised important new problems. Up to the summer of 1938 petroleum units had developed without a formal pattern. Should these and new units be coordinated into a system and organized as a separate retail petroleum service? How best could these petroleum units be integrated with the operations of the local G.L.F. stores and Agent-Buyers?

It was apparent to McConnell that the petroleum program could not be satisfactorily developed without a clear-cut plan. In a G.L.F. School on June 20, 1938, McConnell said, "There isn't much question but that we are going to build petroleum distribution in G.L.F. The question that I am raising . . . is whether the petroleum distribution service should be entirely cooperative or whether it should be built part cooperative and partly through private distribution as in our farm supply distribution system. . . . I lean very strongly toward a cooperative system. . . ."

To find out how to best proceed he directed E. H. Fallon, then a District Manager, to study petroleum retail operations and suggest ways of improvement.

Fogg recalls that:

the petroleum program under Stuart Miller's direction was then being aggressively developed. However, it was clear that this was quite a different program compared with other retail operations. How could it be fitted in? District men didn't know a thing about it so we decided to bring someone to study the darned thing, and that's how Ed Fallon was given the job. Following the study Stuart centered his work on the wholesale end with Ron Fitch helping him on transportation problems, while Ed developed the distribution end. (Interview, with author, June 3, 1958)

On July 21, 1938, while Fallon was working on this assignment, McConnell issued the following announcement on Petroleum Distribution:

It is important that in developing a sound, long-time program for the distribution of petroleum products we do not make mistakes in the early stages of the development that will hamper it later on when we have more experience and can really formulate a sound program. It seems to me undesirable at this time to attempt to groove petroleum products in G.L.F. without additional experience.

From the limited observations that I have been able to make, I believe that it is probably desirable to at least plan and work toward a hundred per cent cooperative distribution of petroleum products as far as bulk distributing stations are concerned. Simply stating that we will make this distribution a hundred per cent cooperative does not mean that we can ignore the present G.L.F.

distribution system. Present Patrons' relations to existing Service Stores and Agent-Buyers must be taken into consideration.

In view of the above, I realize that there will inevitably have to be some exceptions to a hundred per cent cooperative distribution on petroleum products. I, however, believe that recognition of this now will prevent many costly mistakes in the set-up of the distribution system.

In order to handle this situation, I am proposing the following, some part of which is already underway.

(1) That we continue setting up the petroleum units, until experience proves otherwise, as separate corporations with common stock owned by the Holding Company.

(2) For the time being, Ed Fallon, representing the *whole* distribution system, will collaborate with Stuart Miller in setting up any new bulk stations.

(3) In setting up any bulk distribution and carrying on any present petroleum operations, these men will work with the following people:

(a) District Men in the territory in charge of Agents
(b) District Men in the territory in charge of Stores
(c) Agent-Buyers or Stores affected in the area
(d) The personnel of now-existing bulk plants.

(4) A committee composed of Misty [Fogg], Scottie [Campbell] and Frank [Naegely] will work with Ed and Stuart in the development of the distribution system.

Six months' operation with this personnel should put us in position to make some decisions on distribution.

It might just as well be recognized now that the setting up of a separate corporation to manage the distribution system of petroleum may be the only practical solution to this whole problem. And further, any system of distribution to be successful, must leave the responsibility for Patrons' relations in charge of the Districtmen.

After spending three months "visiting with directors, G.L.F. officials, district managers, and riding on trucks with Farm Service men," Fallon recommended the establishment of a separate retail Petroleum Distribution Department for the following reasons:

First, I found that the petroleum business was highly specialized. I did not feel that a manager of a G.L.F. Store could spend only a part of his time on the petroleum business and make a success of it. . . .

Second, the facilities to handle feed differ from those needed to handle gasoline, and in no way can be compared.

Third, I found that the area serviced by a bulk plant would cover an average of ten stores and agency areas. When the petroleum business was operated by one store within the area, it often created hard feelings between the various service agencies, as the boys on the trucks did not always stick to the delivery of petroleum products. Sometimes they had to talk feed, seed and fertilizer because the farm patrons asked about these items.[4]

In October, 1938, the Petroleum Distribution Department, as recommended, was set up in G.L.F. Farm Supplies, Inc. and Fallon was placed in charge.

[4] E. H. Fallon, "Your Job in Petroleum Distribution," in brochure issued by G.L.F. Petroleum Distribution Department, *Your Job and You*, October 30, 1941.

Fallon saw his first need as men. "From an operator's standpoint," he later reported,

I considered that the most important job was to man the department with good men: I believe that the average business is about as good as the employees in it. I began interviewing a great many men and carefully selecting the men we could use. At the beginning I thought it necessary to ask a few good store managers to help the department get started because of their experience. I do not think I was wrong in doing this.[5]

There was this advantage in drawing on G.L.F. personnel. These men were not only of proven compatibility, and competence, but they knew the philosophy and methods of G.L.F. They could help keep this program in line with general G.L.F. objectives, and help gain support for it within the Institution.

The immediate success of the Petroleum Distribution Department reflected Fallon's ability to lead and train men. Its high morale facilitated its rapid growth.

With manpower assured, Fallon began to build volume through the establishment of area bulk-plants, selected to cover G.L.F. territory. The rapidity of progress is shown by the following figures:

		Volume	
	Bulk Plants	Gallons	Dollars
1937-38	10	2,044,803	381,105
1938-39	18	6,117,500	850,745
1939-40	25	11,807,164	1,610,386
1940-41	32	18,920,237	2,513,439

The pattern of areawide services established by the Petroleum Department raised the problem of patron or member control. While the members of the stores were served by advisory committees, the petroleum units were set up to serve the members of a number of stores, and somewhat the same type of situation was developing around G.L.F. marketing units. While the need for membership control of the petroleum units was recognized, it was not deemed desirable to have these independent of the store committees already serving the same clientele of members. In a few areas patrons' councils had been set up by marketing units, and there was some sentiment for the formation of such councils to represent petroleum users.

In a brochure, "How G.L.F. Operates," issued in June, 1939, McConnell said:

The wholesale unit handling petroleum products is Farm Supplies. . . . Its present source of supply is United Cooperatives. . . .

[5] "Your Job in Petroleum Distribution," cited above.

Distribution of gasoline and kerosene is through bulk stations operating tank trucks for direct delivery to the farm. . . .

The operation of these bulk stations is quite different from the operation of community services on feeds, seeds, fertilizers, and other farm supplies. Each bulk station requires a relatively high fixed asset investment as compared to the initial stage of a G.L.F. Service Store. The distribution area of these bulk gas stations is not on a community basis but on an area basis, carrying in most instances a number of communities. . . . A single bulk gas station may [service] the patrons of a dozen community services. . . . These bulk stations at the present time operate without Patrons' Committees, although they may have, and some will have, Councils selected from the patrons. . . .

The relationship of the petroleum operations to the G.L.F. program as a whole was further clarified on August 3, 1939, by a statement of "G.L.F. Membership Policy as it Relates to Marketing and Petroleum Distribution." This statement pointed out that:

(1) Patron Committees representing members by communities are already established around G.L.F. Agent-Buyers or G.L.F. Service Stores. Policy Committees around marketing and gas units are not needed inasmuch as the patrons already have representatives. Groups of patrons acting as councils may or may not be needed. If they are needed, they should be established to counsel with management rather than to act as legal representatives of patrons.

(2) Experimental use of councils composed of farmers at certain locations should be made. Such groups should be selected by the management rather than elected by the patrons. They need not be qualified as voters. They need not be stockholders. They should be users of the service. Marketing or petroleum management in selecting them should have one thing in mind, that is to keep the operation working in the interest of farmers and keep it practical.

(3) Marketing and petroleum distribution men must keep in mind that the management of patrons' relations is under G.L.F. District Men in charge of G.L.F. Agent-Buyers and Service Stores. They should plan to handle their membership responsibilities through the present established membership organization in those areas in which they operate. Annual G.L.F. community meetings, committee meetings, and meetings of Agent-Buyers and Store Managers are the means through which reports should be made to patrons and their representatives. The closest kind of relationship between the District Men in charge of membership and the managers of these operations is necessary. This should be District Men's responsibility.

The above policy statement shows how carefully G.L.F. management watched to see that this new program did not get out of hand and break down existing lines of responsibility, while every encouragement was given to its proper growth within the institutional framework.

With the air cleared, the Petroleum Distribution Department proceeded to set up Petroleum Councils around each bulk plant, made up of one representative from each store and agent-buyer's committee in the area served. This system of representation proved practicable from the beginning and has become established in G.L.F. petroleum operations.

The morale of the employees of the Petroleum Distribution Department was high from the outset. Care was taken to select employees who were competent and cooperative, and the opportunity for rapid expansion gave job advancements which created optimism. Fallon fully appreciated the value of enthusiastic workers, as he worked unceasingly to create an *esprit de corps* in his staff. Monthly meetings were held in each plant, and two schools were held each year, one in Ithaca, and one in the field. At the same time Fallon realized that the petroleum program must be kept in line with the program of the G.L.F. as a whole—that it could not be developed as an elite group within the G.L.F. staff. This did not preclude him from experimenting with personnel policies and procedures that were not commonly used throughout G.L.F.

In 1941 a brochure was prepared for employee training purposes in the petroleum distribution department entitled, "Your Job and You," which later was revamped and used throughout the G.L.F. This publication carried a foreword by H. E. Babcock which expressed his conviction that well-qualified and loyal employees were indispensable to G.L.F. success. Fallon's own article on "Your Job in Petroleum Distribution" told the story of what the department was trying to do. He stressed the point that employees were partners with the patrons, and that the organization would crumble if the balance got out of line. The other material in the brochure gave the employee information on personnel policies, the group insurance program, the availability of health insurance, and the credit union. Of special interest was a section entitled, "Meet your Employer—the G.L.F." which answered fifty-five basic questions on G.L.F. Fallon said that "It is necessary for you to have the answers to these questions in order to have an understanding of the organization you work for." The last question was: "What is the future of the men in the Petroleum Department?" The answer given was:

> The Petroleum Department is new and growing. As it expands responsible jobs will have to be filled. Who will fill them depends on the men themselves. It has always been the policy of G.L.F. to promote men in the organization who have shown themselves to be qualified by training and experience.

The soundness of this policy was reflected in the phenomenal growth of the petroleum operations as shown above.

Five years after the Tompkins G.L.F. Cooperative, Inc., had modestly begun to give service, McConnell in his annual report for 1940-41 could say:

> The Petroleum Distribution Service of G.L.F. is strictly beyond the experimental stage. Thirty-two G.L.F. Bulk Petroleum Stations . . . are operating throughout the territory. G.L.F. has become one of the very large purchasers of petroleum products on the Atlantic Seaboard. . . . This year this system will handle 30 million gallons of petroleum.

Whether or not G.L.F. patrons, in the future, in order to carry on this business more effectively, or at all, will need to build pipe lines, own transport fleets of trucks, terminal water facilities, or oil refineries is still to be determined. The essential thing, however, is that if these facilities are needed and required, the distribution system of petroleum products now being built will furnish them with an outlet and thus safeguard the investment and services.

This statement was made just before the attack on Pearl Harbor. When war came the G.L.F. was in position to meet the extraordinary demands of its members for petroleum service.

CHAPTER 24

The Defense Period

. . . Farmers must never forget they are considered one of the main
spokes in the defense wheel.
J. A. McConnell, *G.L.F. Stockholders' Meeting, November 6, 1941*

THE G.L.F. had just completed a good year when war broke out in Europe in the late summer of 1939. Volume in dollars was down a little from the year before but the tonnage of supplies and products handled was only slightly less than in the peak year 1936-37. Savings of $1,465,000 for the year were the highest in the history of the Exchange.

What would be the effects of the war and would this country become involved? No one could be sure but a condition of widespread anxiety set in as leaders in Government and industry called for preparedness measures. Top officials in the G.L.F. followed the situation closely so as to be in position to act should the need arise. However, the lull following the conquest of Poland engendered complacency and a belief that this country somehow might not be seriously affected.

While Mr. McConnell did not cry "Wolf," he never ignored the contingency of war. In his address to the annual meeting in November, 1939, he warned that a world war or continuance of the war then going on in Europe might result in a very much higher price level which would require the retention of more savings for working capital and an interruption of patronage refund payments.

As the "Sitzkrieg" or "Phony War," as it was called in this country, wore on, the G.L.F., like other business organizations, almost forgot the war in Europe. This complacency was shattered by the rapid invasion of Norway in April, 1940, followed by the "blitzkrieg" conquest of the Lowlands in May and France in early June which left England in a desperate and seemingly almost hopeless situation.

What did this trend of events mean to the G.L.F.? How should G.L.F. key employees react to this situation?

THE CHALLENGE OF COMING EVENTS

Mr. McConnell gave his answers in a talk to G.L.F. District Men and Department Heads on June 18, 1940. This talk, entitled, "Can We as G.L.F. People Adjust Ourselves to the Coming Events?" nipped defeatism in the bud and gave the G.L.F. a fighting philosophy for the difficult period ahead. The spirit and content of this talk can best be given by extensive quotation.

Sweeping revolutionary changes in the world . . . have been on the march for several years. . . . The average man has not comprehended this. . . . The realists who were willing to face facts were discounted and discredited. . . . Winston Churchill . . . is an example of one of the realists . . . it is interesting to note how a nation turns to a realist when a crisis finally comes. . . .

McConnell then set the stage for a consideration of the present situation, by saying:

When the British and French were defeated in Scandinavia, this country got a little nervous. You could notice that just a few people began to wonder if all was as serene and safe as they had thought. Then when Germany hit Belgium and Holland and took them within a few days, the world woke up with a start, including the United States. . . .

All this leads to some inescapable conclusions. One is that each and everyone of us is going to be affected in some way or another. We may be in war soon . . . whether or not, we cannot escape the fact that we are going to prepare for war at a tremendous rate. . . .

For a nation that is as unprepared as the United States, getting ready for such wars as are being fought today means great changes in our whole economy. . . . All of the productive machinery in this country has to be called upon . . . farms, factories, capital, labor, transportation and mines. Every person will be affected directly for years to come. . . .

Every single one of us, if we are going to stay in G.L.F. has got to face the facts, no matter how unpleasant they are. We must form a personal philosophy which will carry us through the next few weeks, months, and perhaps years. No one with a defeatist attitude can possibly face the future and be any good to himself or to this organization.

Now the test of each individual will come. First, whether he's able to play on a team that doesn't always win and still continue to play a good game. Whether he can take defeat as well as victory. Whether he lets the march of world events . . . get him down where he can't carry out the day's work for G.L.F. Whether he can take the mental and spiritual shocks which are sure to come and the hardships that go with them and still deliver instead of becoming a whiner and a crybaby.

In my opinion, we are going to change from a world where security, the rights of the individual and a high standard of living for everyone, regardless of performance, will give way to a world in which we'll fight for our very existence and the right to attempt to achieve in some degree security, personal liberties and some of the things that are richly possible under a democratic form of government by a people who realize the responsibilities that go with self-government. Personally, I am not downhearted. . . .

Somebody is going to run the farms and industries of this country. A portion of them are being run by G.L.F. I think we are the best qualified group in the world to continue running it. . . .

There must be, in times like these, constant planning, both for the individual and for the organization. If I can keep this Institution looking ahead, planning, and working and then be willing and alert enough to change its plans as re-quired by day-to-day developments, I feel that I will have done what can be done in a critical situation. . . .

What does all this add up to in planning? . . .

Increase the working capital by selling an issue of one million to two million dollars of preferred stock to provide for improvement of plants and facilities and for a rising price level.

Repair and remodel immediately present facilities to make them as efficient as possible, increasing capacity and reducing unit costs.

Study new sources of supplies and possible substitutes for patrons' needs.

In consideration of young men being drawn into government service—women and older men should be employed for clerical work. . . .

Limit new services and the development of old services to the fundamental needs of farmers. . . .

If we can leave here . . . with our courage high, our objectives clear and some idea of how to proceed to attain these objectives, the week will be the most valuable one of the succeeding year. . . . I want to give you as a group a philosophy and get you in a frame of mind . . . where you will face what is coming with courage and perhaps to some degree, a certain grim pleasure. . . . I'm not downhearted. I hope you won't be. I think real democracy is worth fighting for but I doubt if we can preserve it unless we fight for it. . . .

We have a job to do right here at home. . . . When the country needs us in other fields, it will probably tell us. In other words, don't become so concerned with what you can't do much about that you fail to carry on your own work.

This talk ripped away any lack of concern or defeatism that may have existed in G.L.F. ranks, and replaced it with a vigorous fighting philosophy that gave new strength to the organization.

In the next eighteen months—until the attack on Pearl Harbor—the G.L.F. continued to get ready, and when the challenge finally came it was conditioned both in morale and physical resources.

Although the tense world situation continued during the summer and fall of 1940, and throughout 1941, this was not manifest in business op-erations. The deadlock between Germany and England even led many to hope that through some miracle this country might not become involved. Although prices and costs rose and governmental controls and defense efforts increased the G.L.F. was in good position to adjust to these factors without disturbing its basic services.

When the G.L.F. stockholders met in Syracuse on October 24 and 25, 1940, the immediate danger had largely subsided and attention was fo-cused on more apparent present problems. However, Manager McConnell pointed out that the drift toward war was beginning to have an effect on G.L.F. He saw the need of building needed plants, getting out of debt, conserving earnings and taking other steps to be able to meet a crisis should it come. "Personally," said McConnell, "I should hate to face the coming years as a farmer without G.L.F. to meet the many problems that are sure to arise."

The fiscal year 1939-40 had been the best in G.L.F. history. With inflated prices volume of purchases had increased from $32,994,620 in 1938-39 to $40,245,501 in 1939-40, while net savings had increased from $1,476,715 to $2,086,677. Tonnage was also up to 1,326,000 as compared with 1,109,000 the year before.

PROGRESS IN TWENTY YEARS

One of the highlights of the annual meeting in November was an address by President Leigh G. Kirkland who compared the present assets and liabilities of the G.L.F. with those of 1920 when the G.L.F. was formed.

Among the assets in 1920 he stressed "fighting enthusiasm, determination and a group of young executives who wouldn't be licked."

Among the liabilities he listed lack of experience, lack of finance, lack of credit, lack of facilities, lack of supplies, and many other lacks.

In contrast he found in 1940 a first class cooperative institution supported by a group of enthusiastic, intelligent, loyal and confident farmers; with a group of trained executives and a record of achievement. He saw serious problems ahead and said, "Don't let the picture lull you into a sense of security. . . . The challenge that faced this organization in 1920 still stands. . . ."

McConnell in his report placed emphasis on the problems of 1940. "To have," he said, "one must prepare to hold. . . . G.L.F. is a tremendous business. It is a direct challenge to hundreds of competitive forces. . . . Make no mistake, this organization is not beloved by anyone except ourselves."

McConnell then turned to the essential jobs in G.L.F. and the means for carrying on the job. The importance of education was being recognized by the establishment of the School of Cooperative Administration with H. E. Babcock as Director.[1]

McConnell also thought it important to emphasize the significance of feed in G.L.F. operations—the principal supply item handled and the main source of earnings. "G.L.F. is still a cow and hen feed cooperative. *Seeds, fertilizer, Family Foods, and other farm supplies will flow economically through G.L.F. only as long as it keeps itself efficient in its main life line, that is principally feed.*"

McConnell also felt impelled to explain the place of the Holding Com-

---

[1] The G.L.F. School of Cooperative Administration, which formalized and extended the employee educational program previously carried on by the University of the G.L.F., was opened on October 15, 1940, by Leigh G. Kirkland, President of the G.L.F. The principal speaker was Edmund Ezra Day, President of Cornell University. W. G. Wysor, General Manager of the Southern States Cooperative, Inc., dedicated the main auditorium—named Bibbins Hall in honor of Arthur Leal Bibbins—*to self-help, fair dealing and good citizenship.*

pany in the G.L.F. He said that "Certain interests are continually pointing out that there must be something sinister and dishonest in the conduct
of the affairs of G.L.F. They whisper that this must be true because the
G.L.F. has a Holding Company."

He pointed out that the G.L.F. Holding Company was "a wholly-owned
subsidiary—entirely responsive and subservient to the G.L.F. Exchange
through its board of directors." It was a mechanism for financing—nothing
more nor less.

With regard to patronage refunds he warned that "it is obvious that
we are entering upon a very troubled sea." He proposed setting up large
reserves and earmarking them for the patrons of the year until danger had
passed.

Many other problems were pressing—especially the relationship with
organized labor. McConnell promised that he would do everything within his power "to prevent any labor monopoly from dominating G.L.F.
plants." This problem was to erupt in a serious strike the following year.

McConnell summed up his talk with an analysis of the present and
future place of G.L.F. in agriculture.

Why is it that many country dealers and other suppliers to farmers thoroughly hate the name of G.L.F.? It is not because these men are afraid of an
"ism" or a social movement. It's because farmers are using it as an effective
pacemaker.

G.L.F. has also had its effect in a social way. Improve the economic condition of any group of people, and to that extent you improve their social welfare. . . . It has had its effect in broadening the vision and outlook of farm
people. There is no other way that I know of in which the farm boy can project
himself through all the operations of industry and commerce so effectively as
through active membership in G.L.F.

The future of G.L.F. is whatever farmers wish to make it.

The preparedness program began to really affect G.L.F. operations in
1941. It showed up in rising prices, increasing scarcities of critical materials, pressure on labor supplies, and a proliferation of government controls and regulations.

Getting Ready

When McConnell again met with his department and district heads
on June 23, 1941, a great change had taken place. Looking back almost
one year to a day, he recalled that then:

Poland, Norway, Belgium, and Holland had been nicely butchered and hung.
The same process was under way with France. Most of the people qualified
to have an opinion, believed that England was prostrate and could be finished
off by Germany at will. England, however, rose from the ashes and for a year
has put up an increasingly strong battle. This has given the United States an

unexpected respite to look the situation over, continue our social reforms, and finally, to begin to effectively prepare for giving aid to England, and, for war.

Then after enumerating the many events of the past twelve months McConnell closed with the comment,

The trend is unmistakable. [It is] . . . almost a rushing current toward war.

Among the changes "close to home" he listed:

(1) The United States Government has clearly taken control of the milk price-fixing machinery in this State.
(2) Farmers have voted a wheat allotment with all of its implications.
(3) The Government has become the one big handler of corn in the United States. . . .

While McConnell observed with concern an increasingly "well-defined current . . . leading toward State Socialism," he urged that "we cannot indulge in violent recriminations against the administration. After all, this is our country and this administration was put in power by a majority of the so-called intelligent voters. . . . We are in a situation where increasingly direct Government action comes into the day-to-day operations."

McConnell saw no good in bitter cynicism, for that "makes us as individuals, ineffective." He held to the hope "that when the real test comes, the nation will sort of jell and act as a unit."

To McConnell the job of the G.L.F. was unmistakably clear. "We must continue to be an effective group in carrying out services to farmers."

The failure to do this would lose for farmers "the best bulwark possible against farmers losing the right to think, to act, and to live as individuals. . . . for [the G.L.F.] is the best means of self-expression and of raising the sights of farm people that has ever been developed in any society known to man. . . . In time of war," McConnell went on, "the cooperatives are the only means farmers have of exerting any influence in public planning."

While McConnell was thus endeavoring to condition the minds of key personnel he saw two immediate problems. A serious labor dispute was brewing at the Buffalo Mill which could immediately create an emergency. Defense inventories had to be built throughout the territory before the heavy winter feeding season.

THE BIG STRIKE

The threatened strike at the Buffalo Mill became a fact on July 1. The issue was clearly drawn. The G.L.F. refused to renew a contract which gave the Union control in hiring labor and demanded the right to have a voice in the quality of labor employed in its Mill. For fourteen weeks the Mill was closed until a new contract was signed which was satisfactory to both parties.

The strike was a significant event in G.L.F. history for two reasons:

1. It led to the establishment of better relations between the G.L.F. and Union labor as evidenced by a long no-strike record which followed.

2. It caused the G.L.F. to develop alternative manufacturing outlets so that it would not be dependent upon any one mill for supplies.

The desirability of decentralizing mill operations had become immediately apparent as the strike began to affect farmers. On July 23 the Board of Directors instructed the Annual Community Patrons' Meetings to vote on the following question:

Shall this Cooperative proceed to develop enough feed mixing plants to provide for the entire feed requirements of its patrons; these plants to be so located that if necessary they can be operated by patrons themselves?

The response to this question gave G.L.F. management the full support of its members, and it was not long before local facilities were taxed to the utmost in grinding and mixing feed.

When the strike was over conditions could never be the same as they had been before the strike, and new mill facilities which had been planned for the Buffalo Mill were found to be not needed.

In his annual report to the Stockholders' Meeting on November 6, McConnell dealt at length with the effects of the strike. He admitted that it had been costly but he was proud of the fact that service had not been seriously impaired. He emphasized that G.L.F. was not anti-labor and offered publicly with the full approval of his Board "to sit down, anywhere, any time, with responsible Union and Government labor leaders in an attempt to work out a program which will fully guarantee the recognition of unions, the right to bargain collectively, proper working conditions, and a wage scale commensurate with what farmers are able to pay."

McConnell felt that "If there is anything this strike has taught G.L.F. it is not to get too many eggs in one basket. . . ." "Most businesses," he said, "carry a form of insurance called 'Use and Occupancy' as a protection for the business against plant disasters. I'm now convinced that the best form of 'Use and Occupancy' insurance for G.L.F. is enough decentralization of facilities, so that the stoppage of no single plant [by strike, fire or other disaster] can stop the flow of materials through the G.L.F. services."

At this time the attack on Pearl Harbor was but one month ahead. The defense program was beginning to have an increasing effect on agriculture. Supplies of materials, such as nitrogen for fertilizers, needed for war industries were becoming increasingly scarce, and inflationary pressures were forcing prices up. The G.L.F. was following these developments closely and was taking steps to meet any problem that might arise.

During the defense period the G.L.F. was also strengthening its organization structure. In March, 1940, the General Manager had recommended to the Board that some better method be adopted for nominating directors other than those nominated by the Grange and Farm Bureau. The Dairymen's League had given up its right to nominate directors.

McConnell proposed the division of G.L.F. territory into nominating districts, two in New Jersey, two in Pennsylvania and three in New York State. This would give a board of 13 directors, including the six nominated by the Grange and Farm Bureau for New York State.

This proposal was accepted and the bylaws were amended to make the plan effective, at the Stockholders' Meeting in 1941. This change was a step forward in giving recognition to the advisory committeemen in electing directors, in that it extended the system used in New Jersey and Pennsylvania to New York State.[2]

Personnel Administration also required attention. A Cornell Doctoral dissertation by John Marshall O'Brien, *The Management of Labor Relations in the Cooperative Grange League Federation Exchange, Inc.*, (1939) had stated that "the methods of employee management are practically the same as those used when the G.L.F. was in its infancy." O'Brien described the existing state of personnel administration as follows: "G.L.F. has no formal personnel administrator or manager, nor is there any one person, or group of persons, whose duties and responsibilities are thought of in terms of formal personnel procedure."

As a result of his study he urged "the establishment of a formal, centralized personnel system" under the direction of a personnel administrator "empowered with the authority commensurate with his tremendous responsibilities."[3]

Although this study undoubtedly had a decided influence on top management thinking, little was done along the lines suggested until July 1, 1941. By this time preparations for war had made the need of a better

[2] At the Annual Meeting in 1942, another significant change was made in the bylaws of the Exchange. It provided that all shares of common stock owned by G.L.F. in retail operations were to be "held in trust" by G.L.F. for the farmer patrons of such retail cooperatives. This made clear that the G.L.F. intended to be the servant of its patrons rather than the master. Another provision in the revised bylaws made this clear by giving any retail cooperative serving G.L.F. patrons the right to divorce itself from the G.L.F. should it vote to become independent. The G.L.F. welcomed a test of this bylaw provision in early 1944 when the G.L.F. retail cooperative at White Oak voted to withdraw from the G.L.F. However, the vote was not honestly made, and it was declared invalid by a second meeting of the patrons. No other attempt has been made by a local G.L.F. retail cooperative to free itself from the parent organization.

[3] This comprehensive audit of G.L.F. personnel procedures was made with the full cooperation of G.L.F. officials. C. W. Sadd, then in charge of the University of the G.L.F., represented the General Manager as contact man in helping O'Brien make all necessary arrangements within the G.L.F. Sadd informs me that there were "a few spots where some of the people thought we were prying into some things that were not our business." Letter, to author, January 12, 1959.

coordinated system of personnel administration more obvious and more acceptable. At that time H. E. Shackleton was made Director of Personnel Relations. In announcing Shackleton's appointment McConnell said: "He will assist Mr. H. E. Babcock in running the G.L.F. School of Cooperative Administration and, as his title indicates, will deal with personnel relationships throughout the entire Exchange." Although this was but a modest step toward a more advanced system of personnel administration, it served G.L.F.'s emergency requirements. In Chapter 43 we will see how this rather informal arrangement gradually evolved into a well-articulated program of personnel management.

For two years the G.L.F. had been preparing itself to meet the supreme test of war. When the Pearl Harbor attack came, it was as ready, in resources and determination, as any organization could be.

IV. STRENGTHENING THE STRUCTURE, 1940-1950

CHAPTER 25

The G.L.F. Helps Win the War

The finest effort is called for on the part of all G.L.F. people today.
J. A. McConnell, *January 1942*

PEARL HARBOR did not catch G.L.F. flatfooted. Instead, it unleashed all of the pent-up energies of the organization. Jim McConnell gave the lead to all G.L.F. workers in a statement carried in the *G.L.F. Week* of December 13, 1941, "Your Business and the War":

This country will have to make some tremendous adjustments to move over to a real wartime economy. . . . In the meantime, there are a few things to be done: (1) Keep your inventories as high as your finances will permit. . . . (2) Keep your prices as nearly as you can on the market. (3) Keep feed orders at the Mill well ahead. (4) Keep shoving superphosphate out on farms. (5) Remember that the defense feed storage program is available . . . I look for some serious tie-ups in transportation before spring.

At this time McConnell announced that the schedule of the G.L.F. School of Administration had been canceled. "While this adjustment is being made I consider it inadvisable to pull G.L.F. people away from their operations even for a few days."

On January 5, 1942, McConnell called the District Managers together to mobilize all forces to meet the crisis. He opened his talk with these words:

For over two years this country watched the storm clouds of war building solidly along the horizon, much as we oftentimes, on a hot summer afternoon, watch the building-up of a tremendous thunder shower. We hoped it would go around, much the same as a thunder shower often does. We saw it coming, we felt sure it would hit, and still we seemed powerless to close the windows and put ourselves in shipshape to weather the storm. It took Pearl Harbor to make us realize that the storm had hit. We are at war.

Experience the preceding summer in attempting to increase feed storage on farms had proved that "while the time was right to do this in terms of cold logic, psychologically we could not make it stick."

McConnell was concerned with getting every ounce of support for the war effort from every G.L.F. employee. He called the services of G.L.F. just as essential as manning the boats, the airplanes and the guns.

He did not overlook the importance of membership work, for it was essential to help members meet their problems. "But," he declared, "I want to be sure what good membership work is." In calling a series of meetings with District Managers and the operating men in G.L.F. "to better adapt G.L.F. to the present needs of farmers," he saw immediately ahead problems in keeping transportation channels open; in meeting shortages of burlap, feed, fertilizer, and many other supplies; and in getting labor to man the facilities.

The need for preserving the G.L.F. as an Institution was stressed. "In order to preserve it, it first must be made effective through the war effort. That's what we are going to devote our main time and effort to from now on." To preserve it he saw the need of keeping it adequately financed, not only to do the service job but to take the shock of adjustment when the war was over. "We have got the job of keeping this Institution adequately financed in spite of hell and high water. . . . I expect to call for action and get it. . . . When the signal is called I know that people will respond cheerfully to the needs of the times."

On January 29, 1942, McConnell followed up with a printed letter to all G.L.F. Committeemen, in which he said, "Now that we are at war it is essential that an effective war machine be built. . . . Cooperatives like G.L.F. assume a positive significance in these times." He admitted that one could not see far enough ahead to make any very definite plans, but it was clear that work in certain vital areas could make the G.L.F. "useful during the war," and "an effective instrument after the war." These "vital" areas were membership, finances, community facilities, and materials.

(1) *Membership.* To maintain strong membership he advocated "no let-down in meetings with the farmers and their employees although they might be cut down to save travel."

(2) *Finances.* The rise in the general price level and the need for carrying larger inventories had thrown a tremendous load on the working capital. The G.L.F. would require more working capital to meet the emergency ahead and to stand the shock of adjustment at the end of the war. "There are two ways to get additional capital. By the sale of 4 percent Holding Corporation Stock and by retaining earnings. Both methods will be used. . . . Patronage dividends will have to be declared for this year in some form other than cash."

(3) *Community Facilities.* "The community warehouses, storage bins, grinders, mixers, and marketing facilities are now and will continue to be the farmer's primary line of defense not only in meeting our war emergencies but in defending ourselves against the entrenchments of other aggressive groups in our society."

(4) *Materials.* All evidence indicated that it was going to be difficult to obtain the materials needed to run farms efficiently. The farm, itself, was held to be the best place to carry future requirements of feed, ferti-

lizers, and other supplies. This was not hoarding but "just good defense procedure" to help relieve pressure on transportation agencies in the bleak months ahead.

As the G.L.F. swung into action one of the problems was to replace and train men lost to the Army, to keep facilities operating effectively. Although shortages in supplies, equipment and manpower were general they were met by improvised methods, substitution, and make-do.

Every effort was made to get the G.L.F. on a war footing. For example, a "Save That Bag!" program was designed to help meet the bag shortage[1] and a simplified fertilizer program was adopted to eliminate little-used fertilizers.

In March "alert areas" were organized to handle emergency community problems, for it was recognized that many problems could best be met locally by informal organizations of the members. These "alert area" groups mobilized the G.L.F. to the grass roots and made a contribution of great value to the war effort.

In the early summer the G.L.F. set up a Community Transportation Plan. This involved obtaining pledges from farmers owning trucks so that if the railroads should be tied up, G.L.F. could call on these farmers to move supplies into the community.

While G.L.F.'s energies were being devoted to war problems, a disturbing development briefly challenged the foundations of Northeast agriculture. In an attempt to get dairy farmers of the Northeast to join its District 50, the United Mine Workers of the C.I.O. began an intensive membership campaign with paid organizers. These organizers promised higher prices for milk through collective bargaining with no increase in consumer prices.

As the success of this drive, and its extension to other products, could have emasculated the long-established cooperative enterprises of this region, they cooperated in March, 1942, with the general farm organizations in the area to set up a defensive organization known as "Free Farmers, Inc."

Its principal objective was to inform farmers of the implications in the "District 50" plan. Thousands of farmers signed Free Farmers pledge cards "to fight to the end attempts to bring American farmers and the marketing of farm products under the control or domination of United Mine Workers of America." In turn, Free Farmers, Inc., agreed to pay pledges for loss or damage "caused by strike, riot, civil commotion, or malicious damage" resulting from carrying out the pledge. As the welfare

---

[1] See R. B. Gervan, "Save That Bag!" *News for Farmer Cooperatives,* March, 1942. Few now recall how serious the bag shortage was in 1942.

of the Northeast dairy farmer was a primary concern to the G.L.F., its board of directors fully endorsed Free Farmers, Inc., and pledged it necessary organizational and financial support. The Dairymen's League was one of the G.L.F.'s parents, and the success of the "District 50" drive would have largely destroyed the League's cooperative effectiveness. The G.L.F. could not stand by while one of its parent organizations was concerned.

While the "District 50" campaign was largely stopped in 1942, it cropped up again in 1943 before final collapse.[2]

To conserve capital a plan for distributing patronage refunds in Participation Certificates was approved by the Board of Directors at its June, 1942, meeting. Shortly after this, McConnell released a printed statement on "G.L.F. Patronage Refunds, 1941-42," for staff and members.

This stressed "the need of keeping all of this year's earnings in your cooperative in order to keep it effective." G.L.F. was to distribute refunds in the form of a security—a Participation Certificate—instead of following the usual practice of paying the patronage refunds in cash. "In effect, by use of Participation Certificates, G.L.F. is borrowing money from its membership to use in carrying on the business."

The rate of interest on the Participation Certificates had been set by the Board of Directors at 4 percent. After January 1, 1943, the certificates were to be convertible into G.L.F. Common Stock, at the option of the holder. Members were to be issued regular G.L.F. Common Stock (voting); while non-member purchasers, for statutory reasons, were to be issued G.L.F. Class B Common Stock (non-voting), a new type of stock.[3]

Although the certificates were not negotiable, to facilitate sale or transfer, the G.L.F. was prepared to purchase these certificates at face value from men who found it absolutely necessary to convert them into cash. Members were encouraged to convert their certificates into Common Stock as soon as possible after January 1, 1943, "in order to keep the ownership of G.L.F. in the hands of the actual users." Moreover, the G.L.F. would eventually call all of the certificates not converted into Common Stock.

The record for 1941-1942 was good. There was a substantial increase in volume of business, measured both in tons and dollars, and savings reached $2,700,000 as a result of steadily rising commodity prices and lower costs of maintaining inventories.

To meet the growing need for capital the Board of Directors set aside substantial reserves before distributing $1,600,000 in patronage refunds. Moreover, even the bulk of this amount was to be retained for use as

[2] The full story of this dramatic incident is unfolded in the 1942 and 1943 issues of the *American Agriculturist*. Of special interest are the full-page advertisements of the Dairymen's League which fought District 50 with all its resources.

[3] The Board, in September, 1942, increased Common Stock from one to five million dollars. Provision was made for 200,000 shares of this ($1,000,000) in Class B.

operating capital through issuing it to patrons in the form of Participation Certificates rather than in cash.[4]

Significantly, McConnell concluded his 1942 annual report by saying, "G.L.F. is a big cooperative and we must have means of dealing with . . . great forces . . . G.L.F. is a federation of local, independent community cooperatives, local dealers and wholesale services, highly decentralized as to local activities, but closely correlated together . . . to get results."

Up to this time the G.L.F., through its Holding Corporation, had exclusively financed the G.L.F. retail stores. In March, 1943, the Board adopted a policy under which each retail unit would sell preferred stock to its patrons, and, if desirable, pay patronage refunds on such preferred stock. This paved the way for a substantial degree of patron ownership in these community facilities, and recognized their growing importance. It also broadened the G.L.F.'s capital base.

Throughout the war years the G.L.F. was vigilant to see that government programs did not encroach on the right of farmers to serve themselves. Of particular concern to the G.L.F. was a lime and phosphate distribution program of the Agricultural Adjustment Administration. McConnell dealt with this problem in his Annual Report for 1942.

Little by little, the United States Government, through the Agricultural Adjustment Administration, is by-passing and making useless the country dealer and the farmers' cooperative as a handler of lime. The same practice is being started with superphosphate. . . . *I challenge the policy of Government in respect to the necessity and wisdom of such a course. I am pointing out that through Triple A, the Department of Agriculture is gradually establishing in every farm community in this nation, a distribution system completely under the control of government.*

McConnell saw nothing in the war emergency that required such government action that could "be stopped only by sharp resistance of farmers themselves."

This public expression of the G.L.F. could not be ignored, and after several months of negotiation the Agricultural Adjustment Administration worked out an experimental program for New York State which gave the farmer a free choice of distribution agency in obtaining his lime and phosphate for conservation purposes. McConnell considered this an important achievement. "As far as I know," he said in reporting to the Board on September 30, 1943, "this is the first indication that the forward march of Triple A toward the control of the distribution of farm supplies has been checked."[5]

[4] For a full account of how this campaign was presented to G.L.F. members, see "Ploughing Back Wartime Dividends," in *News for Farmer Cooperatives*, for March, 1942.

[5] It is of interest that the G.L.F. later helped effectively to block government sponsorship of cooperative fertilizer manufacturing facilities proposed under a bill sup-

The G.L.F. missed no opportunity to build *esprit de corps*. In November, 1942, an attractive pamphlet, *The Spirit of the G.L.F.*, was issued, with a foreword by Babcock declaring, "G.L.F. is a fighting unit in the country's front line of food production." Members were urged to enlist in the "B.F.I.," short for "Bureau of Farm Ideas," and pledge themselves to send in suggestions to help G.L.F. meet war problems.

The growing shortage of feed had become a serious problem by December 26, 1942, when McConnell informed all patrons by printed postcard that the G.L.F. and other large cooperatives were discontinuing certain formula feeds because of the critical shortage of high protein ingredients. He announced that during the emergency ingredients would not be shown on the G.L.F. feed tag although the formula for each lot of feed would be obtainable from service agencies.

The lead article in the *G.L.F. Week* of January 11 explained that the supply of burlap feed bags was dangerously low. Patrons were asked to conserve and return bags for re-use, and to accept delivery in cotton bags.

To meet the continuing feed emergency, the G.L.F. took an active interest in setting up at this time the Feed Industry Council, comprised of representatives of the feed dealers, farmer-owned cooperatives, and nutritionists from the agricultural colleges. The Council was to serve as a fact-finding body to investigate feed supplies and needs, and work with government agencies on feed industry problems, and develop programs for the more effective use of feedstuffs. General Manager McConnell was named Chairman.

On February 17-18, representatives of the Feed Industry Council and the U. S. Department of Agriculture worked out an agreement for a voluntary protein conservation program which was publicized in a joint statement by Secretary of Agriculture Claude Wickard and James A. McConnell, as Chairman of the Council. They pledged their organizations to explain the plan to farmers so that feed manufacturers and distributors might conserve protein and help farmers use feeds properly.

As the feed shortage intensified during the spring, many feed distributors in the Northeast restricted their supplies to established customers. This caused many farmers to turn to the G.L.F. for feed, and it was difficult to deny them service. This placed a heavy burden on the G.L.F. and made it clear that feed rationing was needed. On June 7, G.L.F. put into effect an allotment program.

In announcing the plan to all G.L.F. employees, McConnell called feed

ported by the American Farm Bureau Federation. At that time, October 1945, the Board in a unanimously adopted resolution declared "the fertilizer industry of the United States, including farm cooperatives, has demonstrated its ability . . . to adequately meet the farm fertilizer demands of the nation. . . ."

allocation one of the most crucial tests in the history of the G.L.F. "For twenty years we have claimed that people could do things for themselves through cooperation. . . . If there ever was the chance to prove this to the hilt we have the chance now in doing a bang-up first-class job of handling feed allocations." He went on to say, "G.L.F. didn't ask for feed rationing. . . . We tried to avoid it as long as we could, but it is here . . . and carries its own priority, which is AA-1. Unless we meet it squarely and lick it our membership-ownership program will fail. We must accept the logic of events and place feed allocation at the top of the list of immediate jobs now facing G.L.F. . . . Unless we do we will have neither membership nor ownership."

Under the feed allocation program, G.L.F. Mills issued coupons to service agencies for each ton of feed allotted and these coupons were surrendered when feed was ordered. No feed was to be furnished to new patrons. The plan was built on the assumption that it would be handled in the local communities through individual service agencies, and they were urged to handle the program so effectively that it would increase the appreciation of G.L.F. patrons for local G.L.F. service. It was up to each service agency to distribute its allotment of feed among patrons, and individual allotments were worked out for each agency with district managers in collaboration with G.L.F. Mills.

To carry on the plan effectively, joint committee meetings were held throughout G.L.F. territory where answers were given to questions on how to carry out the program. To the question, "Why doesn't G.L.F. allot feed clear down to the patron and save me all of these headaches?" the answer was given, "Nobody in G.L.F. is smart enough to work out a program that will be fair to all G.L.F. farmers. Only in the local community can the needs of the individual farmers be balanced against available supplies to arrive at a fair basis for distribution."

It was the job of each service agency to work with his local committee and district manager in stabilizing its feed operations on an allocation basis, in accordance with general standards for meeting patrons' feed requirements. This program was continued throughout most of the war, and even into the post-war years.

The allocation program was running smoothly when McConnell presented his report at the Annual Meeting on November 5, 1943, for he did not stress the feed problem. Instead, he gave major attention to the "pattern being developed," through "operations," "membership activities," "member ownership," and "research," the four legs of "the G.L.F. Service Platform."

The year had been good from the standpoint of volume and savings which reached new highs. Capital was again being conserved by the issuance of patronage refunds by Participation Certificates, but McConnell thought payment of patronage refunds in cash might be resumed "not this next year but possibly in the summer of 1945."

Most of the needs of members were being met although priority ratings were in effect on many supply items. The Farm Supplies system of seven central warehouses, providing weekly service to local communities, was making supplies available where most needed. Although the manpower regulations were "hurting," G.L.F. was maintaining an effective force of trained personnel.

During 1944 the attention of the G.L.F. was focused on building a sense of member-ownership and of planning for the future. McConnell preferred not to think of this as "special post-war planning" which was the theme of the day, for he believed that all successful concerns should plan several years ahead under all conditions. He saw in the developing research program the kind of planning needed. The new P & C Family Foods program, the recognition of local community services, and the new attitude in membership work were all closely related to this new research approach. These important developments are fully treated in the chapters which follow.

G.L.F. was now operating with high effectiveness. In the face of war-time restrictions, it was finding supplies and getting them to members. It was changing feed formulas repeatedly to make use of available ingredients. It was also giving real help to farmers on their marketing problems. Of most immediate concern was the maintenance of petroleum supplies to enable farmers to operate their tractors. To take care of patrons' needs it was necessary to move, at heavy loss, petroleum by tank car from the Middle West and Southwest and by barge from the Great Lakes and canal system. The courageous way G.L.F. met this emergency gained both support and goodwill for the petroleum operations.

The record for 1943-44 was impressive. With prices rising, volume increased in almost every activity and savings reached $5,616,590. As a result, G.L.F. resumed payment of patronage refunds in cash. The amount so distributed amounted to $4,184,157, which still left $1,055,241 for reserves after dividends on common stock.

Growth was less marked in 1944-45, for the upward trend in prices had been temporarily arrested. In March, McConnell reported to the Board that "the whole feed situation has pretty well straightened out," although this optimism was to be shortlived. However, it was a year of uncertainty, with many fearing a postwar recession.

With the war over, G.L.F. was much stronger than when the struggle began. This was registered by phenomenal growth in volume and assets during the four war years, and by great extension and expansion of G.L.F. retail services as shown on the following page.

Year	Wholesale Supplies Volume		Value of Products Marketed
	In Dollars	In Tons	
1940-41	$ 48,960,219	1,457,813	$ 3,394,535
1941-42	66,446,421	1,525,360	5,581,305
1942-43	86,002,352	1,638,346	8,605,091
1943-44	114,013,013	1,880,966	12,462,956
1944-45	107,879,517	1,755,060	12,094,220

G.L.F. Exchange

		Distribution of Net Margins		
Year	Total Net Margins	Dividends on Stocks and Certificates	Patronage Refunds	Reserves and Undistributed Margins
1940-41	$1,943,566	$ 97,174	$1,124,469	$ 721,923
1941-42	3,084,182	108,228	1,470,427*	1,505,427
1942-43	3,775,751	201,257	2,027,219*	1,547,275
1943-44	5,616,590	377,192	4,184,157	1,055,241
1944-45	2,689,519	471,380	1,846,614	371,525

* In participation certificates.

G.L.F. Exchange

Year	Total Assets	Percent in Net Worth	Growth in Number of Stockholders
1940-41	$12,871,998	53.5	29,552
1941-42	17,440,392	56.5	28,869
1942-43	20,391,084	66.	31,658
1943-44	24,237,268	65.	49,934
1944-45	23,568,616	74.	60,378

Growth in Retail Stores

Year	Number	Total Assets	Volume In Dollars	Volume In Tons	Net Margins	Retail Preferred*	Margins Retained
1940-41	160	$3,767,211	$25,086,680	722,831	$ 803,629	$ 132,295	$1,063,990
1941-42	170	5,658,319	36,144,319	850,909	1,167,681	132,565	1,749,777
1942-43	177	7,257,141	44,185,937	895,257	1,389,763	1,927,425	1,166,750
1943-44	181	8,707,150	60,386,603	1,026,683	1,978,046	2,046,908	1,818,308
1944-45	194	9,467,620	59,374,617	1,073,474	1,325,672	2,022,658	2,136,616

* Stock held by farmers.

Growth of Retail Petroleum System

Year	Bulk Plants	Total Assets	Volume In Dollars	Volume In Gallons	Net Margin	Margins Retained
1940-41	32	$558,224	$2,513,439	18,920,160	$ 79,721	$ 4,451*
1941-42	37	808,800	4,585,893	30,704,237	145,303	152,645
1942-43	45	841,654	5,742,431	35,568,202	157,163	309,720
1943-44	45	871,433	6,759,973	41,238,587	213,446	444,839
1944-45	45	429,655	6,845,254	42,963,273	209,652	639,496

* Denotes loss.

This rapid growth had not been without cost. Educational work had been seriously curtailed, and many other basic programs had been set aside, or de-emphasized, "for the duration." For one thing, the pressure for supplies had forced G.L.F. to place less stress on quality.

McConnell recognized the need of conversion back to peacetime conditions in his annual report for 1945. "I know I am representing Board policy when I say that . . . for the next year or two, perhaps three, G.L.F. will . . . forget everything except carrying out its own functions in . . . establishing high quality standards, living up to those standards, getting efficient operations [and] building strong community cooperatives. . . ."

The G.L.F. was also moving forward in other ways. A comprehensive pension plan for employees, developed under the leadership of Silcox, was now getting established. The reorganization of services at the community level was well under way under the direction of Ed Fallon, and the responsibilities of local Committeemen in their relations with G.L.F. District Managers were at last codified in a *Committeemen's Handbook*. To McConnell, its issuance was "one of the most important events . . . in recent times."

It is also significant that in January, 1945, the G.L.F. subscribed $200,000 for a school of nutrition building at Cornell University, to be named Savage Hall, in honor of Professor E. S. Savage—the father of the open-formula principle, the foundation stone of the G.L.F.—who had died on November 22, 1943. Thus, G.L.F. recognized its great debt to Savage with a memorial that would help perpetuate his lifetime interests which were shared with G.L.F.

Based on its record of service during the war and its strength as the war ended, McConnell was justified in his confidence that the G.L.F. could meet any problems that might arise.

CHAPTER 26

Research to the Front 1943-45

G.L.F.'s research is restive, curious, and game to take on anything in the way of experiment which a wild-eyed patron or a crazy employee may suggest. . . .
                    H. E. BABCOCK's *Address to Service Agency School,*
                                    November 12, 1944

S PEAKING TO THE BOARD OF DIRECTORS on April 12, 1943, General Manager McConnell said, "Some companies reach maturity and 'dry up' because they have no program for future development." He proposed that G.L.F. have a well thought-out and well-balanced plan of research.

In a way, research was embedded in the G.L.F. Its founders had conceived of the G.L.F. as an instrument to bring research results of the land-grant colleges home to farmers, and G.L.F. had made use of research from its formation. The feed program was built on the research leadership of Professor Savage. Similarly, G.L.F. drew on Cornell research in drawing up specifications for fertilizer, oil and other items. As far back as 1925 Babcock had joined in a research experiment to test the value of feeds, and when he resigned as General Manager in 1937 he did so partly in order that he might devote more time to research.

The new emphasis on research thus did not come as a bolt from the blue. The G.L.F. was expanding rapidly and in many directions, and there was an interest in finding out how to make new programs work. For example, much careful thought had gone into the marketing and petroleum programs, and various ideas were being tried out. G.L.F. had been one of the first cooperatives to see the possibilities of frozen food locker plants and, after a considerable amount of investigation, it had opened one of the first plants of this kind, on a pilot study basis.

Probably the most important element leading toward greater emphasis on research was the restless, inquiring spirit of H. E. Babcock, who, freed from the responsibilities of general management, was able to devote his attention to the development and promotion of ideas. The School of Nutrition of Cornell University sprang from Babcock's research-oriented mind in 1941.[1]

He used his farm, Sunnygables, as a laboratory to test out a home

---

[1] It is significant that Babcock served as Chairman of the Board of Trustees of Cornell University, from 1939 to 1946. See Ruby Green Smith, *The People's College,* pp. 109-110.

freezer and for experiments with grass silage, permanent pasture, Birdsfoot trefoil, electric fence controllers, rubber-mounted farm equipment, winter barley, weed control in grain by dusting and spraying, the development of better pasture mixtures, farm storage for feed and grain, the doodlebug, the buck rake, and standards for farm equipment.

Whether or not Babcock sold McConnell the idea of setting up a research department is of little importance for the two men saw eye to eye on its need. At any rate, the research program was tailormade for H. E. Babcock and might not have been started without his availability as Research Director.

The Program Takes Shape

Babcock unveiled his plans for the research program at a G.L.F. Managers' Conference on September 28, 1943. Significantly, he opened his talk by saying. "The final goal of all G.L.F. research must be to support the broad objective of self-expression which farmers seek through their cooperative."

Believing that the time was ripe for farmers to take an inventory of their satisfaction with the G.L.F., he proposed "audits of membership thinking on goods and services." Babcock had been much impressed by a study recently completed by Cornell Professors Dwight Sanderson and W. A. Anderson on the attitude of members toward their cooperatives, and this no doubt suggested how the G.L.F. might make somewhat similar studies. He paid tribute to the Cornell study by saying, *"I am quite sure that this survey resulted in setting ahead and increasing the emphasis on G.L.F.'s program of member ownership."*

As a follow-up to the earlier Cornell study, G.L.F. was also developing with Professors Sanderson and Anderson a project which would "ferret out and disclose the attitudes of farm women toward cooperatives in general and the G.L.F. in particular."

Another project would examine the possibilities of community freezer-locker plants. Although G.L.F. was keeping well informed in this field through experimental use of home boxes and by studies being made at the Geneva Experiment Station, more research was needed. Babcock pointed up the problem by saying, "G.L.F. cannot stand pat on a development in which so many of its members are interested, nor can it drift blindly into the construction and operation of community freezer locker plants and the manufacturing and distribution of home freezer boxes."

G.L.F. was meeting this problem by actively working with two committees of the Cornell School of Nutrition: the first, to develop a blueprint of a model freezer-locker plant to be built in conjunction with the cooperative food store in Ithaca; the second, to deal with all processing techniques to be used in the new plant and related technical questions.

G.L.F. was concerned with another processing problem—how to receive and slaughter animals that could not be handled by the community freezer locker plants being planned for processing fruits and vegetables. Babcock saw the need for livestock packing houses since "G.L.F.'s projected chain of super markets will need to handle meats in order to run a balanced operation" and because "cull dairy cows, cull ewes, and cull chickens, to say nothing of beef, pork and poultry for meat, are important sources of farm income to members of G.L.F." To gain experience a pilot packing house was already in operation. It was to be used "not only to learn how to institute new techniques in the handling of livestock and poultry products, but also to train a skeleton personnel to handle larger operations in the future."

A project was nearing completion, under the leadership of Arthur J. Wells, on the uses and limitations of Patrons' Pantries in selling food through retail stores. These were large display rooms in service stores with girls in charge. There were two definite opinions on how farm supplies could be best distributed. One group favored setting up specialized stores for farm supplies other than feed, seed and fertilizer. The other held that supplies of all types should be handled best in one operation. To resolve this conflict of opinion a complete farm supply store was to be operated on an experimental basis.

In much the same manner a community farm repair shop was to be established "to determine the practicability of farmers in a communtiy utilizing their Cooperative G.L.F. to supply themselves with the men and equipment to repair their farm machinery and in off seasons to make gadgets which they need for the farms." It was also planned to experiment in the operation of some community owned service equipment like paint spray rigs and combines.[2]

Babcock summarized his program by saying that these projects were all designed to widen the use which G.L.F.'s member-owners make of their organization. He had authorized these projects to "carry out the wishes of farmers who believe in free enterprise and self-help."

In this preview of his research program Babcock pointed out that he had inherited research done by various G.L.F. operating units costing some $65,000 annually. He declared: "I intend to work closely with the individuals who are responsible for these activities with the object of preventing duplication and of gradually building a carefully correlated program of research for the Institution as a whole."

[2] Mr. McConnell, in reading the draft of this chapter, notes here that "G.L.F. and H.E.B. used research as a blow-off valve. Many things were kept on a pilot basis this way and proven or discarded."

On September 30, Babcock, in reporting to the Board of Directors, said: "The beginning of G.L.F. research must be the relationship with the patron member at the community level. G.L.F. research, for the most part, should not go along the line of gadgets. It should strive for a pattern of services at the community level."

On October 13, he presented "an outline of research activities for the G.L.F." for Board approval. This outline, here given, shows the broad scope of the work to be done and its estimated burden on the research fund:

OUTLINE OF G.L.F. RESEARCH

% Research Fund		
10%	#1	*Patrons' Attitudes* (men-women-youth)
		1-A Toward Cooperation
		1-B Toward Cooperative Responsibilities
		1-C Toward G.L.F. Financing
		1-D Toward G.L.F. Community & Area Services
	#2	*Patrons' Services at Community & Area Levels*
50%		2-A Farm Repair Shop
		2-B Farm Supply Store
		2-C Farm Machine Service
		2-D Family Food Pantry
		2-E Freezer Locker Plant
		2-F Family Foods Super-market
		2-G Diner or Restaurant
		2-H Farmers' Market
		2-I Lumber Yard and Farm Woodlot Services
		2-J Egg Station
		2-K Canning Factory
		2-L Cold Storage & Freezer
		2-M Grain & Bean Elevator
		2-N Flour Mill
		2-O Livestock Packing Plant
		(others to be added from time to time)
10%	#3	*Services to Communities*
		3-A Territory-wide
		3-B Area-wide
5%	#4	*Personnel and Labor Relations*
10%	#5	*Specifications*
5%	#6	*Equipment and Devices*
5%	#7	*Position, Performance and Forecasts*
5%	#8	*Public and Government Relations*
100%		

In submitting this outline, Babcock suggested that attention be directed to the fields of work under the eight major projects "to decide whether the ground is covered to your satisfaction. . . . My idea is that adequate research in the areas listed should provide you with the basic information you need to decide most policies which will come before you."

Babcock proposed to place these projects and sub-projects under the direction of special committees with a common recording secretary.

"*It is my thought,*" said Babcock, "*that by careful selection of commit- tees a large number of G.L.F. junior executives may be broadened in their experience and tried out for their abilities.*"

The research program was given further encouragement by the General Manager in his address to the Annual Stockholders' Meeting on November 5, 1943. McConnell referred to research as one of the four legs which supported the G.L.F. service platform. He said:

We are not building a cooperative just for today, but one which will be of continuing service. The stability and continuing usefulness of this service plat- form depends, in a large degree, on how effectively we use this leg of the plat- form in conducting research, not on gadgets and raw materials, but rather on methods of performing community services.

In answer to the question, "Where is G.L.F. going?" he saw many changes ahead which would show up "largely at the community level."

Like Babcock, McConnell was particularly interested in the possibilities of freezer locker plants in the marketing of cull dairy cattle. "We cannot do the farmer any good in this field until we have learned how to run freezer-lockers and how to tie up local slaughter houses with them."

G.L.F. thinking was changing rapidly with respect to the type of facili- ties needed for handling feed and other supplies. No longer would small buildings and hand labor suffice. "Today we have to start thinking of a more complete service, which includes not only formula feeds but grind- ing services, seed treating services, lime spreading services, and the Lord only knows what the future may require. . . . The sheer volume of business is forcing us to change our methods."

McConnell posed the problem coming from this situation by saying: "No one in G.L.F. has yet designed the various types of buildings and facilities that we now need in different size communities. Work is being done on this problem, but it has not reached the blue print stage."

McConnell then turned to the problems involved in providing farm families "with items of food which they do not themselves produce." He pointed out that G.L.F. in its marketing operations was engaged on a large scale in canning operations, flour operations, and cereal operations, and said, "It is no longer a question of 'Shall G.L.F. enter the food busi- ness?' *When it decided to enter the field of marketing it was in the food business.*" Nevertheless, he pointed out:

The whole method of G.L.F. food distribution to farmers as well as food distribution to city people—which is part of our marketing program—is still to be determined. We cannot lightly dismiss it by saying that the food which

G.L.F. handles in its marketing operations cannot be distributed to farm families, because the present feed store through which G.L.F. members are served is not suitable for handling food. It may or may not be. Perhaps by slight modifications, it can be. It may, however, require a complete new distribution system. Our research job is to keep an open mind and find out.

Another problem of much concern to G.L.F. management was how to provide hardware service, or service on supplies other than feed, seed and fertilizer. To answer this question G.L.F. was exploring "how to operate a community farm supply store on commodities other than feed, seed, and fertilizer." Of related interest was the problem of providing parts and repair service on farm machinery—a matter of great moment to farmers due to materials and labor shortages.

A Research Job for Everybody

With the stage set by McConnell at the annual meeting, Babcock set the program in motion with an inspiring address at the December Managers' Conference. He named the committee members for the eight major projects and for the 24 sub-projects. He called on every G.L.F. man to be a research man. The author, who was present at this conference, recalls vividly the enthusiastic response. The G.L.F. was to be a hive of research activities operating in all parts of G.L.F. At this time Babcock's thinking on how the research was to be done was still in flux.

As the various research committees began to function, they rapidly found that research calls for special abilities, training, attitudes and approaches which could not be provided through group procedures. Some succeeded in finding significant work to do while others, after a meeting or two, languished and then folded up. As Babcock later explained:

Experience revealed that this approach involved (1) too many committee meetings; (2) too many people; (3) too many projects. [It was found] that few people possess a genuine research point of view and that the tendency of many of the persons involved was to manipulate projects to substantiate foregone conclusions rather than to seek comprehensive information as a basis for plans and policies.[3]

It would be wrong to assess this experience as a failure, for it had the virtue of forcing G.L.F. management personnel to think as a team, an ob-

[3] As reported by Committee of Eastern States Farmers' Exchange, November 14 and 15, 1944, Silcox, in reviewing the research program, at a Service Agency School, November 12, 1944, explained that: "Many of these committees, after several meetings, arrived at the conclusion that there was no research problem of immediate or future importance. As Chairman of a Committee on Transportation Services, I recommended, after several meetings, that our committee be discharged because most of our problems were operating problems which were being solved in our day-to-day activities."

jective from the beginning. Babcock saw the research program as a means of keeping G.L.F. management "alert and on its toes," and he considered this "by-product" of great significance. This early "cut and try" experience also helped determine the areas where research could best be applied, and those who could make most use of it.

RESEARCH PROJECT NO. 1

No time was lost in getting Project No. 1 under way, to determine the attitude of farmers toward their Cooperative. On January 31, 1944, Babcock stated that the committee in charge of this project was employing teams of three, consisting of outstanding farmers with college experience in making farm management surveys, to work in typical territories. One month was to be spent on gathering information in the field and two months were to be devoted to its analysis. Then the report was to be made to the committee which represented top management. Babcock said the main objective was to keep G.L.F. on the beam and not allow it to go sour.[4]

In the next few weeks plans were tightened up. One team of four under the leadership of George H. Maughan, was to gather the desired information in seven selected communities scattered throughout G.L.F. territory in New York State. The selection of the four-man team was an important part of the plan. Each man was "a real farmer with callouses on his hands." None had been previously employed by G.L.F. One was a patron of a G.L.F.-managed store and a committeeman for the store. Two were patrons of G.L.F. Agent-Buyers, and one was not even a G.L.F. patron.

To facilitate the work of the four-man team a printed questionnaire was designed, coded for tabulation and analysis. The technical work involved in drafting questionnaires, tabulation, analysis and reporting results was largely entrusted to Warren A. Ranney. Altogether 1,139 farmers, patrons and non-patrons, provided information for the study. The survey was made from farm to farm and was not built on mailing lists or any other arbitrary, pre-determined guides.[5]

The work on the survey proceeded according to plan, and Mr. Babcock was in position to report to the Board of Directors on June 12, 1944. No record of Mr. Babcock's report is available, but he drew on two documents resulting from the study. The first was a tabulation of the answers ob-

[4] In talk to staff of Farmer Cooperative Service, Washington, D.C.

[5] The procedure followed was outlined in an illustrated brochure, entitled, "What's the Boss Thinking," issued by the G.L.F. in June 1954. It explained the objects and methods of the study, but gave no results. "The men who did the field work in this survey went into each community with a free hand. Their only job was to come out with a good sample of the cross-section attitudes in the community."

tained from the interviews. The second was a narrative report written by the four-man team at the conclusion of the field work.

The principal point stressed by Mr. Babcock was that the survey revealed great lack of information by patrons interviewed on all aspects of the G.L.F. It is significant that the Board took immediate action to correct this situation. "Before Mr. Babcock left the meeting it was decided that G.L.F.'s educational program should be thrown into high gear again, and Ed Fallon was called. He entered the room as Manager of Petroleum Division Service, and left it as the Director of G.L.F. Education."[6]

The survey team's narrative report dramatized the results of the study. It gave the central idea of the auditing squad as follows:

G.L.F. has made unusual progress on the matter of growth and has done a great job as a price and quality stabilizing service to farmers. Now is the time for (a) a much clearer expression of G.L.F. aims; (b) the development of a better sense of ownership and loyalty; (c) an educational program at the farm level.

It supported these views in reverse order by saying, "Lack of interest and information in matters of general cooperative philosophy and in such details as the aims and usefulness of G.L.F. is very noticeable amongst the farmers themselves. *Education is necessary and at the farm level.*"

On the second point the report held: "Farmers have had little interest in the details of G.L.F. financing. . . . This may be a good time to develop the idea of 'ownership in proportion to use' because this, in itself, teaches the need for responsibility in financing."

On the first point, the survey disclosed that farmers realized that they need to cooperate and that "practically all were emphatic about it." However, "it was disappointing that more of them did not think of G.L.F. as the cooperative furnishing that opportunity." This interesting challenge was given: "Do G.L.F. activities fail to conform to this definition of cooperation? Could it be that G.L.F. to them is an Institution that furnishes a friendly service, free of obligation, but also lacking the power to hold them together or defend their cause?"

The squad had this to say on the need for keeping the farm point of view:

[6] As reported by C. N. Silcox to the Annual Stockholders' Meeting, November 3, 1944. Under Fallon's energetic direction the G.L.F. School of Cooperative Administration was soon carrying on an aggressive educational program for employees and committeemen throughout G.L.F. territory, using as a text book a manual comprised of articles by key executives—*You and G.L.F.* Working with H. E. Shackleton, Director of Personnel, a decentralized program was developed which placed responsibility for conducting educational work in the division personnel directors. Fallon gave the program overall planning correlation and leadership. He enlisted the full cooperation of all executives and especially district managers and supervisors in the hundred and more schools held.

It is easy for those who manage and direct cooperatives to develop and perfect methods, and to acquire habits of thinking. . . . What was once an organization managed on a contact-basis becomes one run on the basis of self-confidence. . . . The institution that becomes fat and soft needs to take off its coat and shirt and grapple again with the real elements of its business.

This was straight thinking expressed in language that couldn't be ignored. There was no disposition to challenge the final statement of the report: "We believe that G.L.F. stands in a critical, pivotal era of its development."

While Research Project No. 1 held the center of the stage work was "humming" on the other research projects.

RESEARCH PROJECT NO. 2

The work relating to community services under Research Project No. 2, was largely carried on under Sub-Projects, each supervised by a committee. Babcock took an interest in them all but he leaned heavily on Dr. Maurice Bond, on leave from Cornell University, for help. Dr. Bond recalls that the research on this project stemmed from the following questions: "What services is G.L.F. rendering? What services are needed? Are the services well coordinated? Are there duplications or omissions which need attention?"[7]

One of Bond's jobs was to get together a group of managers and supervisors to discuss the kinds of services available. He recalls that "some were on the defensive, while others were active and forward-looking" and that "one of the accomplishments that came from this work was the determination of those with imagination and foresight who could be moved into positions of greater and greater responsibility. It was interesting to see how able and promising young men grew and blossomed before the challenges set forth—while others shrank away."

Following the conferences in Ithaca, Bond with representatives of the Committee, traveled to communities where the views of farmers, store managers, Agent-Buyers and others were obtained. As a result, in many cases new facilities and new activities were brought into the community services offered by G.L.F. Bond believes that these reviews presented a real challenge to the persons responsible for community services that were then being provided, and helped bring about their better integration. He expressed this view as follows:

I am sure it was quite a stimulation to the local managers and supervisors to have this overall inquiry by persons representing the central management of the cooperative. It is a real stimulant to an able person to be challenged by

[7] Letter to author, of August 16, 1953.

central management to think of the overall services of the organization in a community rather than continue to limit his interests to that of meeting the standards of operation of his particular division or unit.

Without doubt this research emphasis contributed to the establishment of the G.L.F. Farm Service in early 1945 to achieve a better coordination of retail services.

From this early exploratory work also came the idea of setting up model community centers where various services would be provided under one general management. This idea was to be given a trial in 1945.

During all of this time, Babcock was busy spreading enthusiasm for the various research projects that were getting under way. He met with the various committees and gave them not only moral support but many ideas.

Babcock himself was a little dismayed by the genie he had let out of the bottle. In July, 1944, when Milliman advised him that Mills had set aside $50,000 for seed research he replied, "I don't know whether I am thrilled or depressed by this information. My mixed state of mind arises, I guess, from the fact that there are so many activities going on in G.L.F. under the name of research that even I, who should know about them all, haven't them all in mind. What worries me is that I am afraid many of these so-called research projects will not be productive."

He went on to say, "While $50,000 for seed research is a lot of money, it still could be poured down a rat hole pretty fast."

However, Babcock was undaunted. He proposed to Milliman that he work with Bibbins on a plan of seed research, and offered this suggestion: "The two greatest agricultural assets of the Northeast are its pastures and its hayfields. How about research aimed at providing pastures in July and August and hayfields which will produce year after year without reseeding."

The Revised Program

By the process of the survival of the fittest some of the projects were winnowed out while greater emphasis was placed on others. On August 7, 1944, Babcock, following consultation and clearance with the Management Committee, boiled down the G.L.F. Research Program into five major projects, each under the supervision of a special committee: I. Audits; II. Community Services; III. Specifications for Goods; IV. Equipment and Devices; V. Patrons' Welfare.

Under Project No. I, Audits, Babcock explained that the quest of this research was not so much information as "tested methods of making various audits."

Five kinds of audits were proposed. The first was designed to find out the attitude of all farmers toward G.L.F. Now that this type of audit had been tested it could be applied quickly on any of numerous problems. The second audit was designed to develop a method to audit the attitudes of G.L.F. Committeemen. The third audit was to "discover ways to make institutional audits of cooperatives' financing more informative and more understandable to farmer directors." The fourth audit was to evaluate the adequacy of *community services* used by farmers, the theory being that this would "rally local support for additions or improvements" and give "dimensions to the exhibit of undeveloped opportunity for cooperative growth." The fifth audit on goods and services proposed to find out how well farmers were satisfied with particular goods or services.

It was the aim of the research division to have tested methods worked out for all five audits by 1950.

Under Project No. II, Community Services, there was to be "a full-scale tryout of completely servicing cooperatively the farm family needs of two types of communities."

The first test was to be tried out at Cobleskill, New York. Here the G.L.F. was to acquire a 10-acre plot of ground suitably situated for rail and highway facilities and design, install and operate 10 service units, to include (1) farm supply store; (2) farm equipment repair shop; (3) lumber yard; (4) freezer locker plant; (5) producer-consumer super market; (6) producer-consumer diner; (7) cattle auction; (8) petroleum service; (9) egg auction; and (10) slaughterhouse. This A-type project would call for an investment of around $200,000. Plans were also under way for a B-type project to be installed at Canandaigua which would embrace all of the A-type installations plus (11) fresh fruit and vegetables, (12) wheat and bean elevator, and (13) canning and freezing plant. The facilities for the B-type project would cost about $1,000,000.

Babcock was anxious that these projects should not be looked upon as "model plants." It was not the aim of G.L.F. to prove that these two installations were of themselves practical and should be copied in other counties. Rather, the aim of this full-scale tryout of facilities was "to find answers to the complex problems of integrating planning, administering and operating the components of these installations."

Babcock pointed out that this project interlocked with the audit research on community services, for the problem of raising the several levels of a given commodity involved first an audit of existing and needed services. Next came plant planning to guide the placement of new or relocated service facilities. Then followed the engineering work to make efficient, sound and economical use of highways, railroads, electric lines, water mains, sewage disposal, heating plants, and to adapt these to the terrain of the area or areas involved. Then would come the planning and perhaps remodeling of buildings to house the facilities involved. Finally, working arrangements would be needed for supervising accounting, employment, and policy-making involving a complicated problem of local interests and patronage.

From these two types of complete community service institutions G.L.F. would aspire to learn how to plan and operate more or less complete units to be installed where need and impetus required. Babcock rated this the most pressing area for G.L.F. study.

Research Project III, *Specifications for Goods and Services,* was designed to improve quality standards and was to be carried on largely through the operating departments.

Research Project No. IV, *Equipment and Devices,* was to be a hopper for stimulating all sorts of gadget ideas, "crazy notions," and products of Yankee ingenuity which might help farmers. This work was being carried on in collaboration with colleges and industrial companies. Studies were being made, for example, of a hay blower machine, a feed piler for community use, egg-cartoning equipment, and rubber-tired farm equipment.

Project No. V, *Patrons' Welfare,* covered broad areas of research designed to raise living standards for all farmers, whether or not members of G.L.F. Here Babcock's interest was intense. The number one project in this area centered around the "Mother Zero" super-locker plant being built in Ithaca. Its object was to find the "ultimate pattern of frozen food servicing for Northeastern communities." Babcock reported that $250,000 had been jointly subscribed for the work by public utilities, manufacturers of freezer equipment, Cornell University, and the G.L.F. It was Babcock's thought that "this rather enormous experiment" would go far in pointing out the extent to which farm and city families could buy and use home freezer units in preference to renting central lockers, and the degree to which a central processing plant will service foods stored at home. . . ." He thought that such information would help locker plants avoid costly oversize or undersize capacities.

The second project under "Patrons' Welfare" was to develop an Animal Products Marketing Service. Babcock called this "by far the most important single project." He thought Northeastern dairying was reaching "its optimum development," and that dairy farmers needed a "whole new income supplement of large promise." The problem called for a combined system of production, slaughter, freezing and marketing.

Another Patrons' Welfare project aimed to increase and stabilize Vitamin A content in alfalfa feed products. Another was trying to find better controls for mastitis—"the greatest single leak in Northeastern farming."

Thus, Babcock's report indicated that the multi-purpose research program prescribed a year earlier had been telescoped into five rather carefully defined areas of research which could be given specialized attention.

At this time Babcock was endeavoring to make the G.L.F. "research conscious." He believed G.L.F. research would produce all sorts of "by-products" which probably would "do more to keep G.L.F. Management alert and on its toes than any activity which G.L.F. has yet undertaken."

In a talk to a Service Agency School on November 12, 1944, he defined research as "the difference between accepting things as they are and doing something about them," and then pointedly remarked: "Research is not for people who prefer the certainty of what is to the uncertainties of change."

He then asserted: "G.L.F.'s research is restive, curious, and game to take on anything in the way of experiment which a wild-eyed patron or a crazy employee may suggest, provided only that upon careful examination the idea promises to contribute to patron or public welfare."

This statement registered the highwater mark of Babcock's research thrust.

It is not possible here to discuss the experience of the various research committees as they tried to develop worthwhile programs. It was a period of "reaching for the moon," and there was much disillusionment and frustration. Some of the operating personnel found the approach practical—others wanted "to get on with the job." As time passed, the less practical ideas were sloughed off, leaving as a hard core the work on attitudes, community services, and a group of projects of a general character which were identified as being related to patrons' welfare.

In November, 1944, a committee from Eastern States Farmers' Exchange inspected the G.L.F. research activities being carried on at Babcock's Sunnygables Farm, Cornell University, and at local G.L.F. facilities. In exhibiting the artificial insemination center then being constructed, Babcock pointed out that this represented coordinated effort on the part of the State Experiment Station, Cornell University, and the G.L.F. Babcock explained that the G.L.F. was involved only as a promoter or "catalyst"—a spur to get the program going. He pointed out that "New York was becoming spotted with small, struggling breeding associations. G.L.F. leadership was thrown into a drive to re-plan the whole State's program and "do it right" before it was too late.

Impressed with the vigor of G.L.F.'s research program the committee summed up its report as follows:

It is very evident that G.L.F. by no means considers its destiny to be in the farm supply field alone. . . . Apparently G.L.F. philosophy is that the cooperative's major obligation is to improve farm income and farm living standards by every reasonable means business acumen, courage, imagination and adventure can devise . . . and to root this philosophy in an impatient, inquisitive, thoroughly-aroused, well-informed membership. G.L.F. dreams boldly in its high command and vigorously strives to alert its total community to the responsibilities of making these dreams come true.

In his report to the Annual Meeting in November, 1944, McConnell discussed postwar planning, a topic then under general discussion. McConnell held that planning should be a continuing function, not necessarily one for a special purpose. Defining research as a "find-out-how-to-do-it program," McConnell went on to say:

G.L.F. has never made a move in its specifications for supplies without leaning heavily on the research of colleges and experiment stations and private corporations. Recently the G.L.F. Board of Directors instructed me to organize our own research division. Under competent direction it is mobilizing its power behind the kind of research that is peculiarly needed in G.L.F.—the kind not available to it elsewhere.

In reporting to the Board in December, Babcock proposed that the research program be further simplified and made more realistic by dropping from the program, Projects II and IV, *Specifications for Goods,* and *Equipment and Devices.* He had come to believe that "the research under these two projects should be left with the operating divisions subject to such correlation and influence by the Director of Research as the General Manager might wish to establish."

This position was logical in that the operating divisions could not relinquish control over research related directly to their areas of service. For example, it was natural for Soil Building to experiment with the use of paper bags and the bulk spreading of lime and fertilizer.

From its establishment in 1936, Farm Supplies had carried on or encouraged research to provide supplies that would best meet farm needs. Some of the first work of this type done was started at the suggestion of Director Harry Bull to develop a satisfactory and economical electric milk cooler. Work on farm freezer boxes was carried on for years in close cooperation with H. E. Babcock and led to their widespread use. Much of this research was conducted jointly with college personnel or technicians in supplier firms.

To direct this program most effectively, V. A. Fogg, President of G.L.F. Farm Supplies, sent out to all members in June, 1944, an attractively printed and illustrated publication called "What's Your Idea?" It was in reality an elaborate consumers' survey designed to find out what kind and type of supplies and services farmers wanted and in what form. A return postal card was provided for replies on specific questions relating to the farm freezer, portable compressors, poultry equipment, farm tools such as shovels and pitchforks, electric fence controllers, laminated rafters, electrical supplies, household appliances, bottled gas, and paint spray service. "What's Your Idea?" not only helped the G.L.F. to provide supplies and services that would meet farming requirements, but did much to advertise G.L.F.'s ability to furnish them. It is significant that a high proportion of the members cooperated by sending back the cards with their ideas.

In view of this experience, Babcock could feel that this area of research was being well handled.

The Audit of Goods

G.L.F. benefited from experience gained in its audit of patrons' attitudes in planning its audit of goods and services. When this work was started in late 1944 an office for handling the administrative problems of such research was operating smoothly under the direction of Warren A. Ranney.

A decision of considerable importance was made in the planning stage of this project, when it was decided to limit the study to an audit of goods and forego combining with it an audit of services.

The basic objective of this audit was to test and develop certain practical techniques, through which G.L.F. patrons could appraise and report the comparative value and fitness of the goods bought through the cooperative and suggest changes as they might desire.

The first problem was to define the scope and limits of the study. It was decided to ask each patron interviewed to evaluate all products purchased from a G.L.F. retail outlet, whether it was a G.L.F. commodity or one approved by the G.L.F.

The questions used to find out what patrons thought of each commodity bought through the G.L.F. were built around these specific questions:

1. How does the quality of this item compare . . . ?
2. How does the price compare . . . ?
3. Are you satisfied . . . ?

If the patron's rating was less than good for any commodity the patron was asked, "How can this item be changed?"

It was first planned to confine the study to New York State, but after field work was completed in New York it was decided to expand the coverage to New Jersey and include additional questions.

To obtain the information required for the audit in New York State, G.L.F. undertook to obtain the part-time services of over 100 teachers of vocational agriculture. This arrangement worked well, for the teachers were well trained and informed in the agricultural conditions of the area.

Those interviewed were selected largely by the enumerators from the patronage refund list to obtain a fair proportion of those who could be rated as good, bad, or indifferent patrons. The actual field work was conducted during the period December 15, 1944, to January 20, 1945, when farmers were mostly at home and able to devote time to answering questions.

On June 22, 1945, two printed reports were submitted by Babcock relating to the audit of goods. The first was called "Patrons' Report to Management," and the second, "1945 Audit of Goods." The first was a generalized presentation of some of the things that had been found in connection with the audit. In general, the report provided a wealth of data that could be used by G.L.F., in improving operations.

The other report provided patrons' opinions on the type of service they were getting on various commodities. The two reports together largely met the objective of the audit, to give patrons an opportunity to tell management what they thought of G.L.F. goods in terms of quality, price, and results.

In the introduction to these two reports Babcock pointed out that one of the problems any large cooperative must face is that of maintaining first-hand contact with its patrons. While Babcock thought the results obtained from the audits were important, he considered of equal importance the development of a technique through which management could keep itself better informed on the needs and attitudes of members. In the words of Babcock, "Once G.L.F. can build a system through which patrons periodically can report to management on how it is doing there will be little question of the end result. Both patron and management will benefit through an improved and more sensitive relationship."

Warren Ranney, who directed this project, points out that "This particular audit, a very complex job, demonstrated that a project must be carefully planned from the initial stages straight through to the very end. This discipline in planning and organizing and anticipating the bugs certainly has taught us a great deal about conducting surveys, and this information has been of considerable value to us ever since."[8]

The Audit for Committeemen

A natural outgrowth of the earlier audit of patrons' attitudes was an audit of G.L.F. Committeemen attitudes. Mr. Maughan, the leader of the first audit team, was convinced of the need for this, and Babcock gave him a relatively free hand in developing plans for a committeemen's audit. The aim was to interview a large proportion of the committeemen and this was done through the winter and spring of 1945.[9]

[8] Letter to author, of June 16, 1955.
[9] Warren A. Ranney writes me that he helped Maughan with his original "modification of the schedule used in the study of farmers' attitudes. In October, 1944, Maughan pre-tested a mimeograph form of the schedule by interviewing committeemen located

The study was made in accordance with a shot-gun pattern, although some plans were made to obtain representative coverage. The field team was composed of five men, three of whom had worked on the previous study of farmers' attitudes.

The field work was done from November, 1944, through March, 1945. Most of the interviews were conducted at Service agencies because of wartime conditions. Generally, each committeeman was interviewed separately by one member of the research squad.

The report on this survey, was solely the work of Maughan. Warren Ranney simply tabulated the data and delivered it to Maughan. "He took it from there. He loved the first job and he wanted to continue. Ed saw no harm, so authorized the money needed and Maughan was off again. Ed suggested that we give Maughan a free hand without worrying too much about the results."[10]

This observation shows Babcock's peculiar point of view. He became interested in the idea and gave Maughan a free hand. A more meticulous research director would probably have kept a tighter grip on Maughan's methods which were reflected in the somewhat didactic way Maughan reported results.

The report on this study was presented as a paper for a Managers' Conference, August 28, 1945. However, the report was more an expression of Maughan's thinking than an analysis of the data which was presented in table form. In brief, these tables brought out these following pertinent facts: (1) About a third of the committeemen were "not sure" that G.L.F. belonged to them; (2) Many of the committees met but a few times a year; (3) About one-fifth of the committeemen were "not sure" whether the G.L.F. was democratic; (4) Many committeemen were not often consulted by the Manager; (5) The committeemen had little or only partial control over local G.L.F. policies; (6) Few committeemen were given an understanding of their responsibilities when they became committeemen.

The preparation of a Committeemen's handbook to help them to better understand their responsibilities and relationship to G.L.F. was one important outcome of this study. (See p. 254.)

Babcock's Research Testament

On March 1, 1945, while these projects were in progress, Babcock presented a more complete statement of G.L.F.'s research program. Significantly, emphasis was placed on research for public welfare "in such fields

---

in Tompkins and adjacent counties. Following this, he made further modifications, and I then had his schedule printed." Letter, to author, July 18, 1955.

[10] Ranney, the same.

as human nutrition and such processes as that of freezing and storing food in home and community zero storage."

G.L.F. had recently provided a building on the Cornell campus for the first school of nutrition in honor of the memory of Professor Savage. (See p. 254.) It was "making available to this school for laboratory work a small slaughterhouse, a frozen locker plant, a bakery, a food store, and a restaurant—facilities which it too will utilize for research work."

Babcock then made clear that "not all of G.L.F.'s research has to do with tangible things. An important phase of it is designed to answer the question of how G.L.F. Directors may always retain control of the organization." He continued:

. . . Obviously, elected farmer directors cannot control a great business like G.L.F. . . . unless they are in possession of certain facts on which they can safely base decisions.

Some of the facts which G.L.F. directors need to know themselves, independently of what employees may tell them are:

1. What is the trend of public opinion toward G.L.F.?
2. How do farm people regard cooperation and G.L.F. in particular?
3. What are the wishes of G.L.F. committeemen and are they being observed?
4. What are the reactions to G.L.F. Community Services?
5. How adequate to the needs of the communities they serve are the local facilities of G.L.F.?
6. Are the goods and services which patrons get through G.L.F. as good or better, cost considered, as they may get through other channels?

At present, the main research job in G.L.F., as it relates to the independent gathering of information for G.L.F. directors, is to develop the questionnaires and the methods of inquiry through which G.L.F. directors may in the future, in a moment's notice, quickly and accurately secure the facts they need.

This program was demonstrating its value and was being extended.

The third general area of research was designed "to learn what constitutes adequate community service through G.L.F., how such services may be democratically administered and how they may be financed and managed." To find the answers G.L.F. was undertaking "a projection of all the possibilities of G.L.F. Service" at Cobleskill, New York. ". . . The site will be surveyed. The buildings to go on it will be carefully planned in relation to one another, and the management of offices will be by a special research committee which will be free to try out innovations and develop new techniques in operations and in local management."

In his last statement on the G.L.F. payroll, on June 30, 1945, Babcock gave his final views on G.L.F. research. He was concerned over the tendency in G.L.F. to classify men as good operators, poor operators, visionaries, and dreamers. He thought this bad, as some of the best operators were "fairly good at dreaming, too." He didn't want either the operators or dreamers to dominate the other.

Likewise he saw a conflict growing up between research and operations, and said: "A mature organization should possess enough poise and stability so that research, even of the most radical character, can be conducted until it is completed and conclusions drawn *without upsetting the normal trend of operations.*" He left this legacy to his successors:

Originality, intuition, and pioneering built G.L.F. If the organization ever gets so big, so complex, and so dead on its feet that it can't be original, that it can't be made to take the initiative, that it is afraid to pioneer, then I sincerely believe that its significance to a patron-member will begin to decline.

THE PROGRAM IN RETROSPECT

Several things were accomplished during the two years that Babcock was actively in charge of the research program.

1. The audit surveys largely met the purpose of finding out how G.L.F. patrons and Committeemen felt toward their organization and its services, and gave management a guide on patrons' and Committeemen's thinking.

2. Attention was focused on the need for improving retail service and laid the foundations for greater emphasis on better coordinated community service.

3. The studies made in the field of public welfare helped the G.L.F. think through its relationship to these activities.

4. The research effort gave impetus to many other important developments. By working with them on research studies, it increased the support of the land-grant colleges in New York, Pennsylvania and New Jersey. It stimulated interest in the objectives and values of agricultural cooperation.

5. It taught G.L.F. a great deal about the relationship of research to sound determination of policies and developmental work. Although much of the program was visionary in the overall, it led to many practical programs. It should be noted that many "screw-ball" ideas were tried and tested which were not put into effect.

6. It did much to subject policy questions to more vigorous analysis.

7. It had great influence on executive development. It released the energies of the more gifted and energetic, while it demonstrated the unfitness of others for leadership.

In the words of Warren A. Ranney, who was most intimately associated with Babcock in the actual conduct of the research program, "It stimulated a lot of creative thinking and broadened the horizons of a lot of men."[11]

[11] Letter, to author, of June 16, 1955.

CHAPTER 27

Across the Board with Marketing

*It is no longer a question of: Shall G.L.F. enter the food business?
When it decided to enter the field of marketing it was in the food
business.*

JAMES A. McCONNELL, *November, 1943*

CHAPTER 22 traced G.L.F. marketing developments through the 1930's.
During this decade, marketing became established as a major G.L.F.
activity. In the next decade we will see how this program proliferated under the influence of Babcock's "across-the-board" marketing philosophy,
how it was accelerated by war and postwar inflationary influences, and
how it was finally stabilized. This chapter will deal with marketing expansion during World War II.

On January 3, 1940, Babcock maintained in a letter to the Board of Directors that the G.L.F. was destined to expand its marketing services.
When the Board met in February he proposed a program for marketing
development which was promptly adopted. Babcock favored letting down
on the emphasis being given to purchasing so that a real beginning could
be made in the field of marketing. At this time pressure was coming from
the patrons for a wide variety of marketing services.

In his annual report to the stockholders in October, 1940, McConnell
pointed out that the volume of products sold for farmers during the fiscal
year totaled $3,300,000. A canning factory had been started July 1 on an
experimental basis at Waterloo, and G.L.F. Stores and Agent-Buyers were
distributing "a surprisingly large proportion" of the output of this factory.
He observed that:

> Cooperative selling in G.L.F. is far beyond the experimental stage. There is
> still plenty of experimenting to be done, but I expect that selling of farm prod-
> ucts in G.L.F. will steadily grow in volume from this point. . . . There have
> been developed certain principles upon which to base a procedure which
> seems to offer some promise that we may eventually expect to achieve some
> very tangible and favorable results.

Babcock set forth these principles later in the meeting. He advocated
an "across-the-board" approach to marketing through performing as many
as possible of the various steps involved in taking a product from producer
to consumer.

In February, 1941, Sadd reported to the Board that marketing was showing a steady increase and that the Waterloo canning plant was coming

274

along quite well.[1] At Rome, New York, the G.L.F. had joined with the Consumer Distribution Corporation in sponsoring a cooperative food store, an experiment which soon demonstrated that G.L.F. objectives could not be realized without full control of policies.[2]

When the Board met in May, Babcock advocated "delivery of goods to the consumer when he wants them, where he wants them, and in the form that best suits his need." Holding that the risk of failure in cooperative marketing "varies indirectly with the number of services performed," he urged G.L.F. "to increase, wherever practical, the number of services it performs." McConnell presented two projects for consideration: Construction of a store at Ithaca to be rented to a consumers' cooperative, and establishment of a cooperative food store at Batavia.[3] Both projects were approved as worthy experiments.

In the fall of 1941, Babcock assured the Board that the G.L.F. was not plunging hastily or blindly ahead into marketing in that a clear and definite philosophy governed the moves being made. The food store at Batavia had now been organized under the name, "Cooperative P & C [Producers and Consumers] Market, Inc." Under the plan, the G.L.F. provided all of the initial capital, but savings were to be shared by producers and consumers in accordance with their deliveries or purchases, and Cooperative G.L.F. Farm Products, Inc., was to provide management.[4] It was contemplated that similar units would be set up in other localities. This first P & C Market was launched with great fanfare as an experiment to bring producers and consumers into the same business on a partnership basis, but the real objective was to get a start in the retail food business.[5]

The growing importance of marketing was reflected in the annual report of the General Manager, presented to the Stockholders' Meeting on

---

[1] During the first year this plant was leased. It was purchased outright by the Holding Corporation on April 12, 1941.

[2] See J. A. McConnell, "Pancakes on Consumers' Plates," *Cooperative Digest,* June 1941.

[3] G.L.F. had encouraged both proposals as a means of getting experience in the retail food business. At Batavia a group of farmers were pressing for a canning plant. "Jim McConnell told the folks if they would support a super-market G.L.F. would eventually support them with a canning factory. This was the very beginning of P. and C." Letter of C. W. Sadd, to author, December 21, 1954.

[4] This ambitious plan of sharing savings was never completely effected, although patronage refunds were paid consumers in the form of "customers' rebates." Customers claimed them by turning back cash register tapes. Letter of C. W. Sadd, September 22, 1958.

[5] According to C. W. "Happ" Sadd, the man most involved, in that he was President of Cooperative G.L.F. Farm Products, Inc. "Ed's interest was to demonstrate his theory of marketing. Mine was to see why chain buyers act the way they do and to see first hand, what makes a chain tick." Letter to author, of September 22, 1958. Sadd had been rebuffed by the chain stores and he was determined to prove that farmers could run them.

November 6, 1941. In the section of the report devoted to cooperative selling, Mr. McConnell said:

For twenty years G.L.F. farmers have been engaged in taking over the performance, one by one, of many of the services in connection with the movement
of raw materials to their farms. . . . These raw materials, brought to farms
through G.L.F. purchasing services, are then converted into milk, eggs, meat,
vegetables, flour, and other food products. These food products then move
through the same series of services from the farm to the ultimate consumer;
thus is completed the final phase of services in the movement of goods from
producer to consumer. . . . In G.L.F. we describe this as cooperative selling.

After explaining how G.L.F. was applying this philosophy in selling
eggs, he said: *"While the procedure may be somewhat different, in the
handling of other commodities, such as wheat, beans, potatoes, fruit and
vegetables, the same basic principle, namely, performance of a series of
services, underlies the handling of each commodity."*

McConnell was well satisfied with G.L.F. progress, to date, in cooperative selling. "We have now gone far enough in setting up these selling or
marketing services to know definitely that instead of being hazardous undertakings . . . they are, on the contrary if properly manned and operated,
safe operations." He went on to say: "I confidently forecast that, as the
years go on, the volume of business done by G.L.F. in cooperative selling,
commonly referred to as 'marketing,' will gain on that of cooperative purchasing and eventually should outrun it by millions of dollars annually."

Then he added a word of caution:

The establishment of a canning factory or a dry beans plant, or any other
food processing plant as self-contained units, is a mistake, without, at the
same time provision is made for the performance of all of the essential services
which must be done in order to carry a crop to be marketed from the field clear
through to the consumer. . . . Establishment of G.L.F. food factories without
an assured distribution system that will work with these factories is like trying
to operate a reaper and binder to cut and tie grain without having made provision for the knotter which does the tieing. . . . If we are to succeed in this
job we must get away from the concept, so widely held, that the solution of
cooperative selling lies in the field of prices. It does not. The solution is in the
successful performance of the series of services needed in moving goods from
farm to consumer.

Although interest in marketing expansion was temporarily diverted by
the attack on Pearl Harbor, McConnell noted in his annual report for
1942 a growing use of the marketing division by farmers. He felt that the
program was succeeding in view of the "steady decline in the number
of letters from farmers advising me how terrible is the G.L.F. marketing
service."

When the Board met on January 18, 1943, McConnell recommended the appointment of a marketing committee to make a complete study of the marketing situation. While there was unanimous approval it is significant that one director cautioned that there should be a limit to services rendered—that it was not possible to follow all products to their logical end—from producer to consumer.

The Board at this time adopted a policy to provide for the self-development of marketing operations: "Whenever an operation in the G.L.F. system passes beyond the experimental stage and in case the operation is participated in directly by farmers and is carried on primarily for the benefit of said farmers it shall be proper to segregate the business by incorporating the same. . . ."

This policy was designed to build up local financial and membership responsibility for specific marketing enterprises. On April 12 the Board approved a recommendation from McConnell "that the Marketing and Budget Committees should work on a plan for the segregation of all marketing activities into separate groups."

Marketing was now expanding at a spectacular rate. The volume of cooperative selling for the fiscal year ending June 30, 1943, exceeded $13 million as compared with $8,200,000 for the preceding year, and $4,930,000 for the year before that.

In his report for 1942-43, McConnell said, "While [marketing] doesn't offer services to as many farmers as purchasing—and never will—it is now large and continues to grow." Then he went on to say:

> The whole method of G.L.F. food distribution to farmers as well as through distribution to city people—which are a part of our marketing program—is still to be determined. We cannot lightly dismiss it by saying that the food which G.L.F. handles in its marketing operations cannot be distributed to farm families because the present feed store through which G.L.F. members are serviced is not suitable for handling food. It may or may not be. Perhaps by slight modifications it can be. It may, however, require a complete new distribution system. Our research job is to keep an open mind and find out.
>
> We are beginning to find out some things. . . . There is no mystery about the operation of the food business. It's a case of learning the business and seeing: First, whether we want to operate a food business at the community level and how extensively; and then determining what type of facilities are needed, whether it is the office of the feed store or a pantry in the feed store, or a complete and separate food store.

Appended to the report were some "cooperative selling notes" which described the marketing developments during the preceding year. The canning plants were growing in volume and G.L.F. canned foods were now stocked in 75,000 retail food stores scattered from Coast to Coast. The Government was the largest single purchaser of G.L.F. canned goods, and G.L.F. employees now in the armed services had reported eating them in several foreign lands. Bean volume was up to an all-time high, with the United States Government being the largest buyer.

Consumer food services of the G.L.F. were now being conducted by "Cooperative P & C Family Food Service, Inc.," under the general direction of Cooperative G.L.F. Farm Products, Inc.[6] The wholesale grocery business of Products had grown "like Topsy" since it began handling canned goods for G.L.F. Stores and Agents, and in March, 1943, a wholesale grocery service had been opened in Syracuse to serve 100 G.L.F. service agencies in the Syracuse area, two P & C retail food stores, and 75 independent grocers in the city of Syracuse. The G.L.F. now had almost two years of experience in operating food stores and they "gave promise of being one of the greatest developments in the G.L.F. marketing program."

At the December 13, 1943, meeting of the Board, Sherman Peer, General Counsel, reported that P & C Family Foods Service, Inc., had grown well beyond the experimental stage. It was now a retail food business serving non-farmer patrons, and he believed that its growth as an integral part of the G.L.F. might endanger the G.L.F.'s tax-exempt position as a farmer cooperative association. This was also the view of W. L. Bradley, G.L.F.'s Tax Counsel. McConnell, Peer and Sadd were directed to study the problem and present a plan for its solution.

At this time food-processing and marketing were fast coming to the front in G.L.F. There was great interest in the possibilities of frozen food locker plants, and the Board was even giving serious consideration to the purchase of a food chain-store system. With the expansion of food stores, freezer lockers, and canning plants, in accordance with across-the-board doctrine, apprehension grew that marketing might get out of control. Babcock's research program poured fuel on the fire for all kinds of ideas were proposed by the "research committees." (See p. 267.)

When the Board met, April 3, 1944, McConnell called a halt. He reported that the G.L.F. was not interested in taking over a chain of supermarkets and going into the grocery business. However, he saw possibilities in livestock marketing, and Sadd at this meeting pointed out that "investigation indicates an opportunity to market cull livestock." The Board authorized the purchase of a site for a packinghouse.

Many requests were now coming in for help in the development of local canning plants, and a policy was needed to guide G.L.F. management. It was agreed that G.L.F. would hold token control, but that the sponsors were to be responsible for financing 50 percent of the fixed assets. Sadd believed that six to eight plants, strategically located, could serve as pacesetters, and he favored getting this program under way.

In view of the persistent fear that the operation of P & C Family Food

[6] C. W. Sadd was President of both corporations. The name was changed from Cooperative P & C Markets on January 4, 1943.

Service, Inc., endangered the G.L.F.'s Federal income tax exemption, the Board decided on June 30 to reorganize it on an independent basis. McConnell was on leave of absence due to illness when this decision was made, and up to this time he had not been convinced that separation was necessary.

However, he had not watched the development of P & C as a G.L.F. activity without some concern. At a District Managers' Conference, April 14, 1943, he had expressed the view that because of tax implications "P & C should be set up as a new organization, not a subsidiary of G.L.F., independently financed, but correlated by the same board of directors." Under the plan of separation worked out, G.L.F. lost direct control of P & C development.

With P & C operations divorced from the G.L.F., marketing resumed a more normal pattern. The G.L.F. continued such essential marketing functions as assembling, transportation, wholesaling and processing, while the P & C Family Foods, Inc., undertook to carry the product to the ultimate consumer. Fortunately, the break was made before the P & C Family Foods Service had become a well-established G.L.F. activity so it resulted in little change in G.L.F. operations. In the separation C. W. Sadd, President of G.L.F. Products and Cooperative P & C Family Foods Service, Inc., became General Manager of the new organization, Cooperative P & C Family Foods, while Ray Flumerfelt, Vice-President, became President of G.L.F. Products.

The Annual Report indicated that cooperative marketing volume had increased to $15,736,000 in 1943-44. It contained the following statement from the Board's marketing committee, comprised of J. C. Corwith, Chairman, Jacob E. Ameele, Earl Clark, and Clayton G. White: "Our whole program is aimed at building sound marketing facilities which will set the pace in efficiently moving products from G.L.F. farm to the consumer to the end that the producer may receive a fair return and that the consumer shall get as much real food value as possible for his money."

In this annual report Silcox also called attention to a number of interesting achievements in marketing: Community egg stations had been set up in six more upstate areas. The first unit in livestock marketing had been started with a slaughter plant at Clyde, New York. Of this he said, "This field of marketing will be thoroughly explored as it promises to farmers improved opportunities for the selling of cull dairy cows and hens." Silcox pointed out that patronage refunds on marketing had become the rule rather than the exception; that the 20,000 farmers using G.L.F. marketing service had received the going price and, in addition, would divide cash patronage refunds of about $250,000.

He declared that the requests from farm communities for the extension of existing marketing services and for new marketing services indicated satisfaction with present performance and promised a tremendous future development.

Silcox also insisted that separation of the P & C from the G.L.F. did not mean that the G.L.F. had lost its interest in marketing at the level where the producer meets the consumer. "Far from it," he declared, "the operation of P & C will always remain within the sphere of G.L.F. influence."

In January, 1945, Flumerfelt gave an optimistic report to the Board on the future of marketing. At this time the Board rescinded action which had granted Cooperative P & C Family Foods, Inc., the right to use G.L.F. brand labels. It was appreciated that G.L.F. could not yield such an important right and impair its ability to regain it.

At the May, 1945, Board meeting McConnell noted with some concern how marketing activities could get out of hand. The following statement represented, if not a reversal of Babcock's philosophy, at least a precaution on its use:

There has been some talk of establishing here at Ithaca a bakery and a diner. The minute we start such establishments down here you have gone clear 'across the board' in wheat marketing. If we aren't careful a lot of men in G.L.F. will say that that has established a policy and will want a bakery and restaurant in every town in the state. I bring this out as an example of how easy it is to confuse research and policy.

Later in the same talk Mr. McConnell raised this question: "Can G.L.F. distribute food through Agent-Buyers and Stores?" McConnell said that "For the last few years G.L.F. had been hammering out a food distribution policy for its stores and agents' system. . . . We tried everything." He indicated that a current study was not favorable to distribution of food through service stores.

McConnell also gave consideration to this question, "What is the relation between G.L.F. and the Cooperative P & C Family Foods, Inc.?" He had come to certain conclusions:

1. There has been established within G.L.F. boundaries a new farmers' cooperative which primarily is engaged in marketing farmers' products.
2. P & C is independent of G.L.F. to whatever extent the P & C Board of Directors may wish. However, they are 'closely allied' and have a 'powerful influence' on each other.
3. There is coming into prominence in the farmer cooperative world of this area a 'relatively young, aggressive,' new group of farmers tied in with the P & C.
4. There is coming a new development in food distribution in the area which is significant in that it is farmer-directed.
5. G.L.F. has a big financial interest in P & C. While G.L.F. started and developed P & C to a certain stage, it has been decided that G.L.F. and P & C can develop along parallel lines but as independent organizations. However,

G.L.F. has incurred a responsibility for P & C 'which it cannot shed quickly and completely, and which it does not desire to. This responsibility is accepted.'

McConnell went on to say that while the G.L.F. intended over a period of time to get its P & C investment returned, "G.L.F. is more interested in service returns than in financial returns."

In a report on Farm Products operations, June 26, 1945, Flumerfelt said, "I feel that we have gone a long way toward laying the groundwork for successfully marketing farm commodities." This report is presented in some detail to show the status of marketing at the close of the war.

Canning operations had been financially successful. However, with construction costs continuing to advance, a proposed canning plant at Batavia was being postponed until economic conditions warranted. However, it had seemed desirable to set up a plant at Macedon, New York, under the name, "The Macedon Food Company." This plant was scheduled to go into operation in late July.

While progress of the canning plants had been successful so far, they had been favored by war conditions. Flumerfelt doubted whether canning could maintain its present volume in the postwar period but he believed that freezing would probably show a rapid growth.

Flumerfelt believed that there were also opportunities in marketing fresh produce. He said, "For the last six or eight years we in G.L.F. have talked about marketing fresh produce for G.L.F. patrons all over G.L.F. territory. . . . During this time we have done very little to render this necessary service."

He held also that the G.L.F. system of service agencies, developed over the past twenty years, offered tremendous advantages to a well-organized marketing service in that they could furnish the farmer with his production supplies and offer him a market for his produce.

Moreover, the experimental milling operations at Hemlock, Coudersport, and Churchville, and the bean marketing program were giving good results.

Based on the experience of the small livestock slaughtering plant at Clyde which had been leased to the Cooperative P & C Family Foods, Inc., on April 15, 1945, Flumerfelt said, "There appears to be a real opportunity for a cooperative to improve livestock marketing conditions for farmers in G.L.F. territory. However, until the present meat crisis is over it will be very difficult to make constructive moves in this direction."

Likewise, he saw opportunities in poultry marketing. To get some experience in dressing and freezing poultry a small poultry dressing line had been installed at Clyde in conjunction with the Clyde cold storage operations.

Flumerfelt concluded his report by saying:

There are two definite moves that Farm Products must take in order to be successful in the postwar period. (1) Begin to advertise our products under G.L.F. label in various markets through the country; and (2) Set up a quality control in the research division, directly responsible to management in order that we will have uniformity of production and constantly be developing new products from raw materials produced by our patrons.

It will be observed that this program was, on the whole, conservative in tone although optimistic in character.

The annual report for 1945 indicated that the marketing volume now amounted to $15,168,000, even with P & C volume removed from the marketing operations. In a separate report on marketing, Flumerfelt said, "During the past year our marketing patrons have increased in number and we have reached a new high in volume of units handled." After paying all operating expenses there had been net margins from marketing of about $75,000. While the marketing program was thus running along satisfactorily, certain problems were beginning to show up. The canning plants were still operating successfully, but the competition was gaining in strength as war demands subsided. On the whole, Flumerfelt believed that the marketing program was in a strong position because of its diversified character.

In his report, Mr. McConnell devoted no specific attention to marketing, as he was concerned with immediate problems of adjustment confronting the G.L.F. now that the war had closed. However, President Frank Smith, in his report, said, "We realize that demands on the G.L.F. for new marketing operations will be tremendous." He also stated that the G.L.F. policy on marketing was that:

We should never get more than one step ahead of our outlets. To be specific, when we can sell the full production of the three canning factories now in operation we will consider a fourth. When we can sell the full production of four factories we might consider a fifth if there is a service to be rendered.

Babcock's farewell address to the stockholders was published in this same report. In emphasizing the importance of improving the American diet, he urged the completion of the Ithaca food center by the addition of a bakery and a restaurant.

When these two pilot plants are built and in operation, the Ithaca food research center will then be comprised of the following facilities: A community slaughterhouse; a processing, freezing, and Zero storage plant with both individual lockers and bulk Zero storage space for wholesale and quantities of frozen food; a bakery for the preparation of breadstuffs, pastries, preserves and the like, to be either frozen or sold fresh; a supermarket for testing consumer reactions to all kinds of foodstuffs and the techniques of handling them; and a restaurant for a final check on consumer reactions. . . . This food center is unique in three particulars. It provides complete facilities for the best possible handling of locally grown foodstuffs. It provides Cornell University's School of Nutrition with a fine laboratory for studying food-handling techniques and consumer reactions. It provides G.L.F. with a series of pilot operations through which it can learn what to do and what not to do in its marketing of human foods.

Although the G.L.F. had gone a long way across the board in marketing it did not then take this final step. With more conservative economic forces being generated by the fear of a postwar depression G.L.F. thinking was reverting to the immediate problems of servicing the primary needs of G.L.F. members.[7]

[7] This will be brought out in Chapter 33.

CHAPTER 28

The Member-Ownership Program

What I want to point out to you is that, as farmers, we should not only use the G.L.F., but we should own and control it just as we own our farms, the cattle, the hens and the machinery we use to operate with.

M. E. (SCOTTY) CAMPBELL
October, 1943

FOR SOME TIME the G.L.F. leaders had been concerned with the ebbing of a sense of membership consciousness. To many patrons the G.L.F. was just another feed and farm supply company. This problem was intensified by war conditions which restricted membership meetings.

During the thirties the G.L.F. had placed emphasis on increasing volume through attracting patronage by services rendered. As the New York State law permitted a cooperative to consider as a member any farmer who purchased or marketed $100 worth of supplies or products through the organization, a large number of farmers automatically became G.L.F. members, and the meaning of membership lost vitality. Moreover, little was done to encourage farmers to buy stock.

After the initial drive for stockholders, no great effort was made to increase their number, and after 1925 emphasis was placed on expanding volumes to lower costs. Patrons were considered more important than stockholders, as evidenced by the elevation of the word "patron" while the words "member" and "stockholder" were played down.

As a result of this policy of indifference toward stock ownership few new patrons acquired membership stock, and the number of stockholders fell off as members died or gave up farming. On June 30, 1942, there were only 28,869 stockholders, compared with 33,500 on June 30, 1932.

The emphasis on building volume had served the immediate interests of the G.L.F. in establishing itself. However, it tended to de-emphasize the importance of the membership tie. Legally speaking, the stockholders held the voting control, and this threatened difficulty if the interests of stockholders and patrons were to diverge. The danger became apparent in 1932 when a group of stockholders attempted to gain control, and it led to the working out of a plan whereby the local committeemen, elected by patrons, regained effective control through their concentrated stock ownership. Thus the principle of control by stockholders was nominally preserved although the patron members elected the committeemen who held the stock in their behalf. This move strengthened control by stock ownership but it did nothing to encourage patrons in general to become stockholders.

The necessity of more work in membership education became apparent in the late thirties. The charge of John Daniels in a G.L.F. University lecture that the G.L.F. was vulnerable as a cooperative because of the weakness of the membership tie cut deeply. (See p. 202.) G.L.F. thinking in regard to membership was further shaken by the Cornell studies made about this time under the direction of Professors W. A. Anderson and Dwight Sanderson in the Department of Rural Sociology, which found that many G.L.F. patrons felt little sense of direct loyalty to the organization. Of particular importance was a doctoral dissertation by J. Edwin Losey, "Membership Relations of a Cooperative Purchasing Association," completed in August, 1940. This was really a case study of the G.L.F.'s membership relations.

Losey found that "the complex organizational scheme of the G.L.F. was beyond comprehension to a majority of those interviewed. . . . Farmers constantly personified the organization as 'it' or 'they' and rare were the instances of 'our' and 'we.'" He concluded that "the casual and automatic feature of patron membership is a detriment to the creation of a 'sense of belonging' which is a well-established factor in the acceptance of responsibility."

By showing the membership ignorance of the G.L.F. this study disclosed the need for a more tangible identification of membership with ownership, although no change was recommended in the requirement for membership.

Although the weakness of the membership tie was apparent, it was not easy to bring about a change.[1] Few farmers saw the need of buying common stock when the rights of membership came to them automatically through purchase of G.L.F. supplies.

The need to conserve capital in 1942 provided an opportunity to change this situation. By paying patronage refunds for 1942 in the form of participation certificates which could be converted into common stock after January 1, 1943, an easy and patriotic way was provided for the acquirement of common stock.

This action, however, was justified primarily as a safety measure to protect the G.L.F.'s solvency in event of a severe price decline rather than as a means of increasing stockholder-ownership. In announcing this plan in a special report to G.L.F. patrons, there was this statement: "This year, because of rising prices and higher operating costs and the need for

---

[1] In his annual report for 1939-40, McConnell recognized that "the number of stockholders is slowly and steadily declining." He held that this was "undesirable" and that "any farmer who believes in G.L.F. should have a few shares of G.L.F. common stock, as a matter of good, common cooperative practice."

much larger inventories to protect patrons' needs, your organization requires more working capital. Your Board of Directors has therefore decided to pay your patronage refund in the form of a security—a G.L.F. participation certificate." It was believed that most certificates would eventually be redeemed in cash rather than converted into common stock. The certificates were to bear interest at 4 percent and be considered "in effect, loans."

However, the use of participation certificates to encourage stock ownership was not overlooked. In a printed leaflet, "G.L.F. Patronage Refunds, 1941-42," issued in July, 1942, Manager McConnell stated: "In order to keep the ownership of G.L.F. in the hands of the actual users it is desirable that as high a percentage of certificate holders as possible convert their certificates into common stock. . . ."

Later, in his October report at the Annual District Meetings, McConnell pointed out that conversion of participation certificates into stock would "spread the ownership of G.L.F. in a large way into the hands of the present members of G.L.F." and he went on to say, "This is highly desirable."

Although provision was made for conversion of participation certificates into common stock, it was not pushed and at the end of the fiscal year, 1943, the number of stockholders stood at 31,658, as compared with 28,869 the year before.

During this time the war was emphasizing the importance of having a loyal, well-informed membership. In addressing the District Managers on June 1, 1943, McConnell declared: "Membership and cooperative thinking must be revitalized." He held that a principal weakness in G.L.F. was a lack of understanding on the part of the great rank and file of farmers of its strength and possibilities. He attributed the absence of "membership consciousness" to the fact that so many G.L.F. members had never been called upon to make a decision in regard to membership. He indicated that this condition was to be remedied by a new membership program to increase the ownership interest of members.

When the Board met, later in June, McConnell proposed the inauguration of an active member-ownership campaign, and M. E. (Scotty) Campbell presented a well-conceived program with a goal of 100,000 member owners. The Board endorsed the program in principle and Campbell's appointment as Director of Member Relations, to get the job done.[2]

It was recognized that the member-ownership plan would help meet

[2] The success of this program was to have a far-reaching effect. Several years later, Sherman Peer, General Counsel, said, "Unwittingly, it paved the way for G.L.F. to adopt later the plan of paying wholesale patronage refunds to owner members only and thereby in consequence it gave up deliberately exemption from Federal income taxes." *Digest of G.L.F. Board Actions,* 1940-50, pp. 29-30. See also Chapter 34, "The Income Tax Decision."

the growing need of the G.L.F. for equity capital as a basis for its extensive borrowings. The ownership interest of G.L.F. members had gradually declined while business volume expanded until it had become embarrassingly thin. It was becoming apparent that the financial health of the Institution required more membership investment to support its growing need for capital.

Another factor which influenced the Board to favor the plan was the belief that G.L.F.'s right to Federal income tax exemption would be better protected if members were owners as well as users. This was considered something that should be insured against in view of a growing demand for a tightening up of the so-called tax exemption available to qualifying farmer cooperatives.

The 1943 membership program for G.L.F. was brief:

1. Get every G.L.F. member to become a substantial owner of common stock.
2. Convert outstanding participation certificates into common or non-voting stock.

The new member-ownership program was presented in detail at a staff conference in late June. At this meeting McConnell called attention to G.L.F.'s growing need for working capital and the fact that under the policy that had prevailed in the past a farmer-patron became a patron-member as soon as he used the organization to the extent of $100 in any one year. This arrangement, said McConnell, was so automatic that very few of the 177,000 who used the organization realized that G.L.F. was anything but another feed and supply company.

McConnell declared:

Starting now, a new policy is going into effect. All effort is going to be directed toward making patrons realize their responsibility in being patron stockholder members as well as users. Every G.L.F. patron is going to have to make a decision as to whether he wants to be a stockholder member or not. This is going to be accomplished partly through paying of all patronage dividends in the form of participation certificates. A great deal of encouragement is going to be directed toward patrons turning their participation certificates into common stock.

During the next few months the member-ownership program was vigorously pushed, under the leadership of Campbell. He reviewed progress to date at a Managers Conference, September 27-28. A special school had been conducted to train junior executives in G.L.F. membership thinking. Letters to emphasize the importance of membership ownership had been sent out with interest and dividend payments; reports on the program had been carried in the G.L.F. Week; a report had been issued listing holdings of participation certificates by communities; material had been prepared for use of employees in carrying on the campaign.

Campbell then outlined further steps to be taken. A poster on the member-ownership program was to be made available to all service agencies, with a pamphlet to explain how it could best be used. Regional schools were to emphasize the program. A contest was to feature accomplishment and conversion of participation certificates, and goals for member-ownership were to be set up for each community. These goals were being set up to establish the amount a member should invest in the G.L.F. organization, based on his holdings of cows and hens, and acres of cropland.

Campbell stated that as the program was designed both to raise money and to solidify membership support, two terms aptly described it: "member ownership" and "member participation."

In his annual report for 1943, McConnell, in emphasizing the significance of the member-ownership program, said, "The only objective of member ownership is to have a large body of stockholders, with sufficient investment on the part of each one so that they feel a sense of ownership and responsibility."

McConnell was very much disturbed at this time by the general public's misunderstanding of cooperatives, and he believed that the member-ownership program—by demonstrating that farmers were supporting G.L.F., not only with their patronage but with their funds, would help improve public understanding and relations.

During the year the campaign to increase member ownership gave very satisfactory results. In a talk for a service agency school in March, 1944, Campbell reported that more than 5,000 new stockholders had been added. He indicated that the goal was 50,000 total stockholders by July 1, 1944, with 100,000 the goal for the next two years. He said, "Our over-all goal in our membership campaign is that every worthwhile patron in G.L.F. territory be an owner-member of the G.L.F. through ownership of common stock and a supporter of his local service. . . ." The goal of 50,000 stockholders by July 1 was almost reached, for the number stood at 49,934 on June 30—an increase of 18,000 for the year.

At a school for local cooperatives served by the G.L.F., attended by the writer, in October, 1944, Campbell gave a complete report on the member-ownership program. In this talk he pointed out that during the first few years of the G.L.F. the sense of ownership on the part of members was all that kept the institution going. He said there was little else for these original owners to tie to. These men had made investments in the G.L.F. and they wanted results. This point was well made. Without question, the significant economic stake of farmers in the G.L.F. during its formative years helped maintain their interest and support until the organization got on its feet.

Bordentown Feed Mill

Caledonia Bean Plant

TEXAS CITY TANKER AT ALBANY TERMINAL

PETROLEUM BULK STATION

WARNERS SEED PLANT

ITHACA SERVICE STORE TODAY

FARM STORE AT HUNTERDON, N.J.

Farm Supplies Warehouse, Owego, N.Y.

At Weedsport Egg Station

McConnell saw the need of re-establishing the sense of ownership among those served by the G.L.F. In his annual report for 1943-44, he termed "the fact that more and more farmers are taking it for granted" as G.L.F.'s "greatest weakness."

To encourage G.L.F. member investment a large cash refund was made for the first six months of 1943-44, and many patrons were encouraged to buy a few shares of common stock. The issuance of cash patronage refunds for the full fiscal year was followed with a vigorous campaign to "mop up" as much of it as possible in sales of common stock.

For many years the limit on individual holdings of G.L.F. common stock had been placed at one thousand shares. On May 15, 1944, the Board reduced the limit to one hundred shares. "It was the thought," said Campbell, "that our voting and control stock should not be considered investment stock and it should only be owned by farmers and users of G.L.F. services."

In line with this thinking, a strenuous effort was made to acquire all outstanding stock no longer in the hands of active users. As a result, several thousand of the original stockholders gave up their holdings of common stock. Campbell considered it significant that the present stockholders were gradually becoming an active user group.

A common sight at this time at a G.L.F. Service Agency was a locally-made "membership thermometer" which recorded the status of member-ownership for the community.

Up to this time the main object of the membership-ownership program had been to increase the proportion of patron-members who were owners of G.L.F. stock. It had brought a new vitality to the meaning of membership, but there had been no change in legal basis of memberships which largely rested on the purchase of $100 worth of supplies through the G.L.F.

A new impetus was given the member-ownership program in 1946 and 1947 when McConnell and others in the G.L.F. began to see the possibility of settling the federal income tax controversy in so far as it related to the G.L.F. by changing the basic requirements for G.L.F. membership. (See Chapter 34.) Without the member-ownership base built up during the three or four preceding years, it is doubtful whether the G.L.F. could have undertaken the drastic change in program called for by its decision in November, 1947, to pay income tax on non-member business. It would have been unwise, if not disastrous, to give up the federal income tax exemption before the G.L.F. largely represented a body of active owner-members.

The decision of the G.L.F. stockholder body to limit membership to those holding stock was made at the Annual Meeting in November, 1947, to go into effect on July 1, 1948. To bring about this significant change by July 1, 1948, a strenuous campaign for new stockholder members was carried on in the spring.[3]

The growth in the number of owner-members and the value of their stock holdings are here given for the years from June 30, 1943, just after the member-ownership program was adopted, to June 30, 1949, one year after it became the basis of membership in the G.L.F.:

As of June 30	Owner-Members	Common Stock Holdings
1943	31,658	$1,549,105
1944	49,934	4,487,170
1945	60,378	5,383,935
1946	59,440	5,874,735
1947	57,532	6,121,550
1948	72,438	7,422,540
1949	105,151	8,445,260

It will be observed that the number of member-owners declined slightly in 1946 and 1947 following the conversion of participation certificates to stock, and almost doubled in the next two years.

Thus, within a six-year period, a revolutionary change was made in the basic membership structure of the G.L.F. This change, in the words of Manager McConnell, "made membership mean something."

[3] Campbell's articles in the *G.L.F. Week* as the campaign drew toward its close, reflect the intensive and skillful effort put into this campaign by Campbell and the field force. The *G.L.F. Week* of July 12 stated that membership stood at 83,000 on June 30, 1948, an increase of over 8,000 in the last week of June. Many of the new stockholders were not registered until after June 30, so they do not show up in the year end official figures.

CHAPTER 29

Farm Service Lifted Up

On this judgment I make my decision, namely, to lift Farm Service Management from its role of functional division and make it an overall administrative agency. . . .

JAMES A. McCONNELL
January 4, 1945

W AR CONDITIONS placed great responsibilities on the men who represented the G.L.F. in dealing with farmers. Although there was much teamwork throughout the organization there was no coordinating center except the general manager's office.

The need for better central direction of retail service was emphasized by the work of the research committees. It was clear that a farm community could best be served only by full coordination of the available retail services.

To meet this problem, McConnell made T. E. Milliman Director of Community Services on April 3, 1944. McConnell's main concern at this time was to determine how local services could be better coordinated, and Milliman was given the job of finding out how this could best be done. In pointing out to the Board the need for administrative correlation of the various local services, McConnell said: "Heretofore, this has been done by the General Manager. With the variety of services now being rendered and the tremendous increase in business it is impossible for him to do the job adequately." On December 4, 1944, McConnell reported to the Board that the position of Director of Community Services was working out "very satisfactorily."

Convinced by Milliman's work that a basic reorganization of the G.L.F. at the community service level was needed, McConnell, on January 16, 1945, proposed to the Board that Farm Service management be "lifted up" so that it would become a management corporation for all divisions concerned with providing community services. T. E. Milliman was to serve as President of the new corporation, with Ed Fallon as its Executive Vice-President.

Even prior to this, on January 4, 1945, McConnell had already authorized Milliman to proceed with the reorganization of the administrative machinery of G.L.F. to provide services at the farm level "efficiently and without confusion." He made his thinking clear in his instructions to Milliman:

291

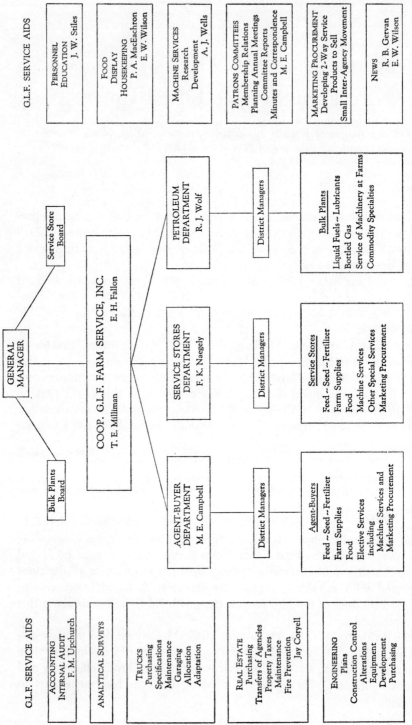

FIGURE 4–G.L.F. FARM SERVICE, INC., ORGANIZATION CHART, APRIL, 1945

. . . It seems that we should return to the original concept which Babcock, our founding General Manager, had when he conceived of the development of Farm Services in its original stage. He has often told me that it was never his intention to have Farm Service Management grow up as a subdivision but rather as an administrative cooperative, owned by all eligible community agencies as it matured, under which functional divisions could be developed and handled. In my judgment . . . his original conception of this is correct. On this judgment I make my decision, namely, to lift Farm Service Management from its role of functional division and make it an over-all administrative agency under which as many functional divisions as needed may be developed.

It is generally agreed that our present administrative machinery, while performing efficiently and orderly in the past, is no longer adequate to handle community services as they are now being projected, developed, and organized. Various functions such as engineering and accounting cut across all the divisions in community services. Many skilled men (specialists) in certain fields are needed by all divisions. It seems unsound and unwise, for instance, to try to develop two groups of food specialists to serve two different divisions such as Agencies and Stores, when both can be served by the same group if the administrative machinery is properly organized.

He went on to say, "It is my wish that all men concerned in this field give you the utmost cooperation in carrying out this reorganization, as this is fundamental if G.L.F. is to go forward."

The formation of the new corporation was approved on March 19. Its name, "Cooperative G.L.F. Farm Service, Inc.," had been chosen from 182 suggestions. It was to harmonize and direct all retail activities of the G.L.F., and Cooperative G.L.F. Farm Stores, Inc., the management corporation for G.L.F. Stores, was to be retired.

In presenting the plan of organization for Cooperative G.L.F. Farm Service to the Board of Directors on April 4, 1945, Milliman stated that "energy" had been applied to adapt the existing field service structure to achieve the best correlation of effort without making organic changes. As President, he was to report directly to the General Manager on policies, trends, public relations and new developments, while Fallon, as Executive Vice-President, would direct operations.

The plan of organization provided for three operating departments, each with a vice-president in charge.

The G.L.F. Stores Department would continue to give supervision to the Stores and provide them with accounting service.

The Agent-Buyer Department would continue to work with Agent-Buyers through its own district managers.

The Petroleum Products Department would likewise direct the work with the bulk plants.

Although these departments were to continue, with little change, the work done with Agent-Buyers, Service Stores, and petroleum units, they were to be coordinated at the top through the President of Cooperative

G.L.F. Farm Service, Inc., rather than the General Manager. This represented a major change in organization.

An important feature of the plan was provision for common services to all three departments through staff units to be designated as Service Aids. Each Service Aid was to provide specialist assistance in a given field, such as accounting or personnel, and departments or individual units using the assistance were to share in the cost. In effect, each Service Aid was to become a small department providing specialist service, although the man placed in charge was usually designated the Service Aid.

The role to be performed by the Service Aids was not clear-cut when the plan was adopted. It was recognized that it would take some time to determine what Service Aids were needed and how they could best function.

The form of organization thus made use of the line and staff concept of organization. The heads of the three operating departments were primarily line officers, while Service Aids were to furnish them with certain staff services.

Milliman concluded his report by saying, "Farm Service is already functioning as a full-fledged G.L.F. division, although it will not assume its full corporate status until July 1." He was sure that this program would increasingly improve the effectiveness of the men operating in the field— "the sole objective of this G.L.F. division."

With Farm Service well launched, McConnell, on July 1, 1945, placed Fallon in full charge so that Milliman could direct the research program developed by Babcock. (See p. 314.)

The formation of G.L.F. Farm Service gave McConnell great satisfaction. In reporting to the Board of Directors on September 10, 1945, he said, "If the retail division is properly conceived, organized and administered it will cover up practically all of the mistakes that we can make elsewhere. One of the most needed things in G.L.F. has been taking place within the last year."

Time was to justify McConnell's enthusiasm.[1]

[1] How Farm Service grew is continued in Chapter 31.

CHAPTER 30

Postwar Readjustment

We must start planning and thinking now rather than on V.J. Day to the end that war thinking, planning and action be shed as fast as possible. . . .

JAMES A. McCONNELL
June 26, 1945

IN THE NEXT six chapters we will see how the G.L.F. met the problems of the postwar adjustment during the inflationary period which came to an end with the economic recession that became evident in late 1948. This chapter describes how the G.L.F. dealt with the more general problems of readjustment. The following chapter will show how G.L.F. Farm Service reorganized retail operations to meet postwar needs. The next four chapters deal with significant developments that call for separate treatment—new approaches in marketing and research, the simplification of operations and structure, and the moves which culminated in the giving up of federal income tax exemption as of June 30, 1948.

THE WAR'S EFFECT

The G.L.F. had practically doubled in size to meet the needs of farmers during the war. Part of this expansion reflected inflation, but a substantial part represented real gains, measured in units of feed, fertilizer, petroleum, and other supplies and farm products. This abnormal growth had greatly changed the character of the organization. The G.L.F. had increased in power and prestige and in the range of its activities, but not without heavy costs in the quality of service provided farmers and in the attitudes of its personnel.

At G.L.F.'s Silver Anniversary Meeting on June 26, 1945, McConnell described conditions as the war closed. Plants and equipment were run down. Employees were war-weary, tired, and not up to par. There was much confusion in thinking. He said: "We must start planning and thinking now rather than on V.J. Day, to the end that war thinking, planning and action be shed as fast as possible. . . . Management must start to deal with war effects now."

In looking ahead, McConnell could not understand why so many, both in and out of the G.L.F., were so critical of its operations. He had come to the conclusion that what people do not understand, they suspect. He concluded that "G.L.F.'s limitations as to size, scope and breadth of services will in the future probably be determined not by its ability to operate many services efficiently, but rather by its ability to keep its directors, its employees, and . . . community leaders . . . sure of where it is going and why. . . . G.L.F. can go no faster with safety than it can consolidate its position in public opinion."[1]

He was concerned that many employees appeared to be more interested in developing new services than in maintaining top operating efficiency. He said, "We should take at least two years and concentrate on efficient operation. We should analyze and study service at the retail level and then back up what we decide to be our job."

In the June Managers' Conference, McConnell stressed the need for employee education. He said:

I want, within rather broad lines, to give the . . . [School of Cooperative Administration] its assignment for this coming year. *It is teaching the fundamentals of good service at the retail level.* This means going back to the simple things—good housekeeping, good record-keeping, inventory control, handling credit within a given policy, intelligent ordering, good patron relations—in fact, the kind of service that a farmer needs and expects from his G.L.F. Store and from his G.L.F. Agent. On these simple, fundamental management principles at retail will G.L.F. establish clearcut leadership pleasing to farmers.

At this same conference, McConnell called attention to a trend that was to become very important in the next few years—the use of G.L.F. to sponsor cooperatives or organizations to achieve important ends, rather than attempt to provide all possible services itself. To stress the point that G.L.F. already had a substantial record as a sponsor of other cooperatives, McConnell reviewed how the G.L.F. had worked with G.L.F. Service Stores and G.L.F. Petroleum Cooperatives to give them legal and financial independence. Referring to Cooperative P & C Family Foods, Inc., he said: "Here we have sponsored a cooperative which is legally independent and rapidly getting into a position to become finan-

---

[1] The G.L.F., like other farm cooperatives, woke up in 1944 to the fact that interests opposed to farm cooperatives had been "propagating misinformation so persistently" that the public was coming to accept it. Recognizing that concerted counteraction was required to provide the public with fair information on the organization and operation of farm cooperatives, the G.L.F. had joined with other farm cooperatives to revitalize and place on a year around basis the American Institute of Cooperation, which had been dormant during the war. To get this program going, G.L.F. had agreed to help underwrite it for a three-year period.

The G.L.F. was also coming to see that radio could be effectively used to inform members and the public on agricultural affairs and G.L.F. services. At a Managers' Conference on August 28, 1945, Bruce Gervan reported that after five years of experiment the G.L.F. Information Service had started on August 1 a five-day a week network program, "The World at Noon." Later we will see how this program developed. (Pages 354-357.)

cially independent." He then said: "From this, the student of cooperative development in this area will be able to predict pretty closely many things which will probably happen in the next generation within this territory." The formation of the Empire Livestock Marketing Cooperative, which was incubating at this time, soon was to give point to this statement. (See p. 319.)

(See p. 319.)

FEELING THE WAY

The problems confronting the G.L.F. were perplexing. The clock could not be turned back, for the G.L.F. had become a changed organization in the five years of war. Basic values of employees, and even of members, had to be re-established in the face of an uncertain future. Many economists of standing were predicting a serious postwar depression such as followed World War I, while others saw a pent-up demand that would continue boom conditions for several years. It should be recalled that, as the war closed, the demand for farm products remained high, and many supplies needed by farmers for production—especially feed, fertilizers, steel products and petroleum—were in short supply.

Although the expansion of the G.L.F., brought about by the war, called for new plant and equipment to serve members adequately, costs for construction seemed abnormally high; and the G.L.F. knew from experience that overhead costs must be kept to a minimum. It was apparent to G.L.F. management that the times called for prudent investment only where this was essential to maintain or strengthen operations.

The Directors deemed four steps immediately necessary to get the G.L.F. back into line:

(1) Revise and remake specifications on farm production supplies.
(2) Check quality controls.
(3) Adjust wholesale facilities to current and future needs.
(4) Bring community services to an efficient level.[2]

As the G.L.F. had built its reputation on the high quality of its supplies, it is not surprising that attention was promptly directed toward restoring quality to pre-war standards. During the war, substitute ingredients or materials had to be used and less care could be given to plant operations. As a result, many products handled at the close of the war were not "up to what farmers wanted."

To meet this problem the Board of Directors set up a standing committee on quality control, composed of Directors Earl Clark and Clifford Snyder, to review and revise quality specifications for goods and services. During the fall and winter this committee held a series of quality control

[2] President Frank Smith in report to stockholders, October 30, 1945.

hearings throughout the organization to examine carefully every G.L.F. commodity and service. The vigilance shown by this committee gave members confidence that G.L.F. quality, in McConnell's words, "was coming back from the war."

The G.L.F. School of Cooperative Administration was now operating with high effectiveness under the direction of Dr. Karl D. Butler. At a Managers' Conference in January, 1946, McConnell said, "We are quite well satisfied with the program as it has worked out for the education of employees. It is adapted to our needs. It is broad. It is consistent and sustained. It implements policy and does not try to make policy. . . ."

The avowed objectives of the school at this time were "(1) To teach employees cooperative fundamentals and the usefulness and the use of G.L.F. commodities and services; (2) To foster honesty, courtesy, self-reliance, and the spirit of cooperation among employees, and between employees and patrons; (3) To teach the value of resourceful, informed and articulate farm people as a vital force in American life; (4) To perpetuate the spirit of G.L.F. among employees, Agent-Buyers, patrons and the public; (5) To train teachers and help develop leaders."[3]

At a Managers' Conference on January 31, 1946, McConnell called attention to two factors giving trouble. (1) Price ceilings on important raw materials were causing less and less to reach the market at legal ceiling prices. (2) Manufactured articles were not yet flowing freely to market. He then said, "There you have it. Ninety percent of our effort is devoted to handling commodities and naturally we are in great distress because of these two factors."

At this conference, Silcox explained that the G.L.F. had decided to support the liability insurance program sponsored by the New York State Grange, rather than enter this field. Urged by the G.L.F. executives, the Grange had dropped the requirement that insured persons be members of the Grange. Silcox stated that this was another example of "how the G.L.F. will work with existing farm organizations which are owned and controlled by Northeastern farmers."

THE PROBLEM OF CONTROL

For several years McConnell, as General Manager, had been struggling to control the conglomerate operations of G.L.F. The war made it apparent that the system needed a controller who would think in terms of the total needs of the organization. This action was postponed until May,

[3] Karl D. Butler, "Learning by Doing," *News for Farmer Cooperatives*, March, 1946. This article gives a comprehensive picture of the work of the school as then carried on. See also pamphlet issued by the G.L.F., in July, 1946. *The G.L.F. School of Cooperative Administration.*

1946, when Charles E. Dykes, then serving as Controller for the Holding Company, was appointed Controller for the Exchange. At that time McConnell said: "As G.L.F. multiplies its functions and its operations, a continual critical examination of operational and accounting methods is required to avoid pyramiding and wasteful operations in manpower and money."[4]

Perhaps McConnell believed that a controller could help determine policy on inventories and reserves, matters of much concern at that time. Until conditions cleared he favored maintaining larger than normal inventories to insure continued services and the preservation of the cash reserves built up during the war to meet severe price declines. He expressed his thinking as follows: "The ability to keep a stream of production goods flowing to farmers is so tied up with large inventories that they are, in practice, inseparable. The greatest danger is that we will be lulled into a sense of security and dissipate our [financial] reserves, thinking that we have reached a permanently higher price level. Possibly we have, but of course reserves will do no harm. They can always be released."[5]

McConnell also strengthened central executive power and freed himself of operating detail in June, 1946, when he took over the direction of Mills, following the resignation of its President, A. L. Bibbins, and made C. L. Dickinson Assistant to the General Manager. At the same time he relieved himself of a major responsibility by shifting Karl Butler from education to research so that he could place T. E. Milliman in full charge of marketing operations. As feed was the heart of G.L.F. operations, the significance of these actions could not be overlooked.

McConnell then saw two main challenges confronting the G.L.F.:

(1) . . . how to fit operations to a very high wage rate per hour and an ever-decreasing number of hours per week.

(2) . . . how to expand facilities to meet the new demands . . . when it is almost impossible to build and when building costs are so much higher than pre-war.[6]

The G.L.F. was gradually liquidating wartime activities. This was evidenced in September, 1946, by the sale of the Crown Point Lumber Mill which had served a need during the war but could not be continued as a profitable operation for members under peacetime conditions.

In accord with its policy of working with other organizations on problems of common concern, G.L.F. joined with other major farm organizations in the Northeast to set up the Northeast Farm Foundation in the fall of 1946. Its object was to conduct and promote research relating to

[4] *G.L.F. Week,* May 1, 1946.
[5] Letter of J. A. McConnell, to author, of March 25, 1946.
[6] Letter, to author, of June 19, 1946.

Northeastern agriculture and keep Northeastern farm leaders currently informed on national problems as they might affect Northeastern agriculture.[7]

A PERSPECTIVE FOR PLANNING

McConnell placed G.L.F. planning in perspective in his address to the Annual Meeting of Stockholders on October 30, 1946. He pointed out that the direction of the G.L.F. required an understanding of two facts: "(1) The market—the place where our food is consumed—its character, size, and location. (2) Our main raw material—grass and hay."

He then characterized the market of the G.L.F. as "the golden horseshoe," because of its great productivity and purchasing power. McConnell termed this horseshoe with the heel at Buffalo and the tips at Philadelphia and New York City—embracing one-fifth of the nation's population—a great G.L.F. asset if dealt with wisely.

According to McConnell, crop production conditions in G.L.F. territory made dairying the "must" industry for serving this market, although limited areas were suitable for such cash crops as fruits and vegetables. He saw great opportunity for poultry production, if skillfully managed.

With this background he then turned to the problem of supplying the feed needs of dairy and poultry farmers. He recognized that this would require modernization and mechanization at a cost of from 8 to 10 million dollars, but he advocated waiting to the extent possible for a break in prices which "was sure to come" in view of the present high construction costs.

McConnell's concept of "the golden horseshoe" had convinced him that G.L.F. research should be confined to the fields of agronomy, animal and poultry nutrition, and human foods to help farmers produce and market the foods needed by consumers. Moreover, he saw in it guidance for G.L.F.'s marketing operations. "If G.L.F. is to market foods in volume to the people living [within the horseshoe] . . . we must have access to them through stores."

He pointed out that with G.L.F. canneries and other food marketing facilities now valued at $2 million G.L.F. could not dispose of more than 7 to 8 percent of its marketing output through its own agency and store system. This explained why the marketing of food had been taken out of the farm supply purchasing system—where it stirred up the resentment of

---

[7] G.L.F. took a leading position in establishing the Foundation, and for a time General Manager McConnell served as Chairman of its Board. R. L. Culver, a G.L.F. director, was its Administrative President, from February, 1947, to March, 1948. A. B. Genung served as Economist from February, 1948, to October, 1956, when the Foundation ceased operations and during this period it issued a monthly bulletin on matters of interest to Northeastern farm organizations.

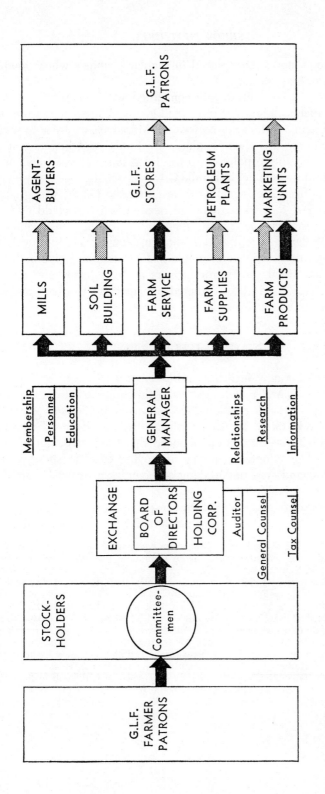

FIGURE 5—THE G.L.F. SYSTEM, DECEMBER, 1946

established food stores—and placed in regular channels where food was consumed in large quantities.

G.L.F. at this time was deeply concerned with the problem of disposing of its increasing output of canned goods. Army orders were being cut back and urban outlets were essential. Moreover, contrary to popular belief, the country was then "loaded with foods" and buyers could be "choosy." This condition pointed up the importance of good commercial relations with those who might handle G.L.F. products.

It was clear from McConnell's address that the G.L.F. was gradually accepting the fact that construction of needed facilities could no longer be postponed. In fact, plans were being made for the construction of a new million dollar feed mill at Bordentown, New Jersey, to absorb local grain and ingredient supplies available in that area, and give better and more economical feed service for farmers in New Jersey and on Long Island.[8] The Board had also instructed management to check and thoroughly modernize all fertilizer plants.

STAYING CLOSE TO SHORE

The pressure for new facilities and services was becoming intense in the spring of 1947. McConnell dealt with this in an article in the *G.L.F. Week* for May 19, 1947, entitled, "A Time to Stay Close to Shore." He feared that G.L.F. might tie itself up "with fixed assets costs" to a point where it couldn't compete. He announced that the Board, upon his recommendation, had adopted a policy of staying close to shore on fixed assets planning and was undertaking no avoidable expansion until the economy was more stable.[9]

A significant change in feed formula policy was announced in the *G.L.F. Week* for July 7, 1947. Henceforth its flexible formula feeds would

[8] Since *1933* the G.L.F. had tried various arrangements to lower feed costs for its New Jersey and Long Island patrons—barge shipment down the Hudson, contract with a concern in New York City, production through a cooperative association in Mt. Holly, and purchase of this plant. In December, 1946, this plant was sold back to the Burlington County Farmers Cooperative Association, with agreement to obtain feeds through it until a new plant could be built. G.L.F. bought the land for the new plant at Bordentown, N.J., on March 1, 1946, construction was started in early 1947, and operations begun in late 1948. An important consideration in building the plant was the market this would give for grains grown in the New Jersey area. Grain prices were then comparatively low in New Jersey as outlet to market grain was very limited. Letter of Herbert J. McClain, to author, of December 2, 1959.

[9] A few months later, McConnell pungently observed: "It is difficult to fight an effective rearguard action when the attack from the front is three times as strong as it is from the rear. This is another way of saying that we have got to keep hammering our boys that a drop in price is eventually coming." Letter, to author, of November 29, 1947.

be shipped under a tag which would list ingredients without giving pounds of each. McConnell stressed that this did not mean going to a closed formula, as the open formula would be available to all patrons through their service agencies. The change was designed to avoid the "rigidity" inherent in buying toward the formula and to permit "sorting the market" for bargains. This change of policy did not apply to mashes and Super-Exchange, Super-Test, and Dry and Freshening Rations would continue to use the public formula tag.[10]

At this time rising costs were giving G.L.F. much concern. In announcing a campaign to reduce costs, in the *G.L.F. Week* for July 28, 1947, McConnell said: "As a result of analyzing, planning and adjusting . . . we can take a budget to our Board next June, lower in both total and unit costs, without curtailing essential services or stopping progressive action."[11]

HONOR TO SAVAGE

The dedication of Savage Hall, the headquarters building for the Graduate School of Nutrition of Cornell University, on October 10, 1947, demonstrated G.L.F.'s public spirit. It commemorated the memory of Professor Seth Savage, the father of the open-formula idea upon which the G.L.F. was founded, and provided facilities to carry on his work in the field of nutrition—a primary concern of the G.L.F. Moreover, it was made possible by a gift of $200,000 voted by the G.L.F. directors on January 18, 1945.[12]

The commemoration exercises were impressive, with speeches by Governor Thomas E. Dewey, Dean W. I. Myers, H. E. Babcock, Representative Clifford Hope, Chairman of the House Committee on Agriculture, and many others. After paying tribute to the late Professor Savage as "a great teacher and a great leader," G.L.F. President Frank Smith said: "We make this investment in a Nutrition Building at Cornell because

[10] In announcing the new policy, McConnell said, "Any institution which survives and remains effective must service the principle of practical flexibility. . . . Change is the order of the day. I got my first lesson in top policy management watching H. E. Babcock, as General Manager, step in and introduce the principle of flexibility, thus taking G.L.F. out of an untenable position."

[11] In the *G.L.F. Week* of July 22, he had already observed: "It is time to do our level best to cut handling costs on commodities and be sure that the farmer has the opportunity to take the minimum of services."

[12] In transmitting the gift to Cornell President Edmund Ezra Day, General Manager McConnell had said, "The Board asked me to convey to you its recommendation that the headquarters building it is providing be named Savage Hall in memory of the late Professor E. S. Savage, whose leadership was largely responsible for the establishment of the School of Nutrition." See *G.L.F. Week*, January 22, 1945.

we believe that in no other place can the forces of research, education, industry and agriculture be brought together so effectively in the general interest of the public."[13]

BIG DECISIONS AHEAD

The growing importance of local advisory committeemen in G.L.F. affairs was reflected in a report called *Facts and Figures,* issued for their use prior to the 1946-47 Annual Meeting. In the preface McConnell pointed out that the report was designed to give G.L.F. "policy-makers" basic facts so that as delegates at the annual meeting they could deal more effectively with policies. Three important questions of policy were outlined: (1) The proposed change in membership qualification which would determine whether G.L.F. would give up its federal income tax exemption; (2) A plan for simplification of G.L.F. structure; (3) and a plan for increasing permanent capital.

Several interesting facts were reported. Since July 1, 1946, G.L.F. had sold three plants, while it had established two fertilizer plants, and started construction on the feed mill at Bordentown, New Jersey, and on a farm supply warehouse at Trenton, New Jersey.

However, the three plants sold were not lost to the G.L.F. as they were acquired by cooperative organizations in which G.L.F. held membership. At Fort Wayne, Indiana, the G.L.F. sold its Allied Seed Company plant to Select Seeds, Inc., and, as one of its seven members, was to continue its management under contract. The second plant, a basket factory at Orchard Park, New Jersey, had been acquired during the war to meet special war needs. This was sold to a newly-formed cooperative, The Orchard Park Cooperative, comprised of G.L.F. and three other regional cooperative organizations as members. The third plant, the Farm Supplies Research Laboratory at Ithaca, was acquired by United Cooperatives, Inc., of which G.L.F. was an established member. Thus, these transactions gave G.L.F. full use of these facilities at reduced cost, while it made them available to other farmer cooperatives.

One of the most thwarting problems of the G.L.F. during and after

---

[13] Babcock, in his address, gave McConnell credit for originating the idea of the School of Nutrition at Cornell, while Governor Dewey, in turn, remarked, "Mr. Babcock picked up the ball and ran with it, and the result is that we have a School of Nutrition." (See *G.L.F. Week,* October 20, 1947.) As a matter of record, McConnell got the idea of a school for research and teaching in the field of nutrition from a conversation with Dr. Paul Manning, biochemist with the Peebles Company. He recounted this conversation in a letter to Babcock, then President of the Board of Trustees of Cornell University, on June 3, 1941, in which he said: "Knowing how you and Day think on these things, the idea took hold of me." It is of interest that the Cornell School of Nutrition was established on June 16, 1941.

the war was to maintain a source of petroleum supplies. In late 1947 the situation grew so bad that the G.L.F. joined with other cooperatives to purchase an oil tanker to transport petroleum from Texas. This soon led to the joint acquisition of a refinery in Texas. This experience is discussed in Chapter 37.

The initial postwar inflationary explosion following the war had taken place by July 1, 1948, when the new membership policy went into effect. (See p. 335.) The next two years were to test G.L.F.'s ability to meet a period of declining prices in the commodities in which it was vitally concerned. Before going on to the problems of this later period, which will be considered in Chapter 36, it is essential that we observe how other developments were also changing the character of the G.L.F.

CHAPTER 31

Farm Service Steps Out

*We have reorganized ... Farm Service, to ... do the best job possi-
ble for G.L.F. patrons and at the same time put the retail division into
the over-all G.L.F. organization so that it meshes at all points.*

EDMUND H. FALLON
June, 1946

THE UNIFICATION of retail services, as described in Chapter 29, now
demonstrated its value. With retail operations under one head, concentrated attention could be given to common problems. This reduced
organizational friction and permitted the best use of manpower.

Fallon was the ideal man to direct the new program. He had demonstrated his leadership capacity and drive in developing the petroleum
service and in revitalizing the employees' educational program. He was
in tune with both the field and central management.

On June 27, 1945, he reported to a Managers' Conference that recon-
version to peace had already started. He called attention to the great
changes, brought about by the war, to be taken into account. In the retail
stores the tonnage of supplies handled had nearly doubled since 1940.
Operating costs per ton had increased from $1.80 to $3.00. The number of
retail employees had grown from 583 to 930, and 75 percent of those at the
end of 1945 were not employed in 1940. The number of items on the price
list had expanded from 1,318 to 3,526.

Fallon saw several needs—new buildings and new facilities; a breather
in new items handled; training of personnel, especially of returning veteran employees; and improved public relations at the community level.

He anticipated intense competition for farmer business. "We must be
alert to many changes that will take place as they affect farmers, such as
feeding practices, agronomy, quality, labor-saving devices for the farmer."
Farm Service was getting ready to meet these changes. Service Aid programs had already been set up for Engineering and Real Estate (Jay Coryell); Accounting (Fred Upchurch); Personnel and Education (Seeber
Tarbell); and Food (Phil McEachron); and the others called for by the
plan were being "lined up." Each Service Aid program was being organized by a special committee made up of the wholesale or retail agencies
directly involved in its proposed activities.

Research and experiment during the war had shown that merchandising
of farm supplies required specialized attention. To meet this need, a Farm

Stores Department was set up in July, 1945, under the direction of Arthur J. Wells, who had a flair for promotion and merchandising, and excellent experience in retail distribution as a store manager and fieldman.

The new department called for pioneering ability, for it had to build its own local service facilities and furnish them with trained management. However, each farm store was to be owned by a local store corporation and under the supervision of its patron committee.

In reporting to the Board in September, 1945, Fallon explained that the Farm Stores Department had been created to recognize the merchandising needs of farm supply items which were growing in importance with the expansion of mechanized farming. He pointed out that the service stores had not been aggressive in handling farm supplies and equipment since their primary concern was providing service on feed, seed and fertilizer which accounted for 85 percent of all G.L.F. business. The proper handling of farm supplies called for trained personnel and specialized equipment for display and storage. He said: "We have merely distinguished the farm store from the service store." Wells, as Director of the Farm Stores Department, was to harmonize the farm store and service store programs.

At a Managers' Conference, November 29, 1945, Wells described how retail operations were being correlated through a retail committee on farm supplies. This committee, composed of William Ellsworth for Service Stores, E. S. Griffith for Agent-Buyers, and himself for Farm Stores, was working in cooperation with the Farm Supplies Division on the selection of farm supplies to be offered Service Agencies. It was providing advance order programs for such items as steel roofing, farm freezers, bale ties and packages. It was recommending retail prices on all items, dealing with complaints, and cooperating with the Farm Supplies Division in keeping Service Agencies informed on such matters as the availability of supplies. The committee was also helping retail agencies to improve their facilities, and giving them leadership in merchandising through planned commodity programs and suggested displays.

When Fallon reported to a Managers' Conference on June 31, 1946, the existing Service Aids were operating well and plans were being made to add Service Aids to achieve better wholesale-retail coordination in handling feed, fertilizer and seed. These posts were soon filled.

The progress of Farm Service during its first year was reflected in its reports at the June, 1946, Managers' Conference. Fallon pointed out that "adequate knowledge of useful product information is necessary at all levels of Farm Service in order that it can properly be presented to patrons in each community." He said that the streamlining of personnel education, the development of specialized personnel, and the effective correlation of commodity and promotional programs were essential to accomplish this purpose. Using the Ithaca G.L.F. Service as an example he showed how extensive counseling services were being given to farmers, while serving their supply and marketing needs, and he held that this was one of G.L.F.'s most important functions.

Fallon laid stress on the work of Farm Service in helping farmers with their marketing problems. "The greatest need, as expressed by patrons in certain areas, continues to be for assistance in marketing the crops they produce." He pointed out that Farm Service had responded to this need by setting up a marketing procurement unit to aid patrons in assembling their products for markets as developed by G.L.F. Farm Products.

M. A. Brink, in charge of Marketing Procurement, then explained how Farm Service would work with Farm Products. The Marketing Procurement unit was to deal with farmers on all marketing operations performed through the retail system. It would help local community service agencies with personnel and facilities problems related to marketing and give them advisory service. It would thus correlate all local marketing activities with those of the sales department of Farm Products so that farm products of the right kind and quality could be moved at the right time to the advantage of the producer. Brink made it clear that the Marketing Procurement unit would not supersede or operate independently in any way from Products. It would look to Products for help and leadership in such main services as buying, cleaning, grading, packing, or pricing.

Other Farm Service reports brought out that repair service was being provided for G.L.F. mechanical equipment in all communities, that a maintenance system for trucks had been established, and that the larger service agencies were now providing many specialized services.

Fallon summarized the presentation by saying: "It is now general policy in the Retail Division to departmentalize and specialize. . . . We have reorganized the Retail Division, Farm Service, to meet the changing conditions which took place during the war, in order to do the best possible job for G.L.F. patrons and at the same time fit the Retail Division into the over-all G.L.F. organization so that it meshes at all points."

At the Managers' Conference, October 2-3, 1946, Fallon reported the appointment of C. E. Dayton as Service Aid for feed and of P. A. MacEachron as Service Aid for seed and soil building items. Thirty-six Service Agencies now had separate departments to handle farm supplies, with separate supervision and records. Although all building possible was being curtailed, the Engineering Department had a million dollar construction program under way.

Fallon also reported a significant new development which was to grow in importance. A merchandising committee had been created under the chairmanship of Dayton to strengthen merchandising methods within the G.L.F. The committee was also to correlate merchandising programs of the retail and wholesale services. It had prepared an attractive two-color booklet, *One Dozen Ways*, to emphasize the essentials of good merchandising, which was distributed at this meeting. *One Dozen Ways* gave merchandising a real boost. It emphasized such things as the need of good housekeeping, adequate display facilities, commodity calendars, planned merchandising programs, arrangement of displays, posting of price and commodity information, encouragement of patrons' early orders, using the mail to keep patrons informed, making use of facilities and handling patron relations. The twelfth way was "What's Your Idea?." This question was designed to encourage the Service Agencies to find ways to put ideas into use.

Later during the meeting, Dayton defined merchandising in G.L.F. as ". . . the art of letting the patron know what is available to him through the G.L.F., and making it so attractive that he makes the decision to use his own cooperative's services rather than someone else's."

One of Farm Service's most difficult problems in the postwar period was to establish close working harmony with the wholesale divisions and, particularly, with G.L.F. Mills, Inc. McConnell had worked on this problem through use of committees and by stationing fieldmen at the mills to achieve better coordination, but it had not been entirely solved. In fact, the problem had been somewhat aggravated by the rapid expansion of retail manufacturing facilities during the war. Fallon's appointment of Dayton as Feed Service Aid was designed to meet this problem. He was well suited for this position. As a district manager he had served as Chairman of the Dairy Feed Merchandising Committee, and during the war he had worked closely with Mills on feed allocation problems. Under his leadership, greatly improved mill-retail relationships were established.

Phil MacEachron, as Service Aid for Soil Building and Seeds, likewise established close liaison between wholesale and retail operations in handling fertilizers and seeds.

Another serious need in retail distribution after the war was to correct some of the bad personnel practices which had grown up under wartime conditions. In a retail service conference at Syracuse in January, 1947, Seeber Tarbell, Service Aid for Personnel and Education, graphically described "the mess" left by the war. He saw the following problems needing attention: (1) Certain managers had taken advantage of an extremely democratic system of supervision and management; (2) others had been conditioned, by lack of adequate help and extreme pressures of work, to perform only the day-to-day routine essentials; (3) the managerial capacity of other men had not kept pace with the size and complexity of present-day operations; (4) "Horatio Alger" success during the war years had caused many managers to become self-centered and self-satisfied.

To correct the situation, Tarbell proposed (1) a closer working relation-

ship between District Managers and Committeemen; (2) better selection of
men for specific jobs; (3) better organization of employees in the assignment of definite responsibilities; (4) better employee training, and (5)
closer contact between employees and management.

At this same conference, Ralph Dudley of the Service Store Department, called attention to the weaknesses that had crept into retail operations. He saw the need of (1) better accounting records to give standards
for efficiency; (2) more attention to established goals; (3) more study of
operations in the light of changing conditions; (4) getting patron committees to become more operation-minded; (5) giving salary raises to those
who deserve them. He concluded his talk by saying: "We are in a new
era and . . . it is time to tighten our belts."

The emphasis on farm stores had caused many service stores to give
more consideration to the merchandising of farm supplies. In many service stores, farm supply departments were being set up, rather than separate farm stores. Ellsworth reported that the problem was to determine
whether volume justified setting up a separate farm store or a farm supplies department.

A pamphlet, *G.L.F. Farm Service,* issued in January, 1947, gives us this
picture of the organization at that time:

Farm Service correlates the activities of all service agencies. Within Farm
Service are four operating departments; one for each kind of community retail
service . . . Agent-Buyers . . . Service Stores . . . Petroleum Plants . . . Farm
Stores. Each Department is similarly organized . . . Divisions of responsibility
are clearcut. Each manager or owner of a community service is responsible to
his district manager or supervisor. The supervisor is responsible to the director
of his department and these directors are in turn responsible to the head of
Farm Service.

As a further step in correlating the retail departments and assisting individual
retail service agencies, eight members of Farm Service personnel have been
designated as Service Aids. There is an aid for: (1) Feed, (2) Seed and Soil
Building; (3) Marketing Procurement; (4) Real Estate and Engineering; (5)
Accounting and Internal Audit; (6) Personnel and Education; (7) Membership
Relations and (8) Motor Transportation.

Each of these Service Aids first discusses all matters of policy with the department head concerned. After the policy has been cleared and the department
head has given permission, the Service Aid man may then work directly with
the district manager or the local agency manager as the need arises.

All department activities within the division are correlated through the Farm
Service Executive Committee, comprised of E. H. Fallon, President; C. E.
Dayton, Feed Service Aid; R. J. Wolf, Director of Petroleum Department; J. W.
Stiles, Director of Service Stores Department; M. E. Campbell, Director of
Agent-Buyers Department; and A. J. Wells, Director of Farm Stores Depart-
ment.

At this time there were 362 Agent-Buyers, including 44 Community Cooperatives; 217 Cooperative Service Stores; 54 Cooperative Petroleum Bulk

Stations; and 12 Farm Stores. Twelve more Farm Stores were waiting for Government approval to build.

The pamphlet then described the work of the Service Aids and how they might be used. This statement conveys the "staff" character of the Service Aid program. It was to facilitate operations—not engage directly in them. For example, the Service Aid for Personnel and Education was to direct training and education of employees. The educational programs were to be correlated with all divisions and planned in cooperation with department heads, their assistants, and district managers. It was clear that the Personnel and Educational Service Aid had no authority over department heads or personnel. His functions were restricted to study, guidance, coordination and leadership in the personnel field.

Few changes were made in Farm Service during the next year, although a Service Aid program for merchandising was set up under E. J. Biggie.

In addressing a Managers' Conference on December 18, 1947, McConnell expressed satisfaction with the way Farm Service had fulfilled expectations. He said:

Today, Farm Service sits in the position of reflecting to policy management in G.L.F. and to the heads of wholesale divisions an accurate picture of the requirements of G.L.F. Stores, G.L.F. Gas Stations, plus the set of facts needed to determine the policy of G.L.F. as it applies to the farmer. . . . Farm Service is in so responsible a position toward farmers and toward the G.L.F. today that not to handle it well would be very serious.

He continued:

I now want to point out that G.L.F. has the greatest management system of community services ever devised, either in proprietary business or in farm cooperative circles. It is great because it combines local over-all policy through a professional management system.

McConnell was concerned with but one problem. He thought that too often, in dealing with local committees, those in Farm Service had concerned themselves with defending their right to manage. He urged those in Farm Service to "sell this system" of management on a positive basis to farmers.

In a report to the Board of Directors in January, 1948, Fallon stated that the Farm Service Department then supervised 425 Agent-Buyers, 61 Petroleum Units, 230 local Service Stores, and 38 Farm Stores. He pointed out that many manpower moves had been required in the Farm Service Division since the end of the war, but that the men had now settled into their jobs. He indicated that the next big objective was to qualify farmer members as stockholders by June 30, when the new membership program would become effective.

The importance of the Agent-Buyers as distributors of G.L.F. supplies was not overlooked in Farm Service. The work with Agent-Buyers had been aggressively carried on by M. E. Campbell, with 12 District Managers. At the conference in January, 1948, Campbell indicated that the Agent-Buyers still accounted for 45.3 percent of G.L.F.'s wholesale volume, although 75 Agent-Buyer points had been converted to service store points since 1940. He estimated that their retail sales exceeded $70,000,000, and that 80 to 85 percent of the supplies handled were obtained through G.L.F. He called attention to the fact that the Agent-Buyers were using from $12,000,000 to $15,000,000 in their businesses, and that they were doing a good job especially at the smaller points where it was uneconomical for service stores to operate.

During 1948, the work of the Merchandising Committee was intensified under the leadership of Biggie as Service Aid for Merchandising. Publication was begun of *The Builder,* a monthly house organ to bring good merchandising ideas and information to the attention of the retail service agencies and others concerned with expanding use of G.L.F. commodities and services. The *Builder* made effective use of animated cartoons, testimonials, contests and illustrations to promote such things as better displays, farm calls, new merchandise offerings, use of newspaper ads, warehouse housekeeping, and better timing of sales effort.

The pamphlet, *One Dozen Ways,* developed by the Merchandising Committee, had suggested that every Service Agency develop a commodity calendar to know *what* to offer and *when.* The idea took hold that there was a time to order, a time to have meetings, a time to begin a commodity sales program, a time to have sales, a time to reduce inventories, and a time for stock-selling drives. *The Builder* promoted this idea and out of it grew the Planned Action Program, which has become an established institutional device for planning and timing merchandising efforts. The first action calendar was issued in June, 1949, for use in 1949-1950.[1]

The following facts give some idea of the growth of Farm Service operations in the three years from June 30, 1945 to June 30, 1948:

The number of service stores grew from 194 to 227, and their sales volume from $59,374,617 in 1944-45 to $99,031,674 in 1947-48. Their total assets rose from $9,467, 620 to $16,543,641, while their fixed assets (at cost) rose from $3,506,647 to $7,911,367. Their preferred stock, representing membership investment, increased from $2,122,658 to $3,359,570, while they increased retained savings from $2,136,686 to $3,475,687. The net margins of the service stores were $1,325,672 for the year 1944-45 and $1,801,705 for the year 1947-48.

[1] According to Paul Taber, this was largely "Fallon's baby." He saw the need of advance planning for meetings and commodity drives, and had plan charts developed for each major commodity showing sales by weeks over a period of a year. These were then used to develop plans which could be shown on a calendar for ready reference. Biggie worked closely with Fallon on the original development of this program. Letter of Paul Taber, to author, October 6, 1958.

Petroleum operations also reflected marked expansion. The number of bulk plants increased during the three-year period from 45 to 57, while their sales volume increased from $6,845,754 in 1944-45, to $12,395,127 in 1947-48. The total assets of the bulk plants increased from $1,008,585 to $1,858,159, while their fixed assets (at cost) grew from $929,655 to $1,926,195. The net margins of the bulk plants were $209,652 in 1944-45 and $252,484 in 1947-48.

During this period the number of Agent-Buyers declined from 475 to 446 as more Agent-Buyer units were converted into service stores.

The reorganization which took effect on July 1, 1948, had little effect on G.L.F. Farm Service for, in practice, it had operated as a Division from its formation. The form of G.L.F. Farm Service was now set and was to remain largely unchanged until 1953.

CHAPTER 32

Research Settles Down

A clear understanding of the main characteristics of our agriculture gives us an idea as to where our research interests lie.

JAMES A. McCONNELL
October 30, 1946

BABCOCK'S RETIREMENT AND RESIGNATION as Director of Research came just as World War II was closing and interest was shifting to post-war adjustments. By this time the research program had lost much of its momentum. Babcock had become primarily interested in the promotion of his ideas for better nutrition, dramatized by his concept of the Ever-Normal Refrigerator.

Research under Babcock had given the G.L.F. a needed shot in the arm. McConnell, responsible for administration, sensed that it could now be de-emphasized. He therefore placed Milliman in charge and tied the program more closely to his office. He re-directed the survey work on attitudes to studies relating to commodities to be carried on by a staff known as the Farm Management Group.[1]

Milliman's approach to research was reflected in a report to a Managers' Conference on August 28, 1945. He explained in some detail how the project in unified management of community enterprises was going forward on a nine-acre tract at Cobleskill. (See p. 265.) The freezer locker plant and small community slaughterhouse were authorized and would soon be available. The other facilities—a feed, seed, and fertilizer store, and a machine service and hardware establishment—were planned to follow. A manager for the entire project was to be carefully selected.

Freezer-locker-slaughterhouse research was being carried on at the Mother Zero plant. It was now losing money, and Milliman held that prudence would indicate the wisdom of waiting out the research before undertaking such service at other points.

He wanted it understood that the experimental dairy cattle auctions—

[1] The Farm Management Group consisted of technical agricultural specialists. Their job was described at the June 1946 Managers' Conference as follows: (1) To carry on a continuous appraisal of the performance of G.L.F. goods on the farm; (2) To report farmers' changing needs; (3) To help on complaints relating to goods and services; (4) To assist the Information Division on farm practice problems; (5) To make studies for the General Manager; and (6) To serve as a task force in the field of public relations. At this time the group consisted of F. K. Naegely (Dairy Specialist), John Huttar and John Vandervort (Poultry Specialists), Forrest Mather (Farm Crops Specialist), and Warren A. Ranney (Information and Survey Specialist).

then much in the news—did not mean that G.L.F. was entering the cattle marketing business. In fact, these G.L.F. dairy cattle auctions, after careful dissection and diagnosis, could be catalogued as failures. However, he thought that they might encourage other cooperatives, including milk organizations, to examine the facts and make their decision on what to do. Consideration was also being given to the development of an Ithaca restaurant and bakery. If the idea was tried out it would be purely a research experiment.

It was clear that the scope of the research program was gradually narrowing; that Milliman was tidying up and bringing to completion the various projects that had been started by Babcock.

On November 14, 1945, McConnell gave an important talk at a staff conference, entitled, "Defining and Defending Our Cooperative Frontiers." Declaring that the research frontier must be protected, he said: "The necessity of research is obvious to any mature business organization. Its fundamental nature is just beginning to be recognized in cooperative circles." It was his view that G.L.F. was still in the formative stage in determining just how to apply research. He was inclined toward the idea of promoting the use of research in certain desirable directions rather than undertaking it.

He thought that the operating divisions could carry on the research needed within their divisions but he pointed out, "There is research of another character." This other kind of research needed to be headed up under one man who could "evaluate, prod, and, if necessary, finance." He said, "If research in a cooperative is to be effective, it must come under a man with a very broad vision, experience and knowledge of the agricultural problems of the area covered, as well as the activities of the cooperative."

McConnell apparently was thinking of research that could be done by land-grant colleges or others, with G.L.F. encouragement and financial support. He was moving away from the idea of the G.L.F. having a separate operating research department.

He further expressed his views on research and development in a conference report on January 31, 1946:

We have had several years now of considerable and, at times, intense activity along this frontier. Actually, we have been doing research in methods of research. I think we have learned but are still searching.

At the Managers' Conference in June, Milliman reported as follows on the trends in G.L.F. research:

Developments which apply to operations can best be handled by the operating departments. An illustration of this is a development of the Chemical Division of lime and fertilizer-spreading equipment over a period which has now reached ten years. Another illustration is the creation and long operation of the Kem Fee process of seed treatment by the Seed Division.

The establishment at Cobleskill of a series of community services, grouped in one lot, was the application of an idea furnished by Mr. H. E. Babcock while Director of Research. . . . As his successor, I inherited and enlarged the committee which, in turn, chose Cobleskill. The committee decided upon a single manager for the various operations. This, in itself, constitutes a major piece of research, due to the fact that the G.L.F. managerial pattern on community services is strictly one of specialization. . . .

No new operations . . . are being conducted or contemplated at Cobleskill. This removes the necessity of research or pioneering on the individual operations, themselves, and leaves the whole development in its new aspect, one of research in management. . . .

Since Cobleskill is a Farm Service operation and the pattern is set, there is no need for the Research Department, as such, to continue functioning in control of it. Accordingly, your General Manager and Research Director made the decision to withdraw Cobleskill from the research field, as such, and leave it as a development project. That is the way it is now.

The frequent and concentrated attention given to Cobleskill problems by the Community Services Research Committee has resulted almost imperceptibly in a change in viewpoint toward the establishment of additional facilities at farm trade centers. . . .

Milliman continued:

There is now a consciousness of the desirability of grouping enterprises where possible and of operating in concert as a whole farmers' institution, as contrasted to independent functioning of departments. . . .

Milliman then reviewed the problem of farmers during the war years in maintaining equipment and the decision to establish at Owego a machine shop at which (a) machines of various kinds might be repaired and an inventory of supplies and parts maintained; (b) tractors and certain other equipment might be rented by farmers; and (c) custom services performed for farmers.

Milliman summed up:

. . . We regard the Owego research as completed. . . . We have learned a considerable list of facts, including:

(1) Repair services to equipment cannot be maintained for farmers at a cost low enough to suit them. . . . A machine shop operating on its own at competitive rates is apparently incapable of self-support.

(2) The rental of equipment such as tractors and tractor attachments is a deal of considerable service to farmers in time of equipment scarcity but one which can with difficulty be made to be self-supporting. . . .

(3) Custom services in the form of field baling, tractor plowing and harrowing, and combining grain are bad losers when conducted by a cooperative, which must observe all of the present-day regulations, such as Social Security, Workmen's Compensation, and several others . . . .

He saw some possibilities in the use of large-size, heavy-duty equipment but, in general, he believed that custom services could be better and more economically rendered by others.

Milliman concluded that the real field of research within the G.L.F. system lay in the great opportunities for agronomic advancement of the Northeastern farmer.

Recognizing this fact, this cooperative has turned more and more to the stimulating and the support of land-grant colleges in the development of better crops, better methods, better seeds, better fertilizers, better feeds and feeding, and better farming.

Karl D. Butler, who was at this time taking over the job of Director of Research, said: "Much of what we call research in G.L.F. is more than that. It might more properly be called application or development."

He made it clear that the research program was being cut down and cut back. "It is my belief that there is a real need for coordination and understanding within the organization and between Departments regarding research. I believe that our present trend toward more grants to colleges and cooperation with industry is proper."

McConnell supported this position in his 1945-46 annual report when he summed up research policy as follows:

It is to promote investigation in the fields of human foods, agronomy, and poultry and dairy cattle nutrition, and to do this primarily in the land-grant colleges. This is now done largely in those colleges in the area where we farm and market. At these institutions are highly trained research key people who can direct specific projects. This policy avoids building of research facilities, laboratories, etc., and acquiring permanent staffs which may be difficult to direct and maintain, as well as over-costly.

For the past five years the cost of research in G.L.F. has averaged about $65,000 per year. At the present time this appears to be adequate.

Then McConnell said: "We should distinguish clearly between research and quality control work." He also said: "Possibly because G.L.F. research policy has not been clearly explained and publicized, there has resulted some honest and sincere criticism on the part of farmers, of the G.L.F. Board's appropriations for research purposes."

The revised G.L.F. research program, as outlined by Butler, in December, 1946, provided for a G.L.F. Research Board comprised of major executives representing the various activities of the organization to work with the Director of Research who was to serve as Chairman. This Board was to develop over-all policy within management. It was to be kept fully informed on all development and quality control work in all departments. The Director of Research was charged with the responsibility of coordinating research throughout the G.L.F. and of serving as a focal point for research, quality control and development so that there would be no misunderstanding. He was "to coordinate but not dominate all G.L.F. research activities."

The objectives of the program were stated as follows:

1. To make use of every known resource and to seek out new information which will benefit Northeastern agriculture.

2. To bring research problems to the attention of land-grant colleges, industry, and other research institutions.

3. To help develop and maintain a spirit of "research consciousness" among key G.L.F. executives and the Board of Directors.

Butler expressed G.L.F. policy on research even more succinctly at a Managers' Conference in June, 1947: It is "to *stimulate and support existing outside research facilities wherever possible rather than duplicate or conduct research in our own right.*" While he recognized that G.L.F. did a great deal of quality control and development work through the laboratory and pilot operations of Farm Supplies, Soil Building, Mills and Farm Products, he termed these strictly departmental functions.

These policy statements served to bring the research program into better balance with the other activities of the organization. A breathing period was called for after the breathless period of innovation which research under Babcock had stimulated.

It should also be borne in mind that the period following the war was filled with uncertainty and that McConnell was, understandably, concerned most directly with stabilizing operations and lowering operating costs. He saw the extravagance which had crept in with the war and early postwar inflation, and his first interest was to tighten up on operations all along the line.

The spirit of adventure and experiment which had characterized G.L.F. research during the war years was thus muted by the day-by-day necessities of management, and research interest was to remain largely static until the late fifties when new problems again called for fresh research approaches.

CHAPTER 33

Re-Appraisal of Marketing, 1946-50

Any marketing undertaken by the G.L.F. should be of a nature that fits or meshes into G.L.F. operations.

JAMES A. McCONNELL
Report to G. L. F. Directors
December, 1947

MARKETING WAS A bouncing baby at the war's end. (See p. 282.) President Smith, in his annual report for 1944-45, said: "We realize that demands on the G.L.F. for new marketing operations will be tremendous." He then said:

The policy of your Board of Directors on marketing is that we should never get more than one step ahead of our outlets. To be specific, when we can sell the full production of the three canning factories now in operation we will consider a fourth, and when we can sell the full production of four factories, we might consider a fifth if there is a service to be rendered.

FORMATION OF EMPIRE LIVESTOCK MARKETING COOPERATIVE

It will be recalled that in June, 1945, McConnell directed attention to a trend in G.L.F. toward sponsoring cooperatives to achieve important ends. At this same meeting Ray Flumerfelt, in charge of G.L.F. marketing operations, said, "There appears to be a real opportunity for a cooperative to improve livestock marketing conditions for farmers in G.L.F. territory." However, he added, "Until the present meat crisis is over it will be difficult to make constructive moves in this direction."

The need for a better livestock marketing system for New York farmers had long been recognized, and during 1943 and 1944 it had been the subject of much discussion in the G.L.F. Research Committees.

To get experience in livestock slaughtering and distribution, Farm Products had opened a small slaughtering plant at Clyde in 1944. Due to difficulties in operating under O.P.A. price regulations, this plant had been leased to Cooperative P & C Family Foods, Inc., on April 15, 1945.

Soon after this a "constructive" move, called for by Flumerfelt, came with a meeting at Ithaca in July between McConnell and Babcock, representing G.L.F., and Eugene Forrestel, Clayton White, and Palmer Flournoy, representing the Buffalo Livestock Producers' Association, to consider the desirability of a statewide livestock marketing organization to be sponsored by all interested groups.

319

This led to a meeting at Batavia in August with representatives of the College of Agriculture and P & C Markets to explore the possibilities of "organizing a committee and deciding what organizations should be interested." It was agreed that a sound livestock marketing program could be developed only by the true cooperative effort of livestock producers, marketing agencies, consumer agencies, farm organizations, and the College of Agriculture.

Following consultation with these groups, a meeting was held in Ithaca on December 21, 1945, attended by representatives of the following organizations: The New York State College of Agriculture, the New York State Grange Patrons of Husbandry, the New York State Farm Bureau Federation, the Dairymen's League Cooperative Association, The Cooperative Grange League Federation Exchange, the Cooperative P & C Markets, and the Producers' Cooperative Commission Association of Buffalo.

It was unanimously decided that a livestock marketing cooperative should be set up, with directors chosen from the five cooperatives represented, and a committee was appointed to develop plans for a permanent organization. The recommendations of this committee, with minor modifications, were adopted at a follow-up meeting held on January 5, 1946, and the Empire Livestock Marketing Cooperative was born.[1] Its purpose was to establish a network of livestock markets in the area served by the sponsoring organizations to meet the needs of producers and consumers.

Empire was initially financed by the sale of non-voting stock to the sponsoring organizations. G.L.F.'s investment in Empire amounted to $30,210 on June 30, 1947. As of June 30, 1948, it stood at $91,210.

In a Managers' Conference, January 31, 1946, McConnell reported that the Empire Livestock Marketing Cooperative was being formed to handle the surpluses of cull dairy cattle and other livestock in the territory. He also indicated that a companion organization, the Empire Packing Cooperative, to be sponsored by the Dairymen's League, P & C, Producers' Livestock Association of Columbus, Ohio, and the G.L.F., would establish a packing house at Syracuse. He said: "This will be built by G.L.F. and rented and operated by P & C."

In developing plans for the Empire Livestock Marketing Cooperative it was agreed that the packing house was needed to serve the P & C stores. This was in line with Babcock's across-the-board theory of marketing that the product should be moved cooperatively from producer to consumer. As it did not seem feasible to combine the operation of a slaughter house with an auction system of markets, dependent upon the good will of

[1] For more information on formation of Empire Livestock Marketing Cooperative, see "Empire Co-op," *Cooperative Digest*, May, 1946, and article by its manager, Raymond V. Hemming, "Progress in Marketing Livestock Cooperatively in the Northeast," *American Cooperation*, 1954.

existing slaughterers, it was decided that the meat slaughtering corporation would be set up as a subsidiary by P & C Markets. Although this organization—Empire Packing Cooperative—was incorporated, it never constructed the slaughter house although land was acquired for this purpose under a 99-year lease from the Central New York Regional Market Authority.[2]

The success of the Empire Livestock Marketing Cooperative in the next few years demonstrated how G.L.F. could work with other organizations to develop a service of value to its members.[3] In this way the G.L.F. realized an objective without assuming all of the financial cost and bearing all of the financial risks involved.

REALISM INCREASES

The reports given at the June, 1946, Manager's Conference show how G.L.F. Farm Products was attempting to correlate marketing activities within the whole G.L.F. system "keeping in mind that the ultimate goal of the marketing development is to better serve the farmers for whom we work." The decision had been made not to sell processed foods and vegetables through G.L.F. stores and agencies, since this was impairing business relations with established wholesalers. Plans were made to use brokers outside of G.L.F. territory.

The new program was giving good results. The A & P Company had agreed to stock a full line of G.L.F. labeled products in its stores in G.L.F. territory, and R. N. Goddard, who was supervising the three canning plants for G.L.F. Farm Products, said, "The sales stream has started to flow and is headed in the right direction."

The Board had also decided that all commodities produced by farmer-owned G.L.F. canning plants and sold in G.L.F. territory must carry the G.L.F. label. Goddard said, "By the policy of selling the G.L.F. label we will be prepared for that time when the food demand will be lessened considerably." Moreover, it was recognized that consumer advertising would be needed to sell and establish the G.L.F. label.

Goddard made another interesting point. He estimated that some $75 million was invested in fruit and vegetable processing plants in G.L.F. territory while the G.L.F. had only one million invested in these plants.

[2] According to C. W. Sadd, the Manager of P & C Markets at this time, "No one ever came forth with the finances to build a slaughter house and, personally, I never had any great interest in one, nor did I feel that it was a good operation for P & C. Consequently, the idea died a natural death and P & C has utilized the corporation and the land under lease for construction of its warehouse and official headquarters." Letter from C. W. Sadd, to author, April 3, 1956.

[3] See H. H. Hulbert, "Empire Livestock Sells Under Hammer," *News for Farmer Cooperatives,* February, 1950.

He said, "To have a proportionate amount to their investment to purchasing for farmers, G.L.F. would need to have an investment in fruit and vegetable processing plants of $20 million." Thus the G.L.F. had not entered the marketing field with a full realization of all it would take in resources to do the job efficiently. Although problems ahead were anticipated, the extent of the changes which might be called for was yet little appreciated.

At this time, as noted above (p. 308), the Farm Service Division under Fallon was also assuming larger local responsibilities in marketing through its Marketing Procurement Service.

In his annual report for 1945-46, presented at the annual meeting on October 30, 1946, McConnell dwelt at length on the problem of marketing. He pointed out that the early food handling of G.L.F. was largely a purchasing service for its farmer membership, with distribution through G.L.F. stores and agents; that even when the first canning factory was acquired, G.L.F. stores and agents had been able, for the most part, to dispose of its output in the rural area. This situation had changed with the aggressive expansion of G.L.F. marketing facilities and, as a result, the G.L.F. agency and store system "could not dispose of more than 7 to 8 percent of the present marketing output." The G. L.F. could no longer "kid" itself. It was necessary to establish good commercial relations and remove causes of friction. "Incidentally," he said, "the controversy over the tax status of farmer cooperatives has not helped develop market outlets."

McConnell was leading up to this general point—that it was wise to take the marketing of food out of the purchasing system in G.L.F. and place it in regular food channels so as to get distribution where food was consumed in large quantities, namely, in metropolitan areas.

It is obvious from this general statement that G.L.F. was going through a change of thinking with regard to marketing. It was in the process of separating marketing from purchasing operations. McConnell's comments set the stage for a more realistic recognition of marketing problems.

During the next year marketing volume reached an all-time high of $17,837,000. In his annual report for 1946-47, McConnell said: "Certain types of marketing done by G.L.F. have unquestionably proven their worth." He thought that egg-marketing should be considered a "worthwhile, permanent operation within the G.L.F. framework." Moreover, he believed that marketing of wheat, buckwheat and beans, along with the utilization of locally-grown feed grains, was an activity that the G.L.F. should continue. He called attention to the fact that "all of these products are either non-perishable or else go to market every day, . . . [so that] G.L.F. has been able to focus effectively on the problems of marketing them." On the other hand, he pointed out that the marketing of fruits and vegetables was presenting difficult problems involving processing and brand advertising—"new in the experience of G.L.F."

Up to this time the heavy demand for food, following the war, had obscured the marketing problems for fruits and vegetables. The difficulties began to show up when the Government withdrew from the market and G.L.F. had to learn to market in competition with well-established brands. McConnell then said: "In the light of these developments, we are re-examining our policy of marketing in the field of fruits and vegetables. It may have to be changed drastically."

BACK TO FUNDAMENTALS

There was a lengthy discussion of the marketing problem when the Board met in December, 1947. McConnell said:

That there have been major mistakes in policy is now apparent. I expect that blame for most of these mistakes will have to be laid in my lap. Certainly the Board has a right to expect that when management asks for an appropriation to buy or revamp a canning factory that we know what we are doing. The only excuse that I can offer is that the marketing of fruits and vegetables and the operation of canning factories is not in my own experience. Therefore I had nothing within my own experience to draw on in arriving at recommendations.

McConnell then pointed out that Tom Milliman had been placed in charge of marketing after its present form and policy were fairly well fixed. An attempt had been made to make the existing system work rather than to examine critically the whole setup from the standpoint of immediate change in policy. He said: "We seem to have had the idea that we were committed to marketing of fruits and vegetables and could not back out or change direction. . . . Management is approaching this today from a different base. Namely, we can quit or we can change direction according to what we think is best."

With regard to canned goods he said:

I think we should look this one over. . . . I am not suggesting that we back out but I am pointing out that we should not be too proud to do so. . . . It may be that G.L.F. should sell these canning factories or its interests to local cooperatives. This sale might mean taking a substantial loss in the sale of the plants.

Looking backward he felt that some of the decisions made with regard to going into marketing were marginal. He said: "From the moment we . . . took on one canning factory we were subject to pressures from various groups to take over or build canning factories." He went on:

H. E. B., then Marketing Counsel, the Board of Directors, and myself, all became concerned as to where we might wind up but we were unable to stop the procession until we finally had three canneries. . . . One of the most familiar sights for a time in the Ithaca Hotel dining room was a group of farmers from some county and a group of G.L.F. men talking about building or buying a canning factory at some point. The momentum on canning factories was so great that it was difficult to stop. . . .

He continued:

Then the tax problem in connection with marketing started us in another direction. Our G.L.F. people were generally unable to distinguish between marketing and operating grocery stores. . . . G.L.F. was oriented to tax exemption to a point where it required a major reorganization. The Board had no liking for the so-called grocery business and under the tax pressure was not reluctant to cut it loose. [See p. 279.]

He then said:

I realize that we are looking at canning factory marketing today during a declining demand for canning goods and also a declining—up to the moment at least—price level for these same goods. It is not too easy to keep objective and draw sound conclusions at such a time. However, as I review the history of G.L.F. operations in canning I can honestly say that up to this moment it has never grouped with other marketing or with purchasing. . . .

These questions concerning marketing have not arisen because of possibilities of big losses this year. They come because of some criticisms from farmers, but more because of the feeling on the part of myself and others in G.L.F. not directly concerned with marketing that the marketing of fruits and vegetables and the operating of canning factories . . . can never be conducted successfully enough to warrant its being carried on.

McConnell then presented the following recommendations:

That the Board conduct its own investigation.

That the corporation, Farm Products, be merged with the parent G.L.F.

That on the basis of this report here today, Mr. Milliman, Chairman of the marketing group, be asked to submit to the Board at an early date a complete report embodying recommendations as to over-all future marketing policies. Then, on the basis of the Board's own investigation and Mr. Milliman's report and recommendations we should determine policies in marketing based on the following principles:

1. That they be of real service to farmers.

2. That G.L.F. marketing activities when they include heavy investment and substantial risk should serve large groups of farmers rather than a few. This probably means localizing canneries as to ownership and risks.

3. That any marketing undertaken by G.L.F. itself should be of a nature that fits or meshes into G.L.F. operations.

It is of interest that the canning operations had paid their way up to this time. However, the sellers' market for canned goods was beginning to give way and trouble was anticipated. McConnell saw the need of a thorough analysis of the situation in the light of broad G.L.F. interests.

The special committee which the Board set up to study the canning operations reported on January 12, 1948. It recommended that the canning plants be continued for the present; that a qualified canner be employed; that the plants be operated on a competitive basis; and that a G.L.F. name brand be established. Communities were to be given an opportunity to assume ownership of the plants, when desired, at a figure that would permit them to operate efficiently.

At this meeting Milliman took the position that the canning division could eventually carry its full burden of costs under a "strengthened and improved sales program" with "continuing investment improvement" in canning operations.

However, the market outlook continued to deteriorate and at the annual meeting on October 28, 1948, Milliman said that no thought was being given to marketing expansion; that refinement, consolidation, and improvement in efficiency was the order of the day. He held that the actual selling was now needed more than at any time in the history of the Marketing Division, and that it was being pushed and strengthened. Significantly, neither General Manager McConnell nor President Smith made any statements on marketing in their reports. Volume of marketing had fallen from the year before to $16,736,000.

On December 3, 1948, McConnell reported to the Board that Milliman was being relieved of his marketing duties so that he could give full attention to G.L.F. research activities. McConnell proposed that Fallon be temporarily assigned these duties in view of his strong organizing ability and wide experience in the distribution system which was needed to straighten out the marketing operations. The Board accepted this recommendation.

Milliman gave his final views on marketing in a report to a G.L.F. Managers' Conference on December 18, 1948. He indicated that the first canning operation was started at Waterloo in 1939; that during the next six years anything that was of sound edibility was sold easily and that, as a result, G.L.F. had found it unnecessary to establish high quality standards. A thoroughgoing revamping of quality procedure had been found necessary, and as losses piled up, an attempt had been made to streamline operations. He favored a policy of getting raw products consigned for processing in the way that eggs were consigned to G.L.F. for marketing. With regard to policy being formulated on marketing he said: "If policy is to wash it up—fine. It is certain that G.L.F. can establish favorable reputation and a good line of outlets in canning more quickly than our competition did in their day. The decision is not whether the G.L.F. can do it but whether G.L.F. wants to do it."

The Canning Plants Go

At the meeting of the Board on January 6, 1949, McConnell reported that the Marketing Division had recommended the closing of the Waterloo canning plant and its subsequent sale, if possible. It was estimated that Waterloo would lose $325,000 during the next three years if the G.L.F. continued to operate it. Plans were being made to dispose of this property.

On February 28, 1949, McConnell recommended that the G.L.F. should largely base its operations on deflationary factors appearing in the economy. He recommended discontinuing the Macedon canning plant and the sale of the Bloomsburg plant to local farmers or closing the plant, in view of the steady decline in the market for canned goods. This recommendation was accepted by the Board. At this meeting a committee was set up, with Fallon as chairman, to study every function and activity in G.L.F. to see if it was essential. (See Chapter 36.)

Plans for the dismantling of the Marketing Division were presented by McConnell to the Board on April 15, 1949. He proposed that the Egg Department be transferred to the Retail Division under the supervision of Fallon, and that the flour milling and dog food operations be transferred to the Mills Division under the supervision of Silcox. The auction and produce associations had already been turned over to the P & C. He admitted that "the ultimate aim" was to eliminate entirely the Marketing Division as a separate operation.

The use of the G.L.F. label came up for reconsideration, since P & C desired to make use of the label in its distribution program. McConnell held that the G.L.F. label under longtime policy should be restricted to G.L.F. operations. There was general agreement on this position.

In the *G.L.F. Week* for April 25, 1949, McConnell reported that the canning plants had been discontinued. He stated that the decision had been made in January and February but that outstanding contracts had made impossible an earlier announcement. He then went on to say:

Canning requires a very large investment for fixed assets and working capital which must be furnished by thousands of farmers who have no direct interest in cannery crops. With the deflationary period ahead G.L.F. must be sure that the use of capital is directed in such a way that the maximum number of farmer-members are served efficiently in the field of both distribution and marketing. When this principle is understood it becomes clear why it has been necessary for the Board of Directors and management of G.L.F. to take steps to discontinue the G.L.F. canning plants.

Although this was a logical decision, in view of the losses shown by the canning plants in 1947, there is some question of whether these operations could not have been nursed back to health and placed on a firm foundation. As one G.L.F. employee later expressed this: "Jim McConnell will not stand for any red figures and he got the axe out pretty fast—maybe too fast. I am personally of the opinion that if the canning plants had kept their quality and management up to snuff when the going was too easy they would still be in operation."[4]

FROM THE BOTTOM UP

At the meeting of the Board on May 26, 1949, McConnell reported that the Marketing Division as a Division no longer existed. In the *G.L.F. Week* for May 30, 1949, he announced that all G.L.F. marketing activities had been transferred to the Farm Service Division, and that "with the decision to discontinue canning, the remaining marketing activities are essentially of a community nature."

On October 1, 1949, most marketing and processing activities, except those relating to egg distribution, were centralized in a newly formed Co-operative G.L.F. Marketing Service, Inc. This fitted into McConnell's conception that a program should be related to those who were served by it. The new program was designed to serve the western New York area where marketing operations were extensive. It was a program based on the principle of working from the bottom up.

In reporting to the Board on December 5, 1949, Fallon said that the objective of the marketing operation was to be a pacesetter. He maintained that marketing should supplement purchasing and be an area service under farmers' control. He recommended setting up a committee made up of farmers in western New York who would recommend policies and principles for the marketing operations in that area.

At this meeting C. W. Sadd gave an extensive report on P & C operations as they were being financed to a large extent by G.L.F. Sales volume had now grown to $6 million. He thought the difficulties in getting the organization under way had been due to confusion in thinking as to what

---

[4] The following statement by C. N. Silcox throws further light on G.L.F. thinking at this time: "After our experience in operating canning factories which we are now bringing to a close because we feel they require too great an investment for too small a number of farmers who are being served, I have some questions in my mind which are still unanswered. Farmer cooperatives can build just as modern and efficient plants as proprietary businesses. They can operate them just as cheaply per unit as competition. The skilled, experienced management to do all of these things is readily available for farm cooperatives. The great difficulty is the actual marketing of the finished product. That is, to get the commodity into the regular channels of trade at prices which will make fair returns to the growers. What sort of research job could be laid out on this problem? The right answer would be worth millions of dollars to marketing cooperatives. A few cooperatives have been successful in this work. What is the secret of their success?" Letter of C. N. Silcox, to author, of May 13, 1949.

kind of program was wanted. He said, "We talked about an agency system of stores, G.L.F., and independent, and a P & C owned system of stores." He added:

These were the postwar planning days. Due to the short supplies during the war it had been necessary to decentralize buying; when the supply situation turned around, exactly the reverse policy was needed. At the beginning an attempt was made to make the P & C both a consumer co-op and a producer co-op and it wouldn't work. We started to work with inexperienced, inferior personnel. There was little or no business volume to begin with, and it was necessary to buy going businesses at a premium, also quite a lot of expensive, secondhand equipment.

"However," Sadd said, "these difficulties are behind us. (1) We know the kind of business we want to operate. It is a chainstore type of business with emphasis on the brands of farmer cooperatives. (2) We have a fairly tight operating and experienced personnel." This report suggests that the G.L.F. made—in 1944—a wise decision which was stumbled into more than made when it divorced itself from P & C operations and let them develop independently.[5]

On June 15, 1950, McConnell reviewed with the Board the marketing program for western New York being carried on by the Cooperative G.L.F. Marketing Service, Inc. Both he and Fallon favored a farmer board for this corporation instead of an employee board. He thought that the G.L.F. Board should name one man on the Board of the Cooperative G.L.F. Marketing Service, Inc., for liaison purposes. J. D. Ameele was chosen.[6]

A somewhat similar policy board for G.L.F. Egg Marketing Department was set up on October 18, 1951, with one member named from the Exchange Board of Directors.

During the next few years, marketing in the G.L.F. was to "mark time" under the stewardship of G.L.F. Farm Service. However, economic forces were at work which would bring marketing back to the center of the stage, in 1958. (See Chapter 46.)

[5] In a meeting of the Board on November 29, 1954, President Corwith said: "It is now evident that no chain store can do the job in marketing that was first thought could be done in marketing local products."

[6] The G.L.F. Week of December 11, 1950, announced the appointment of Millard Brink, formerly Marketing Procurement Aid, as Director of Marketing Operations. Brink had been on leave of absence for the past three years to help develop markets for the Empire Livestock Marketing Cooperative.

CHAPTER 34

The Income Tax Decision

As soon as the G.L.F. adopts the policy of limiting patronage refunds to members only, it automatically gives up its legal right to Federal income tax exemption.

JAMES A. McCONNELL
G.L.F. Annual Meeting
Syracuse, N.Y., October 30, 1947

THE PROBLEM OF operating under the law granting Federal income tax exemption to agricultural cooperatives became increasingly difficult as the G.L.F. grew in size and corporate complexity. The problem was intensified by the increasing number of patrons who were not farmers. The law required that the farm supply activities could not qualify for exemption if more than 15 percent of those served were non-members and non-farmers. As the burden of complying with this requirement increased, G.L.F. officials began to question whether the advantages of the tax exemption were greater than the costs.

This attitude of doubt was increased in the early forties, with the concerted drive to repeal the tax exemption which was launched by those opposed to farmer cooperatives. The allegation that farmer cooperatives were not paying their fair share of taxes had a considerable impact on the general business community during this period when tax rates were rising rapidly to meet war costs. It struck a sensitive nerve in the G.L.F.

The entire problem was complicated by the lack of public knowledge on farmer cooperatives. It was difficult for the average person to understand the status of farmer cooperatives under the Federal income tax law, because they did not understand the basic distinction between cooperative corporations and other business corporations.[1]

[1] This distinction is still not fully understood by many people. A farmers' marketing or purchasing cooperative is a voluntary organization of producers, formed and operated along democratic lines for the purpose of supplying services at cost to its members and other patrons, who contribute both capital and patronage. To carry out the operation-at-cost principle, a properly organized cooperative obligates itself by contract to distribute to patrons in proportion to their use of the cooperative's services any amounts accruing from operations in excess of expenses and permissible reserves. The use of this contract by cooperatives is the basic reason why they usually have less tax to pay than an investor-type corporation, whether or not they qualify for "exemption" under the Federal statute. Throughout the years the courts and the Internal Revenue Service have held that the existence of this legally binding contract prevents funds covered by it from becoming income to the corporate entity for tax purposes.

Regardless of the justice of the attack, the charge that cooperatives were "tax-dodgers" inclined G.L.F. officials to question whether the adverse effect on public opinion of operating under the exemption was not greater than the nominal advantages derived. While the first effect of the organized pressure against the tax-exemption was to determine the Board in June, 1944, to "resist all attempts toward taxation," the question was at least opened up for further consideration.

In a talk to a G.L.F. conference in January, 1946, C. N. Silcox pointed out that farm cooperatives, in defending their position as cooperatives against those who would "destroy" them, should not blind themselves to the need of "a possible adjustment of Federal income taxes" because of the tremendous need of the government for increased tax revenue.

McConnell gave but passing attention to "the drive to tax patronage refunds" in his annual report for 1944-45. He maintained that any attempt to tax patronage refunds "other than in the hands of the farmer himself would result in their disappearance by pricing."

In October, 1946, McConnell gave the Board of Directors a full analysis of the problem as he then saw it. The Directors were so favorably impressed that they instructed him to present it later in the month at Syracuse in his annual report to the delegate body.

His statement expressed so well the entire problem at that time in the light of G.L.F. interests that it is given here in some detail. In opening up the subject, McConnell called attention to the wide difference of opinion on the income tax question, even among cooperative leaders. However, he maintained that one did not "betray his profession by being honest about it."

McConnell then listed the charges made against farm cooperatives:

(1) That private business in the same fields cannot successfully compete with farm cooperatives, because business profits are taxed heavily and farm cooperatives are exempt from Federal income tax.

(2) That they are permitted under the Federal tax laws and regulations, to capitalize net margins, and with this tax-free and easy capital, are constantly expanding into new business not directly related to farming.

(3) That cooperatives are a threat to free enterprise because, with the use of this tax-free capital, their competition eventually eliminates private business, and destroys the profit system.

(4) That through cooperatives, the Communists and reformers are working to destroy the American way of life.

McConnell then went on to emphasize that:

The main defense of the cooperatives against these charges is that since purchasing cooperatives cannot make a profit unto themselves, but only operate to reduce the cost of material to their membership, their net margins, therefore, cannot be subject to Federal income taxes; and that marketing cooperatives, as agencies of their members, operate under the obligation to pass on to members all the proceeds received by them, less cost of doing business.

McConnell then discussed the question from the standpoint of G.L.F.'s record. He refuted the charge that the G.L.F. had capitalized its net margins by saying that the policy had been established in 1936 "of pricing at the market and annually, after setting up prudent reserves, paying net margins, if any, to patrons in cash as a patronage refund." He stated that under this policy the G.L.F. system had distributed since 1936 just over $24 million to its members as patronage refunds. He then made the point that since 1936 farmers had invested new capital in the G.L.F. to the extent of about $11 million. He said, "Not because of tax regulations but because of good membership requirements, the G.L.F. Exchange has put farmers' investment in G.L.F. on a voluntary basis." He went on to say, "At no time in its history has the amount of this tax exemption been a significant factor in the development of the G.L.F. Exchange."

McConnell then proceeded to give his thinking, based on more than 20 years of experience, on the relation of farmer cooperatives to taxation. He introduced his views by saying:

This statement is not an apology for the present or past position of G.L.F., nor is it an attack on the sincere views of many other cooperative and business people. It is a considered statement of the case of G.L.F. as a farmer cooperative in a field which has been stirred to a white heat of controversy during the past few years.

(1) *Free enterprise.* The farmer cooperative is a legitimate, organic, and beneficial part of a free enterprise system. An increasingly specialized and scientific type of agriculture makes it necessary. By no stretch of the imagination can the aims and objectives of farmers in belonging to cooperatives be said to be socialistic. . . .

(2) *Soundness of farm cooperatives.* The influence and volume of business of bona fide farmer cooperatives will continue to grow in this country, not because of Federal income tax exemption but rather because of two developments taking place since 1920.

The first development was that farmer cooperatives were finding ways to finance themselves on a voluntary basis through sales of stock. The second was the improvement in professional management. McConnell gave it as his considered opinion that "farmer cooperative management is as efficient, as skillful, as enterprising, and as well-trained and capable as that of private industry in the same field." He then continued:

(3) *Refunds not taxable.* It is my belief that a true patronage refund, based on use rather than invested capital, returned to farmers or members is, in fact, a reduction of costs to the member and should not be subject to taxation, except in the hands of the farmer, as it now is.

(4) *Taxation of retained margins.* If other monies retained in a cooperative

corporation except revolving funds in common use by many cooperatives, which are in effect a loan, are subjected to taxes no greater than those paid by straight business corporations, certainly G.L.F. would not be adversely affected when we consider the freedom of action that this would give us in our co-operative business operations.

(5) *Need for reserves.* It is my belief that the present so-called tax-exempt status of cooperatives, requiring them to pay all net margins in good years with no chance to set aside adequate reserves essential for protection of the members' investment and the members' service, will in years of disaster, seriously embarrass and could even wreck a strong cooperative, such as G.L.F. . . .[2]

(6) *Public relations.* . . . Farmers are a part of the business life of the nation. They cannot afford to be in bad repute with their customers. They are engaged in commerce and they have to deal with the people who carry on the commerce of the nation. Cooperatives do not operate in a vacuum, contrary to what so many cooperative purists assume. The standing of this farm cooperative in the estimation of the general public is being hurt, and probably to the real detriment of our necessary relations with business and consumers. Thousands of worthwhile people erroneously have been led to believe that G.L.F. is a tax-dodger, without realizing that cooperatives are the instruments of farmers to aid them in producing and marketing food.

I do not believe that we can afford to make our relations with our customers and with our business associates difficult and hard to handle and our position costly to defend.

McConnell then summarized by saying:

It seems to me that the bad public relations and the lack of freedom in our own business, when balanced up against the savings in taxes which might arise from operating on a tax-exempt basis in the future will amount to a net loss. . . .

No attempt was made to come to a decision at the annual meeting following McConnell's forthright presentation of the issues. The G.L.F. at this time was concerned with developing full agreement on the part of all persons related to the G.L.F. management and members so that should a decision be made it would have the united support of all elements of the organization. The G.L.F. came nearer to a decision when, at the April, 1947, meeting of the Board, it was decided to sound out all committeemen in G.L.F. territory on the advisability of giving up tax exemption. A letter was sent to them over the President's signature which called for no reply but which inferentially gave committeemen an opportunity to express themselves. In effect, the letter asked:

Can G.L.F. do a better job for its members for the long pull, operating as a Federal income tax exempt cooperative under strict regulations, or would it

[2] It should be noted that the Federal income tax statute provided that exemption shall not be denied "any association because there is accumulated and maintained by it a reserve required by State law or a reasonable reserve for any necessary purpose." The G.L.F. was unduly strict in interpreting this provision of the law and could have properly accumulated larger reserves for necessary purposes if it had elected.

be better to pay Federal income taxes on moneys remaining in the cooperative after patronage refunds have been paid and a nominal reserve set up.[3]

During the next several months the value of the income tax exemption was carefully weighed against its cost. A factor that helped G.L.F. come to a decision was the growing concern over the increasing number of non-farmer patrons. Figures presented to the Board in June, 1947, showed that only about 115,000 of the 354,000 patrons were bona fide farmers.[4] As a tax-exempt cooperative, G.L.F. had to maintain accounting records of the business of all patrons and return them refunds on it. This not only imposed a heavy accounting load but there was always the danger that the volume of business with non-member, non-producer patrons would exceed the 15 percent limitation and result in the withdrawal of the income tax exemption. No one can understand the G.L.F.'s decision to give up the tax exemption unless account is taken of the administrative burden which compliance imposed.

The problem came to a head when the Board met in September. After a careful weighing of pros and cons, it was decided to relinquish exemption, as proposed by McConnell, subject to the approval of the decision by the stockholders at their meeting in October. The policy was to be effected through changing the requirements for membership in G.L.F. By paying patronage refunds to members only, who must be holders of common stock, the exemption would become automatically void.[5]

Thus when McConnell gave his report to the annual meeting it was understood that G.L.F. was giving up tax exemption. McConnell introduced the subject by saying:

As soon as the G.L.F. adopts the policy of limiting patronage refunds to members only, it automatically gives up its legal right to Federal income tax exemption. This act, of itself, does not put the G.L.F. on record as either for or against the present statute which gives farm cooperatives, who conform with certain rules and regulations, tax exemption from Federal income tax. The decision, or so it seems to me, is that G.L.F. needs, and must have . . . a change in membership policy. It cannot make this change without giving up tax exemption.

Earlier in his report, McConnell described the proposed new membership policy, under which "a member shall be a farmer who owns voting stock and patronage refunds will be paid to members only. . . ." This policy, he declared, should have the following effect:

---

[3] As condensed by Sherman Peer, *G.L.F. Digest*, 1940-1950, p. 67.

[4] Many of these non-member, non-producer patrons were only casual purchasers.

[5] The desire to spread holdings of common stock under the member-ownership program pointed the way for this decision. See Chapter 28, "The Member-Ownership Program."

(1) Put all membership in G.L.F. on a voluntary basis. Every person who has become a member will have done so by means of his own decision.

(2) Save substantial money and thousands of man-hours now spent in doubtful record-keeping. . . .

(3) Make it possible to carry on the necessary education of membership much more effectively because it can be confined to farmers who have the interest to be members. . . .

(4) Provide a large potential reservoir of working capital as needed and supplied by the farmers who are making use of the institution.

Then McConnell observed:

I am old-fashioned enough to believe that membership in the G.L.F. should carry with it benefits that can be secured only by being members. I don't see why the farmer membership of G.L.F. should carry on its back a couple hundred thousand other people by giving them the full benefits of membership when they are not members, either because they do not want to be or because they are not farmers.

McConnell was not greatly concerned about the cost of giving up the tax exemption. On this he said:

It is my belief that the payment of Federal income taxes by the G.L.F. Exchange will not change particularly the amount of refunds payable to members in accordance with the business done by each member. There will be taxes, yes, but I believe they can largely be made up for in the savings in the cost of doing business on the one hand and the greater freedom of action on the other.

He anticipated this offsetting advantage. The decision "should permit the establishment of permanent reserves after taxes, reserves needed to safeguard not only the services but also the very substantial financial investment that thousands of farmers already have in G.L.F."

McConnell's views were endorsed by action of the delegate body on October 30, 1947, who voted 2,636 to 204 to define clearly membership and pay patronage refunds to members only, and thereby automatically to give up Federal income tax exemption.[6]

---

[6] This decision was made just as the Committee on Ways and Means of the House of Representatives was about to hold hearings on proposed revisions of the Internal Revenue Code with reference to cooperative organizations. These hearings provide a full record of the views of those who at this time favored or opposed changes in the income tax treatment of farmer cooperatives. C. N. Silcox represented the G.L.F. and presented on November 14, 1947, a full explanation of the conditions that had led the G.L.F. to voluntarily give up its income tax exemption status. In this statement Silcox maintained that during the preceding fiscal year it was necessary to maintain patronage records on 344,224 names of people who made purchases through the G.L.F. and that of these some 96,000 were non-farmers. As the non-farmer members represented only 7.3 percent of the dollar volume, the G.L.F. operations were within the limitation that not more than 15 percent of the volume of purchases could be made for non-member non-producers. Silcox estimated that the cost of maintaining patronage records and issuing the refunds for the 344,000 patrons was $450,000, and that this would be reduced by three-fifths through restricting membership to stockholding farmers and giving up tax exemption. In his presentation, Silcox emphasized

This decision was not to become effective until July 1, 1948. This would give the G.L.F. time to carry on a campaign to get farmers using G.L.F. services to become G.L.F. members, and permit the G.L.F. to make accounting arrangements and otherwise adjust its operations to the needs of the new policy. The campaign for members was favored by the fact that only through membership could one henceforth obtain patronage refunds and benefits, and by July 1, 1948, a large proportion of the farmers qualified to become members had in fact become members.

The decision to alter the basis for membership so as give up automatically the right of Federal income tax exemption was, as shown by this chapter, not abruptly made without full deliberation and acceptance throughout the entire organization. The G.L.F. had to be sure that it was in the long-run interests of the institution.[7]

In addressing a G.L.F. Managers Conference on December 18, 1947, McConnell made clear that the decision would not impair the G.L.F.'s cooperative character.

> We are being accused today by people who do not like us and by people who do not understand us of having given up our cooperative character. We could do that by the way we operate. The challenge is to operate more than ever so that policy is determined at the farm level and implemented at the retail and wholesale levels. . . . This is a good program to tie to because it is something that is worth while. . . .

McConnell agreed that the requirements for tax exemption had served as a guidepost in keeping G.L.F. operations geared to the agricultural field and he held that "we must substitute our own policies" to achieve this end. "I propose," he added, "that we really develop some statesmanship in our decisions with which to replace Government direction."

---

that his statement concerned itself with explaining the operations of the G.L.F. in that other cooperatives differed in their philosophy, methods and operations. No views were expressed on proposed changes in the Internal Revenue Code relating to tax-exempt organizations. For full statement and discussion of the G.L.F. position see: *Revenue Revisions, 1947-48, Hearings before the Committee on Ways and Means, House of Representatives, Eightieth Congress, First Session on Proposed Revisions of Internal Revenue Code*, Part 4, Tax-Exempt Organizations (Cooperative Organizations), November 4 to 26, 1947, pp. 2451-2477.

[7] There was no doubt in McConnell's mind. In a letter to the author on November 17, 1947, he said: "If there is any one thing that I feel reasonably sure of after 25 years in G.L.F., it is that cooperatives must have a membership which is dependable in specific terms. Otherwise they cannot stand up against the criticisms which are leveled at them by their critics. As to whether or not our move will strengthen membership consciousness, I have no way of knowing until we have tried it. Personally, I think it will."

CHAPTER 35

Simplifying the Structure

Beginning July 1, the G.L.F. Exchange will again start doing business for the first time since 1931.

JAMES A. MCCONNELL
June, 1948

AT THE OUTBREAK of World War II, the G.L.F. was a network of subsidiary corporations, held together through a holding corporation controlled by the parent organization—the Cooperative G.L.F. Exchange, Inc. Ten years later the major activities were grouped in wholesale and retail divisions, under heads directly responsible to the General Manager of the G.L.F. The holding corporation had become a subsidiary to assist in property and financial management.

The need for simplification of the G.L.F. structure had become evident in the thirties. Yet, at that time, the G.L.F. was in an experimental period with new activities arising and there was much to justify use of separate autonomous corporations to fix responsibility for specialized operations and obtain the maximum response in initiative. This program would have broken down had it not been for strong central management and a system of interlocking directorships comprised largely of management personnel which knitted the corporations together. Moreover, all of the corporations had the same secretary, and the records were open to each other.

In time the disadvantages of a conglomerate group of corporate enterprises became apparent. Corporations for special purposes were set up so frequently and disbanded so rapidly that it was hard for even insiders to know whether a corporation was in existence or what its functions were.

The way in which the G.L.F. was organized and operated made it vulnerable to the attacks of the *Rural New Yorker* and other critics. The establishment of the University of the G.L.F. and the G.L.F. School of Cooperative Administration was designed in part to explain the G.L.F. to itself.

Members also had difficulty in knowing their relationship to the G.L.F. They had faith that its leaders were interested in their welfare but they took only an apathetic interest in its organization, operation and management. They didn't look upon the G.L.F. as their responsibility.

It was doubly hard for others to understand how the G.L.F. was organized and operated. Business firms had to deal with so many agencies carrying the G.L.F. name that they couldn't know what relationship they bore to the parent organization.

As G.L.F. activities widened, the problem of administration for the system as a whole became more difficult. McConnell felt this pressure and in February, 1941, he recommended that the Board appoint a committee to study how the G.L.F. could be simplified.

Little came from this committee. For one thing, it concerned itself with minor matters such as whether the official name of the G.L.F. should be shortened. As most of the various corporations had become, to some extent, vested management interests, it was difficult for those in charge to see the desirability of change. Moreover, the problem of simplification lost its urgency as war problems increased.

However, McConnell did not loosen his grip on this problem and, as opportunity permitted, he took steps leading toward its solution. For example, the member-ownership program, started in 1943, gave definite meaning to membership and moved the organization toward a single standard for membership. The establishment of the G.L.F. Farm Service, Inc., in 1945, clarified the relationship of wholesale and retail activities and, in effect, simplified and unified retail services. By bringing together all retail activities under one head, responsible to the General Manager, Farm Service gave a counterbalance to the wholesale corporations, and raised the question of whether it would not be desirable to combine the wholesale services under one head in much the same way.

The gradual perfection of the Member Committee system gave the Committees stature and a clearcut function. This centered control of the organization in the committeemen and, in turn, they took a greater interest in how the organization was set up and how it functioned. The preparation in 1944 of a committeemen's handbook, which set forth procedures of G.L.F. operation, was also an important device for clarification of G.L.F. methods.

STANDARDIZATION OF PATRONAGE REFUND PROCEDURES

Another step toward simplification came with the standardization of patronage refund payment procedures. When G.L.F. began paying patronage refunds in 1935, a system was adopted whereby each wholesale corporation paid separate refunds on the supplies it handled in cents per ton of feed or per ton of fertilizer, or per dollar of farm supplies.[1] This

---

[1] The great variety of farm supply items handled made impractical payment of refunds by commodity.

plan was confusing although refunds were paid in one check, and it made each wholesale corporation seem more significant than the parent organization.

By 1944, with the great increase in number of members and the variety and volume of supplies handled, the problem of handling patronage refund payments had grown to be a burdensome problem and something had to be done about it. A system appropriate for the relatively simple conditions of 1935 had become a strait jacket.

Then, G.L.F. was keeping records for some 300,000 patrons as a basis for calculating patronage refunds. These refunds had to be distributed through two types of retail outlets—Service Stores and Agent-Buyers. The problem was further complicated by the determination of patronage refund payments in accordance with physical and dollar volume.

For 1944-45, the following G.L.F. refunds were paid: $1.40 per ton on feed; 4% on seed; $2.20 per ton on fertilizer; 6% on dust and fertilizer.

If a farmer were served by a Service Store he would receive two patronage refund payments. One would represent the refunds paid by the G.L.F. while the other would cover the refund by the local service store. The two payments were recorded on one check and paid through the local service store. The problem was made more confusing by the different ways in which the patronage refund was calculated by the wholesale corporations. G.L.F. Mills paid a refund of a certain amount per ton of manufactured feed or a certain percent on seed, and G.L.F. Soil Building paid a per-ton refund on fertilizer. A refund from G.L.F. Farm Supplies was determined according to dollar volume of purchases. The retail agencies' refund was simply calculated to cover the dollar-volume of all purchases by a patron.

A patron of an Agent-Buyer received only the refund from the G.L.F. which was distributed through the Agent-Buyer. The problem of G.L.F. in paying refunds to patrons served by Agent-Buyers was identical with that in paying them through the Service Stores.

This system had grown in complexity with the desire of the G.L.F. to reflect equitably savings from its diverse operations to the farmer. In a report to the Board of Directors in December, 1944, Charles E. Dykes, Controller of the Holding Corporation, said, "The items of information given with each patronage refund check three or four years ago were five. This increased to 16 in 1943, and to 30 in 1944." This problem called for solution and McConnell asked Ed Fallon to study the problem because of the mounting perplexities and costs in handling patronage refunds at the retail level.

It soon became obvious that changes in procedure could not be made at any one point when they concerned the entire G.L.F. system. A committee was appointed, under the chairmanship of C. E. Dykes, representing wholesale, and F. M. Upchurch, retail, to study the whole matter of patronage refund payments from the standpoint of longtime effects on G.L.F. records, costs, and membership relations.

This committee found that, as more and more commodities came under the refund plan, the existing basis of paying on commodities was leading to increasing confusion in the minds of farmers, was cumbersome to a point where payments were months behind and, in addition, was costly both as to money and manpower. This committee recommended to the General Manager that all G.L.F. corporations adopt the dollar-volume basis for patronage refunds. Furthermore, the group recommended that each major wholesale division pay its own rate of refund. It was also recommended that the wholesale units pay patronage refunds in lump sums to various cooperative service stores so that the wholesale patronage refund could be added to the retail patronage refund. The wholesale refund to patrons of agent-buyers would be paid as heretofore, with checks drawn to the patron for distribution through the agent-buyer or independent local cooperatives.

The G.L.F. Board of Directors considered these recommendations on May 14 and 15, 1945, and unanimously adopted the following resolution:

The management is authorized for the fiscal year 1945-46 to instruct retail units to keep records of patrons' purchases on a dollar-volume basis rather than on commodity and dollar volume to the end that when deemed advisable patronage refunds be paid throughout the G.L.F. system on dollar volume only.

On June 9, 1945, McConnell issued an institutional statement which announced that the shift to the dollar-volume basis for paying refunds would become effective on July 1, 1945, to cover the fiscal year 1945-46. In this statement he indicated that refunds should be paid as simply as possible and should meet the main objective of getting money saved back to the patron to whom it belonged. McConnell, in this memo, estimated that at least $300,000 in bookkeeping and other costs would be saved annually by this change, without taking into consideration its intangible advantages.

The decision to pay patronage refunds on dollar volume, as contrasted to commodity volume basis, was not lightly made, for there were many in G.L.F. who felt that the refunds should reflect savings made on specific commodities or groups of commodities. There was much variation in savings between commodities, and it was felt that these savings should be reflected directly to the patron in proportion to their purchases of them. On the other hand, it was admitted that this philosophy, carried to the extreme, would call for a separate refund on every commodity and elaborate accounting procedures at prohibitive cost. Moreover, a greater refinement in patronage refund procedure would be confusing to patrons who cared little how the refund was calculated.

Although the solution of this problem was dictated by practical cost consideration, it led to a broader conception of G.L.F. service. As long as patronage refunds were paid by commodities, many farmers thought of themselves as buyers of specific G.L.F. commodities rather than as patrons of the G.L.F. as a whole. They missed the "over-all aspect" of cooperative service.

By placing patronage refund payments on a total dollar-volume basis the G.L.F. achieved a practical combination of simplicity and equity in terms of total membership. As a matter of fact, as the services of the G.L.F. were available to all, the proportion of various commodities purchased did not vary appreciably among the membership as a whole.

SIMPLIFICATION OF ELECTORAL PROCEDURE

Another development leading toward simplification was an improved procedure for electing directors. Prior to 1940, there was one system for electing directors in New York and another system in Pennsylvania and New Jersey. In that year provision was made for nomination of three directors for New York State by chairmen of patrons' committees, so that seven directors were nominated, while three each were nominated by the New York State Grange and New York Farm Bureau Federation. While this system provided a more representative procedure and recognized individual patrons throughout the territory, it still gave dominant representation to New York State.

This imbalance was, to a large extent, corrected in November, 1946, when the articles were amended to give about equal recognition to members in all parts of the territory in electing directors, while still recognizing the valuable support of the New York State Grange and New York State Farm Bureau.

Effective July 1, 1947, the territory would be divided into ten numbered directoral districts: Two for New Jersey; two for northern Pennsylvania; and six for New York State. The term of office would be changed to two years, and even-number districts would nominate a director in the even years and the odd-number districts in the odd years. Under the plan, the New York Grange and the Farm Bureau would relinquish their right to nominate three directors for three-year terms and accept the right to nominate two directors for two-year terms. Thus, each of the farm organizations would nominate one director each year. In effect, these directors would become directors-at-large. This would give a total of 14 in place of 13 directors, of whom 10 would be elected, in effect, through district nominating meetings.

Although this represented a marked improvement, it did not satisfy all.

Figure 6—G.L.F. Board of Directors Nominating Districts

In view of this sentiment, General Manager McConnell proposed at the Annual Meeting in October, 1948, that a committee of members be appointed by the President to examine and study the ways and means by which directors were nominated and elected.

This committee,[2] appointed by President Smith after a careful study of past experience and current viewpoints, reported the following year that representation was about as equitable for each section of G.L.F. territory as it was possible to make it. The committee found the directors nominated by the Grange and Farm Bureau to be "in effect, Directors-at-Large," and helpful to the objectives of the G.L.F. Although voting by mail ballot was increasing, the committee did not think that this seriously

[2] The members were: David G. Agne, Oneida, N.Y.; Harold Blakesley, East Aurora, N.Y.; Harold B. Everett, Flemington, N.J.; Maurice Russell, Carbondale, Pa.; Rowland M. Sharp, Rhinebeck, N.Y. (Chairman); and Paul Taber, Ithaca, N.Y. (Secretary).

affected the election of directors as nominated by districts or by the farm organizations. It was considered as furnishing a way through which members could voice their views. Thus the electoral machinery was found to provide, in effect, a delegate system.

Divisions Replace Corporations

During the war period G.L.F. became increasingly concerned with its public relations and more and more sensitive to the charge that it was not responsive to the direction of farmers. The allegations that cooperatives were not paying their share of Federal income taxes were hard to refute as long as cooperative operations were unduly complex.

The difficulty of explaining the G.L.F. setup was spotlighted at the Hearings before the Committee on Ways and Means in November, 1947, when Mr. Silcox was presenting G.L.F.'s view with regard to the taxation of farmer cooperatives. Finding it very difficult at one point to explain the G.L.F. corporate set up, he said, "To the layman who has not watched G.L.F. develop over a period of 27 years, the corporate setup may be confusing." He admitted that to outsiders the G.L.F. was a very complex system "although the explanation is really very simple when one understands the functions of the various corporations and the reasons for the system."

These various forces gradually made it evident to McConnell and his colleagues that administrative efficiency required the merging of all the G.L.F. operating corporations into the G.L.F. Exchange and their replacement by functional operating divisions. This would involve the subordination of the Holding Corporation so that it would become largely a property-holding corporation.

McConnell outlined his ideas to the Board on September 8, 1947. He gave the following advantages for simplification of the corporate structure:

> Our corporate structure is confusing to farmers, to operators, to directors, and to the outside public. . . . Functions now performed by the present operating subsidiaries can be grouped under divisions of the Exchange and performed equally as well. . . . It is my judgment, based on experience, that subsidiary corporations tend to operate as entities instead of as part of a whole. Using subsidiary corporations to carry out functions tends to build up corporate consciousness in employees, farmers, and the general public. . . . I believe using subsidiary corporations unnecessarily complicates financing and record-keeping. . . . When we begin to function as a non-exempt cooperative we can deal with the Treasury in a more cleancut manner.

The Directors were agreed on the importance of this major change, and plans were worked out to put it into effect with the opening of the new fiscal year, July 1, 1948. The changeover required a considerable amount of preliminary planning. It was decided that the Holding Corporation would loan the Exchange money to carry on the business of Mills and the other wholesales to be merged. The Exchange would become debtor to its wholly-owned subsidiary and would guarantee payment of the Holding Corporation's obligations to banks.

At its January, 1948, meeting, the Board authorized merger of G.L.F. Mills, Soil Building Services, Farm Supplies, Farm Products, and Farm Service Corporations with the Exchange, by the simple method of purchase at par of their outstanding shares from the Holding Corporation.

At the annual Managers' Conference in June, 1948, just before the new plan was put into effect, McConnell answered the question, "Why are we changing direction?" He said:

Beginning July 1, the G.L.F. Exchange will again start doing business for the first time since 1931. At that time the various wholesale functions of G.L.F. were organized and grouped under subsidiary corporations for operational purposes. The G.L.F., as far as operations were concerned, became in reality a holding company, and placed all functions except policy in fully owned subsidiaries. Now, after nearly twenty years, it has been decided to eliminate subsidiary corporations as far as possible. Since G.L.F. stores are owned in trust only for management purposes, this will not affect their corporate structure or their corporate relations to G.L.F. Why are we changing direction?

1. The first [reason] is a matter of broad public relations. The farmer has never understood the corporate structure of G.L.F. as the multiple corporate feature was introduced. What he could not understand he distrusted. Not even the Board of Directors has been able to keep corporate structure straight.

2. The second reason is the unsound pricing methods which are resulting from the pyramiding of corporate overhead. Assessments and rentals determined in advance are built into our pricing regardless of competitive positions.

3. The third reason for a simplified corporate structure is to permit the free flow of money to the point in G.L.F. where most needed. . . . We have many occasions when one division in G.L.F. is in serious trouble while other divisions are getting along easily. . . .

4. The final reason is as we get to operating I believe we will be able to eliminate much duplication of record-keeping and accounting and financing procedures.

McConnell then pointed out that "some men in G.L.F. may be concerned that the consolidation means a shift in policy as to centralization of authority." He did not fear this. In fact, the new plan, in his opinion, would give a better balance between centralization and decentralization.

The new structure of the G.L.F., effected by the simplification, is shown by the organization chart on page 365.[3]

[3] When the G.L.F. went on to an income tax paying basis on July 1, 1948, it was necessary to file a prospectus for the sale of G.L.F. securities. The prospectus of the Cooperative G.L.F. Exchange, Inc., of August 19, 1949, succinctly explains the changes that took place as a result of the reorganization.

CHAPTER 36

Operation Cutback

*We face a very difficult job in converting from inflation to deflation,
but convert we must or the countryside will be strewn with the bones
of another great cooperative failure.*

JAMES A. McCONNELL
General Manager
March 2, 1949

IN THE BOOM following the war, G.L.F. had reluctantly expanded facilities and services to meet the pent-up growth needs of the organization. Most of these investments were needed but still there was a tendency for expansion to get out of control.

McConnell expressed his conviction that good times could not last much longer, on May 17, 1947, in his article, "A Time to Stay Close to Shore." He urged caution in further expansion "until we have a more stable economy to deal with." (See p. 302.)

By early 1948 it seemed clear that a recession was developing. An article by Silcox in the *G.L.F. Week* for March 22, 1948, entitled "Recession or Depression," reflected a mood of caution which was beginning to permeate G.L.F. management personnel.

This mood was softened somewhat by the annual report for 1947-48 which indicated that wholesale supply sales had increased from the year before by $21 million while marketing volume had increased by over $2 million. Savings amounted to $4,876,000, as compared with $3,298,000 for the year before; while cash patronage refunds amounted to $3,496,000 as compared with $2,701,000 for the year before. These figures could not help but regenerate a spirit of optimism even in the face of economic trends which were far from encouraging.

The complacency registered at the Annual Meeting, October 28-29, 1948, was shortlived. On January 6, 1949, McConnell reported to the Board that the United States was already well into a business recession. The need for tightening up operations all along the line was indicated.

By deliberately changing its pricing policy to break the upward march of feed prices, G.L.F. demonstrated how it could help farmers lower their costs. Instead of following its usual policy of pricing at the market regardless of cost and returning the overage in patronage refunds, the G.L.F. decided in January, 1949, to hold feed prices until new crop prospects plus supplies on hand brought them down. To do this, G.L.F.

announced a reduction in feed prices of $3.50 per ton under the preceding week. G.L.F. recognized that if it were to follow the market up with the large volume it represented prices would go even higher and it was prepared to price on the basis of its ingredients costs for a period of sixty days if necessary.

Within two weeks after the price cut was announced, a nationwide break in grain and ingredient prices took place and Northeastern dairymen and poultrymen were thus saved millions of dollars as a result of this pricing leadership.[1]

The situation in marketing which had mushroomed following the war was giving the G.L.F. most direct concern. In particular, the new canning facilities which had been acquired hastily without careful consideration of longtime needs could not be operated profitably. We have explained in Chapter 33 how this problem was handled.

However, to safeguard basic G.L.F. interests a decisive change in direction was also called for. To help meet this problem, General Manager McConnell, on March 2, set up a Survey and Budget Committee, consisting of E. H. Fallon, Chairman; C. N. Silcox, V. A. Fogg, J. C. Crissey, and C. E. Dykes, Secretary. He directed it to "review and study G.L.F. functions to accomplish the following: 1. To eliminate duplication. 2. To cut out obsolete functions. 3. To relocate various functions, where it is possible to do so, to the end that expense may be lowered or worthwhile decentralization take place."

In his directions to the General Committee and the sub-committees to be formed, McConnell said: "These committees face rather difficult situations because while they deal with functions, they will inevitably have to deal with human nature. We face a very difficult job in converting from inflation to deflation, but convert we must or the countryside will be strewn with the bones of another great cooperative failure."

The Survey Committee, in taking over its assignment, was aware that "in an organization with so many commodities and services, there is always the possibility of dissipating the energies of personnel through unbalanced or conflicting programs." It therefore adopted the following yardstick to measure the organizational efficiency of the G.L.F.: "How does each division, department and individual contribute to the attainment of the basic purpose of G.L.F. working for farmers?"

In beginning its work the Survey Committee enlisted the cooperation

[1] See Annual Report of G.L.F. for 1948-49. See also Lacey F. Rickey, "G.L.F. Called a Halt on Feed Prices," *News for Farmer Cooperatives*, April, 1948. Rickey concluded his article by saying: "This cooperative was willing to take some financial risk in this attempt to halt the increasing costs of production of milk and eggs in this area. . . . Unlike nearly everyone else, it was willing to take courageous action to buck the trend. . . ."

of Division and Department Heads. In a letter to the Chairman of the Sub-Committees, who were generally Division and Department heads, it said:

It is expected that the Committee will impartially point out to the General Manager your recommendations where economies can be made. We hope to be analytical and thereby stimulate sound economies. It is not the intention of this Committee to be arbitrary; to sit as a Court of Justice; to say that this man must be fired; or that this expense must be cut any given amount.

Each Division and Department Head was requested to report to the Committee:

1. What moves and what economies can you make immediately in your Department? List these and the dollars saved.
2. What moves and what economies can you make in your Department not later than July 1, 1949?

Those who were to develop information for the review of the Committee were instructed to have it ready for presentation within a few weeks.

The report of Survey and Budget Committee, presented to the Board on May 20, found that 142 jobs could be eliminated without impairing general G.L.F. efficiency. The Committee proposed that there be no salary increases in 1949-50 except for promotions or noteworthy cause, and that all expenses for traveling and telephone service be reduced. Moreover, the Committee recommended as a general policy that the G.L.F. free itself to the extent possible from certain non-productive outside investments amounting to over $3,200,000 which represented a burden on the commodity departments. (See Chapter 37—The Outside Investments.)

The Committee also proposed "that consideration be given to establishing Director terms at three years rather than two, in the interest of less meetings, therefore economy, and a longer term for a Director to way-wise himself."

Another recommendation proposed that "the heads of the operating divisions be constituted a committee to review all G.L.F. commodities and to designate as *basic commodities* those items which furnish farmers the best means of cutting costs and on which G.L.F. can do the best job."

A corollary proposal was that "all promotional effort be confined to these basic commodities, except at those retail points which are equipped and manned to handle a broader line effectively."

The Committee was of the opinion that more attention should be devoted to increasing volume. It therefore proposed that a study be made to bring about a reduction in time devoted to membership and public relations, conferences and schools in the hope that more of this time could be spent in obtaining volume.

The proposed cutback did not call for the discharge of workers so much as their transfer to more vital operations.

The Committee estimated that the adoption of its various recommendations would result in savings of about 2 million dollars, or about 10 percent.

The preparation and reception of this report had a tonic effect throughout the organization. It was like a dash of cold water after a hot bath. It arrested and turned back a tide of upward expenses and undisciplined actions.

For some time McConnell had felt the need of an Assistant General Manager who could relieve him of operating detail. With the tightening up of operations called for, this need became urgent, and the Board created the position of Assistant General Manager "to assume duties largely in the field of operations." The appointment of C. N. Silcox was announced in the *G.L.F. Week* of April 25, 1949. He was to continue as Manager of the Mills Division.

While the Survey and Budget Committee was preparing its report, steps had been taken to close out the Marketing Department. On May 26, when Fallon presented the Committee's report to the Board, McConnell announced that the Marketing Division "no longer exists" and that "the functions retained will be transferred to the Farm Service Division."

Facts presented at the June Managers' Conference were encouraging in the face of lower prices which reduced dollar sales volume. Tonnage of formula feeds, grain and ingredients was up, feed quality was being strictly controlled, and the new feed mill at Bordentown was tending to stabilize feed markets in New Jersey. Seed volume had been unexpectedly good. Soil building commodities, except superphosphate, registered a healthy tonnage gain, and the number of lime spreading units had increased by 50 percent. The Farm Supplies Division which had doubled volume in the past three years was decentralizing its accounting and order departments to reduce expenses and better control orders and inventories. The new G.L.F. Farm Freezer and G.L.F. Egg Washer had been well received by patrons. Bulk fuel volume was rapidly expanding, with the near completion of four new marine terminals, and the enlargement of the Newburgh terminal. The retail services were all functioning well.

The *G.L.F. Week* for June 27 quoted Silcox as saying at the Managers' Conference: "Our organization is in fighting trim—really set to do a job of serving farmers." During the next few months the G.L.F. was to keep up the pressure on efficiency, economy, and volume-building.

The effect of the recession and the lower farm prices was reflected in the record for the fiscal year, which closed June 30, 1949. Volume fell from $154,600,000 in 1947-48 to $142,199,000 in 1948-49, although total tonnage was up from 1,805,000 to a new high of 1,952,000 tons. Net margins fell from $5,132,000 to $3,374,000. This was the first year under the new membership policy under which G.L.F. gave up tax exemption. To meet an income tax payment of $921,000, it was necessary to reduce patronage refunds from $3,572,000 to $1,067,000, and the amount added to reserves from $910,000 to $628,000.

When the stockholders met in October, 1949, the G.L.F. was on a full economy basis. To cut expenses the annual meeting was streamlined, and attendance was restricted. Even the Annual Report was issued in abbreviated form.

McConnell's report, which he aptly called "Strength Through Sound Planning," met the challenge of deflation head-on. He took the "cold realistic position" that "the general price level will continue downward for a period of years, as it has after every great war." This situation had not come as a surprise. McConnell pointed out that for two years the G.L.F. had been getting ready for "operating in a tight operating economy," and that it was "in fine operating shape." He supported his position with fourteen points:

(1) Our manpower . . . has been brought up to par. . . . (2) We . . . are now operating on a safer price-level. . . . (3) We have taken about 10 percent out of operating costs. . . . (4) We have gotten out of an untenable position by changing from a tax-exempt to a taxable cooperative. (5) We have reorganized and simplified our corporate structure. . . . (6) All our wholesale divisions are in good shape. . . . (7) Our membership program has been brought into focus. . . . (8) Our finances are sound, our credit is excellent. . . . (9) No purchasing cooperative can be strong without volume of business. G.L.F. has it. . . . (10) We have a fine distribution system. . . . (11) The G.L.F. has a wonderful policy group in its committeemen. . . . (12) Throughout the years . . . this cooperative has developed specifications on its feeds . . . and other supplies . . . which . . . insure members of the most suitable supplies that can be secured. (13) G.L.F. has developed scores of valuable industry and business connections. . . . (14) Our G.L.F. personnel . . . has been trained to think primarily of service to farmers. . . .

To meet the "trying times which may be ahead," McConnell proposed that reserves be increased even if this reduced patronage refunds and that membership-ownership be increased through a program to sell to G.L.F. members an additional $5 million of common and $2 million of preferred stock, or $7 million in all. To further this increase in membership-ownership, the Board raised the amount of common stock limitation for individuals from 100 to 400 shares or, in other words, from $500 to $2,000. The limit on preferred stock per individual was raised to 250 shares, or to $25,000 in value.

During the next year the full energies of the organization were devoted to this stock-selling effort, with the result that some 4½ million dollars in new capital came in from farmer members. At the next annual meeting, on October 26, 1950, McConnell said: "This is a magnificent response from membership and an amazing demonstration of confidence in the policies of G.L.F." President Smith said at this same occasion: "The financial standing of G.L.F. has been placed on a basis calculated to withstand shocks resulting from troublesome times ahead."

Other highlights for 1949-50 were reported by Assistant Manager Silcox. Local service units had increased their facilities to provide more efficient and economical use of home-grown feedstuffs, and a strike at the Buffalo plant had again demonstrated the value of such facilities. By shipping some 200 carloads of barbed wire direct from point of manufacture to farmers, G.L.F. had shown the flexibility of its wholesale system, and saved farmers $270,000. A new fertilizer plant constructed on deep water at Albany promised substantial freight savings, while another plant was being built to broaden fertilizer service. A new seed warehouse was under construction at Bordentown, New Jersey, to assure better service for southeastern G.L.F. territory. An elevator was being built at the Bordentown feed mill. This would permit taking advantage of local grains and ingredients. A careful study of freight costs, which totaled $12 million a year, promised better use of shipping facilities.

Although the deflationary conditions continued to prevail in 1949-50, the G.L.F. was better adjusted to meet them, with the result that G.L.F. made a better record in 1949-50 than it did the preceding year. Although volume in dollars declined from $142,199,000 to $141,920,361, reflecting a lower level of prices, volume in tons increased from 1,952,000 to 2,155,000, another all-time high. Greater efficiency in operations was reflected in a growth in net margins before provision for taxes from $3,374,252 to $4,036,991.

The disposition of these net margins is of interest:

	Year ended June 30, 1949	Year ended June 30, 1950
Patronage refunds	$1,067,322	$1,119,485
Dividends on capital stock	757,474	972,038
Retained as addition to reserves	628,456	846,475
Provision for Federal income taxes	921,000	1,099,393

This was the situation when the Korean War broke out and unleashed great inflationary forces. However, G.L.F. could be proud of its record under its "Operation Cutback." This is shown by the condition of the organization on June 30, 1950, just before the close of the fiscal year. In a report to the June Institutional Conference this comparison was made. Compared to the situation that prevailed a year before, the current ratio was now 4 to 1 as compared to 3.5 to 1. The organization's net worth, due to the stock-selling campaign, stood at 72 percent as compared with 63 percent the year before. It had reduced general overhead expenses during the fiscal year by $446,000, or more than 10 percent. Long-term debt had been reduced by $2,536,000, while net operating capital was increased by $2,450,000.

Thus the G.L.F. took advantage of the postwar fall in prices to strengthen its financial position and make strategic improvements in its facilities to serve its members.

With the resumption of inflation at the outbreak of the Korean War, G.L.F. was basically much stronger than it had been two years earlier.

CHAPTER 37

The Outside Investments

G.L.F. has a number of investments in related businesses. These have been made for much the same reason that a farmer invests in G.L.F. itself . . . to accomplish something that can better be done in collaboration with others.

JAMES A. McCONNELL
November 22, 1949

PRIOR TO 1948, G.L.F.'s outside investments had raised little comment. They were reasonable in amount and they were generally accepted by members and the public as essential to the achievement of organization objectives.

The abrupt rise in these investments in 1948 and 1949—as economic conditions deteriorated and as losses began to show up in the canning operations—made them a matter of considerable concern.[1]

On June 30, 1947, the outside investments totaled $1,534,212. One year later they amounted to $5,472,811, while on June 30, 1949, they were $9,990,370.[2] To see what happened we must compare changes in the principal investments for the years from June 1, 1947 to June 1, 1950.

The table on page 352 shows that during these years the increase in these outside investments was modest except for Petrol Refining, Inc., Rural Radio Network, Inc., and Robinson Airlines, Inc. The way these investments came about and how they grew requires explanation.

PETROL REFINING, INC.

To understand how the G.L.F. became financially involved in Petrol Refining, Inc., we must go back to the problem of G.L.F. in maintaining petroleum service during and after the war.

In the early forties G.L.F. was obtaining its petroleum from a major refining company. As war demands for petroleum products increased, it was impossible for this company to continue its service to the G.L.F.— just when G.L.F.'s requirements were increasing. This forced G.L.F. in

---

[1] See comments of the Survey Committee in May, 1949, p. 346.

[2] A substantial part of this increase reflected a change in recording non-current advances to G.L.F. service corporations brought about by the 1948 reorganization. If such advances had been included as of June 30, 1947, the outside investments would have then stood at $3,228,690.

Selected Investments	1947	1948	1949	1950
Fertilizer Mfg. Cooperative	$ 175,433	$ 184,291	$ 191,267	$ 201,533
United Cooperatives, Inc.	230,600	295,900	328,900	345,600
Cooperative P & C Family Foods, Inc.	704,630	704,640	939,640	939,640
Empire Livestock Marketing Cooperative	30,210	60,210	87,710	87,710
Select Seeds, Inc.	108,000	108,000	108,000	108,000
Robinson Airlines, Inc. (Mohawk)	50,100	60,102	172,602	258,579
Petrol Refining, Inc. (Texas City)	—	447,420[1]	3,785,000	4,685,000
Rural Radio Network (Northeast)	—	—	631,000	784,000
Totals	$1,298,973	$1,860,563	$6,244,119	$7,410,062
Non-current advances to G.L.F. Service Corporations[2]	—	$2,971,380	$2,815,321	$1,523,873
Other[3]	235,239	640,868	930,930	809,320
Totals	$1,534,212	$5,472,811	$9,990,370	$9,743,255

[1] Tanker "Four Lakes," Inc. Absorbed by Petrol Refining, Inc.
[2] Prior to 1948, all advances were listed as current on the financial statement.
[3] Includes Mortgages Receivable, Stock in Springfield Bank for Cooperatives, U. S. Treasury Bonds, and numerous minor investments.

1942 to obtain supplies on the open market at premium prices. (See p. 252.) Moreover, to facilitate such purchases it was necessary to lease a storage terminal at Utica. Within the next two years, additional terminal storage was leased at Buffalo, Rome, Syracuse, Plattsburg, Albany, and Tremley Point to permit the purchase of petroleum in barge-load quantities. In February, 1944, the G.L.F. purchased its first terminal storage at Newburgh, N.Y. In 1948, with the growing need for terminal storage to maintain year-round deliveries and increasing difficulties in renting it, G.L.F. undertook construction of new terminal storage facilities at Tonawanda, Brewerton, Ogdensburg, and Rochester, and enlarged its Newburgh plant. These facilities, representing an investment of over $1 million, were all completed during 1949.

Of more importance than terminal storage and essential to its effective use, was a dependable source of petroleum supply. Although the supply situation had improved following the war, it again became very tight in 1947, and the G.L.F. found it difficult to obtain supplies from major companies even under supply contracts. To meet requirements of patrons, other sources had to be found.

G.L.F.'s first step toward obtaining an interest in a supplier company was relatively modest. It consisted of loaning the Petrol Terminal Corporation approximately $450,000 in early 1948 to enable this company to acquire from the United States Maritime Commission a T-2 oil tanker, "Four Lakes," and thus assure delivery of petroleum products via the Gulf of Mexico from its refinery in Texas.[3]

One step led to another. The president and principal owner of the Petrol Terminal Corporation, E. M. Callis, became interested in acquiring a second war surplus refinery at Texas City, Texas. As this was beyond his resources, he proposed that G.L.F., the Southern States Co-operative, Inc., and the Pennsylvania Farm Bureau Cooperative Association, Inc., join with Petrol Terminal Corporation as equal partners in forming a new corporation, Petrol Refining, Inc. In view of the tight petroleum supply situation, this proposal was attractive to the three cooperatives and, on August 17, 1948, Petrol Refining, Inc., was formed, with E. M. Callis as President and General Manager. Soon afterwards the topping facilities at the Beaumont refinery were removed and installed at the Texas City Refinery and a Houdry catalytic unit was added, along with storage tanks.

As part of the transaction G.L.F. paid $1,095,572 in cash and turned over its interests in the T-2 tanker, "Four Lakes," for 15,000 shares of common capital stock in Petrol Refining, Inc. It was also necessary for G.L.F. and the other three stockholders to guarantee payment on a mortgage given to the U. S. Maritime Commission which involved a contingent commitment by each of $275,000. The G.L.F. also accepted a contingent liability of $625,000 under a performance bond given the Venezuelan government to assure a supply of crude oil. Thus, within a few months, G.L.F. had become deeply involved in a petroleum company not yet in effective operation.

The enthusiasm of the cooperative partners was shortlived. Within a few months the market turned abruptly from a condition of shortage to one of surplus, and with the decline in the price of refined petroleum products the Venezuelan crude commitments became a source of embarrassment and their cancellation or adjustment became essential if the refinery was to operate without loss.

It was soon found necessary for the G.L.F. and the other two cooperatives to invest more money if they were to protect what they already had invested. In the spring of 1949 the four stockholders each purchased $100,000 more in capital stock, while the G.L.F. and the Southern States Cooperative each contributed $900,000 in cash for preferred stock in

---

[3] The Petrol Terminal Corporation itself had recently been set up to purchase a war excess refinery at Beaumont, Texas. Under the deal the Petrol Terminal Corporation agreed to supply a large part of G.L.F.'s petroleum requirements for five years, commencing February 13, 1948. Moreover, G.L.F. also guaranteed the balance of the purchase price of the tanker under a purchase money mortgage for $1,194,000. See Prospectus of Grange League Federation Exchange, August 19, 1949.

Petrol Refining, Inc. After months of negotiation, the Reconstruction Finance Corporation, in June, also loaned Petrol Refining $5,600,000, guaranteed by each of the stockholders. As of August 19, 1949, the G.L.F. had also outstanding to Petrol Refining short-term loans amounting to approximately $1,300,000.[4]

This investment of nearly $5 million in Petrol Refining, Inc., within little more than a year, during a period of financial stringency, placed a great strain on the G.L.F. and was no doubt partly responsible for the drive to sell more G.L.F. common and preferred stock in 1949 and 1950. As we will see in Chapter 38, the problems of Petrol Refining, Inc., were to grow worse before they were eventually settled. Now let us turn our attention to another outside investment that "turned sour"—the Rural Radio Network, Inc.

The Rural Radio Network, Inc.

The G.L.F. began to use radio in the late thirties. Its value was demonstrated during the war when it was difficult to hold membership meetings. A five-minute script called "The Farm Front" was then prepared to provide timely information on supplies and services available to farmers through the G.L.F. This was presented each Monday morning on about ten stations which covered most of the G.L.F.'s territory. This program laid the foundation for a more comprehensive broadcasting program.

After careful study, a 15-minute daily program was developed in 1945, and presented six days a week over an informal network created by renting wire lines. This program featured general and agricultural news under the title "The World at Noon." It was welcome and attracted a wide audience, but its cost was high and its coverage did not reach members in Pennsylvania or New Jersey.

Just as the war ended, F.M. radio took the center of the stage. In 1945 there were 48 F.M. licensed stations. By the end of 1948 there were 682. F.M. radio gained immediate popularity for two reasons. It provided opportunity for opening up new stations. It promised more reliable reception.

F.M. radio seemed to offer G.L.F. what it was looking for—a network of broadcasting stations that could serve a large portion of its territory at reasonable cost. F.M. could pick up and rebroadcast without the use of telephone, and this would yield substantial savings in operations. One of the difficulties in using A.M. stations lay in the fact that they were not adapted to farm audiences. As they were dependent upon commercial

---

[4] For more complete information see the Prospectus of the Cooperative Grange League Federation Exchange, issued on August 19, 1949. See also the account of W. G. Wysor, former General Manager of the Southern States Cooperative, in *The Southern States Story*, pp. 103-104.

advertising revenue they catered to urban listeners in heavily populated areas.

The G.L.F. at this time was enamoured with the idea of working with others on programs of mutual interest—as evidenced by its participation in the formation of the Empire Livestock Marketing Cooperative and similar organizations. It thus looked with favor on the establishment of a radio network which would embrace all of the member organizations of the New York State Conference Board. This idea began to take shape during 1946 following research supported by the G.L.F. and the Dairymen's League.

In December, 1946, the G.L.F. directors considered a proposal to set up a Rural Radio Foundation to direct rural radio service which would have as members the state's principal agricultural organizations. The plan was approved and $10,000 appropriated as an initial outlay.

The Rural Radio Foundation was to be a non-profit organization made up of the agricultural organizations who were members of the New York State Conference Board. It was to be the sole owner of a subsidiary operating corporation, The Rural Radio Network, Inc., and any profits from the operation of the network were to be paid into the Foundation for use in research and education for the benefit of the member organizations.

The Rural Radio Foundation was incorporated on March 18, 1947. It was to own and operate a main studio in Ithaca and a network of six Class B F.M. stations. Its initial operations were to be financed by the G.L.F. and the Dairymen's League.

When the G.L.F. Board met in April, 1947, it considered an extensive report on the possibilities of rural radio service. Membership in the Foundation was approved and $200,000 was appropriated to assist in setting up the program.

To help the Rural Radio Network get under way the G.L.F. gave a leave of absence to R. B. Gervan, head of its Information Service, so that he could serve as Manager of the Rural Radio Network until it was well established. The Network was incorporated on June 3, 1947, and the G.L.F. and the Dairymen's League provided it with capital by each loaning $200,000 on demand notes.

During the next few months arrangements were made to get the network into operation. In December, Gervan reported on progress to date, at a G.L.F. Managers' Conference. He presented a map showing the six locations where F.M. radio stations were to be erected. He hoped that broadcasting could be started in the spring. He stressed that this would be the first farmer-owned network in the world, and he thought it would become "the farm and home paper of the air." He believed that the program would have a "tremendous impact on the G.L.F."

Success of the rural radio network required a good F.M. radio for listeners and in anticipation of a great expansion in the use of F.M. radios, G.L.F. had begun experimental work with manufacturers to supply a modestly priced combination AM-FM table model set to be sold through G.L.F. stores and agencies.

At the December meeting, J. W. Crofoot of the Farm Supplies Division reported that G.L.F. would have this model available for distribution before broadcasting was begun. He indicated that none of the existing F.M. radios gave adequate reception in rural areas and that a radio would be made for the G.L.F., based upon specifications shown desirable by research.

The network went on the air in June, 1948, and almost at the same time a campaign was launched to sell the G.L.F.'s AM-FM model at a retail price of $87.50. Various promotional materials were made available for use by the retail agencies—posters, banners, and an illustrated booklet.

The Rural Radio Network was beset with difficulties from the start. Farmers were not accustomed to F.M. radio broadcasting, and their acceptance was slow. Most already had A.M. broadcasting sets and hesitated to buy the new G.L.F. AM-FM table model radio until the superiority of F.M. reception was demonstrated, and the programs of the network were well established. Moreover, at that time it was necessary to use a rather complicated antenna to obtain F.M. reception. This was not only a nuisance but it added $10 to $15 to the cost.

Problems arose in programming and, with few listeners, substantial operating revenues from advertisers were not forthcoming. As a result, losses began to accumulate as did inventories of the radios. From the opening of the network in June, 1947, to April 30, 1949, the accumulated operational deficit amounted to approximately $442,000. Both the G.L.F. and the Dairymen's League found it necessary to increase their advances and by May 31, 1949, the network was indebted to the G.L.F. for $631,000 and to the Dairymen's League for $365,000, evidenced by 4 percent demand notes.[5]

Although the G.L.F. AM-FM model performed satisfactorily, it was considered expensive and to move the initial supply of 2500 it was necessary to sell about one third of the radios at a cut price before the line was discontinued in 1950. The loss to the G.L.F. amounted to about $50,000.[6]

In July, 1949, the Rural Radio Network modified its earlier policy of operating "a self-sustained broadcasting service" to that of operating "a network sales and programming service." This increased its coverage by

[5] See Prospectus of the Cooperative Grange League Federation Exchange, August 19, 1949.
[6] Letter of R. B. Gervan, to author, December 11, 1959.

means of affiliated stations. An operating agreement was made with Cornell University whereby the University Station WHCU-FM became the key station of the network.

As of August 31, 1950, the accumulated operational deficit totaled approximately $665,000.[7]

Several problems had plagued the Rural Radio Network from the start. FM Radio was new and its advantages had been oversold. It had to be introduced and established with the public. Not only were there technical difficulties in getting the network established but, at the same time, a largely untested product—the radio itself—had to be introduced and sold. Although the plan for Rural Radio Network was carefully developed, probably insufficient time and research were given to a consideration of the problems that would be involved.

At the same time, television was becoming rapidly more prominent. By the end of 1947 nineteen television stations were on the air, and a year later the number had increased to 50. By 1949 television had become a national institution. During this year the number of television stations doubled while the number of sets distributed increased fourfold. As G.L.F. territory was well served by metropolitan TV stations, G.L.F. farmers were quickly attracted to this new medium and less interested in F.M. radio.

Another factor also checked the rise of F.M. The Federal Communications Commission began opening up new areas to A.M. stations, thus giving greater coverage to A.M. broadcasts. This took away one of the main advantages which the G.L.F. had counted on for its F.M. network.

A later chapter will show how this program was salvaged and put on a practical basis.

Mohawk Airlines, Inc.

The location of G.L.F. headquarters at Ithaca proved a handicap as the organization grew in size and relationships. Rail service to and from Ithaca was notoriously inadequate, and valuable time was lost in maintaining field and business contacts.

G.L.F. therefore took an active interest when Cecil S. Robinson and other Ithaca promoters formed Robinson Airlines in 1945 as a non-scheduled airline flying between Ithaca and New York City, with a few two-passenger planes. This soon developed into scheduled intra-state operations serving Ithaca, Buffalo, Binghamton and New York City. In December, 1946, G.L.F. was persuaded by Mr. Robinson to invest $50,100 and help him get a permanent certification for the airline. During the

[7] See G.L.F. Prospectus October 10, 1950.

next few years Robinson Airlines gradually became established with G.L.F.'s backing. In this way G.L.F. assured itself of modern transportation and helped establish a service of value to the entire Northeast.[8]

THE OUTSIDE INVESTMENTS UNDER FIRE—1949

The outside investments were of little public concern until August 19, 1949, when full information was made a matter of public record through the issuance of a prospectus which, under the law, was required of G.L.F. as an income tax-paying corporation. As an exempt cooperative, the G.L.F. had not been required to file stock offerings with the S.E.C.

The prospectus was pounced upon by interests critical of the G.L.F. who spread the word that G.L.F. was wasting farmers' money. McConnell recognized the force of this attack in a statement that he prepared for the convenient reference of Board members, key employees and district managers on "the outside investments."

He opened his statement by saying, "G.L.F. has a number of investments in related businesses. These have been made for much the same reason that a farmer invests in G.L.F.—to accomplish something that can better be done in collaboration with others. They are service investments rather than investments for profit. Each one, however, has been made with the intention that it would pay its own way financially, in addition to carrying out the service objectives." He then said, "Practically every investment that has been in effect for an extended period of time has proved to be financially sound."

McConnell then reviewed the origin and status of each major investment and its importance as a service facility of the G.L.F., and brought out the fact that except those in Petrol Refining, Rural Radio Network and Robinson Airlines, all of the investments were in a healthy condition.

The investment in Petrol Refining, Inc., was giving most concern. The refinery had been closed and he could not then tell whether it would be possible to "eventually work it into the black" or whether it would have to be disposed of at a loss. He then said, "G.L.F.'s investment is $2½ million in stock and $2,185,000 in debentures. This is the one investment in

---

[8] In July, 1952, Robinson Airlines took the name, Mohawk Airlines, Inc. Mohawk Airlines now serves, with a permanent certificate of Public Convenience and Necessity, some 34 cities through 21 airports located in the states of New York, New Jersey, Massachusetts, New Hampshire, Pennsylvania, Maryland and Connecticut. G.L.F.'s investment as of June 30 for the following years was as follows: 1948—$60,102; 1949—$172,602; 1950—$258,579; 1951—$512,510; 1952—$733,035; and 1958—$709,060. Although the airline eventually received substantial support from the International Business Machine and Endicott-Johnson Store Corporations, the airline was firmly established when these firms invested their funds. G.L.F. now holds almost 39 percent of Mohawk's capital stock.

the lot in which substantial losses have already been suffered and which looks unfavorable for the future." He was not without hope, however, for he added, "It is not G.L.F.'s long-term policy to operate a refinery, but a quarter interest in one to protect our supply may prove to be sound."

With regard to the investment in the Rural Radio Network he said, "G.L.F.'s investment is $697,000 in first mortgage bonds, representing about two thirds of the total capital of Rural Radio." He admitted that if Rural Radio were to be liquidated at that time the loss would be substantial but he believed that it would eventually achieve a sound financial position and provide an invaluable facility.

G.L.F.'s investment in Robinson Airlines, Inc., was then $172,602 in stock and $36,000 in notes. In McConnell's opinion the "difficult shakedown period" was over and it promised to provide a valuable service. Even if the company were to be forced into liquidation he saw no great danger of loss.

After recounting this investment experience McConnell expressed his philosophy by analogy. "Like a football team, a live organization must make play after play. The plays are made to gain ground. Sometimes a play will be thrown for a loss. The team is judged, not by the occasional loss, but by the net yardage gained and the touchdowns made." He thought it significant that the G.L.F. system had realized since 1935 a net of $55,000,000, while it had lost on the canneries and other discontinued operations $1,800,000.

In the chapter to follow we will show how the G.L.F.'s outside investments were gradually stabilized and brought under better control.

V. REDESIGNING FOR GROWTH, 1950-60

CHAPTER 38

The Korean War Interlude

The Korean War has completely blanked out the strong deflationary forces of a year ago.

JAMES A. MCCONNELL
1949-50 Annual Meeting

WHEN THE KOREAN WAR broke out in July, 1950, McConnell recognized that new assumptions would be needed for future planning.[1] He ruled out the possibility of a total global war as compared with a series of satellite wars which would accelerate inflationary forces. "We are at swords' points with an implacable, strong enemy," said McConnell. "Preparedness for war will be substantial and at an increasing tempo."

The G.L.F. was in good shape for the emergency. The stockselling campaign had provided needed capital and the cutback of 1949 had placed the organization in first-class operating trim. Moreover, from World War II it had achieved the know-how to deal with the unexpected. With basic economic trends moving toward lower farm prices the Korean War was taken in stride.

In a way, the next two years were like an Indian Summer for the G.L.F. While operating conditions were made easier by the abnormal war demand for supplies and services, it was realized that winter was coming. These were the last years of Jim McConnell's management, and he used them to prepare the organization for the more difficult years he saw ahead.

To understand this period in G.L.F. history we must realize that the index of New York farm prices rose from 237 for 1950 to 274 for 1951 and to 281 for 1952; while the index of prices for articles bought by farmers

---

[1] The death of H. E. Babcock also marked a new era in the life of the G.L.F. just as the Korean War began. Babcock had been the living symbol of the G.L.F.—the man who got the enterprise under way. McConnell voiced the feeling of all in his expression of tribute in the *G.L.F. Week* for July 17, 1950: "Many things can truly be said about Ed Babcock as a great leader of thought and action. He was noted in the field of agriculture. In the realms of science, education, business, nutrition, and farming he was the most broadly based man I ever knew. The key to his achievements, however, was in his ability to inspire people to have confidence in themselves and to carry through. He was always available to everyone with a problem or in trouble. His wise counsel and inspiration to hundreds of people was one of the main reasons why he was so effective in carrying out ideas based on a sound knowledge and experience. He left his mark on the country in the form of ideas and organization. This is important. But far beyond that was his contribution in the form of influence on the minds and character of people. His disciples are almost countless."

rose from 256 for 1950 to 282 for 1951, and to 287 for 1952.[2] Thus, during these years both farm prices and prices of farm production supplies rose appreciably.

In the July 31 issue of the *G.L.F. Week,* the heads of the wholesale divisions gave their views on the problems which war would bring. They reported sufficient supplies on hand or available to meet strains and saw no need for panic buying.

The ability of the G.L.F. to meet almost any problem was shown in August when a strike occurred at the Buffalo Feed Mill. Immediately the full standby facilities of G.L.F. Stores and Agent-Buyers were thrown into high gear. When the strike was settled, McConnell wrote to Silcox: "Occasionally there comes a time when one can really evaluate an organization. G.L.F. was so efficient in maintaining a stream of feed during the longshoremen's strike that what could have been a real emergency looked to be just an easy game."[3]

When McConnell addressed the annual meeting of the stockholders on October 26, 1950, he said, "The Korean War has for the moment at least blanked out the strong deflationary forces of a year ago, and set in motion strong inflationary forces."

He used this occasion to indicate that a general manager's report should deal with fundamental policies which keep a service organization strong. This year, as top policy, he stressed building, maintaining and strengthening the committee system. After lauding the G.L.F. Member Committees as "the Power Plant in G.L.F.," and "unique in corporate and cooperative practice," he gave the member committee system credit for keeping G.L.F. "a dynamic, progressive organization."

Silcox, as Assistant General Manager, reported that the G.L.F. had set an all-time record during the preceding year in volume of farm production supplies and in products marketed. An outstanding development had been the recent increase of local service facilities to give more efficient and economical use of home-grown feedstuffs. More grinders for grain, more blenders for molasses, more storage tanks and bins for storage of ingredients were providing a more complete and well-rounded service and giving patrons a chance to cut feed bills.

With regard to marketing, he said: "We have laboriously and with some admitted mistakes arrived at the conclusion that most marketing activities must be tied closely to the local community service." With the sale of the canning plants, G.L.F. marketing operations were now broader in scope and more members were being served with less financial risk.

He reported an outstanding farm supply achievement which was to

[2] Source: *Farm Economics,* New York State College of Agriculture, March, 1959.
[3] See C. N. Silcox, "G.L.F. Spirit Delivered the Feed," *G.L.F. Week,* September 4, 1950.

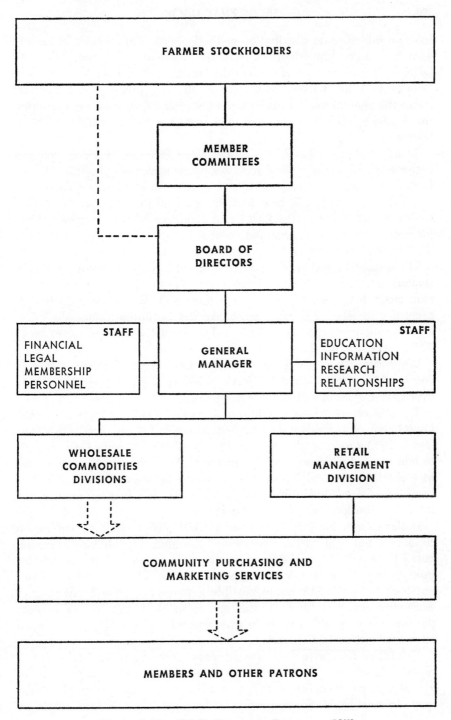

FIGURE 7—THE G.L.F. EXCHANGE, DECEMBER, 1950

have an influence on distribution methods. Some 300 carloads of barbed wire had been shipped direct from the point of production to G.L.F. farmers. These cars were put on side tracks at strategic locations and farmers took the barbed wire rolls off the car, saving about $270,000 under the general market price. This operation, Silcox said, demonstrated the flexibility of a system where sales were not tied to wholesale warehouses.

At this time the G.L.F. was modernizing facilities to serve members better and at lower cost. New fertilizer plants were being built at Albany, N.Y., and Union City, Pa., and a seed warehouse was under construction at Bordentown, N.J. The new Bordentown feed mill was proving that a central mixing plant on the East Coast could pay off in lower feed prices for nearby farmer members; and construction of a new grain elevator at the Bordentown feed mill had been approved.

The financial position of the G.L.F. was at "an alltime high." The substantial investments of farmer members during the past two years in common stock had reduced bank borrowings and "any losses which it is necessary to take . . . would not shake the institution financially." The current ratio now stood at 3.53 to 1, while the net worth had increased to 70.55 percent of total assets.

While the size of the Federal income tax bill was beginning to give concern, Silcox pointed out that savings in record-keeping were offsetting over half of the amount of the taxes paid.

The stiff competitive conditions of 1949 and 1950 had emphasized the importance of merchandising to maintain volume and keep costs low, and in 1950 a merchandising committee of district managers was created to improve G.L.F. merchandising methods. The report of this committee in early 1951 stressed how efficiency could be improved through bulk handling of feed and other commodities—not only in manufacture and retail distribution, but also on the farm.

Dollar volume for 1950-51 reached $163,011,466, the highest volume on record. Net margins from operations amounted to $5,103,026, as compared to $4,055,020 for the preceding year. The high savings for 1950-51, even after a Federal income tax payment of $1,752,970, and dividends on stock of $1,084,816, made possible a patronage refund payment of $1,245,635, and an addition to the reserves of $1,041,898. The savings for the fiscal year would have been even greater had the G.L.F. not rolled back feed prices in February.

This interesting price development was covered by Silcox in the annual report. Management had found appreciation of inventory so great under a continually advancing market that savings appeared more than adequate to meet requirements for dividends on stock, patronage refunds, reserves and taxes. In view of this situation it was decided to roll back feed prices. "This would reduce the payment of excess profit taxes, which is entirely proper," Silcox explained, "and also stabilize feed prices to G.L.F. farmers and all farmers, thus making milk and egg production more profitable. It also represented an opportunity for G.L.F. to regain feed leadership in certain communities and to give to its competitors, particularly those with batch mixing facilities, some real price competition." "Because of the roll-back," said Silcox, "G.L.F. feed prices during February and March, 1951, were from $3 to $4 per ton on dairy feed, and from $7 to $8 per ton on mash below the market price, with the result that the market price was forced to move toward G.L.F. prices." He maintained that this "pricing play" saved G.L.F. farmer members at least a million dollars "and had an influence on the processing trade of the entire nation." He added: "As long as the spirit of G.L.F. exists, there will always be price competition, whether there are government price ceilings or not. "

Since 1949 the G.L.F. had been providing financing assistance to selected Agent-Buyers under an experimental program. Ed Fallon, in reviewing this experience for the Board of Directors on June 18, 1951, pointed out that it had resulted in improved services to farmers or continuation of existing services. In his opinion, this program was raising the morale of the Agent-Buyer system and strengthening working relations with financed Agent-Buyers. The Board approved extension of this program up to a ceiling of $600,000.

The growing emphasis on merchandising was highlighted at a Farm Service Conference in September, 1951, when recognition was given to Service Agency managers who were winners in the 1950-51 merchandising contest. They were ranked on their ability to (1) balance merchandising activities with service and operations; (2) merchandise to fit the needs of users of G.L.F.; and (3) encourage employees to spend more time on merchandising.

On October 18, 1951, a Policy Board of Directors for the G.L.F. Egg Marketing Department was set up by the G.L.F. Board of Directors. It was patterned somewhat on the G.L.F. Marketing Service Board, with a member appointed from each of the eight egg-marketing areas, plus one member from the Exchange Board of Directors.

A New Course Set

Although on the surface all was well, McConnell was becoming disturbed by the underlying trend. The burden of non-productive outside investments continued to be heavy and the scramble for supplies had encouraged hoarding, with the result that inventories had increased by almost $10 million during 1950-51. Moreover, with the tight labor situation, costs were generally rising and this was greatly increasing working capital needs. How to find the money to carry on G.L.F.'s expanding operations had become a serious problem. This problem had been aggravated by the increase in the Federal income tax rate to 52 percent, since payment of tax was required on amounts paid as dividends on stock and on amounts set aside for reserves.

McConnell was now convinced that there would be a business recession soon after the close of the Korean War, and he wanted the G.L.F. to be ready for it. He set forth his views in a talk to a Farm Service Conference on September 10, 1951, which he called "The Importance of a Sound Financial Policy in a Topsy-Turvy World."

He saw G.L.F. in a state of high acceleration and riding for a fall unless abrupt changes were made. He emphasized that G.L.F. had always made its boldest moves when it was strong financially, as an organization's fighting courage and fighting spirit were directly related to its financial security.

In considering G.L.F.'s financial needs, McConnell dealt with the system as a whole. He held that if the Stores could meet more of their own needs for capital this would relieve the burden on the Exchange. He had come to the conclusion that the cheapest way of increasing the G.L.F. pool of capital, outside of additions to reserves, was through an increase in Store preferred stock, as most of the stores—as farmer cooperatives—were exempt from Federal income tax and thus paid no tax on dividends on preferred stock. He favored selling Store preferred stock even if this should cut down investment in G.L.F. common and preferred stock.

McConnell was primarily concerned in this talk with presenting overall strategy for meeting the problems ahead. He set up three objectives: (1) to speed up inventory turnover; (2) to cut out the cost of carrying inventory for supplies not needed; and (3) to reduce the debt structure.

THE OUTSIDE INVESTMENTS STABILIZED

This is a good place to review G.L.F. experience with the outside investments since late 1949 when we left Petrol Refining, Inc., in a precarious condition and Rural Radio Network, Inc., continuing to lose money. These investments had continued to be a source of anxiety to G.L.F. management. Not only did they represent a burden in non-productive assets but they absorbed a great amount of time and thinking that could not be devoted to other important problems. They had this good effect—they forced G.L.F. management to give more careful attention to long-run financial planning.

First, let us see what happened to Petrol Refining, Inc.

In November, 1949, the refinery at Texas City was shut down because of operating losses. By this time the cooperative partners had lost much of their confidence in Mr. Callis. Disturbed by the state of affairs they had succeeded in placing an experienced oil man on the Board of Directors—George Taber, Jr., a former president of Sinclair Refining Company. On Taber's recommendation, an audit was made which justified immediate action to protect their interests. On March 31, 1950, they succeeded in forcing the resignation of Mr. Callis as President and General Manager. By that time the operating deficit amounted to $6,950,000. Soon afterward, on June 22, 1950, V. A. Fogg of the G.L.F. was elected President "to bring some sense out of chaos."

The most immediate problem of Petrol Refining, Inc., was to free itself of burdensome supply contracts. According to Fogg, "The lawsuits in the offing for commitments for Venezuelan crude and domestic crude as well as for product were staggering. We laid our cards on the table as honestly as we knew how and were able to work out a few reasonable settlements."[4]

This was helpful but it didn't solve the main problem. In Fogg's words, "We checked into selling the plant but found that it was regarded to be only junk, and if we had gone bankrupt our corporation loss plus selling the plant at junk value, plus the forced sale on the tankers, plus all the possible grab for commitments, would have put us somewhere between 13 and 15 million dollars in the hole. The sum was so staggering that we just had to find some way of working out of it."[5]

The *Prospectus* of the G.L.F., dated November 10, 1950, indicated that the properties were being maintained in good operating condition and could resume production without delay, and that three possible courses of action were being considered by Petrol Refining, Inc.: (a) Reopening the refinery as a supply source for its member cooperatives; (b) reopening the refinery for production under processing contracts; and (c) the lease or possible sale of the refinery. Fortunately, the company's tankers were operating on a break-even or better basis under charter contracts.

Fortunately, the government then needed aviation gasoline. The cooperatives, by having control, seized this opportunity and agreed to pro-

[4] V. A. Fogg, to author, April 15, 1959. The *G.L.F. Prospectus* of November 10, 1950, reported that the Venezuelan contract had been canceled on October 13, 1950, without payment of penalty.

[5] The same.

duce the product under a contract which provided for the cost of necessary equipment. They then changed the name of the company to Texas City Refining, Inc., and employed William Fetter to get the plant into operation.[6]

In March, 1951, Texas City Refining, Inc., undertook the processing of crude for an independent refinery and shortly after this began producing refined products. As a result of the resumption of the refining operations and the continued profitable operations of its tankers, the financial position of the refinery began to show steady improvement, as will be indicated later in this volume.[7]

It has been impossible here to reflect the gravity of the situation which confronted the three cooperative partners in this enterprise from 1949 to 1951. Failure would have dealt these organizations a serious blow in prestige as well as in dollars. By meeting the problem energetically, intelligently and courageously, they turned near disaster into an outstanding achievement and demonstrated the power of united action. Credit must go to V. A. Fogg, who as President gave leadership to the three cooperatives; to Fetter who provided able professional management; and to the three general managers, J. A. McConnell of the G.L.F., W. G. Wysor of the Southern States, and H. S. Agster of the Pennsylvania Farm Bureau Cooperative, who contributed the full support of their organizations and personnel when the going was hard.

In July, 1949, the Rural Radio Network had modified its earlier policy of operating a self-contained broadcasting service to that of operating a network sales and programming service. Under this plan, which increased coverage by means of affiliated stations, the Cornell University radio station became the key station of the network. This brought about a reduction in operating costs, but it was not possible to develop sufficient operating revenues to place the network on a paying basis.

As of September 30, 1951, the accumulated deficit from June, 1947, totaled approximately $839,000. On that date the network was indebted to the G.L.F. for $900,000, and to the Dairymen's League for $365,000, evidenced by 4 percent demand notes.[8] Although this investment was a source of embarrassment to the G.L.F. during these years, it helped provide a service of great value to the organization, and the burden was not oppressive or dangerous. As noted in Chapter 39, the G.L.F. took over full control of the Rural Network in 1953 and removed it from the category of outside investments.

[6] Fetter had college training in refining and was the manager of the petroleum department in the Pennsylvania Farm Bureau Cooperative Association.

[7] For a full account of developments during this period see the *G.L.F. Prospectus,* dated November 18, 1952.

[8] For more complete information see *Prospectuses of G.L.F.,* dated November 10, 1950, and January 18, 1952.

FINANCING GETS EMPHASIS

In view of the urgency of the financing problem, McConnell gave it primary attention in his annual report for 1950-51, which he entitled, "Financial Policy—A Management Keystone." He said, "I want to deal with financial policy because it is the keystone of successful management in any business, whether individual or cooperative. . . . I am very much concerned to see that we maintain a strong financial position to meet any kind of times that may face us a few years from now." He indicated that financial policy would be the main consideration in the regional meetings to be held during December and January. He said these meetings "are very important at this time. Decisions can have a tremendously beneficial effect on the G.L.F. during the next two, three, or four years. We look forward to an adjustment and not an easy one."

G.L.F. was beginning to feel the great burden of high taxes, and he pointed out how this affected financing fixed assets. He said, "Under the present tax law, for every dollar we earn to pay off debt we have to earn approximately another dollar for the federal government and this dollar comes first." He also pointed out that the sale of common and preferred stock involved a tax bite which doubled the cost of the money to G.L.F. "For that reason," he said, "It's time to be cautious about going into debt."

He indicated that as farmers became mechanized and changed the type of farming it was requiring tremendous change in the character of retail facilities, and that G.L.F. had been modernizing its plants ever since the close of World War II, so that they were generally in excellent condition. He believed that G.L.F. could afford to take it easy for a while but he did not want to stop G.L.F. progress or expansion. He said, "I don't want to see G.L.F. back into the storm cellar and operate under a fear psychology. . . . The way to freeze G.L.F. and make it impotent is to over-restrict use of capital."

For the past year and a half, G.L.F. had maintained high inventories under a threat of shortages. McConnell thought this danger was past and that it would be better to be out of something once in a while than to tie up millions of dollars in larger-than-needed inventories.

In referring to the seed program he indicated that as most of the ideal seed-producing areas were in the far Northwest the G.L.F. had to operate in that area, and a new seed-cleaning warehouse had been put into operation at Caldwell, Idaho. The use of fertilizer and demand for fertilizer were increasing and a new fertilizer plant at Albany had been completed during the past year. Limestone spreading had grown about 40 percent in volume over the preceding year. Better than 90 percent of this lime was being spread directly on the field by 128 lime and fertilizer-spreading trucks operated by various G.L.F. local services. The Bordentown elevator had been completed and would soon be in operation.

There had been a great increase in farm supplies sold during the preceding year—from about $12 million to $18 million, or an increase of about 50 percent. To take care of supply orders, huge tractor trailers, carrying about 30,000 pounds of farm supplies were being used.

President Frank Smith, in his report for 1950-51, referred to the great improvement in such local G.L.F. services as grinding and mixing, high analysis fertilizers, reproduction of better seeds developed by plant breeders, fertilizer spreading, and dependable egg marketing; and attention being directed to the bulk delivery of feed. He also defended the considerable sums of money tied up in other investments on the grounds that they had been made to supply G.L.F. patrons with certain commodities and services which management believed G.L.F. should not supply on its own because of the heavy financial requirements for fixed assets and operations and for manpower. He called attention to the fact that the investment in the Petrol Corporation was no longer in great danger.

In his report, Silcox pointed out that a careful study of supplies purchased by G.L.F. patrons showed that bulk handling offered the greatest opportunity for economy and efficiency in shipping, storing, processing and mixing feed and fertilizer. The development of the bulk feed program would require an investment on the part of service agencies and farmers.

The report of the Treasurer, E. V. Underwood, indicated that the current ratio for 1950-51 had fallen to 2.10 to 1, while the net worth ratio had fallen to 61. Both inventories and receivables were up by over $5 million. Because of higher rates, the income taxes were up about $650,000, and this fact was giving concern. A complete study of financial needs, projected for five years, was currently being made. "From that study," Underwood said, "it will be determined how much additional capital will be needed and recommendations will be made as to the type of that financing."

The need for financial planning was emphasized in the series of regional meetings held in December, 1951, and January, 1952. Thus the whole organization was keyed to the problem of improving its financial position. As a result, steps were taken to curb unnecessary expansion of fixed assets, and a better control was achieved over inventories and other operating costs.

McConnell's concern over the emerging capital problem in 1951 had caused him to direct Charles E. Dykes, Controller, to undertake a comprehensive study of G.L.F.'s finance needs and sources of capital. The results of this study, completed in 1952, left no room for complacency.

One of the facts brought out was that the total amount of money used by G.L.F. had approximately doubled every five years since 1935, while assets had been growing less liquid since 1944. One of the most significant facts disclosed was the downward trend of retained margins since 1938. During the years 1945-46-47, margins had not been retained for fear that this would endanger G.L.F.'s tax exemption, and these were years of substantial savings. Dykes commented, "Retained earnings have not kept pace with growth." It was also brought out that while there had been healthy growth in unit volume during recent years, net margins had been declining and this made the attainment of operating savings more difficult. Moreover, the current ratio had been declining since 1940, and a downward ratio of total assets to sales was unfavorable.

To meet these disturbing trends Dykes recommended that larger margins be taken if possible; that no funds be expended for fixed assets until available through stock or savings; that applications for appropriations be accompanied by a forecast of savings or margins; that warehouses be better controlled; that debt financing not be used for new capital until the balance sheet was greatly improved; that there be a planned schedule for amortization of assets financed by debt; that $7,500,000 in new capital be raised through sale of stock by the Exchange and Stores; and that patronage refunds be paid in equity stock.

Although these measures were not all taken, the report emphasized the need for a revision of financial policies, and put the spotlight on the need for long-range financial planning.[9]

In June, 1952, a Petroleum Division was set up under the direction of V. A. Fogg. Its separation from the Farm Supplies Division was logical in view of the continued growth in volume and significance of petroleum and the different and specialized problems involved in handling petroleum products. Moreover, this freed Fogg to give more concentrated attention to the petroleum problems arising in connection with the Texas City refinery. Glenn Edick became manager of the Farm Supplies Division.

The various divisions were now all working to increase efficiency. The Farm Supplies Division was moving an increasing percentage of supplies direct from manufacturer to the retail stores, thus saving on wholesale warehousing and distribution costs. In 1951-52 service agencies had spread 325,000 tons of lime directly on the land with 145 lime-spreaders. The separation of seed operations from feed operations was giving a new impetus to the seed service. A new dry bean processing plant was being constructed at Caledonia at a cost of $175,000. A business management service was being developed for Agent-Buyers. Bulk feed delivery was beginning to

[9] The general findings of this study were presented at the American Institute of Cooperation in August, 1952. See Charles E. Dykes, "Financing Cooperatives Tomorrow." *American Cooperation,* 1952.

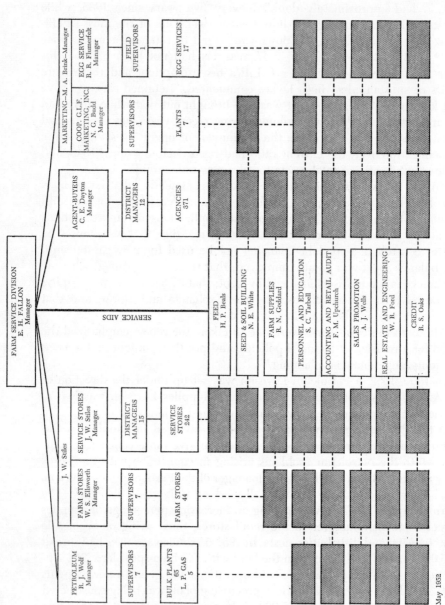

May 1952

Units which use this Service Aid

take hold, and this was requiring expenditures for bulk distribution facilities, and a delivery truck was being developed to facilitate bulk handling. Many of the retail service stores were building more modern facilities.[10]

Considerable progress was made in getting the G.L.F. into better financial shape during 1951-52. Largely through reduction of receivables and inventories and by curtailing expenditures, it had been possible to reduce total assets by $4,600,000, and current bank borrowings by $5,000,000, with a resulting lower cost for interest. The current ratio had increased from 2.1 to 1, to 3.1 to 1, while net worth jumped from 61 percent in 1951 to 68 percent in 1952. More importantly, plans had been made to insure continued financial health.

The new capital needs, estimated at around $9 million for the next five years, were to be met by the continued sale of common and preferred stock; by adding at least a million dollars a year to retained margins; and by financing the balance through a long-term commitment from the Springfield Bank for Cooperatives.

The financial situation of the Exchange was also improved by the increasing sale of preferred stock by the Stores which made it possible for them to assume a still larger share of the financing of the system as a whole.

One thing was giving the G.L.F. cause for concern—its inability to build capital reserves. In 1951-52, net margins, before provision for patronage refunds and income taxes, were lower than for the preceding year, although sales were higher than ever before. Under the bylaws formula that existed for distribution of net margins, G.L.F. was forced to pay a patronage refund of $1,556,876, and could add only $47,110 to reserves for contingencies and operating capital. It was apparent that this mandatory provision for paying patronage refunds when net margins exceeded $3,500,000 was throttling the ability of the G.L.F. to build free capital in the form of additions to reserves.

This situation is explained by the figures on page 376.

The decline in reserves was of great concern to McConnell. In his report, as Executive Vice-President, to the 1951-52 annual meeting, he said: "G.L.F. has a financial problem. The problem is not one of getting the

---

[10] "Progress is being made on the bulk feed delivery program, and many farmers are being served by bulk trucks. We have a number of the large expansion trucks and we find that they have many bugs in them yet. We are working on a small unit which can be used for both bulk and bag feed and will be of value to the smaller points which cannot afford the expensive jobs. The unit is not perfect but it works, and improvements will be made as we go along. Along with the equipment development must come many changes in facilities on the farm for accepting bulk delivery. The bulk delivery program appears to be sound and is evidently here to stay." Jay Coryell, in charge of G.L.F. Facilities Engineering Department, in letter, to author, of September 15, 1952.

	1949–50	1950–51	1951–52
Net margin	$4,036,991	$5,125,320	$4,379,970
Patronage refund	1,119,085	1,245,635	1,556,876
Net margin (before payment Federal Income Tax)	2,917,906	3,879,685	2,823,094
Less Federal Income Tax	1,099,393	1,752,971	1,597,890
Net margin (after Federal Income Tax)	1,818,513	2,126,714	1,225,204
Dividends on capital stock	972,038	1,084,816	1,178,094
Reserves	846,475	1,041,898	47,110

money to operate with, but rather one of getting money from the right sources so that we aren't taxed to death." He held that it would be financial suicide "to continue a policy of no reserves for long." He was of the opinion that the only way to build the $1 million necessary for reserves was "to quit paying a patronage refund until the Exchange has earned in any one year, at least $5,000,000."[11]

In line with his thinking, the bylaws were amended at the 1951-52 annual meeting so that patronage refunds would be paid only if the net margins were more than $5 million. It was apparent to the G.L.F. that this requirement, if set too low, would prohibit the G.L.F. from building "free capital" in the form of additions to reserves. The new provision, in effect, tied the hands of the G.L.F. in the other direction and made almost impossible paying out savings in patronage refunds. As will be noted later (Chapter 41), this also was to prove unsatisfactory.

Problems of inflation and finance had dominated G.L.F. thinking during the Korean War period. The next few years were to call for a fundamental re-assessment and revision of the G.L.F. procedures and practices.

[11]McConnell's election to the newly created post of Executive Vice-President was announced by President Smith on October 24 at the annual meeting. At this time Silcox was named General Manager. Under the new position McConnell would be "the chief policy officer of the G.L.F." In February, 1954, he resigned as Executive Vice-President to become Administrator of the Commodity Stabilization Service, and a year later he was named Assistant Secretary of Agriculture.

CHAPTER 39

Redirection

Come what may, depression or prosperity, Democrats or Republicans, hell or high water, we must operate G.L.F. in the best interests of its members.

CHARLES N. SILCOX
G.L.F. Annual Meeting
October 25, 1952

T HE ABOVE STATEMENT was made by Silcox as he took over the reins of management from McConnell just before the national election.

Silcox was well qualified for the position. Since 1922, when he came to work in the Seed Department, he had helped develop and reorganize marketing operations, instituted the employee insurance program, and served as Secretary of the G.L.F. Holding Corporation, and of many of its subsidiary corporations. During the war and postwar period he had represented the G.L.F. in Washington contacts with various government agencies, and since then he had directed the Mills Division and served as Assistant General Manager. No one had a better grip on the G.L.F. from bottom to top.

As Silcox and McConnell had worked closely together for many years, it was assumed that no great change would occur in managerial direction. However, there was a pronounced difference in the temperament and approach of the two men. McConnell, to a great extent, worked through people, while Silcox relied to a greater extent upon organization and system.

In taking over as General Manager, Silcox realized that G.L.F. was entering a new era. The Korean War had run its course and deflationary forces were gaining in strength. Silcox favored a continuation of the cautious policy of the past year to delay action on the building of fixed assets except where they were needed to render essential services. He saw a new generation coming into the Exchange with ideas quite different from those who had built the organization, and he recognized the need of guiding them in the right direction.

He did not under-estimate the difficulties in making adjustments to the conditions lying ahead. In his report to the Annual Meeting he called attention to the fact that a large part of the G.L.F. staff, including employees, supervisors, and even junior executives, had never lived through adversity in business conditions. He said: "A new generation has been growing up in what has been called 'good times.' These people must be conditioned to meet adversities before they can be asked to make sudden changes in their thinking."

To achieve this end, Silcox announced that management was undertaking studies of the organization and operation of the G.L.F. to "determine if we are getting the most out of (1) employee effort and skill; (2) the use of the money which patrons have provided; (3) the buildings, machinery and equipment; (4) supplies and equipment." He added, "We must determine whether operating costs are as low as possible, yet sufficient to cover the services rendered."

One of Silcox's first acts as General Manager was to appoint Fallon Assistant General Manager. In announcing this appointment, he said, "Close relationships between the wholesale purchasing divisions and the retail distribution services are necessary for the most effective operation of G.L.F. Mr. Fallon, as Assistant General Manager, will direct the operating policies of community services in close association with the General Manager who will continue to direct wholesale operations. . . . Mr. Fallon will also take part in the development of institutional operating policies." This change gave recognition to the growing importance of retail operations and gave them equal standing in the General Manager's office.

Another harbinger of things to come was an announcement by Fallon in the *G.L.F. Week* for November 17, that G.L.F. Farm Service Division had canceled the regional committee meetings "in view of an intensive analysis being made of G.L.F. organization and procedures at all levels to improve operating efficiency." Taking into account the importance usually attached to this series of regional meetings, the significance of this action "to free men for this important job" could not be overlooked.

Fallon indicated that the analysis would lead to action in three areas. 1. Methods, including materials handling, money use, facilities and organization. 2. Volume building. 3. Personnel, including selection, job training and productivity per employee. Fallon declared: "G.L.F. is a sound and aggressive organization. It's our business to keep it that way."

While the survey was being made, Silcox gave his views on the problem of financing the G.L.F. in the January *G.L.F. Week*. His main concern was to explain the need of reserves and the bylaw passed at the Annual Meeting which provided that patronage refunds would be paid only if margins exceeded $5 million. He said: "For the long pull this is a certainty. Only a soundly financed business can produce earnings and only out of margins can patronage refunds be paid. Building a strong reserve policy is in the long run the best patronage refund policy."[1]

[1] Members' Edition of *G.L.F. Week,* January, 1952. At this time Silcox considered the problems of membership and financing of most importance to cooperative manage-

In the *G.L.F. Week* for February 2, Silcox gave his views on operating problems in the G.L.F. He stressed the need for facilities necessary to serve the growing needs of farmers. He emphasized the importance of such services as storing, grinding, mixing, and bulk handling of feeds; and lime and fertilizer spreading.

The results of the studies instituted by Silcox in the fall were reported at a Farm Service Conference held on March 17. Fallon, in a keynote speech, called attention to the big changes that had occurred in operations during the past year. There had been a drop of about 50 percent in net margins, and formula feed volume was off nearly 5 percent. Wholesale and retail costs were rising. According to Fallon, this did not mean that G.L.F.'s growth had come to an end. It simply meant that the period of rapid expansion was over and that G.L.F. was now engaged in a shakedown of organization, methods, and policies. He interpreted the present as a period of consolidation of forces and of gains made in the past. He saw, lying just ahead, one of the most challenging and interesting periods in G.L.F. history.

Silcox, in summarizing the conference, said: "Each man [must] accept the fact that we are on the downward side of an economic cycle." He didn't know how serious the change would be but he felt that "the wise and prudent man will get ready for the worst."

He then reviewed the problem of maintaining volume in major supplies and services. He hoped that "an awakened personnel" would be able to turn in better than an average record. A study of the fixed assets in the light of the economic trends indicated that "for the time being we probably need add nothing to retail facilities to supply commodities or services within a radius of 40 or 50 miles of existing wholesale facilities." He thought that one of the most important considerations was to maintain and improve present facilities in efficient operating condition and to gain greater productivity from present facilities. Turning to the problem of financing, he said, "It is important that we remain flexible in our financing program, always with a plan ahead but ready to change with the times and in keeping with the type of business in which G.L.F. is engaged."

The economic situation was emphasizing the need for qualified em-

---

ment. "While many of the problems of a farm cooperative are exactly the same as those of a proprietary business, membership and finances in a farm cooperative are distinctive." With regard to membership he said: "A new generation of young farmers has grown up—who will not support cooperatives simply because of what we did in the past. They have new problems and new ideas." The tax laws were making financing more difficult. He asked: "Should farm cooperatives go into debentures or raise more money through capital stock or set aside necessary amounts in surplus? What are the advantages and disadvantages of allocated or unallocated surplus?" Letter, to author, of February 2, 1953.

ployees. Silcox recognized that better men would be needed to operate bigger and better facilities with a declining price level. He thought that the job-evaluation program then being developed would enable G.L.F. to determine fair ranges of pay for each job classification and thus give employees a greater incentive to improve performance. He held that programs to help employees make personal adjustments were a major responsibility of management. (See Chapter 43.)

Silcox believed that the times called for strong management to provide enough capital to meet competition, to make adjustments to changed conditions, to develop proper operating policies, and to see that fixed assets were not top-heavy or inventories excessive. He said, "Business management must plan, act, and measure results, . . . for with a declining price level adherence to sound business methods becomes more difficult and is increasingly important."

He then said, "Up to this point, we have analyzed the situation and diagnosed the problem." More business was to be the answer. "What we do in volume building and merchandising will determine the future of the G.L.F. . . . Are we simply going to float downward with the stream; can we paddle fast enough to hold our own; . . . do we have the mental ability, the physical effort and the desire to make gains during an unfavorable business period?"

He saw two ways to maintain volume during a declining price level: "(a) obtain new business from non-buyers, or (b) solicit business from present members on the commodities they are not now buying from G.L.F." Moreover, he held that the potential was great in that G.L.F. had only 35 percent of the total feed volume, 29 percent of the total fertilizer volume, 10 percent of the total farm supplies volume, and 20 percent of the total gasoline volume. He said, "Because of the above conclusions it is our plan to give active leadership to all service agencies so that they may become more active in merchandising. We think it is important to start in this direction immediately."

Silcox concluded his statement by saying, "These reports and the summary have presented an atmosphere in which you are going to work in the next month, year, or maybe five years. Management will try to keep that atmosphere as healthy as possible. Your operations will determine how successful we are in meeting the challenge." He was conditioning the entire organization for the energetic steps needed if a crisis was to be avoided.

The severe drop in feed prices, mentioned above, confronted G.L.F. with a major policy problem. As he later explained:

It was evident that there was no opportunity to make earnings of more than $5 million, the level at which under the new formula patronage refunds might be paid. It was also evident that to make any large sum on feed would simply be taking this money out of the pockets of farmers and giving half of it as corporation income taxes to the government. Therefore G.L.F. followed the markets down rapidly and gave members the lowest possible prices.[2]

According to Silcox, this policy saved Northeastern farmers millions of dollars because competition was forced to do the same thing, and as a result gave Northeastern farmers the most favorable feed prices in the country. He pointed out that it was consistent G.L.F. policy to provide farmers with quality products and services at the most reasonable cost, and that high margins were not a G.L.F. goal.[3]

At this time the G.L.F. also removed a source of operating embarrassment by acquiring the Dairymen's League interest in the Rural Radio Network for a fraction of its investment. The Rural Radio Foundation was then discontinued and the Rural Radio Network became the Northeast Radio Corporation, a wholly-owned subsidiary of the G.L.F.[4] This action gave G.L.F. greater freedom in operating the Network, and led to more satisfactory programming service. One of the first steps taken was to increase use of AM stations.[5]

In April, Silcox reported to G.L.F. members on "Your G.L.F. Today."[6]

He said: "It appears that Northeast agriculture is in a period of price adjustment which is beginning to put a squeeze on farmers between high costs of production and lower farm income." While tonnage was holding up, dollar volume was off appreciably, and net margins promised to be lower than for any year since World War II. The main cause for lower dollar volume and lower margins was the sharp decline in feed prices, which was fortunately benefiting farmers.

Every effort was being made to adjust the institution to the changing times. "In boom times an inefficient farm or inefficient business can still operate fairly successfully. But, when times get tough, a tight, stream-

[2] *G.L.F. Week*, Members' Edition, August, 1933.

[3] "The roll-back on feed prices which I have referred to above has been one example of how strong farmer cooperatives like G.L.F. are saving farmers millions of dollars. These savings do not show up on the fiscal balance sheet in the form of high margins and large patronage refunds. They are, however, very real savings for farmers who take advantage of them and this type of saving is one of the primary purposes behind the founding and continuing growth of G.L.F." *The same.*

[4] See *G.L.F. Week* of April 20, 1953. Up to that time the G.L.F. had invested about one million dollars in the Rural Radio Network. It ceased at that time to be an outside investment.

[5] With improvements made in operations the accumulated loss of Northeast Radio Corporation amounted to only $17,600 for its first 21 months under the new management, according to the *G.L.F. Prospectus*, dated March 31, 1955. The *G.L.F. Prospectus*, dated July 25, 1958, showed that the Northeast Radio Corporation was at last operating on a break-even basis. This corporation was sold in 1959 under an arrangement which provided broader coverage.

[6] Members' Edition of the *G.L.F. Week*.

lined, efficient operation is the only solution either for the farm business or for the business serving farmers."

Silcox then announced that a thorough analysis and study of G.L.F. organization and operations had been under way since the preceding summer. He reported that the early phases of the study had been completed and that some of the conclusions were already in effect. He added: "Meanwhile, the study is continuing and will not let up until we are sure that G.L.F. is operating in the most productive and effective way possible to serve farmers' needs and save farmers' money."

This study had been started as an experiment in the Buffalo feed mill in 1951. Silcox, as head of Mills, was concerned with feed mill operating costs, and this led to the employment of George H. Elliot and Company, a consulting engineering firm, to make a time and motion productivity study. The results of this work for Mills had been so "startlingly favorable," to use McConnell's words, that he and Silcox had decided "to take the entire G.L.F. through the process."[7]

It was apparent from this report to members in April that some major organizational changes were in the offing. The announcement of a reorganization to decentralize retail activities on May 18 therefore came with little surprise. Discussion of this significant change will be deferred to Chapter 40.

Silcox was firmly in the saddle when he addressed the June Institutional Conference on "The Challenge Ahead." He admitted that "some people might say that we have had almost a negative policy in G.L.F. during the past two years, and that there was some truth in this for there had been a reversal from saying yes to no." He gave credit to Mr. McConnell for picking just about the right time to reverse expansion tendencies in inventories and facilities. He said: "What a catastrophe could have occurred had we not changed the trend in G.L.F. operations about two years ago! We did not retreat. We simply stood our ground, consolidated our position, and got ready for the next phase of operations."

He thought that some very worthwhile results had come from the productivity studies, especially through raising the question of why things were being done in a certain way, and why they couldn't be done better. He stressed the importance of asking "Why?," "Why?," and again, "Why?."

As a result of the fall in prices for goods sold, G.L.F. dollar volume for supplies was only $154,185,698 for the year ending June 30, 1953, compared to $164,345,431 the preceding year. However, the value of products marketed went up from $19,387,113 to $21,247,571.

[7] Address by J. A. McConnell, Institute of Modern Management, Chicago, February 9, 1954.

The net margin was only $3,346,848, or over a million less than in the preceding year. No attempt was made to pay a patronage refund, but $716,493 was retained as an addition to reserves.

With new capital invested by members and better use of funds, the current ratio improved from 3.1 to 1, to 4.4 to 1, and farmers' ownership rose from 67.9 percent to 72.7 percent of total assets. Silcox took pride in this improvement in financial status during his first year of management.

CHAPTER 40

Decentralization of Retail

When any organization gets too highly centralized and frozen into a pattern . . . the answer is decentralization.
CHARLES N. SILCOX, *Report to Institutional Conference, June 11, 1953*

As THE G.L.F. grew in size and complexity, the concentration of retail administration in one central office called for attention. Experience had shown that the plants in the wholesale divisions could be effectively managed on the spot within the limits of general policies, and there was a growing belief in G.L.F. management circles that the principle of decentralization could be applied advantageously in distribution and membership contact.

This view was supported by the comprehensive analysis, finished in early 1953, by George H. Elliot and Company. It proposed a complete plan of decentralization "to give authority to those capable of exercising it and yet retain control in the hands of those ultimately responsible."

This plan provided the basis for a complete reorganization of the G.L.F. retail system which was presented by General Manager Silcox in the *G.L.F. Week* of May 18, 1953, under the title: "G.L.F. Keeps Pace With the Times."

He opened his statement by saying: "Last summer, under the leadership of J. A. McConnell who was then General Manager, a thorough study of G.L.F. organization and operations was instituted. The objective was to determine whether there were ways in which this cooperative could be made more efficient, more economical, more effective in serving our farmer members in the difficult times which lie ahead."

He made it clear that the recommendations from the study had been carefully considered and that they were not being adopted verbatim. Several had been modified, postponed, or rejected. He was careful to point out that "the naming of specific men to specific positions was not part of the work done by the Elliot Company," and that "the selection of the individuals has been done entirely by myself and by the other executives responsible for specific functions."

According to Silcox, the plan involved two "somewhat radical" changes in the retail system:

1. The territory was divided into three areas. This represented a new operating principle.
2. The six operating departments of the Farm Service Division were con-

NORTHEASTERN

CANANDAIGUA

NEW HARTFORD

ITHACA

WESTERN

SOUTHEASTERN

SOMERVILLE

FIGURE 9–G.L.F. DISTRIBUTION AREAS

solidated into three divisions—Petroleum, Egg Marketing, and Service Agencies —and given the same status as wholesale divisions. This involved placing the Agent-Buyers, Service Stores, Farm Stores, and Marketing Departments under the Manager of the Service Agencies Division. The Petroleum and Egg Marketing Departments were elevated to Divisional status.

The changes in top management, designed to give effect to the plan, were not drastic. Two new executive positions were set up: *Director of Retail Operations,* and *Director of Wholesale Operations.*

The Director of Retail Operations would supervise the three retail operating divisions. Fallon was to hold this position in addition to his position as Assistant General Manager.

The Director of Wholesale Operations, not yet named, would supervise the wholesale operating divisions: Soil Building, Mills, Seed, and Farm Supplies.

Thus, all line operations were to be headed by executives responsible to the General Manager.

The major change in organizational emphasis was in the greater recognition given retail operations by placing Petroleum and Egg Marketing on a par with the wholesale divisions. To some extent this was counterbalanced by the consequent weakening of the Service Agencies Division.

The Petroleum Division, with Ronald Fitch as Manager, would now be responsible for all petroleum operations except for bulk procurement which was left in the Farm Supplies Division. Terminals and transports would now be the responsibility of the Petroleum Division.

The Egg Marketing Division was to be managed by R. R. Flumerfelt. This operation would be little changed but the function of egg marketing was now to have divisional status.

The Service Agencies Division, with J. W. Stiles as Manager, would now cover work with all Agent-Buyers, Service Stores, and Farm Stores, and all marketing other than eggs.[1] Stiles was to have a central control staff located in Ithaca, but operations were to be decentralized and handled through three largely autonomous area offices. The territories of District Managers for Agent-Buyers and Service Stores were to remain unchanged, but they were to report to the Area offices. Those placed in charge of the Area offices were Charles Riley, Western Area; Garland Clarke, Northeastern Area; and Nelson Houck, Southeastern Area.

In directing the work of the three retail divisions, Fallon was to be assisted by the following four staff departments:

The Sales Promotion Department, with A. J. Wells as Director, would continue substantially the work of the existing Promotion Department, but it would have additional long-range planning responsibility in the field of sales strategy.

The Member Relations Department, with C. E. Dayton as Director, would be responsible for all relations with members at the retail level, including local meetings. Policies on member relations would continue to be established by the Board of Directors and the General Manager.

The Facilities Engineering Department, with Donald Miller as Director, would handle construction and other engineering work for the whole retail system.

The Industrial Engineering Department, a new department created by the plan, would apply industrial engineering techniques to retail operations. In June, Harold Smith was given the job of organizing this Department.

Administrative functions, other than operations, were grouped into six departments, responsible directly to the General Manager. Three of these

---

[1] One result of this change was a de-emphasis in the work with retail stores, as the Service Stores Department had been the strongest Department in the Farm Service Division.

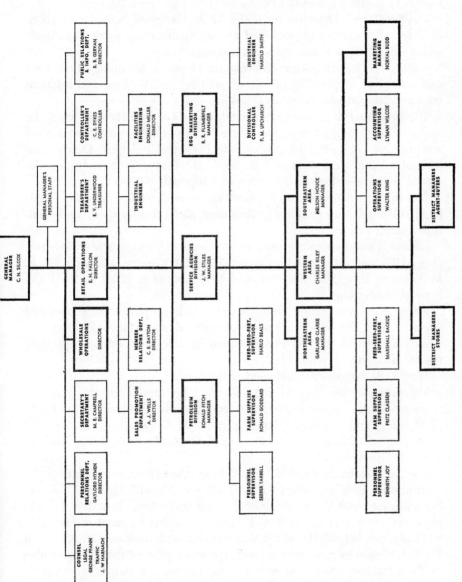

FIGURE 10—G.L.F. ORGANIZATION CHART, JULY, 1953

were new: The Secretary's Department; the Public Relations and Information Department; and the Personnel Relations Department.

The Secretary's Department, under M. E. Campbell, would be responsible for all records but, as noted above, membership work, previously under Campbell, was made a retail function.

The Public Relations and Information Department, under R. B. Gervan, would be responsible for all advertising, publications, and relations with government and the general public.

The Personnel Relations Department, under Gaylord Hymen, would be responsible for employment procedures, wage administration, education, and training. The establishment of the Personnel Relations Department recognized that personnel was so important that its administration deserved "being elevated to the status of a top staff position."[2]

The three remaining staff departments were the offices already under Legal Counsel George Pfann, Treasurer E. V. Underwood, and Controller C. E. Dykes.

Likewise, no changes occurred in the General Manager's personal staff. C. L. Dickinson continued as Assistant to the General Manager; T. E. Milliman as Research Director; and J. C. Huttar as Head of the Farm Management group.

Every effort was made to realign staff rapidly to put the new plan into effect so that the organization could settle down. Many jobs were involved and it was difficult to select men for key posts without upsetting the morale of those passed by.

More staff assignments followed rapidly.

For example, on May 27 the following key appointments were announced for the newly-formed Service Agencies Division: Harlo Beals, Feed, Seed and Fertilizer Supervisor; R. N. Goddard, Farm Supplies Supervisor; F. M. Upchurch, Divisional Controller; and S. C. Tarbell, Personnel Supervisor.

Staffing was nearly finished by mid-June when Silcox gave a talk to the Institutional Conference on "The Challenge Ahead." He used this occasion to interpret the meaning of the reorganization. He stated that the main objective was to place G.L.F. in a position to meet unfavorable economic conditions. He added that the reorganization was imperative if the G.L.F. was to grow and expand. He was confident that the new plan of decentralized operations would give employees a better opportunity, than previously available, to prove their ability.

This frank explanation of why the reorganization was necessary did

---

[2] However, it was recognized that labor relations required specialist attention, and responsibility for all wage negotiations and similar problems in working with organized labor was continued under the Director of Employee Relations for the Mills Division. This position had been set up in 1952. (See Chapter 43.)

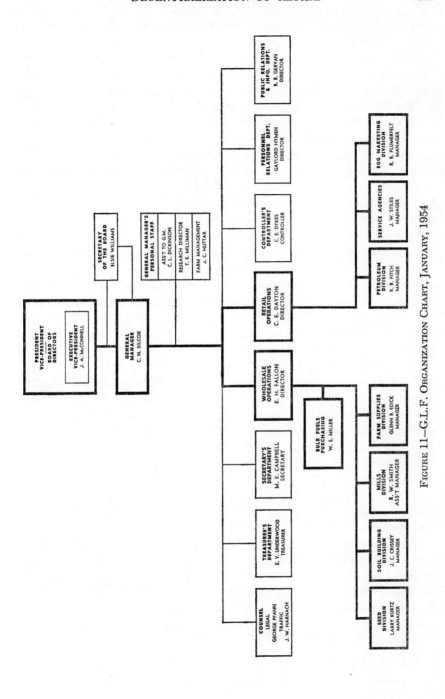

FIGURE 11—G.L.F. ORGANIZATION CHART, JANUARY, 1954

much to gain support necessary to make the plan function effectively. Figure 10 shows the organization chart at this time.

During the next few months the initial stage of reorganization was rounded out by other key appointments. For example, in the *G.L.F. Week* of September 14, G. W. Hymen, Director of Personnel Relations, announced the selection of W. A. Ranney as Manager of the Education and Training Section. He would be responsible for all educational and training programs for employees throughout the Exchange.[3]

One of the main jobs during the summer and fall months was to set up and establish good working procedures for the three Area offices. This involved many difficult problems and decisions. Men and their families had to be moved to new locations and a new set of methods had to be installed. Selection of the best men for each one of the posts involved serious personnel adjustments and retraining on the job. Moreover, it was not always easy to convince those who were not selected for the positions desired by them that the reorganization was necessary.

Fallon continued as Director of Retail Operations until December, 1953, when he was made Director of Wholesale Operations in addition to his post as Assistant General Manager. The appointment of C. E. Dayton to succeed Fallon as Director of Retail Operations completed the central administrative structure called for by the plan of reorganization. Figure 11 shows the organization chart as of January, 1954.

The delay in shifting Fallon permitted him to complete the reorganization of retail operations. Dayton's appointment now enabled him to turn his organizing abilities to the problems of Wholesale. The new position placed him in position to interpret and apply retail changes to Wholesale, and to examine the problem of how to use the wholesale divisions to best help the retail divisions through programs of coordinated action.

The posts of both Fallon and Dayton were to be primarily administrative rather than operational. They were expected to correlate activities and interrelationships of the wholesale and retail divisions.

In announcing Fallon's new appointment, Silcox stated that the Director of Wholesale Operations would perform many of the functions formerly handled by the General Manager. He was to work with the wholesale division managers on long-range planning, development of facilities, conformance with budgets and development of policy. The Director of Retail operations would work along similar lines with managers of the retail divisions.

Silcox said:

---

[3] Since 1945 educational and training programs had been largely the responsibility of the separate divisions.

The size and complexity of G.L.F. operations makes it necessary to divide the various functions into several divisions. One of our great challenges has been to give division managers the freedom and power they need to operate effectively and at the same time to achieve harmony and teamwork among the various divisions.

He was confident that:

The method we have now established is going to produce even better correlation than we have had in the past. . . . Every service—for feed, seed, or any other item—must flow smoothly all the way from the point of procurement to the member's farm. All the steps that have been made in reorganization have been aimed toward expediting that flow.

In *Farming with G.L.F.* for December, 1953, Silcox said, in reflecting on his first year as General Manager, "The most drastic and most important change we have made . . . is the establishment of three Area retail offices. This continues a long-term trend toward decentralization. . . . The purpose of this move is to take as many decisions as possible out of Ithaca and place them nearer to the point where the service actually takes place."

He had little patience with those who felt that the G.L.F. was growing "too big," an expression which he felt should be answered. It was big, he declared, because members were making greater use of its services and if that were the case, he observed, "Let's make it bigger. There is a great deal of good in bigness through voluntary use."

Such a radical change was not made without strain. The new Area offices had to be set up and new procedures and responsibilities established.[4] Men needed to be retrained and old habit patterns broken. While many found the adjustment difficult, the logic of the reorganization was gradually accepted. The G.L.F. could not turn back.

[4] A large part of the load in setting up the Area offices had fallen on Jerry Stiles, as Director of the Service Agencies Division. His report for the year ending June 30, 1954, given in *G.L.F. Facts and Figures*, is thus of special interest. "The G.L.F. fiscal year, 1953-54, has been largely one of reorganization, adjustment and development. The move was one of the most drastic realignments of responsibilities and jobs in the history of G.L.F. but the past few months have seen it rapidly develop into a smooth functioning team of division and area line and staff management."

CHAPTER 41

Easing the Cost-Price Squeeze

In a cooperative there is a time for volume building. There is a time for making net margins. There is a time for setting aside reserves. There is a time for paying patronage refunds. . . . Now is the time for emphasis on those services which cost you the least and give you the greatest returns.

CHARLES N. SILCOX, *Annual Report for 1953-54*

A S FARM PRICES declined, with abundant production and more normal conditions of demand, while costs of farm supplies remained high due to strong demand for materials in industry, farmers increasingly complained of the cost-price squeeze. The change in the farm situation is portrayed by a comparison of trends in prices of farm products with prices of production items as shown by index numbers.[1]

As farmers endeavored to cut costs by restricting purchases, competition was keen for the available business. Emerging from a period of optimism, farmers were gloomy, and they looked to the G.L.F. or any other source for help. To meet this problem, the full energies of the G.L.F. were directed toward reducing farmers' costs for feed and other supplies.

In April, 1954, the G.L.F. announced that on May 1 it would launch a campaign to aid dairymen in combating the cost-price squeeze in the months ahead. Margins taken on many important feed, soil-building and farm supply items were to be slashed. A new 14 percent Grassland Dairy Feed was to be priced at $9 a ton below Milk-maker.

At the June Institutional Conference, Silcox said:

We have been shaping our operations to efficiently and economically . . . [increase] the use and usefulness of G.L.F. . . . It has been a period of test and trial but I think the new machine is working efficiently. Our job now is to get the best results out of it. . . . We have come to the point of no return to the easy days . . . when the major problem was to get supplies to fill what seemed like an unlimited demand.

For a long time the emphasis had been on operations. "Now," he said, "if we are going to make farming more profitable, we must help and en-

[1] Source: *Farm Economics,* New York State College of Agriculture, March, 1958.

Year	New York Farm Prices	Price of Articles Farmers Buy
1952	281	287
1953	243	279
1954	226	281
1955	225	281
1956	230	286
1957	249	296

courage farmers in the development of better farm practices. . . . The opportunity to increase the use and the usefulness of G.L.F. lies in our hands. A new challenge to serve a new type of farming with new methods is here. Can we meet it? I think we can."

Throughout the summer of 1954, the G.L.F. searched for new ways of reducing distribution costs. In a talk on "Planning for Better Cooperative Distribution," given at the American Institute of Cooperation meetings at Cornell University in August, Fallon pointed out how farmer cooperatives must keep up to date to give the best possible service to farmers. He thought that the great opportunity for improvement lay not *within* operating units but *between* operating units, or in the steps that can be by-passed between raw materials and the farmer, or between farmer and consumer. He maintained that this could be done by: (1) bringing farm production supplies as close to the farm as possible; (2) by-passing as many facilities in handling as possible; (3) recognizing obsolete facilities and consolidating units where necessary to lower costs; (4) pooling carlot orders and improving packaging; (5) providing mechanical equipment to help farmers use services; and (6) pricing to give farmers transportation advantages based on their location.

At the Annual Meeting in October, Silcox made it clear that G.L.F. was going to do everything possible to help farmers produce more efficiently and economically. He held that: "The agronomy program of farmers stands out as being most important in this tightening farm economy. I mean the production of more and better homegrown grains and roughage on your farms."

To help members lower costs the adoption of bulk-handling methods was accelerated. Bulk handling equipment for loading feed and fertilizer was installed at all of the mills and plants. To lower the cost of lime spreading, inefficient spreading units were rapidly replaced. Development of a bulk milk tank for use on the farm was pushed.

The trend toward bulk handling to reduce costs called for modernization of facilities by the local service agencies. On this, Silcox said, "As we learn more about the handling of bulk feed, the handling and spreading of bulk fertilizer and lime, the local investment in equipment for these purposes will go up. These are all tied in with better farm management, and while the total investment is large, the savings made for farmers are correspondingly large."

Silcox expressed G.L.F.'s concern for the farmer's plight in the following words:

In a cooperative there is a time for volume building. There is a time for making net margins. There is a time for setting aside reserves. There is a time for paying patronage refunds. . . . Now is the time for emphasis on those services which cost you the least and give you the greatest returns. . . . The present is not the time for making large or even average margins in wholesale and retail operations.[2]

He continued, "The policy of the time for G.L.F. operators, both at wholesale and retail, is to be close, tight pricing." This statement made G.L.F. policy clear. The full energies of the G.L.F. were to be devoted to rendering essential services at a minimum of cost to farmers.

The need for this policy was obvious in the spring of 1955. Few, except the old-timers, could remember when dairy and poultry farmers were more hard pressed or more discouraged.

The Price Discount Plans

At this critical time Silcox conceived a novel plan, while on vacation in Florida, to give members $5.00 a ton discount on purchases of manufactured feed. This was not an entirely new departure, for the G.L.F. had frequently used price policy to reflect price advantages direct to farmer patrons. It differed in that it was set up as a formal program and restricted to members. The reasoning back of the plan was fully explained by Silcox in the *G.L.F. Week* for April 18, 1955.

The G.L.F. had made sufficient margins by early spring to cover dividend payments on stock and to provide for a modest reserve and the amounts required for Federal income tax. Thus, G.L.F. was in position to make margins for the remaining months of the fiscal year which could be used either to pay a modest patronage refund or to reduce prices paid by members for feed. Silcox proposed this latter course as being in the best interests of farmer members.

The program gave G.L.F. Service Agencies an opportunity to build good will. They welcomed it as a way to demonstrate that their organization was up on its toes in serving the needs of its farmer members. It offered proof that by good management savings were being reflected to members at a time when reductions in farm costs were needed. It emphasized the efficiency of a large organization which could return three quarters of a million dollars in the form of a discount. It gave farmers something to think about and discuss. As President Frank Smith said, "The plan gives dairymen concrete evidence that the G.L.F. is attempting to help them in the price-cost squeeze."

The Members Feed Discount (or M.F.D.) program ran for seven weeks and during that time some 5,000 farmers joined the G.L.F. in order to get its benefits. In June, M. E. Campbell reported to the Institutional Confer-

---

[2] The bylaw which required net margins of $5,000,000 before patronage refunds could be paid was rescinded at this Annual Meeting. Thus, G.L.F. would have freedom of action the following year.

ence that the Members Feed Discount had been the most outstanding program in the interests of G.L.F. membership since the early 1920's. He pointed out that members had received over $700,000 from it and said, "It was a heck of a time to sell a G.L.F. membership but it was easier to get a $5.00 bill from him so you could discount his feed bill $5.00 per ton."

The plan had obvious weaknesses but these were considered of little importance in view of its main advantages. Some farmers complained that it violated the principle of treating all members alike as some patrons were but nominal users of feed and only feed purchasers could benefit from the plan. Others complained that any farmer could get the benefit of the discount by taking out a membership. They felt that the benefits of the plan should be restricted to those who were members of the G.L.F. before the plan was announced.

Without doubt, the plan gave the G.L.F. a competitive advantage over other feed concerns who were unable to quickly develop effective counter measures. Although some criticized the plan as being a sales gimmick, the rank and file of members appreciated the help thus given them by G.L.F. The plan had several major advantages. (1) It gave the benefit to the members when a general reduction in prices would have gone to non-members as well. (2) It gave immediate help to farmers rather than year-end help to them in the form of patronage refunds. (3) It distributed net margins accumulated on feed to purchasers of feed rather than to purchasers of all supplies. (4) It reduced substantially the income tax liability of G.L.F. for that year. (5) It served as an effective advertising and promotional medium. (6) It demonstrated the power and the push of the G.L.F. at a time when farmers were demanding relief.

Silcox devoted his column in *Farming With G.L.F.* for June, 1955, to the results achieved by the Membership Feed Discount. It had been years, he said, since the G.L.F. members and employees had talked so enthusiastically about a G.L.F. program.

He answered the question, "Why did G.L.F. take this action?" by quoting a young Pennsylvania farmer, "G.L.F. must occasionally prove by action that it is not just another feed company. It must show its members that the operation of this big business is not more important than the purpose for which it is operated."

Silcox then pointed out that the years 1954 and 1955 had been hard years for farmers and that the toughest time of year for them was in the spring when their cash outlays were greatest. The discount "seemed the most effective means of putting a few extra dollars in the pockets of farmers when they needed it most. . . ."

Silcox answered the charge that the plan was not fair to all members by claiming that it had "reached nearly all of the members on an equitable basis." He thought that this criticism was "mainly the result of misunderstanding."

He ended on this note of cheer, "I believe the squeeze on Northeastern farmers is pretty well over. If we stick together . . . the months ahead will be better and farmers can look forward again to a strong and prosperous agriculture."

However, the optimism was shortlived. Although there was a slight improvement in farm prices during the summer of 1955, this did not loosen the grip of the cost-price squeeze. There was to be no quick return to farm prosperity and farmers were to have no alternative except adjustment to a lower level of prices with continuing high costs.

With conditions in the spring of 1956 fundamentally the same as for the year before, it is not surprising that the price discount plan in modified form was used again.

The new plan "to ease the cost-price squeeze" was announced in the *G.L.F. Week* for April 2, 1956, under this heading, "The Members Spring Discount Unveiled."

The M.S.D., as the new plan was called, differed from the M.F.D. in that it was a straight 4 percent discount on all formula feeds and fertilizers, field and grass seed, and all farm supplies. It did not apply to such low margin items as feed ingredients, scratch feeds, lime and superphosphate, or to locally-mixed feeds.

The M.S.D. thus silenced the complaint of the preceding year, since it applied to other basic commodities as well as feed, and since it retroactively also covered early orders of fertilizer and seed.

Although the plan was well publicized it was not received as favorably as the earlier M.F.D. This was partly due to a general rise in feed prices that occurred during the period the plan was in force, which favored the criticism of competitors that G.L.F. prices were raised to cover the discounts.[3] Moreover, in the spring of 1956, competitors were better able to counter the M.S.D. plan for it did not come to them as a complete surprise.

Even though the plan was not quite so successful as that of the year before, it attracted some 5,000 new members and gave farmers some $700,000 that otherwise they would not have obtained.[4]

[3] The general rise in feed prices, coming just at this time, placed the G.L.F. in a somewhat embarrassing position, although there was nothing to the charge that it was caused by the G.L.F. As costs for ingredients went up, G.L.F. had no alternative but to raise prices. If it had lagged it would have dissipated reserves and, moreover, it would have had to replace inventories later at higher prices. If it hadn't raised prices with the industry it would have had to raise them later under probably even more difficult conditions.

[4] This is on the assumption that no patronage refund would have been paid in this year, an assumption which cannot be verified.

Silcox was well pleased with these results. In the August issue of *Farming With G.L.F.*, he raised this important question: "Have we found a means of benefiting members which is quicker, more economical, efficient and equitable than the patronage refund?"

He listed the following advantages for a members price discount over a patronage refund: "(1) It is effective at a time when farmers most need cash to pay their bills . . . ; (2) The costs for record-keeping are small . . . ; (3) the element of surprise has an important effect on the whole farm supply industry; (4) a members' discount can be applied exactly to the profitable commodities. . . ."

The enthusiasm of Silcox for a price discount as compared with a patronage refund, however, was not shared by all members. Many had long been accustomed to patronage refunds and they looked upon the discount plan as a palliative and no real substitute for a patronage refund which reflected total savings for an annual period.

When the local committeemen were given an opportunity to indicate at the fall regional meetings whether they preferred the discount plan to payment of a patronage refund, a large proportion favored a patronage refund.

One feature of the discount plan still caused considerable membership resentment—the fact that the discount was available to any farmer who paid $5.00 for a share of membership stock. Many long-time members of the G.L.F. felt that the benefits of the G.L.F. discount plan should be restricted to those who were members when it went into effect.[5]

The Board, on August 6, 1956, developed a policy statement to deal with this problem. Because of its importance, this is given in full:

It is the judgment of the Board that a person must be a member of this cooperative to receive a patronage refund—such patronage refund to apply only to business transacted while a member. It is the further judgment of the Board that a person shall not be eligible for special *institutional* price discounts offered to members and shall not receive such special price discounts unless he is a member of the cooperative at the time the announcement of such program is made.

Therefore as a matter of policy for guidance of management in dealing with members of this cooperative it is

Resolved: That membership privileges or benefits existing in or offered by this cooperative shall not attach to events, conditions or transactions prior to actual admittance to membership, and no patron shall be entitled to, or exercise any of the rights, privileges or benefits of this cooperative in connection

---

[5] On the other hand, M. E. Campbell, Director of Membership Relations, saw an advantage in making the discount available to non-members as soon as they became members for this encouraged farmers to join the G.L.F. and give it the added strength of their membership.

with events, conditions or transactions of an institutional nature which occur prior to admittance to such membership or after disqualification as a member.

In presenting this policy to the stockholders at the annual meeting, President Corwith said, "It is the judgment of your Board that membership is a year-round job. Users should be given a chance to know the benefits of membership so that when special programs come they will not have to qualify at the last minute."

With a considerable improvement in farm prices in 1957, conditions were not so psychologically favorable for the use of a discount plan, and a patronage refund was again paid.

In looking back over these experiments in pricing it is well to remember that they were the product of unusual times and that they served a valuable purpose in the life of the organization. Like so many developments in G.L.F., they were experimental in character and they tested a procedure that could be employed again should needs require its use. During 1955 and 1956 the main concern of the G.L.F. was to ease the cost-price squeeze. Although the discount plan may be criticized from the standpoint of orthodox cooperative theory that savings should be reflected in patronage refunds so as to reflect advantages to all patrons, it helped maintain cooperative vitality during a period of farmer unrest. This vitality was shown by the action of the Board when it restricted the plan in response to the views of members.

CHAPTER 42

Renovation for Change

We don't have to be told that agriculture is changing rapidly. You
may be sure G.L.F. is keeping the pace.
CHARLES N. SILCOX, *Farming in G.L.F.*, April, 1957

UNDER Silcox's management from 1953 to 1957, the G.L.F. was thoroughly overhauled and renovated to meet changing agricultural needs. It was a period of systematic improvements and of continuous search for ways to improve efficiency and to provide members with desired services.

A new generation of farmers had developed during the war and postwar years. Having not personally helped build the G.L.F., it lacked paternal feeling. The new group measured the G.L.F. more in terms of immediate self-interest than in terms of its long-run value to the agriculture of the Northeast.

As indicated in the last three chapters, this was a period dominated by the cost-price farming squeeze. Gone were the easy days of inflation and almost automatic growth. Farmers were restive and they were not content with old methods of service—no matter how good they had been.

The G.L.F., like any long established organization, had developed habits that were hard to break. Member support was usually taken for granted and it was difficult for G.L.F. personnel to realize that it was now necessary for a thorough re-evaluation. McConnell had set the stage for the work of renovation, but the actual job of renewal fell squarely on his successor, Silcox, who was ready for the challenge.

In this chapter we will examine how the G.L.F. met certain problems under these new conditions.

PROTECTING THE RIGHT TO MANAGE

One of the problems of change involved relationships with organized labor. In October, 1953, the G.L.F. undertook a study to increase efficiency in the Buffalo elevator. The G.L.F. wanted "to test the practicality of unloading a grain car with a crew of six men, as compared to the practice then followed of unloading two cars with a crew of ten men. All employees had been informed that no employee would lose his job as a result of a study of this type."[1]

[1] "The Facts Behind the Strike in Buffalo," *The G.L.F. Week*, December 14, 1953.

However, when employees were asked to perform the work required to test the plan they refused to comply. The G.L.F. reasoned that, since this was a reasonable request from management, it had no recourse except to discharge them.

As a consequence of this action, members of the elevator workers union who were members of the International Brotherhood of Longshoremen, picketed the Buffalo Feed Mill. The mill workers, who were members of the A.F. of L. American Federation of Grain Millers, refused to cross the picket lines and the plant had to shut down.

G.L.F.'s position on the dispute was presented as follows by Silcox: "The management of any business has not only the right but the duty to run its business as efficiently as possible. Responsible labor unions recognize this right. Respect of management for labor's rights and respect of labor for those of management are the foundation stones of good industrial relations."[2]

Although the union members at the Mill returned to work on November 9, a basic agreement with the International Brotherhood of Longshoremen and its Local 1286 was not reached until January, 1955. The new contract outlined fully G.L.F.'s right to manage. The agreement stated:

Except as otherwise provided in this agreement, the management of the elevators, the direction of the working force, the fixing of the size of crew, the assignment of work, the direction of the order and manner of doing work, designation of part of the plant in which any operation is to be performed, the right to hire, suspend or discharge for cause, the right to transfer within the elevator, or lay off due to lack of work, and in general all other usual functions of management are reserved to and are vested exclusively in the Employer.

In return, the G.L.F. agreed to rehire those discharged at the elevator with full reinstatement of their employee privileges.[3]

FARMING WITH G.L.F.

A paramount problem of the G.L.F. during this period was to keep members actively interested in their own organization. To help solve this the G.L.F. in October, 1953, introduced an attractively-designed and well-illustrated quarterly, digest-size, 32-page membership magazine, *Farming With G.L.F.* Its object was to "keep farm people informed about G.L.F. commodities and services and what was going on in the organization itself . . . [so as] to help farmers make better use of their coopera-

---

[2] The same.

[3] Herbert J. McClain, letter to author, October 1, 1959. While the plant was closed, G.L.F. members were supplied with feed from the Albany and Bordentown Mills and from local service agencies with mixing facilities.

G.L.F. FEEDS THE CHAMPIONS, TOO!

WORLD CHAMPION

All-Breed Fat Record
Brown Swiss Milk Record

LEE'S HILL KEEPER'S RAVEN 171673
34,850 Milk   1579 Fat   365-3X

The Lee's Hill Farm herd, New Vernon, N. J., has been fed exclusively on G.L.F. Super Test since 1926. Nearly fifty records over 1,000 pounds of fat have been made during that time.

WORLD CHAMPION

Guernsey Milk Record

HADDON'S M. IDA 1245498
28.787 Milk   1235 Fat   365C-3X

Haddon's M. Ida of Grayce Farms, Dalton, Pa., is the first Guernsey on AR test ever to produce over 100 pounds of milk a day. While making this record, Ida was fed 9,125 pounds of G.L.F. Super Test.

WORLD CHAMPION

Living Lifetime Milk Record

KORNDYKE BEETS JANNECK SEGIS 2065418
276,176 Milk   9921 Fat

This is "Old Nit's" record to April 20. The Clark Bowen herd, Wellsboro, Pa., has won the State top production award seven out of the last eight years. G.L.F. Super Feeds have been fed for 30 years.

WORLD CHAMPION

Sr. 3 yr. Guernsey Milk Record

FAIRLAWN ACTOR'S FAITHFUL 1505608
23,298 Milk   911 Fat   365C-3X

This senior 3-yr.-old record also places Faithful 19th for milk production in the entire Guernsey breed. Faithful, as well as Ida and the 140 other Guernseys at Grayce Farms, is fed G.L.F. Super Test.

The right combination of breeding, management and feeding produced these championship records. More milk in the Northeast is produced *on G.L.F.* than on any other feed.

G.L.F. DAIRY FEEDS

Quality That Pays Off on the Farm

ADVERTISEMENT, JULY, 1958

tive and be more effective in establishing its policies and developing its services." Silcox made use of this organ to give members frank expressions of his views. In the first issue he said, *"Farming With G.L.F.* is an effort to bring the spirit of G.L.F. right into the farm homes of its members. . . . We want you to know what we are thinking about, what we are planning to do, and what we are doing to meet your needs in farming." For several years this magazine served a useful purpose in informing members on new G.L.F. services and developments.[4]

Another constructive step was the formation in 1953 of the G.L.F. Insurance Company to provide insurance for G.L.F. facilities. Prior to this time the G.L.F. had built up a fund of over one million dollars in a fire insurance pool which provided coverage for its retail facilities and some marketing plants. The new company made this service generally available to all properties in the G.L.F. The following year its services were extended to G.L.F. agent-buyers and related cooperatives.

With the growth of farm stores and farm store departments, the G.L.F. farm supplies line had expanded to include a large number of miscellaneous household and novelty items which were not in keeping with G.L.F.'s basic aim, the serving of farmers' vocational needs. The boom conditions of the Korean War period had accelerated this development until it was questioned whether the time and effort given to the handling of these non-farm items was not impairing emphasis on G.L.F.'s basic services and doing more harm than good in patron and public relations.

Following a careful analysis of this problem, G.L.F. decided in August, 1953, to stop handling all items on which it could not perform any special service in price or quality. As a result, "white goods" such as washers and refrigerators (but not freezers); and various household items, such as clocks, irons and food mixers, which were commonly referred to as "pots and pans," were largely eliminated from the G.L.F. line. To rate continuance, commodities had to meet three requirements: (1) They had to be in character with the G.L.F.; (2) they had to be essential to farm production; and (3) they had to add to the efficiency or to savings in the operation of a farm business. In line with these requirements, the petroleum division stopped handling bottled gas since it was primarily purchased by town people.[5]

To render better service and to gain experience the G.L.F. was at this time installing pilot granulation equipment at the Lyons Fertilizer plant.

---

[4] Publication ceased following the reorganization of 1957. It was costly to prepare and distribute, and membership interest in the publication was not sufficient to warrant its continuance.

[5] Although the G.L.F. line has greatly expanded since 1953, its offerings in 1960 are more basically associated with agriculture, except for lines associated with its lawn and garden business.

Granulation was being accepted by farmers and seemed to answer certain physical application problems.

The feed plants were rapidly getting into position to load bulk feed for direct farm delivery, and a new marine leg was being planned for the Buffalo feed mill which would greatly reduce grain unloading costs.

Plans had been made for a G.L.F. seed warehouse in the San Joaquin Valley of California to provide improved seed service, and in June, 1954, to further improve the efficiency of seed operations, all western seed procurement activities were centered at Fort Wayne, Ind., under the management of L. D. Kurtz, while seed department activities in G.L.F. territory were placed under the management of J. A. MacEachron at Ithaca.

In March, 1954, the completion of the Buckeye Pipe Line made possible direct movement of petroleum products from tankers unloaded at Carteret, New Jersey, to northern Pennsylvania and southern New York, through recently constructed G.L.F. pipeline terminals at Vestal, New York, and Dupont, Pennsylvania. With the closing of this "missing link" all G.L.F. territory could now be served with petroleum products from the Texas City refinery.

In view of the many changes taking place within the G.L.F., it seemed desirable to review fundamental principles and policies and bring them up to date for the guidance of employees and members, in a pamphlet entitled, "G.L.F. Principles and Policies," which was issued early in 1954. At this time Silcox said, "There are certain fundamental principles and policies in G.L.F. which will never be changed. G.L.F. is by tradition and character a farm organization."

To stimulate farm supply business the farm supply warehouses held a series of V.B. (Volume Building) Days in the early months of 1954. Most of the service agencies came to see model displays of supplies and equipment and obtain commodity and servicing information from the wholesale buyers and warehousemen. This program placed emphasis on knowing the merchandise and services available through G.L.F. and did much to tie wholesale and retail operations more closely together. It was used even more effectively the following year.

Personalized Service

In addressing the Institutional Conference in June, 1954, Silcox emphasized how the "use and usefulness of G.L.F." could be increased. He saw market research as a most important tool for gaining information necessary to meet farmers' needs. He thought of market research as "simply a matter of finding out what farmers need to aid them in carrying on good farm practices." He considered the new "personalized service" program being developed by the Service Agencies Division as a form of "market research" in that it would study and develop "an intimate knowledge of all the key farmers in each community." He continued, "Think how fortunate we are to have as our market the same farmers who own and control the G.L.F., the farmers who use G.L.F."

While Silcox thus recognized the importance of market research, he did not then see it as a function of G.L.F.'s research program. However, his remarks indicated that he was coming to understand its importance, and this helped lay a foundation for an expansion of the research program in 1955 to include market research.

The "personalized service" program, launched in July, 1954, recognized that more contacts should shift from the store to the farm as farms grew larger and fewer. The objective of this plan was stated as follows: "Each service agency [will] study and develop an intimate knowledge of the farm needs for all key farmers in [its] community. This close liaison should be continuous and a sincere attempt [should be] made to satisfy their individual farm needs."

This change in emphasis to help each farmer choose the right G.L.F. commodity or service to fit his needs required leadership and employee training programs. It also called for a modification in the merchandising approach by giving more emphasis to farm calls.

With costs of retail distribution increasing, the G.L.F. also began to encourage self-service—or self-selection of supplies by patrons. An experiment to determine the practicability of this type of merchandising, especially in speeding up retail service, was initiated in several stores in 1954 and 1955, and the lessons from this experience were published in a report prepared in 1956. Since that time a number of the retail service agencies of G.L.F. have adopted self-service facilities to some extent.

CAPITAL STOCK STABILIZED

With lower prices and smaller inventories, the need for working capital was greatly reduced. Moreover, the steps which had been taken to increase equity capital and reserves had placed the Exchange in an excellent financial position. On June 30, 1954, the current ratio was 3.6 to 1, and members' ownership amounted to 72 percent of the total assets. Under these circumstances, the Board decided to stabilize the amount of stock outstanding by calling the Holding Corporation's 5 percent preferred stock; by stopping the sale of the Exchange's 4 percent preferred stock; and by limiting sales of Exchange common stock to 100 shares per member. This program was designed to reduce the burden of interest costs on stock, balance membership ownership, and achieve tighter management control.

The F.F.A. Crop Demonstrations

The G.L.F. has long recognized that its members tomorrow are the rural youths today. In the 1930's, T. B. Clausen, then in charge of G.L.F. membership relations activities, attempted to build a youth auxiliary known as the G.L.F. of Tomorrow. This served a useful purpose in attracting the interest of rural youth to G.L.F. activities but it was never developed into a permanent program. Moreover, the G.L.F. has always taken an active interest in the programs of the Future Farmers of America and of the 4-H Clubs and helped them whenever possible.

In the early 1950's Warren A. Ranney, who had built up close relations with the teachers of vocational agriculture in research and educational activities, saw the desirability of working out a program with the Bureau of Agricultural Education in the New York State Education Department which would further the joint interests of the F.F.A. chapters and the G.L.F.

The F.F.A. chapters were at that time interested in crop demonstrations as a means of gaining experience in better farming methods. Ranney saw that at a reasonable cost G.L.F. could sponsor this program and help increase its effectiveness. Under the plan developed, the local G.L.F. service agency would cooperate with the local F.F.A. chapter interested in carrying on a crop demonstration, by providing seed, fertilizer or other supplies with a value of $30 or less, to be used in the demonstration. The G.L.F. would also provide cash prizes and other awards to stimulate interest in the program. This program was eventually worked out in 1953 and 1954 for New York State. Since 1956, it has also been carried on in New Jersey and in parts of Pennsylvania.[6]

[6] 156 F.F.A. Chapters participated in the program in 1959. Of these, 132 were in New York, 8 in New Jersey, and 16 in Pennsylvania. In announcing the New York State program for 1960, R. C. S. Sutliff, Chief of the Bureau of Agricultural Education, New York State Education Department, said: "The F.F.A. Crop Demonstration program was introduced in 1953 in cooperation with the Cooperative G.L.F. Exchange to aid in bridging the gap between the agricultural experiment stations and the farms of the State. The primary purpose of the program is to encourage and recognize F.F.A. Chapter achievement in planning, developing, conducting, and making effective educational use of a crop demonstration which is designed to emphasize the value of using approved and recommended practices in growing specific crops. . . . The Crop Demonstration program is one of the most valuable chapter activities available for improving the teaching of agriculture and promoting cooperation between agricultural teachers and other agricultural and educational leaders."

LAWN AND GARDEN DEPARTMENTS SPRING UP

The G.L.F. had long handled grass seed, fertilizers and similar products of interest to suburban residents, but it had done little to stimulate this business. In the early 1950's it began to grow in importance as industrial centers spread into the surrounding country. Some of the G.L.F. Service Stores found that this type of business largely offset the loss in volume occasioned when farms were made into suburban homes.[7]

By 1954 several Service Stores had set up lawn and garden departments and, in 1955, several specialized Lawn and Garden Centers were operating in connection with G.L.F. Service Agencies. This activity was given encouragement by the Board of Directors in December, 1955, and since then it has grown rapidly. This is shown by the following sales figures:

1953-54	$ 714,248
1954-55	818,159
1955-56	2,013,562
1956-57	2,694,879

Since 1955 the G.L.F. has held an annual fall trade show to exhibit the kinds of lawn and garden products available the following year. These shows have been increasingly well attended by G.L.F. wholesale and retail representatives.

OUTSIDE BUYING RESTRICTED

In 1954 many service agencies were obtaining supplies from non-G.L.F. sources. The practice had begun during the Korean War when certain supplies were scarce, and it was well rooted. Vexed by this problem, Silcox called together the retail executives most concerned, and they agreed that outside buying should be strictly limited to one of the following situations: (1) when supplies available from G.L.F. wholesale services were inadequate; (2) when standard items of equal quality could be purchased at cheaper cost than through G.L.F. wholesale sources; or (3) when commodities needed locally could not be obtained through G.L.F. wholesale sources.[8]

[7] The *G.L.F. Week* of March 8, 1954, carried a report on the lawn and garden business of the Nassau Store at Hicksville on Long Island, which stated: "The lawn and garden volume on Long Island is steadily increasing, in all agencies, but the store that has pioneered in this field is in Nassau." Sales of $260,000 reported for the six weeks September 1 to October 15, 1953, included 51 tons of lawn seed, 20,000 bales of peat moss, 447 tons of lime, 678 tons of fertilizer, and $16,250 worth of garden supplies.

[8] For more complete information see C. N. Silcox, "Buying for Farmers," *G.L.F. Week* of September 13, 1954. See also supporting articles which stressed the slogan: "Let's Buy the G.L.F. Way," by C. E. Dayton and E. H. Fallon in the *G.L.F. Week* for September 20, September 27, and October 4.

Green Tag Specials

A new merchandising publication was also introduced in the summer of 1954—the *Catalogue of Values*. It was a streamlined version of *Patrons Purchasing Guide*, which had taken information on G.L.F. merchandise into farm homes since early in the forties. Produced with a saving in makeup cost of some $30,000, it featured "Green Tag Specials" which were items selected for promotion with a green tag notation showing the amount of the saving. For example, the price of an electric fence controller, listed at $21.35, was reduced to $14.95 by the green tag. The success of the *Catalogue of Values* in stimulating sales led to another for the following year, but with the rapid growth of personalized selling techniques the Catalogue was discontinued in 1957.

I & R Work Centered

With the rapid adoption of mechanical equipment to reduce farming costs, the service agencies found it necessary to employ more and more Installation and Repair men. The growth of this activity led in 1954 to the appointment of a Central I & R supervisor to better correlate and develop I & R programs.

During this year the Farm Supplies Department also placed a sales engineer in each area service office as a technical assistant to the Area Farm Supply Supervisor. His job was to work directly with the Service Agencies and farmers as a consultant in the layout and installation of specialized equipment, and assist on problems relating to irrigation systems, ventilators, hay drying fans, and laminated rafters. However, his main function was to teach managers and agents, and other employees, the technical fundamentals required to effectively install mechanical equipment and explain its use to G.L.F. patrons. This work called for close contact with Extension Service agricultural engineers and representatives of the utility companies.

In 1955 the addition of bulk milk coolers to the commodity line brought a major change in G.L.F.'s method of handling mechanical equipment. This was certification of G.L.F. agencies to handle large mechanical items. The certificate defined responsibilities of the agency in providing trained employees to properly service the commodity, in providing critical repair parts and in providing essential equipment for installation and service men. This program has grown until it now covers bulk coolers, stable cleaners, silo unloaders, and pipeline milkers.

In May, 1957, a formalized I & R training program was started at

Alfred University, the New York State Agriculture and Technical Institute, to give G.L.F. men a working background in installing and trouble-shooting techniques. The first schools dealt with problems of refrigeration and farm wiring.

BUILDING EXTENSION PARTNERSHIP

In January, 1955, an interesting conference brought together New York County Agents and G.L.F. District Managers.[9] Its object was to clarify and improve relationships. In opening the meeting Silcox said:

G.L.F. must give special attention to market analyses in farming. By 'market analysis' I mean the needs of farmers to carry out better farm management. What goods and commodities are needed? What services must go along with them? What new equipment and gadgets are required to carry out better farm management?

In doing this job, G.L.F. must itself do a great deal of practical teaching right along with the teaching of the County Agricultural Agents and the Extension Service of the College. There can be no sharp line of demarcation between the two.

You might say that the work of County Agents and Extension workers is a little more in the field of pure education, while in G.L.F. we apply it more specifically to the use of G.L.F. commodities and services for better agriculture.

In response, Dean W. I. Myers said: "The G.L.F. is a vital part of New York agriculture because it's owned and controlled by farmers. It is one of the most important allies of the College and our Extension Service in helping farmers steadily improve the efficiency of their food production."

He also said:

I think we need G.L.F. for at least four important reasons:

(1) . . . to make available to farmers properly the supplies and services recommended by the College, based on recent research. . . .

(2) . . . [to serve] as the pacesetter in working out new and better ways of providing these services at lower costs. . . .

(3) . . . [to process and provide] supplies and services needed by farmers in efficient operations, but which are not attractive to companies which operate primarily for the profit of the stockholders. . . .

(4) . . . to provide vigorous and constructive leadership in all programs to improve the agriculture of the state and the welfare of farm people.

He concluded by saying, "The College and the G.L.F. are natural allies working for the same people, responsible to the same people, and to the same public . . ."

[9] Much of the material presented at this conference was brought together in a folder under the title, *G.L.F. Reference Manual for County Agents*, issued by the G.L.F. for the use of county agents in March, 1955.

Research Amplified

In announcing the appointment of Dr. Keith Allred, a trained agronomist, as Research Assistant, in November, 1954, T. E. Milliman, Director of Research, said: "Research activities have been growing in this cooperative and are now out of all proportion for administration by one man."

A few weeks later it was announced that J. W. Stiles, Director of the Service Agencies Division, would join the Research Department on January 15, as Assistant Director, and would become Director on April 1, following Milliman's retirement. Although not a trained research scientist, Stiles was well qualified to administer the G.L.F. research program. He was interested in the application of research to his own farm and he knew G.L.F. methods and problems from long and varied experience. He had excellent contacts with Directors and operating personnel, and with the State agricultural colleges with whom he would be working.

When Stiles took over as Director of Research, Silcox was greatly interested in the possibilities of farm testing as a way of insuring that newly developed products would meet the practical needs of G.L.F. farmers. In April the Board passed the following resolution on this subject:

> Resolved: that this Board hereby approves of conducting farm testing of G.L.F. goods and services, specifically on farmers' farms in cooperation with the colleges, specialists in G.L.F. Divisions, and practical farmers. This Board is opposed to the ownership of a research farm by G.L.F.

At the June Institutional Conference, Stiles reported on "How Research Helps Fit G.L.F. for Today's Farm Needs." While he stated that "the objective of the Research Office is to stimulate, promote, approve and coordinate research work," he also indicated that the research program was being broadened to include farm testing and other direct projects as needed.[10]

During the next year Stiles explored how a practical farm-testing program might be carried on. Then, in October, 1956, E. C. Charron was given the job of getting the work under way and, as this work grew, he was designated as Manager of Applied Research. In the beginning, major concern was given to the testing of new products before they were added to the product line. However, this work was soon expanded to provide information on farmers' experience with various commodities and services and their possible interest in proposed programs. Some 60

[10] In the annual report for 1954-55, Silcox stated that a program was being planned to "test under practical farm conditions, the goods and farm practices developed by research." He declared, "The G.L.F. farm-testing program will be the final check before the product or farm practice is recommended by G.L.F. . . . [so that G.L.F.] will be as sure as humanly possible that what it recommends is right."

"applied research" projects of this type now have been conducted, ranging from tests of feeds and feeding programs to adaptation studies for various hybrids and a program for building a prefabricated poultry house.

MARKET RESEARCH BEGUN

G.L.F. also began to give serious attention to market research in 1955, with the appointment of Robert B. Child as Survey Supervisor in the newly-formed research department.[11] He was to help determine farmer opinion of G.L.F. commodities and services.

To develop plans and techniques for this work, Child first studied on the spot the market research programs and methods of various companies and cooperatives. One of his first jobs was to help plan and conduct the committeemen's attitudes surveys of 1956. The work in market research has gradually broadened to include studies of almost any operation where information is needed. For example, it has been used to develop knowledge of sales potentials for various commodities and services. While much of the work is done for G.L.F. by market research agencies under contract, many of the major studies are supervised or conducted by Child, whose title was changed to Market Research Manager.

In 1958 the requests for studies were coming in so rapidly that a market research priorities committee was established, consisting of the Director of Research, the Director of Distribution, the Director of Wholesale, and the Sales Manager. This committee has not only helped direct the research effort to the areas of greatest need, but it has greatly increased the appreciation of top management on how market research can be used to improve operations.

COLLEGE RESEARCH EXPANDED

As G.L.F. expanded its own research program it did not reduce support given to research in the land-grant colleges. In fact, as the G.L.F. came to better appreciate how research could help it meet problems, the interest in outside research increased. In 1954-55, grants to the three land-grant colleges in its territory totaled only $53,000, as compared with $115,000 for 1956-57 and $141,000 for 1957-58. In 1956-57, a report on G.L.F. research projects supported by G.L.F. listed over 40 active college projects dealing with such subjects as bean breeding, calf feeding, ear corn silage, farm wiring, potash fertilization, residues in milk, meat and

[11] While studies of a market research nature had been made by W. A. Ranney and others in G.L.F. since the early 1940's, there had been no sustained effort in this field.

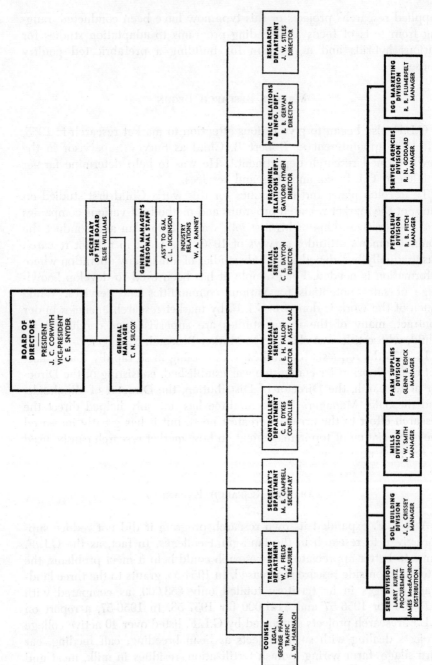

FIGURE 12—G.L.F. ORGANIZATION CHART, SEPTEMBER, 1956

BOARD OF DIRECTORS
PRESIDENT
J. C. CORWITH
VICE-PRESIDENT
C. E. SNYDER

SECRETARY OF THE BOARD
ELSIE WILLIAMS

GENERAL MANAGER
C. N. SILCOX

GENERAL MANAGER'S PERSONAL STAFF
ASST TO G.M.
C. L. DICKINSON
INDUSTRY RELATIONS
W. A. RANNEY

COUNSEL
LEGAL
GEORGE PFANN,
J. W. HARNACH
TRAFFIC

TREASURER'S DEPARTMENT
W. J. FIELDS
TREASURER

SECRETARY'S DEPARTMENT
M. E. CAMPBELL
SECRETARY

CONTROLLER'S DEPARTMENT
C. E. DYKES
CONTROLLER

WHOLESALE SERVICES
E. H. FALLON
DIRECTOR & ASST. G.M.

RETAIL SERVICES
C. E. DAYTON
DIRECTOR

PERSONNEL RELATIONS DEPT.
GAYLORD HYMEN
DIRECTOR

PUBLIC RELATIONS & INFO. DEPT.
R. B. GERVAN
DIRECTOR

RESEARCH DEPARTMENT
J. W. STILES
DIRECTOR

SEED DIVISION
LARRY KURTZ
PROCUREMENT
JAMES MacEACHRON
DISTRIBUTION

SOIL BUILDING DIVISION
J. C. CRISSEY
MANAGER

MILLS DIVISION
R. W. SMITH
MANAGER

FARM SUPPLIES DIVISION
GLENN E. EDICK
MANAGER

PETROLEUM DIVISION
R. B. FITCH
MANAGER

SERVICE AGENCIES DIVISION
R. N. GODDARD
MANAGER

EGG MARKETING DIVISION
R. R. FLUMERFELT
MANAGER

eggs, weed control, pasture renovation, grass silage and poultry equipment. The report provided information on the objectives of the research, results, and listed the project leaders in the colleges with their counterpart leaders in the G.L.F. By having representatives keep in close touch with the research being done, G.L.F. has been in position to get the maximum benefit from it without delay.

The Soil Test Plan

In the April, 1955, issue of *Farming with G.L.F.*, Silcox reported that committeemen had shown great interest in soil testing in the series of winter regional meetings. They had agreed that G.L.F. should actively promote the practice, working in cooperation with the Extension Service. In line with this sentiment, a "members' soil test plan" was announced on July 2 in the *G.L.F. Week*.

Under the plan, which was to run until July 1, 1956, the G.L.F. would pay the $1.00 testing fee for each soil sample submitted by G.L.F. members to State college laboratories in G.L.F. territory. The mechanics of the plan were simple. The service agencies would obtain official soil test boxes from the county agents. These boxes would be distributed to members on request. The member would return the box with his sample, taken according to directions on the box, to the service agency which would forward it to the State college laboratory for analysis. The findings from the laboratory would be sent to the member's county agent, with a copy to the service agency. The county agent would make his recommendations to the farmer.

In announcing the plan Silcox said that it was the long-term intention of G.L.F. to stimulate and encourage the use of this public service by members as a means of improving their agronomic practices. He emphasized that the plan had not been adopted for the purpose of promoting sales of lime and fertilizer, although this might result.

Although the soil test plan was announced in July it was not vigorously promoted until October when it was made one of the "Big 2" items on the merchandising calendar. It was then publicized through a full page advertisement in the *American Agriculturist*, advertisements in local papers and a feature story in *Farming With G.L.F.*, and by a large G.L.F. brochure for special use of service agencies. This included statements on the value of the plan from N.C. Brady, Head of the Agronomy Department of Cornell University; William H. Martin, Dean of the College of Agriculture and Director of Agricultural Extension at Rutgers; and H. R. Albrecht, Director of Agricultural Extension at Pennsylvania State University; and G.L.F. leaders. The slogan was coined "Test—Don't

Guess!" The plan was well received from the beginning, and it has since become an established G.L.F. service.

THE RETAIL FINANCING PLAN

For some time the G.L.F. had been concerned by the growing burden involved in financing the retail service stores. Although the stores now met a large part of the cost for their expanding facilities through the sale of Store preferred stock, they still relied heavily on the G.L.F. for funds to carry on operations. To meet this problem a plan was worked out with the Banks for Cooperatives in 1955 under which they would make separate term loans to individual G.L.F. Service Stores, although the G.L.F. held legal control of each Store through ownership of the common stock.[12]

The first loan to a G.L.F. retail service store was arranged with the Baltimore Bank for Cooperatives in the fall of 1955, and by June 30, 1959, some 50 individual loans had been executed with the Springfield and Baltimore Banks for Cooperatives, aggregating $3,200,000. This program has relieved the Exchange from a considerable financial burden while at the same time it has strengthened the sense of independence of the Stores.[13]

MEMBERSHIP RELATIONS WORK ACTIVATED

Under the reorganization of 1953, the position of Director of Member Relations was attached to the Service Agency Division. However, the importance of this work was not fully developed until August, 1955, when Seeber C. Tarbell was made Director of Member Relations. In announc-

[12] In making a loan to a store the banks have required the consent of both preferred and common stockholders. The loans are therefore obtained by the G.L.F. after approval by the Service Store Committee. If the real and personal property is to be mortgaged to the Bank, preferred stockholder approval is required and this is customarily solicited at the local annual meeting. According to Treasurer W. J. Fields, it was inevitable that use would be made of the substantial assets of the store system to support its own debt requirements—rather than depend fully on the Exchange. "In effect, the Exchange had been using its equity and borrowing power not only to support its own debt requirements, but the debt requirements of the entire retail system whose assets were free of outside encumbrances. This could become particularly burdensome as the Exchange had to increase its equity capital to support additional debt lines." W. J. Fields, letter to author, May 14, 1959.

[13] Fifty-two loans have now been completed with both banks. Five have been paid in full and seven applications will be completed by June 30. Eleven more stores are candidates and expect to consummate loans during 1960-61. A Service Store automatically becomes a candidate when it reaches the point of requiring term funds in excess of $25,000 and has an earning capacity to amortize the loan in from ten to fifteen years. W. J. Fields, letter to author, of February 10, 1960.

ing his appointment, C. E. Dayton said: "It is only logical that member relations should receive high priority in G.L.F."

Tarbell brought to this position broad experience throughout the G.L.F., a friendly personality and an inquiring mind. One of his first actions was to examine the effectiveness of the membership meetings, and in the next two years various experiments were carried on to make them more useful. Recognizing the importance of the Committeemen in the G.L.F. structure, he began to consider how the committees could be made more effective. Just at this time Stiles, as Director of Research, saw need of a survey of committeemen's attitudes similar to that made under Babcock in 1944. He believed that there were many weak spots in G.L.F.'s methods of working with committeemen, as well as a lack of understanding of functions on the part of both management personnel and committeemen. As a result of their mutual interest, Tarbell and Stiles designed a comprehensive research project to study the attitudes first of store committeemen and later those of agent-buyer committeemen.

These studies, completed during 1956, provided much valuable information on how the G.L.F. could improve its day-to-day operations to better meet farmers' needs. The results of the studies were taken back to each local committee by the district manager, and this gave all of the committeemen an opportunity to frankly consider with G.L.F. representatives the problems disclosed by the survey of particular interest to them. Of more importance, the studies showed that G.L.F. management attached great significance to the views of the committeemen, and the way the committees operated, and this gave the committeemen a higher sense of institutional responsibility. Thus these studies strengthened the G.L.F. at the grass roots.

Tarbell took advantage of G.L.F.'s awareness of the importance of member relations by planning a two-day member relations clinic at Aurora in October, 1956. Its objective was "to review and appraise member relations and procedures in G.L.F. in terms of a new generation of farmers and employees." It was a select gathering, comprised of the President, General Manager, other G.L.F. directors and executives, and several outside leaders in cooperative member relations work. For the first time in G.L.F. history, attention was directed exclusively to member relations problems in G.L.F. If nothing more, the clinic drew attention to a field too much neglected in the past.

AN EXPERIMENT WITH DEBENTURES

In early June, 1956, the G.L.F. gave its members an opportunity to buy a ten-year 4 percent subordinated debenture. The avowed object of the issue, which was limited to $2,000,000, was to provide members with a way of investing in their own business, since the Board in 1954 had voted to maintain the outstanding securities at a level of approximately $24,000,000, and there was little opportunity for them to buy shares of stock.[14]

Within five weeks some $400,000 in debentures were sold. The amount outstanding was $1,201,400 on July 1, 1957, and $1,481,300 on July 1, 1958. This was not a bad showing in view of competitive interest rates. Besides providing needed capital at low cost, debentures gave the Exchange useful experience in another method of financing.[15]

"Quality That Pays Off on the Farm"

In opening the June, 1956, Institutional Conference, Silcox stated that "quality" would be "the pitch for 1956-57." He was concerned that many of the newer employees did not fully realize that quality was a G.L.F. cornerstone. He made clear his meaning by saying:

G.L.F. quality must not be too high to be practical. It must not be so low that farmers are cheated. It must be obtainable in the market place, and when we cannot get it in the market place, we work with suppliers to find ways whereby they may produce the quality of goods G.L.F. demands. We are not looking for diamonds and we will not accept junk. The most simple statement is that G.L.F. shall have a degree of quality specifications that pays off in practical farming.

Throughout 1956-57, G.L.F. kept up the pressure to establish in the minds of its employees and members that "quality" in the lexicon of the G.L.F. meant "quality that pays off on the farm."

The Large User Problem

As farms declined in number and grew in size, the problems of serving them changed. Large users demanded specialized services to fit in with their farming operations. This raised a problem. Could the G.L.F. as

[14] See W. J. Fields, "Debentures vs. Capital Stock," *American Cooperation*, 1956, page 344. The use of debentures was not favored by the G.L.F. as a major means of providing debt capital in view of the liability that would be incurred in maintaining a market for them under its long-established policy of providing every G.L.F. security with a market, a sound book value, and an assured good return. W. J. Fields, letter to author, May 14, 1959.

[15] For a full description of these debentures see Prospectus of the G.L.F., July 25, 1958, pp. 20-21. It should be kept in mind that as debentures represent a debt, interest paid on them is an expense and as such is not subject to Federal income tax. Thus, to the extent that debentures replaced the issuance of common stock, they reduced the income tax burden by the amount of tax that would have been paid if capital had been obtained through the issuance of stock.

a cooperative give the kinds of services demanded by large users and at the same time provide an equitable service to all farmers, whether large or small? Any preferential treatment to large users—not considered fair by the small users, would cause small users to turn against their association. On the other hand, unless service was geared to their needs, large users could not be expected to stay with the cooperative, and their presence helped keep down costs for the small user.

The G.L.F.'s answer to this problem was to give large users the type of service they required, taking into account the cost of serving them. If it cost less to serve a large user he was given the benefit of the lower cost in the prices charged him.[16]

Sharpening the G.L.F. Image

Up to this time the G.L.F. had made little effort to create an institutional image, and there was a great variety in signs, stationery and labels used by different divisions of the G.L.F. Not only was this costly, but it gave a confused impression. The Department of Public Relations and Information had begun to work on this problem and a new G.L.F. seal and a standard form for letterheads was in effect by the end of 1956. These changes were so popular that it was decided to mark all G.L.F. buildings, trucks, packages and commodities to make them easily identifiable as related to the G.L.F. System. In February, 1957, this plan was broadened to cover all commodities and facilities throughout the G.L.F. system.[17]

The G.L.F. Agency Corporation

As farms were crowded out by urban expansion, it became increasingly difficult in many areas to maintain effective service to members through existing local service stores. In some cases service stores were consolidated to maintain sufficient volume for efficient operations but in other cases this was not possible.

In some of the urbanized areas the service agencies met this problem

[16] For an interesting discussion of the way G.L.F. met the large-user problem, see R. N. Goddard, "G.L.F. Fits Service to Big and Little Users," *News for Farmer Cooperatives*, October, 1957. Goddard pointed out that the G.L.F. must serve big farming operations, little ones, and medium-sized ones, and that G.L.F. had found it desirable to adhere to the principle that all services should be charged to the recipient, commensurate with their costs and that by adhering to this policy for all users the G.L.F. was able to avoid charging the large user for services he did not need or desire.

[17] "This is a long-range program to develop standards for package labels, stationery and office forms, signs, trucks and signatures for all G.L.F." *The G.L.F. Week* of February 7, 1957.

by expanding lawn and garden business with non-member urban patrons. This arrangement was satisfactory as long as the volume of non-member patron business was of only minor importance. However, it was not a satisfactory solution in those areas where the volume of non-farmer business largely supplanted the farm supply business with farmers. If savings were made, they belonged to the dwindling number of members who were still farmers, while the risk and effort in providing the service had to be borne by the G.L.F. as a whole. Moreover, as a farmer cooperative, the G.L.F. did not wish to change its membership qualifications to include city dwellers as members—for their interests in the total program of the G.L.F. as a farm organization were but nominal.

To meet this problem, the G.L.F. in 1957 set up a subsidiary—the G.L.F. Agency Corporation. This corporation was designed to own and manage local service facilities in communities which no longer could be maintained as independent G.L.F. farm supply centers.

The plan permitted the G.L.F. to maintain farm supply service for the farmers remaining in the community while providing services desired by urban consumers. Any savings from these operations would accrue to all members of the Exchange, including those served by the Agency Corporation.

Under this arrangement the G.L.F. could expand its volume of business in those lines of interest to urban consumers, and thus decrease costs of providing members with such services. This arrangement also enabled the G.L.F. to serve farmers who would have been cut off from G.L.F. services if no arrangement were made for local service.

In November, 1957, the Agency Corporation took over the business of a G.L.F. agency, the Farm Cooperative Exchange of Morristown, N.J. If the G.L.F. had set up a service store it would have been dependent upon lawn and garden business to live, and the number of members to be served did not justify this type of operation. Soon afterward, the Nassau Cooperative G.L.F. Store at Hicksville, N. Y., which had lost most of its farmer members through encroachment of the suburbs, was reorganized as a service facility of the Agency Corporation. This type of operation will no doubt grow where farming gives way to suburban developments.

Marketing Comes Back

Under the plan of Area decentralization put into effect by the reorganization of 1953, marketing, except for eggs, was concentrated largely in the Western Area, and during the next few years marketing operations in this area were actively developed, with the encouragement and direction of the special Board of Directors for Marketing. The new Caledonia plant, opened in 1954, had greatly improved bean processing, packaging and marketing methods, with the result that G.L.F. had become one of the largest packaged bean distributors in the Northeast. With the increase in corn as a crop, the G.L.F. had also become a large handler of surplus corn, and by 1957 it was handling over a third of the grain sold from the farms of New York State. G.L.F. egg marketing was now a well-established G.L.F. activity and G.L.F. was now the largest egg-handling cooperative in the eastern part of the United States. These developments showed that marketing was far from dead in the G.L.F. In his last Annual Meeting report, in October, 1957, Silcox said: "We believe that the greatest future opportunities for farm cooperatives exist in the field of marketing. G.L.F. stands ready to discuss this with any producer groups which need help in present operations or future planning." It was clear that G.L.F. was thinking more of getting the marketing job done than of doing the entire job itself.

CHAPTER 43

The Advance of Personnel Administration

. . . Our most valuable asset is our people, because it is the caliber of our people and the quality of their judgment that determine how well our farmer-members benefit from the capital and facilities which they have entrusted to us.

CHARLES N. SILCOX, *October 25, 1955*

IN EARLIER CHAPTERS we have seen how personnel administration in G.L.F. grew in importance while McConnell was General Manager. Under the management of Silcox it was to achieve full institutional status.

Under McConnell, each Division largely handled its own personnel problems, with a minimum of coordination through the Central Personnel Office. In Chapter 31 we saw how the G.L.F. Farm Service Division developed an effective personnel program under this policy which gave a wide scope for initiative.[1]

This informal and decentralized system of personnel administration had worked quite well when business was booming but it was not suited to the tighter operating conditions prevailing at the close of the Korean War. McConnell recognized this fact, and plans were already under way to strengthen personnel procedures when Silcox took over as General Manager in November, 1952.

The modernization of personnel administration did not come without a struggle. It was hard for many who had grown up under the informal personnel relationships that had long prevailed in G.L.F. to accept the necessity of systematic personnel procedures throughout the entire organization.

Moreover, the reorganization of 1948, by making the G.L.F. one organization rather than a federated system of organizations, placed emphasis on the need for uniform institutional policies that would tie all parts of the organization together. It was apparent that a well-integrated concern

---

[1] In December, 1948, Personnel Director H. L. Shackleton expressed this policy in a memorandum for management on the functions of the G.L.F. Central Personnel Office: "Our job is to act as counselor and coordinator, working with the divisional personnel representatives and management in the development and administration of personnel. Once the policy is established, the responsibility for its execution and correlation is with the Central Personnel Office." With the division personnel departments well established, McConnell shifted Shackleton to other work. In announcing the change he said: "Mr. Shackleton came to G.L.F. as Personnel Director when there was a great need for this work. . . . He aided in supervising and developing personnel departments of the G.L.F. These are now well manned with people trained to carry out this particular problem. . . ." *G.L.F. Week*, September 12, 1949.

required a well-coordinated system for dealing with personnel functions. The new Federal and State laws regulating employment conditions were also making it advisable to handle certain payroll and institutional benefit programs on a coordinated basis.

The disrupting effects of the Korean War placed emphasis on the need for a better system of personnel administration. The war confronted G.L.F. with an increase in personnel turnover, labor shortages, the necessity of employing many workers with sub-standard skills, and the need to comply with new government rules and regulations. These developments had brought a great change in the composition and character of the working force. This is shown by the fact that only half of the employees at the end of the war had four years or more of service. Those who had built the G.L.F. were no longer a majority and the newcomers saw the G.L.F. as a source of employment rather than as a cause of personal significance to themselves. Competitive salaries and fringe benefits had become matters of increasing concern—and with the boom in business while agriculture lagged, it was not easy for G.L.F. to attract its share of "the bright young men" needed for future growth.

PERSONNEL OBJECTIVES DEFINED

In 1950 C. L. Dickinson, the Assistant to the General Manager, asked G. W. Hymen, Manager of the Central Personnel Office, to prepare a statement of objectives for G.L.F. personnel administration. Hymen produced a memorandum in March, 1951.[2] In addition to endorsing the need for a written statement of personnel policy and the need for adequate administrative tools he suggested three "long-run objectives" to help develop a better work force: 1. Establishment of more definite hiring standards. 2. Better wage and salary administration. 3. Better measurement of personnel effectiveness.

Under the first, he said:

We should set as a goal to be reached within the next three or four years the establishment of more definite hiring standards in G.L.F., particularly in the field units. This recommendation encompasses the use of proven techniques such as standardized tests in the selection of personnel. I would like to make the observation that a very high percentage of our present work force has entered G.L.F. through our retail division where, to my knowledge, no examination or test other than a physical exam is used. I think we do a good job in selection. I think we could do even better and make better use of the abilities of our workers if we knew more about their apparent capacities. We don't buy seed of unknown quality or quantity. We should approach personnel in the same manner.

[2] Gaylord W. Hymen, letter to author, March 21, 1958.

Under his second heading, Hymen advocated immediate attention to job analysis and evaluation. He also observed that the administration of fringe benefits could be better coordinated.

Under the third heading, Hymen concerned himself with the development of measures to check the value received from "personnel dollars." It was his belief that until standards of performance were set up it would be difficult to distinguish between mediocre and superior performance.

Although there is no record that this memorandum directly influenced policy, it set forth a philosophy which was rapidly gaining acceptance within the G.L.F. high command. The need to increase efficiency was awakening G.L.F. management to personnel administration deficiencies.

A step toward clarification of personnel work came in December, 1952, with the establishment of the position of office manager. Previously there had been no clear distinction between personnel and office management activities.[3]

The productivity studies in the Mills Division, (see Chapter 38) showed the need for job evaluations and an organization analysis so that employees would know for what they were to be held responsible. This work was completed in 1952. As an outcome of this work Herbert J. McClain, the director of employee relations for Mills, was made responsible for all G.L.F. dealings with organized labor. This centered another important area of personnel administration.

THE "YOU TELL US" SURVEY

A new approach in personnel administration was also coming from the Farm Service Division. This division had been striving continuously to improve its personnel efficiency, and any idea that seemed feasible was given a trial. In 1951, Jerry Stiles, then Director of Retail Stores in the Farm Service Division, became convinced that an employee attitude survey would help the Farm Service Division find ways to improve the efficiency of its personnel. He discussed this idea with Earl Brooks, Professor of Industrial Relations at Cornell University, who welcomed an opportunity to develop plans for a survey of this type. Working with Warren Ranney and Seeber Tarbell, Personnel Supervisor for Farm Service Division, two 12-page printed questionnaire schedules were developed—one for employees and one for managers. Each was given the

---

[3] At the request of C. L. Dickinson, G. W. Hymen, on September 18, 1952, had submitted recommendations for the organization of office manager and personnel work in the Ithaca G.L.F. offices. Hymen stressed the need for centralizing and coordinating personnel work.

title, "You Tell Us." These questionnaires were then filled out at meetings held in March, 1952.

The questions were designed to find out how the employee viewed his work and his general relations with G.L.F. To encourage candid answers the employee was not asked to give his name. The stated purpose of this employee-opinion survey was "to give every G.L.F. employee in the Farm Service Division an opportunity to tell us exactly how you feel about G.L.F. as a place to work." A summary of results was to be distributed to all employees so that they could measure their opinions against those of their co-workers.

The employees welcomed this opportunity to express their opinions. The results were presented in a little pamphlet called "You Told Us," issued in April 1952. In an introduction to this pamphlet, Fallon stated that the results were being sent out just as they had come off the tabulating machines. In general, the replies showed a warm feeling toward the organization. Certain information was also of great interest to management. For example, many of the employees claimed that they were not kept informed on how they were doing. Some thought that they were not receiving as much instruction as they needed in undertaking new work.

One fact was made clear. More educational work was needed on the principles of management and supervision. To meet this need a series of training conferences was held to develop frank discussions with employees on how personnel problems could be better handled.

The significance of this work was indicated a year or so later by a study by Miss Geraldine Senderoff, a Cornell graduate student working with Professor Earl Brooks. Her primary interest was in the values that had been derived from the series of training conferences which was conducted following the employee-attitude survey. In March, 1954, Miss Senderoff interviewed approximately 20 of the store managers who had participated both in the survey and a follow-up supervisory training conference. Her general conclusion was that the opinion survey and the follow-up conferences were greatly appreciated by G.L.F. employees as a means of self-development.

The employee attitude survey and the conferences which followed did much to awaken G.L.F. leaders to the importance of personnel procedures and their influence on employee morale. It helped condition the entire organization for the far-reaching organizational changes and procedures ushered in by the reorganization of 1953.

In 1952, Hymen, at the request of Fallon, conducted an experimental study in the Farm Service Division to acquaint supervisors with the principles and mechanics involved in job evaluation and to determine

its usefulness. This work, involving some 75 or 80 interviews in the
Farm Service Accounting Section, showed how certain management practices could be improved through job evaluation.

It will be recalled from Chapter 40 that the organization survey for the
Mills Division had led to a similar study for the entire G.L.F. and that
this, in turn, had led to the major reorganization of May, 1953, with the
establishment of a Personnnel Relations Department at the executive staff
level. As Director of this new department, Hymen was given broad responsibilities over such personnel policies as selection, training and development, safety, and wage and salary administration. However, the
plan did not bring all personnel work together in one office, since personnel
supervisors for each division would deal directly with divisional personnel matters. In effect, the Director of Personnel Relations was to be a
coordinating officer with no direct authority over the personnel directors
in the separate divisions. He thus had to gain their concurrence for recommended programs, and any personnel instructions relating to the institution as a whole could be given only by the General Manager through
the division directors who were responsible for operations.

It is important to realize that the reorganization of 1953 recognized the
line and staff concept throughout the organization. The Personnel Relations Department was set up as a staff office to help the line officers carry
on operations. With lines of responsibility fixed by the reorganization,
work was continued by the management consultant firm in assisting the
Department set up job descriptions for all employees except in retail units
where only managers were included.

In his report for the year ending June 30, 1954, Hymen stated that 900
interviews were conducted with employees in various jobs throughout
the operating territory. He indicated that the executive job evaluation
program had covered 135 jobs and that the evaluation of executive positions had been done by a committee appointed by the General Manager
with the assistance of the consultant firm. Hymen anticipated that management executives would soon have the benefit of this program in administering their respective compensation programs.

Many administrative problems arose in the transitional period following the establishment of the Personnel Relations Department in June,
1953. The job of consolidating personnel services which had been identified with other offices required time and explanation. Moreover, it was
not easy for operators who had been accustomed to handling personnel
in their own way to accept institutional direction. Prior to the reorganization, changes affecting personnel had come from within the G.L.F. Following it many oldtimers came to feel that their fitness was being gauged
by an outsider with little appreciation of the contribution that they had

made to the G.L.F.'s growth and development. While some took the job evaluation graciously, others gave it but lip service support.[4]

The problems of wage and salary administration gave most concern. In the minds of many, wage and salary policy was confused with job evaluation. As a high job grade immediately became a prestige factor, many were dissatisfied with the evaluations of their jobs. As the job evaluations were largely made by an outsider, many veteran employees feared that the G.L.F. was growing bureaucratic and losing the personal warmth that had long characterized employee relations. Although the new system gradually gained acceptance, it left a residue of bitterness in the minds of many. Some of the difficulty was inescapable, but part was the result of lack of participation by the employees in the formulation of the program and of the "long-drawn-out" way it was put into force.[5] It may be argued that arbitrary and "outside" action was called for to effect a change of this magnitude. If so, a prolonged weakening of the excellent morale which had long been a source of G.L.F. pride was part of the price paid.

STEP-UP IN TRAINING PROGRAMS

Following the Korean War, G.L.F. was greatly influenced by the nationwide interest in executive development programs. Most of the younger executives in G.L.F. had grown up with the institution and lacked knowledge of the trends in modern management thinking. As a first step to remedy this condition, G.L.F. sent E. H. Fallon to the Advanced Management Program of the Graduate School of Business Administration, Harvard University, in the fall of 1953. In subsequent years several others were sent and many additional men were given the opportunity to undertake similar training programs provided by the American Management Association, the Cornell School for Advanced Management, or some similar institution.[6]

Thus, within a few years many of the younger executives could compare G.L.F. management methods and personnel with those of other businesses.

---

[4] Hymen states that the reactions ranged from "unqualified acceptance to passive resistance, to overt blocking of certain company-wide personnel programs." G. W. Hymen, letter to author, of March 21, 1958.

[5] The reader should keep in mind that the beginning of this program came with a major upheaval, namely the reorganization of 1953 and that it continued for several years until the job evaluations were completed. "There was just too much change to digest at one time." Letter of Seeber Tarbell, to author, November 11, 1959. Another observer has referred to this period as one of "turmoil, unrest and uncertainty."

[6] A little pamphlet that Fallon issued for Farm Service employees after he returned from Harvard illustrated how the men who were sent to school brought home ideas and put them to work. Its object was to make clear the concept of line and staff organization and the importance of good principles of supervision.

This program, which was developed under the leadership of W. A. Ranney, Supervisor of Education and Training, reached a high point in the 1955-56 fiscal year when 274 G.L.F. employees were enrolled in various training courses, executive development programs, and professional conferences of an educational nature. The tuition cost for this instruction totaled $29,532. This did much to gain acceptance for ideas that would have otherwise seemed radical.

For several years the retail divisions had felt the need for a training program to orient the new employees. In the early 1950's this need was explored by the personnel directors in the retail division with W. A. Ranney, then in charge of employee training. This group developed the concept of a basic corpus of information which would give every new employee a working knowledge of G.L.F. objectives and practices through a series of one-day schools. The program was formalized in 1954 through the inauguration of Basic I and Basic II schools for all new employees. The Basic I school was a one-day program covering the history, organization and purposes of the G.L.F. The Basic II school was also a one-day program which covered information on sources of supplies, specifications for commodities, quality control procedures, and types of G.L.F. services. Training materials were specially developed for these schools, and they have become a standard part of G.L.F.'s employee training program.

The Manpower Development Program

The frank opinions of the Elliot survey, the widespread interest in advanced management training, the growing complexity of management, and the knowledge that a new general manager would be selected in a few more years all served to emphasize the fact that G.L.F. needed to take steps to insure an adequate supply of competent management personnel. This problem was brought into sharp focus at a meeting of staff and divisional managers at Cooperstown, N. Y., in August, 1954. For two hours consideration was given to the question of whether an institutional program of manpower development should be launched. The interest shown in this question led to a two-day meeting the following August with this as the sole subject. Soon after this, in October, 1955, Silcox issued a memorandum to all management personnel to launch formally the G.L.F. Manpower Development Program. The memorandum stated that the directors and management considered it "good business to put positive value and sustained emphasis on a systematic program of manpower development."

The G.L.F. Manpower Development Program called for a sincere belief in the following propositions:

1. That our most valuable asset is our people, because it is the caliber of our people and the quality of their judgment that determine how well our Farmer-Members benefit from the capital and facilities which they have entrusted to us.

2. That it is our obligation to determine and forecast periodically the manpower needs of G.L.F. and at the same time to evaluate the performance and potential of the resources available to meet these needs.

3. That it is our responsibility to develop and understand the specifications and requirements of each job we supervise, and then use proved methods and judgment to select the best qualified candidates for each job.

4. That manpower development is primarily our obligation to help each subordinate learn to cooperate with others, to respect and be respected by his associates, to improve his own performance on his present job, and to take advantage of opportunities to develop his own abilities and potential fully.

5. That each supervisor is accountable for the development of subordinates and that his own performance as a supervisor will be judged on how well he can develop people and get things done through people.

6. That each supervisor, by his sense of values and by the nature of his own example and practices, creates the climate under which the self-development of his subordinates flourishes or perishes.

7. That each supervisor should actively participate in helping his people improve their performance by working with them to (a) develop a clear statement of what is to be done; (b) develop standards of what results will be considered satisfactory; (c) check actual performance against the standards that have been set; and (d) recognize (1) performance that is satisfactory or outstanding and, (2) performance that needs improvement. And when improvement is needed, it is then his responsibility to work out corrective action and the follow-up necessary to improve performance.

At this time Silcox established a Manpower Development Committee "to be responsible for maintaining the spirit and institutional nature of G.L.F.'s Manpower Development Program."[7]

The primary device to implement the Manpower Development Program was the Performance Review Guide. This was to be used by supervisors in reviewing the performance of their subordinates. Under the plan a supervisor was to confer annually with each of his employees in regard to the employee's performance and ways to improve it. If necessary, follow-up interviews would be made. A record of all interviews was required.

Each performance review was to be based on four steps: (1) Advance preparation for review discussion. (2) The discussion itself. (3) A writeup of what was agreed upon during the discussion. (4) The subsequent follow-up which was intended to make sure that the agreed-upon plans were being carried out. The procedure was to be only a means to an end.

[7] C. N. Silcox, Chairman; E. H. Fallon, Vice-Chairman; Warren Ranney, Executive Secretary; and Professor Earl Brooks, Consultant. The other members were C. E. Dayton, C. E. Dykes, and G. W. Hymen.

"The payoff," according to the Guide, was to be "the action taken to help each individual develop himself."

An important part of the Manpower Development Program was an inventory of manpower needs and resources. Each supervisor was required to make an annual inventory for each of his employees. This inventory was to give such information as years of service, age, health, education, growth record, and performance. Its primary purpose was to develop candidates for specific positions and to highlight characteristics needing improvement.

The Manpower Development Program was also designed to give emphasis to education, training, and personnel recruitment practices required to augment the supply of men qualified "to man the G.L.F."[8]

Although the Manpower Development Program represented a constructive step forward in personnel administration, some employees saw it as a further step toward bureaucracy. The timing was unfortunate in that employees were restive following the reorganization and installation of job evaluation. However, the program has gradually gained acceptance as performance reviews and manpower inventories have been modified in the light of practical experience. (See Chapter 45)

The principal problems which arose with these major changes in personnel administration came from their methods of application more than their content. They were put into effect with inadequate advance indoctrination and with insufficient adaptation to the practices which had long prevailed, at a time of economic uncertainty, and fears were aroused that the G.L.F. was becoming an impersonal organization dominated by efficiency engineers. As a result, the immediate advantages that would have been derived from a wholehearted acceptance of their need was largely lost. A sustained effort was required to overcome resistance which could have been avoided by a more patient and perceptive approach.

Although employee morale had been bruised under the impact of rapid change following the reorganization of 1953, there were many offsetting advantages of long-run benefit. Within a period of five years the G.L.F. had adopted a modern system of personnel administration adapted to its needs. A revolution in personnel administration could not come without strains and stresses. Time would permit modifications to make the changes generally acceptable.

[8] See Warren A. Ranney, "The Man in Management," *American Cooperation*, 1956, pp. 373-381, for a review of this program after one year of experience.

CHAPTER 44

Reorganization for Selling

The growing competition for a farmer's business . . . dictates what management must do . . . the goal for the next year is increased volume with a profit to members and decreased cost per unit.
CHARLES N. SILCOX, *June, 1957, Institutional Conference*

O N JUNE 5, Silcox opened the 1957 Institutional Conference by saying: "The purpose of this conference is to plan ahead." While conditions had not changed much during the past year, he saw the business climate as more favorable to agriculture, although he held out little hope for any long-run major improvement in agricultural conditions. Farmers were constantly increasing their productivity and cutting their costs as the only way to remain in farming.

Turning to 1957-58, Silcox held that the present situation of G.L.F. farmers and their future prospects dictated very clearly the job of running G.L.F. Changes in farming had made the bigger farmers keener buyers and competitors had changed their pricing and selling methods. There was developing a life and death struggle for the farmer's patronage. Therefore G.L.F.'s goal for the next year was to be "increased volume with a profit to members and decreased cost per unit." He said, "These [facts] are so self-evident that they should be crystal clear to every G.L.F. employee."

Silcox made clear that the G.L.F. system was not falling apart, but he was concerned that the rate of growth was declining. Surveys showed that "on many commodities we have not been holding our own in percentage of the total volume of business available." With wholesale and retail facilities capable of handling 10 to 20 percent increases in volume, and with direct labor the only increased cost, it was clear that an increase in volume was needed to increase productivity.

He thought the same kind of opportunity for expansion existed throughout the G.L.F. Holding that decreasing unit costs could come only through better planning and wise spending, he said, "This program of decreasing unit cost is going to start right in the General Manager's office."

This conference set the stage for the reorganization for selling which was announced by E. H. Fallon, on June 17, 1957, in the *G.L.F. Week.*[1]

---

[1] Plans for the reorganization were well under way at the time of the conference but key decisions had not been made and announcement would have been premature and

According to the announcement, a new merchandising division was being formed "to supervise all G.L.F. sales activities."

Fallon said, "This new division is being established to gear the G.L.F. organization to our No. 1 objective—volume building." Ronald N. Goddard, former manager of the Service Agencies Division, was to be head of the Merchandising Division. It would include all personnel with a direct responsibility for sales effort and would combine several departments formerly attached to other divisions. It would tie together commodity specialists, farm supplies purchasing and warehousing, advertising, and sales promotion.

The activities of the new division and all other retail divisions were to be correlated by a Director of Distribution, Glenn E. Edick, former manager of the Farm Supplies Division.[2] Under the Director of Distribution there would be six retail divisions: Egg Marketing, Petroleum and the new Merchandising Division, and the three Area offices which were each now to have divisional status.

The Central Service Agencies Division was discontinued and the Area Division Managers in effect became assistant directors of distribution.

The plan of organization is shown in Figure 13.

Fallon said, "Our General Manager, C. N. Silcox, has given us the goal of 'volume at a profit to the member.' To meet this goal we must have a substantial group of men who spend 100 percent of their time working on volume. We are not adding men. We are regrouping our forces so that the sales people will be working on sales full time and operations people will spend all their time on operations."

"This move," he said, "is a recognition of changing conditions in agriculture and in our national economy. I am confident that it will enable G.L.F. to do a better job of anticipating and meeting farmers' needs."

The June 24, 1957, issue of the *G.L.F. Week* announced the filling of several important executive positions in the Merchandising Division. M.

---

unsettling. The plan apparently became more comprehensive as it was put into effect. It was presented to the Board of Directors on June 24 simply as a reorganization for sales emphasis. Mr. Silcox explained the purpose of the reorganization in a letter to the author, dated July 30, 1957: "This reorganization shifts a little of the emphasis which we had in operations, for the last fifteen years, over into the field of selling to build volume and cut unit costs. My definition of selling as applied to this work is 'Selling the use of the G.L.F.' so that members will know more about the goods and services which are available. . . . Enclosed is an organization chart which shows how this is set up, with two lines of flow from the Director of Distribution. One group operates, and the other sells. We kept our plans for reorganizing the Retail Division very confidential until after the Institutional Conference because we did not wish to upset any of the men who were being shifted around." As a matter of fact, the grapevine during the June conference was already speculating with regard to the scope and significance of the pending changes.

[2] C. E. Dayton, former Director of Retail Services, became Assistant Secretary of the Cooperative G.L.F. Exchange, Inc., responsible for membership relations.

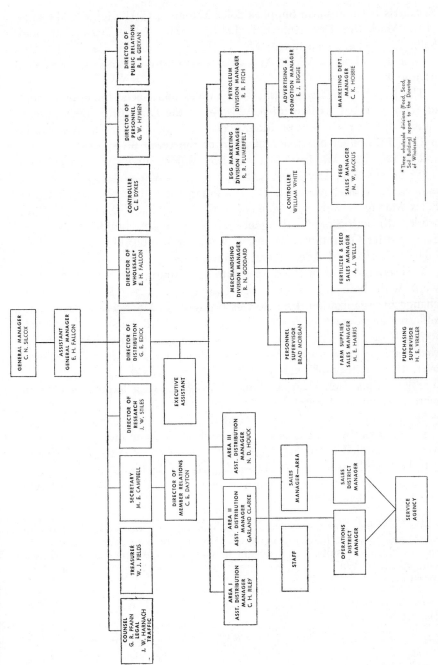

FIGURE 13–G.L.F. ORGANIZATION CHART, JULY, 1957

E. Harris became Farm Supplies Sales Manager; C. H. Hobbie, Manager of the Marketing Department; E. J. Biggie, Manager of Advertising and Sales Promotion Department; M. W. Backus, Manager, Feed Sales Department; and A. G. Wells, Manager, Seed and Soil Building Sales Department.

The July 1, 1957, issue of the *G.L.F. Week* announced the appointment of Seeber Tarbell as Executive Assistant to the Director of Distribution. Edick said, "In his new position, Seeber will take a very active part in putting into effect our reorganization of the retail divisions."[3]

The July 22, 1957, issue of the *G.L.F. Week* named Area Sales Managers for the three Divisions: K. S. Joy, Area I; William English, Area II; and N. E. White, Area III. District Operations Managers and District Sales Managers were also named. The District Sales Managers would work with both Stores and Agent-Buyers on volume building programs. The District Operations Managers would be responsible for operations in both Stores and Agent-Buyer communities.

This separation of the field force into two groups, each of which would work with both Stores and Agent-Buyers, represented a significant change in organization. Prior to this the District Managers were responsible for all contact work with Stores and Agent-Buyers for given territories. Under the new plan there would be two District Managers for each territory—one responsible for operations and one for selling. Moreover, the territory of each District Manager would be approximately doubled. Thus each District Manager would serve a larger territory, in more of a specialist way.[4]

M. E. Harris was made manager at this time of the reorganized Farm Supplies Department. Under the change it would handle several products formerly handled in the Soil Building Division: insecticides, farm chemicals, lawn and garden materials, shells, grit and bedding.

During the next few months the new program became a fact. On October 11, Silcox said:

We have just about completed the job of putting the reorganization into effect and throwing it into gear. It will probably take six months or more to see any definite results. . . . In truth, it is more a regrouping of men than a reorganization. We have simply sorted men into two groups: salesmen and operators.[5]

[3] One of Tarbell's first jobs was to help develop job descriptions for the new positions set up by the reorganization.

[4] This separation of the field force may be compared to the "separation of the sheep from the goats" put into effect by Ed Babcock in 1935—when the field force was divided into two groups—one to work with Stores and the other with Agent-Buyers. (See Chapter 19.)

[5] Letter of C. N. Silcox, to author, October 11, 1957.

In his address to the annual meeting on October 24, Silcox said that the problem up through the Korean War was to have a supply of goods to meet the needs of a rapidly growing farm business. Now with conditions changed and the inefficient farm supply dealer out of business, problems were coming from competition. He said:

G.L.F. must meet and will solve these problems. The recent reorganization of our retail division into a streamlined distribution system is one step in doing the job. In describing this change we have used the phrase "sell—to serve better." We are going to do a job of selling G.L.F. as a farmers' cooperative institution. We intend to tell members of all of the goods and services which are available. We will try to sell members the idea that if management knows what goods and services members want, we have an organization which can supply these needs. To do this, we have simply sorted out those men who are the best salesmen of ideas, the best merchandisers of goods, and have given them this new sales responsibility. We have placed in another group those men who are the best operators of facilities and services, the most capable in controlling inventories, credit, etc. This group will have charge of operations.

The material that was developed by Fallon for use in the regional annual meetings in the fall of 1957-58, placed emphasis on two major operating problems in G.L.F.—building additional volume and decreasing operating costs so as to obtain satisfactory savings. These were stated to be the problems throughout the G.L.F. at wholesale and at retail.

In presenting information on levels of revenue necessary to keep G.L.F. sound and progressive, Fallon pointed out that methods of decreasing costs through mechanization and added volume had not brought a sufficient reduction in costs. He admitted that in some commodities, such as dairy and poultry feeds, G.L.F. had actually lost in its share of the market since 1950, while farm supplies and seed had about held even. Increases had come only in petroleum, fertilizer, and egg and bean marketing. The problem was accentuated for feed, because the growth of local mixing was resulting in a drop of G.L.F. formula feeds, and it was these feeds that provided a large percentage of the margins needed by the G.L.F. Exchange. More and more services were being rendered at retail, and often at a loss. This was placing pressure on retail operators to recoup such costs in higher margins.

Then he raised the question, "What are we doing about these problems?" The answer was: "First we have established goals—short-range and long-range. Second, we have reorganized from top to bottom for selling. . . ." He pointed out: "We now have a sales organization and an operating group." These were to be closely correlated but each would have a distinctive job to perform. Although this sales organization was organized only to the district manager level, it recognized that the key

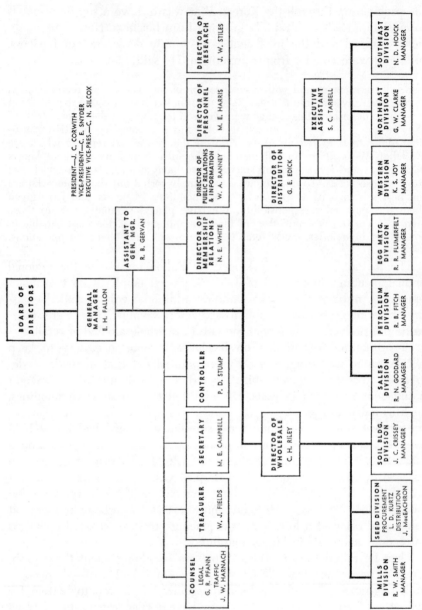

FIGURE 14—G.L.F. ORGANIZATION CHART, FEBRUARY, 1958

to increasing sales was continued activity at each store and agency. Lower cost per unit was to be the goal. The object was to make each service pay its way.

This was the state of affairs when Silcox turned over the full management to Fallon in November, 1957. At this time G.L.F. was restive. The reorganization had been disturbing. In the rapid shuffle of personalities two men well known in the G.L.F.—C. E. Dayton and C. L. Dickinson—had resigned because they were not satisfied with the jobs assigned them. Shortly afterwards, C. E. Dykes, the Controller, left the organization to accept a more attractive offer.

Silcox recognized that the burden of carrying on the new program with its emphasis on selling called for aggressive, dynamic leadership over a period of time. Since his retirement was imminent, he welcomed the appointment of Fallon as General Manager, and his own appointment to the position of Executive Vice President, recently vacated by McConnell.[6]

In the *G.L.F. Week* for December 10, 1957, Fallon, as General Manager, announced the following appointments to complete his management team: Charles Riley, Director of Wholesale; Bruce Gervan, Assistant Secretary and Assistant to the General Manager; Warren Ranney, Director of Public Relations and Information; M. E. Harris, Director of Personnel Relations; Bradford Morgan, Manager of Farm Supplies Department, to follow M. E. Harris. Kenneth Joy succeeded Riley as Western Division Sales Manager.

The appointment of N. E. White as Director of Membership Relations, to be effective as of April 1, 1958, was announced in the *G.L.F. Week* of January 6, 1958.

With these changes, reflected in the organization chart as of February, 1958, the reorganization for selling was largely completed.

---

[6] Silcox had paved the way for this change by placing Fallon in charge of operations in January, 1956. Thus Fallon had been performing many of the functions of a general manager since that time while at the same time he had been increasingly concerned with policy problems.

CHAPTER 45

The New Look

*"We must keep up with change if cooperatives are to remain strong
enough to serve members well."*

EDMUND H. FALLON

June, 1957

A NEW ERA in the G.L.F. opened in November, 1957, with the appointment of E. H. Fallon as General Manager. The preceding three general managers had been partners in building the G.L.F. almost from its start. Fallon had over twenty-five years of experience, but he was only fifty years of age, and he represented the new generation. He came to the position with a reputation for getting things done and, as he had served in all parts of the G.L.F., he was well aware of its strengths and weaknesses.

Fallon was not afraid of change, for he recognized that changes created challenges and that challenges created opportunities. He had expressed this philosophy in the June, 1957, Institutional Conference. He saw the following opportunities: (1) To fit services and commodities to the farm. (2) To improve member use. (3) To apply research results faster. (4) To develop coordinated cooperative marketing services. (5) To develop, promote, and apply new marketing ideas. (6) To eliminate unnecessary functions and jobs, and apply new methods. (7) To promote better use of credit. (8) To serve large farms as well as average farms. (9) To deal with employees as individuals.[1]

The reorganization for selling was largely completed when Fallon became General Manager. His immediate problem was to build throughout the whole system confidence in the new program. In a letter sent to all members on January 29, 1958, he said: "Your cooperative is in excellent financial condition." He reported that the recent series of 44 regional committee meetings had shown interest in the increasing trend toward bulk feed; the improvement of installation and repair service; and G.L.F.'s plans for dealing with integration and marketing. He stressed volume building through farm calls, lowering of costs, and the need to work closely with members. He ended with this personal comment:

To be chosen General Manager of G.L.F. is a great honor and a great challenge. I will do my best to justify the confidence of the Board of Directors. To the best of my ability I intend to see that G.L.F. is operated at all times in

[1] "The Door to Opportunity," *Cooperative Digest*, June 1957.

the interests of farmers. Our products and services must fit the needs of the individual farm—that is the only place where a cooperative's value can be measured.

A few weeks later, on March 3, Fallon addressed a letter to "My Associates in G.L.F." He reported that overall dollar volume was 1 percent under the same period for the preceding year, and 6 percent under the set goal. Net margins were down 41 percent. This pointed up the need for increased effort to build volume and reduce controllable expenses. He indicated that plans were in the making to enable G.L.F. to grow. Emphasis was to be placed on "(1) membership, (2) personnel, (3) sales effort by all people in G.L.F., (4) control of expense, (5) further development of our marketing services, and (6) a major G.L.F. forage plan."

These letters made clear Fallon's determination to see that G.L.F. was serving farmers at optimum efficiency.

The Emphasis on Sales

The reorganization for selling had been through its shakedown period when Fallon became General Manager. The problem was to make it work.

The main effect of the change was to increase emphasis on volume building through more farm calls and more aggressive sales drives. It intensified trends which had been evident for several years.

In August, 1957, the new emphasis was reflected in a two-day school in sales methods for district managers, store managers, farm contact men, and other selected personnel, with Jack Lacey, famous for his "Hot Button" sales technique, as instructor. A special group was given additional instruction so that they could pass the training on to all retail personnel in special schools set up for this purpose.

One of the problems in going all out for selling was to give it a meaning which would not be offensive to G.L.F. members. The following definition was finally agreed upon: "Searching out and filling the needs and wants of farmers in a manner that establishes confidence and brings to more and more farmers the benefits that come through maximum use of their own cooperative."

Prior to 1957, the G.L.F. had found it desirable to concentrate sales drives for given commodities at specific periods of the year. They came into being because of the need to focus the attention of all personnel on the really important commodities and services. These programs have been more carefully designed and carried out since the Sales Division was formed.

The first major promotion of this type was the "Go Bulk—Go G.L.F."

feed program carried on in the fall of 1957. Television, radio, and advertisements in farm papers were all used to attract interest, and synthetic sponges were used as handouts on farm calls.

Other important promotions have been: The Fall Feed Missile Program, 1958; The Spring Feed Program, 1959; The Fall Feed Jet Program, 1959; and The Crop Needs Jet Program, 1959.

These campaigns are built with military precision in seven stages under a count-down plan, starting 180 days before a program is to start. In the early stages the preliminary planning is done. In Stage 4, with 100 days before the plan goes into effect, the Advertising and Sales Promotion Plan is submitted to the Sales Manager for approval. In Stage 7, with 20 days to go, the Advertising and Sales Promotion Department completes distribution of merchandising material, plus employee information and materials.

A good illustration of a campaign of this kind was the 1959 Fall Feed Jet Program. After the plan was perfected through the process described above, it was "kicked off" with top executives calling on farmers with agency salesmen to sell feed and the complete G.L.F. service package. The objective was to increase G.L.F. dairy, stock, and poultry formula feed purchases by 10 percent over the comparable period a year before, and progress was to be measured by volume summaries at specified times while the plan was in effect.

Preliminary instruction for employees was provided through area feed schools, and a specially prepared manual which included sales features, information on sales incentives, advertising and sales promotion devices, ideas for displays, sample advertisements, and suggestions for use in farm calls.

This plan featured sales incentives for agency salesmen, with prizes valued at $500 for the leading salesmen in each of the three areas.

The Fall Feed Missile Program for 1958 featured a family bonus plan, under which G.L.F. Mills provided $2.00 in patron coupons for every ton of G.L.F. formula dairy, poultry, or stock feed purchased during the period of the campaign. These coupons were redeemable in G.L.F. farm and home hardware items. Although competitive concerns criticized the plan as a sales gimmick it put the spotlight on G.L.F. feeds and was well received by members. Some 150,000 tons of feed were sold under the plan. The cost in face value of coupons was $300,000, although cost to G.L.F. in value of commodities was but $265,000.

In 1958, the Sales Division developed a Volume Incentive Program, known as the V.I.P. Under this program payments were made to store managers, agent-buyers and sales personnel for volume increases over the preceding fiscal year on feed and fertilizer and farm supplies. A base was worked out for each service agency in terms of volume the preceding year. The plan worked in this way. A payment of $1.00 per ton was paid for feed and fertilizer tonnage increases over the base. If an agency had a base of 1,000 tons and made an increase of 100 tons it yielded an incentive payment of $100. For farm supplies, 1½ percent was paid for dollar purchase increases over the base. This plan was well received by agency personnel but, like most incentive programs, it gradually lost its effectiveness and it is not being used in 1960-61.

In 1958 the G.L.F. developed a Mill-to-Farm Plan to meet the needs of the big user who does not require local service. Under the Mill-to-Farm Plan carloads of feed are shipped direct to the farmer's siding or delivered in truck loads to the farm from the mill. The user thus gets his feed at plant prices plus delivery cost. This plan has met the needs of many large users and retained their patronage for the G.L.F. It has benefited all patrons in that tonnage makes possible low cost feed manufacturing. Under the plan a payment is made by the Mills Division to the local service agency for maintaining local contacts with Mill-to-Farm patrons.

The emphasis on volume building since 1957 has not been fully reflected in increased volume. Competition for the farmer's business has been strong, and it has called for great effort to hold the significant position attained. However, the general trend, except for marketing, in recent years has been upward, as shown by the following net volume data for the G.L.F. Exchange:[2]

Year ending July 30	Commodities purchased by patrons	Products marketed for patrons	Total net volume
1956	$143,075,466	$19,972,545	$163,048,011
1957	149,119,854	18,756,057	167,875,911
1958	148,434,827	20,922,831	169,357,658
1959	157,687,892	19,667,765	177,355,657

[2] Information for fiscal year ending July 30, 1960, was not available when this was written, but data for the first 8 months indicate that they will show a slight decline in purchasing volume from the preceding year. Fallon attaches great importance to direct selling on the farm. He writes me as follows: "The large farmer today can buy almost anything he wants at or near the wholesale price. He rarely comes into the store. His business is actively solicited by every feed company and other supplier. He has to be sold, and sold on his own farm. This underlines the need for trained men capable of meeting the farmer on his own ground and selling him face-to-face on G.L.F. feeds or other commodities. We have around 100 full-time salesmen, and about 200 others, including many store managers, who spend a substantial share of their time on farm calls. Keeping this sales force trained, informed, and on the job is one of our most important projects. The same factors which make personal selling so vital reduce the value of traditional merchandising methods. Advertising and sales promotion have their place, but in agriculture it is a different and less important one today than 10 or 20 years ago." Letter of May 9, 1960.

THE NEW ATTITUDE IN PERSONNEL ADMINISTRATION

Fallon's appointment as General Manager gave an immediate lift to G.L.F. morale for it was well known that he measured personnel administration in terms of its ability to achieve G.L.F. objectives.

One of his first actions was to place M. E. Harris in charge of personnel administration. Harris brought to the position practical experience in G.L.F. operations. He understood how to get people to work together. He subordinated system to the achievement of results. Immediately, steps were taken to loosen up some of the procedures that had given employees irritation. While job interviews, performance reviews, and manpower inventories were continued, they were made more informal and were better adjusted to the attitudes of G.L.F. employees. Those in direct charge of operations were consulted and kept informed. "Manpower development" quietly became "Management development." As a result, there was an immediate improvement in G.L.F. morale.

Harris had been placed in charge of Personnel Administration to gear it more closely to operating needs. In July, 1959, this transition had been made and he was transferred to the position of Operations Supervisor of the Distribution Division where his special abilities were urgently needed.

Seeber Tarbell was well qualified to succeed Harris as Director of Personnel. He was experienced in G.L.F. personnel and administrative procedures and he had a strong liking for people. He had served as Assistant Manager and Manager for several Service Stores, as a Service Store District Manager in two territories, as Personnel Supervisor of the Farm Service Division, and its successor, the Service Agencies Division. His experience as Director of Member Relations for the Retail Division from 1955 to 1957, and as Assistant to the Director of Distribution for the past two years, gave him a comprehensive knowledge of the entire organization.

Tarbell, like Harris, subscribes to the view of Fallon that personnel administration must be carried on largely to help operators meet their responsibilities. Tarbell believes that a good personnel man should aim to work himself out of a job. He holds that the burden of "so-called" personnel work will be lessened if good personnel practices are followed by operators. He is now studying how the G.L.F. pension system can be modernized to better meet the needs of employees.

The emphasis throughout the organization on volume building since 1957 led to an expansion of incentive plans. The major plan of this kind, the V.I.P., as described above, was an overall volume-building incentive paid to all retail employees for volume increases in G.L.F. formula fertilizers, formula feeds, and farm supplies commodities. A somewhat comparable plan, known as the V.C.C., or Volume-Credit-Cost plan, was used until 1960-61 by the Petroleum Division. Although it has been difficult to measure the benefit of these and other incentive plans, it is recognized that they have given emphasis to the importance of volume building.

All incentive plans are reviewed by the Institutional Incentive Committee, with the Director of Personnel Relations as Chairman. Any incentive program representing total payments of more than $100 per plant or store requires the approval of the committee. After a plan is developed and approved by the Director of Distribution or the Director of Wholesale it is presented to the Institutional Incentive Committee where it is tested for compatibility with general and specific institutional objectives and measured against stipulated requirements. All award payments not requiring committee approval must be reported to the incentive committee with an evaluation of results. While incentive programs are correlated through the Director of Personnel they are largely developed and administered by sales and operating executives.

Many problems have come up in the use of incentive plans. They have proved costly to administer and they have tended to overemphasize volume building to the detriment of well-balanced operations. Moreover they have soon lost their effectiveness. Most G.L.F. executives now believe that there is little need for elaborate programs of this type in view of the provision for merit increases under the G.L.F. salary plan which encourages employees to work for raises and promotion to higher paying jobs.

Membership Work Gains Standing

Under the reorganization for selling, the problem of maintaining membership support took on a new significance, for there was danger that the pressure for getting volume might cause members to think of themselves more as customers or as stockholders than as responsible owner-members. It was apparent that sustained effort would be needed to strengthen the membership tie.

Fallon recognized that this situation called for a Director of Membership Relations who could infuse the whole organization with a new spirit of membership consciousness. He found this man in N. E. White, who had demonstrated marked ability to gain support for various programs.

One of White's first problems was to gain employee acceptance for the idea that membership relations was a matter of the utmost practical importance. He stressed this point in a carefully prepared talk given at the 1958 Institutional Conferences held in June and July. In these talks he made clear that good member relations gave an organization a competitive advantage. He said:

We are now dealing with a group of second generation members. The first generation found it fun building the G.L.F. The second generation finds that maintaining the G.L.F. is routine. . . .
We have G.L.F. as an economic magnet, not a membership magnet. We have the new employee—the employee of 1958—coming with the G.L.F. because he feels that it is an outfit that is going places and therefore . . . good for him. And we have the new farmer buying from G.L.F. for the first time in 1958 because he feels, for example, that his best buy in bulk feed is from the G.L.F. In both cases membership as we think of it is far down the list.

With this background, White undertook to prove that membership was a cooperative asset. He was interested in getting employees to recognize that it would pay them to give more support to membership work. He maintained that it should be looked on as a part of all programs and woven into the fabric of day-to-day jobs. He summarized by saying:

Membership is good business. This is the only point we wish to make. . . . Why? Because we must first believe that there is a payoff. Only then will we work on a membership project. If your objective is a better job you should work on membership. It will be good business for you. Weave member relations into the fabric of your day-to-day work. It will be good business for you. Broaden and magnify your views of membership. It will be good business for you. Raise it up on the scale of your objectives. It will be good business for you. . . . Those who work with members will find members working for them if the leadership is straight and true.

With the discontinuance of *Farming With G.L.F.* in 1957, there was no regular means of providing members with current G.L.F. information. As an experiment, the publication for G.L.F. employees, the *G.L.F. Week*, was sent to a selected group of members. It was so well received that it is now being sent regularly to 25,000 members selected by their local service agencies.

After the reorganization of 1957, the Membership Relations Department was given custody of all membership records. In January, 1960, it was made responsible for the promotional phase of the members insurance program. This relationship is logical, as this program, which is explained below, was designed as a membership service.

Under White's leadership there has been a steady improvement in membership meetings and in the meetings of member committees. He has obtained the close cooperation of the Directors of Personnel who are responsible for handling membership affairs in the various area offices. By placing all meetings and general membership contacts under the supervision of the Director of Member Relations a unified member relations program has at last been developed.

Fallon places great emphasis on membership work. In reporting to the Board of Directors on February 2, 1960, he said:

Farmers are becoming more critical; competition is the keenest in history; it takes more business to cover rising costs; and business is harder to get. . . . To keep G.L.F. alive, vigorous and effective for farmers, we must explore and probe. One of the great challenges is communication with members. Leadership and information on communication to farmers will be stepped up.

The Members Group Insurance Plan

In his report to the annual meeting on October 29, 1958, Fallon announced that the Board of Directors had approved a plan through which G.L.F. soon would make available to members group health, accident, and life insurance protection.

For many years, group life and medical insurance had been available to G.L.F. employees, and members had inquired whether this service could be provided for them. In view of this interest, G.L.F. had studied the problems involved and the degree of probable support for a program if adopted. It was found that a practical plan could be developed for providing members with group health, accident, and life insurance protection and that many wanted this service. The plan was to be available only to G.L.F. members and any savings were to go to the participants through lower rates or refunds.

In launching the plan on January 5, 1959, Fallon called it "the biggest membership project ever undertaken by G.L.F." Not only was it available to members but it provided coverage for their families and employees. The insurance would be underwritten by the Travelers Insurance Company of Hartford, Connecticut, with the G.L.F. acting as Trustee.

The plan was scheduled to become effective on April 1, 1959, and Seeber Tarbell was placed in charge of the campaign to enroll the members. It was a Herculean job to get the signup required to place the plan in operation, for those who contacted the members had first to be well trained so that they could explain how the plan would work for the individuals concerned.

Although most of the actual contact work with members was to be done by G.L.F. store managers, agent-buyers, and district managers, with some specially assigned personnel, it was necessary that practically all employees be well-informed on the plan. In the various training conferences approximately 1,200 employees received instruction from representatives of the Travelers Insurance Company, or R. C. Rathbone, Inc., the insurance brokers who acted as consultants on behalf of G.L.F. in working with Travelers on the program's development. The bulk of the solicitation work was done by about 800 of these G.L.F. representatives who called on approximately 90,000 members.

The Dairymen's League cooperated by permitting members of the G.L.F. who were League members to pay their premiums through milk check deductions, and similar arrangements also were worked out with other firms who handled the milk of G.L.F. members.

When the campaign closed on April 1 about 22,000 members had taken out policies for themselves, their families, or their employees. These policies provided health and accident coverage for over 55,000 individuals and life insurance at a value of $60 million.[3]

THE 5-STAR FORAGE PLAN

G.L.F. has long believed that anything good for the farmer is good for the G.L.F. From its beginnings G.L.F. has supported college research to help farmers increase the productivity of their fields and livestock. The interest of G.L.F. in farming efficiency has also been emphasized by its soil testing and liming programs. For many years a recognized G.L.F. objective has been to increase the efficiency of forage production.

In the summer of 1957, Fallon, then Assistant General Manager, appointed a committee under the chairmanship of J. W. Stiles to develop a long-range forage program for the G.L.F. This committee, after several months of meetings and discussions with college representatives, developed and recommended a program which was launched in May, 1957, as the G.L.F. 5-Star Forage Plan.[4]

In presenting the plan, Fallon said: "There is no more promising source of dairying profits than a good forage program. To help dairymen plan and carry on such a program, G.L.F. has developed a 5-star forage plan, based on the research and teaching of our state colleges. It is a long-range program, because forage production is a long-range project."

The five-star forage plan emphasized:

1. *Soil-testing.* Knowing what the soil needs to grow the crop you want. . . .
2. *Liming and fertilization.* Lime is absolutely basic . . . . Then comes fertilization according to test. . . .
3. *Seeds and seeding.* The right seed in the right field.
4. *Weed and insect control.* Protecting the crop from its enemies is increasingly important.
5. *Harvesting.* That means harvesting at the right time, and for hay or grass silage, the right time is early.[5]

In a letter to members in the dairy business, explaining the plan, Fallon said, "G.L.F., as your cooperative, stands ready to work with you in sup-

---

[3] For a full description of the way this program was inaugurated, see Ken Keoughan, "At Last—For Members, Group Insurance." *Cooperative Digest,* April 1959.
[4] After the plan was developed, Fallon named a permanent committee under the chairmanship of R. B. Gervan to put it into effect.
[5] See R. B. Gervan, "Everybody's on the 5-Star Bandwagon," *G.L.F. Week,* April 13, 1959.

plying the commodities, services and information to carry out these practices."

The G.L.F. took immediate steps to implement this program under the aggressive leadership of A. J. Wells, Sales Manager, Seed and Soils Building in the Sales Division. In June it ran 12 hay-drying demonstrations and in July field demonstrations were set up for various commodities and practices.

Although the plan was well launched in 1958, it did not receive wide promotion until April, 1959, when it was made a continuing institutional campaign. At that time, R. B. Gervan said, "First, last, and above all, good forage practices make for solvent G.L.F. members and a stable, prosperous agriculture. And that's what G.L.F. is here for—to contribute to the economic welfare of Northeastern farmers."

While it is not possible to measure the value of a plan of this type, it is the belief of G.L.F. executives that it has greatly stimulated the adoption of better forage practices and demonstrated the G.L.F.'s interest in improving the income of those it serves. Incidentally, it has emphasized G.L.F.'s ability to provide the supplies, services and information needed to carry out the recommendations of the plan.

EXPANSION OF EQUITY CAPITAL

It will be recalled that the G.L.F. Board of Directors decided in 1954 to hold stock ownership at the then existing level and to finance expansion largely through savings, reserves and increased borrowings.

In accordance with this policy, preferred and common stock holdings had been kept at approximately $24,000,000 from June 30, 1954 to June 30, 1958, while long-term debt had been increased by $3,141,000, and retained margins by $5,694,000. Although membership investment (net worth) increased in these 5 years from $39,705,000 to $43,380,000, or by $3,475,000, the value of net worth to total assets fell from 72 percent to 66 percent.

In the spring of 1958 the Directors decided that it was time to again strengthen the equity position of the Exchange, and the issuance of more common and preferred stock was authorized. Several factors explain this change of policy. More credit was being granted to increase or hold volume. Marketing operations were requiring more capital. Inflation had brought higher costs for goods and facilities. Moreover, it appeared that integrated agricultural programs including contract farming might require use of more capital. At this time the amount of common stock that could be held by a member was increased from $500 to $2,000 to give members an opportunity to have a more significant investment interest in their organization.

Under this new policy, stock holdings were increased by about $2 million in 1958-59. As a result of this and an increase in retained margins for the year of about $1 million, the ratio of stockholders' ownership (net worth) to total assets was raised to 68 percent on June 30, 1959.

Steps also were taken to improve the equity position of the retail stores through the sale of more store preferred stock in stores where the debt ratio had become heavy in relation to the equity capital. The sale of such stock amounted to $800,000 by June 1, 1959.

To help the retail stores and agencies build up necessary reserves and otherwise strengthen their financial position, the Directors of the Exchange authorized a 2 percent discount on sales to all retail service agencies for a period of several weeks in early 1959. While this served to reduce the net margin of the Exchange for the year it also reduced the Exchange's income tax liability in this amount. The Board recognized that the stores and agencies as an integral part of the G.L.F. system could make better use of the savings for the benefit of members than the parent organization.

THE PROBLEM OF EXPENSE CONTROL

The upward trend in expenses has been of growing concern to the G.L.F. From 1954-55 to 1957-58 net expenses increased almost a million dollars a year. Although this trend reflected new and expanded operations, it could not be continued without ultimate disaster.

A "hold-the-line budget" reduced the increase in expenses to a nominal amount for 1957-58. The problem of expense control has become more acute in 1959-60 as dollar volume has fallen off despite strenuous efforts to maintain or increase it. This has caused Fallon to order a major cost reduction campaign. By June 30, 1960, every division, service and function will be carefully reviewed to reduce costs to a minimum in the 1960-61 budget. To achieve a better continuing control over expenses a flexible budgeting system is also being installed which will better relate expenditures to changes in business volume.

The problem of expense control also has been a matter of increasing concern in the retail service stores. The emphasis on selling given by the reorganization of 1957 weakened attention to operations, with the result that costs expanded more rapidly than revenue. To remedy this condition, M. E. Harris was made Director of Retail Service Operations under the Director of Distribution, on July 1, 1959. In this position Harris worked directly with the Area and District Managers and Operations

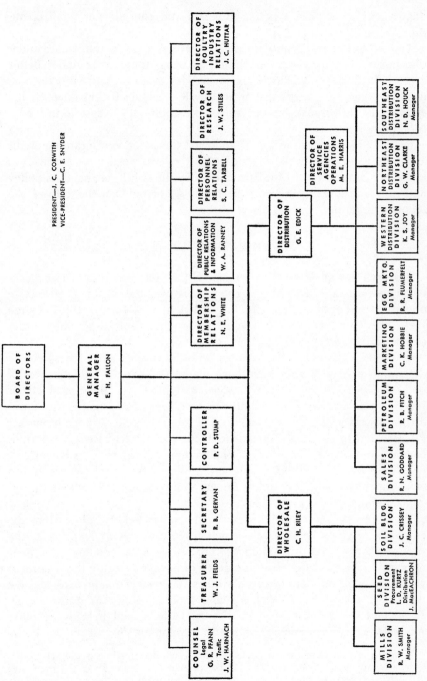

FIGURE 15—G.L.F. ORGANIZATION CHART, NOVEMBER, 1959

Supervisors to achieve a better direction and control over retail operations.[6] (See Figure 15.)

The control of credit and inventory costs required his immediate attention, and procedures were instituted to bring these costs under better
control. In both cases Harris endeavored to establish and enforce more
definite policies to meet current needs. He recognized that uncontrolled
costs could eat up margins and impair the ability of the system to render
continuing service.

From 1938 to 1958, the G.L.F. followed the practice of granting credit
as a service to worthy patrons provided they balanced their accounts in
full every thirty days. In the Spring of 1960 the G.L.F. changed its policy
and now considers an account past due if not paid on the 15th of the
following month.

RESEARCH POINTS THE WAY

Research has again become a major G.L.F. interest. It is at last recognized that an effective research program is essential to G.L.F.'s effective
operation and future. The operating divisions now turn to the Research
Department for assistance in evaluating programs and in planning future
activities.

Since 1955 the G.L.F. has made increasing use of market research to
determine policy. Studies have been made to determine effectiveness of
various G.L.F. supplies and services, potentials for new products or
services, adequacy of information channels, and factors motivating farmers as buyers. The increasing number of requests for assistance in market
research led to the establishment in 1958 of a market research priorities
committee, with the Director of Wholesale as Chairman. This committee,
which meets regularly to evaluate and implement research proposals, is a
valuable device for developing research-mindedness throughout the organization.

Work in applied research has also demonstrated its value. Here the
emphasis is given to research which tests, analyzes and appraises the
performance of farm production items or practices under actual conditions
to help G.L.F. meet the changing needs of farmers. During the past three
years some 60 applied research studies have been made to determine
degree of acceptability of feeds and feeding programs, farm supply
equipment items, drugs and medicants, various seed hybrids, or other
products. The "70 before 60" project to develop an efficient poultry house

[6] Under the realignment of functions in April 1960, described on p. 458, Harris became Director of the Sales Division. At the present time, June 1960, the three area
distribution offices are being reorganized to achieve more effective retail operations.
(See Chapter 47.)

suitable for the needs of G.L.F. members is now being farm-tested under the supervision of the Manager of Applied Research.

The Director of Research is now held responsible for the effective performance of the research function as it is applied throughout the G.L.F. He correlates all G.L.F. research activities and is the center for research contacts with the agricultural colleges, government and industry. The research grants to the colleges, which continue to be very important, relate mostly to areas of broad interest to farmers in the Northeast such as forage production, corn breeding, poultry and animal nutrition, and fertilizer requirements. Members of staff closely follow the work on such projects so that findings may be applied in G.L.F. operations as soon as possible.

In August, 1958, Dean W. I. Myers, of Cornell University, commented as follows on the value of the G.L.F. research grants:

> The research grants of the G.L.F. are of great value to us and to the farm people of the State because they help us to finance a more vigorous program of research on the projects which the G.L.F. thinks are most important to its members. . . . The G.L.F. does not get any selfish advantage from its gifts since the results of all research are made available to all farmers and the public as soon as possible.

The budget of the Research Department for 1959-60 was $256,000, and of this, $128,850 was earmarked for grants to state agricultural colleges. When the amount provided for research in the operating departments is added, the total funds provided for research activities approximated $400,000.

The present views of the General Manager relative to research are as follows:

> I believe that the tremendous expansion in research expenditures, both public and private, in recent years is largely responsible for the increase in farm productivity, the technological advance in industry, and the upgrading of our standard of living. Research in agricultural production must be continued and research in marketing greatly expanded. It doesn't necessarily follow that a farm cooperative must spend great sums for basic research. The cooperative can be more effective by helping to shape the direction of basic research, keeping on top of the results, and translating these results into new and improved products and services. It is hard sometimes to determine where research leaves off and development begins, but I think our emphasis should be mainly on development.[7]

LONG-RANGE PLANNING

The rapid changes in Northeastern agriculture have emphasized the need for long-range planning. With Fallon's active encouragement, every G.L.F. division has set up 5-year goals. Long-time plans have been developed for petroleum, egg marketing, lawn and garden, and various other operations. These plans are flexible projections. They provide guide

[7] Letter of E. H. Fallon to author, of May 9, 1960.

lines for budget planning and they anticipate problems that may arise. Their main aim is to keep the organization forward-minded and alert to change.[8]

[8] Fallon considers long-range planning "very important" and "very difficult." His views follow: "We spend a great deal of time on long-range planning. . . . The way things are changing in agriculture, we don't undertake to plan much beyond five years. Our planning takes the form of trying to establish direction and goals, along with general, broad plans for reaching the goals. Detailed plans are made and changed as we go along. For example, a year ago we adopted a five-year growth plan for the Petroleum Division. . . . The present price squeeze has modified our current action program, but not our basic plan." Letter, to author, of May 9, 1960.

GENERAL MANAGER FALLON REPORTING TO MEMBERS AT 1959
ANNUAL MEETING

EXHIBIT AT 1958 ANNUAL MEETING

JAMES W. HARNACH
Traffic Counsel

R. BRUCE GERVAN
Secretary

WILLIAM J. FIELDS
Treasurer

GEORGE R. PFANN
Legal Counsel

PHIL D. STUMP
Controller

JARED W. STILES
Director of Research

SEEBER C. TARBELL
*Director of
Personnel Relations*

NATHANIEL E. WHITE
*Director of
Membership Relations*

WARREN A. RANNEY
*Director of
Public Relations
and Information*

PRESENT TOP MANAGEMENT OF G.L.F.

CHARLES H. RILEY
Director of
Wholesale

GLENN E. EDICK
Director of
Distribution

RONALD N. GODDARD
Director of
Marketing

GARLAND W. CLARK
Manager, Northeast
Distribution Division

KENNETH S. JOY
Manager, Western
Distribution Division

NELSON D. HAUCK
Manager, Southeast
Distribution Division

PRESENT TOP MANAGEMENT OF G.L.F.

RICHARD W. SMITH
Manager,
Mills Division

JAMES L. MACEACHRON
Manager, Seed
Distribution Division

L. D. KURTZ
Manager, Seed
Procurement Division

JOHN C. CRISSEY
Manager, Soil
Building Division

MILTON E. HARRIS
Manager,
Sales Division

RONALD B. FITCH
Manager,
Petroleum Division

ROY R. FLUMERFELT
Manager, Egg
Marketing Division

JOHN C. HUTTAR
Director of Poultry
Industry Relations

CALEB K. HOBBIE
Assistant Director
of Marketing

PRESENT TOP MANAGEMENT OF G.L.F.

CHAPTER 46

Toward an Integrated Marketing Program

> *I put these two words—marketing and integration—together be-*
> *cause I believe that any integration program is going to have market-*
> *ing as a part of it, and that more and more of our marketing activities*
> *are going to have some elements of integration.*
>
> EDMUND H. FALLON, *August, 1958*

T HE REORGANIZATION for selling had recognized the potential significance of marketing a wider range of farm products by setting up a
separate marketing department in the Sales Division to deal with all farm
products except eggs, which were being handled in the Egg Marketing
Division. In view of Fallon's long interest in this field, a more vigorous
program could be anticipated.

Although G.L.F. was committed to do something about marketing, it
was difficult to know what to do. One thing was clear—the problem required careful study. While these studies were being made, Fallon directed his attention to the allied problem of vertical integration which
was then expanding rapidly in farming areas everywhere in the nation.

THE CHALLENGE OF INTEGRATION

To understand the importance of this problem to G.L.F. we must
realize that integration through contract farming had the entire agricultural industry in ferment. There were many who feared that if not arrested or controlled through cooperatives it would largely destroy the
independence of farmers.[1]

G.L.F. first encountered integration in late 1956. At that time it had
joined in a small broiler-contracting operation in order to protect a block
of feed volume and gain some experience in this rapidly expanding form

---

[1] For the classic statement of this issue, which was a call to arms for farmers, see
Carroll Streeter's article, "Who Will Control Farming?" *Farm Journal*, February,
1958. For a general interpretation, see "Contract Farming and Vertical Integration in
Agriculture," Agriculture Information Bulletin No. 198, U. S. Department of Agriculture, July, 1958. Under the contract farming type of vertical integration the farmer
contracts to produce broilers or other products under stipulated conditions for an
agreed-upon return. Farm production is thus controlled by the integrating firm rather
than by the farmer as an independent entrepreneur. For a complete explanation see
the author's articles, "Cooperatives and Integrated Agriculture," (June 23, 1958), and
"The Effects of Integration on Marketing of Farm Products," (November 20, 1958),
Mimeographed, Farmer Cooperative Service, United States Department of Agriculture.

of economic integration. The initial success of the program, plus continued grower interest, led to the development of a second experimental program in the spring of 1957. While this experience was being obtained, integration through contract began to spread to egg production in the Northeast.

As long as integration had been confined to broiler production it was of only minor concern, for this industry was not well developed in G.L.F. territory. Integration of egg production was a different matter. It was apparent that a widespread expansion of integration of laying flocks by feed companies or marketing firms would threaten G.L.F.'s feed volume and curtail its egg marketings.

Recognizing the danger in this situation, the G.L.F. Board of Directors, in February, 1957, had expressed opposition to integration as it was then being practiced. In view of the urgency of the problem, President Corwith had authorized Fallon, as Assistant General Manager, to explain this policy in a printed letter to G.L.F. Committeemen. In this letter, dated March 1, Fallon said:

G.L.F. was established and has been built on the principle of voluntary use. Members make their own decisions from day to day whether they wish to use the services of the cooperative. The integration contract deprives the farmer of this freedom of choice. For the duration of the contract—usually three years —he is under legal obligation to use only the stipulated brand of feed, to get his chicks from a specified hatchery, to market his eggs through the designated outlet. This concept is contrary to the philosophy of G.L.F. . . .

The problems of the poultry industry are severe and deepseated. The individual poultryman is hard pressed to stay in business. G.L.F. as an organization whose membership includes tens of thousands of such poultrymen does not believe these problems will be solved by integration, as it is currently being proposed. Contracting with an egg producer for supplying his feed and disposing of his eggs does not provide any permanent answer to the squeeze between production and egg prices.

Fallon then stated G.L.F.'s program to meet the needs of poultrymen in working out of the present situation:

It is G.L.F's intention to mobilize all the facilities at its command to assist the poultrymen in working out of the present situation. These include: 1. Supplying the best possible feeds at the lowest possible cost. This includes use of bulk and other packaging economies; use of nearby grain; use of market "buys" as they become available. 2. Continuing development of our marketing service through more candling and cartoning, a sound quality program and increased promotion. 3. Promotion of eggs and poultry products. The Board of Directors has authorized a substantial promotional program beginning March 1. 4. Offering management assistance to members. 5. Collaborating with agricultural and financial groups in the development of constructive credit programs. 6. Working against legislative proposals and administrative programs which would raise the cost of feed.

The letter closed with this statement, "It is the firm conviction of the G.L.F. Board and management that the problems of the poultry industry can be solved through voluntary action, and that only through voluntary action can poultrymen retain control of their own business."

This firm declaration of G.L.F.'s determination to resist the practice of integration unless it could be harmonized with its program of working for farmers can be given a considerable amount of credit for slowing down the spread of the contract farming type of integration into the Northeastern egg production area. It indicated that G.L.F. was not going to permit itself to be integrated out of the egg business.

Although the G.L.F. was opposed to integration in egg production as then practiced, it was not blind to the factors that made the plan attractive to many producers. In order to get more experience it stepped up its experiment in broiler contracting.

When the Board met in February, 1958, it re-affirmed its experimental financing of patrons for selected products such as broilers, replacement pullets and insecticides. In this way it modified the strong stand taken against integration the preceding year. Later in the spring it approved in principle a proposed research project on the contract feeding of hogs.

Fallon had gradually become convinced that contractual integration was part of an economic process that could not be resisted. He therefore gave his attention to ways in which the process could be made to work for the G.L.F. and its members. He presented his views to the G.L.F. Board on May 5, 1958, in a statement entitled, "How Integration or Contract Farming Will Affect G.L.F. and the G.L.F. Member."

In this statement, which was approved by the Board, Fallon declared that the G.L.F. always moved with the times. He referred to the spread of integration which had grown to the point where 90 percent of the broilers grown in the United States were now produced under contract. He indicated that about a year earlier attempts were made in G.L.F. territory to develop integration contracts with egg producers, and that the Board took a position in opposition to the type of integration then being proposed. He also indicated that, since then, integration of laying flocks had made very little progress in the Northeast although it was growing rapidly in other areas.

In view of the growth of integration in almost all segments of agriculture, Fallon believed that it was time for G.L.F. to find ways and means of dealing with it. He recognized its appeal to many farmers but he feared that if integration encouraged expansion there might be more product than the market could absorb.

He answered the question, "What can farmers do as integration advances?" by saying, "If integration is a coming trend, and I believe it is, it seems far better for farmers to control it through their organizations than to have the control pass into the hands of commercial feed companies or chain stores or other outside interests."

He then reviewed G.L.F. experience with integration. He reported that no money had been lost on its experimental broiler contracting program and that the contract was a model for competition. He mentioned that G.L.F. also had a small experimental program in turkeys and one in raising of pullets for resale.

Fallon foresaw that vertical integration might bring some changes in long-established policies. "We have a policy that says patronage is voluntary and no contracts or commitments are required. Yet we already have some contracts with farmers. There are situations where a contract or an agreement or a commitment of some sort is a great protection to a farmer." He also believed that integration might even strengthen membership relations. He held that serving a member who was feeding turkeys under a marketing agreement could prove to be a much closer and more enduring relationship than serving a member who bought feed from G.L.F., as the spirit moved him. He said, "Farmers today choose to join G.L.F., but G.L.F. will have to choose the farmers to work with it on integration."

He also saw integration by contract as a way of protecting volume. He said: "In integration agreements you tend to get a large block of business in a single transaction and get it nailed down for a long period of time. This means relatively low sales cost." Moreover, he thought that marketing developments would be greatly influenced by the spread of integration. He saw it expanding such things as bulk service and the bypassing of all unnecessary steps in distribution. He concluded by saying that he did not feel that the G.L.F. should rush headlong into integration but neither should the G.L.F. run and hide from it.

It was clear from this statement that G.L.F. was committed to an extension of its experiments in integration and, in August, 1958, the Sales Division set up a Livestock Contracting Department, under Harold G. Smith, to supervise contractual programs. When the Board met in October it instructed management to use its own judgment in dealing with broiler contracting as this was no longer to be considered an experiment. The Board took another step in integration at this same meeting by approving the purchase of a Poultry Processing Plant at Hinsdale, New York.

In his annual report to stockholders, on October 23, Fallon explained how this plant came to be acquired: "Many of our broilers have been going through a small processing plant in Hinsdale. . . . The owner was about to close this plant. . . . There appeared to be no one else interested in operating [it]. G.L.F. management then recommended, and the Board approved, that G.L.F. purchase this plant, install some additional and modern equipment, and use it as an experimental pilot plant."

Fallon then said: "While our broiler contract is to date our only active integration project, we are now developing a plan for turkeys, another for pullet rearing, and one for hogs. We have under consideration an even more far-reaching plan. This is a contract or agreement with egg producers."

He made it clear that this was to be an experimental program. He said: "We have no intention of making a contractual arrangement a requirement for marketing eggs through G.L.F. If the contract works out, the farmer will still have a choice—whether he wishes to operate under an agreement or simply to market his eggs as he sees fit, from week to week, as he is now doing." Fallon was sure that integration was advancing in agriculture, and his concern was that farmers control it through their own cooperative so as to preserve their independence.

As G.L.F. became more deeply involved in the Hinsdale processing operation, problems began to develop. The plant was found to be obsolete and poorly located, and expenditures for modern machinery could not be justified by the market outlook. G.L.F. therefore closed the plant in October to stop further loss.[2]

Although optimism for integration was dampened by the closing of the Hinsdale plant, the programs under way were continued, but reduced in scale. This experience demonstrated that integrated operations require careful advance planning and administration if they are to give desired results.[3]

G.L.F. has learned much from its experiments in contractual integration. Out of this experience has recently come a "share the risk" plan of growing broilers whereby the hatchery, the processor, grower, G.L.F. Exchange, and the Service Agencies all participate as risk-bearing partners. This plan is now being used in a limited area. If it proves generally satisfactory it will be more broadly used.

Another late development has been the introduction of an Egg-Feed Agreement which is being tried out on a limited basis. It is not a plan for complete integration since G.L.F. will not own nor manage the flocks. Its

[2] In announcing G.L.F.'s decision to close the plant, Glenn E. Edick, G.L.F. Director of Distribution, said the action was being taken because the "uncertain state of the broiler industry precludes investing at this time in the expansion and mechanization necessary for effective operation." *Olean Times Herald*, October 3, 1959.

[3] In 1959, the boom went out of broiler contracting, and since then farmers have been more skeptical of integration contracts in all parts of the country. The rapid expansion of broiler contracting resulted in over-production and low prices, and brought a shakedown throughout the entire industry. G.L.F. was fortunate in not being more heavily involved.

object is to tie together the use of G.L.F. feeds with the marketing of eggs. Under the agreement the producer will receive 1 cent per dozen premium for all Grade A eggs marketed. In brief, the producer agrees to meet certain conditions in producing eggs of required quality, while G.L.F. agrees to pay a fixed return for eggs in relation to the market. The costs of the program are to be shared by the Mills and Egg Marketing Divisions and by the Service Agency. It is hoped that this plan will improve returns to producers, increase the volumes of feed and other production supplies, and provide a consistent supply of quality eggs for distribution.

New Approaches in Marketing

As G.L.F. gained more experience in integration through contractual arrangements with producers, Fallon saw its application to programs for marketing farm products.

At the meetings of the American Institute of Cooperation, in August, 1958, he said: "I put these two words [marketing and integration] together because I believe that any integration program is going to have marketing as part of it, and that more and more of our marketing activities are going to have some elements of integration." He saw a much closer tie-in developing between purchasing and marketing, and predicted that this trend would snowball in the next few years.

In his annual report, October, 1958, Fallon declared that the need was "tremendous" in the field of marketing. He also stressed that G.L.F. was deeply committed in this field with a marketing volume of 22 million dollars in the Exchange, and another eight million in the Service Agencies. After pointing out that G.L.F. was endeavoring to improve services in marketing eggs, grain and beans, and that members were pressing G.L.F. to experiment with the marketing of potatoes, fruits, vegetables and onions, he said, "We are trying to develop methods of working with other cooperatives, both regional and local, in the development of marketing." Moreover, he foresaw much marketing improvement through integration which he defined as "the tying together, under common ownership or control, of two or more production, processing or marketing functions in the movement of commodities from the raw material stage to the ultimate consumer."

That marketing was fast becoming a major G.L.F. interest became clear in March, 1959, when Fallon gave a carefully prepared talk on "Some Challenges in Marketing New York State Farm Products." In this talk, presented at the regional marketing meetings, he dealt with the changing patterns in marketing, the products being produced and the markets available for them. He said: "No longer can we look at the nearby metropolitan markets as 'ours' exclusively. Everybody has a desire for them; everybody has a stake in them; everybody has a right to them. We are going to have to fight for our share of them." He pointed out that the total value of products marketed by N.Y. State farmers amounted to about $825 million, with dairy products accounting for approximately half of this amount. Livestock and livestock products, including poultry, were next with $179 million. Grain and hay accounted for $36 million; greenhouse and forest products for $57 million; and various fruits and vegetables for $135 million. He emphasized that New York was a significant producer of fifteen main fruit and vegetable crops.

Fallon saw this situation of great advantage to G.L.F. or any other organization which could serve as a "middle marketer," in providing the marketing services between the producer and the retailer. He said, "The cooperative which is going to do a satisfactory job of marketing for its members has to carry out the functions and meet the specifications that we have listed as belonging to the middle marketer." These were: setting up specifications for the final product, procurement, processing, quality control, packaging, storage, promotion, selling, financing, and product development.

He maintained that cooperatives had a great role to play if their leadership was willing to step up on the stage and play it. He called marketing "perhaps the greatest challenge that the leaders of this state have faced in forty years."

He did not believe that G.L.F. could, by itself, meet all of the problems in marketing. He said, "We want to work with any group where we can be constructive in contributing to progress in marketing the crops of this region. . . . In a word, we want to help those farmers and those organizations who are willing to help themselves."[4]

The subject of marketing was given a prominent position in the June Institutional Conference. Fallon gave much the same talk he had given at the Regional Marketing Conferences but under the title, "New Direc-

---

[4] The experience of the Orleans G.L.F. Farm Products Cooperatives, Inc., at Albion, New York, indicates how G.L.F. has worked with a local group of farmers on a marketing program. This organization was set up in July, 1946, with grower ownership and G.L.F. management, to provide improved marketing service for farm produce, mainly apples and onions. In 1951 it built a cold packing plant to process sour cherries, financed by the sale of preferred stock, and in 1959 it constructed a freezer storage to better handle the pack. Since 1953 it has provided complete G.L.F. farm supply service. During the 13 years of operation this cooperative has paid out over $170,000 in cash dividends and refunds, and accumulated a reserve of over $100,000. The manager attributes its success largely to the fact that, from the beginning, grower money has financed the fixed assets. He believes that the sense of ownership has been a major factor in building grower support. Harlan Harvey, letter to author, of March 23, 1960.

tions in Marketing." C. K. Hobbie, Manager of the Marketing Division, then reported on how the policy enunciated by Fallon was being put into effect in one area of marketing through an exploratory study of the fruit and vegetable processing industry in New York State. The object was to "develop a profitable marketing organization controlled by farmers, adequate in size to bargain more effectively with purchasers of fruits and vegetables."

He explained that, following a meeting of key farm leaders, marketing organizations in the area had been surveyed with the assistance of a marketing consultant firm experienced in packing and processing. This preliminary work was now nearing completion, and it would be followed with a study of the feasibility of merging cooperatives to make efficient units for serving farmers. This was admitted to be "an extremely complex endeavor."

After Fallon's talk and Hobbie's report, T. E. Milliman, who was in the audience, said, "This is the first concept of marketing I have ever had confidence in. I am a veteran with scars. I like the way you are going at it—microscopic evaluation of factors. Getting all possible teamwork with others." However, he urged caution in not taking anything for granted and in seeing that producers' interests were protected. His experience in developing a marketing program for fruits and vegetables following the war gave emphasis to his statement that G.L.F. was at last approaching this problem in a proper way.

In October at the annual meeting, President Corwith indicated that in August the Board had authorized an investment of $100,000 in the Seneca Grape Juice Company of Dundee, New York. He said, "This merits some explanation inasmuch as it sets a new pattern of cooperative effort to improve marketing." The Seneca Grape Juice Company had worked out a management contract with the Westfield Maid Grape Company in 1958. This arrangement had been satisfactory and it was thought that it might do the same sort of job for two small apple processing cooperatives. To help it meet this added responsibility, G.L.F. had agreed to invest $100,000 in common stock in the Seneca Grape Juice Company provided certain conditions were met. Corwith then said, "G.L.F. made this investment to help stabilize the apple processing industry in Western New York, through an investment in a company which had proven management . . . and sales ability."

Fallon's drive to improve agricultural marketing methods was well received. In January, 1960, the New York State Horticultural Society, the Empire Potato Club, and the New York Vegetable Growers Association presented him with a citation for his leadership in bringing about an understanding of marketing problems and in devising means for their solution.

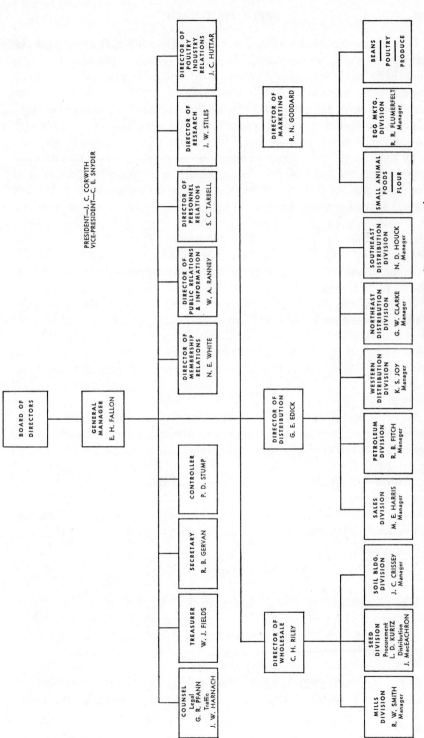

FIGURE 16. G.L.F. ORGANIZATION CHART, MAY, 1960 (PRELIMINARY)

On that occasion—the annual meeting of the State Horticultural Society—he gave a talk entitled, "The 1960's—Feast or Famine for New York Fruit and Vegetable Growers," in which he pointed out that if farmers were to go into "middle-marketing" they must be as good as the best in the field. He saw two areas in the marketing of fruits and vegetables where farmers could become more effective. The first was through bargaining associations, which could do much to bring about more orderly marketing, and reduce competition among farmers. The other big area was in the field of processing which he preferred to describe as middle-marketing, because it represented more than processing. He saw several ways for going further into processing: through direct purchase of a company; by establishing a company; by indirect purchase over a period of time as had been done by growers in acquiring the Welch Grape Juice Company; or by having processing done under contractual agreement, as G.L.F. was doing through its investment in the Seneca Grape Juice Company, an operating processing firm.

None of these possibilities offered a panacea but they provided hope. Fallon summed up by saying: "I can see no prospect of a great boom for fruit and vegetable growers in the 1960's. Nevertheless, I believe this can be a period of steady, substantial progress. We have . . . many natural advantages. We are close to market; the crops we are providing are those that are most in demand, and we are a deficit area for most fruits and vegetables."

He was confident that New York farmers would find the leadership and the means to make real progress in marketing in the 1960's. But he warned that this could be done only through the working together of all agricultural forces. He said: "It is time for the leaders of New York agriculture to sit down around a table and discuss how they can best pool their power, their ideas, their brains and their imagination to do a more effective marketing job for farmers." With G.L.F. support for unified marketing assured, its attainment no longer seems chimerical.

The New Marketing Set-up

The reorganization of 1957 had placed all marketing activities under the Director of Distribution. This arrangement did not provide for clearcut attention on marketing problems, and it also weakened administration of supply distribution operations.

This situation was remedied through a realignment which became effective in April, 1960. It removed all marketing activities from supervision by the Director of Distribution and placed them under the supervision of a Director of Marketing, of equal status with the Director of Wholesale and the Director of Distribution. The revised organization chart is shown in Figure 16.

This change recognizes the growing importance of marketing operations in G.L.F. and provides for their orderly development.

CHAPTER 47

The G.L.F. Today

*G.L.F. is primarily an instrument set up by farmers to provide them
with commodities and services.*

> From Statement of
> G.L.F. Institutional Objectives

U P TO THIS POINT I have endeavored to explain how the G.L.F. came
into being, how it has grown in strength and character, and how it
has adapted itself to the tremendous changes of the past forty years. This
chapter presents a cross-section view of its structure and operations as of
1960.[1]

BASIC PRINCIPLES AND POLICIES

The basic principles on which the G.L.F. was founded remain essentially
unchanged today. It is an agricultural cooperative, whose ownership and
control are vested in its farmer members. Its sole purpose is to serve them
by supplying efficiently and economically the farm production supplies
they need and providing the best market for their farm products. The
principles under which the organization operates have been tested and
proven by time and were reaffirmed in these terms in 1954.

1. G.L.F. is primarily an instrument set up by farmers to provide them with
commodities and services. Therefore, service takes precedence over patronage
refunds and over return on investment but not to a degree that would endanger
financial stability.

2. G.L.F. services, both in purchasing and marketing, are available to anyone
on equal terms based on services rendered.

3. G.L.F. aims to be a pacesetter in quality, price, and service in every commodity handled.

4. It is not G.L.F. policy to achieve a monopoly or near monopoly in any of
the items it handles, or in any community it serves. It is G.L.F. policy to secure
sufficient volume to achieve the most efficient use of facilities and to make available the best possible service to patrons.

5. Each line of commodities and services, once it is past the experimental
stage, is expected to pay its full share of handling costs.

THE MEMBERS

Any person engaged in the commercial production of agricultural products in G.L.F. territory can be a member by buying a share of common

[1] It does not contain information on the size and scope of G.L.F. operations, for
this is available in Appendices D and E.

stock at a cost of $5.00. There are about 118,000 G.L.F. members and of them approximately 75 percent are in New York State, 15 percent in northern Pennsylvania, and 10 percent in New Jersey. Most of the members operate dairy or poultry farms, although many produce specialized cash crops.

Thus about three-fourths of the farmers in G.L.F. territory hold memberships in the Cooperative G.L.F. Exchange, although some are not active or full users of its services. About half of the members account for more than 90 percent of G.L.F.'s total volume of business.

G.L.F. members each have on the average an equity interest in the Exchange of about $400, although their individual equities vary with their investments in G.L.F. stock and their contributions to the reserves according to their patronage. In addition, many members hold substantial equities in G.L.F.-managed retail facilities.

Members obtain supplies and services through retail facilities of five principal types: 1. G.L.F. retail service stores. 2. G.L.F. petroleum distribution corporations. 3. G.L.F. agent-buyers. 4. Independent local cooperatives. 5. Specialized marketing units.

The 226 G.L.F. retail service stores are cooperative corporations, managed by the G.L.F. under a "management agreement" with the members committee for a local store. The fee for management and accounting service is currently set at a maximum of 15 percent of payroll expense. The Exchange holds all of the common stock in trust for the local members who own all of the preferred stock. Member committees, which perform the general functions of a local board of directors, are elected at annual meetings of the members.

The 65 petroleum distributing corporations are managed by the Petroleum Department, with the assistance of a local patron petroleum advisory council comprised of representatives from the member committees of the service stores and agent-buyers in the territory served. About 65 percent of G.L.F.'s wholesale volume is developed through these service stores and petroleum distributing corporations.

The 245 agent-buyers are independent dealers authorized to distribute G.L.F. products and to furnish G.L.F. services in the areas where G.L.F.-managed local cooperatives are not in operation. The agent-buyers maintain records of G.L.F. members' purchases so that Exchange patronage refunds can be paid to them direct. G.L.F. members in the community served by an agent-buyer meet annually and elect a member committee to represent them in dealings with the G.L.F. Exchange and the agent-buyer.

The 20 independent local cooperatives are locally controlled farmer cooperatives who use the G.L.F. as a source for supplies and services. Technically, they are agent-buyers, for they operate under modified agent-buyer franchise agreements. However, they differ in that they are locally supervised by their own boards of directors.[2]

The agent-buyers and local independent cooperatives account for about 35 percent of the G.L.F.'s total wholesale supply volume.

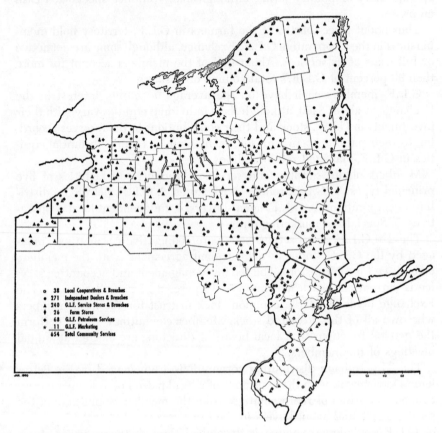

o	38	Local Cooperatives & Branches
•	271	Independent Dealers & Branches
▲	240	G.L.F. Service Stores & Branches
♦	26	Farm Stores
✦	68	G.L.F. Petroleum Services
★	11	G.L.F. Marketing
	654	Total Community Services

FIGURE 17—G.L.F. COMMUNITY SERVICE AGENCIES, JANUARY, 1960

The marketing units which serve members are operated by the G.L.F. Egg and G.L.F. Marketing Divisions. These units do not have separate membership committees but the functions of membership committees are performed for the units in these groups by councils comprised of members who use their services. These councils elect an Egg Marketing Policy

---

[2] In some cases the member committee is separate and distinct from the local board of directors. In other cases the local board serves as the member committee. The member committee has distinct responsibilities in regard to the G.L.F. Exchange. Patronage refunds are not commingled with the refunds of the local cooperative. Refunds from the G.L.F. are paid direct to each G.L.F. member. N. E. White, letter of April 29, 1960, to author.

Board and a Marketing Policy Board. These Boards advise the G.L.F. Board of Directors on matters relating to marketing but they have no local or administrative power.[3]

The G.L.F. members control the G.L.F. primarily through the actions

LEGEND

● 4 Feed Plants
★ 7 Seed Plants (4 at Ft. Wayne, Plymouth, Ind.; Bakersfield, Calif. & Caldwell, Idaho)
○ 14 Fertilizer and Chemical Plants (1 at Baltimore, Md.)
◆ 8 Farm Supply Warehouses
▲ 12 Petroleum Terminals
□ 10 Marketing Plants

FIGURE 18—G.L.F. OPERATING FACILITIES, MAY, 1960

of the member committees of the local stores and agent-buyers. These committees represent them in maintaining effective local service, in selecting nominees for the G.L.F. Board of Directors at district nominating

[3] To achieve liaison, the G.L.F. Board of Directors appoints one of its members to each Board. According to an article in the April, 1959, *Egg Business*, a monthly publication issued by the G.L.F., "The Egg Marketing Policy Board works with the Egg Marketing Division management to recommend operating procedures for the entire Division. . . . This in-between group—the Policy Board—is of vital importance. These 10 men insure an organized, two-way flow of ideas between members and management. They make sure that producers' weight is felt on the scales of decision. Conversely, Policy Board members are able to bring into focus for Councilmen and other poultrymen the 'big picture' as seen through the eyes of G.L.F. marketing specialists."

meetings, in voicing their views at regional and annual meetings, in voting at the annual meeting for directors, or on institutional policies. Members also have an opportunity to express control through mail ballot or in direct voting at the annual meeting for directors, or for or against proposed changes in policies. Moreover, they also have a primary influence on management by giving or withdrawing their patronage. A decline in the use of a service is a vote for its improvement or discontinuance, while an increase in volume registers member satisfaction.

To intelligently control the G.L.F., members must be well-informed on its services, commodities and methods. They obtain their knowledge of the G.L.F. through a wide variety of sources: Radio, T. V., direct mail, newspaper and magazine articles and advertisements, the *G.L.F. Week*, *Egg Business*, the annual report, special reports, contacts of patrons with G.L.F. employees, and various kinds of meetings where G.L.F. programs and plans are presented and discussed.

The G.L.F. provides members with broad and varied services. It helps them obtain the type and quality of supplies desired to best serve their needs. It helps them in marketing their farm products. It performs many services of value to them in their farming operations. For example, the insurance program provides members with group insurance at reasonable cost. It is hard to put a value on these various services which help the members meet their farming problems in the most economical and efficient manner and which add to satisfactions of farm living.

Members also receive benefits in the form of direct savings. From time to time they receive patronage refunds either through the Exchange or through their local service stores. As of June 30, 1959, these have totaled $52,689,087 since the G.L.F. was formed. In addition to their direct savings reflected in cash patronage refunds, members during this period have increased their ownership interest in the Exchange and the local G.L.F. Stores by $39,108,723 through retained margins.

Even more significant have been the savings to members resulting from the price-influencing effect of the G.L.F. Since prices to members reflect only the costs of maintaining and strengthening the institution, it provides a standard of pricing which gauges the fairness of charges for all farm services. Price-reducing benefits are thus diffused to all farmers in G.L.F. territory.

The Exchange also provides a safe investment for farmers in their own business. Cash dividends on capital paid by the combined G.L.F. system amounted to $22,596,467 as of June 30, 1959.

A major benefit to members has come from representation on matters relating to agriculture. The G.L.F. system of organizations gives farmers an opportunity to participate in affairs pertaining to their industry. It helps build farm leadership and increases farmers' economic understanding. Its encouragement of research has also been of general benefit to Northeastern agriculture.

The G.L.F. not only renders a wide variety of useful economic services for its members but it also joins with other organizations to promote programs of common value. The Empire Livestock Marketing Cooperative, the P & C Food Markets, the Mohawk Airlines, and many similar organizations or activities have come into existence largely through the sponsorship or encouragement of the G.L.F.

The Board of Directors

Although the ultimate strength of the organization resides in its members, the governing power of the organization is expressed through its democratically-elected Board of Directors. The members look to the Board to represent their broad interests which must be organized and centered in one place. The Board formulates policies and sees that these policies are made effective by G.L.F. employees. The Board secures an annual outside audit by a recognized accounting firm and uses the budget process to maintain control over programs and expenditures. It also provides for continuing management through selection of its General Manager and officers.

The procedure for nominating the Directors through meetings of member committeemen, held in electoral districts, provides men who are carefully selected to represent the basic interests of the membership. It is difficult to appraise the quality of a Board of Directors, but it is significant that the G.L.F. Board is generally recognized as being comprised of men of high principles, good judgment, and special competence. They are conscientious in the performance of their duties, and rarely miss a Board meeting. They serve without compensation except for per diem and travel expenses while on official business.

The Board is comprised of 14 Directors, 10 of whom are selected to represent 10 designated electoral districts. (See Figure 6, p. 341.) Two of the other four are nominated by the New York State Grange, and the remaining two by the New York Farm Bureau.[4] These four Directors give representation to two of the farm organizations who helped found the G.L.F. The third, the Dairymen's League, voluntarily gave up its right to nominate Directors.

The Directors meet in scheduled meetings for two or three-day periods six to eight times a year, with the Manager and other officers present. They employ the Manager and the Secretary, Treasurer, Controller, and General Counsel, although the latter four officers are responsible to the General Manager. They place on the General Manager full responsibility for execution of all Board policies.

[4] This is the present name of the New York State Farm Bureau Federation.

In February, 1958, the directors approved a statement which defines the respective functions of the Board and the General Manager. This indicates that the Board and General Manager are to work closely together to represent the interests of the members. It declared: "The Directors are trustees of the interests of the farmer-stockholders who own and use G.L.F. Each Director represents all members, not simply his own district, nor any specific commodity interest. . . . The Board is responsible for policy, management for operations. The Board of Directors is responsible for: (a) determining the policies under which G.L.F. shall operate; (b) authorizing the general line of commodities and services which are offered by G.L.F.; (c) selecting the general officers and the general manager; and (d) supervising and holding management accountable by means of an annual budget and annual outside audit and periodic reports from management."

This statement holds that "Principles are the fundamental cornerstones of a corporation," while "policies are the ground rules or guides which interpret these principles and put them into action." The principles can be changed only by the members through revisions of the bylaws.

The statement makes clear that the Directors make all decisions on policies.[5] The Manager is authorized to take whatever action is necessary to execute these policies.

The statement of relationship also contains an interesting provision designed to safeguard communications: "[Top] management has the responsibility of informing the Board of actions which may be expected to have important effects in public, membership, or personnel relations."

During the past forty years G.L.F. has achieved a highly effective Board-Manager relationship. Continuous liaison with the General Manager is maintained by the President of the organization. The General Manager keeps him closely informed on programs and operations so that he can evaluate them in the light of G.L.F. policies.[6]

In carrying on its work the Board makes use of several committees. Of primary importance are the Executive and Budget Committees.

[5] "The Board is a freezer of recommendations and principles into policy. Once the Board acts officially in respect to certain recommendations or principles, and makes them policy, they remain as guide lines to the institution. . . . More than any Board I've ever known, this Board performs the functions of a board the way a board is supposed to. It has no pressure coming from a concentrated stockholding; the members are active farmers whose main source of funds come from their own farming operations. They are not professional directors as so often is the case yet they are well enough grounded to be effective in moulding general policy." Letter of James A. McConnell, to author, of April 11, 1960.

[6] McConnell also remarks on this: "My Board . . . was of tremendous value to me in counseling and in meeting emergencies. A strong Board gave me courage and determination." He also said: "The Board furnishes a backdrop, so to speak, against which management projects its ideas and recommendations . . . very important." Letter of April 11, 1960.

The Executive Committee is composed of the President, Vice President, Chairman of the Budget Committee, and two other members. It represents the Board between regular meetings but is used sparingly, as a special meeting of the full Board is called on any matter of great importance.[7]

The Budget Committee of seven, which includes the President and Vice President as Ex Officio members, works closely with the Controller (the G.L.F. Budget Director) and operating executives in developing the annual budget and in checking up on performance under it. The members of this committee keep themselves well-informed on all G.L.F. operations.

The Service and Quality Control Committee is composed of C. G. White, Chairman, and the entire Board of Directors. This Committee is responsible for maintaining G.L.F. quality standards.

Five committees, with three or four members each, carry on a continuing detailed study of the important divisions, which involves annual inspection of facilities used and interviews with key operating personnel. These committees are designated: 1. Mills; 2. Soil-Building; 3. Farm Supplies; 4. Retail Services; and 5. Marketing. The members are rotated annually so that over a period of years most directors get a close working knowledge of all parts of the organization.

The G.L.F. as an Operating Organization

How is the Exchange organized to do its job? We will now look at the G.L.F. as an operating organization.

As chief executive in the G.L.F. structure, the General Manager must put into effect the policies and achieve the objectives set by the Board of Directors. It is important therefore that we see how the General Manager and his operating staff meet this total responsibility.

As shown by the Chart of Organization, Figure 16, G.L.F. is organized to perform wholesale, distribution, and marketing functions. The services relating to the procurement, manufacture and wholesaling of feed, fertilizer and seeds, are grouped under a Director of Wholesale Operations. All services relating to distribution of supplies or services to farmers are supervised by the Director of Distribution. As we will see later, the Director of Distribution is also responsible for wholesale functions performed for farm supplies and petroleum products under integrated programs. The Director of Marketing is responsible for all marketing operations, although some marketing activities are carried on jointly with the Area Distribution Divisions.

In an organization as comprehensive as the G.L.F., there are many functions that must be centrally administered. Those on the top line of

[7] For more complete information see Section 7 of Article II of the Bylaws, given in Appendix A.

the organization chart help the General Manager carry on the general job of management. With the Directors of Wholesale, Distribution, and Marketing, they make up the Manager's staff. Let us briefly examine their duties.

The Secretary. The Secretary is responsible for maintaining all of the official records of the organization. He schedules Board Meetings, executes corporate documents, records minutes of the Board and Stockholders' Meetings, and keeps track of all the corporate records of the organization and its subsidiaries. He supervises procedure for the election of Directors. He functions also as Assistant to the General Manager and represents him as a member of various committees.

The Treasurer. The Treasurer is responsible for the custody and control of all money and securities and for the development and implementation of financial planning for the Exchange and its subsidiaries. As chief financial officer of the Exchange he assists and advises the General Manager on the general financial affairs of the institution. He supervises and controls all corporate borrowing, the hypothecating of securities, the encumbering of property, and the concentration and redistribution of institutional funds as they flow between wholesale and retail operations. The primary objective of the Treasurer is to maintain the financial strength of the organization.

The General Counsel. The General Counsel advises the General Manager and the Board of Directors upon the legal implications of policies and operational proposals. He is responsible for performing legal services for the G.L.F. and all of its subsidiary corporations. He handles or supervises a substantial amount of commercial and contract legal work for the various G.L.F. affiliates. He represents the G.L.F. in dealings with the Securities Exchange Commission; the National Labor Relations Board; the Federal Communication Commission; the Federal Trade Commission; the Bureau of Internal Revenue; various State Departments in New York, Pennsylvania, and New Jersey; and other administrative agencies.

The Traffic Counsel. The Traffic Counsel coordinates the work of separate traffic departments in the operating divisions. He negotiates freight rate adjustments; attends rate-making conferences; maintains relations with carriers and regulatory bodies; advises management on plant location, significant developments in transportation and coordinates and assists the training and development of traffic department personnel.

The Controller. The Controller function in G.L.F. encompasses responsibilities for: (1) general accounting; (2) internal auditing; (3) taxes; (4) financial reporting; (5) methods and systems; (6) industrial engineering; (7) facilities engineering and real estate; and (8) office management. The Controller is responsible for the data processing center, central payroll, maintenance of buildings and grounds, servicing of the G.L.F. School and the general management of the headquarters office properties. He is the chief accounting officer of the G.L.F. as well as its budget director. He carries on his responsibilities through a staff of specialists and 9 division controllers.

Director of Personnel. The Director of Personnel is responsible for maintaining good personnel practices and performance. He formulates and supervises policies relating to such employee matters as selection and placement, management development, compensation, benefits, communications, safety, and regulations involving personnel. He is also responsible for initiation, coordination and control of approved personnel policies, working through line or staff personnel as the situation requires. Matters involving organized labor and labor contracts for all divisions are delegated to the Director of Employee Relations of the Mills Division.

Director of Member Relations. The Director of Member Relations is responsible for seeing that the interests of members are properly recognized in the operations of the G.L.F. It is his job to see that members are kept properly informed and given an opportunity to actively participate in the affairs of the organization. The Director of Member Relations is responsible for the maintenance of all membership records, the planning and conduct of membership meetings, promotion of the members' insurance program, and similar activities relating to the membership.

The Director of Research. The Director of Research is responsible for correlating, coordinating and directing all G.L.F. research activities. He is responsible for searching out research opportunities and supervising research programs to enable the G.L.F. to meet rapidly changing industrial and agricultural conditions. As indicated in Chapter 46, the direct research work done by the G.L.F. is primarily of two types: (a) applied research, which is designed to put into effect research findings of colleges or other research institutions; or (b) market research, which is carried on primarily to determine market potentials and opportunities.

Public Relations and Information. The Director of Public Relations and Information is responsible for helping the General Manager establish and maintain basic policies and procedures essential to good internal and external communication and relations. He assists the staff and division managers in carrying out these policies and procedures, in keeping with the principles, character and current objectives of the G.L.F. He maintains liaison with the government agencies, agricultural colleges, civic organizations, and others on matters of interest to G.L.F. All institutional publications, such as *G.L.F. Week,* the Annual Report, the Directory, Calendar of Events, annual meeting literature, and similar materials are issued under his direction. His primary function is to recommend meas-

ures and disseminate information which will strengthen the standing of
the G.L.F. with the public and enhance its good will.

The Job of the General Manager

There is no written job description for the position of General Manager. He must interpret broad policy and see that the organization as a
whole functions smoothly and achieves desired results. He must set an
example and obtain the cooperation of all employees in meeting institutional objectives. He must see that all parts of the organization run
smoothly. He must see that programs are kept moving. He must have a
system for reviewing the performance of those who report direct to
him. Moreover, he must represent the G.L.F. in many public matters and
meetings.

The General Manager uses a number of standing committees to help
him manage. These committees study, review, and recommend, but do
not make management decisions, for this responsibility cannot be delegated. Important committees of this type are the Planning Committee, the
Sales Board, the Fixed Assets Committee, and the Methods and Systems
Policy Committee.

The Planning Committee, instituted in February, 1958, is composed
of the General Manager, Secretary, Treasurer, Controller, Director of
Wholesale, and Director of Distribution. In a way, it serves as a cabinet
for the General Manager. It receives periodic reports from operating
divisions and occasional reports from staff departments, and considers
major plans and programs. Any significant program goes before the Planning Committee before it is submitted by the Manager to the Board. The
member insurance plan, for example, was developed by the Planning
Committee before it was presented for Board approval.

The Sales Board is composed of the General Manager, Director of Distribution, Director of Wholesale, the Secretary, and the Manager of the
Sales Division. It meets monthly to consider plans for major sales programs.
Each month, sales results for the previous month are reported and compared with volume goals. Reports on major sales programs that have been
completed are also given. The Sales Board reviews the advertising budget,
and approves or modifies the Planned Action Calendar. It is also the group
which reviews proposals for major new commodity lines.

The Fixed Assets Committee is composed of the Treasurer, Traffic Counsel, Director of Distribution, and Director of Wholesale. All proposals for
fixed assets expenditures in excess of $25,000 have to be presented to this
committee before they are taken to the Board of Directors or the Retail
Board.

The Methods and Systems Policy Committee, under the Chairmanship
of the Controller, considers systemwide applications of advanced tech-

niques. For example, this committee carefully considered the advisability of establishing centralized inventory control for the farm supplies warehouses before a data processing system was installed.

The General Manager also makes use of special committees as needs arise. For example, the 40th Anniversary Committee made the plans for celebrating the 40th anniversary. The Forage Committee developed the Five-Star Forage Plan. The Integration Committee has worked out various problems arising from integration.

Reference here should also be made to the Retail Board although technically it is not part of the General Manager's apparatus.

The Retail Board serves as the Board of Directors for all Service Stores, petroleum plants and marketing units which are technically incorporated subsidiaries of the G.L.F. Exchange. The Retail Board is composed of G.L.F. executives, selected by the Board of Directors upon the recommendation of the General Manager. Its officers are W. J. Fields, President, and R. B. Gervan, Vice-President. Although he is not a member of the Retail Board, the General Manager serves as its Chairman.

The Retail Board performs all the legal acts that are necessary in the operation of these subsidiary retail corporations. This may involve chartering, dissolving, or merging corporations; granting authorization for borrowing and mortgaging; and making appropriations for fixed assets. The Retail Board usually adopts the recommendations of the member committees which serve as informal boards of directors for the stores or other subsidiary units. However, frequently, proposals are returned to the local committees for further study and revision before acceptance.

Now let us see how the wholesale, distribution, and marketing operations are performed.

THE WHOLESALE SERVICES

The Director of Wholesale is responsible for all of the activities of the organization relating to the procurement, processing, manufacturing, and wholesale distribution of feeds, fertilizers, insecticides, and seeds. He supervises and coordinates the three specialized wholesale divisions: the Mills Division, the Seed Division, and the Soil Building Division. The managers of the wholesale divisions are responsible for a wide range of activities in the field of research, development of specifications, purchasing, formulation, production, quality control, commodity information, pricing, transportation, storage and delivery to retail.

The Mills Division. The Mills Division is of great importance in the G.L.F. since feed accounts for over half of G.L.F.'s business volume. The Mills Division, with headquarters at Buffalo, N. Y., operates major feed plants at Buffalo, Albany and Binghamton, N. Y., and at Bordentown, N. J. These mills have quality control laboratories, bulk-loading facilities, truck-loading facilities, elevator storage, modern quality-control laboratories, and other facilities essential to perform effective service. In recent years, Mills has been handling an increasing proportion of feed in pelleted form, and bulk operations have steadily grown in importance. Superintendents at each mill report to a production manager who, in turn, reports to the manager of the Mills Division.

The Seed Divisions. The Seed Division is currently split into two parts. All western operations, which are primarily related to procurement, are supervised by the Manager of Seed Procurement, located at Fort Wayne, Indiana. Distribution and other seed operations within the G.L.F. territory are the responsibility of the Manager of Seed Distribution, located at Buffalo. These coordinate parts of the Seed Division report separately to the Director of Wholesale. The Seed Procurement Division supervises the operations of seed plants in Bakersfield, California; Caldwell, Idaho; Plymouth and Fort Wayne, Indiana. The Seed Distribution Division supervises plants in Buffalo and Warners, New York, and Bordentown, New Jersey.

The Soil Building Division. The Soil Building Division operates 12 fertilizer plants plus one chemical plant in G.L.F. territory. These plants are operated under the general direction of a production manager with a plant superintendent in charge of each plant. He reports to the manager of the Soil Building Division, located at Ithaca, who is in charge of all soil building operations. The G.L.F. is also part owner of a fertilizer manufacturing cooperative at Baltimore. The Purchasing Department of the Soil Building Division is located in New York City. The Division maintains a quality-control and research development laboratory in Ithaca. Much of its work is related to insecticides.

The Distribution Services

The managers of the five divisions which are responsible for distribution of products to farmers report to the Director of Distribution. Since each division is an operating unit within itself, the Director of Distribution must keep balance between them in services, sales and operations. This system of organization allows for specialization both in sales and operations.

Two of the divisions which report to the Director of Distribution also perform related wholesale functions. Thus, the Sales Division both procures and distributes farm supplies, while the Petroleum Division procures petroleum products and distributes them to farmers through its own system of retail agencies.

The three Area Distribution Divisions are strictly retail divisions in that they direct and supervise retail operations for specified territories.

Let's look more closely at the way the Sales Division operates.

The Sales Division. The Manager of the Sales Division is held responsible for overall administration of G.L.F. sales policies and procedures, and for liaison relations with the Wholesale Divisions. The Sales Division has four departments.

Of major importance is the Farm Supplies Department which distributes farm supplies to retail agencies. Prior to the reorganization of 1957, this department was known as the Wholesale Farm Supplies Division. It purchases all farm supplies merchandise and supervises the eight wholesale farm supplies warehouses which provide weekly delivery service to each retail agency. It operates four garages which develop, build, and repair special equipment such as bulk-feed trucks, lime-spreaders, and petroleum trucks. It supervises the installation, repair and parts services for mechanical equipment.

All purchasing for the Farm Supplies Department is supervised by a Director of Purchasing. His counterpart is the Farm Supplies Sales Manager who is responsible for moving farm supply commodities from the agency to the ultimate consumer. Five commodity technical men who provide assistance to retail agencies through sale and service of mechanical items report to him.

The Seed and Soil Building Sales Department is headed by a seed and soil building sales manager who has the responsibility of developing sales volume for these commodities. He has a staff of technical field men located throughout G.L.F. territory. His department serves as a bridge between the Seed and Soil Building Wholesale Divisions and the retail service agencies that help the wholesale divisions get their supplies into the hands of farmers.

The Feed Sales Department is the third operating department. The manager of the Feed Sales Department is responsible for developing sales policies and programs for G.L.F. formula-feed and related feed items, and maintaining liaison between the Mills Division and the retail agencies. His staff includes three poultry specialists.

The three commodity sales managers implement their programs through the Sales Managers in the three Distribution Divisions who, in turn, work through the district sales managers and the retail agencies.

Each Sales Division Manager is also assisted by a personnel supervisor and a controller who is in charge of accounting for the Division. The personnel supervisor is expected to provide leadership in sales training for the area divisions.

The Advertising and Sales Promotion Department provides leadership in sales and advertising programs on all Exchange commodities. It is made up of advertising and sales promotion specialists for various products and it also maintains the mailing service. It prepares and places space and broadcast advertising, produces pamphlets, brochures, point-of-sale and other advertising aids, and publishes specialized publications such as *Egg Business.*

The Petroleum Division. This division provides an integrated whole-sale-retail petroleum service. It distributes products to patrons from 65 bulk plants and two branch plants. Each of these bulk plants is a separate corporation having an advisory council composed of representatives of the Member Committees in its operating territory. The wholesale Department of the Petroleum Division operates 8 G.L.F.-owned terminals, while 6 others are used on a lease basis. These terminals, located on the waterways and pipelines in the G.L.F. area, make possible the use of liquid products from the Texas City Refinery. This Division operates through 7 territory district managers who supervise retail distribution operations. Each district manager has a territory of from 9 to 10 bulk plants and one or two terminals. All of the bulk plants now have burner service departments, and a few are experimentally distributing petroleum products through filling stations.

The Three Area Divisions. The reorganization of 1953 set up three area retail divisions. These are now known as the Western, Northeast and Southeast Distribution Divisions. Each area division has a Distribution Manager in charge, assisted by a Division Sales Manager, Operations Manager, Personnel Supervisor, and a Controller.

Prior to the reorganization of 1957, all of the district field managers reported to the area manager. Some worked direct with Stores while others worked with Agent-Buyers. Under the reorganization, the same field manager works with Stores and Agent-Buyers, segregated according to function.

One group is designated District Operations Managers, and they report direct to the District Distribution Manager. The District Operations Managers are responsible for maintaining sound local operations. They help plan needed facilities and advise on finances, services, personnel, equipment, and other related business problems. They aid with training programs and assist in planning and conducting meetings. They work with the local member committees and local managers to maintain the membership support and public relations essential to a sound cooperative business serving local needs.

The other group of district managers are designated District Sales Managers, and they report to the Area Sales Manager who supervises all sales activities within the area. The District Sales Managers are responsible for the volume of G.L.F. commodities distributed in their districts. They work with the local service agencies in meeting volume objectives. They help plan volume building programs and advise the local managers or agents on display, advertising, mailing lists and farm calls. They are also responsible for surveys of community volume potentials and for developing special commodity programs.

This method of dual field organization calls for skillful coordination of the work of the District Operations Managers with that of the District Sales Managers. This is a major responsibility of the area distribution manager.[8]

THE MARKETING SERVICES

An organizational change in April, 1960, placed all general marketing operations under the supervision of a Director of Marketing who, like the Directors of Wholesale and Distribution, reports direct to the General Manager. (See Figure 16, p. 457.) Marketing covers procurement, processing and sale of farm products.

Under the plan of organization, which has not yet been fully developed, the Director of Marketing will be assisted by a Controller and a Sales Manager. The Manager of the Livestock Contracting Department, who formerly reported to the Manager of the Sales Division, will now report to the Director of Marketing. This is a logical arrangement in that this department deals with integrated marketing programs involving the use of contracts with livestock (including poultry) producers.

The primary work in marketing will be carried on by commodity divisions or marketing departments, with one man in complete charge for each commodity. These will cover (a) eggs, (b) poultry, (c) beans, (d) flour and cereals, (e) produce, and (f) small animal foods. This form of organization provides for specialized attention to each distinct type of marketing activity.[9]

The Egg Marketing Division. This Division will operate eight centrally located stations where eggs are graded according to quality; candled and cartoned for delivery to supermarkets. The recently installed electronic grading, candling and packing machine at its Weedsport

---

[8] A significant change occurred in the organization of the area offices while this chapter was in galley proof (June 1960). It eliminates the dual District Manager set-up and reverts to the former system under which the District Manager is responsible for both sales and operations. Under the new plan the area Division Managers are assisted by a staff consisting of (1) Controller, (2) Farm Supplies Sales Manager, (3) Feed-seed, Fertilizer Sales Manager, (4) Personnel and Membership Manager, (5) Operations Manager, and (6) Credit Manager. The District Managers report direct to the area Division Manager. This plan in no way de-emphasizes sales effort and continues sales responsibility in the Sales Division. It is believed that the plan will meet the following objectives: (a) better and more direct supervision, (b) clear-cut lines of authority, (c) more time to work more with agent-buyers, (d) more time to work with committees, (e) good general acceptance by employees and committees. It is estimated that the plan will achieve more effective administration with a saving of approximately $75,000 in travel and personnel costs.

[9] Letter of Ronald N. Goddard, Director of Marketing, of May 5, 1960, to author.

plant promises to save thousands of dollars in lowered costs. The Egg
Marketing Division is now experimenting with producer agreements to
provide premiums to those producers who deliver regularly a high quality
product.

The Bean Division. This Division will operate the two bean-processing
plants. Its services are well established in Western New York where beans
are an important crop.

The Flour Department. This department now manufactures and sells
a specialty flour from locally produced grain. It has a steady but modest
volume of business.

Produce Department. This department will be responsible for marketing onions and later other fresh produce. It operates through G.L.F.
Produce, Inc.

Pet Foods Department. This is a specialized department now producing pet foods for members and non-members. It deals with a specialty
trade and requires specialist direction.

As indicated in Chapter 46, the G.L.F. is now working with other
groups to develop a better marketing system for fruits and vegetables.
This effort will no doubt be intensified by the Director of Marketing.

In this chapter I have endeavored not only to show how G.L.F. carries on its work but also to convey something of the spirit with which the
work is done. The final chapter will consider briefly G.L.F.'s capacity to
meet the problems lying ahead.

CHAPTER 48

To Meet the Future

I see plenty of problems ahead for G.L.F., but I see a dynamic, experienced managerial team to meet them, backed by a well-balanced Board of Farmer Directors and supported by a well-informed membership of farmers.

> James C. Corwith
> President of the G.L.F.
> In letter to author, April 10, 1960

THIS BOOK has endeavored to show how a great farmers' cooperative was born, and how it grew and matured. It illustrates how farmers can organize to carry on large affairs essential to their wellbeing. As we come to the end of our story the question naturally arises, "Where does the G.L.F. go from here?"

The answer, of course, depends upon many things beyond the cooperative's control or the farmer's control. But it also depends upon the ability of the organization itself to meet the great economic, agricultural and social challenges that lie ahead.

The 40-year record gives much assurance that G.L.F. will be able to solve problems as they arise. The organization has already survived a technological revolution in agriculture and demonstrated the capacity to adapt its structure and operations to continually changing needs.

The environment in which the G.L.F. now operates is far different from what it was in 1920. Then there were 273,000 farms in the territory now served. The average size of farm was 102 acres and the average farm represented an investment in land and buildings of $6,624.

Our latest census figures, for 1954, show only 158,000 farms in this same area, or only 58 percent of the number in 1920. On the other hand, the average size of farm has increased to 131 acres, or by 28 percent, while the average investment per farm has increased to $16,139, or by 144 percent.

This change is even more strikingly illustrated by data for the township of Dryden, New York, over a forty-year period, as given on the next page.[1]

These facts explain partially why the G.L.F. is so different today from what it was forty years ago, and there is every reason to expect a continuation of these trends in the years ahead. The number of farms will

[1] See *Farm Economics*, Cornell University, March 1959, pp. 5749-5752.

	1917	1957
Number of farms	159	65
Total acres per farm	148	225
Cows per farm	10	35
Pounds of milk sold per cow	4,412	8,493
Cash receipts per farm	$ 2,338	$17,223
Cash expenses per farm	$ 1,302	$13,879
Capital investment per farm	$10,300	$46,000

no doubt continue to decrease, while their average size will increase. There will be fewer economic units engaged in farming, but they will be more specialized and more mechanized.[2] The process of economic integration will continue to expand—either from the farm forward, or backward to the farm.

One of the striking things about the G.L.F.'s ability to meet its problems in the past has been its flexibility. It has not only adjusted to change but it has often led in the changes. It has always been an innovator. It has started many new ideas and new methods which are now accepted practices with cooperative and other business organizations. These have been described in this book and I will not recapitulate them here.

The G.L.F. is a good demonstration of democracy in action, and it is perhaps more democratic today than at any time in its history. It has learned how to operate effectively under centralized direction and, at the same time, it has devised procedures to insure democratic control.

While G.L.F. has recognized that competent business administration is essential to effective cooperative organization and operation, it has understood that intelligent membership administration is of equal importance in building and maintaining a strong *cooperative* business enterprise.

Throughout its existence the Board of Directors has assumed responsibility, whenever necessary, as was demonstrated in the managerial crisis of 1922. Without interfering with prerogatives delegated to management employees, it has seen that these responsibilities were accepted and met.

From the beginning, the G.L.F. has manifested a high sense of civic responsibility. Its large-scale support of public research has been unique among cooperative organizations. Few business groups have done as much for the general welfare of agriculture.

G.L.F. has great assets as it goes into the future. These include: well-defined objectives, oriented to serving farmers; established principles and

[2] See talk by Dr. L. C. Cunningham, of Cornell University, at Northeastern Dairy Conference, April, 1960, *Dairy Farm Adjustments in the Nineteen Sixties,* (typewritten).

policies; democratic membership control and good membership support; dynamic leadership; competent operating management; able and conscientious directors; high quality standards for its products and membership services; a deep-seated respect for research and planning; a strong financial structure; excellent *esprit de corps;* a well-developed sense of civic and community responsibility; a form of organization forged on the anvil of experience; and the momentum given by a long record of accomplishment.

As a good heritage helps build a strong family, the record of the G.L.F. gives great promise of its ability to meet tomorrow's problems.

APPENDICES

APPENDICES

APPENDIX A

Certificate of Incorporation and By-Laws

Certificate of Incorporation

(As Amended)

WE, THE UNDERSIGNED, all being persons of full age, and at least two-thirds citizens of the United States, and one or more of us being residents of the State of New York, desiring to form a cooperative corporation pursuant to the Business Corporations Law of the State of New York, and more particularly as provided for in Article III, Sections twenty-five to thirty-eight inclusive, of said Law [now Article VII of the Cooperative Corporations Law] do hereby make, sign, acknowledge and file for that purpose, this certificate, as follows:

First—The name of the proposed corporation is *Cooperative Grange League Federation Exchange, Inc.*

Second—The purposes for which it is to be formed are:

(1) To purchase as a going concern, acquire, take over, continue, carry on, enlarge, expand and otherwise avail of the assets, property, good will and business of the New York Grange Exchange, Inc., a corporation duly organized and existing under and by virtue of the laws of the State of New York and carry forward the same in the manner and for the purposes herein set forth, such acquisition to be accomplished by purchase or such other lawful means as may be found available and expedient.

(2) To engage in and conduct business with special reference to supplying needs of members of the New York State Grange Order of Patrons of Husbandry, the Dairymen's League Cooperative Association, Inc., and the New York State Federation of County Farm Bureau Associations and other farmers and agricultural producers in the State of New York and adjacent regions and throughout the territory and possessions of the United States and elsewhere, who shall be its patrons and for whom it shall do business, and to that end primarily for the mutual help and benefit of its shareholders, employees and patrons, to conduct a general producing, manufacturing and merchandising business on the cooperative plan, in articles of common use, including farm products, food supplies, farm machinery and supplies, and articles of domestic and personal use, and buying, selling or leasing homes, or farms for members.

To the ends aforesaid and in furtherance of the said business and enterprises so by it to be conducted and carried forward, and for the purpose of fulfilling and accomplishing the same, it shall have, enjoy and exercise the following specific powers insofar as the same or any thereof shall be incidental and necessary to the exercise of the powers hereinbefore set forth, but the specific powers hereinafter enumerated shall in no wise constitute or be construed as constituting any curtailment or limitation of the general powers enumerated above.

(3) To produce, manufacture, buy, acquire, rent, exchange, lease, rebuild or repair and otherwise deal in and with, at wholesale and retail, either as princi-

483

pal or agent or on consignment, commission or otherwise, any such articles, supplies, commodities or things as may be so necessary or useful including plows, harrows, harvesters, binders, reapers, mowers, rakes, headers, shredders, presses and agricultural machinery of all kinds; wagons, tools and implements of all kinds; twine and wire for use with all or any thereof, together with repair parts and devices, materials and articles used or intended for use in connection with any of the same. Also tractors, motors, boilers, engines and all means for generating, transmitting or using powers; automobiles, carriages, and all other vehicles, belting, packing repair parts, devices and the like fully and in the manner as above more particularly set forth.

(4) To produce, make, acquire and deal in and with groceries, meats, fish, hardware, dry goods, furniture, drugs, medicines, boots and shoes, provisions, fertilizers, farm and household supplies and personal effects of every kind and nature, paint, putty, lead and oils; plumbers, blacksmiths, mill, foundry, steamboat, tramway, miners, machinists and all other supplies and fixtures, metals and material; fibres, rubber, gums, resins and oils of all kinds, and their products; coal, wood and other fuel; lumber, timber, stone, brick, tile, cement, sand, lime, plaster and building material of all kinds; dynamite, gunpowder and other explosives; sporting goods and amusement supplies, including books, papers, newspapers, periodicals, publications, pictures and moving pictures, together with frames, equipment, supplies, booths, projecting machines and all other accessories necessary or useful in connection with the same or any thereof.

(5) To produce, raise, purchase, sell, trade and deal in, store, mill, grind, blend, prepare, warehouse, forward and ship grains, cereals, feeds, flour, bran, hay, grass, clover, alfalfa, fruits, vegetables, milk, cream, butter, cheese, sugar, tobacco and generally all products of the soil and things produced therefrom or useful to be handled or dealt in, in connection therewith, and the derivatives of or products from the same.

(6) To apply for, obtain, register, purchase, lease or otherwise acquire, and to hold, own, use, operate under and introduce, sell, assign or otherwise dispose of any and all copyrights, trademarks, tradenames, design patents and rights used in connection with or secured by design patents of the United States, or of any foreign country, or protecting or to be protected by the copyright or design patent laws of the United States, or otherwise, and to use, exercise, develop, rent, license in respect of, or in any manner turn to account such copyrights, trademarks, tradenames, patents, licenses and the like or any of the same.

(7) To apply for, receive, register, take assignment of, or otherwise acquire, hold and operate under licenses, and grant licenses and sub-licenses in respect of, pay and receive royalties and emoluments for the use of, sell, assign, lease or otherwise dispose of patents, patent rights, letters patent or any thereof, issued by the Government of the United States or by any other Government or authority; as also applications for patents domestic or foreign, processes and formulae, secret or otherwise, including improvements on any of the same; useful or deemed by it to be useful, in or in connection with the said business or the manufacture or use of the articles or things so to be acquired, manufactured, dealt in, utilized or disposed of by said corporation.

(8) To purchase, subscribe for, acquire, hold and dispose of stocks, bonds and evidences of indebtedness of any corporation, domestic or foreign, and to issue in exchange therefor its stocks, bonds or other obligations, and while

owner of any such stocks, bonds or other obligations of any other corporation, to possess and exercise in respect thereof all the rights, powers and privileges of individual owners or holders of the same, and to exercise any and all voting powers thereupon, or by reason of such ownership. To aid in any manner permitted by law, any corporation or association issuing any bonds or other securities or evidences of indebtedness or stock so held by this corporation, and to do any act or acts, thing or things, to protect, preserve, improve or enhance the value of any such bonds or other securities or evidences of indebtedness or stock, so far as permitted by the Business Corporations Law.

(9) To purchase or otherwise acquire all or any part of the business, good will, rights, property and assets of all kinds, and assume all or any part of the liabilities of any corporation, association, partnership or person engaged in any business, included in the powers or objects of this corporation. To acquire and take over as a going concern, and to carry on the business of any person, firm, association or corporation engaged in any business which this corporation is authorized to carry on, or, in connection therewith, to acquire the good will, and all or any part of the assets, and to assume or otherwise provide for all or any of the liabilities of the owner or owners of such business.

(10) To adopt such means of making known the benefits of cooperation and the advantages offered by this corporation and the products dealt in by it, or anything produced, handled or manufactured in the course of its business, as may seem expedient, and in particular by advertising the same through the press, magazines, books, circulars and publications of all kinds whatsoever, including photographs, motion pictures and works of art and by the publication, exhibition and distribution of the same, or any thereof.

(11) To purchase, lease, or otherwise acquire, erect, construct, improve, hold, occupy, use, manage, rent, sell or otherwise dispose of lands, plants, mills, factories, stores, warehouses, machine shops, dwellings, buildings, and all other property, real, personal or mixed, wheresoever situated, and to mortgage, exchange and dispose of the same.

(12) To conduct upon said property or therein, any and all of the activities and enterprises aforesaid, and to provide warehousing and cold storage facilities, bonded or otherwise in all their branches, in connection with the said business or any and all the products, goods, manufactures and articles as aforesaid, and to issue certificates, warrants, warehouse and other receipts, negotiable or otherwise, to persons dealing with the company in any such respect, and to make advances or loans upon such or any property stored, warehoused, transported or to be so dealt in by or with it; to construct, purchase, take, lease, own or otherwise acquire any wharf, pier, dock or works capable of advantageous use in connection with such property or business or commonly undertaken or carried on by warehouse men, or accessory thereto or any thereof, including the acquisition, holding, rental, improvement and conveyance of lands under water and riparian, dock and maritime rights, and rights in docks, drydocks, wharves, piers, basins, derricks, elevators, warehouses, manufactories, stores, shops, tracks and other structures thereon, or on any of the same, and to rent, lease, and convey the same.

(13) To acquire in any manner, ranches, ranges or farms for the production or handling of cattle, sheep, horses, swine, and all other animals, and to secure, purchase, erect or otherwise acquire, abattoirs, and all other buildings necessary or expedient in connection therewith for the storage and handling of the products of the same.

(14) To cause or allow the legal title, estate and interest in or to any property acquired, or to be acquired, or used, employed or controlled by the company in any manner to be registered, held or carried in the name of or by or through any other person, company or companies, as agents, nominees or trustees for this company, or upon any other terms or conditions which may be considered for the benefit of this company, and to control, direct and manage the affairs of any such company, agent, nominee or trustee, or take over and carry on the business of the same, either by acquiring shares of stock thereof, or any other securities, or otherwise in any manner whatsoever as shall be necessary or expedient; and generally to conduct, own and carry on its said business so far as involves ownership of, or interest in any and all real property in the State of New York and throughout the territory of the United States and generally as, and in such manner as may be deemed advantageous by its board of directors, and as may be authorized by the Business Corporations Laws and generally by the laws of the State of New York.

(15) To enter into, make, perform and carry out contracts with any person, firm, corporation, private, public, municipal or body politic, under the government of the United States or any State, Territory or Colony thereof, or any foreign government, so far as and to the extent that the same may be done and performed under Article III of the Business Corporations Law.

(16) To act as agent and representative of and in conjunction with its business as aforesaid and the business of any and all other corporations so as aforesaid dealing with it or engaged in manufacture, production, distribution or other enterprises in connection with the same or any thereof, and likewise in connection with said or any of such business, as house, factory, boat or warehouse, engineers or builders, sanitary or electrical engineers, contractors and erectors, gas fitters, fuel agents, decorators, auctioneers, cabinet makers, purveyors of machinery, goods, domestic and other supplies, food commodities, wares and merchandise, periodicals, photographs, photo-plays and literature and as farmers, stockmen, dairymen, market gardeners, nurserymen, florists and wholesale and retail dealers in feeds, grains, fertilizers and seeds, and as distributor, jobber and wholesaler of and in respect to any goods, wares, or merchandise dealt in or with, by it.

(17) To borrow money for its corporate purposes; to make, accept, endorse, execute, issue and deliver bonds, debentures, notes, bills of exchange or other obligations; to mortgage, pledge or hypothecate any stocks, notes, bonds or other evidences of indebtedness, and any other property owned or held by it, and to lend money with or without collateral security, so far as necessary for its business; to make, accept, endorse, execute and issue promissory notes, bills of exchange, bonds, debentures, and other obligations, from time to time, for the purchase of property in or about the business of the company, and to secure the payment of any such obligations by mortgage, pledge, deed of trust or otherwise.

(18) To make any guarantee respecting dividends, stocks, bonds, contracts or other obligations arising out of or connected with its business or affairs so far as the same may be permitted to corporations organized under the Business Corporations Law.

(19) To do all and every thing incidental and necessary for the accomplishment of any of the purposes or the attainment of any of the objects or the furtherance of any of the powers hereinbefore set forth, either alone or in association with other corporations, firms or individuals.

(20) The foregoing clauses shall be construed both as objects and powers; and it is hereby expressly provided that the foregoing enumeration of specific powers shall not be held to limit or restrict in any manner the powers of the corporation.

Third—The amount of the capital stock shall be Thirty Million Dollars ($30,000,000.00).

Fourth—The number of shares of which the capital stock shall consist is four million, one hundred thousand (4,100,000) shares, of which one hundred thousand (100,000) shares shall be 4% Cumulative Preferred Stock of a par value of One Hundred Dollars per share and three million, eight hundred thousand (3,800,000) shares shall be common stock of a par value of Five Dollars per share and two hundred thousand (200,000) shares shall be Class B common stock of a par value of Five Dollars per share.

The designations, preferences, privileges and voting powers of the shares and the restrictions or qualifications thereof are as follows:

(a) The holders of the 4% Cumulative Preferred shares shall be entitled to receive, when and as declared by the Board of Directors of the Corporation, out of any assets of the Corporation available for dividends pursuant to the laws of the State of New York, preferential dividends at the rate of four per cent (4%) per annum and no more, payable annually, semiannually or quarterly on such days as may be determined by the Board of Directors before any dividend shall be declared or paid or set apart for the common stock.

(b) Holders of 4% Cumulative Preferred Stock in the Corporation shall not be entitled to vote for directors nor to participate in the meetings or management of the Corporation nor to vote in a proceeding (1) for mortgaging the property and franchises of the corporation pursuant to Section 16 of the Stock Corporation Law, (2) for guaranteeing the bonds of another corporation pursuant to Section 19 of the Stock Corporation Law, (3) for sale of the franchise and property pursuant to Section 20 of the Stock Corporation Law, (4) for consolidation purposes pursuant to Sections 86 or 91 of the Stock Corporation Law, (5) for voluntary dissolution pursuant to Section 105 of the Stock Corporation Law, (6) for a change of name pursuant to the General Corporation Law or pursuant to Section 35 of the Stock Corporation Law, nor otherwise, except in statutory proceedings as to which their votes are required by law and their right to vote cannot be waived or surrendered by the provisions of this Certificate.

(c) Upon the dissolution or other termination of the corporation or its business, or the distribution of its assets, the holders in order of priority of 4% Cumulative Preferred Stock shall first receive the full par value of the same, together with any and all cumulative dividends accrued and unpaid to the date of such distribution and payment, and all of the property, assets and resources of the Corporation shall be applied and employed to that end, and thereafter the funds remaining shall be distributed among the holders of the common stock and patrons as provided by law and this certificate and, saving as above provided, the 4% Cumulative Preferred Stock shall not be entitled to any dividend or distribution from or interest in the property of the Corporation.

(d) The Corporation shall be entitled from time to time to retire the whole or any portion of its 4% Cumulative Preferred Stock upon payment of all accrued dividends and the amount of One Hundred Dollars ($100.00) for each share so purchased. Such retirement shall be effected by payment out of the surplus, if any, of the Corporation but no preferred stock shall be redeemed for cash under circumstances which would produce any impairment of the capital or capital stock of the Corporation. Such retirement or redemption of stock can only be effected on three months' notice, and, if a partial retirement, by drawing by lot, in the manner provided by the by-laws. The amount of the preferred stock or the common stock may be increased from time to time as authorized by vote of the common stockholders and under amendment of the certificate of incorporation and by like vote and amendment preferred stock with a lower rate of dividend, or other classes of preferred stock hereby authorized may be issued but no stock shall be issued with rights prior to the preferred stock herein authorized.

(e) The common and Class B common stock shall have the same designations and privileges as originally specified in the certificate of incorporation as if there were no classification, *except* the Class B common stock shall have the qualification that such shares shall not be entitled to vote at any meeting of the stockholders for any purpose except as otherwise required by Statute of the State of New York.

Fifth—The City of Ithaca, in the County of Tompkins, and State of New York is the place in which the principal office of the Company is to be located, but it shall have power to conduct its business in all of its branches, or any part thereof, in any of the states, territories, colonies or dependencies of the United States, including the District of Columbia, and in any and all countries foreign to the United States; and to establish and maintain offices, agencies or branches in any thereof.

Sixth—The duration of the corporation is to be perpetual.

Seventh—The number of its directors shall be fourteen (14). Directors shall serve for a period of years each as hereinafter designated and until their successors are elected and have qualified, a majority of the directors qualified and acting shall constitute a quorum for the transacting of business at any meeting. Directors shall, in so far as practical, be chosen from among stockholder members in the following organizations or groups.

New York State Grange, Order of Patrons of Husbandry—Two (2) for 2 years each.

New York State Farm Bureau Federation—Two (2) for 2 years each. Patrons of all G.L.F. agencies which are qualified agents of this cooperative—Ten (10) for 2 years each.

Nominations for such directors may be proposed by said groups under such terms and conditions as are provided from time to time by the By-Laws of this Corporation and not inconsistent with the Cooperative Corporations Law of the State of New York. Immediately after this Amendment to the Certificate of Incorporation has been adopted, for each director whose term of office for which elected shall expire, there shall be elected a Director to serve for two years or until his successor is elected and qualifies.

Nominations by the organizations or groups above specified shall not preclude nomination from the floor at any Stockholders' Meeting at which directors are to be elected nor preclude nomination and election of a candidate eligible as a stockholder of this corporation irrespective of whether he is or is not affiliated with any particular nominating group, but in so far as possible full recognition shall be given the particular qualifications established by long practice by each group and the particular classification set forth in the original Certificate of Incorporation as amended.

In case any dispute shall arise between nominating groups as to their respective rights or privileges, the Board of Directors of the Corporation shall hear and determine the issue and its determination shall be binding on stockholders and all nominating organizations.

Eighth—The names and post office addresses of the Directors for the first year are as follows:

Names	Addresses
William L. Bean	McGraw, N.Y.
Sherman J. Lowell	Fredonia, N.Y.
Raymond C. Hitchings	Syracuse, N.Y. R.D.
New York State Grange, Order of Patrons of Husbandry.	
Niles F. Webb	Cortland, N.Y.
Harry Bull	Campbell Hall, N.Y.
John C. Griffith	Salamanca, N.Y.
Dairymen's League Co-operative Association, Inc.	
H. Edward Babcock	Ithaca, N.Y.
Arthur L. Smith	DeRuyter, N.Y.
Harry L. Brown	Waterport, N.Y.
New York State Federation of County Farm Bureau Associations.	

Ninth—The names and post office addresses of the incorporators, and the number of shares which each agrees to take, are as follows:

Names	Post Office Addresses	Shares
Frank W. Howe	Syracuse, N.Y.	20
William L. Bean	McGraw, N.Y.	30
Richard Hall	Syracuse, N.Y.	30
H. Edward Babcock	Ithaca, N.Y.	30
Raymond C. Hitchings	Syracuse, N.Y.	30
Niles F. Webb	Cortland, N.Y.	30
Robert L. Speed	Slaterville Springs, N.Y.	30

Tenth—The following provisions are adopted for the regulation of the business and conduct of the affairs of the corporation:

(1) No transaction, right or liability entered into, enjoyed or incurred by or in respect of the corporation shall be affected by the fact that any Director or Directors of the corporation are or may have been personally interested in or concerning the same, and each Director of the corporation is hereby relieved of and from any and all disability which otherwise might prevent him from contracting with the corporation for the benefit of himself or any firm, association or corporation, in which in anywise he may be interested.

(2) All corporate powers, including the effecting of the sale, mortgage, hypothecation or pledge of the whole or any part of the corporate property, shall be exercised by the Board of Directors of the company, except as otherwise expressly provided by law.

(3) No dividend shall be declared or paid by the corporation which shall impair its capital or capital stock nor while its capital or capital stock is impaired. Subject to such limitations, the corporation may declare and pay dividends not to exceed six per cent on its common and Class B common capital stock, but only from net earnings arising from the business of the corporation.

(4) So far as permitted by law, the Directors may hold meetings outside of the State of New York.

(5) The corporation may use and apply its net margins accumulated, other than those required by law to be reserved, to the purchase or acquisition of property, and as authorized by the Cooperative Corporations Law of New York, may purchase or acquire its own capital stock, from time to time, and to such an extent, and in such manner, and upon such terms, as its Board of Directors shall determine.

(6) The Board of Directors may, from time to time, sell any or all of the unissued capital stock of the corporation, whether the same be any of the original authorized capital or of any increase thereof, without first offering the same to the stockholders then existing, and all such sales may be made upon such terms and conditions, as by the Board may be deemed advisable, and may restrict a purchase, sale, distribution, transfer, owning and holding of stock as fully and to the extent authorized by the Cooperative Corporations Law.

(7) The Board of Directors, from time to time, shall determine whether, to what extent, at what times and places, and under what conditions and regulations, the accounts, books and papers of the corporation, or any of them, shall be open to the inspection of the stockholders and no stockholder shall have any right to inspect any account, book or paper of the corporation, except as expressly conferred by law, or authorized by the Board of Directors or the stockholders.

(8) Being an agricultural marketing and purchasing corporation formed and operated under the Cooperative Corporations Law of the State of New York, only persons engaged in the production of agricultural products who hold common stock in the corporation and, if the by-laws so provide, cooperative corporations of persons engaged in the production of agricultural products, whether organized under the laws of the State of New York or any other state, shall be eligible for membership in the corporation. The terms and conditions of membership shall be prescribed by the by-laws; provided, however, such by-laws shall not be inconsistent with this Certificate of Incorporation as amended.

(9) The Corporation shall distribute or allocate to each member, as a patronage refund for each fiscal year, either in cash, stock, evidences of indebtedness, or equity or services, a portion of the net margins of the Corporation for the fiscal year under such terms and conditions as are prescribed from time to time by the by-laws of this Corporation, provided that nothing contained in such by-laws shall be inconsistent with this Certificate of Incorporation or with the laws of the State of New York.

(10) Voting powers at any stockholders meeting under the statute are limited to the common stockholders of record as disclosed by the books of the Corporation.

In witness whereof, we have made, signed and acknowledged this certificate, in duplicate, this 22nd day of June, 1920.

WILLIAM L. BEAN
NILES F. WEBB
RICHARD HALL
H. EDWARD BABCOCK
RAYMOND C. HITCHINGS
ROBT. L. SPEED
FRANK W. HOWE

STATE OF NEW YORK⎫
County of Onondaga ⎬ss.
City of Syracuse ⎭

On this 22nd day of June, 1920, before me personally appeared William L. Bean, Niles F. Webb, Richard Hall, H. Edward Babcock, Raymond C. Hitchings, Robt. L. Speed, Frank W. Howe, to me known and known to me to be the individuals described in, and who executed the foregoing Certificate, and they duly acknowledged to me that they executed the same.

Leslie G. Abbott,
Notary Public.

The original above Certificate of Incorporation was filed in the Office of the Secretary of State of New York on the 25th day of June, 1920. Various certificates of amendment to the Certificate of Incorporation were duly filed in the Office of the Secretary of State as follows:

(a) Change of Location of Office, Increase of Number of Directors, Nomination of Directors, and Change of Certain Provisions filed . . .December 9, 1932

(b) Change of Method of Nominating Directors filed . . .November 27, 1940

(c) Increase of Capital Stock and Number of Shares and Classifications thereof filed . . . . .November 21, 1942

(d) Increase of Capital Stock and Number of Shares filed . . . .
. . . . .November 22, 1944

(e) Change of Number of Directors and Change of other Powers and Provisions filed . . . . .December 9, 1946

(f) Change in Powers and Provisions relating to Requirements for Membership and Formula for Payment of Patronage Refunds or Price Adjustments filed . . . . .July 1, 1948

(g) Certificate of Increase of Capital Stock and Number of Shares . . . .
. . . . .November 24, 1948

(h) Change in Powers and Provisions relating to the Payment of Patronage Refunds and Certificate of Increase of Capital Stock and Authorization of New Class of Stock filed . . . . .November 20, 1951

By-Laws

(As Amended November 15, 1932, as amended October 25, 1940, and as amended February 12, 1941, October 31, 1946, July 1, 1948, October 21, 1948, May 26, 1949, June 19, 1951, November 28, 1951, September 15, 1952, October 17, 1952, October 24, 1952, October 22, 1954 and May 5, 1959)

ARTICLE I
Meetings of Stockholders and Members

Sec. 1. The annual meeting of stockholders of this corporation shall be held at the time and place designated by the Board of Directors and set forth in the notice of meeting. Notice of the time, place and special business to be transacted at such meeting shall be given the stockholders by mailing not less than ten or more than twenty days prior to such meeting, postage prepaid, a copy of such notice directed to each stockholder at his address as the same appears on the books of the Corporation.

SEC. 2. Special meetings of stockholders, other than such as at the time may be regulated by statute, may be called by a majority of the Directors or by a majority of the stockholders of the Corporation by a writing duly signed specifying the time, place and purpose of the meeting. A notice of such special meeting specifying the purpose for which it is called shall be given by mailing a copy of such notice to each stockholder in manner similar to that required for the annual meeting, and no business other than that so stated shall be transacted at such meeting.

SEC. 3. At all meetings of stockholders, the stockholders present shall constitute a quorum, and at any regularly called meeting of stockholders, the written vote of an absent stockholder signed by him shall be received and counted, provided he shall have been previously notified in writing of the exact motion or resolution upon which such vote is taken and a copy of the same is forwarded with and attached to his written vote, except that no votes of absent stockholders shall be received and counted for or against by-law amendments reported to the annual meeting of stockholders pursuant to Section 16 or 111 of the Cooperative Corporations Law.

SEC. 4. Two inspectors of election shall be elected at each annual meeting of stockholders to serve for one year thereafter and at the next annual meeting, and if any inspector shall not be present or shall decline to serve, the stockholders shall elect an inspector in his place.

SEC. 5. At the annual meeting of stockholders the following shall be the order of business:

1. Calling the roll or noting those present.
2. Proof of proper notice of meeting.
3. Reports of Officers.
4. Reports of Committees.
5. Election of Inspectors of Election.
6. Election of Directors.
7. Miscellaneous business.

SEC. 6. At all meetings of stockholders all questions—except questions the manner of deciding which is otherwise regulated by statute—shall be determined by a majority vote of the stockholders present in person or voting by mail as above provided. No voting by proxy shall be permitted.

SEC. 7. The common stock of the corporation shall be issued only to persons engaged in the production of agricultural products and cooperative corporations of such producers. "Persons," as used in limitation of eligibility for membership, shall include individuals, partnerships, two or more individuals having joint or common interests, corporations and associations.

No subscription for common stock of the corporation shall be accepted and no certificate issued any person until such person has been certified by the Membership Committee as being qualified for membership in the corporation within the limitation prescribed in the Certificate of Incorporation, as amended, and these by-laws. No common stock shall be transferred without the written consent of the corporation endorsed on the certificate of stock. The Membership Committee shall consist of 5 employees of the corporation, each appointed by the Board of Directors to hold office until such appointment is rescinded or the successor appointed and qualified.

The Membership Committee shall approve or reject stock subscriptions and applications for transfer, and shall, within the limitations prescribed by the Cooperative Laws of the State of New York, the Certificate of Incorporation, as amended, and these by-laws, determine the eligibility of subscribers or transferees for membership in the corporation.

In any case where factual information concerning the occupation of a subscriber or transferee is insufficient to determine eligibility, the matter shall be referred by the Membership Committee to the G.L.F. Member Committee in or near the community in which the subscriber resides for report and recommendation as to eligibility.

SEC. 8. Holders of, and accepted subscribers to, common voting stock of the corporation who are engaged in the production of agricultural products shall be members of the corporation and their names entered on the membership roster kept by the Secretary, together with the date of membership. Each member as entered upon the membership roster shall be entitled to all the rights and privileges and assume all of the obligations of membership in the corporation as prescribed by the Certificate of Incorporation, the bylaws, and the Cooperative Corporations Law of the State of New York.

Subscribers in default on subscription payments, members ceasing to be common stockholders, and persons otherwise eligible who decline membership in writing shall, upon affirmative action of the Membership Committee cease to be members and their names stricken from the membership roster with a notation of the date on which they cease to be members.

SEC. 9. Members as hereinabove defined shall be eligible to attend agency G.L.F. meetings whenever called and vote for the election of members of the G.L.F. Member Committee to be chosen from among those who do business with the agency concerned. Such members may elect not fewer than six nor more than nine G.L.F. member committeemen to represent them in all matters affecting their relationship with this corporation, its subsidiaries and qualified agencies. Committeemen must be G.L.F. members to qualify for election. G.L.F. Member Committees shall be organized as a group having a Chairman and Secretary, shall keep minutes of their meetings and actions taken thereat. Each member of the G.L.F. Member Committee shall be entitled to attend any stockholders meeting of this corporation as a stockholder and have one vote thereat on each question presented to the meeting, without regard to the number of shares owned by said committeemen. Stockholders voting in person shall not vote any shares by mail.

Each G.L.F. member committeeman shall receive such proportion of his disbursements reasonably incurred incident to attendance at stockholders meetings, to be paid him from such sources as the Board of Directors and the agency concerned may from year to year determine in recognition of the agency service and the service of the G.L.F. member committeeman to the G.L.F. members dealing with the agency.

SEC. 10. (a) Definitions.

(1) *Member*—The term "member" as used in this Sec. 10 of Article I includes only members of the Corporation.

(2) *Contract patron*—The term "contract patron" as used in this Sec. 10 of Article I includes non-members who have entered into patronage refund contracts with the Corporation as authorized by Sec. 11 of Article I.

(3) *Net margin*—The "net margin" of the Corporation shall be the gross receipts of the Corporation for the fiscal year reduced by all operating expenses of the Corporation for the fiscal year. Such operating expenses shall include cost of goods, overhead, interest, maintenance, depreciation, obsolescence, depletion, bad debts, taxes other than Federal income and excess profits taxes,

and other proper costs, all as determined in accordance with sound corporate practices and sound accounting principles, but shall not include any patronage refunds. In no event, however, shall net margin include either "net capital gain" or "net capital loss" from sale or exchange of assets as such terms are defined in the Internal Revenue Code, or Federal income and excess profits tax adjustments.

(4) *Non-member margin*—The "non-member margin" shall be the portion of the net margin derived from business with non-members other than contract patrons, determined by multiplying the net margin by the percentage of gross volume of business transacted which is attributable to business with such non-members.

(5) *Member's and Contract Patron's pro rata share*—Each "member's and contract patron's pro rata share" shall be computed by multiplying the amount of volume subject to refund attributable to each member or contract patron by a rate determined by dividing the total refund or reserve to be allocated, as the case may be, by the total amount of volume subject to refund.

(6) *Non-margin volume*—The term "non-margin volume" is used to refer to that portion of the gross volume of the Corporation for any fiscal year which, when compared with the costs incurred in its realization, does not result in any net margin either (1) because services are initially rendered at cost, or (2) because the net margin which was contemplated never materialized.

(7) *Non-member volume*—The "non-member volume" shall be that portion of the gross volume of the Corporation for any fiscal year which is attributable to business with all non-members except contract patrons.

(8) *Volume subject to refund*—The "volume subject to refund" shall be the gross volume of the Corporation for any fiscal year reduced by (1) non-margin volume and (2) non-member volume to the extent that such volume is not included in non-margin volume and increased by (3) the overall average percentage of markup to reflect an equivalent volume at the retail price level.

(b) The Board of Directors may set aside each fiscal year, from the net margin of the Corporation, such reserves as the Board of Directors in its discretion deems necessary for the efficient prosecution of the Corporation's business; *provided, however,* that no amounts shall be so set aside which are not reasonable in amount, giving due regard to the purposes thereof. The amounts so set aside shall be referred to as "reasonable reserves."

(c) Except to the extent, if any, to which the Corporation shall be required under its Certificate of Incorporation or the laws of New York to pay or set aside amounts in excess of what would remain after the payment of patronage refunds as provided in this Paragraph (c) of this Section 10 of Article I, the Corporation shall be obligated at the close of each fiscal year to pay to members and contract patrons, pro rata, as provided in Subparagraph (a) (5) of this Section 10 of Article I, in cash or its equivalent, patronage refunds in the following amount or such greater amount as shall be required by the Certification of Incorporation of the Corporation:

All net margins over and above (1) amounts set aside by the Board of Directors, as provided in Paragraph (b) of this Section 10 of Article I, as reasonable reserves, and (2) amounts, not to exceed 6%, paid or set aside for payment as dividends on issued and outstanding capital stock, shall be distributed as patronage refunds, provided that the amount of patronage refunds payable hereunder shall not exceed the net margins remaining after deducting the non-member margin.

The amount of patronage refund thus determined shall be increased or decreased to the extent necessary to enable the obligation for the payment of such refunds to be expressed as a percentage of volume subject to refund to the nearest one-tenth of a percentage point of such volume.

The Corporation shall be absolutely liable for the payment of each member's and contract patron's pro rata share of the patronage refund so determined without further action on the part of any officers or directors of the Corporation.

Each member and contract patron shall be entitled to his respective pro rata share of any patronage refund paid on G.L.F. distributed goods regardless of whether such goods were purchased from a G.L.F. Agent-Buyer, a G.L.F. local cooperative corporation or otherwise.

(d) The Corporation shall enter into such contracts, undertakings and understandings with G.L.F. Agent-Buyers, G.L.F. local cooperatives and others as may be necessary and proper to insure that the pro rata rate share of such patronage refunds paid on G.L.F. distributed goods will be duly allotted and/or distributed to members and contract patrons.

(e) The Corporation shall maintain records sufficient to afford permanent means for allocating to each member for each fiscal year such member's pro rata share of all amounts retained by the Corporation as reserves. The Board of Directors shall determine the manner and form in which such allocations of such amounts shall be made.

Sec. 11. If authorized by the Board of Directors, the corporation may contract to pay and pay patronage refunds to persons transacting business with it other than members, provided the amounts of such patronage refunds are determined upon the same basis and under the same terms and conditions as those of members and, provided further, that any such contract with non-member persons shall be entered into prior to the accumulation of any gross income subject to the charge of such patronage refunds.

The Board of Directors may prescribe such additional terms and conditions as they may, in their judgement, deem necessary for the execution of the patronage refund or price adjustment contracts with members and non-members, provided that nothing contained in such additional terms and conditions shall be inconsistent with the Certificate of Incorporation, as amended, and these by-laws. Any net margins not distributed in cash may be used for such proper corporate purposes as shall be determined by the Board of Directors, including, but not limited to, the maintenance of required statutory reserves, allocations of working capital, contributions to sinking funds to meet future corporate long-term indebtedness, acquisition of fixed assets, development of building fund reserve for expansion or replacement, reserves for price decline or to capital surplus.

ARTICLE II

DIRECTORS

SEC. 1. The Directors of this Corporation shall be elected by ballot at the annual meetings of stockholders, to serve for two years respectively as specified in the amended certificate of incorporation, and until their successors shall have been elected and duly qualified. The directors shall be chosen by a plurality of the votes cast.

SEC. 2. Whenever a director representing the member stockholder group is due to be nominated as the candidate of that group, the method of placing him in nomination shall be as follows:

The States of New York and New Jersey and the Counties of Bradford, Carbon, Columbia, Crawford, Erie, Lackawanna, Luzerne, McKean, Monroe, Northampton, Pike, Potter, Sullivan, Susquehanna, Tioga, Wayne, and Wyoming in the State of Pennsylvania shall be divided into ten districts numbered from One (1) to Ten (10) inclusive, and until otherwise defined shall be as follows:

NEW YORK STATE

District 1. Western New York comprising the Counties of Allegany, Cattaraugus, Chautauqua, Erie, Genesee, Livingston, Monroe, Niagara, Orleans, Wyoming.

District 2. West Central New York comprising the Counties of Cayuga, Chemung, Ontario, Schuyler, Seneca, Steuben, Tioga, Tompkins, Wayne, Yates.

District 3. Central New York comprising the Counties of Broome, Chenango, Cortland, Madison, Oneida, Onondaga.

District 4. Northern New York comprising the Counties of Clinton, Essex, Franklin, Hamilton, Herkimer (northern half), Jefferson, Lewis, Oswego, St. Lawrence.

District 5. East Central New York comprising the Counties of Albany, Columbia, Fulton, Greene, Herkimer (southern half), Montgomery, Otsego, Rensselaer, Saratoga, Schenectady, Schoharie, Warren, Washington.

District 6. South Eastern New York comprising the Counties of Delaware, Dutchess, Nassau, Orange, Putnam, Rockland, Suffolk, Ulster, Westchester.

PENNSYLVANIA

District 7. Western Pennsylvania comprising the Counties of Crawford, Erie, McKean, Potter, Tioga, Warren.

District 8. Eastern Pennsylvania comprising the Counties of Bradford, Carbon, Columbia, Lackawanna, Luzerne, Monroe, Northampton, Pike, Sullivan, Susquehanna, Wayne, Wyoming.

NEW JERSEY

District 9. Northern New Jersey comprising the Counties of Bergen, Essex, Hudson, Hunterdon, Middlesex, Morris, Passaic, Somerset, Sussex, Union, Warren.

District 10. Southern New Jersey comprising the Counties of Atlantic, Burlington, Camden, Cape May, Cumberland, Gloucester, Mercer, Monmouth, Ocean, Salem.

The foregoing Districts may be altered from time to time by the Board of Directors providing the District(s) concerned at meetings of the Chairman of Member Committees called and held as provided in this section, shall consent hereto or providing all Districts concerned shall request alteration.

In addition to the nominees of the New York State Grange and Farm Bureau Federation, each District shall nominate one (1) representative each year in which a vacancy is due to arise in the District concerned.

Beginning with the year 1947, the nominating group shall be those Member Committee representatives in the odd numbered Districts; namely Districts 1, 3, 5, 7 and 9, and

Beginning with the year 1948, the nominating group shall be those Member Committee representatives in the even numbered Districts; namely Districts 2, 4, 6, 8 and 10.

In each year commencing in 1947, the New York State Grange, Order of Patrons' of Husbandry and the New York State Farm Bureau Federation may nominate one director each.

At least thirty (30) days but not earlier than sixty (60) days before the date set for a Stockholders Meeting the Secretary of this Corporation shall notify the individual Chairman of each Member Committee of each agency in the several Districts concerned that a District meeting is to be held at a convenient time and place set by the Board of Directors. The notice shall be mailed at least ten (10) days prior to date of meeting and shall state that the meeting is called for the purpose of making a nomination of a candidate to be the nominee of the G.L.F. members of the particular District for Director of this Corporation. The Chairman of each Committee or his alternate is hereby authorized to attend said Meeting as the representative of all G.L.F. members of the agency for the purpose of voting on a nominee and for such other purposes as may be outlined in the notice.

Said District meeting shall be organized by the selection of a Chairman and Secretary thereof and proceed to the election of a nominee and such other business as may properly be brought before the meeting. Upon the selection of a nominee, the President and Secretary shall immediately certify the nomination to the Secretary of the Exchange and may accompany the same with a short biographical sketch of the person concerned. Whereupon, the Secretary of this Corporation may and if the certification is received by him thirty (30) days or more prior to the date set for the Annual Meeting, shall enclose with the notice of such Annual Stockholders meeting a statement of each District nomination so made, including the name and residence of each nominee, the Group or District so nominating each, the term to be filled, the name of his predecessor in office and also a form of ballot drawn to vote at such meetings for the person(s) so nominated. He shall also include a synopsis of any biographical sketch of the nominee submitted. Other nominations may be made from the Floor at the Stockholders Meeting. In case other nominations are made from the Floor in opposition to any candidate nominated by any Group or District, the person placing a candidate in nomination shall at the Meeting state to the Stockholders assembled in what classified group the nominee is placed by him for the purpose of clarifying and simplifying the stockholders' choice of candidates for particular Group or District.

No other nominations or forms of ballots or written votes for directors shall be mentioned in or enclosed with such notice.

Sec. 3. Vacancies in the Board of Directors occurring during the year, caused by death, resignation or otherwise, shall be filled for the unexpired term of the Director so retiring and until a successor shall be elected, by a majority vote of the remaining Directors at any regular meeting of the Board.

Sec. 4. In case the entire Board of Directors shall die or resign, any 10 stockholders may call a special meeting in the same manner that the President may call such a meeting, and Directors for the unexpired term may be elected, at such special meeting in the manner provided for their election at annual meetings.

Sec. 5. Subject to the provisions of the Certificate of Incorporation and amendments, and of these By-Laws, the business of the Corporation shall be managed and conducted by the Board of Directors. The Board may adopt rules and regulations for the conduct of its meetings and for the management of the affairs of the Corporation and additional By-Laws consistent with the laws of the State of New York and with these By-Laws. A majority of the members of the Board, qualified and acting, shall constitute a quorum for the transaction of business.

The Board of Directors by a two-thirds vote of a quorum present at any meeting, may amend or suspend these By-Laws provided however that Section 2 of Article II, hereof, and the provisions in Sections 1 and 2 of Article I, hereof, requiring the mailing of a notice to stockholders of all stockholders meetings, shall not in any way be so amended, altered or suspended.

SEC. 6. Regular meetings of the Board of Directors shall be held at least four times in each year. One such regular meeting shall be held within two months following the adjournment of the annual stockholders meeting. The Board shall also meet whenever called together by the President upon three days' notice, duly given to each director. On the written request of five directors, the Secretary shall call a special meeting of the Board, giving notice thereof to each Director. Meetings of the Board shall be held at the principal business office of the Company in the City of Ithaca unless some other place within the States of New York, New Jersey or Pennsylvania be designated in the call for meeting pursuant to order of the President.

SEC. 7. The Board of Directors shall have the power to appoint, in its discretion, an Executive Committee to consist of such number of Directors as the Board shall determine. The Board may designate the Chairman of such Committee, and fix the number of members thereof necessary to constitute a quorum for the transaction of business, as well as the number of members whose concurrent action shall be necessary for any action by such Committee. The Board may delegate to such Committee all or any of the powers of the Board which may be lawfully delegated, and thereupon such Committee may—in the intervals between the meetings of the Board—exercise the powers so delegated. The Executive Committee shall have no power, however, to declare dividends or to remove any officer elected by the Board of Directors. Vacancies in the Executive Committee shall be filled by the Board of Directors, and, subject to the instructions of the Board, such Committee may fix its own rules of procedure and the time for its meetings. All action of the Executive Committee shall be reported to the Board of Directors at the meeting of said Board next succeeding the taking of such action, and unless then approved shall thereupon cease to be effective.

SEC. 8. Without assent or other action of the stockholders, unless otherwise expressly provided by law, the Board of Directors may purchase, acquire, hold, lease, mortgage, pledge, sell and convey such property, real or personal, without as well as within the State of New York, as the Board of Directors may from time to time determine; and in payment for any property, issue or cause to be issued stock of the Corporation, bonds, debentures, or other obligations thereof, secured or unsecured.

ARTICLE III
OFFICERS

SEC. 1. The Board of Directors, at their first meeting following the annual meeting of stockholders in each year, shall, by a majority vote, choose from their number a President and a Vice-President, and shall also elect a General Manager, a Treasurer, a Controller and a Secretary, and may elect a General Counsel. Officers, except the President and Vice-President, need not be directors or members. Each such officer shall serve for one year and until his successor is elected and has qualified. All officers shall be subject to removal at any time by affirmative vote of a majority of the whole board of directors.

Any two offices except those of President, Vice-President or General Manager may be held by one person.

The Board may also elect such other officers as it shall deem necessary who shall have such authority and perform such duties as from time to time may be prescribed by the Board.

Sec. 2. Officers, including the chairman of the Executive Committee, shall receive such compensation as the Board of Directors may prescribe. The Board may also provide for the payment to Directors and members of Committees appointed by said Board, of stated fees for attendance at meetings of the Board or of such committees, and shall have power, in its discretion, to provide for and to pay to Directors rendering unusual or special service to the Corporation, special compensation appropriate to the value of such service.

Sec. 3. The President shall preside at all meetings of the Board of Directors, and shall act as temporary chairman at, and call to order, all meetings of the stockholders. He shall represent the Board of Directors in the exercise of general policy supervision over the affairs of the Corporation. He may also sign certificates of stock and execute contracts in the name of the corporation when duly authorized thereunto.

Sec. 4. In case of the absence or disability of the President or the vacancy of that office, the Vice-President shall perform all of the duties of the President.

Sec. 5. Subject to the Board of Directors, the General Manager shall be the chief executive officer of the corporation and shall have general charge of its business and jurisdiction over its employees. He shall keep the Board of Directors fully informed and shall freely consult them concerning the business of the corporation in his charge. He may sign and execute all authorized contracts, checks or other obligations in the name of the Corporation and may sign, together with other duly authorized officers, all certificates of shares of stock of the Corporation. He shall do and perform such other duties as from time to time may be assigned to him by the board of directors.

The General Manager shall appoint and discharge such assistant general managers, managers of Operating Divisions, district and local retail managers, agents and other employees as he shall deem necessary and advisable to carry out the conduct of the business of the Corporation. The General Manager may set up such Operating Divisions and Departments within the Corporation as he may deem proper and may delegate such of his powers and duties to the appointed managers of such Operating Divisions, district and local retail managers and agents and other employees as he shall deem necessary in the efficient conduct of the business of the Corporation; provided, however, that he shall at all times be responsible to the Board of Directors for the proper discharge of his powers and duties, whether delegated or not.

Sec. 6. The Treasurer shall have the care and custody of all of the funds and securities of the Corporation and shall deposit the same in the name of the Corporation in such banks or depositories as the Directors may select. He shall disburse the funds of the Corporation as may be ordered by the Board, taking proper vouchers for such disbursements, and shall render to the General Manager and Directors an account of all his transactions as Treasurer and the financial condition of the Corporation. In addition, he shall perform such other duties as may from time to time be prescribed by the General Manager. He shall, when authorized, by the Board of Directors, borrow money for the sole use of the Corporation and give its notes or other obligations therefor, and as collateral for any such loan or loans, hypothecate any securities owned by the Corporation, provided, however, that notes and obligations of the Corporation shall only be executed in the manner prescribed in these by-laws. He may, with the General Manager, sign certificates of stock. He shall give bond in such amount as the Directors may require.

Sec. 7. The Secretary shall keep the minutes of the Board of Directors and also the minutes of meetings of stockholders; he shall attend to the giving and serving of all notices of the Corporation and shall sign and affix the seal of the Corporation to all certificates of stock when signed by the General Manager and to other papers and instruments when duly directed thereto; he shall have charge of the seal of the Corporation, of the certificate books and of such other books and paper as the Board may direct; he shall attend to such correspondence as may be assigned to him and shall perform all the duties incident to his office. He shall also keep a stock book containing the names, alphabetically arranged, of all persons who are stockholders of the Corporation, showing their places of residence, the number of shares of stock held by them respectively, the times when they respectively became the owners thereof, and the amounts severally paid thereon, and such books shall be open for inspection as prescribed by law. In addition, he shall perform such other duties as may from time to time be prescribed by the General Manager.

SEC. 8. The Controller shall perform all of the duties incident to the office of Controller, including the institution and maintenance of adequate accounting policies and practices, internal audit, taxes, forecasting, budgeting and methods and systems. In addition, he shall perform such other duties as may from time to time be prescribed by the General Manager.

SEC. 9. Whenever, in their opinion, the business of the Corporation may require, the Board of Directors may appoint assistant Treasurers or assistant Secretaries and may assign to such officers prescribed powers and duties in aid of the General Manager, the Treasurer or the Secretary, respectively.

SEC. 10. A majority of the stockholders, present at any regular or special meeting, duly called, which notice of meeting shall set forth the nature of the proposed investigation to be made, may remove any Director or officer for cause, and fill the vacancy. Written charges must be made and signed by not less than twenty-five stockholders, filed with the Corporation, and a copy thereof served upon the accused, together with written notice specifying the time and place set for the hearing of the same. At such hearing no matters other than such as are embraced in charges presented as above shall be considered, or voted upon or made the basis of any action, unless upon written consent signed by the person affected.

Service of the required notice shall be made personally or by registered mail duly received within the United States, or by such method as is provided for service in Supreme Court actions in cases wherein a defendant is without the State of New York or personal service cannot be obtained, publication to be made in a newspaper published in Tompkins County and which shall be complete thirty days before the date of hearing.

The hearing shall be before the stockholders at the stockholders meeting, and the vote on such removal may be had only in person. The accused may appear in person and be represented by counsel, and may require that witnesses giving testimony be sworn; the stockholders may authorize the Chairman of the meeting to be the sole judge of the admissibility of evidence and the procedure of the trial.

SEC. 11. In case of removal by the Directors of officers or employees, at pleasure, as provided in the Stock Corporations Law, or otherwise, no notice or hearing shall be necessary, but such procedure shall be entirely in the discretion of the Directors.

SEC. 12. Any officers elected or appointed by the Board of Directors may be removed at any time by the Board, but the Board nevertheless may contract for a definite period of employment for any officer or agent. All vacancies in office shall be filled by the Board.

Sec. 13. All contracts and agreements purporting to be the act of the Corporation shall bear thereon the seal of the Corporation and shall be signed by the President, one of the Vice-Presidents, the General Manager, the Treasurer or the Secretary, or by any two said officers or person or by persons acting in a representative capacity, when duly authorized thereunto.

ARTICLE IV
Capital Stock

Sec. 1. Certificates of stock shall be signed by the President and by the Treasurer or Secretary, numbered and registered in the order in which they shall be issued, and the seal of the Corporation shall be affixed thereto. All certificates shall be bound in books and shall be issued in consecutive order therefrom, and in the margins of the books shall be severally entered the names of the persons owning the shares represented by said certificate respectively with the number and date of each certificate. All certificates exchanged or returned to the corporation shall be marked cancelled, with the date of cancellation and each shall be pasted in the certificate book from which it was issued, opposite the memorandum of its issuance.

Every certificate shall state on the face thereof the kind and class of shares which it represents, and shall state on the face or back thereof all of the designations, privileges and voting powers of the shares of each class which the corporation is authorized to issue, and the restrictions or qualifications thereof.

Sec. 2. Transfers of shares shall be made on the books of the Corporation by the holders in person or under power of attorney duly executed, witnessed and filed with the corporation, and upon the surrender of the outstanding certificate or certificates of such shares. The corporation shall have the right to purchase at par and dividends accrued any common or Class B common shares of the stockholder offered for transfer, or the common or class B common shares of any deceased or retiring stockholder, or any stockholders who shall have purchased from or sold to the corporation or one of its agencies or affiliates goods of the value of less than $100.00 in any one corporate year.

In case of a liquidation of this cooperative or other distribution of its assets, the holders of the 4% Cumulative Preferred shares shall be entitled to receive on surrender of their shares the par value thereof only plus accrued dividends, if any, before any distribution shall be made to the common and Class B common stockholders. Thereafter the common and Class B common stockholders shall be entitled to receive on surrender of their shares the par value thereof only plus accrued dividends, if any, for the current year and the residue of net margins, if any, shall be distributed only to the members of this Cooperative pursuant to the provisions of these By-Laws and the Cooperative Corporations Law of the State of New York.

Sec. 3. No stock of the Corporation held in its Treasury shall be issued, unless such issue shall have been first authorized and approved by vote of the Board of Directors of the Corporation.

Sec. 4. The transfer books of the Corporation may be closed by order of the Board of Directors for a period not exceeding thirty days, before any meeting of stockholders and until the day after the final adjournment of such meeting. The transfer books of the Corporation may also be closed for a like time before the payment of any dividend.

ARTICLE V
Dividends and Reserve Funds

Sec. 1. Dividends on the capital stock of the corporation shall be declared and paid as provided by law and by the Certificate of Incorporation out of the reserve for dividends established in accordance with Section 10 of Article I of these by-laws as often and at such times as the Board of Directors may determine.

Sec. 2. The corporation may use and apply the net margins not distributed as cash patronage refunds or price adjustments or any other funds as permitted by law to the purchase or acquisition of property and to the purchase or acquisition of its own capital stock, from time to time and to such an extent and in such manner and upon such terms, as its Board of Directors shall determine, and shall be authorized by law.

ARTICLE VI
Seal

Sec. 1. The seal of the Corporation shall be circular in form, with the words "Cooperative Grange League Federation Exchange, Inc." on the circumference, and the words "Corporate Seal 1920" "New York" in the center.

ARTICLE VII
Checks, Bills, Notes, Etc.

Sec. 1. All checks, drafts, bills of exchange, notes, orders for the payment of money and other negotiable instruments of the Company, shall be made in the name of the Corporation, and shall be signed by the President or any Vice-President, the Secretary, Treasurer or Assistant Secretary or Assistant Treasurer or any one of them. The Board of Directors may also delegate to other officers or agents the power to sign or countersign such instruments. No officers or agent of the Company, either singly or jointly with others shall have the power to make any bill payable, note or check or other negotiable instrument or endorse the same in the name of the Company, or contract or cause to be contracted any debt or liability in the name or on behalf of the Company, except as provided in these By-Laws and as authorized by the Board of Directors. Bills of exchange, checks, notes and other negotiable instruments received by the Corporation shall be endorsed for collection by such officers or agents as may be designated by the Board of Directors for that purpose.

ARTICLE VIII
Stock Owned by the Company in Other Corporations

Sec. 1. Stock owned by this Company in other corporations shall be voted in the name of this Corporation by such officer or officers as shall be delegated thereto by resolution adopted by the Board of Directors of this Corporation.

Sec. 2. All shares of common capital stock owned by this Cooperative or by its subsidiary, Cooperative G.L.F. Holding Corporation, in retail Cooperative Corporations organized under Article 7 of the Cooperative Corporations Law shall be deemed to be owned, held and voted in trust only for the benefit of the members of such cooperatives respectively. All G.L.F. employed personnel having to do with the operations or management of such cooperatives or holding an office therein or serving as a director thereof are hereby charged with the responsibility of administering their duties solely in the interest of the members of said cooperatives.

SEC. 3. Whenever a cooperative defined as above, shall cease to become indebted to this cooperative or its said subsidiary or shall have made satisfactory arrangements to secure payment of said indebtedness,—the Member Committee may by a majority vote of all its Committeemen submit the question of independent ownership to the members at a meeting thereof to be duly called and held on a day not less than 10 nor more than 20 days after notice is mailed. The members entitled to notice shall be those defined as such under the by-laws of such cooperative. Said notice shall clearly state the time, place and object of the meeting. The proposition to be voted on may be stated to be "Shall the members of (name of cooperative) take over control and/or management of this cooperative?"; or may state whatever modification of this proposition is proposed. In case a majority of the members entitled to vote on such proposition shall attend said meeting in person and at least two-thirds of those members in attendance shall vote in favor of the proposition, then a contract shall be made between the owner of the shares of stock outstanding and the Member Committee of the cooperative concerned who shall be deemed to be representing the entire membership thereof, covering the following provisions:

(a) The owner of the common stock will agree to cause a meeting of the Board of Directors of such cooperative to be held, at which meeting the Board will declare a patronage dividend to all members of the cooperative in the form of shares of its common stock to be issued, however, to the then members of the Member Committee—one committeeman—one share in *trust* however as per the provisions of a Declaration of Trust hereinafter set forth. The owner will also take resignations of all directors then in office and elect as a new board the Member Committeemen then in office, each to serve for the unexpired term for which each was elected by the members. The owner will also amend the By-Laws to conform to changes herein provided.

(b) Owner will also agree to take action to cause the old shares of common stock theretofore issued to be redeemed by such cooperative at face amount.

(c) The Member Committee as representatives of their members, shall sign the proposed Declaration of Trust; shall constitute the sole stockholders and be the first Board of Directors under the new order.

(d) Said Declaration of Trust shall conform substantially to the following:

DECLARATION OF TRUST
on behalf of Members
of

....

....

We, the undersigned, constituting the sole common stockholders of the above named Cooperative, hereby certify:

Each of us is a stockholder of record of said cooperative.

We declare that we hold said shares in Trust for the benefit of the members of this cooperative located in its trade area and constitute ourselves individually and collectively, Trustee(s) of said shares.

We severally covenant that, whenever we vote said shares, we will to the best of our ability, vote the same at meetings of stockholders and members of this cooperative in the interest of the patrons for whom we are acting as Trustees. We further agree to elect for directors only such members as may be duly designated by the membership at regular or special meetings of members as their choice for directors.

In case any one of us should die or cease to be a member of the Board of Directors, the share in the name of each of us respectively shall pass to our successor director, nominated by the members at any meetings of the members or to a successor elected by the Board to serve for the remainder of an unexpired term, and we now certify that we have each endorsed our share for transfer in blank and delivered the certificate to our local Secretary or Chairman for safe-keeping and hereby irrevocably constitute and appoint our Secretary or Chairman, our Attorney in Fact to make the transfer when a successor is elected and consents to serve as Trustee. Consents shall be signified by the signing of this Declaration of Trust or by such other means as may hereafter be adopted.

Actual ownership of said trust shares of this cooperative is by this instrument and by corporate action, vested in all members of this cooperative located in its trade area at any given time and are held in trust for them by the trustees under the provisions of this Declaration of Trust.

As stockholders of this cooperative we will, through the Board of Directors, annually call an assembly of members as defined in the by-laws to meet as a membership body at a convenient place and time for the purpose of choosing nominees for election to the Board of Directors to succeed any who by death or expiration of term shall cease to be directors; to receive reports and to transact such other business as may be required.

This Declaration of Trust may be amended, altered or terminated by unanimous action by the then trustees hereunder and ratification by a majority of the members present and voting at a membership meeting called on at least three days' notice. The notice of the meeting shall state clearly the proposed action to be taken by the Trustees.

(e) The contract shall provide in substance that in case the cooperative concerned votes to discontinue both control and management and also elects to discontinue handling G.L.F. commodities, then the officers, Board of Directors and owner shall cause the letters G.L.F. to be eliminated from the corporate name by appropriate action before the transfer is made and the Member Committee shall agree that if after the transaction is consummated, the cooperative elects at any future time to discontinue handling G.L.F. commodities they, or their successors, as sole trustee stockholders, will take the necessary steps to eliminate said letters from the corporate name.

SEC. 4. Upon the completion of the foregoing or such modification thereof as may be mutually satisfactory to the parties concerned, such cooperatives shall be classified as having a status independent of management and/or control as the case may be, by this cooperative or any of its subsidiaries, or its or their employed personnel except as such cooperatives by independent action may see fit to enter into a contract with respect to management, audit or for other services as it may in its sole discretion determine to be advantageous to its patrons.

ARTICLE IX
AMENDMENTS

SEC. 1. These By-Laws may be amended, altered or added to, as set forth in Article II, Section 5 thereof, and also at any meeting of stockholders by a vote of a majority of the stockholders voting in person or by mail whose stock shall remain outstanding and shall not have been called by order of, or pursuant to vote of the Directors for redemption, and who shall otherwise be entitled to vote, who act either in person, or by mail, providing the substance of the proposed amendment shall have been duly inserted in notices duly given of such meeting.

ARTICLE X
NOTICE AND WAIVER OF NOTICE

SEC. 1. Whenever under the provisions of these By-Laws or of any of the statutes of the State of New York, the stockholders or Directors are authorized to hold any meeting after notice or after the lapse of any prescribed period of time, such meeting may be held without notice and without such lapse of time by written waiver of such notice signed by every person entitled to notice or by his attorney thereunto duly authorized. At any meeting of the Board of Directors at which every Director shall be present, though held without notice, any business may be transacted which might have been transacted if the meeting had been called and held on notice.

* * *

I, M. E. Campbell, Secretary of Cooperative Grange League Federation Exchange, Inc., certify that the foregoing is a true copy of the original Certificate of Incorporation and By-Laws as amended in November, 1932, October, 1940, February 12, 1941, November 21, 1942, November 22, 1944, October 31, 1946, July 1, 1948, October 21, 1948, May 26, 1949 (effective July 1, 1949), June 19, 1951, November 28, 1951, September 15, 1952, October 17, 1952, October 24, 1952, and October 22, 1954.

M. E. CAMPBELL

G.L.F. Directors

PAST AND PRESENT G.L.F. DIRECTORS

Organization or district represented[1]	Name	Date Elected	End of Service
Grange	Bean, W. L.	June 28, 1920	Feb. 6, 1922
Grange	Lowell, S. J.	June 28, 1920	July 1, 1921
Grange	Hitchings, R. C.	June 28, 1920	Feb. 1, 1932
Dairymen's League	Webb, N. F.	June 28, 1920	Jan. 10, 1930
Dairymen's League	Bull, Harry	June 28, 1920	Oct. 30, 1945
Dairymen's League	Griffith, J. C.	June 28, 1920	Feb. 5, 1923
Farm Bureau	Babcock, H. E.	June 28, 1920	Jan. 31, 1921
Farm Bureau	Smith, A. L.	June 28, 1920	Feb. 2, 1931
Farm Bureau	Brown, H. L.	June 28, 1920	Feb. 4, 1924
Farm Bureau	Porter, F. L.	Jan. 31, 1921	Sept. 4, 1938
Grange	Kirkland, George	July 1, 1921	Feb. 1, 1932
Grange	Walrath, E. J.	Feb. 6, 1922	Oct. 31, 1946
Dairymen's League	Burden, H.	Feb. 5, 1923	Feb. 5, 1937
Farm Bureau	Burritt, M. C.	Feb. 4, 1924	Feb. 4, 1929
Farm Bureau	Kirkland, L. G.	Feb. 4, 1929	Dec. 25, 1942
Dairymen's League	Utter, Fred	Feb. 3, 1930	Oct. 24, 1940
Farm Bureau	Smith, F. M.	Feb. 2, 1931	Oct. 22, 1953
Grange	Corwith, J. C.	Feb. 1, 1932	Active
District 9, N.J.	Snyder, C. E.	Nov. 15, 1932	Active
District 10, N.J.	Heritage, R. L.	Nov. 15, 1932	Oct. 24, 1940
District 8, Pa.	Culver, C. B.	Nov. 15, 1932	Dec. 4, 1937
District 7, Pa.	Benson, H. L.	Nov. 15, 1932	Nov. 5, 1941
Grange	Hubbard, W. C.	Nov. 14, 1933	Oct. 19, 1936
Grange	Clark, Earl	Oct. 19, 1936	Active
District 2, N.Y.	Welles, J. S.	June 28, 1937	Oct. 21, 1954
Farm Bureau	Ameele, J. D.	Nov. 1, 1938	Oct. 21, 1954
District 8, Pa.	Culver, R. L.	Nov. 1, 1938	Active
District 4, N.Y.	Atwood, J. L.	Oct. 24, 1940	Oct. 26, 1950
District 10, N.J.	Davis, T. W.	Oct. 24, 1940	Oct. 30, 1945
District 7, Pa.	Moulton, L. H.	Nov. 6, 1941	Oct. 30, 1942
District 1, N.Y.	White, C. G.	Jan. 18, 1943	Active
District 7, Pa.	Hummer, George	Nov. 5, 1943	Oct. 22, 1953
District 6, N.Y.	Mapes, W. S.	Oct. 30, 1945	Jan. 20, 1946
District 6, N.Y.	Rich, W. H.	May 20, 1946	Active
District 3, N.Y.	Creal, H. L.	Oct. 31, 1946	Active
District 10, N.J.	Bibus, H. W., Jr.	Oct. 31, 1946	Active
District 5, N.Y.	Albright, M. C.	Oct. 31, 1947	Nov. 7, 1950
District 4, N.Y.	Orrin Ross	Oct. 26, 1950	Active
District 5, N.Y.	Milburn J. Huntley	Oct. 25, 1951	Active
District 7, Pa.	Paul R. Smith	Oct. 22, 1953	Oct. 20, 1955
Farm Bureau	Harold G. Soper	Oct. 22, 1953	Active
District 2, N.Y.	Harold A. Giles	Oct. 21, 1954	Active
Farm Bureau	Morris T. Johnson	Oct. 21, 1954	Active
District 7, Pa.	Roy S. Bowen	Oct. 20, 1955	Active

[1] Districts were first set up in 1932 for New Jersey and Pennsylvania, and later for New York. The districts have been re-numbered from time to time and the district numbers now in effect are used.

APPENDIX C

Price Movements, 1920-59

PRICES RECEIVED AND PAID BY FARMERS IN NEW YORK
AND UNITED STATES, 1920-59
1910-14: 100

Year	Prices Farmers Received		Prices Farmers Paid[1]	
	New York	United States	New York Dairymen	United States
1920	219	211	201	214
1921	151	124	150	155
1922	141	131	146	151
1923	147	142	162	159
1924	134	143	165	160
1925	150	156	169	164
1926	163	145	170	160
1927	153	139	174	159
1928	161	148	177	162
1929	159	146	170	167
1930	149	125	163	151
1931	105	87	138	130
1932	79	65	116	112
1933	82	72	105	120
1934	99	90	116	120
1935	102	109	121	124
1936	113	114	124	124
1937	115	122	136	131
1938	98	97	130	124
1939	101	95	127	124
1940	111	100	128	124
1941	129	124	142	133
1942	157	159	171	152
1943	199	193	208	171
1944	217	197	230	182
1945	231	207	243	190
1946	259	236	268	208
1947	261	276	287	240
1948	290	287	308	260
1949	249	250	300	251
1950	237	258	296	256
1951	274	302	328	282
1952	281	288	350	287
1953	243	258	346	275
1954	226	249	343	281
1955	225	236	346	281
1956	230	235	352	285
1957	241	242	363	296
1958	248	250	376	293
1959	243	240	387	298

[1] Prices of articles farmers buy includes those for commodities, interest, taxes, and wage rates.

Source: Farm Economics—New York College of Agriculture, Cornell University.

G.L.F. Operating Statistics

DOLLAR VOLUME, G.L.F. SYSTEM, 1924-25 TO 1958-59

| Fiscal Year Ending June 30th | Wholesale Exchange Consolidated | Retail | | Total G.L.F. System |
		Service Stores	Bulk Plants	
1924-25	$ 6,635,364	$ —	$ —	$ 6,635,364
1925-26	8,208,208	459,392	—	8,667,600
1926-27	10,778,174	943,193	—	11,721,367
1927-28	19,066,118	2,242,214	—	21,308,332
1928-29	24,684,730	3,735,657	—	28,420,387
1929-30	29,239,098	6,449,576	—	35,688,674
1930-31	24,071,832	7,645,024	—	31,716,856
1931-32	16,783,451	6,661,165	—	23,444,616
1932-33	16,244,993	7,485,759	—	23,730,752
1933-34	23,927,595	12,511,456	—	36,439,051
1934-35	24,261,900	16,011,107	—	40,273,007
1935-36	25,501,940	13,974,110	—	39,476,050
1936-37	41,158,517	21,551,463	75,318	62,785,298
1937-38	35,147,471	18,596,940	381,105	54,125,516
1938-39	32,994,620	18,011,050	850,745	51,856,415
1939-40	40,245,501	22,464,651	1,610,386	64,320,538
1940-41	48,960,219	25,086,680	2,513,439	76,560,338
1941-42	66,446,421	36,144,319	4,585,893	107,176,633
1942-43	86,002,352	44,185,937	5,742,431	135,930,720
1943-44	114,013,013	60,386,603	6,759,973	181,159,589
1944-45	107,879,517	59,374,617	6,845,254	174,099,388
1945-46	108,903,923	71,242,707	7,145,449	187,292,079
1946-47	128,459,726	80,081,788	9,180,897	217,722,411
1947-48	151,339,483	99,031,674	12,395,127	262,766,284
1948-49	144,145,525	93,157,279	14,443,295	251,746,099
1949-50	141,944,802	91,949,033	15,456,661	249,350,496
1950-51	163,001,466	106,328,155	17,023,285	286,352,906
1951-52	183,732,534	124,688,883	18,960,563	327,381,980
1952-53	175,435,269	121,987,178	19,606,181	317,028,628
1953-54	166,872,990	110,583,228	20,725,233	298,181,451
1954-55	165,426,856	110,588,950	21,786,142	297,801,948
1955-56	163,810,913	105,330,835	23,286,673	292,437,421
1956-57	167,882,441	113,318,724	25,627,523	306,828,688
1957-58	169,357,000	113,227,000	25,867,000	308,451,000
1958-59	177,355,657	122,017,751	28,436,337	327,809,745

TOTAL ASSETS, G.L.F. SYSTEM, 1924-25 TO 1958-59
(WITHOUT ELIMINATIONS)

Fiscal Year Ending June 30th	Wholesale Exchange Consolidated	Retail Service Stores	Retail Bulk Plants	Total G.L.F. System
1924-25	$ 945,041	$ —	$ —	$ 945,041
1925-26	944,605	78,340	—	1,022,945
1926-27	1,187,947	167,378	—	1,355,325
1927-28	1,494,051	351,520	—	1,845,571
1928-29	3,281,260	358,798	—	3,640,058
1929-30	4,825,199	696,635	—	5,521,834
1930-31	3,714,516	839,545	—	4,554,061
1931-32	4,186,387	735,584	—	4,921,971
1932-33	5,072,178	850,719	—	5,922,897
1933-34	5,678,084	965,581	—	6,643,665
1934-35	5,503,403	1,252,838	—	6,756,241
1935-36	5,445,729	1,312,014	—	6,757,743
1936-37	7,554,640	2,052,067	33,975	9,640,682
1937-38	7,132,826	2,015,079	125,061	9,272,966
1938-39	8,281,150	2,381,045	323,050	10,985,245
1939-40	9,429,256	2,861,067	517,324	12,807,647
1940-41	12,871,998	3,767,211	694,698	17,333,907
1941-42	17,440,392	5,658,319	1,157,422	24,256,133
1942-43	20,391,084	7,257,141	1,153,150	28,801,375
1943-44	24,237,268	8,707,150	984,352	33,928,770
1944-45	23,568,616	9,467,620	1,008,585	34,044,821
1945-46	24,363,584	10,919,535	1,175,550	36,458,669
1946-47	30,468,940	14,494,707	1,740,325	46,703,972
1947-48	40,524,878	16,843,641	1,858,189	59,226,708
1948-49	43,244,159	17,417,903	2,163,310	62,825,372
1949-50	46,199,778	19,170,204	2,342,365	67,712,347
1950-51	58,486,912	24,822,941	2,957,756	86,267,609
1951-52	55,382,083	25,739,236	2,438,694	83,560,013
1952-53	53,253,488	27,046,923	2,840,453	83,140,864
1953-54	55,419,478	31,091,277	3,325,539	89,362,294
1954-55	58,130,816	33,176,578	3,948,578	95,255,972
1955-56	63,269,703	33,935,947	4,360,511	103,566,161
1956-57	65,438,711	39,094,477	4,886,626	109,419,814
1957-58	65,668,000	42,401,000	5,178,000	113,247,000
1958-59	67,900,455	44,974,330	5,593,972	118,468,757

MEMBERS INVESTMENT, G.L.F. SYSTEM, 1924-25 TO 1958-59

Fiscal Year Ending June 30th	Capital Stock	Retained Earnings	Total
1924-25	$ 774,457	$ 101,221	$ 875,678
1925-26	815,878	124,018	939,896
1926-27	858,742	326,132	1,184,874
1927-28	906,540	691,433	1,597,973
1928-29	1,027,635	1,211,551	2,239,186
1929-30	1,771,615	1,056,383	2,827,998
1930-31	1,959,040	983,950	2,942,990
1931-32	1,965,345	1,381,781	3,347,126
1932-33	1,973,580	2,038,676	4,012,256
1933-34	1,976,490	2,548,757	4,525,247
1934-35	1,946,825	2,626,425	4,573,250
1935-36	1,786,035	2,642,172	4,428,207
1936-37	1,772,715	3,658,336	5,431,051
1937-38	1,734,770	4,298,081	6,032,851
1938-39	1,733,720	4,891,246	6,624,966
1939-40	1,732,835	5,417,182	7,150,017
1940-41	2,074,730	6,002,290	8,077,020
1941-42	3,957,947	7,933,601	11,891,548
1942-43	8,100,832	8,769,632	16,870,464
1943-44	9,732,455	10,332,889	20,065,344
1944-45	11,559,844	10,679,543	22,239,387
1945-46	11,782,872	10,796,154	22,579,026
1946-47	12,818,930	10,489,116	23,308,046
1947-48	16,480,910	16,569,910	33,050,820
1948-49	18,395,680	18,105,002	36,500,682
1949-50	22,745,415	20,093,974	42,839,389
1950-51	24,953,715	23,464,297	48,418,012
1951-52	30,203,625	26,054,740	56,258,365
1952-53	32,560,140	26,207,237	58,767,377
1953-54	33,105,335	28,233,036	61,338,371
1954-55	32,850,815	29,757,844	62,608,659
1955-56	32,988,335	31,588,755	64,577,090
1956-57	32,823,145	33,483,083	66,306,228
1957-58	32,869,000	35,222,000	68,091,000
1958-59	35,850,310	37,490,488	73,070,798

DISTRIBUTION OF NET MARGINS, G.L.F. SYSTEM, 1924-25 TO 1958-59

Fiscal Year Ending June 30th	Net Margins	Patronage Refunds	Federal Income Tax[1]	Dividends on Stock	Retained Margins
1924-25	$ 48,277	$ —	$ —	$ 45,994[2]	$ 48,277
1925-26	48,608	1,711	—	47,077	180*
1926-27	214,538	8,284	—	49,495	156,759
1927-28	451,386	15,504	—	50,982	384,900
1928-29	627,395	21,603	—	59,740	546,052
1929-30	86,152	29,473	—	92,245	35,566*
1930-31	65,327	—	—	120,622	55,295*
1931-32	596,051	—	—	123,042	473,009
1932-33	855,959	7,384	—	127,167	721,408
1933-34	920,611	29,205	—	126,778	764,628
1934-35	671,499	42,217	—	127,079	502,203
1935-36	1,092,105	359,368	—	111,020	621,717
1936-37	1,918,493	679,850	—	97,951	1,140,692
1937-38	1,306,986	430,357	—	96,071	780,558
1938-39	1,932,646	1,151,746	—	95,268	685,632
1939-40	2,796,431	1,628,275	—	95,195	1,072,961
1940-41	2,826,916	1,593,135	—	104,926	1,128,855
1941-42	4,397,366	1,925,662	—	116,026	2,355,678
1942-43	5,322,677	3,932,425	—	208,991	1,181,261
1943-44	7,808,082	5,559,104	—	466,085	1,782,893
1944-45	4,224,843	2,807,290	—	552,487	865,076
1945-46	5,352,959	4,267,775	—	601,409	483,775
1946-47	5,275,973	3,663,795	—	643,737	968,441
1947-48	7,274,136	4,476,273	—	794,793	2,003,070
1948-49	5,435,206	2,059,335	938,531	918,138	1,519,202
1949-50	6,424,503	2,183,540	1,121,583	1,151,915	1,967,465
1950-51	8,998,591	2,626,953	1,758,169	1,305,306	3,308,163
1951-52	7,704,969	2,431,842	1,651,354	1,617,277	2,004,496
1952-53	4,609,609	1,192,958	1,518,540	1,731,039	167,072
1953-54	7,825,332	1,585,595	2,740,612	1,783,979	1,715,146
1954-55	7,471,186	1,708,125	2,494,363	1,742,991	1,525,707
1955-56	8,236,377	1,935,949	2,680,830	1,753,602	1,865,996
1956-57	8,467,393	2,056,580	2,750,814	1,741,926	1,918,073
1957-58	7,664,408	1,112,757	3,087,201	1,738,657	1,725,793
1958-59	8,353,348	1,157,055	2,962,301	1,922,371	2,311,621

[1] Not subject to federal income tax until July 1, 1948.
[2] Dividend paid in 1924 calendar year.
* Denotes loss.

WHOLESALE PURCHASING VOLUME, G.L.F. EXCHANGE,
1929-30 TO 1958-59

Fiscal Year Ending June 30	Feed (tons)	Fertilizer (tons)	Seed (tons)	Petroleum (gallons)[1]	Farm Supplies (dollars)
1929-30	562,895	44,894	5,767	—	527,608
1930-31	532,333	49,446	6,582	—	453,894
1931-32	546,520	54,815	6,796	—	374,022
1932-33	576,005	87,656	7,634	—	372,014
1933-34	672,061	119,058	8,975	—	469,441
1934-35	583,698	125,728	7,101	—	413,685
1935-36	719,849	111,118	9,241	—	816,823
1936-37	798,347	285,457	9,925	—	974,596
1937-38	776,098	263,779	9,504	—	1,588,100
1938-39	797,420	244,832	10,171	—	2,512,854
1939-40	857,733	376,660	11,546	—	3,504,454
1940-41	949,549	383,465	12,599	—	5,533,761
1941-42	997,145	348,952	14,017	—	4,669,510
1942-43	1,201,556	271,105	19,709	—	3,907,780
1943-44	1,342,620	318,366	20,783	43,103,000	5,540,976
1944-45	1,195,543	330,356	16,719	45,139,049	6,584,251
1945-46	1,062,818	354,850	19,661	49,650,687	7,709,497
1946-47	1,031,239	371,831	19,554	58,772,626	11,240,829
1947-48	1,060,515	422,493	18,530	70,422,504	11,945,062
1948-49	1,133,023	485,771	16,383	75,625,429	12,435,086
1949-50	1,251,128	529,642	19,095	86,918,442	11,682,797
1950-51	1,257,015	604,708	20,966	90,273,162	18,050,107
1951-52	1,325,985	718,088	20,028	93,372,397	15,195,128
1952-53	1,284,814	728,349	19,927	100,270,683	14,684,415
1953-54	1,308,891	724,105	20,406	104,050,088	13,983,876
1954-55	1,307,171	758,608	20,468	110,850,531	14,203,674
1955-56	1,328,817	763,884	20,824	117,434,977	15,996,193
1956-57	1,287,093	839,782	19,506	121,160,031	16,721,554
1957-58	1,284,558	787,550	19,304	127,428,579	20,679,000
1958-59	1,305,424	815,723	20,361	139,878,734	22,897,000

[1] Volume in gallons not reported until 1943-44.

MARKETING VOLUME, G.L.F. EXCHANGE, 1940-41 TO 1958-59

Fiscal Years Ending June 30	Eggs (cases)	Grain (bushels)	Beans (cwt.)
1940-41	183,696	541,603	99,574
1941-42	295,456	401,617	107,450
1942-43	406,713	311,818	138,411
1943-44	636,109	134,139	169,819
1944-45	476,334	665,394	152,212
1945-46	366,863	825,515	140,480
1946-47	406,157	801,363	189,219
1947-48	473,782	1,243,269	184,376
1948-49	452,910	1,815,959	198,905
1949-50	591,540	1,316,162	186,075
1950-51	571,511	2,647,199	223,769
1951-52	666,845	3,166,458	273,778
1952-53	704,709	3,089,437	277,901
1953-54	760,459	1,858,949	343,932
1954-55	864,972	1,368,427	355,802
1955-56	910,318	1,528,117	355,784
1956-57	925,242	2,228,655	315,411
1957-58	897,172	2,462,990	361,926
1958-59	865,224	2,116,524	410,182

SERVICE TONS OF RETAIL STORES,* 1949-50 TO 1958-59

1949-50	1,043,901
1950-51	1,337,234
1951-52	1,580,206
1952-53	1,467,621
1953-54	1,690,091
1954-55	1,689,358
1955-56	1,780,888
1956-57	1,848,279
1957-58	1,924,301
1958-59	2,009,210

* "Service tons" represent one ton of "equipment service" for a patron. For example, a "service ton" records one ton of grinding, mixing, trucking, drying or lime-spreading service. It does not include commodity tonnage. One ton of a commodity grown by a farmer can produce several "service tons." If a store-owned truck picked up and delivered a ton of corn and trucked it to a G.L.F. Store this would give one "service ton." If the corn was then ground this would represent another "service ton." If mixed with other ingredients for feed, another "service ton" would be produced. "Service tons" thus reflect operator's time, equipment time, management time and record keeping time. They measure the use of G.L.F. retail services. (Information provided by Frederic M. Upchurch, Assistant Controller, October 30, 1959.)

WHOLESALE VALUE OF SUPPLIES DISTRIBUTED BY G.L.F. FOR THE FISCAL YEARS ENDED JUNE 30, 1958 AND 1959

Commodities	1958	1959
Feed, grain, flour, and cereals	$ 82,648,956	$ 86,920,727
Fertilizer and lime (including shells, bedding, etc.)	16,851,369	16,815,208
Petroleum products	17,665,495	18,966,230
Tires, tubes, and auto supplies	2,449,502	2,961,915
Seed and seed potatoes	7,683,250	7,809,373
Hardware (tools)	659,979	600,159
Refrigeration equipment	1,805,370	1,934,532
Farm equipment and parts	3,525,685	4,144,003
Steel and other metal products	3,198,626	3,491,238
Building material, paint, and roofing	2,484,443	2,582,609
Insecticides, sprays, and farm chemicals	4,485,582	5,140,081
Containers and package materials	553,134	507,261
Rope and twine	1,228,004	1,259,141
Lawn and garden equipment	1,390,014	1,788,758
Miscellaneous	1,340,412	1,341,257
Total	$147,969,821	$156,262,492

VALUE OF FARM PRODUCTS MARKETED BY G.L.F.[1] FOR THE YEARS ENDED JUNE 30, 1958 AND 1959

Commodities	1958	1959
Eggs	$ 12,706,046	$ 10,738,473
Fruits and vegetables	903,017	1,261,969
Grain	6,728,890	5,954,223
Beans	3,430,184	3,823,115
Onions	—	172,710
Miscellaneous	723,906	1,375,952
Total	$ 24,492,043	$ 23,326,442

[1] Includes marketing by service stores.

NUMBER OF RETAIL UNITS, G.L.F. SYSTEM, 1925-26 TO 1958-59

Fiscal Years Ending June 30	*Service Stores*	*Bulk Plants*[1]	*Agent Buyers*[2]
1925-26	5	—	—
1926-27	12	—	—
1927-28	21	—	—
1928-29	29	—	—
1929-30	68	—	—
1930-31	74	—	—
1931-32	91	—	—
1932-33	119	—	—
1933-34	129	—	—
1934-35	137	—	—
1935-36	142	—	—
1936-37	146	5	—
1937-38	148	10	—
1938-39	149	18	506
1939-40	153	25	520
1940-41	160	32	510
1941-42	170	37	502
1942-43	177	45	503
1943-44	181	45	497
1944-45	194	45	475
1945-46	208	49	468
1946-47	218	56	443
1947-48	227	57	446
1948-49	230	64	428
1949-50	231	65	412
1950-51	234	75	410
1951-52	245	75	401
1952-53	244	75	390
1953-54	245	75	385
1954-55	240	69	365
1955-56	238	65	328
1956-57	232	66	320
1957-58	231	65	317
1958-59	231	65	310

[1] No program prior to 1935.
[2] Not reported until 1938-39.

NUMBER OF STOCKHOLDERS AND EMPLOYEES, G. L. F. SYSTEM,
1936-37 TO 1958-59

| Fiscal years ending June 30 | Stockholders | | | | Employees |
	Exchange Common	Preferred	Holding Corp. Preferred	Service Store Preferred	
1936-37	31,129	—	—	—	1,834
1937-38	30,300	—	—	—	1,625
1938-39	31,528	—	—	—	1,785
1939-40	31,428	—	—	—	2,051
1940-41	29,552	—	—	—	2,520
1941-42	28,869	—	—	—	2,827
1942-43	31,658	—	—	—	3,345
1943-44	49,934	—	—	—	3,650
1944-45	60,378	—	—	—	3,647
1945-46	59,440	—	—	—	4,121
1946-47	57,532	—	—	—	4,123
1947-48	72,438	—	—	—	3,953
1948-49	105,151	—	—	23,203	3,994
1949-50	108,504	—	5,341	22,846	3,929
1950-51	113,658	—	5,488	22,897	4,241
1951-52	118,212	523	5,415	27,352	4,353
1952-53	118,254	1,280	4,888	27,765	4,314
1953-54	115,228	2,162	3,813	27,591	4,367
1954-55	118,149	2,553	2,989	27,125	4,402
1955-56	119,753	2,878	2,723	26,580	4,589
1956-57	117,742	3,066	2,533	25,978	4,626
1957-58	115,275	3,302	2,326	25,416	4,678
1958-59	117,815	3,504	2,122	25,164	4,824

G.L.F. Financial Statements

COOPERATIVE GRAND LEAGUE FEDERATION EXCHANGE, INC.
AND WHOLESALE SUBSIDIARIES
CONSOLIDATED BALANCE SHEETS

	June 30, 1957	June 30 1958	June 30 1959
ASSETS			
Current Assets			
Cash	$ 3,347,413	$ 2,799,183	$ 2,308,553
Accounts Receivable	3,526,754	4,523,526	5,065,542
Notes, Advances and Acceptances Receivable	13,371,900	14,507,237	16,546,263
Allowances for Doubtful Accounts and Notes	102,569*	102,569*	100,000*
Advances on Broilers	102,258	265,112	511,218
Advances on Purchases	921,385	1,210,370	115,980
Inventories	15,983,911	15,440,816	17,336,478
Total Current Assets	37,151,322	38,643,675	41,784,034
Investments (Net)	9,187,624	9,143,241	7,479,901
Fixed Assets			
Land, Buildings and Equipment— Cost	26,219,357	27,288,769	28,603,945
Less, Allowance for Depreciation	8,957,864	9,924,971	10,977,982
Net Total Fixed Assets	17,261,493	17,363,798	17,625,963
Deferred Charges	309,199	516,920	1,010,557
Total Assets	$63,909,638	$65,667,634	$67,900,455

* Denotes red figure

BALANCE SHEETS—continued

	June 30, 1957	June 30, 1958	June 30, 1959
LIABILITIES, CAPITAL STOCK AND PATRONS' EQUITY			
Current Liabilities			
Accounts Payable	$ 3,794,075	$ 4,119,395	$ 4,090,063
Outstanding Checks and Called Certificates	901,220	879,505	712,724
Notes and Acceptances Payable	3,267,313	2,507,516	1,868,736
Dividends Payable	1,075,095	1,072,930	1,170,594
Patronage Refunds Payable	1,000,000	—0—	1,359
Liability Provisions (including Income Taxes)	1,893,777	1,892,539	1,301,820
Accrued Liabilities	1,132,261	1,853,843	2,264,823
Total Current Liabilities	13,063,741	12,325,728	11,410,119
Deferred Credits	2,745	20,902	22,890
Long-Term Liabilities	8,573,068	9,941,302	10,309,200
Capital Stock and Patrons' Equity			
Capital Stock—Preferred	8,835,900	9,108,900	9,436,500
Capital Stock—Common	14,971,820	14,818,830	16,356,765
Reserve for Contingencies and Operating Capital	18,462,364	19,451,972	20,364,981
Total Capital Stock and Patrons' Equity	42,270,084	43,379,702	46,158,246
Total Liabilities, Capital Stock and Patrons' Equity	$63,909,638	$65,667,634	$67,900,455
Net Operating Capital	$24,087,581	$26,317,947	$30,373,915
Current Ratio	2.84	3.14	3.66
Capital Stock and Patrons' Equity (%)	66.14	66.06	67.98

COOPERATIVE GRANGE LEAGUE FEDERATION EXCHANGE, INC.
AND WHOLESALE SUBSIDIARIES
CONSOLIDATED OPERATING STATEMENTS
AND
DISTRIBUTION OF MARGINS

	1956–1957[1]	1957–1958[1]	1958–1959[1]
Net Purchases by Patrons	$149,126,384	$148,434,827	$157,687,892
Net Products Marketed for Patrons	18,756,057	20,922,831	19,667,765
Total Value	$167,882,441	$169,357,658	$177,355,657
Cost of Patrons' Purchases and Products Marketed	147,653,193	148,544,766	155,089,608
Gross Margin on Patrons' Purchases and Products Marketed	$ 20,229,248	$ 20,812,892	$ 22,266,049
Plant and Warehouse Costs	8,223,441	8,950,383[2]	9,479,698[2]
Gross Margin on Purchasing and Marketing Operations	$ 12,005,807	$ 11,862,509	$ 12,786,351
Operating Revenue and Expense (Net)	583,987*	—[2]	—[2]
Total Gross Margin from Operations	$ 11,421,820	$ 11,862,509	$ 12,786,351
General Overhead Expense	6,305,933	7,355,452[2]	7,270,288[2]
Net Margin from Operations	$ 5,115,887	$ 4,507,057	$ 5,516,063
Other Revenue and Deductions (Net)	621,544	437,076	926,633*
Net Margin	$ 5,737,431	$ 4,944,133	$ 4,589,430
Distribution of Net Margins			
Patronage Refunds	$ 999,790	$ 32,105[3]	$ 535[3]
Dividends on Stock	1,251,183	1,250,774	1,355,491
Federal Income Taxes	2,348,306	2,676,698	2,320,394
Retained Margins	1,138,152	984,556	913,010
Total	$ 5,737,431	$ 4,944,133	$ 4,589,430

* Denotes Red Figure.
[1] Fiscal year ends June 30.
[2] Operating Revenue and Expense (Net) no longer used and not identifiable, but are included in Plant and Warehouse Costs and General Overhead Expense.
[3] Adjustment of Prior Years Patronage Refund.

COOP. G.L.F. SERVICE STORES
COMPOSITE BALANCE SHEETS

	June 1957	June 1958	June 1959
(Number of Corporations)	(232)	(231)	(231)

ASSETS

Current Assets			
Cash	$ 1,107,145	$ 1,561,184	$ 1,524,370
Accounts Receivable	7,887,694	8,870,923	10,822,913
Notes and Advances Receivable	3,685,859	3,924,632	4,316,628
Advances on Purchases	189,736	181,466	194,677
Inventories	11,166,087	12,235,893	13,004,983
Total Current Assets	24,036,521	26,774,098	29,863,571
Investments	68,198	77,217	84,097
Fixed Assets			
Land, Buildings and Equipment— Cost	22,327,148	23,481,524	24,095,208
Less Allowance for Depreciation	7,894,806	8,858,799	9,887,141
Net Total	14,432,342	14,622,725	14,208,067
Deferred Charges	557,416	926,892	818,595
Total Assets	$39,094,477	$42,400,932	$44,974,330

LIABILITIES, CAPITAL STOCK AND PATRONS' EQUITY

Current Liabilities			
Accounts Payable	$ 1,885,954	$ 2,429,925	$ 2,142,456
Notes and Advances Payable	10,796,796	12,915,132	13,135,286
Patronage Refund Payable	1,376,863	1,394,033	1,427,512
Dividends Payable	490,743	487,884	566,880
Federal Income Tax Payable	383,043	401,617	571,268
Accrued Liabilities	282,093	341,026	364,815
Total Current Liabilities	15,215,492	17,969,617	18,208,217
Deferred Credits	32,407	28,049	46,704
Long Term Liabilities	1,656,500	1,717,050	2,218,050
Capital Stock and Patrons' Equity			
Capital Stock—Preferred	8,993,075	8,918,645	9,764,920
Capital Stock—Common	17,400	17,250	17,250
Patrons' Equity Reserve	273,552	273,552	273,552
Reserve for Contingencies and Operating Capital	12,906,051	13,476,769	14,445,637
Total Capital Stock and Patrons' Equity	22,190,078	22,686,216	24,501,359
Total Liabilities, Capital Stock and Patrons' Equity	$39,094,477	$42,400,932	$44,974,330

COOP. G.L.F. SERVICE STORES
COMPOSITE OPERATING STATEMENTS
AND
DISTRIBUTION OF MARGINS

	1956–1957[1]	1957–1958[1]	1958–1959[1]
(Number of Corporations)	(232)	(231)	(231)
Net Purchases by Patrons	$105,181,278	$105,050,413	$113,899,155
Products Marketed for Patrons	8,137,445	8,176,555	8,118,596
Total Value	$113,318,723	$113,226,968	$122,017,751
Cost of Patrons' Purchases and			
Products Marketed	100,708,719	100,746,215	108,859,217
Gross Margin on Patrons' Purchases			
and Products Marketed	12,610,004	12,480,753	13,158,534
Operating Revenue (Net)	48,438	4,859,012[2]	5,349,251[2]
Total Gross Margin	12,658,442	17,339,765	18,507,785
Total Operating Expense	10,463,108	15,036,520[2]	15,994,881[2]
Net Margin from Operations	2,195,334	2,303,245	2,512,904
Other Revenue and Deductions	46,728	113,476	561,194
Net Margin	$ 2,242,062	$ 2,416,721	$ 3,074,098
Distribution of Net Margins			
Patronage Refunds	$ 990,226	$ 1,010,657	$ 1,022,563
Dividends on Stock and			
Certificates	490,742	487,884	566,881
Federal Income Taxes	294,396	338,671	494,569
Retained Margins	466,698	579,509	990,085
Total	$ 2,242,062	$ 2,416,721	$ 3,074,098

[1] Fiscal year ends June 30.

[2] Operating Revenues in 1956-57 and Prior Years were reported on a net basis. In 1957-58 and 1958-59 the expenses applicable to Operating Revenues were included in Total Operating Expenses and can not be identified. Therefore, the Operating Revenues are reported on a gross basis.

G.L.F. PETROLEUM COOPS. (BULK PLANTS)
COMPOSITE BALANCE SHEET

(Number of Corporations)	*June* *1957* (66)	*June* *1958* (65)	*June* *1959* (65)
ASSETS			
Current Assets			
Cash	$ 307,093	$ 316,568	$ 372,245
Accounts Receivable	1,081,319	1,313,264	1,585,550
Notes and Advances Receivable	931	–o–	4,137
Advances on Purchases (Merchandise in Transit)	17,025	2,034	6,783
Inventories	647,745	631,372	714,614
Total Current Assets	2,054,113	2,263,238	2,683,329
Fixed Assets			
Land, Buildings, and Equipment—Cost	5,259,209	5,608,962	5,946,748
Less, Allowance for Depreciation	2,514,603	2,789,856	3,126,244
Net Total	2,744,606	2,819,106	2,820,504
Deferred Charges	87,907	96,248	90,139
Total Assets	$4,886,626	$5,178,592	$5,593,972
LIABILITIES, CAPITAL STOCK AND PATRONS' EQUITY			
Current Liabilities			
Accounts Payable	$ 44,968	$ 46,652	$ 31,717
Notes and Advances Payable	2,799,789	2,943,431	2,767,324
Patronage Refund Payable	79,577	83,247	149,253
Federal Income Tax Payable	108,322	71,156	153,403
Accrued Liabilities	7,904	31,440	81,082
Total Current Liabilities	3,040,560	3,175,926	3,182,779
Capital Stock and Patrons' Equity			
Capital Stock—Common	4,950	4,875	4,875
Reserve for Contingencies and Operating Capital	1,841,116	1,997,791	2,406,318
Total Capital Stock and Patrons' Equity	1,846,066	2,002,666	2,411,193
Total Liabilities, Capital Stock and Patrons' Equity	$4,886,626	$5,178,592	$5,593,972

G.L.F. PETROLEUM COOPS. (BULK PLANTS)
COMPOSITE OPERATING STATEMENTS
AND
DISTRIBUTION OF MARGINS

	1956–1957[1]	*1957–1958*[1]	*1958–1959*[1]
(Number of Corporations)	(66)	(65)	(65)
Net Purchases by Patrons	$25,627,523	$25,974,004	$28,436,337
Cost of Patrons' Purchases	21,576,486	21,829,045	23,723,304
Gross Margin on Patrons' Purchases	4,051,037	4,144,959	4,713,033
Operating Revenues	125,807	118,574	129,515
Total Gross Margin	4,176,844	4,263,533	4,842,548
Total Operating Expense	3,733,833	3,978,020	4,205,392
Net Margin from Operations	443,011	285,513	637,156
Other Revenue and Deductions	46,613	18,040	52,665
Net Margin	$ 489,624	$ 303,553	$ 689,821
Distribution of Net Margins			
Patronage Refunds	$ 66,564	$ 69,995	$ 133,957
Federal Income Taxes	108,112	71,831	147,337
Retained Margins	314,948	161,727	408,527
Total	$ 489,624	$ 303,553	$ 689,821

[1] Fiscal year ends June 30.

Acknowledgments

I HAVE MADE many visits to the G.L.F. since July, 1934, when H. E. Babcock opened the doors of the G.L.F. to me as a student of cooperative enterprise. During that first visit I was caught by the magic of Babcock's vision and that was the germ of this book.

It is not possible for me to personally thank the hundreds of persons who have helped explain the G.L.F. to me. I hope that they will feel that the writing of this history expresses my gratitude for their efforts.

I am in greatest debt to James A. McConnell, known as Jim throughout the G.L.F. He, more than any other, has given me the encouragement and sense of high purpose that has made this task a pleasure. For a quarter century I have valued his judgment as a great cooperative leader. As chapters have been completed he has read them objectively for feel and substance.

My debt is also great to the late Charles N. Silcox, who served as General Manager from November 1952 to November 1957, when he took over the position of Executive Vice-President previously held by Mr. McConnell; and to Edmund H. Fallon, who has served as General Manager since November 1, 1957. They have given me unrestricted access to facilities, materials and staff, and abundant amounts of their own time.

For both encouragement and assistance, I am also deeply indebted to Frank M. Smith, President of the G.L.F. from January 1943 to October 1953; and J. C. Corwith, who has served as President since October 1953. Mr. Smith has read many of these chapters in manuscript form, while President Corwith has read them all.

Two others have been of immense help to me: William I. Myers, Dean of the New York State College of Agriculture, Cornell University, 1943 to 1959; and the late Maurice C. Burritt, Director of Extension for New York State, 1916 to 1924, and first G.L.F. Controller, 1924 to 1929. Dean Myers has done all that he could to provide information and insights, and he has read substantial portions of the manuscript. Mr. Burritt made available to me his early manuscripts, records and correspondence and before his death in 1959 he reviewed all of the draft chapters down to 1935.

I also wish to identify personally Mrs. H. E. Babcock, Webster J. Birdsall (New York Department of Agriculture), Walter L. Bradley, Earl Brooks (Cornell University), M.E. Campbell, Elwood Chase, Jay Coryell, Charles E. Dykes, E. R. Eastman (*American Agriculturist*), Verne A. Fogg, Ronald B. Fitch, Jerry Hammond, Fred Hessel, Sherman Peer, Seeber C. Tarbell, C. W. Sadd, Bayard H. Staplin, Jared W. Stiles, E.

Victor Underwood, and E. Curry Weatherby for their kindness in reading and offering suggestions on one or more chapters in draft form. This has been only a small part of the help they have given me over a considerable period of years.

I also desire to thank each of the following for their generous interest and assistance: Harlo P. Beals, Arthur Leal Bibbins (deceased), Edgar J. Biggie, Norval G. Budd, Robert B. Child, Ernest C. Charron, Theodore B. Clausen, John C. Crissey, Garland W. Clark, C. E. Dayton, C. L. Dickinson, Glenn E. Edick, William J. Fields, Ray R. Flumerfelt, (Miss) Bess Goebel, Ronald N. Goddard, Floyd S. Graves, Milton E. Harris, G. W. Hedlund (Cornell University), M. Lyle Holmes, Caleb K. Hobbie, Nelson D. Houck, John C. Huttar, Gaylord W. Hymen, Kenneth S. Joy, Mrs. Peter Kemper (Mary Fennell), Walter P. King, Merrill N. Knapp, L. D. Kurtz, John W. Lloyd, F. A. McLellan (deceased), W. D. McMillan, (Miss) Phyllis McMillan, James L. MacEachron, Thomas E. Milliman, Frank K. Naegely, Will E. Morgan, George R. Pfann, Charles H. Riley, Horace E. Shackleton, Harold G. Smith, Richard W. Smith, (Mrs.) Elsie S. Williams, Frederic M. Upchurch, Arthur J. Wells, Edward W. Wilson, and Nathaniel E. White.

I take pleasure in recording appreciation to Warren A. Ranney for help and insights on research activities under Babcock, for development of statistical charts, and other useful services; to Paul Taber for his patience and good judgment in helping me assemble the photographs used to illustrate this book, and for other invaluable assistance; and to Phil D. Stump for his painstaking provision of statistical information for both the text and appendix.

I am especially indebted to R. Bruce Gervan, Secretary of the Cooperative G.L.F. Exchange, for assembling and developing much needed information and for careful and discriminative reading of the galley proofs for accuracy and interpretation.

Generous assistance was also given me by the following colleagues in the United States Department of Agriculture: Kelsey B. Gardner, Director of the Management Services Division, Farmer Cooperative Service, provided valuable counsel on many important questions and meticulously reviewed my galley and page proofs; while J. Warren Mather, Chief of the Farm Supplies Branch, Farmer Cooperative Service, and Raymond J. Mischler, Senior Attorney, Office of the General Counsel, gave me helpful suggestions on portions of the galley proof.

Over a decade ago my longtime friend and publisher, J. Kenneth Anderson, made initial plans with me for this book. His high standards and warm human spirit have made it a continuing pleasure to work with him.

One other friend has been a source of inspiration to me while writing this book—the late Fred C. Kelly, author of *The Wright Brothers,* and an artist with words and ideas. Over a period of many years I gave him reports on progress and received the benefit of his sage advice.

I wish also to thank Edwin G. Nourse for the joy of working with him on studies of cooperative enterprise since 1926, and for his gracious foreword to this volume.

I am very appreciative also of the help given by my daughter, Mrs. Sheila Knapp Woodard, who assisted me on that "last straw"—the index.

Of course, none of these are to be held responsible in any way.

The endsheet illustration, a typical farm scene in G.L.F. territory, is a reproduction of a painting by Bob Childress of Old Saybrook, Connecticut, and is used with his kind permission.

I could not have completed this adventure without the supporting faith and fortitude of two women—my longtime friend and secretary, Mrs. Jeanne Franklin; and my wife, Carol West Knapp, to whom I have dedicated this book as an expression of my love for her.

Joseph G. Knapp

Index